CW01083164

European Gardens

Like the idea of making gardens, rose cultivation reached Europe from West Asia – and became very popular (*Rosa moyesii*).

European Gardens

History, philosophy and design

Tom Turner

LONDON AND NEW YORK

First published 2011
by Routledge
2 Park Square, Milton Park, Abingdon, Oxon, OX14 4RN

Simultaneously published in the USA and Canada
by Routledge
711 Third Avenue, New York, NY 10017

Routledge is an imprint of the Taylor & Francis Group, an informa business

Designed and typeset by Sutchinda Rangsi-Thompson
Printed in India by The Replika Press Pvt. Ltd., Sonepat, Haryana, India

British Library Cataloguing in Publication Data
A catalogue record for this book is available from the British Library

Library of Congress Cataloging-in-Publication Data
Turner, Tom (Thomas Henry Duke), 1946-
European gardens : history, philosophy and design / Tom Turner.
p. cm.
Includes bibliographical references and index.
1. Gardens--Europe--History. 2. Gardens, European--History. I. Title.
SB451.36.E85T87 2010
712.094--dc22
2010016901

ISBN13: 978-0-415-49684-1 (hbk)

Contents

P.0 The cultivated grape (*Vitis vinifera var. vinifera*), which has hermaphroditic flowers, spread into Europe from West Asia, as did horticulture and the wine-drinking palace civilisation which developed the art of garden design.

Preface

One cannot analyse the design character of European gardens without looking beyond the Mediterranean. This is because horticulture, palace life and city-building developed in the Fertile Crescent before spreading, via Crete, Greece, Egypt and Italy to the forests of Europe. My own garden visits progressed in the other direction: from Scotland to England, to North Europe, to South Europe and then to Asia. This led to a book entitled *Asian Gardens* published in 2010. Starting in the Fertile Crescent might have been more logical but I suspect it would have been less interesting, because I would have known where I was going.

Eight of the chapters in this book were published in a 2005 book, *Garden History: Philosphy and Design 2000 BC–2000 AD*. Its title was wrong, because the coverage was only of West Eurasia from 2000 BCE to 2000 CE. The title of the revised book is therefore *European Gardens*. My discussion of Islamic gardens has moved to *Asian Gardens* and a new chapter on garden origins deals with Neolithic and Bronze Age gardens. Another change to the book is that most of the images now come from digital originals. I took the photographs for the 2005 book on colour negative film and they did not scan and print well. Many of the replacement images were taken by other photographers, whom I thank.

P.1 Diagram of the 'Enclosed Style' from *English Garden Design: History and Styles since 1650*.

In 1986, I included a diagram labelled 'The Enclosed Style' in a book entitled *English Garden Design: History and Styles since 1650* (see Figure P.1). It was drawn to summarise the ideas from continental Europe which influenced England after 1650. Though an over-simplification, the diagram did make the point that post-Civil War gardens in the British Isles were based on ideas which came from continental Europe, including medieval castle gardens and Renaissance palace gardens. The British example which best fits the diagram is Edzell Castle in Scotland (see p. 205 and p. 214), which was one of the first gardens I visited after attending Frank Clark's lectures on garden history. During the seventeenth century, when the Edzell garden was made, it stood on the frontier between the clan system of the Scottish Highlands, then in terminal decline, and the advancing urban civilisation of the Scottish Lowlands. Edzell is a classic example of a 'fringe garden', a microcosm of an ancient tradition:

> *According to the creation myths of Mesopotamia and Egypt, the world began in watery darkness. The gods then made land, light and life – and were honoured in sanctuaries comprising mounds, pools, plants, buildings and terraces. These were the earliest symbolic*
>
> *landscapes and their components, with the sky, remain the compositional elements of garden and landscape design. In the millennia after 3000 BCE, great gardens were made on the fringes of Central Asia. They occupy a belt which, from Sumer, runs west into Europe and east into China. It was a zone of interchange, a landscape in which horsemen encountered farmers and the design of symbolic gardens and landscapes began.*[1]

Future archaeology may prove us wrong but the current view, explained in Chapter 2, is that the world's first settlements were made in the Fertile Crescent and that they were established at the cultural, intellectual and physical interface between the lifestyle of the pastoral nomad and the lifestyle of the settler-cultivators who made the earliest gardens.

Preface to *Garden History: Philosophy and Design 2000 BC–2000 AD* (2005)

My interest in garden history began with the lectures Frank Clark gave to his last student group at Edinburgh University, of which I was a member, in 1969.[2] It continued to grow after I moved to Birmingham in 1971. Since I disliked my lodgings, my car – a VW Beetle stocked with camping equipment – became a mobile home for weekend trips, which often included visits to gardens.

In 1974 Hal Moggridge asked me to prepare a guide for international visitors to Britain, and I drew six garden style diagrams as part of a historical introduction. It is possible that I had seen John Claudius Loudon's diagrams (see p. 280) but I do not think so. I was then working in Sylvia Crowe's London office, for Bill Gillespie, and Susan Jellicoe came for coffee. I asked if she thought my diagrams would be a useful component of the visitors' guide. She looked for a while and said, 'Tom, they're marvellous.' Without this encouragement, the diagrams would surely have been forgotten when the prospective publisher of the guidebook withdrew.

They were resurrected when my wife kindly drew a set of 12 style diagrams for my book, *English Garden Design: History and Styles since 1650*, which was published in 1986. They were then revised (usually for a lecture to Ted Fawcett's students at the Architectural Association) approximately once every five years. Like the cambium in a tree, the diagrams laid down woody tissue (text) inside and bark (examples) outside. The lecture expanded in a similar fashion: it was supposed to be on Loudon but I soon found it necessary to describe the origins of gardening in Ancient Egypt – 'to set Loudon's views in context'.

Researching the text in libraries was a joy, but not a substitute for following the example – and the itineraries – set by Loudon and later garden history tourists. Robert Holden always said I should travel more, and he was right. The garden visits became a logistical challenge and an adventure. Relating my visits to Susan Jellicoe's photographs, Geoffrey Jellicoe's acute observations and Marie-Luise Gothein's narrative became an absorbing occupation, with Loudon often in my thoughts. His sparkling prose and utter freedom from prejudice were examples I should like to have followed.

As I gratefully acknowledge the companionship provided by the words and pictures of those four pioneers, I am aware of how much easier my journeys have been. Loudon's wife relates that:

> *He proceeded by Grodno to Wilna, through a country covered with the remains of the French army, horses and men lying dead by the roadside, and bands of wild-looking Cossacks scouring the country. On entering Kosnow three Cossacks attacked his carriage, and endeavoured to carry off the horses, but they were beaten back by the whips of the driver and servants ... He proceeded to Moscow, where he arrived on the 4th of March, 1814, after having encountered various difficulties on the road. Once, in particular, the horses in his carriage being unable to drag it through a snow-drift, the postilions very coolly un-harnessed them and trotted off, telling him that they would bring fresh horses in the morning, and that he would be in no danger from the wolves, if he would keep the windows of his carriage close, and the leather curtains down.*[3]

P.2 a, b Loudon encountered many hazards in the course of his travels.

I have not found records of how Gothein travelled between 1900 and 1914 but she must have used steamers, trains, trams and cabs. Jellicoe used trains and steamers before the Second World War and added planes and cars afterwards. Having slept through the best part of a rail journey 70 years later, I laughed to read his advice that 'if taking the early train from Innsbruck to Salzburg one should stay awake to see the wonderful view of Melk'.[4] I used modes of transport similar to the Jellicoes', with the addition of a folding bicycle. Except for the occasional mechanical problem it was, for example, great fun to cycle from my home to a London station and then, four hours later, to bump along the Via Appia Antica from Ciampino Airport into Rome. For a cyclist, the best European capitals are Amsterdam and Copenhagen. The worst is Athens. It has smoother roads than Lisbon and Prague (its nearest rivals for the lowest place in my personal list of European capitals ranked for their friendliness to cyclists) but suffers from greater heat, choking fumes, aggressively undisciplined motorists and dogs which rush you with the apparent hope of transmitting rabies.

Note on garden location maps and other web resources

Garden History: Philosophy and Design 2000 BC–2000 AD (2005) contained maps of garden locations at the end of the book. These have been replaced with a web page, http://www.gardenvisit.com/history_theory/european_gardens_companion.

It has links which take the reader to maps, satellite photographs, garden descriptions, additional illustrations, biographies of designers and online garden history texts, including Marie-Luise Gothein's *History of Garden Art*.

CHAPTER 1

Design philosophy

1.0 Repton defined a garden as 'a piece of ground fenced off from cattle … [which] … is, or ought to be, cultivated and enriched by art'.

1.1 a, b Garden walls and fences at Cranborne Manor protect plants from cattle, wind and theft.

Introduction

Humphry Repton, the leading garden theorist of the nineteenth century, defined a garden as 'a piece of ground fenced off from cattle, and appropriated to the use and pleasure of man: it is, or ought to be, cultivated and enriched by art'.[1] His definition has good etymological support. The Indo-European words garden, yard, *garten, jardin, giardino, hortus,* paradise, *paradiso,* park, *parc, parquet,* court, *hof, kurta,* town, *tun,* and *tuin* all derive from the act of enclosing outdoor space. The Old English word *geard,* meaning 'fence', produced our words 'garden' and 'yard'. In American English, an outdoor space attached to a house is known as a yard 'when appropriated to use', and as a garden 'when appropriated to pleasure'. Repton's afterthought, that a garden 'is, or ought to be, cultivated' makes one smile at how little has changed in the long history of gardens and gardening.

Repton described himself as a landscape gardener on his business card (Figure 1.3). He loved views of cattle and one of his primary concerns was the relationship between an enclosed garden and its landscape setting: a juxtaposition of the works of man with the works of nature. The relationship between enclosed gardens and the wider landscape has always been fundamental. As discussed in Chapter 2, the three ancient reasons for enclosing garden space were:

1 to grow plants;
2 to make safe domestic place for family life;

1.2 Humphry Repton loved to see cattle 'animating' a park.

1.3 Repton's trade card. He described himself as a landscape gardener and had a profound theoretical interest in the relationship between buildings, gardens and the landscapes in which they were set.

3 to create places of aesthetic and spiritual delight.

Repton's clients, like their Renaissance and Roman predecessors, were wealthy families who could afford to lavish expenditure on each of the design objectives. But the three objectives have separate histories, separate technologies and separate locational requirements – which result in different types of garden space with distinct characteristics. We must therefore review the theory of garden and landscape design.

Garden theory

A theory is 'a system of ideas explaining something' especially with regard to general principles. Garden design theory explains, or should explain, the 'What, Where, Why and How' of making gardens.[2] 'When and Who' are historical questions. This chapter deals with:

- garden objectives (*why* gardens were made);
- locations (*where* gardens were made);
- garden types (*what* kinds of garden were made);
- aesthetics (*how* gardens were shaped).

Responses to these questions guide composition of the six prime elements used to create gardens and landscapes. They are listed below and represented on the plans

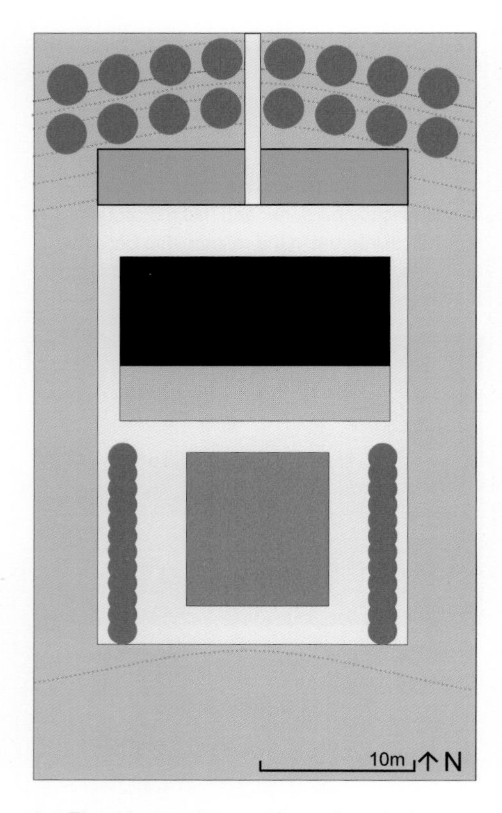

1.4 The primary elements in outdoor design are landform, vertical structures, horizontal structures, vegetation and water. They are composed with regard to the prevailing climate.

1.5 Excellent city plans have been inspired by garden plans. In Paris, hedges become avenues and woodland blocks become urban blocks. When cities have more vegetated roofs (as centre right in Paris), they will become even more like gardens – and even more in need of landscape architects and garden designers.

and diagrams in this book by the colours and symbols shown in brackets (see Figure 1.4):

1. landform (contours);
2. water (blue);
3. vertical structures, e.g. buildings (black);
4. horizontal structures, e.g. paving (yellow for pedestrians, grey for vehicles);
5. vegetation (pale green for grass, bright green for ornamental shrubs, dark green for trees, blue green for non-garden vegetation);
6. climate (indicated by a north point).

Many historic garden designs were inscribed directly onto the ground. Today it is more common to draw on computer screens and use laser equipment to transfer plans to the ground. While architectural styles are best shown in elevation, garden styles are best represented by plans, diagrams and models. To highlight the differences between garden styles, diagrams are best.

Skill in composing the six primary elements is also necessary for the design of towns, making garden design a crucible for town design. Many of the world's best-designed cities were inspired by garden concepts. The word 'tun', from which 'town' derives, means 'fence' in Old German. In Old English 'tun' came to be applied to a cluster of buildings in an enclosure. Designing towns and gardens involves the layout of outdoor space. Sixteenth-century Isfahan, seventeenth-century Paris, eighteenth-century London, nineteenth-century Washington DC and the Garden Cities of the

1.6 Washington DC was planned by Pierre L'Enfant, who had known the Baroque gardens of France as a young man.

twentieth century were composed like gardens, to their immense benefit. Garden design (Figure 1.7) deals with the internal layout of enclosed space; landscape design concerns relationships between enclosures and their surroundings; urban design considers relationships between the elements that comprise cities. The arts are separate but related. In my view, those who shape settlements should hone their skills on a small scale before working on the large scale of landscape urbanism.

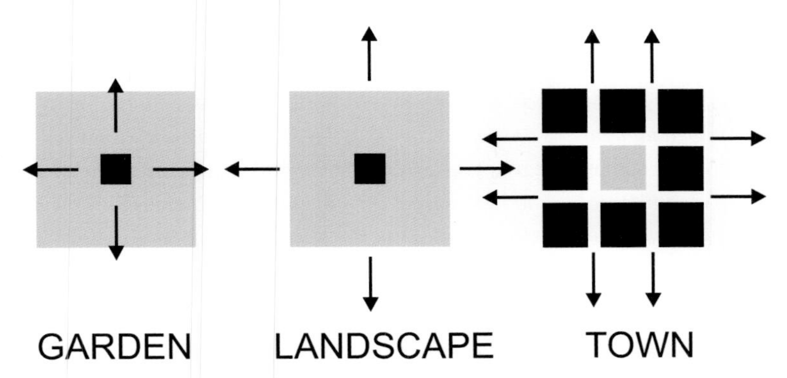

1.7 The relationship between garden design, landscape design and town design.

Design objectives

'Why?' is the first question for design theory. Vitruvius has a pre-eminent position in giving the answer because his writings, *c.*27 BCE, constitute the oldest design manual to have survived. His work, *De architecture libri decem* (*The Ten Books of*

1.8 Inanna equates with Venus – who still lives and reigns in European gardens. She is seen here looking over the Brownian lake at Sherborne Castle.

Architecture), is an accomplished book which, because it reads more like a manual than an imaginative text, is widely taken to be based on earlier works which have not survived. We can view it as an encapsulation of the ancient world's approach to design. Vitruvius was a Roman and is thought to have spent most of his working life in Julius Caesar's army. *De architecture libri decem* deals with design objectives, art and technology. The only building Vitruvius mentions having designed himself is a pagan basilica. Most of his experience was in matters far beyond the scope of what we now would call 'architecture': military structures, defensive plans, clocks, aqueducts, pumps, siege engines and harbours. He makes few remarks on the design of outdoor space. After using the Preface as an opportunity to fawn on the emperor, Vitruvius divides his subject into ten parts. He does not give them names but we can do so:

1. design theory and landscape architecture;
2. materials;
3. temples (Part 1);
4. temples (Part 2);
5. public projects: squares, meeting halls, theatres, parks, gymnasiums, harbours;
6. private houses;
7. finishes and colours;
8. water supply;
9. sundials and clocks;
10. engineering.

The best-known passage, from Book 1, deals with design objectives:

> *All must be built with due reference to* firmitas *[firmness, durability, strength],* utilitas *[commodity, utility, convenience], and* venustas *[delight, loveliness, beauty].* Firmitas *will be assured when foundations are carried down to the solid ground and materials wisely and liberally selected;* utilitas, *when the arrangement of the apartments is faultless and presents no hindrance to use, and when each class of building is assigned to its suitable and appropriate exposure; and* venustas, *when the appearance of the work is pleasing and in good taste, and when its members are in due proportion according to correct principles of symmetry.*[3]

Translation of the three design objectives as 'Firmness, Commodity, and Delight', comes from Henry Wotton's *The Elements of Architecture*.[4] The objectives are of central importance to the art of garden design. For landscape architecture, Ian Thompson has suggested 'ecology' and 'community' as alternatives for *firmitas* and *utilitas*.[5] Thompson also suggests the terms mono-valent, bi-valent and tri-valent for three categories of project. As examples of mono-valent garden projects, a temple garden would focus on *venustas*, a domestic garden on *utilitas* and a plant garden on *firmitas*. Estate gardens, as described below (p. 19), tend to be tri-valent.

1.9 A rare instance of a twentieth-century peristyle garden, at Iford Manor.

Firmitas is necessary to all design and construction. *Utilitas*, the rationale for undertaking a design, has primacy in gardens which provide for bodily comfort and the cultivation of plants. Since the word *venustas,* derives from Venus, Wotton's translation, Delight, is misleading. As a Roman goddess, Venus equates with the Sumerian goddess Inanna, the Akkadian goddess Ishtar, the Semitic goddess Astarte, the Egyptian goddess Isis and the Greek goddess Aphrodite. The ancients believed that aesthetic satisfaction, because it is transmitted from the world of the gods to the world of man, has a spiritual dimension.[6] The personal qualities of Venus became gifts to the human race; she gave girls their loveliness, cities their elegance, gardens their delight. Merely 'utilitarian' gardens may have a high degree of firmness and yet lack grace, charm, beauty and loveliness. Venus and Diana remind us of these qualities and remain the most commonly represented deities in Western gardens. Apollo, symbolising the sun, and therefore divine distance, is even more closely associated with spirituality. He still appears in collections of garden statuary offered for sale, but less frequently than Aphrodite (Venus) (Figure 1.8).

Vitruvius has disappointingly little to say about enclosed outdoor space. In the case of temple enclosures, this may result from the fact that Roman temples, unlike their Greek predecessors, were more often in towns than in sacred groves outside towns. In the case of dwellings, it may be because Vitruvius' life had been spent on army campaign, giving him little experience of domesticity. Book 5, on public projects, has most comment on outdoor space. The following recommendation is for athletics enclosures:

> *This kind of colonnade is called among the Greeks* xystus *because athletes during the winter season exercise in covered running tracks. Next to this* xystus *and to the double colonnade should be laid out the uncovered walks into which, in fair weather during the winter, the athletes come out from the* xystus *for exercise. The* xysta *ought to be so constructed that there may be plantations between the two colonnades, or groves of plane trees, with walks laid out in them among the trees and resting places there, made of* opus signinum *[i.e. paved]. Behind the* xystus *a stadium, so designed that great numbers of people may have plenty of room to look on at the contests between the athletes.*[7]

The Romans used the word *xystus* to mean a garden court but noblemen, like Pliny, would also have exercise grounds on their private estates. Roofed colonnades (peristyles) had many purposes in the Graeco-Roman world. They were used, like trees, to create shelter and shade. Cloister gardens in European monasteries and the forecourts of West Asian mosques are examples of their use to make spiritual space. It is surprising that their popularity has declined. Roofed outdoor space has both utility and beauty.

Location

Where to make gardens is a central issue. It follows the consideration of objectives and precedes the design. Since few owners have left records of how their decisions were made, the analysis of garden location is closer to theoretical archaeology than design history. It is at once apparent that great gardens have significant positions in the wider landscape, often including:

- a significant topographical location;
- a favourable microclimate;
- a planned relationship to water;
- rich soil;
- good views.

The planning of gardens in relation to sites is woefully neglected in the modern world. Officials and developers seem only to care about relationships between money, buildings and cars. Historically, the relationship between buildings, gardens and landscapes was fundamental, as can be illustrated with examples. Queen Hatshepsut's Temple on the edge of the Nile Valley is the world's oldest grand work of landscape architecture and is located in a sanctuary (p. 99). Delphi, high in a valley between the Gulf of Corinth and Mount Parnassus, provides a sense of sacred mystery as well as fresh air and wonderful views (p. 110 and p. 138). The Alhambra sits on a low hill

1.10 A good location – the south-easterly aspect favoured by Repton, together with elevation, shelter and water: Caerhays, Cornwall.

overlooking a river valley surrounded by the Sierra Nevada. The Medici chose sites on the hills round Florence for their houses and gardens (Figure 1.27). Blenheim, like all Lancelot 'Capability' Brown's designs, uses the site as the prime feature of the layout. These places are more than architecture: they are landscape architecture.

Vitruvius explains the Classical approach to site planning, in Book 1, Chapter 4:

> *First comes the choice of a very healthy site. Such a site will be high, neither misty nor frosty, and in a climate neither hot nor cold, but temperate, without marshes in the neighbourhood. For when the morning breezes blow toward the town at sunrise, if they bring with them mists from marshes and, mingled with the mist, the poisonous breath of*

the creatures of the marshes to be wafted into the bodies of the inhabitants, they will make the site unhealthy. Again, if the town is on the coast with a southern or western exposure, it will not be healthy, because in summer the southern sky grows hot at sunrise and is fiery at noon, while a western exposure grows warm after sunrise, is hot at noon, and at evening all aglow.[8]

Landscape designers continue to argue that garden design should receive priority in housing layout and that the character and qualities of the existing site, called the Genius of the Place (see p. 274), should be respectfully consulted on all occasions. Chip Sullivan reviews the influence of climatic design on Italian gardens in his book, *Gardens and Climate*.[9]

Garden types

What type of garden to make rests on decisions about objectives, with owners and designers often looking to pre-existing types (Table 1.1).

Table 1.1 Three classes of motivation have led to the evolution of primary garden types

For the body at rest	For activity	For the spirit
	Primeval enclosures	
Palace garden	Paradise park	Sacred grove
Domestic garden	Hunting park	Temple garden
Vegetable garden	Animal garden	Academy garden
Hofgarten	Botanical garden	Ceremonial avenue
Medicinal garden	Zoological garden	Cloister garth
Public garden	Public garden	Sculpture court
Beer garden	Arboretum	Grotto
Café garden	Alpine garden	City park
City garden	Flower garden	National park

Gardens tend to have more than one category of objective, though temple gardens and beer gardens are usually single-purpose. Versailles was both a work of art and a meeting-place for high society. The Villa Lante, described by Georgina Masson as 'one of the most beautiful in existence',[10] served each of the three main objectives of garden design: it was a work of art, a hunting park and a place for outdoor parties (see

1.11 Growing vegetables was and remains a prime motive for enclosing outdoor space – because they need protection.

1.12 Dining is an ancient use of enclosed outdoor space. From a painting (1578) attributed to *Paolo Veronese* and showing a scene in what may have been the garden in Feltre in the Veneto.

p. 220). Sissinghurst, perhaps the best-loved garden of the twentieth century, served the three objectives in a different manner: it was a work of art, it accommodated family needs and it was a place for the owners to exercise their minds and bodies.

Great parks and gardens combine use with beauty, pleasure with profit and work with contemplation:

> *Utile quimiscens, ingentia Rura,*
> *Simplex Munditis ornat, punctum hic tulit omne.*
>
> He that the beautiful and useful blends,
> Simplicity with greatness, gains all ends.[11]

Productive gardens

The history of gardens is linked to the history of cultivation but, as discussed in the next chapter, the earliest plants to be cultivated were cereals. The spaces in which they were grown, and the methods used, were horticultural in scale but the activity was closer to what we would now call agriculture. The available information on planting in pre-Renaissance gardens suggests that, except in sacred gardens, useful plants were far more common than ornamental plants.

Domestic gardens

Domestic gardens contribute to our well-being. We value places where the old can sit, the young can play and parents can rest. We relish succulent vegetables, ripe fruits, fresh herbs and scents. On hot days we seek shady places that catch the breeze. On

1.13 Sitting outdoors retains its popularity.

1.15 The Orto Botanico in Padua is said to be the oldest botanic garden in the world.

1.14 Munich Hofgarten. T.S. Eliot captured the atmosphere of a court garden: 'Summer surprised us, coming over the Starnbergersee/With a shower of rain; we stopped in the colonnade,/And went on in sunlight, into the Hofgarten,/And drank coffee, and talked for an hour.'

1.16 Horse Guards Parade was the tiltyard for Whitehall Palace, in London, and still has ceremonial roles.

cool days we prefer an outdoor seat with full sun and shelter from the wind. On festive and wedding days we party in gardens. Good domestic gardens accommodate these design objectives in ways that have not changed during the four millennia covered by this book. The best policy is that when land for housing becomes available, gardens and parks should be planned before roads and buildings.

Palace gardens were made by kings and nobles as adjuncts to their living quarters. It was common to muster officials and hold parades in a place which became known as a court (or *hof*). The words court-yard and *Hofgarten* are compounds which, etymologically, mean 'enclosed enclosure', a secular parallel to a 'holy of holies'. In the Baroque period, court gardens were opened to the public as acts of conspicuous consumption, and became available as public open spaces. In the nineteenth century, specialised city gardens, tea gardens, beer gardens, and café gardens were made to satisfy the domestic objectives of garden design.

Plant and animal gardens

Humans have always sought to understand the nature of the world and enclosures have assisted the quest with collections of plants and animals. The earliest spaces of this type were known as *pairidaeza* (literally 'around-wall'). 'Paradise' took on a religious meaning at a later date (see p. 169). Early West Asian kings used their *pairidaeza* for exotic species brought back from military campaigns. Animals could be hunted and guests served with their meat, or vice versa.[12] Rare plants were used in cooking and medicine. Roman emperors kept animals to entertain crowds, a tradition

1.17 Labelled plants attract botanists.

1.18 The Zoological Garden at Schönbrunn is said to be the world's oldest surviving zoo.

1.19 The Temple of Hephaestus, in Athens, has the oldest remnant of a temple garden in Europe. The planting positions, but not the species, were verified by archaeology.

1.20 Berlin's Tiergarten ('Animal Garden') retains more of the character of a wild place than most capital city parks in Europe.

1.21 'Eden' is a superb name for a botanical project.

1.22 Exotic animals have long had a place in gardens.

which lives on in the public bull-fighting arenas of Spain. Monasteries and then universities made infirmary gardens, herb gardens and botanical gardens. With the rise of post-Renaissance science, zoological gardens became fixtures on royal estates, as did aviaries. The peacock, from India, became a popular adornment in Western gardens. New types of plant garden were made in the nineteenth century, including American gardens, Japanese gardens, alpine gardens, arboretums, and pinetums. Animals recovered something of their place in garden design with the reintroduction of aviaries in the nineteenth century and the creation of wildlife gardens in the twentieth century.

Spiritual gardens

Temple gardens are one of the world's oldest and most important garden types. They were made in many parts of Asia, including the Fertile Crescent, India, China and Japan, in which country many examples survive. Their influence on Northern Europe came about through the Romans and Christianity.

The Bible explains the Creation as God breathing life into dust and making a garden:

> *And the Lord God formed man of the dust of the ground, and breathed into his nostrils the breath of life; and man became a living soul.*

And the Lord God planted a garden eastward in Eden; and there he put the man whom he had formed.
And out of the ground made the Lord God to grow every tree that is pleasant to the sight, and good for food; the tree of life also in the midst of the garden, and the tree of knowledge of good and evil.
And a river went out of Eden to water the garden; and from thence it was parted, and became into four heads.[13]

The Koran records that Allah 'seated Himself upon his throne, and imposed laws on the sun and moon'.[14] Scientists explain the creation more prosaically: life on earth began 4 billion years ago and human life began 4 million years ago. The word 'spirit', from the Latin *spiritus* meaning 'breath', is still used to describe the life-force which drives humans and animals. In a religious context, the spirit is associated with the soul. It is that aspect of humans which, because it is immaterial, can survive bodily death. Religions have used gardens as symbols of paradise and, seeking immortality, men have often sought to create things which will survive them: reputations, families, empires, buildings, inventions, works of art – and great gardens.

Ninian Smart identified six dimensions of religious belief:[15]

1. a ritual dimension;
2. a mythological dimension;
3. a doctrinal dimension;
4. an ethical dimension;
5. a social dimension;
6. an experiential dimension.

In ancient times the ritual, mythological and doctrinal aspects of spiritual space were predominant. In the design of Christian and Islamic enclosed outdoor space, the ethical, social and experiential dimensions of spirituality became more significant. Religious objectives lie behind the oldest surviving garden types, which can be described as sacred landscapes. The word 'sacred' derives from the Latin *sacer* meaning 'set off, restricted'.[16] A person or a thing or a place was designated as sacred when it was unique or extraordinary and would be polluted if it came into contact with something non-divine. Sacred places therefore required protection:

The pure state is that which produces health, vigour, luck, fortune, and long life. The impure state is that characterized by weakness, illness, misfortune, and death. To acquire purity means to enter the sacred realm, which could be done through purification rituals, or through the fasting, continence, and meditation of ascetic life. When a person became pure he entered the realm of the divine and left the profane, impure, decaying world. Such a transition was often marked by a ritual act or rebirth.[17]

1.23 The Domain of Amun, filled with temples and planned in relation to the setting sun, was regarded by the Greeks and Romans as the most sacred landscape in ancient Egypt.

In Neolithic times, animist beliefs associated the forces of nature with special landscapes and, at a later date, they became temple sites (Chapter 2). In Egypt, a temple compound with a sacred lake and a sacred grove was conceived as a home for a god-king (pharaoh) to use after his bodily life (Chapter 3). In Greece, a bounded sanctuary with an altar was used for religious ceremonies (Chapter 4). In Rome, where religion centred more on the home, altars were placed in courtyard gardens and towns. In Christendom, an indoor church altar became the ceremonial focus but meditative 'cloister' gardens were made by religious communities (Chapter 5).

1.24 Gardens can be places to contemplate nature and Buddhism became an influence on Europe in the twentieth century. Lumbini, in Nepal, is the Buddha's birthplace.

1.25 The Villa Lante is widely admired as a work of art and has an iconographical programme akin to contemporary painting and sculpture. The Fountain of the Moors has four ferrymen waiting to help passengers over the River Styx to an island on which four athletes hold up the owner's coat of arms.

The temple enclosures of Egypt and Mesopotamia are the oldest surviving examples of sacred gardens. They were planned in relation to the path of the sun, flood plains and other significant astronomical and geographical considerations – so that they helped people understand the nature of the world, the social structures which maintain order, and our Earth's place in the firmament. Art developed as a means of explaining truths to non-literate peoples. When art separated from religion, it retained the role of helping people comprehend the nature of the external world and of the internal world through which it is perceived. This was the 'nature' which artists learned

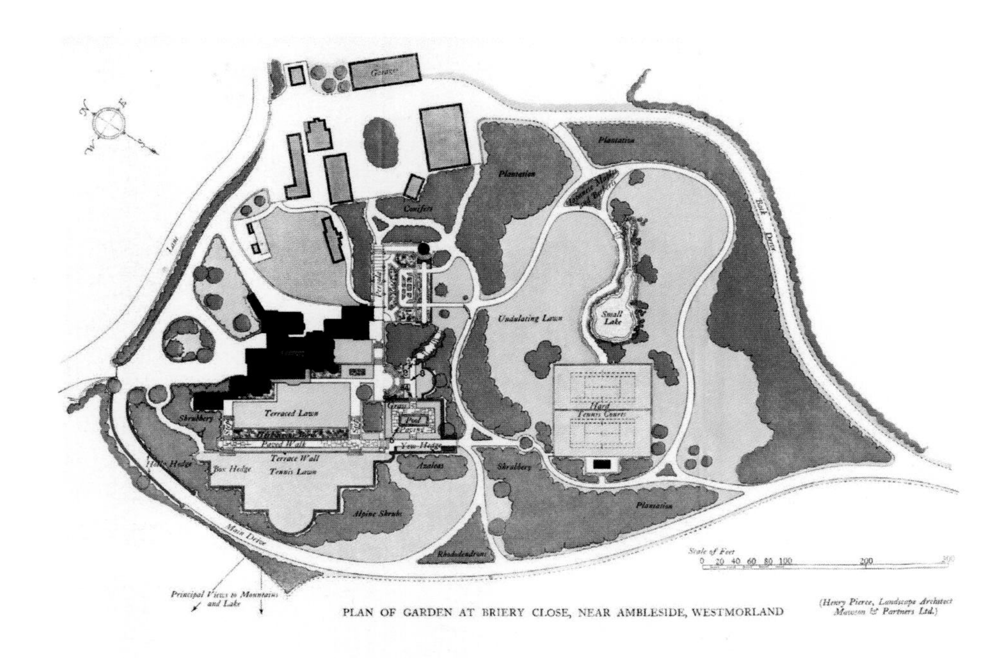

1.26 The wealthy commission gardens with everything – a design by Mawson & Partners for a country villa in North West England.

to 'imitate', as will be discussed below ('Garden aesthetics', pp. 20–4 and Chapter 4). The famous gardens of Renaissance Italy were designed in an equivalent artistic framework to sculpture and painting of the period. In the modern world, a spiritual dimension has become an aspect of certain gardens, rather than a specialised garden

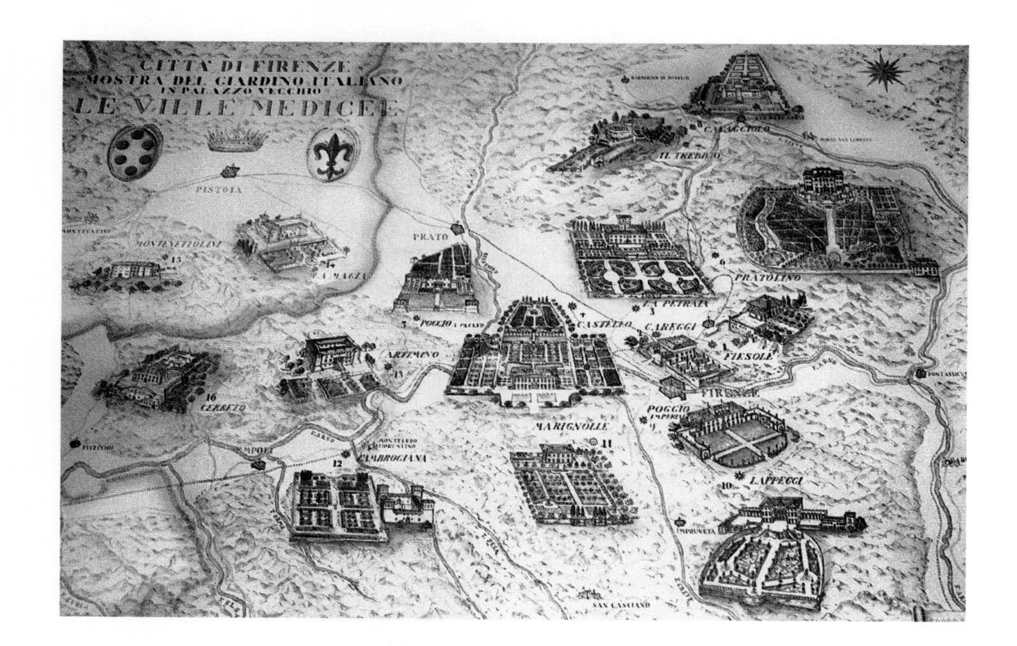

1.27 Medici villas on the hills round Florence, including Castello, Careggi and Pratolino.

1.28 Some public parks still permit horse-riding (Hyde Park, London).

type, leading us to speak of gardens as 'works of art'. The last two gardens discussed in this book (pp. 392–3) were made for museums, one of which is a museum of art.

In the modern world, the best examples of spiritual outdoor space as it was known in the ancient world are the temple pools of India, the cloisters of Europe, the temple gardens of Japan and the national parks of America.

Estates

The rich can have gardens with everything: to satisfy the body, the mind and the spirit. This was true in ancient West Asia, in the gardens made by Europeans who knew the region – and it remains so. Alexander the Great's generals created estates in Macedonia. Roman emperors, following their example, made private villas. The word *villa* was used to describe a country dwelling together with its farm and outhouses. It was a small town and, as *ville*, the word continues to mean 'town' in French. Luxurious villas had domestic gardens, groves of trees and hunting parks. When Roman emperors proclaimed themselves gods, the villas they commissioned were given characteristics previously found in religious sanctuaries. Hadrian's villa (p. 129 and p. 145) can be understood as a representation of the world he knew. Emperors had a fondness for grottoes (see p. 121).

During the Renaissance, Roman villas were studied and excavated, which influenced the new villas made outside the walled castles and towns of medieval Europe. The

1.29 Plato believed that universal forms (the 'ideal' cat) must exist before particular cats can exist.

Medici family were prolific builders and the hills round Florence were spangled with palatial estates. One of the most celebrated, at Pratolino, had a Mannerist garden extending into a hunting park (see p. 209). Francis I built a comparable estate at Fontainebleau, outside Paris; Henry VIII followed his example at Hampton Court, outside London. George Washington was a superb horseman and made a hunting park at Mount Vernon, outside the city he chose as the nation's capital. These are the ancestors of the suburban villas which ring modern cities, often aspiring to characteristics shared with the three Classical garden types. The word 'estate' (from the Latin *status*) refers to the categories of a man's property which define his status.

Garden aesthetics

After decisions about design objectives and types of space, the next set of design issues involves the branch of philosophy known to us as aesthetics.[18] How a garden is formed relates to ideas and beliefs, which brings us to the paradox that garden designers often enclose natural areas and then use natural materials to 'imitate nature'. The most influential interpretations of nature have been:

- the forms which shape the visible world (Ancient Greece);
- the Great Chain of Being, extending from God on high to the humblest organism (medieval Christianity);
- human nature (the Enlightenment);
- everything which is not man (Romanticism and Modernism).

These views are associated with schools of philosophy and attitudes to aesthetics. Bertrand Russell began his *History of Western Philosophy* with the statement that 'Philosophy, as I shall understand the word, is something intermediate between theology and science'. As a mode of thought, Russell believed philosophy to have begun in Greece during the sixth century BCE.[19] The first philosopher to whom Russell devotes a separate chapter is Pythagoras, 'intellectually one of the most important men that ever lived'.

The Pythagorean School originated the belief that 'all things are number' and that mathematics should be 'the fundamental study in physics *as in aesthetics*' (my italics).[20] Pythagoras' discovery of harmonic proportion, in music, was an example of mathematics being used to explain an aspect of nature with aesthetic consequences. Russell wrote that 'those who have experienced the intoxicating delight of sudden understanding that mathematics gives' will understand 'that the pure mathematician, like the musician, is a free creator of his world of ordered beauty'.[21] Designers creating worlds of 'ordered beauty' can have similar experiences.

1.30 Plato's cave analogy suggests we live, like prisoners, able to see nothing but shadows on the wall of a cave.

Plato, doubtless enjoying the same 'intoxicating delight of sudden understanding' as Russell, came to believe in the existence of a perfect world, accessible only to those who explore the natural world with the aid of reason. The belief in a perfect world became known as the Theory of Forms and is explained by Russell as follows:

> *This theory is partly logical, partly metaphysical. The logical part has to do with the meaning of general words. There are many individual animals of whom we can truly say 'this is a cat'. What do we mean by the word 'cat'? Obviously something different from each particular cat. An animal is a cat, it would seem, because it participates in a general nature common to all cats. Language cannot get on without general words such as 'cat', and such words are evidently not meaningless. But if the word 'cat' means anything, it means something which is not this or that cat, but some kind of universal cattiness. This is not born when a particular cat is born, and does not die when it dies. In fact, it has no position in space or time; it is 'eternal'. This is the logical part of the doctrine. The arguments in its favour, whether ultimately valid or not, are strong, and quite independent of the metaphysical part of the doctrine. According to the metaphysical part of the doctrine, the word 'cat' means a certain ideal cat, 'the cat', created by God, and unique. Particular cats partake of the nature of the cat, but more or less imperfectly; it is only owing to this imperfection that there can be many of them. The cat is real; particular cats are only apparent. In the last book of the* Republic, *as a preliminary to a condemnation of painters, there is a very clear exposition of the doctrine of ideas or forms.*[22]

Plato made an analogy between the human condition and life in a cave to explain his theory. Our knowledge of nature is comparable to that of troglodytes, able to look only at shadows cast on a cave wall, never at the forms which cast the shadows. Since artists paint these 'shadows', their work is at a third remove from reality. This led Plato to a low opinion of art, and Iris Murdoch to write a book sub-titled *Why*

1.31 The central portal of the west façade of Notre Dame, Paris, was arranged in a Platonic hierarchy to explain the nature of the world.

Plato Banished the Artists.[23] Plato believed there is something deceptive about art: 'A painter ... may deceive children or simple persons, when he shows them his picture of a carpenter from a distance, and they will fancy that they are looking at a real carpenter.' [24] One doubts if he knew many children who had been deceived but his theory of art was, to say the least, extraordinarily influential.

Plotinus and St Augustine developed a philosophical theory, described as Neoplatonic, from Plato's Theory of Forms. It resolved Plato's objection to painting and had a deep influence on European art (see Chapter 5). The idea was that artists should view many particulars in order to gain the clearest possible impression of the eternal Forms. This became known as the Ideal Theory of Art. The Elder Pliny, writing before Plotinus' time, related that when Zeuxis was commissioned to paint Helen of Troy he organised a parade of naked girls, chose the most beautiful and reproduced the best parts of each in his painting.[25] It resembles the techniques now used by digital artists for glamour magazines.

Encapsulated in the axiom that 'Art should imitate nature', the Theory of Forms came to have a pervasive influence on Western culture. By 'nature' the Neoplatonists meant the world of the Forms, not the everyday visible world. During its long history the consequences of this axiom have varied according to different interpretations of the words 'art', 'imitation' and 'nature'. Developments in religion, philosophy and science produced an endless succession of changes. Before discussing the influence of the axiom on garden design, it is worth pausing to look at some of its consequences for architecture.

Erwin Panofsky explains that 'the High Gothic cathedral sought to embody the whole of Christian knowledge, theological, moral, natural, and historical, with everything in its place' and arranged to manifest the 'uniform division and subdivision of the whole structure', and the separate identity of each part.[26] 'Nature' was understood as a Christian version of the hierarchy of Forms. 'Imitation' was interpreted as the process of manifesting this body of knowledge in the fabric and ornamentation of the cathedral. Thus the central portal of the west façade of Notre Dame in Paris was arranged, visually and structurally, to show the hierarchical relationship between the Damned, the Resurrected, the Apostles, the Virtues, the Saints and the Wise and Foolish Virgins.

Plato's works were studied afresh during the Renaissance by scholars concerned with the roots of Greek philosophy. In 1439, Lorenzo de Medici founded a Platonic Academy in his garden at Careggi, outside Florence (see p. 213). This had important consequences for garden design. After the meeting, Plato's influence shifted from the background to the foreground of Western art. Humanists concluded that Greek and Roman architecture must have been based on mathematical proportions. The relationship between the width of a column and its height, for example, was taken to be based on the mathematics of harmonic proportion. Architecture was made to imitate the Platonic Forms.

Wittkower has shown how the interests of the mathematician, the artist and the designer were linked in the work of a figure such as Alberti, and has explained the degree to which Palladio was influenced by Plotinus and Neoplatonism.[27] Palladio's architecture was based upon the circle, the square and harmonic proportion because they represent the Forms of Goodness, Justice and Harmony. The imitation of these essential Forms was a way of producing buildings which partook of the essence of the universe: they imitated the nature of the world. A.N. Whitehead characterised Western philosophy as 'a series of footnotes to Plato',[28] thus reducing the history of aesthetically-designed gardens to the status of a footnote to a footnote to a footnote.

Neoplatonic ideas lie behind the Islamic and Christian square designs of the Middle Ages and the mathematically calculated 'Cartesian' gardens of the Renaissance. Descartes did not write either on aesthetics or gardening but his use of the 'geometrical method' (i.e. deduction) in reasoning led philosophers and artists to seek self-evident axioms on which to base design. The axiom that art should imitate nature fitted perfectly with a Cartesian approach. 'Nature' was understood, once again, as the essential and universal forms which shape the visible world. We can find the 'geometrical method' in Poussin's use of grids, in Racine's plays, in Le Nôtre's garden designs, and in the formulas which Jacques Boyceau (1560–1633), gardener to Louis XIII, gave for calculating the correct relationship between the length, height and width of an avenue. The latter correspond to the formulas used by Palladio to work out the mathematical relationship between pavements and arcades.

Neoplatonic ideas were current in seventeenth- and eighteenth-century England. They permeate the writings of Dryden, Shaftesbury, Pope, Johnson and Reynolds. These authors tell us that art should imitate nature (see p. 267). Pope expressed the belief as follows in his *Essay on Criticism*:

> *First follow Nature, and your judgement frame*
> *By her just standard, which is still the same:*
> *Unerring NATURE, still divinely bright,*
> *One clear, unchang'd, and universal light,*
> ...
> *Those Rules of old discover'd, not devis'd,*
> *Are Nature still, but Nature Methodiz'd;*
> *Nature, like Liberty, is but restrain'd*
> *By the same Laws which first herself ordain'd.*[29]

In these verses Pope uses 'Nature' to mean the universal forms and rules of proportion which, in Neoplatonic and Neoclassical theory, it is the artist's task to imitate. But

1.32 a, b 'Nature' as the world of universals (above) and 'Nature' as the world of particulars (below).

1.33 The Great Chain of Being, picked out in a yellow, ran from Heaven to Hell, passing through the ranks of archangels, angels, humans, animals and plants.

1.34 a, b The geological specimens in Pope's Twickenham grotto are a survival of Nature, 'unadorned' and 'Nature Methodiz'd'.

Pope also wrote of 'the amiable Simplicity of unadorned Nature, that spreads over the Mind a more noble sort of Tranquillity, and a loftier Sensation of Pleasure, than can be raised from the nicer Scenes of Art'.[30] Here, he uses 'Nature' in a sense close to 'wild nature'. Inserting 'unadorned Nature' into the Neoplatonic axiom revolutionised the art of garden design during the eighteenth century.

The use of 'nature' to mean empirical reality was not an eighteenth-century innovation. J.D. Hunt explains that Cicero conceived wild landscape as a First Nature and the agricultural landscape as a Second Nature so that, in sixteenth-century Italy, gardens could be regarded as a Third Nature.[31] In eighteenth-century England, study of the First Nature was given renewed significance by the philosophical school known as empiricism. There was a steady swing from Cartesian rationalism to the empiricism of Bacon, Hobbes, Locke and Hume. In the nineteenth century, this led to a botanical appreciation of plants (see p. 318). Gardens became an example in the discussion of man's relationship to nature. T.H. Huxley, whose advocacy of evolutionary theory earned him the sobriquet 'Darwin's Bulldog', regarded his garden as a work of art, in contrast to the state of nature which preceded its design.[32]

Summary

Her cosmology is open to question but Dorothy Frances Gurney's ever-popular verse (Figure 1.35) reflects a truth about gardens: their design has been influenced by views of the interrelationships between God, man and nature. The following list gives instances of these relationships and, in brackets, examples of the resultant approach to the design of enclosed outdoor space:

- If gods control the natural world, they should be propitiated through ritual and sacrifice (religious/astronomical compounds).
- If it is natural for kings to become gods after death, they should be provided with temples and gardens for use in the afterlife (temple and pyramid compounds in the Ancient World).
- If the gods of nature intervene in our daily lives, sacrificial offerings should be made in a sacred place, such as an altar in a wood (sacred groves, Classical temples, domestic garden shrines).
- If the natural forms have a godlike existence in a perfect world they should be incorporated into architectural and garden design (Graeco-Roman sacred geometry).
- If the nature of the world is revealed to mankind through religion, then gardens, as places for contemplation, should symbolise the perfection of nature (medieval gardens).
- If the best knowledge of nature comes from the ancients, then modern

gardens should be made in the style of ancient gardens (Renaissance gardens).

- If the natural order is revealed to man through reason, then gardens should be based on mathematical ideas and perspective (Baroque gardens).
- If nature is best interpreted through empirical science, then gardens should exhibit a great range of phenomena: natural, artificial and emotional (Romantic gardens).
- If nature is best understood through scientific analysis, then gardens should be based on the principles of abstraction (Modern/Abstract gardens).
- If our understanding of nature depends on our conceptual framework, then concepts should have a central place in the design of gardens (Postmodern/conceptual gardens).

Modified and combined, the above ideas have generated the styles of garden design which are the subject of this book. The stylistic progression is summarised by the diagrams shown in Figure 1.36.

1.35 Dorothy Frances Gurney's verse contains a truth about garden design: it has been much influenced by ideas about God:

The kiss of the sun for pardon,
The song of the birds for mirth,
One is nearer God's Heart in a garden
*Than anywhere else on earth.**

Note:
* Gurney, D.F., *Poems*, London: Country Life, 1913.

Organisation of the book

The following chapters trace the development of gardens through 12,000 years. For the period from 10,000 BCE to 1400 CE, the discussion is mainly of garden types (e.g. 'temple garden' and 'hunting park'), because there are too few records and too few examples for detailed stylistic analysis. For the period from 1400 to 1700, gardens are placed in the art-historical categories to which they belong (e.g. Renaissance and Baroque). For the period from 1700 to 2000, names relating to styles of garden design are used (e.g. Picturesque and Gardenesque), this being possible because of the fuller records of gardens made in modern times. Art-historical categories are used in the chapter titles to relate garden design to the other arts. It must, however, be recognised that most of the categorisations can be – and have been – deconstructed. As long ago as 1915, Wölfflin wrote: 'We denote the series of periods with the names Early Renaissance, High Renaissance, and Baroque, names which mean little and must lead to misunderstanding in their application to south and north, but are hardly to be ousted now.'[33]

The geographical coverage of the book centres on Europe but with some excursions. Geographically and chronologically, we begin in West Asia. In looking at twentieth-century gardens, work in North and South America is mentioned. Other periods in history and parts of the world, including India, China, Japan, Africa south of the Sahara, Oceania and pre-Columbian America, are not covered because they belong to different traditions: this book is concerned with gardens made under the influence of Western philosophy, with 'Western' meaning 'west of the Persian Gulf'. Reference to

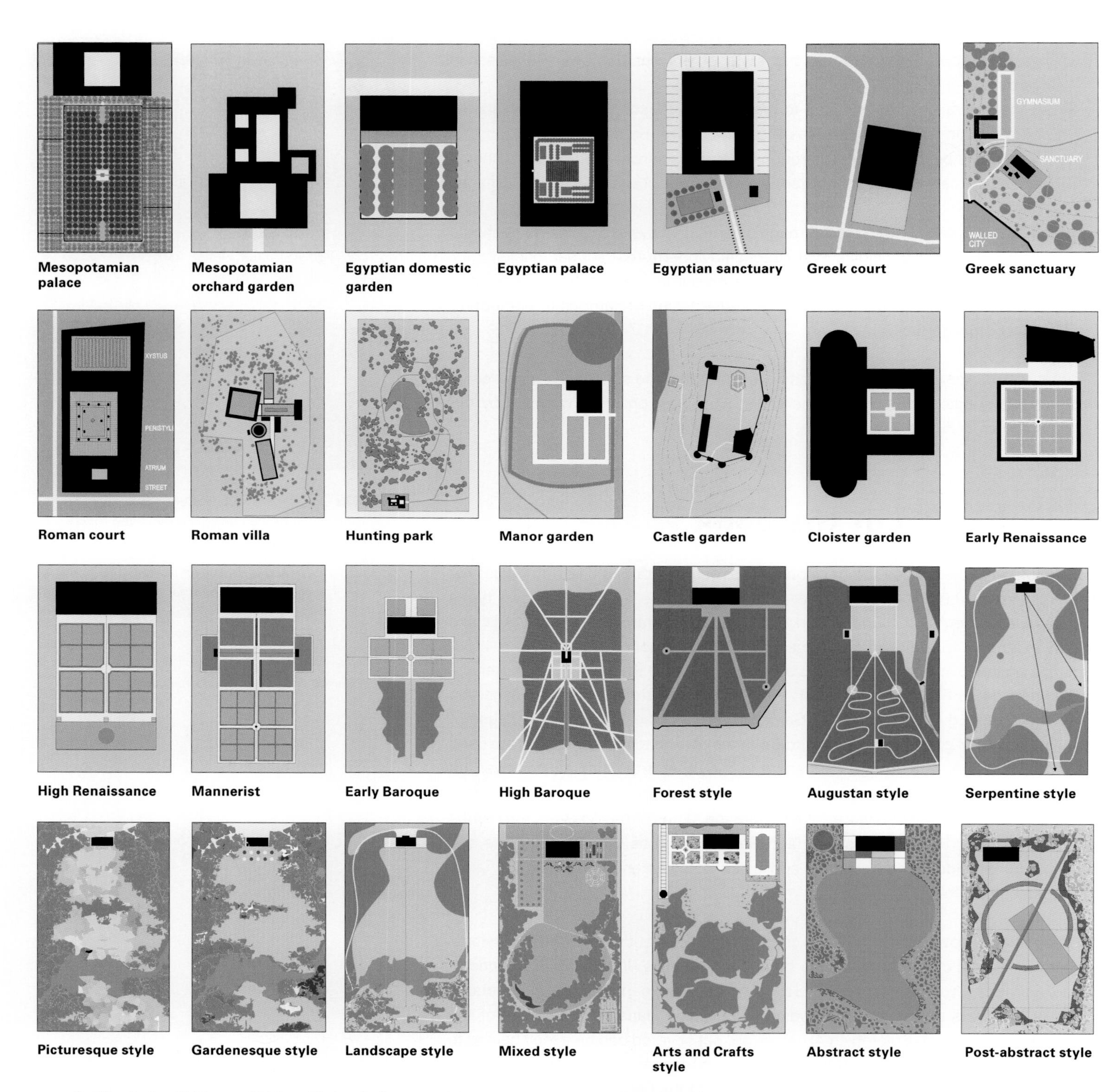

1.36 Garden design 2000 BCE–2000 CE. The early diagrams show garden types and the later diagrams show garden styles.

national characteristics is under-emphasised, partly because garden design has long been an international art and partly because nation-states are of recent origin. Empire-builders, marriage-brokers and travellers have always roamed the world and have often been able to make themselves understood in a widely spoken tongue. At the start of the Roman era they could use Greek in Southern Europe and Celtic in Northern Europe. After the fall of Rome, Latin could be used everywhere in the West for 1000 years. Eventually, it was replaced by French, English and then American.

The nine historical chapters are in two parts with subsections. The first part of each chapter outlines the ways in which social, geographical, philosophical and artistic ideas have interacted to create gardens. The second part of each chapter contains an analysis of garden plans, commencing with a style diagram and giving selected examples. The style diagrams are intended to parallel the elevational diagrams used in synoptic histories of architecture with sections and elevations to show the six compositional elements of buildings (walls, doors, windows, floors, roofs and stairs). Plans with north points show the six compositional elements of gardens (landform, water, vegetation, horizontal structures, vertical structures and climate). Garden and landscape design can be defined as the arts of composing these elements to create commodity, firmness and delight in outdoor space. Key dates are given for examples, relating to their inception, completion, high point or (in the case of Pompeii, for example) their destruction. The date ranges given in chapter titles are inescapably arbitrary.

Since the book covers a wide geographical region and a long period of time, it is sure to contain errors. There is also a little guesswork. As Barry Kemp wrote of his work at Amarna, 'It has proved impossible to write a history of Akhenaten's reign which does not embrace an element of historical fiction.'[34] Speculations of my own are identified as such. Sources are given and the examples are accompanied by quotations which readers can use to find famous accounts of the gardens.[35]

Generally, new plans and new photographs have been used instead of old plans and drawings. Contours are included where they could be obtained. I love old illustrations but they are widely reproduced elsewhere and, because they were drawn in different styles for different purposes, it is less easy to use them to conduct a narrative. The use of colour on plans makes it easier to identify the six great compositional elements of gardens and landscapes.

CHAPTER 2

Garden origins, 10,000–1000 BCE

2.0 Abisko National Park, in Lapland, suggests the character of Europe's Paleolithic landscape at the point when the woolly mammoth was facing extinction. They ate tundra grass in summer and leaves and bark in winter.

2.1 Paleolithic hunters lived in small nomadic bands, moving from place to place in response to seasonal opportunities for hunting, fishing and gathering wild foods.

Source: Illustration from Figuier, L., *L' homme primitif*, Paris, 1870.

Introduction

In 20,000 BCE, North Europe was frozen and its former inhabitants had retreated south. By 10,000 BCE, the ice had melted and some of the land was thinly peopled by nomadic hunter–gatherers. The landscape remained wooded and waterlogged but woolly rhinos and mammoths were facing extinction. A good deal has been learned about the period but it remains pre-historic with no permanent settlements, no farms and no gardens.

Conditions were more favourable in West Asia and, during the fourth millennium BCE, history began at Sumer[1] in the precise sense that this is where writing was invented. Cultivation and settlement developed, *c.*9500 BCE, in the valley between the lands which are now Jordan and Israel. This initiated the Neolithic Age, in which gardening also began. The question this chapter seeks to answer is: when and where were the first gardens made? It is not an easy question, because evidence is scarce and because the archetypal garden of the modern era developed from three distinct prototypes:

1. *Residential enclosures*: Ancient dwellings often had yards. Some may have contained plants but yards were intensively used and often surfaced with clay. The people who cared for them were probably female.
2. *Horticultural enclosures*: When cultivation began, perhaps a thousand years after the first settlements were formed, agricultural crops were grown but

2.2 a, b Charles Darwin owned a highly evolved garden. It was designed for horticulture, pleasure and beauty, as well as being used to further his understanding of nature through scientific experiments.

the scale of operations, and the implements used, were horticultural. The early cultivators are likely to have been female.

3 *Sacred enclosures*: It is thought that places were sacred before enclosures were made or temples built. They were places to make contact with spirits, gods and god-kings. Most priests were male.

This chapter deals with the overlapping histories of residential, horticultural and sacred enclosures, replacing the faulty 'creation myth', I wrote in 2005:

> *The enclosure of outdoor space began* c.10,000 BCE . *Though it can never be known when or where the first garden was made, one can imagine that it was formed by one of our ancestors who, living in a cave, had put up a barrier to protect the family from marauding beasts and brutes. In time, such barriers would have pushed outwards. Branches could then have been laid from rock to ground and branch to branch, creating fenced enclosures to protect domestic animals, to grow food and to enable the family to relax in the glorious sunshine of a Neolithic evening. The first pleasure gardens, surely, were made by women.*[2]

In fact, living in caves was never the norm, settlement predates cultivation and nomads were not cultivators. The origin of domestic gardens in the modern sense of 'enclosed outdoor space attached to dwellings and designed for use and beauty' is best explained by an evolutionary progression – and Charles Darwin's own garden is a fine example of the species.

Darwin was attacked and ridiculed in the nineteenth century for identifying the gorilla and the chimpanzee as 'man's nearest allies'[3] but his belief was confirmed in the twentieth century, by the fossil record and by studies of mitochondrial DNA. *Homo sapiens sapiens* appeared 150,000–200,000 years ago in North East Africa and began to develop skills in language, tool-making, music and art. Our ancestors migrated 'out of Africa' some 70,000 years ago and spread across the globe, replacing Neanderthal man. The migration took place during the last glacial period and modern humans probably entered Europe some 45,000 years ago. Wearing animal skins began about 100,000 years ago, as a response either to northward migration or global cooling. The earliest visual evidence for clothing, on a Siberian statuette, dates from *c.*25,000 BCE.[4]

2.3 The dog was the first animal to be domesticated and is the subject of many garden sculptures (Newby Hall).

The dog was the first animal to be domesticated perhaps as early as 30,000 BCE. The reason for this was hunting. The oldest evidence for the domestication of cereals, *c.*9000 BCE, comes from the Fertile Crescent and DNA analysis of plants indicates that the oldest cultivated grains are natives of this region and South Anatolia. Many theories explain the origins of farming and settlement and since no one theory explains all the evidence, each may have some validity.[5] The Oasis Theory is that as the climate became drier, humans ran short of food and began to settle near water supplies and fish supplies. The Hilly Flanks Theory is that farming began on the flanks of mountains where wild grains could be harvested and stored. The Feasting Theory is that early societies wished to accumulate food for religious festivals and displays of power. The Demographic Theory is that food became scarce as populations grew, so that it was no longer possible to collect sufficient food from the wild, making cultivation a necessity. Paleolithic communities knew how to make clothing and shelters but are unlikely to have enclosed outdoor space until they began making year-round settlements.

Settlement/residential enclosures

Settlement origins

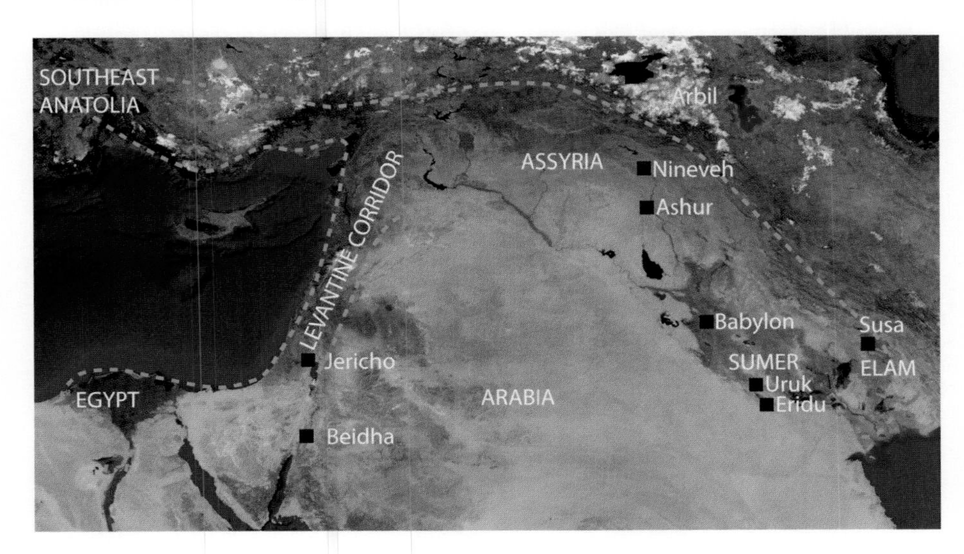

2.4 Agriculture and city-building began in the Levantine Corridor. This area extends from the lower Jordan valley to the Damascus Basin. The rift valley in which it is located was a migration route from Africa to Eurasia. The Fertile Crescent is shown by the dotted green line.

2.5 Beidha is a Natufian settlement, 4 km north of Petra in the Jordan Valley, built in what was then woodland. The dwellings were semi-subterranean with plastered floors and livestock pens.

2.6 The Natufians ground cereals but their grain is thought to have been harvested from the wild.

Source: Illustration from Figuier, L., *L'homme primitif*, Paris, 1870.

The first Neolithic settlements, classified as Natufian, are found in the Levantine Corridor. It is part of the Jordan Rift Valley which runs north from the Red Sea and divides the African and Arabian tectonic plates. The Levantine Corridor was one of the main routes by which humans migrated 'out of Africa'. Well suited to farming and settlement, it had a Mediterranean climate with oak and pistachio woods, wild olives and an undergrowth of wild grasses and grains:

> *The Mediterranean region provided lush herbaceous vegetation which promoted raising herds of domesticated herbivores. Annual grasses with large seeds such as wheat, adapted to local environmental conditions, were domesticated and function at present as one of the basic sources of foot for human kind. Pulses were domesticated too from wild species growing at present in this area. Olives, the fruits of which have been used since prehistoric times, still grow as an important component in the maquis covering the mountainous parts of Israel.*[6]

In Natufian times, the climate of the Levant was wetter than today and a built environment became 'the one feature of the Neolithic world that was entirely new'.[7] A settled life is thought to have become possible through easy access to a wide range of foods: from hunting, from fishing and from gathering fruit, nuts and cereals. Sedentary communities developed, as at Beidha. Flint-bladed sickles were used for harvesting wild grains and shaped stones were used for grinding flour. Storage pits came into use. Round dwellings were built with diameters of 3–6 m. They were semi-subterranean with stone walls and roofs made of brushwood and grass. The dead were buried beneath floors, possibly in disused huts.[8] No evidence of domesticated plants has been found and this is taken as evidence for the Natufians not having been cultivators.

2.7 Jericho has been inhabited since *c.*9000 BCE and the PPNA settlement is on Sultan's Hill. It had a good spring and overlooks the Jordan Valley.

Grains of wild barley are small and connected to the stem by a brittle rachis. Domestic grains are larger and have a thicker rachis, making it easier to harvest grain without the seed falling off. This gives archaeobotanists a means of identifying domesticated plants.[9] Mithen views the early settlers' relationship with wild plants as follows:

> *We have no knowledge of how the Natufian people thought about the plants around them. But in light of the permanence of their settlements, the many mouths needing to be fed, and the abundance of grinding stones, pestles and mortars, wild plants appear to have been managed in a way that we would recognise as cultivation. I suspect that the stands of wild cereals, the groves of nut trees, the patches of lupins, wild peas, and lentils were tended as a wild garden, and that they were manipulated and managed, used in social relations and infused with symbolic meanings.*[10]

Jericho, 170 km north of Beidha, had a good supply of water and was one of the early places where settlement and farming became established. The oldest known settlement dates from *c.*9000 BCE and shows no evidence of cultivation. A new town was built during the Pre-Pottery Neolithic A period (PPNA , *c.*8000 BCE) on a tell site now called Sultan's Hill. It was a 4 ha settlement with a protective wall. The wall is thought to have been a defence against floods, because it does not surround the settlement.[11] Circular dwellings were constructed in mud-brick and there were no streets. The Pre-Pottery Neolithic B city (PPNB, *c.*7000 BCE) had streets and rectilinear houses with mud brick on stone foundations. Rooms were grouped round courtyards. Courtyards were clay-surfaced and used for cooking. Rooms had plastered floors. Emmer wheat, barley and pulses were cultivated in small fields. There is no

2.8 A reconstruction of Çatalhöyök, near Konya. The settlement was on a tell site in what was then a marshy region. There were no streets and cultivation is thought to have taken place outside the boundaries of the settlement.

evidence of aesthetic horticulture or for the existence of the type of space in which it might have taken place.

Çatalhöyük is a famous Neolithic settlement near Konya in modern Turkey. It dates from 6500–5500 BCE and is now a dry tell in agricultural land. When occupied, the terrain was 'that of a marshy flood plain with extensive seasonal flooding and a typically cooler and moist climate'.[12] Communal yards have been found but there were no streets. House walls were shared with neighbours and access to rooms was by ladders from openings in roofs. Ancestors were buried beneath house floors, perhaps after their bones had been cleaned by vultures. Exposure to vultures is known to have been practised in Persia at a later date. There was no space for horticultural activity inside Çatalhöyük but cultivation took place outside the boundary of the settlement.

Mesopotamian cities

Mesopotamian cities were built on tell sites and protected by fortifications. The western shore of the Persian Gulf was home to the Sumerians from 5300–1940 BCE and Uruk (4100–2900 BCE) became the largest city in Sumer. It was protected by a 10 km wall enclosing 435 ha of land. This is 'where history began' in the limited sense that writing was invented in Sumer. Temples were centrally placed and may have had a palatial role in the period before palaces became separate. At a later date, both temples and palaces were designed with courtyards.[13] Tells grew as buildings decayed and were rebuilt, perhaps giving rise to the ziggurat form of later temple mounds.

Sumer is regarded as the place where the characteristics taken to define civilisation first came together. Gordon Childe listed ten characteristics of the 'urban revolution'.[14] The most significant for us, because they created the conditions for aesthetic gardens

2.9 The Uruk countryside is 'a landscape dotted with urban ruins testifying to past intensive settlement, prosperity, and even greatness, today is virtually empty and wholly neglected'.* In ancient times 'swamps, arid steppes, gardens, and fields were continuously interspersed'.** The photograph was taken from the main tell of Uruk and it is possible that future excavations will find evidence of gardens in this region.

Notes:
* Adams, R.McC. and Nissen, H.J., *The Uruk Countryside*, Chicago: University of Chicago Press, 1972, p. 1.
** Ibid., p. 86.

to be made, were cities, monumental structures, writing, farming and kingship. Settlements became organisations ruled by kings who needed power and prestige to maintain civil societies. Temple buildings were dwellings for gods and, since kings were descended from gods, they had a primary role in religious ceremonies. Temple estates owned gardens irrigated by canals. When temple buildings were on higher land, their gardens must have been at some remove. But when temples were on lower land, they could have adjoined gardens. It is a fair assumption that religion influenced the design of the world's first aesthetic gardens. Sumerian kings enjoyed luxurious surroundings, claimed descent from gods and required prestige to organise city-states. Assyrian kings did not regard themselves as gods and palaces became separate from temples.

Private dwellings in Sumer, like royal and sacred enclosures, were attached to walled outdoor spaces but the following comment, from Sayce in 1908, now seems

2.10 Ziggurats reached nearer to the gods as they grew.

2.11 Housing in Ur. The courtyards were used for domestic activities. It is not known if they contained plants but it seems unlikely. The name Gay Street was given by Leonard Woolley in remembrance of his days as an Oxford student.

erroneous. He wrote: 'By the side of the house was an enclosed garden planted with trees and other plants.'[15] The dwellings which have been excavated are on dry hills and their small outdoor yards were used for cooking and storage. In Ur, they have clay tiles and it is known that 'the central space is in most cases a courtyard since it is provided with a system of drainage'.[16] Families must have carried water to their homes but growing plants on hills in a dry country would have been difficult. The gardens mentioned by Gilgamesh are most likely to have been on the low land between the base of the tell and the walls of the city. There is no visual evidence concerning the design of Gilgamesh's gardens but one can imagine them to have been walled orchards with canals and paths. It is known that canals 'routinely flowed through cities as well as alongside them'.[17] Something of the planting in Mesopotamian palace gardens is known from a cuneiform tablet listing the plants used by King Marduk-apla-iddina II, who reigned at Bablyon *c.*700 BCE. The tablets show plants in 16 groups. Many of those which can be identified are edible: onion, garlic, leek, lettuce, dill, origanum, fennel, mint. Some plants have picturesque names: dear-horn-plant, you-strike, bird-dung-plant and slave-girl-buttock-plant.[18] The latter might have been a gourd, used to make containers and musical instruments.[19]

Detailed information on Mesopotamian gardens is a large gap in the history of gardens. Future excavations, or scientific techniques yet unknown, may fill the gap and may reveal that temple gardens and pleasure gardens were influenced by aesthetic considerations, as they were in Egypt. At present, significantly more is known about the gardens of Ancient Egypt, despite the fact that the cities have largely disappeared, because the land on which they stood was subsequently cultivated and washed by flood waters for thousands of years.

2.12 Homer describes Troy as a walled city with an *agora*, an acropolis and a palace, which had a throne room and 50 marble chambers for the king's sons.*

Note:
* Wood, M., *In Search of the Trojan War*, London: BBC Books, 2005, p. 20.

Egyptian cities

Egypt's dynastic history begins at the start of the Bronze Age, *c.*3050 BCE. Records from the New Kingdom (1550–1070 BCE) include the world's earliest visual representations of gardens and some archaeological remains. Unless and until other evidence is found, Egypt can be identified as the first place in the world where private domestic gardens in the sense of 'planted outdoor space designed for use and beauty in conjunction with dwellings' are known to have been made. Many factors contributed to the Nile Valley's suitability for individual domestic gardens: the desert protected the Egyptians from invasion; water was always available from the river; annual floods washed the soil free of salts; the near-rainless climate was ideal for outdoor living. Egyptian garden types and designs will be reviewed in Chapter 3.

European settlements

The lands around the Aegean had Neolithic settlements by 6500 BCE, which, in the main, were small low-density agricultural villages. By the Bronze Age (2000 BCE), the Aegean also had fortified towns. They were stone-built, and architecturally distinct, but with functional similarities to the cities of West Asia. Troy, Tiryns and Mycenae, had centrally located palaces and private dwellings with courtyards. The plants mentioned by Homer (see p. 113) and shown on painted vases are most likely to have been in gardens outside town walls, as will be discussed in Chapter 3. Aegean civilisation developed in the context of trade and other links with West Asia. It was the only part of Europe to have a wine-and-palace civilisation in the Bronze Age. Western Europe had a different settlement pattern.

2.13 A re-created Bronze Age village (made in 1992 at St Fagans in Wales). The buildings are based on archaeological evidence from both Wales and England. It is not known how the space between the round houses was treated in Bronze Age settlements but it may well have been trampled earth, as here.

2.14 Hedeby (or Haithabu) in Jutland was a medieval settlement with dwellings not unlike Neolithic long houses.

From 2500 to 800 BCE, Europe's Bronze Age settlements had rectangular dwellings and, especially in Italy and Britain, circular dwellings. Some settlements were on tell sites and others on open sites. The ratio of built:unbuilt land ranged between 2:1 and 1:3 on tell sites and between 1:3 and 1:15 on open sites.[20] On tell sites, 'there was certainly no room for animal grazing or plant cultivation in the village'.[21] But low density open sites 'could have had garden plots between the buildings, suitable for some cultivation of vegetables and the grazing of a few animals, though not for more extensive grain-crop production which would still have been located outside the built-up area altogether'.[22] There is, however, no evidence of aesthetic horticulture at this time and the safest assumption is that it did not exist. European societies had settlements and chiefs but they did not have a palace civilisation (see p. 38).

Horticultural enclosures

Cultivation origins

The distinction between horticulture and agriculture is of Roman origin. Agriculture takes place in fields (*agri*) and horticulture is 'culture in gardens' (*horti*) involving 'The preparation of land for planting and the tending of crops using only the hoe or digging stick; characterised especially by the absence of use of the plow.'[23] On this definition, horticulture is older than agriculture but, as Harris observes:

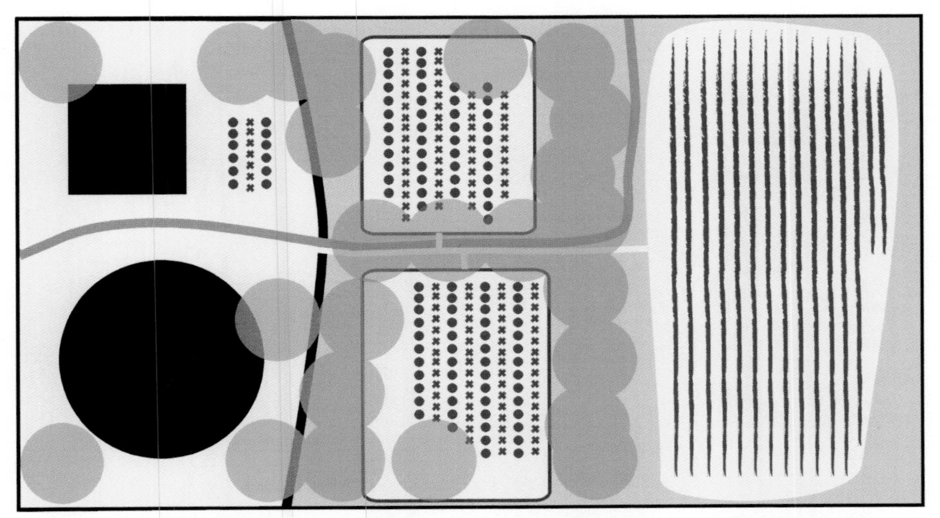

2.15 We now make a distinction between settlements, agriculture and horticulture but in Neolithic times the differences were less marked.

2.16 Ploughs came into use *c.*3500 BCE and the main developments in the next 5000 years involved the use of horses, wheels, iron and mould boards.

> *There is little agreement about what precisely is meant by such terms as agriculture, horticulture, cultivation, domestication and husbandry. This semantic confusion militates against clear thinking about the phenomena we investigate, leads to misunderstanding, and can provoke unnecessary disputes over interpretation of the evidence.*[24]

Plant domestication and cultivation are not things which, like the TV, were invented at a known time and place. Cultivation probably evolved in many places. The ard, a primitive plough, is thought to have come into use during the fourth millennium BCE. 'We do not know when it was first introduced, or where, or by whom.'[25] But we do know that before its invention cultivators used a digging stick or a hoe made from a crooked branch and practised what is called hoe-farming. Seeds were planted in holes or furrows and covered with soil. The first seeds to have been planted are likely to have been cereals and they could have been sown in former grassland, forest clearings or along water margins. Clearing sequential areas of forest for cultivation is known as 'slash and burn' or 'swidden' agriculture but ploughs would not have been able to clear the roots of trees. Clearings could have been protected from grazing animals with barriers made from branches. The use of cultivation techniques to replace wild grassland with domesticated cereal species would have benefitted from protective barriers, as would plots irrigated by diverting river water onto dry soil. But whatever barriers were used have long since rotted away.

Studies of hunter–gatherer communities have revealed much diversity, depending on environmental, cultural and dietary factors. Different ways of life were consequent

2.17 James Tissot, in a painting of *Ruth Gleaning*, illustrates the fact that women were involved with the origins of cultivation.

upon living in forest, steppe, marsh, tundra etc. conditions. Yet with this qualification, a few generalisations can be made. In late-Paleolithic times it was common for nomadic hunter–gatherers to live in bands. They sometimes slept in caves but they knew how to make circular and rectangular huts with branches, skins, bones, grass and leaves. When nomads became farmers, a need for enclosures to separate domesticated crops and animals must have arisen. Circular huts were typical of nomad societies and rectangular huts of sedentary societies.[26] A Paleolithic division of labour is probable, with men hunting and women gathering.[27] The early evidence for plant and animal domestication in West Asia and Europe is reviewed below. Cultivation also began in South America and East Asia but without influencing European gardens.

Cultivation in the Fertile Crescent

The Fertile Crescent stretches from the Mediterranean to the Persian Gulf (see Figure 2.4, p. 31). In the Pre-Pottery Neolithic A period (PPNA, *c.*9000 BCE), the crescent of cultivation included South Anatolia, the Levantine Corridor and North Mesopotamia. By 5000 BCE, it encompassed Egypt and South Mesopotamia. The Fertile Crescent is where civilisation began, probably in this sequence: (1) construction of permanent settlements; (2) plant domestication; (3) farm animal domestication. Lerro suggests that:

> *Women probably led the revolution from foraging to planting because planting is closer to gathering than it is to hunting. They took the lead in seeding, tending, and harvesting the plants. They learned about the healing properties of plants ... Men did the unskilled labor of clearing the brush and preparing the ground while doing occasional hunting.*[28]

2.18 Bronze Age societies practised horticulture and made hoes from crooked sticks. The drawing is charming, but the picket fencing is, to say the least, improbable.

Source: Illustration from Figuier, L., *L'homme primitif*, Paris, 1870.

2.19 The oldest known pictograms for garden. They are written in the cuneiform script of Uruk IV (*c.*3100 BCE, left), in Sumerian (*c.*2500 BCE, centre) and in Old Babylonian (*c.*1800 BCE, right). The word for garden was *sar* in Sumerian and *kiru* in Babylonian.

The availability of cereals was a pivotal factor in the development of settlements, because they are high-energy foods which can be stored. Grains occur naturally in the transition zones between forests and mountains and also between wet and dry zones. Wild grains were harvested and probably flourished when dropped or sown near dwellings and fertilised with human or animal excreta. They would also benefit from being protected from animals. This is a possible origin of enclosures for cultivation but the crops, as noted, were not vegetables or fruits. They were millet, spelt and einkorn wheat. Harris states that:

> *The earliest well attested evidence we have at present for agriculture and pastoralism anywhere in Eurasia comes from the western half of the so-called 'Fertile Crescent' in Southwest Asia: more specifically, from sites in the 'Levantine Corridor' of woodland, moist steppe and rift-valley oases and in the middle Euphrates Valley. Here the remains of domesticated cereals (barley, einkorn and emmer wheat) and pulses (pea, chickpea, lentil) and flax have been dated at such sites as Jericho, Tell Aswad and Tell Abu Hureyra, to the eighth millennium BC.*[29]

The domestication of cereals had many consequences. Permanent settlements could be made, population densities could increase and technical skills could be enhanced. Opportunities to make tools increased and people were able to specialise in their use. It became possible to organise and stratify societies. Food surpluses were stored but they also had to be defended, as did the tools used for their production. Trade took place, leading to a need for records, writing, laws and kings. Rulers benefitted from prestige and stored food for festive displays of wealth and power. The first place where these developments are known to have come together is Sumer, which is also

2.20 In Mesopotamia, cereals were grown in small fields and vegetables beneath the shade of palm trees in orchard gardens (a montage reconstruction). They were called *sar* in Sumerian and *kiru* in Babylonian.

where the first literate culture and the first gardens in written history developed. Scribes cut the ends of reeds to print wedge-shaped marks on damp clay. The marks were used to create pictograms and, at a later date, to create an abstract script. The Sumerian word *sar* meant orchard or garden and was written with a pictogram showing an enclosure (Figure 2.19). One of the world's oldest literary works, the *Epic of Gilgamesh* mentions the presence of gardens in the Sumerian city of Uruk. Here is an extract from Tablet 1:

> *Go up on the wall of Uruk and walk around,*
> *examine its foundation, inspect its brickwork thoroughly.*
> *Is not (even the core of) the brick structure made of kiln-fired brick,*
> *and did not the Seven Sages themselves lay out its plans?*
> *One league city, one league palm gardens, one league lowlands, the open area(?) of the Ishtar Temple, three leagues and the open area(?) of Uruk it (the wall) encloses.*[30]

A 'palm garden' (*sar*) in Uruk was probably an irrigated orchard planted with fruiting and flowering species. It is unlikely to have been attached to dwellings in the manner of modern gardens. Sumerian dwellings were on dry hills, known as tells, raised above the floodplain of the Euphrates. Palaces and smaller dwellings had rooms integrated with enclosed outdoor space. Palace courtyards were used for ceremonies, social gatherings and family life. Yards attached to private houses were used for cooking, work and storage. The 'palm gardens' in the *Epic of Gilgamesh* were probably on low-lying land below the tell on which Uruk was built. This fits with what Kramer identifies as the world's oldest recorded advice on horticulture. He summarises the advice as follows:

> *Once upon a time there lived a gardener by the name of Shukallituda, whose diligent efforts at gardening had met with nothing but failure. Although he had carefully watered his furrows and garden patches, the plants had withered away. The raging winds smote his face with the 'dust of mountains.' All that he had carefully tended turned desolate. He thereupon lifted his eyes east and west to the starry heavens, studied the omens, observed and learned the divine laws. Having acquired new wisdom, he planted the [as yet unidentified]* sarbatu *tree in the garden, a tree shows broad shade lasts from sunrise to sunset. As a consequence of this horticultural experiment, Shukallituda's garden blossomed forth with all kinds of greens.*[31]

Shukallituda may be the first gardener's name in history. The following advice, from a Sumerian tablet, explains how land came to be 'treated as settled' and the hazard of wandering oxen:

> *In days of yore a farmer gave (these) instructions to his son: When you are about to cultivate your field, take care to open the irrigation works (so that) their water does not rise too high in it (the field). When you have emptied it of water, watch the field's wet ground that it stays even; let no wandering ox trample it. Chase the prowlers and have it treated as settled land. Clear it with ten narrow axes (weighing no more than) 2/3 of a pound each. Its stubble (?) should be torn up by hand and tied in bundles; its narrow holes shall be gone over with a drag; and the four sides of the field shall be fenced about.*[32]

Mesopotamian orchard gardens had three tiers of productive plants. Date palms provided the top layer, fruit trees the middle layer and vegetables the lower layer.[33] This type of cultivation is possible only when, as in Mesopotamia and Egypt, there are high temperatures, much sunshine and a plentiful supply of irrigation water. When the Euphrates flooded, it left a deposit of silt which created levees and a fertile flood plain. It was then easy to draw irrigation water through the levee to rich soils. The Sumerian word *sar* is equivalent to the Akkadian word *kiru*.[34]

In Egypt, the earliest evidence for agriculture dates from *c.*5400 BCE. Surprisingly, since Egypt used to be regarded as the cradle of civilisation, this is some 4000 years after the inception of agriculture and 2000 years after the earliest evidence for agriculture in Crete and Greece. Agriculture reached Egypt from West Asia, probably via the Sinai Peninsula, and the plants grown were not native to Egypt. The oldest

2.21 a, b Drawings in the Tomb of Nakht show Egyptians hunting food on the banks of the Nile (top painting), harvesting grapes (lower paintings) and carrying out various agricultural operations.

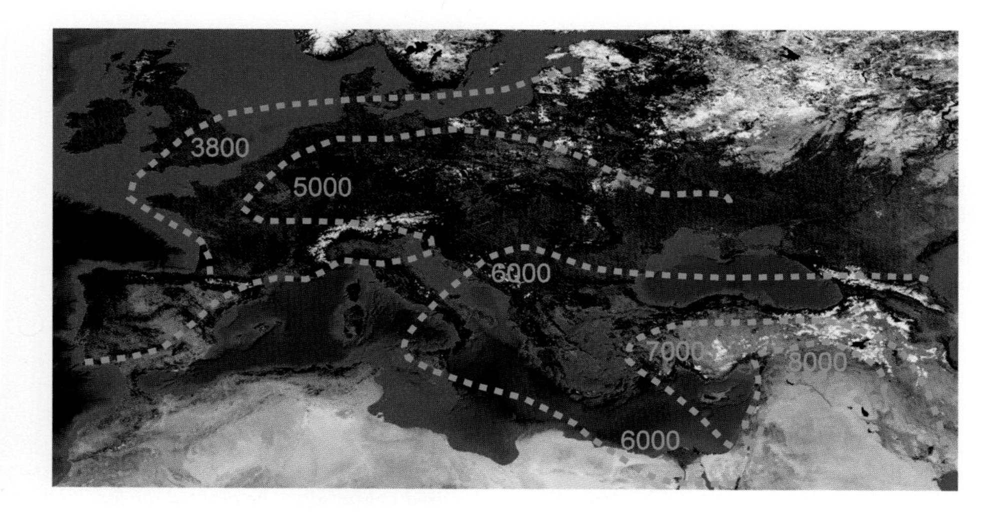

2.22 Wild einkorn, *Triticum boeoticum*, growing on the slopes of Karadag, near Konya in Turkey. This was one of the first wheat grains to be cultivated.

2.23 Agriculture spread into Europe and Egypt after 7000 BCE with the Neolithic package of crops, animals and farming techniques.

evidence for Egyptian agriculture is from the Fayum Oasis and Merimde Beni-Salama.[35] A group of 164 granaries was found in the Fayum containing traces of emmer wheat, barley and flax. Pens, windbreaks, granaries and tools were used.[36] Food was grown on land flooded by the Nile and on additional land watered from basins. Small rectangular plots were used for vegetables and herbs: onions, leeks, garlic, peas, lentils, chickpeas, radishes, cabbage, cucumber and lettuce. Grapes, trained on arbours, were used for eating and for making wine. Figs, pomegranates, persea and other fruits were also grown.[37]

The history, geography and culture of Egypt differ from that of the Mesopotamia. Upper Egypt is a narrow valley cut into a rocky desert. Building stone was freely available. There was a sharp boundary between the Red Land, which was dry, and the Black Land, which was watered by the Nile (see Figure 3.30, p. 90). Floods were predictable annual events. Palaces for living pharaohs were located on the Black Land, built with mud brick, often on low mounds. Mortuary temples for dead pharaohs were built in stone on the fringe of the Red Land. Egyptian palace gardens, as discussed in Chapter 3, are the oldest known domestic gardens in the modern sense. Tomb paintings (see pp. 80–5) show many examples of spaces which fit the description of a garden as 'an enclosed outdoor space attached to a dwelling and designed for use and beauty'. The combination of pools, walks and plants is astonishingly similar to modern gardens, though the building materials and the emphases on food and symbolism in the planting differ.

As shown on the map in Figure 2.23, cultivation and plant domestication spread from the Fertile Crescent. The fact that dispersal had a substantial role in the spread of agriculture is proven by the fact that the plant and animal species used elsewhere all originate in the Crescent: wheat, barley, olives, sheep and goats.

2.24 a, b Franchthi Cave was occupied for 20,000 years and abandoned *c.*3000 BCE. In Neolithic times there were rectangular dwellings on the land which is now a bay.

Cultivation in South Europe

Knowledge of cultivation techniques spread by sea and land to Crete, Greece, Sicily, the Balkans, France, Italy, Spain and beyond. In Greece, the earliest evidence of agriculture comes from the Franchthi Cave in the Peloponnese. The cave itself was in use for 20,000 years and the bones of domesticated sheep and goats have been dated to *c.*7000 BCE.[38] Halstead reasons that crop production in Neolithic Greece was on a small scale but intensive so that it 'may have more closely resembled recent horticulture than agriculture'.[39] Houses near the Franchthi shoreline ('*paralia*') were rectangular. In Neolithic times sea levels were lower and the shore was some 5 km from the mouth of the cave. Food was cooked out of doors and figurines interpreted as fertility symbols have been found. Pistachio nuts were cultivated but not the olive or vine which later became the staples of Mediterranean gardening. Other Neolithic settlements found in Greece were further north, on the rich plains of Thessaly.

The island of Crete had a Bronze Age agricultural civilisation, now described as Minoan, from 2700 to 1450 BCE. The Minoans were seafarers. Their civilisation and their belief systems[40] show evidence of contact with West Asia, as do the species they cultivated: wheat, barley, vetch, chickpeas, grapes, figs, and olives. Cattle, sheep, pigs, and goats were reared. Bees were domesticated. Farmers had wooden ploughs pulled by pairs of donkeys or oxen. Fruits were grown, including figs, olives, dates, pomegranates and quince. There are text references (on tablets in Linear B script) to orchard gardens and the landscape pattern, with palace cities surrounded by farms and gardens, resembles that of Mesopotamia. The Palace of Knossos compares with

2.25 Minoan cities and agriculture developed in the context of trading links with West Asia. Crete had a palace culture and hilltop sanctuaries (Knossos).

2.26 The cultivated olive (*Olea europaea*) was introduced to Greece from the Levant and used in ornamental groves.

the Palace of Mari. Minoan civilisation was overwhelmed by invaders from mainland Greece and after 1450 BCE, Mycenaean Greek culture dominated the island.

Mainland Greece was colonised by farming communities from Western Anatolia (*c.*6500 BCE) and by 6000 BCE farming had reached Italy.[41] The dispersal of language and techniques came about through both trade and colonisation but the dates when Indo-European speakers reached Italy and mainland Greece are unknown. It could have been in the Early Neolithic (*c.*7000 BCE), or the Later Neolithic (*c.*4500 BCE) or even the Bronze Age (*c.*2000 BCE). The earliest evidence for the horse and wheeled vehicles in Greece is 3000 BCE.[42] By the first millennium BCE, plants were appreciated for their aesthetic qualities and Foxhall observes that:

> *It seems very odd the Greeks are not better known for their ornamental horticulture in all its many forms; indeed it has been suggested that the Greeks never made gardens for pleasure ... On the contrary, there is a considerable [body] of documentary, archaeological, and iconographic evidence to suggest that they did.*[43]

She explains that wealthy Greeks owned land outside walled towns which they used to make 'ornamental orchards'.[44] By the fourth century BCE, they were orderly spaces bounded by lines of trees (poplars, olives or plane trees) rather than fences. Pears, pomegranates, apples, figs and olives are mentioned in Homer's description of the orchard of Alcinous (see *Odyssey* Book VII) and Foxhall says they had an understory of rose bushes. Olive oil was used for lighting and as a culinary luxury. In gymnasia it was used for cleaning, massage and adornment. Order and symmetry were valued in orchards as they were in temples. Annual plants were also grown and pulses were important because they could be stored. Cabbage, beets, turnips, celery, onions and garlic were grown and herbs were often collected from the wild.[45] Hesiod describes the plough (ard) *c.*700 BCE.[46] The ancient Greek approach to gardens seems to have been more Mesopotamian than Egyptian.

In Southern Italy, the earliest evidence for Neolithic agriculture dates from *c.*6500 BCE.[47] Italy had more fertile land than Greece and detailed knowledge of Roman cultivation is available from literature, archaeology and the visual arts. Greek farmers used a biennial crop-and-fallow system. The Romans cropped land for two years and then fallowed it for one year.[48] Columella was the author of a famous treatise on agriculture (*De Re Rustica*). It has chapters on soils, vines, fruits, animals and gardens. Columella sees a garden as a place from which we must 'keep out people and animals'[49] and advises a 'living hedge' for this purpose.[50] The plants he expects to be grown within a garden, and for which he provides specific horticultural advice, are predominantly vegetables. His instructions are detailed. For example,

> *Cabbage should be moved when it has six leaves. In such a way that its root shall first be smeared in liquid dung, rolled up in three strips of seaweed, and then pushed home. Doing this ensures that in cooking it mushes quickly, and keeps its green colour without soda.*[51]

The Romans also practised aesthetic horticulture, as discussed in Chapter 4. While Mesopotamian and Greek palace cities were often built on dry elevated sites, the Egyptians and Romans often built their cities and palaces on agricultural land, which made it natural to incorporate planting within their cities and gardens. Geography influenced settlement patterns.

Cultivation in North Europe

Some 20,000 years ago, at the time of the Last Glacial Maximum, North Europe was covered by ice and tundra with the sea approximately 100 m below present levels. By 10,000 years ago Europe was warmer, the average level of the sea was 50 m below present levels and lowlands were densely wooded. Farming skills and the Indo-European languages spread from Anatolia into Europe at an estimated 1.3 km/year and probably more by 'technology transfer' than migration.[52] The Levantine origin of European farming techniques is proved, as elsewhere, by the species used. Emmer wheat, einkorn wheat and barley were the 'founder crops'. Sheep and goats were the 'founder animals'. In Central Europe, people of the Linear Pottery Culture (Bandkeramik) were living in agricultural communities with large rectangular 'long houses' (*c.*5500 BCE). They did not have a palace culture either then or at any point in the prehistoric era.

By 3500 BCE, agriculture had reached North and West Europe and enclosures were in use for the protection of stock and crops. Most of the surviving field boundaries

2.27 Foel Drygarn Trigarn is an Iron Age hill fort in Wales. The sites of 270 houses were identified but, given the hilltop location, horticulture is not likely to have taken place within the settlement. The three cairns are believed to be burial sites.

are in upland Britain, where they are given by the vague name 'Celtic Fields'. 'Celtic' (*keltoi*) is a Greek name for the peoples of North and West Europe. There is no evidence for these peoples having called themselves Celts, or for their having functioned as a community, but the name Celtic is now applied to a group of Indo-European languages and a style of art (La Tène) characteristic of the late Iron Age (450–100 BCE).

The best-known Celtic enclosures are the Iron Age hill forts found in Central, North and West Europe, though 'no archaeologist is satisfied with the term "hill-fort"'.[53] The term is more descriptive of a location and a method of construction than a function. Hill forts are characteristic of the Urnfield culture (*c.*1300–750 BCE), the Hallstatt culture (*c.*1200–500 BCE) and the La Tène culture (*c.*600 BCE–50 CE). Use of hill forts is thought to have been varied: some were permanent settlements, some were occupied seasonally and others were used only in times of strife or to protect valuable items, including tools and cattle. Variations in use led to variations in form. Some hill forts have tight concentric rings; some are semi-circles on sea cliffs; some appear to have been stock pens, for cattle or horses; some were craft centres; others are large enclosures with evidence of round houses, long houses, granaries and underground pits for food storage. Since many of the surviving examples are in inhospitable places, on windswept hills and cliffs, one can only imagine the sites to have been chosen

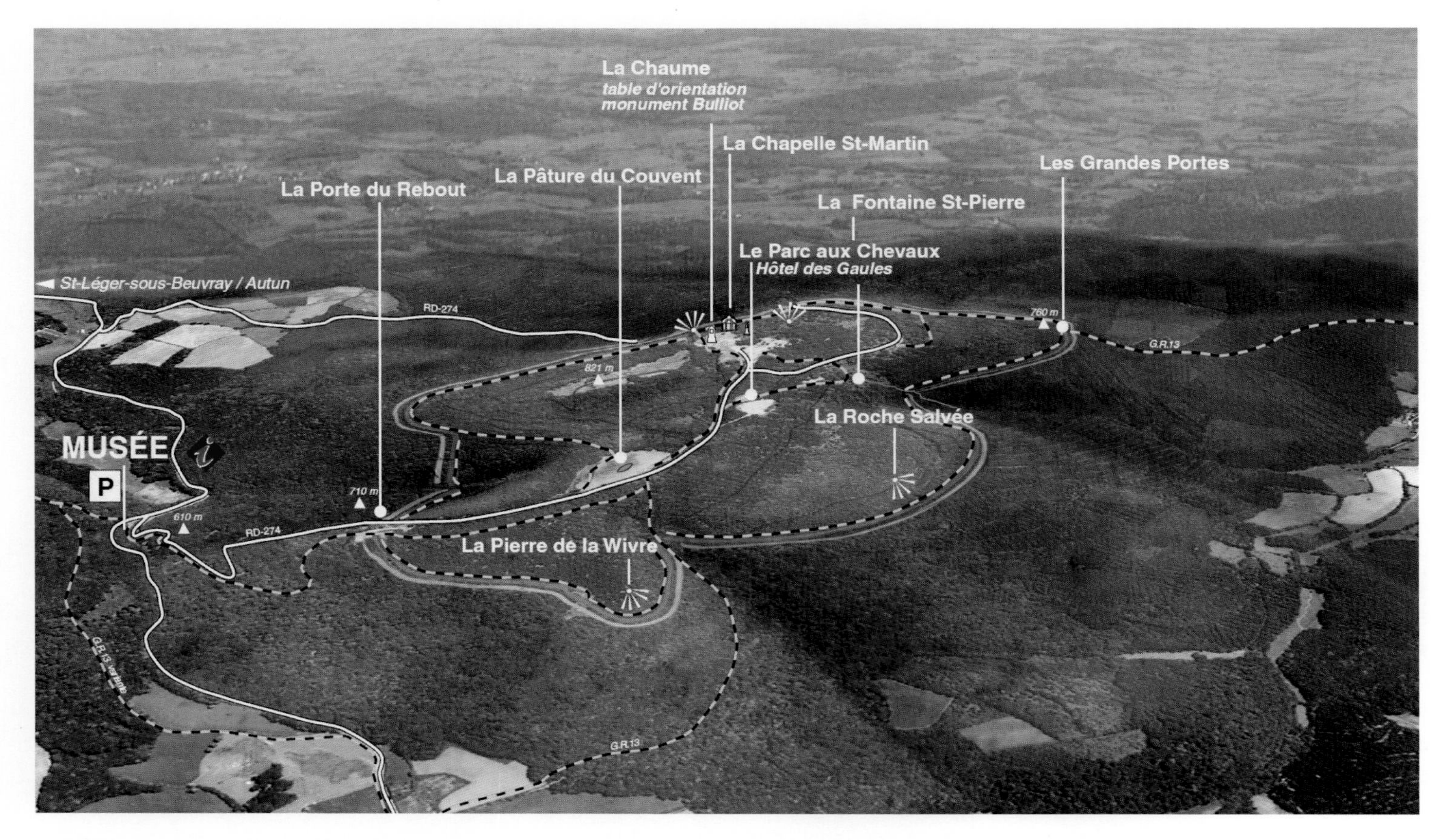

2.28 Bibracte hill fort was the capital of the Aedui and two of Julius Caesar's battles were fought nearby. It was one of the most important settlements in Iron Age Gaul and there was sufficient space for horticulture within the fortifications.

for defensive reasons, assuming the occupants did not have masochistic tendencies. But aerial photography shows traces of circular 'forts' on better land, which is now ploughed. The use of circles and loops for different types of enclosure was influenced by building methods, always adapted to the local landscape. Cultivation probably took place within some enclosures but they did not have palaces or palace gardens.

Bibracte hill fort in Central France encloses an area of 200 ha. It contained a number of structures and the layout is thought to have been low density with 'pastures, orchards and gardens'.[54] Julius Caesar knew the place. His *Commentaries on the Gallic Wars* provide some of the best information on the Celts, whom he called Gauls, but he does not mention gardens or palaces and does not describe a culture in which they might have flourished. Caesar remarked that the Gauls 'for the purpose of avoiding heat, mostly seek the neighborhood of woods and rivers'[55] and 'do not live much on corn, but subsist for the most part on milk and flesh, and are much [engaged] in hunting'.[56] Caesar won the Battle of Bibracte in 58 BCE and went on to conquer Gaul, making himself Dictator in 44 BCE and launching what became the Roman Empire. As it grew, those famous roads carried garden knowledge and practice into Gaul and to the furthest corners of the empire. It was the Romans who spread the art of garden design to Northern and Western Europe and it was very much on the Italian model outlined above and discussed in Chapter 4.

2.29 The Romans spread gardening skills throughout Europe (model of a Roman gardener, from Fishbourne, England).

Sacred enclosures

Paleolithic beliefs and landscapes

Information about Paleolithic beliefs is scarce, because the peoples were nomadic and non-literate. Nor has any record of any Paleolithic language survived. The oldest burials with grave goods date from 100,000 years ago and archaeologists believe that the presence of valuable items in graves 'clearly signify religious practices and concern for the dead that transcends daily life'.[57] The burials were probably not in enclosed spaces, because the tribes were not settlers, but they may well have been at significant points in the landscape relating to camping grounds, topography, events or views.

Art provides some information about prehistoric beliefs and landscapes, though it is non-textual. The oldest cave paintings, at Chauvet in France (see Figure 2.30), date from 30,000 years ago. They are exceptionally beautiful and include half-human-half-animal beasts which are regarded as shamanistic. Shamanism is an Asian name for a category of belief, still found in primitive societies worldwide, in which man is seen as part of nature, distinct but not separate. This makes it possible for places, animals and people to have sacred qualities, with the word 'sacred' used as an adjective to mean 'worthy of respect' and 'worthy of being set apart'. Ingold writes that:

> *For them [hunter–gatherers] there are not two worlds of persons (society) and things (nature), but just one world – one environment – saturated with personal powers and embracing both human beings, the animals and plants on which they depend, and the landscape in which they live and move.*[58]

It is likely that nomadic peoples regarded certain places as sacred, millennia before any monuments were built and that 'the people who built great monuments appropriated the powers originally associated with these locations'.[59] The comment is speculative because the people who chose the sites for 'prehistoric' monuments were, by definition, non-literate. But if the speculation has validity, it follows that the history of religion has given insufficient attention to places, while concentrating on individuals and structures.

Central Asian beliefs

The prehistoric culture of Central Asia developed in a limitless geographical expanse which, despite the paucity of evidence, has attracted much attention from linguists.

2.30 The entrance to Chauvet Cave is at the foot of a cliff in the Ardèche Valley.

2.31 Domestication of the horse turned the Eurasian steppes into an inter-continental highway (photograph of Kazakhstan).

One impetus came from Sir William Jones, an English judge who moved to Calcutta in 1783. Having noticed similarities between Sanskrit, Persian, Latin and Greek, he postulated the existence of an Indo-European language. It is now identified as a parent of the languages spoken by half the world's population. The tribes of Central Asia had no universal religion but

> *shared many common characteristics and traits (polytheism, the belief in a supreme deity, an armed equestrian deity, the veneration of Heaven, Earth, Water, and Fire, the worship of ancestors, meditation in the form of shamanistic practices, both human and domestic animal sacrifice, etc.).*[60]

Their language has come to be called Proto Indo-European (PIE) and the area in which it developed is thought to have centred on the Caucasus region, between the Black Sea, the Caspian Sea and Anatolia. Since the language originated neither in India or Europe, its name is anomalous.

A possible reason for the wide spread of Proto Indo-European is that speakers of the language both domesticated the horse (*c.*4000 BCE) and invented the use of bronze to make bridles.[61] Using four-wheeled wagons to carry tents and supplies, the horse transformed the Eurasian Steppes into an international highway. PIE speakers roamed a land of great rivers, mountains, steppes and forests, fostering their love of nature and a belief that natural phenomena and places were animated and represented by spirits with powers to affect humans. The culture of the PIE speakers, which spread to Iran, India and Europe, is known from linguistic analysis and from verses which were precisely memorised and passed down the generations. This is the origin of the Hindu *Vedas*, the Greek epics and the Celtic sagas. There is continuing debate over the degree to which language and technology were spread by migration, conquest and diffusion. Warriors with chariots, who were not PIE speakers, also invaded Egypt and China. The chariots had been made for hunting and in battle they served as mobile command platforms, not as wheeled cavalry.

The hypothesis in *Asian Gardens* is that when nomads became settlers they retained both a love of wild places and the animist practice of identifying special landscapes as places to interact with the forces which govern the natural world.[62] These may also have been places where holy men took up residence and, at later dates, where temples were built. In Iran, walled enclosures, known as paradises (*paridaiza*) were used to keep plants and animals from faraway places.

Other evidence for a response to landscape character in the identification and subsequent design of sacred places comes from the periphery of Asia. In China, *feng shui* principles were used from early times but not recorded in text until much later. *Feng shui* has the literal meaning 'wind and water'. In India, sacred places became ashrams, monasteries and shrines. The principles for locating Indian sanctuaries with regard to

2.32 *Rishis* are the sages and holy men of the *Vedas* and the *Puranas*, similar to the *sadhus* of today's India. They 'looked upon Nature with the poet's eye ... they reveled also in the gorgeous beauty of dawn and evening, the luxuriance of Indian trees and flowers, the serene majesty of Himalayan mountains, the cascades, the rivers, and the shining lakes. The wonder and mystery of the world inspired their hymns and their religion.'

Source: Mackenzie, D.A., *Indian Myth and Legend*, London, 1913, p. 33, with montage addition of *rishi*.

2.33 A small desert shrine, in Egypt.

hills, water and the cardinal directions are found in the *Vedas* and therefore derive from the pastoral-nomadic culture in Central Asia.[63]

Neolithic beliefs and landscapes

The oldest temple structure yet found in Asia is on a hill (Göbekli Tepe) on the northern border of the Fertile Crescent. It dates from *c.*9000 BCE and is only 30 km from the mountain (Karadag) where wild wheat with the closest DNA to the first cultivated wheat has been found. Göbekli Tepe has circular temples with dry-stone walls and pillars with carved reliefs of animals. As in Paleolithic rock and cave art, there are no representations of plants or flowers. The excavator, Klaus Schmidt, argues that 'First came the temple, then the city.'[64] He connects the site with burial practices and a link with shamanism is possible. The location of Göbekli Tepe on the highest point of a ridge implies the sacredness of the mountain.

The development of settlement and farming led to social groups becoming larger than in Paleolithic times, because a given area of land could support a larger population. Diamond argues that organised religions created social bonds outside family groups, helping to resolve disputes and prevent conflicts.[65] What is thought to be the world's second oldest religious structure, a tower in Jericho (*c.*7500 BCE), is also in the region where farming and settlement began. The earliest textual information about beliefs comes from the cuneiform script of Sumer devised *c.*3500 BCE. In Southern Mesopotamia:

> *Each city and its surrounding area functioned as an irrigated island separated by stretches of desert and swamp. Many of these irrigated 'islands' eventually developed*

2.34 An Apsu tank was commissioned by Sennacherib for the Temple of Assur in the city of Assur. It is now in Berlin.

2.35 Bit Akitu, a house where statues of gods were brought at New Year, was set among cultivated trees 200 m north of the Ishtar Gate, outside the walls of Babylon.

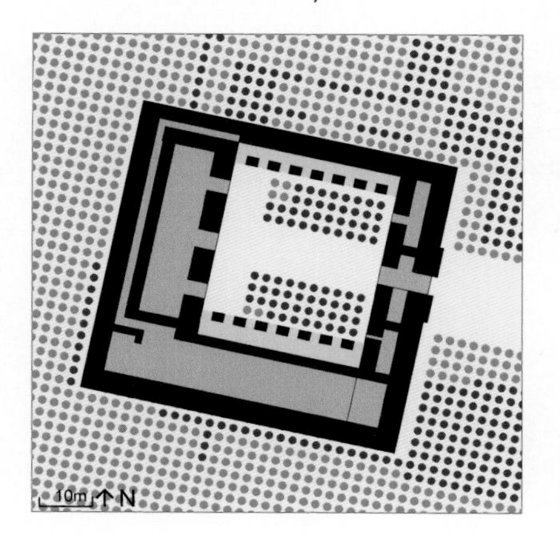

2.36 The Graeco-Roman temple of Garni in Armenia was built on a Neolithic site.

into city-states, which functioned as trade centers and regional shrines. The citizens lived within the city walls and identified with the city.[66]

Fresh and salt water had roles in Mesopotamia's creation myths which, despite name changes, were remarkably consistent over thousands of years. Apsu, god of fresh water, and Tiamet, goddess of salt water, gave birth to lesser gods, including Enki and Nammu, also associated with fresh water, and Marduk, who created mankind from the blood of Kingu. In Babylon, Marduk became the chief god. Apsu represented subterranean fresh water, not river water. Temples had basins or pools to symbolise this water source,[67] also called Apsu or Abzu. An Apsu tank from the Temple of Assur is now in Berlin.[68]

Kramer argued that: 'Sumerian cosomogonic concepts, early as they are, are by no means primitive. They reflect the mature thought and reason of the thinking Sumerian as he contemplated the forces and the character of his own existence.'[69]

2.37 Cape Sounion. Scully argues that site characteristics made places sacred long before they were used as temple sites. He associates horns and a V-cleft with 'the female parts of the goddess in Paleolithic and Neolithic times' (p. 14) and writes that when visiting the temple of Poseidon at Cape Sounion, in Greece, as 'the worshiper mounted toward the colonnade the *stoa* opened a perspective to the right toward the island of Patroclus and the horned promontory opposite ... the sea gleamed with blinding light, with the horns floating above it' (p. 163).

Religious and philosophical ideas have often resulted in aesthetically designed outdoor space which symbolised contemporary thinking about man's relationship with nature, landscape and the universe. In a study of Greek temples, Vincent Scully aimed to show that 'all important Greek sanctuaries grew up around open altars which were normally sited where they are because the place itself first suggested the presence of a divine being'.[70]

From Minoan times onward, Scully identified the key features as an enclosed valley, a gently mounded or conical hill and, on the same axis, a cleft mountain. In Greek times more specific landscape features were associated with individual gods. The Graeco-Roman temple at Garni, in the Caucasus (see Figure 2.36), is built on a site which has Neolithic remains and can be used to illustrate Scully's point that 'the formal elements of any Greek sanctuary are, first, the specifically sacred landscape in which it is set and, second the buildings that are placed within it'.[71]

2.38 a, b Castlerigg Stone Circle seen from the south, above, and across the valley from the north, below. The Circle stands on a classic 'shoulder' site.

When temples came to be built on sacred sites, their planning was similar in many regions. Fox writes that:

> *In my view, the temples in Mesopotamia, Egypt, Israel, and many of those in Greece were unmistakably the same kind of institution. Many of them were built on the same architectural principles, employed the same types of personnel, housed similar ritual functions, and expressed the same conceptual principle: the temple is the god's dwelling, or is spoken of as such. Moreover, the Indian temple, as described in Professor Fuller's article, would in my view be at home in the Near East as well.*[72]

2.39 The Uffington enclosure (*c.*600 BCE) and the Uffington White Horse (*c.*1400 BCE) are thought to have had roles in symbolising tribal ownership of the surrounding landscape.

The oldest monuments in North Europe are the henges and stone circles made from *c.*4000 to *c.*1500 BCE. These circular spaces may be assumed to have had a religious role because they are unsuited to military, agricultural or residential use. Few artifacts, which might indicate their use, have been found. Stone circles were placed at significant points in the landscape. Many were orientated with regard to the summer and winter solstices but claims that they were astronomical observatories have been overworked. It is more likely that they were used on ceremonial occasions, including weddings and cremations, and served as symbols of the territories claimed by recently nomadic tribes. They were built by agricultural societies in the Neolithic period. After a lifetime's study, Burl concluded that:

> *Neolithic and Bronze Age ritual enclosures had a multiplicity of purposes: as family shrines, for seasonal gatherings or as trading-places. Widespread across western Europe in space and time, stone circles are unlikely to have been colleges for dispassionate musings on the nature of the universe. Dancing, drums and drugs may have been the ingredients for the rites.*[73]

Marija Gimbutas, who researched the origins of Indo-European culture, draws attention to the fact that at Callanish there is an avenue of stones and an 'association of standing stones with the sea, rivers, brooks, and wells'.[74]

Uffington is of interest for having both a circular enclosure, misleadingly called a 'castle', and a primitive artwork, the Uffington White Horse (see Figure 2.39). They date from *c*.600 and *c*.1400 BCE. The horse had a central place in Celtic society and may have been used here as a tribal symbol for the community which used the enclosure. Lock argues that White Horse Hill was a religious complex and that the enclosure was a focal point for ceremonial community events linking the people to the place.[75]

Bronze and Iron Age gardens

The earliest text references to temple gardens, as noted above, are on cuneiform tablets dating from the Early Bronze Age in Mesopotamia. Temple rituals are mentioned in hymns and some topographic information has been gleaned from them. They relate to a society with a keen awareness of the distinction between nomads and settlers. During the Uruk Period (4000–3200 BCE) Sumer had temples with temple-owned gardens, symbolic pools and ziggurats with the character of temple-mountains. In Akkad, the 17 kings before Sargon I (1920–1881 BCE) were described as 'tent dwellers' with the term equating to 'nomads'.[76] Hammurabi (1728–1686 BCE) incorporated Sumer into his empire and transformed what had been an unimportant settlement into an imperial capital: Babylon. The language was Akkadian, and hymns celebrating the empire provide information about palace and temple gardens which

2.40 A reconstruction of Babylon, with the Ishtar Gate on the left and the Ancient Euphrates on the right.

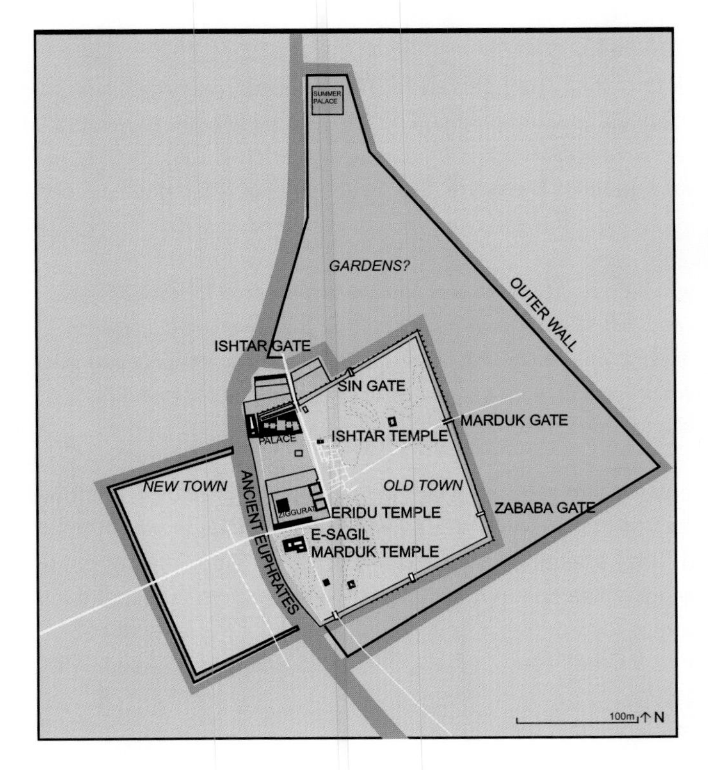

2.41 Plan of Babylon.

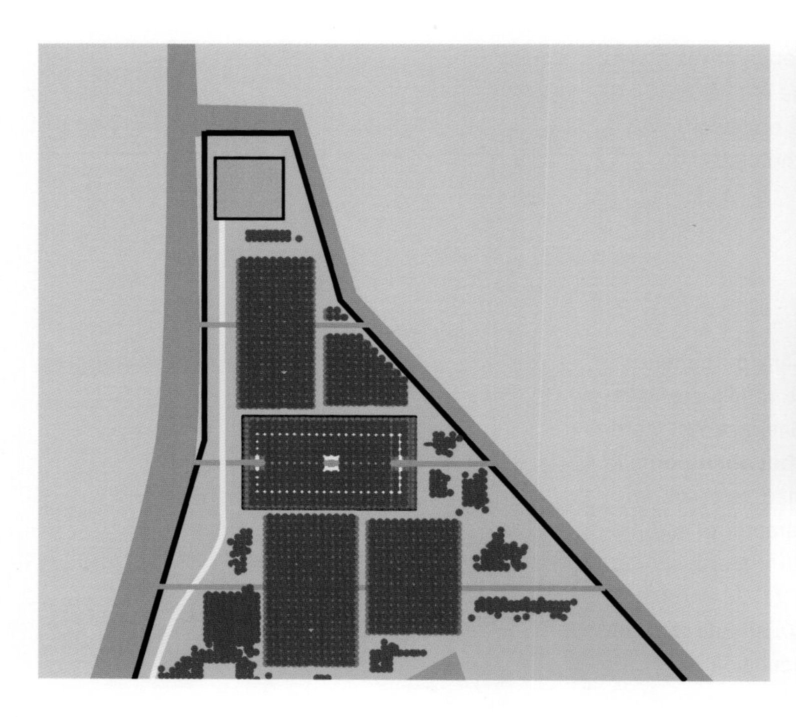

2.42 A hypothesis concerning the character of Babylonian orchard gardens.

2.43 A model of the Ishtar Gate in Berlin's Museum, with a tiled wall from Babylon in the background.

can be related to visual information from carved reliefs. New information comes to light every year but few palaces, few temples and no gardens have been excavated.

Enki's temple in Eridu, was known as E'engurra (the 'Seahouse') or Apsu (the 'Watery Deep'). It is

> *depicted as a large, pure, holy, song-filled 'banquet hall' where pure food for the gods was prepared in large ovens and pure water was drunk from large bowls. In a myth about Enki's organization of the earth and its cultural processes, the E'engurra is depicted as a house whose shade stretches over the marshes; as a place where fishes frolic and birds chirp; where songs are changed and spells recited.*[77]

The E-sagil temple in Babylon, dedicated to Marduk, had two large courtyards: the Grand Court and the Court of Ishtar. Temples were houses for gods in which they were fed and entertained. The Lagas temple had musicians, lamentation priests, singers, acrobats, a diviner and a snake charmer. Courtyards were busy places and their care was an honour. Alittum is recorded as a 'courtyard-sweeper of the Temple of Sin, for 12 days per annum, in the Great Court'.[78] E-sagil also had a Garden of Apsu, with several gates:

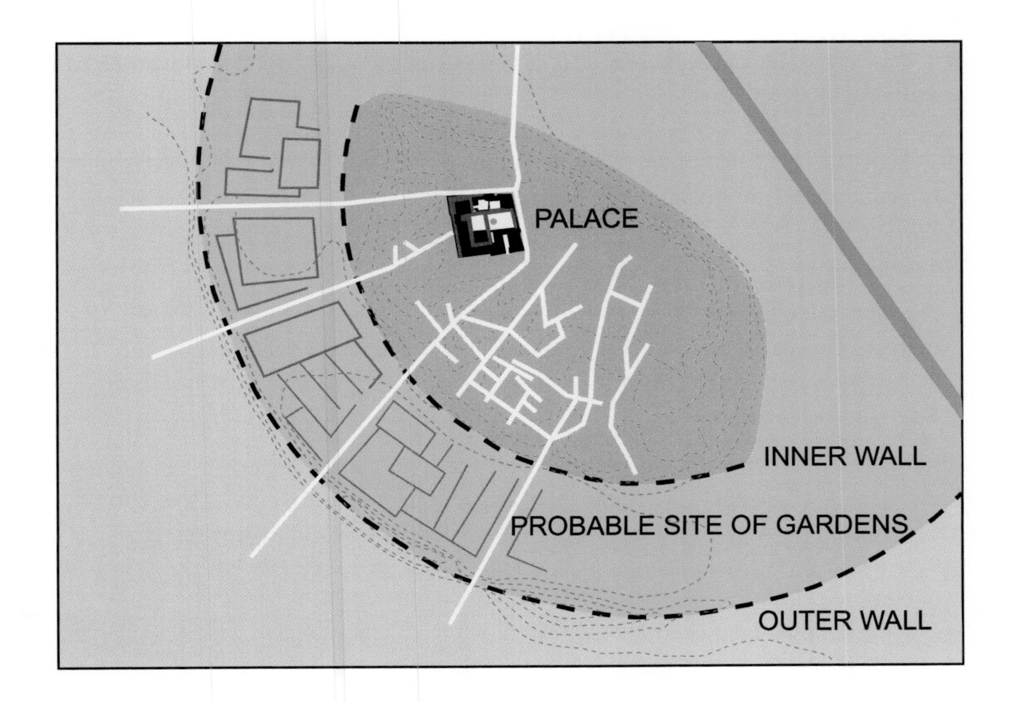

2.44 Mari was a circular settlement. The palace, which has been excavated, was at the heart of the town and had internal courts.

- the Gate of the Garden of Apsu (*Ka-kiri-abzu*) at which 'the mouths of the gods are opened';
- the Gate of the River God (*Ka-Id*);
- the Gate at the Garden's Edge (*Ka-zag-kiri*), also called the gate which opens on to the bank or the Gate of the Trenches.

Canals (*palgu*) were a feature of E-kar-zaginna. The E-kur temple complex had a 'garden of heavenly joy'. E-hursag-sikilla was surrounded by a garden of juniper bushes whose purpose was to supply incense to the cult.[79] Bas-relief scenes show kings and queens dining, in palace temple or gardens.

Mari has one of the most fully excavated and best known Mesopotamian palaces. The city, by the Euphrates in Eastern Syria, flourished until it was sacked by Hammurabi in 1759 BCE. In its final form

> *The entrance gate led through a series of rooms into the main courtyard, which gave access to the shrine of Ishtar and the great sanctuary in the southeast quarter of the palace from which opened the gateway into the official quarters in the northwest. A corridor led from here into a large courtyard with an artificial palm tree of wood clad in bronze and silver at its center and a number of real palm trees.*[80]

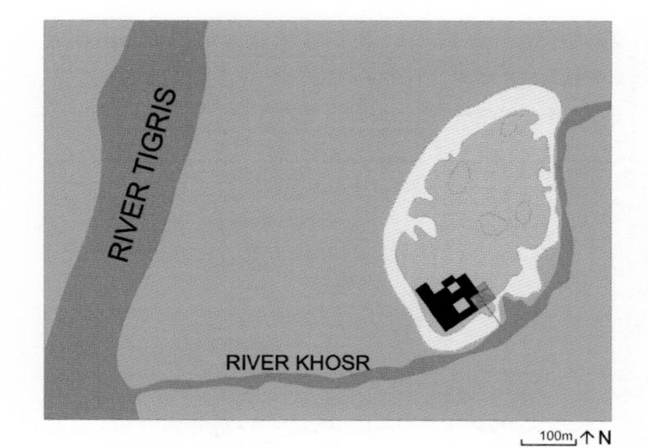

2.45 a A hypothetical reconstruction placing Sennacherib's garden on the hill of Kuyunjik at Nineveh, **b** Sennacherib's palace garden at Nineveh (a bas relief from British Museum, overlaid with colour).

Mari Palace contained private apartments and public audience rooms and was also a centre of production.[81]

Assyria is in North Mesopotamia. It has more rainfall than Sumer and there is both visual and textual information about Assyrian gardens in the Iron Age (1000–600 BCE). Assur-nasir-apli II (883–859 BCE) made gardens by the Tigris using water from the Pati-Nuhsi Canal:

> *The canal-water came flowing down from above to the gardens: the paths [are full] of scent; the waterfalls [glisten] like the stars of heaven in the garden of pleasure. The pomegranate trees, which are clothed with clusters of fruit like vines, enrich the breezes in the garden of [delights].*

It had ornamental and fruiting plants which the king had collected on his travels, including cedar, cypress, box, juniper, myrtle, almond, date palm, ebony, *isssoo*, olive, tamarind, oak, terebinth, *dukdu*, pistachio, *mur*-tree, willow, pomegranate, plum, fir, pear, quince, fig, and grapevines.

Sennacherib made a famous garden in Nineveh which was supplied with water by an aqueduct which came from beyond Jerwan,[82] 65 km from Nineveh. Dally argued that Sennacherib's garden is the place known to history as the Hanging Gardens of Babylon[83] but her view has not been supported by other scholars. Sennacherib's palace was on the south-west section of the hill at Kuyunjik, opposite modern Mosul. There is a bas-relief of these gardens in the British Museum;[84] Figure 2.45 shows a diagrammatic version of the bas-relief and a placing of this design at Nineveh. The 'Hanging Gardens of Nineveh' were enclosed by a wall and supported by vaulted arcades. Within the outer wall were pavilions, flights of steps, trees, flowers, vegetables and channels with flowing water. The gardens appear to have been for walking in safety or for sitting in a pavilion, catching the breeze and admiring the view. They were not 'outdoor rooms' for cooking and eating: this was the role of palace courtyards. The Nineveh gardens had fruits and vegetables. A hand-picked fruit tastes better than any other fruit.

Sennacherib's youngest son, Esarhaddon, reigned from 681 to 669 BCE. He incorporated a pavilion (*bitanu*) in his new palace complex and it was surrounded by a garden described as a *kirmahu*. This word is translated as 'pleasure garden' and distinguished from the older word, *kiru*, used for orchard gardens on the edge of towns.[85] Esarhaddon claimed to have done 'what no king before me had done' in making a large *bitanu* (95 x 31 cubits = 48 x 16 m).

Egypt's most prosperous period was the Late Bronze Age. Under the New Kingdom (1570–1070 BCE), as described in Chapter 3, a variety of garden types took shape. They included palaces and temple sanctuaries which compare with Mesopotamian equivalents. But they were made by a different people with a different cultural herit-

2.46 Genesis 2:7 recounts that 'the Lord God formed man of the dust of the ground, and breathed into his nostrils the breath of life; and man became a living soul' (drawing by von Carolsfeld).

2.47 An illustration to the Song of Solomon. Considering the erotic interpretations placed on the Song, von Carolsfeld's drawing is remarkably chaste.

age in different geographical circumstances. During the Iron Age, Egypt was overcome by Assyria, which had more timber and was able to produce the charcoal needed to smelt iron. In 30 BCE, Egypt became a province of Rome.

Biblical gardens

Biblical chronologists date the creation to *c.*4000 BCE. Archaeologists locate the Age of the Patriarchs in the Middle to Late Bronze Age (*c.*2200–1600 BCE), making this the period to which the two most intensively analysed passages in the history of gardening refer: the Book of Genesis and the Song of Songs. The texts yield information about gardens and are important to three world religions (Judaism, Christianity and Islam).

The Song of Songs, attributed to King Solomon, may have been composed in the tenth century BCE. Also called the Song of Solomon, it is regarded as the most beautiful and the most erotic garden poem in world literature. Its beauty comes from the genius of the poet. Its eroticism comes from the standard Mesopotamian practice of using 'garden' as a metaphor for the female genitalia:

> *A garden enclosed is my sister, my spouse; a spring shut up, a fountain sealed.*[86]

2.48 After giving way to temptation, Adam and Eve were expelled from the Garden of Eden and instructed that 'In the sweat of thy face shalt thou eat bread'. The painting, from *Les Très Riches Heures du Duc de Berry* (Limbourg brothers 1410), shows the Garden of Eden on a circular island with Gothic spires.

> *Awake, O north wind; and come, thou south; blow upon my garden, that the spices thereof may flow out. Let my beloved come into his garden, and eat his pleasant fruits.*[87]

The setting is a palace garden. It was a physical place and a metaphor for female sexuality. 'Fountain' refers to a natural spring and implies that flowing water rather than static water gives life to the garden. The garden in the Song is therefore an enclosure with flowing water and plants. The plants are choice fruits and spices, including pomegranates, henna, nard, frankincense, saffron, calamus, cinnamon and myrrh. Pomegranate was an aphrodisiac. The spices are aromatic and few of them are native so that 'the rarity of the vegetation produced by this fantastic garden suggests the exceptional nature of the woman's beauty'.[88]

The Book of Genesis took its final form in the Iron Age but many of the events are described as though set in the urban civilisation of the Fertile Crescent during the Bronze Age. On Biblical dating, Abraham lived *c.*2000 BCE. As Lemche puts it, the Garden of Eden story 'is unthinkable without its relation to Babylonian religious motifs and associations'.[89]

Let us consider: what *type* of space the author of Genesis had in mind when he described Eden as a garden. The range of vegetated spaces known to him could have included:

- beautiful natural places with wild flowers and fruiting plants;
- mud-walled orchards with cultivated varieties of fruit trees and flowers;
- unwalled horticultural plots with cultivated vegetables and fruits;
- temple gardens (sanctuaries) with sacred plantings and pools;
- palace gardens used for feasting and other pleasures.

The text of the Old Testament was written in Hebrew and the word *gan* ('garden') 'refers to a fenced-off enclosure, particularly to a garden protected by a wall or hedge'.[90] The account that the Garden was 'planted' by God and that Adam's task was 'to dress it and to keep it' imply an enclosure for cultivation. This excludes the Garden of Eden from being conceived as an unwalled wild place and, given the Biblical disapproval of polytheism, the garden in the author's mind cannot have been a polytheist sanctuary with a sacred lake and a sacred wood. Nor is it likely to have been a palace garden. Hamilton interprets 'every tree that is pleasant to the sight, and good for food' (Genesis 1) as 'those that grow wild'. But he sees the plants in the Garden of Eden (Genesis 2) as 'those that grow only as a result of human cultivation through planting and artificial irrigation'.[91] If correct, the 'garden' in Eden was a place for cultivated plants rather than wild plants. We have a better understanding of plant breeding than our Bronze Age predecessors but the distinction between the two types of plant must have been as clear to them as it is to us.

The Garden of Eden is described as having been '*eastward* in Eden' and as having a river which branched into four other rivers, one of which was the Euphrates. This is widely taken to locate the Garden of Eden in Mesopotamia. Many sources confirm the existence of ancient gardens in this region and, as noted above, little is known about their layout. Mesopotamian palace and temple gardens were probably orchards with canals and the best clue to their design may be the palace garden at Passargadae

4 ¶ Theſe *are* the generations of the heavens and of the earth, when they were created; in the day that the LORD God made the earth and the heavens,

5 And every plant of the field, before it was in the earth, and every herb of the field, before it grew: for the LORD God had not cauſed it to rain upon the earth, and there *was* not a man to till the ground.

6 But ‖ there went up a miſt from the earth, and watered the whole face of the ground.

7 And the LORD God formed man † *of* the duſt of the ground, and breathed into his noſtrils the breath of life; and [d] man became a living ſoul.

8 ¶ And the LORD God planted a garden eaſt-ward in [f] Eden; and there he put the man whom he had formed.

9 And out of the ground made the LORD God to grow every tree that is pleaſant to the ſight, and good for food: [g] the tree of life alſo in the midſt of the garden, [h] and the tree of knowledge of good and evil.

10 And a river went out of Eden to water the garden; and from thence it was parted, and became into four heads.

11 The name of the firſt *is* [i] Piſon: that *is* it which compaſſeth [k] the whole land of Havilah, where *there is* gold.

12 And the gold of that land *is* good: [l] there *is* bdellium and the onyx ſtone.

13 And the name of the ſecond river *is* Gihon: the ſame *is* it that compaſſeth the whole land of † Ethiopia.

14 And the name of the third river *is* [m] Hiddekel: that *is* it which goeth ‖ toward the eaſt of Aſſyria. And the fourth river *is* Euphrates.

15 And the LORD God took ‖ the man, and put him into the garden of Eden, to dreſs it, and to keep it.

16 And the LORD God commanded the man, ſaying, Of every tree of the garden † thou mayeſt freely eat:

17 [n] But of the tree of the knowledge of good and evil, thou ſhalt not eat of it: for in the day that thou eateſt thereof, [o] † thou ſhalt ſurely die.

2.49 Genesis 2.

in Iran. It was made at the time Genesis was taking its final form (*c*.500 BCE) and was probably a walled orchard garden.

European sanctuaries

The Aegean civilisation of Crete, Asia Minor and Greece was a palace culture with kings who were almost gods. In Crete, there were both palace shrines and peak sanctuaries which had altars but not temples.[92] Statuettes, paintings and seals suggest that:

> *Minoan goddesses were associated with flowers, trees, snakes, monkeys, and even birds – in short, they were nature goddesses ... For the Minoans, to be a goddess of nature implied being a goddess of life, health, sustenance, healing, technology, and the economy.*[93]

Minoan art shows what appear to be sacred gardens or landscapes which compare with those in Mesopotamia and have both trees and shrines.[94] Peak sanctuaries were predecessors of the sanctuaries and sacred groves in mainland Greece. Minoan, as written in Linear B, is related to Greek. The word *temenos* was used for sanctuaries in Greek and has the literal meaning 'cut out' from the wider landscape. It may be related to the Celtic word *nemeton*.[95] Crete and Greece had, and have, a more varied landscape than the flood plains of the Tigris and the Euphrates.

Scholars find evidence of links between the Fertile Crescent and the Aegean in art, architecture and text. There is 'a fair quantum of proof that Mycenae borrowed certain features of the priest-king system together with the belief in a chief deity at the heart of a theocratic society'.[96] This created a palace society which did not exist in other parts of Bronze Age Europe but which influenced Rome and the subsequent development of 'sacral kingship' – and gardens – in medieval Europe. Though North Europe had settlements, agriculture, religion and chiefs in the Bronze Age, it did not have palaces or palace gardens. One of the earliest and best accounts of North Europe comes from Tacitus' *Germania*, written in 98 CE. The region, inhabited by Germanic, Celtic and Baltic tribes, retained its ancient character through not becoming part of Rome's empire.

> *In their ancient songs, their only way of remembering or recording the past, they celebrate an earth-born god, Tuisco, and his son Mannus, as the origin of their race, as their founders ... All have fierce blue eyes, red hair, huge frames, fit only for a sudden exertion ... Their country, though somewhat various in appearance, yet generally either bristles with forests or reeks with swamps; it is more rainy on the side of Gaul, bleaker on that of Noricum and Pannonia. It is productive of grain, but unfavourable to fruit-bearing trees; it is rich in flocks and herds, but these are for the most part undersized, and even the cattle have not their usual beauty or noble head.*

> *They choose their kings by birth, their generals for merit. These kings have not unlimited or arbitrary power, and the generals do more by example than by authority. If they are energetic, if they are conspicuous, if they fight in the front, they lead because they are*

admired. But to reprimand, to imprison, even to flog, is permitted to the priests alone, and that not as a punishment, or at the general's bidding, but, as it were, by the mandate of the god whom they believe to inspire the warrior. They also carry with them into battle certain figures and images taken from their sacred groves. And what most stimulates their courage is, that their squadrons or battalions, instead of being formed by chance or by a fortuitous gathering, are composed of families and clans. Close by them, too, are those dearest to them, so that they hear the shrieks of women, the cries of infants. They are to every man the most sacred witnesses of his bravery – they are his most generous applauders. The soldier brings his wounds to mother and wife, who shrink not from counting or even demanding them and who administer both food and encouragement to the combatants.

Tradition says that armies already wavering and giving way have been rallied by women who, with earnest entreaties and bosoms laid bare, have vividly represented the horrors of captivity, which the Germans fear with such extreme dread on behalf of their women, that the strongest tie by which a state can be bound is the being required to give, among the number of hostages, maidens of noble birth. They even believe that the sex has a certain sanctity and prescience, and they do not despise their counsels, or make light of their answers.

They assemble, except in the case of a sudden emergency, on certain fixed days, either at new or at full moon; for this they consider the most auspicious season for the transaction of business. Instead of reckoning by days as we do, they reckon by nights, and in this manner fix both their ordinary and their legal appointments ... Silence is proclaimed by the priests, who have on these occasions the right of keeping order. Then the king or the chief, according to age, birth, distinction in war, or eloquence, is heard, more because he has influence to persuade than because he has power to command.

It is well known that the nations of Germany have no cities, and that they do not even tolerate closely contiguous dwellings. They live scattered and apart, just as a spring, a meadow, or a wood has attracted them. Their villages they do not arrange in our fashion, with the buildings connected and joined together, but every person surrounds his dwelling with an open space, either as a precaution against the disasters of fire, or because they do not know how to build. No use is made by them of stone or tile; they employ timber for all purposes, rude masses without ornament or attractiveness. Some parts of their buildings they stain more carefully with a clay so clear and bright that it resembles painting, or a coloured design. They are wont also to dig out subterranean caves, and pile on them great heaps of dung, as a shelter from winter and as a receptacle for the year's produce, for by such places they mitigate the rigour of the cold. And should an enemy approach, he lays waste the open country, while what is hidden and buried is either not known to exist, or else escapes him from the very fact that it has to be searched for.

2.50 Entrance to the Giant's Grave (Hünengrab) at Klein Görnow in North East Germany.

The points to note from the above are as follows:

- History was recorded in verse, as in other Indo-European societies.
- A wild landscape made communications, and therefore kingship, difficult.

- The society was more democratic than in the Mediterranean, with more equality between the sexes.
- Assemblies took place at fixed dates when the moon was new or full.
- There were no cities and no palaces.
- They kept idols in sacred groves.

If community assemblies were held at the summer or the winter solstice, their dates would have been known to tribes who lacked calendars. Henges and passage graves were aligned with the sunrise or sunset on the solstices, days on which there would have been an association with the dates on which their ancestors had held assemblies. In the millennium after Tacitus, North Europe came to have Christian kings with palace gardens and hunting parks. They built cities but sacred groves and pagan statues were destroyed.

Hunting parks

Judging from cave paintings, hunting was the principal activity in Paleolithic societies. It had both economic and sacred characteristics. Axes, bows and spears were used to kill the animals upon which families lived. There are no written records from the period but studies of contemporary hunter–gatherer societies confirm the intuitive point that success in hunting would give an individual high status and power over food supplies, tribesmen and women. This continued when societies became settled. The art and literature of Mesopotamia and Egypt reveal that hunting developed into a royal and noble pastime. Kings used hunting to demonstrate their power. It was both a preparation for war and a recreation. Allsen, in his book *The Royal Hunt in Eurasian History*, writes of 'political hunting'[97] and sees it as 'an ingredient in interstate relations, military preparations, domestic administration, communications networks, and in search for political legitimacy'.[98]

Prehistoric huntsmen drove animals into valleys. Early royal huntsmen used human rings of beaters to contain the animals. Later royal huntsmen used hunting parks which could be re-stocked locally or used to retain exotic beasts, because 'Fabulous beasts can only be slain by fabulous humans.'[99] The developed form of the royal hunt in both East and West Asia was the ring hunt, which continued in China until the nineteenth century. In open country it involved a king and 'thousands or tens of thousands' of beaters. Often soldiers, the beaters formed a great ring centred on an area of flat land. It was progressively closed, with stakes, nets and spears used to stop animals escaping. The king and his nobles then mounted their chariots, entered the ring and slaughtered the animals. A Greek writer, from Bursa in Asia Minor, commented that this was like someone who 'claimed to be fond of war and then, letting slip the chance to engage their enemy, had seized the prisoners at home and put them to death'.[100] Imparked woodland was used in a similar way. The

2.51 Hunting is one of the oldest park uses and remains a near-ceremonial activity in England.

2.52 A ring hunt in China's Mulan hunting ground. The artist (Giuseppe Castiglione, 1688–1766) was a painter at the Chinese court and designed the European section of the gardens in the Yuanmingyuan, Beijing.

hunt demonstrated a king's power over humans, animals and the forces of nature. It legitimated his status.

The earliest records of animal parks come from Sumer. Exotic animals were kept but not for zoological study:

> *Of course the animals had to be managed to some degree, but the idea of the park was to allow the king to hunt on his own private preserve. His favorites were allowed the same privileges as hunting companions.*[101]

The wheeled cart and the chariot originated in the region which can be identified as the homeland of the royal hunt: Turkestan, Iran and North India. The chariot and the ring hunt spread to the Fertile Crescent and China. These were also the first places to have royal and sacred gardens. As noted above, the faiths of Central Asia equated the forces of nature with storms, mountains, forests, rivers and wild animals. The forces of nature were symbolised in gardens. Wild animals were hunted for 'political' reasons. With regard to hunting, Allsen expresses the point as follows: 'Archaic religions such as Shamanism are inextricably tied to hunting because all nature, and most particularly game, is animated by potent spiritual force.'[102] Four-wheeled carts were built for transport and two-wheeled chariots were built for hunting. Military uses came later. Xenophon was the first author to describe the ring hunt. He reports that Cyrus 'had a palace and a large park [*paradeisos*] full of wild animals, which he used to hunt on horseback whenever he wished to give himself and his horses exercise'.

The first enclosed hunting parks may have been accessories for a ring hunt. The eighteenth dynasty Egyptian pharaoh, Amenhotep was a keen huntsman and it is recorded that:

> *He would leave the palace at Memphis in the evening, sail north all night and reach the herd in the early morning. A numerous body of troops, with children from the villages, then surrounded the herd and drove them into a large enclosure, a method also employed in earlier times. On one occasion his beaters counted no less than one hundred and seventy wild cattle in the enclosure. Entering it in his chariot the king himself slew fifth six of the savage beasts on the first day.*[103]

Since killing exotic beasts, including lions and tigers, conferred the highest status, it was natural for them to be kept in what we now call hunting parks. The taste spread to North Europe with the Romans, as part of what became the classic European villa. It had a palace, gardens, farms, and a hunting park which also served as a zoo.

Conclusion

The earliest archaeological evidence for settlement and plant cultivation dates from about 10,000 BCE. The founder crops were cereals. They were grown near settlements in the Levant using cultivation techniques we would classify as horticultural. But there is no evidence for the plots having been private domestic enclosures of the type we now call gardens and nor is there any evidence for their having been aesthetically designed. The life of a farmer was harder than that of a nomad and the *Bible* paints a fair picture of the conditions in which crops were grown: 'In the sweat of thy face shalt thou eat bread, till thou return unto the ground; for out of it wast thou taken: for dust thou art, and unto dust shalt thou return.' Hard work increased the supply of carbohydrates but produced 'an associated general decline in health'.[104] It also ended the nomadic freedom to enjoy wild food and wild landscapes. Before his expulsion, Adam's task had been to 'dress' and keep the Garden of Eden.[105]

2.53 Gustave Doré's engraving of Adam and Eve being driven out of the Garden of Eden to cultivate fields 'in the sweat of thy brow'. Their descendents also learned how to design and make gardens.

The earliest textual evidence for cultivation comes from the eastern tip of the Fertile Crescent: Sumer. The 'gardens' (*sar*) were probably palm-shaded orchards on irrigated land, not vegetated courtyards adjoining mud-brick houses on dry land. Water, shade, flowers, scents and fruit were appreciated but little is known about the design character of Mesopotamian gardens. Future excavations may yield more information. Hunting parks were made in Mesopotamia for reasons which parallel the symbolic objectives for which stately pleasure gardens were made. The oldest visual evidence for the layout of gardens comes from the western tip of the Fertile Crescent and the gift of the Nile is the subject of Chapter 3.

CHAPTER 3

Egyptian gardens, 2000–1000 BCE

3.0 Herodotus described the cultivated land of Egypt as 'a gift of the river'.

History and philosophy

They said also that the first man who became king of Egypt was Min; and that in his time all Egypt except the district of Thebes was a swamp, and ... that the Egypt to which the Hellenes come in ships is a land which has been won by the Egyptians as an addition, and that it is a gift of the river.

(Herodotus)[1]

Herodotus described Egypt in the fifth century BCE as 'a gift' of the River Nile. The inhabited part of the country was, as today, a green-blue ribbon which flowed in a deep valley through a yellow-brown desert. The valley was lush and sheltered. The desert was hot and arid. But at several points in the Palaeolithic era, the desert was wetter and the valley less hospitable. The Sahara had lakes and vegetation. The Nile Valley had jungle, floods, crocodiles and hippopotami. Then, towards the end of the last Ice Age (*c.*10,000 BCE), the Sahara became arid and great floods from Sub-Saharan Africa made the valley even more dangerous. It became, as Herodotus wrote of the time of Min, 'a swamp'. Egypt became depopulated. Prehistoric remains in the valley were washed away or buried in silt. Then, after 9000 BCE, the Sahara became wetter and the Nile more predictable. There is evidence of cattle herding and short-term camps in the Western Desert.

3.1 The valley of the Nile is a blue-green conduit running through a yellow-brown desert.

3.2 The flood plain of the Nile is still cultivated when the water level falls. Water can be brought in channels and retained by low mounds.

Potsherds and stone-grinding equipment have been found with the latter assumed to have been used for crushing wild grain and tubers. Ostrich shells were used for carrying water. At Nabta Playa an astronomical stone circle has been dated to the fifth millennium BCE.

The earliest evidence for agriculture in the Nile valley dates from *c.*5400 BCE (see p. 43) and from this time onward the environment proved well suited to cultivation and settlement. Once a year, from July to September, the river burst its banks and fertilised the valley. As the waters rose, Egyptians withdrew to higher land. At the valley edge, they found cliffs which could be quarried to make stone buildings. The water facilitated transport, as did the Nile. Boats could drift downstream with the current and were blown upstream by the prevailing wind. Annual floods created a summer season when hands and minds could turn to other things than subsistence agriculture. Since the surrounding desert was hostile to invaders, the valley was comparatively easy to defend. It became home to a stable society: Egyptian law and religion endured longer than those of any other civilisation. The system was upheld by pharaohs who were both gods and kings. The dynastic history of Egypt is divided into nine periods:

1. Early Dynastic Period: 2920–2575 BCE;
2. Old Kingdom: 2575–2134 BCE;
3. First Intermediate Period: 2134–2040 BCE;
4. Middle Kingdom: 2040–1567 BCE;
5. Second Intermediate Period: 1567–1550 BCE;
6. New Kingdom: 1550–1070 BCE;
7. Third Intermediate Period: 1070–712 BCE;
8. Late Period: 712–332 BCE;
9. Graeco-Roman Period: 332 BCE–395 CE.

Egyptians interpreted the world through religion, making little distinction between the divine and everyday spheres. Gods represented abstract ideas, natural features and powers of nature, often partaking of each other's capabilities and characteristics.

The pharaoh's task was to uphold *Maat*, which translates as order, truth, balance and justice. His responsibilities therefore extended across what we distinguish as society, nature and religion. He had, for example, to ensure a regular annual flood ('annual' was easy; 'regular' was difficult). Laws and rituals assisted pharaohs in their task of protecting Egypt from danger. Since the duties did not end with his human life, the pharaoh required a mortuary temple with priests, worldly goods and gardens for the millions of years of his afterlife. Some objects, including furniture and jewellry were placed in tombs for use in the afterlife. Others were painted, or written, on tomb walls and papyri. Knowledge of Egyptian gardens thus comes from tombs, archaeological investigations and texts. The oldest settlements with domestic garden-type spaces date from *c.*5000 BCE

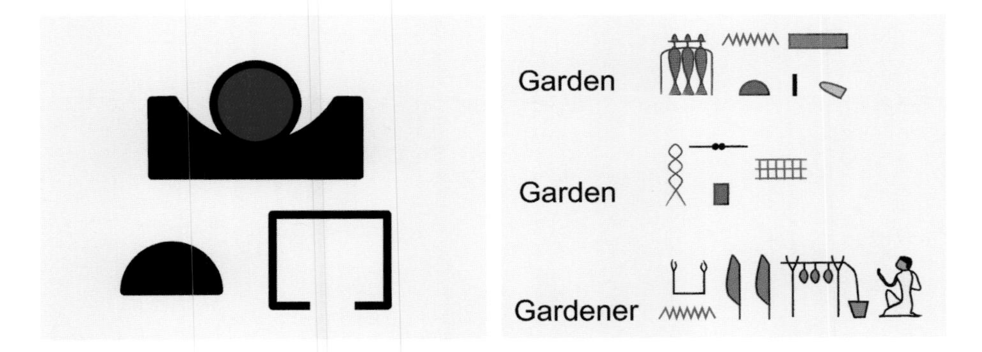

3.3 Hieroglyphic symbols for the setting sun, bread and a tomb.

3.4 The Egyptians had several ways of writing 'garden' and 'gardener'. The first (read as *hent-esh*) uses hieroglyphs for a rack of pots, a ripple of water, a pool, a loaf and a tongue of land. The second (read as *hes-ep*) uses the symbols for twisted flax, a bolt and an irrigated plot. The word 'gardener' (read as *karny*) uses hieroglyphs for upturned arms ('soul'), flowering reeds, a vine on posts and a seated man (the determinative for a man's occupation).

and the oldest visual records of designed gardens date from *c.*2500 BCE. One of the *Precepts of Ptah-Hotep* advises:

> *Thou has cultivated the fields, thou hast (them) surrounded (with hedges?) in front of the furrows, thou has planted sycamores, in walks which bound all the limits of thy dwelling-place. Thou has filled the hand with all the flowers which thy eye has noticed; thou hast supported the most feeble plants for fear that they might happen to fall.*[2]

Without the plans and drawings on tomb walls from the New Kingdom (1550–1070 BCE) we would know little more of Egyptian gardens than we do of gardens in ancient Mesopotamia. But the plans are not easy to read. Wilkinson explains:

3.5 Before the Aswan High Dam was built, the Colossi of Memnon were surrounded by water during the season of inundation. Floods were welcomed as givers of life and tokens of a god's love. The painting is from *c.*1900 and the photograph (Figure 3.47 b, p. 103) *c.*2000.

3.6 The Ramesseum comprised: a home for a deceased pharaoh, a palace for a living pharaoh, a massive food store, a small garden, a sacred lake and a sacred grove. The complex assisted in the task of maintaining order (*Maat*). Hatshepsut's Temple and the Valley of the Kings are in the centre right section of the photograph.

3.7 a, b Avenues interlinked the temple compounds of Luxor and Karnak. They were lined with sphinxes and, presumably, trees.

3.8 The *ankh* symbolised the soul. Called the 'key of life' and the 'key of the Nile', it may represent the unification of the Nile Delta with the Upper Nile Valley (see Figure 3.28).

> *The ancient Egyptian artist represents space and time in his compositions. Space could be shown as one place only, or as several views of the same place. Time could also be indicated as a sequence of events in cartoon style, or by the addition of an inscription, or as one significant moment.*[3]

Ancient Egyptian artists did not understand or use linear perspective. They represented objects 'as known' rather than 'as seen'. This convention has some similarities with the use of symbols in Europe's medieval art but was more sophisticated. A hippopotamus in an Egyptian river scene might be drawn small to indicate either that it was deep in the water or far away.

Hieroglyphs were used as symbols or sounds or both. The word 'sun' was shown as a circle and the word 'lotus' by a pictogram of its flower. The setting sun, together with the symbols for bread (a half-circle) and house (an open rectangle) form a hieroglyph which 'could mean "horizon" as well as "tomb"' (see Figure 3.3).[4] The way in which symbols could be used to express sounds is illustrated by the hypothetical English example of using 'bee-leaf' to write 'belief'.[5] The word 'garden' was written using symbols with garden associations and the phonetic sound *hnt-s/hent-esh* (see Figure 3.4).[6] On drawings, some elements are shown in plan, some (e.g. flowers or buildings) are in elevation and some are symbols. The sycamore fig, drawn as though lying flat on the ground, could be used as a hieroglyph for any tree or could also represent an actual fig tree (see Figure 3.15). These conventions allowed pictorial richness with many layers of meaning.

Egyptian gardens

There was a clear distinction between domestic space, made for the body at rest, and sacred space, made for the spirit (*ka*). Religious awe was the emotion produced by temples: they drew attention to the splendour of the universe, to man's place in creation and to the sacred role of pharaohs in maintaining order. Five Egyptian garden types can be distinguished:

1. fruit and vegetable plots;
2. domestic courtyards;
3. palace gardens;
4. temple sanctuaries;
5. plant and animal parks.

Logic suggests that productive gardens predated luxury gardens, that the first large gardens belonged to kings and that dwellings predated temples. Garden types will therefore be discussed in this sequence.

Fruit and vegetable gardens

Vegetables benefit from walled enclosures and require intensive care, including the classic horticultural activities of weeding and watering. In Egypt, cultivation began *c.*5300 BCE. A fifth-dynasty (2465–2323 BCE) tomb at Saqqara shows the irrigation and cultivation of lettuce. The plant was sacred because its milky sap symbolised the semen of a fertility god, Min. The same tomb has an illustration of a gardener watering the vegetable patch in the royal garden. Another tomb records that the owner was granted 'land property 200 cubits long and 200 cubits wide, enclosed by a wall, equipped, and planted with useful trees; a very large pond is to be made in it, and fig-trees and vines are to be planted'.[7] A cubit was the length of a forearm (0.5 m) so his property was about the size of 40 tennis courts, which is a good size for an orchard with vegetables.

3.9 Ancient Egyptian houses were not unlike modern agricultural dwellings, though more use was made of the roof-space. In Ancient Persia, a man was allowed to shoot an arrow at another man who spied his womenfolk sleeping on a roof.

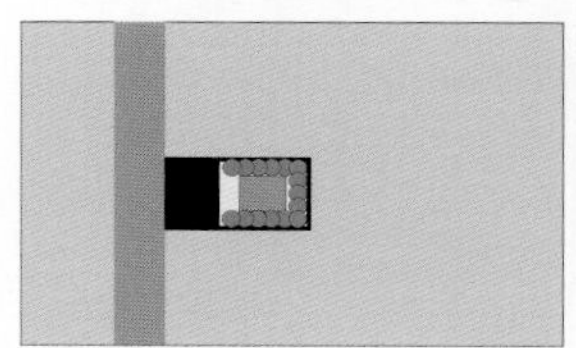

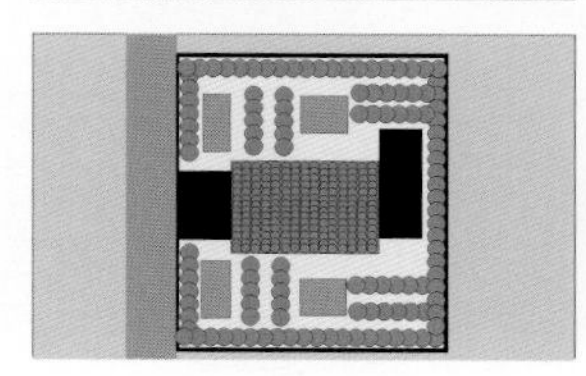

3.10 Conjectural evolution of the Egyptian domestic garden. Poorer people would have used enclosed outdoor space for utilitarian purposes.

3.11 a, b Deir el Medina, a village occupied by the craftsmen who built the royal tombs, has something of the form of the *niwt* hieroglyph (see Figure 3.25).

Domestic gardens

Royal dwellings were built with mud brick, not stone, because they were required only for one lifetime, not for eternity. By the close of the Pre-dynastic period (2920 BCE) Egypt had rectangular houses comprising a room and a yard. Except when built outside the cultivated zone, almost all these structures have been washed away, ploughed or pulverised for use as manure. Egypt is sometimes described as a land without cities but this is mainly because so little evidence of their character survives. The main sources are a few small settlements on non-agricultural land, some models of houses placed in tombs and some paintings of houses which also show private gardens. Archaeologists have, understandably, been more interested in non-domestic architecture. Aufrère and Golvin describe Amarna as 'without doubt the most interesting urban site in Egypt',[8] but in three volumes of reconstructions of Egyptian buildings, their only view of the town is drawn from too great a height to show houses or gardens. As Wildung observes, 'The closest equivalent today of everyday Egyptian architecture can be seen in the mud-brick houses in the Yemen.'[9]

The New Kingdom (1550–1070 BCE) craftsmen's village of Deir el Medina at Luxor is a rare example of a surviving village. It is in the desert because its inhabitants built the tombs in the Valley of the Kings. Water had to be carried to the village by donkey and there was little to spare for plants. For reasons of security, it was a tightly-walled settlement with a single gate, narrow streets and houses with tiny rooms. Kitchens were not roofed, and stairs led to flat roofs used for cooking and for sleeping in hot weather. An even more regimented craftsmen's village was made near the pyramids at Giza. They are not good places for learning about Egyptian domestic gardens.

3.12 a, b David Robert's 1838 drawing, showing Edfu before the temple was excavated, gives an idea of the relationship between stone temples and mud houses in Ancient Egypt, though houses were never built within temple compounds. The photograph shows the excavated temple of Edfu, seen from the Nile.

3.13 Small courtyards used for animals and work are unlikely to have contained plants.

Models and paintings deposited in tombs as grave-goods show one-, two- and three-storey dwellings with rooms and yards. Outdoor steps lead to flat roofs. They correlate with evidence from Amarna to give a picture of Egyptian houses and gardens. Outer walls provided security and privacy. Garden doors opened onto streets. Roofs were brick-vaulted or flat. Columns and beams were made from timber, which was scarce. Open courts were often on the north sides of houses, for shade. Small courts had space only for cooking and eating. Animals were kept in yards at night. Craftsmen used yards as workplaces. Wealthy families had several courts, pools and areas for different kinds of plant. Servants and animals, including cats, donkeys and cows, probably slept in lean-to shelters or open yards. Outdoor living areas were shaded by vines, mats and trees. Water was brought into gardens for horticultural use. At Amarna, many houses had circular wells in their yards.

Water is the first necessity and first luxury for making gardens. It is probable that Mesopotamian garden layouts were based on canals and Egyptian garden layouts on pools, because in Egypt settlements and palaces were built on higher land, to avoid floods. Pools had both functional and aesthetic roles. Water irrigates plants and cools air through evaporation. Keeping fish provides entertainment, food and a means of destroying the larvae of biting insects. Texts from the Old Kingdom summarise the role of domestic gardens and their features: 'I returned from my estate. I built a house and set up doorways. I dug a pool and planted trees.' Symbolic drawings of plants were used as words. Gardens were places for lovers to meet:

3.14 a, b Models of Egyptian houses and a photograph of a mud-brick house, in Iran, with steps to the roof and walled orchards beyond.

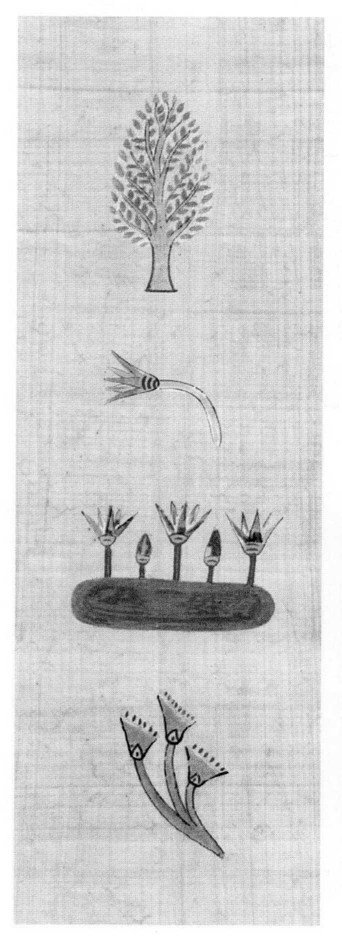

3.15 Hieroglyphic representations of plants were used as words: sycamore – tree; lotus – lotus; lotus pool – lotus pool; papyrus – plant.

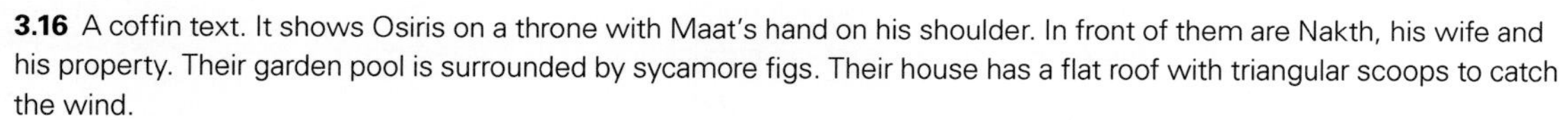

3.16 A coffin text. It shows Osiris on a throne with Maat's hand on his shoulder. In front of them are Nakth, his wife and his property. Their garden pool is surrounded by sycamore figs. Their house has a flat roof with triangular scoops to catch the wind.

I belong to you like this plot of ground
That I planted with flowers
And sweet-smelling herbs.

A surprising fact about the domestic gardens of Ancient Egypt is their similarity to modern courtyard gardens. The plants are also familiar. As in all pre-Renaissance gardens, there was a greater representation of functional than of purely decorative species. Plants known to have been cultivated in Ancient Egyptian gardens include:

Flowers

- corn poppy (*Papaver rhoeas*);
- cornflower (*Centaurea depressa*);
- Madonna lily (*Lilium candidum*);
- mallow (*Althaea ficifolia*);
- mandrake (*Mandragora officinarum*);
- papyrus (*Cyperus papyrus*);
- water lily (*Nymphaea caerulea*).

Food

- apple (*Malus sp.*);
- argun palm (*Medemia argun*);
- carob (*Ceratonia siliqua*);
- castor oil plant (*Ricinis communis*);
- Christ's thorn (*Ziziphus spina-christi*);
- common fig (*Ficus carica*);
- date palm (*Phoenix dactylifera*);
- doum palm (*Hyphaene thebaica*);
- Egyptian plum (*Balanites aegyptiaca*);
- juniper (*Juniperus oxycedrus*);
- olive (*Olea europea*);
- pistachio (*Pistacia vera*);
- pomegranate (*Punica granatum*);
- stone pine (*Pinus pinea*);
- sycamore fig (*Ficus sycomorus*);
- vine (*Vitis vinifera*).

Herbs

- chervil (*Anthriscus cerefolium*);
- coriander (*Coriandrum sativum*);
- peppermint (*Mentha piperita*);
- thyme (*Thymbra spicata*).

3.17 Papyrus (*Cyperus papyrus*).

3.18 The Temple of Ramesses II at Medinet Habu had a small palace and garden. They were built in mud brick and located to the left of the pylon.

Perfume

- henna (*Lawsonia inermis*);
- myrtle (*Myrtus communis*).

Vegetables

- broad bean (*Vicia faba*);
- chickpea (*Cicer arietinum);*
- cucumber (*Cucumis melo*);
- garlic (*Allium sativum*);
- lentil (*Lens culinarus*);
- lettuce (*Lactuca sativa*);
- onion (*Allium cepa*);
- watermelon (*Citrullus lanatus*).

Coffin texts, known collectively as *The Book of the Dead*, were inscribed in tombs for guidance in the afterlife. A famous illustration (see Figure 3.16) shows a royal scribe, Nakht, with his wife. They are standing in front of their house. It has a flat roof with devices to catch the wind. The owners' hands are outstretched in a hieroglyphic gesture signifying worship. Beyond the pool, surrounded by nine sycamore fig trees and four date palms, sits Osiris, god of the dead and of resurrection, with Maat, the goddess of truth and justice, behind him. A tomb was a realm of peace, truth and justice in which to dwell for eternity.

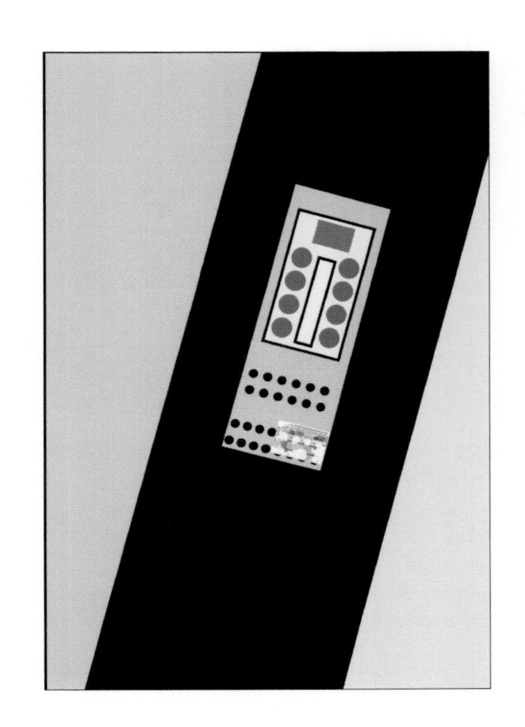

3.19 a, b, c Flinders Petrie commissioned a drawing of the garden painting from the floor of the North Harem (or Harim) at Amarna. **a** Akhenaten and Nefertiti; **b** Petrie's drawing of the pavement with circles marking the columns; **c** a plan to show the painting in relation to the palace (see p. 98).[10]

Palace gardens

Palace gardens were larger than private gardens but were similar in design and function. The word 'pharaoh' means 'great house' (from the Egyptian *per aa*)[11] but few archaeological remains of palaces have been found and almost all are from the New Kingdom. The few include the palaces within the temple compounds of Ramesses II (the Ramesseum) and Ramesses III (at Medinet Habu) which were probably used only for short periods, during coronations and royal visits. More is known of Akhenaten's palace and gardens in his capital city, Amarna. It was built as a new town on virgin land and remains the best surviving example of Ancient Egyptian town planning, despite having been inhabited for only 15 years. Akhenaten worshipped Aten, the sun god, and is thought to be the originator of monotheism. His city stands on the east bank of the Nile, half-way between the modern cities of Cairo and Luxor. The waterside strip was within the zone of cultivation but the greater part of Amarna was in the desert. This allowed more space for gardens and made pools essential. Fragments of mud-brick buildings and courts survive. Akhenaten explained the layout of the town he called Akhetaten:

> *I build the great temple for the Aten, my father, in Akhetaten in this place. And I build the small temple for the Aten, my father, in Akhetaten, in this place. I build the sun-shadow chapel for the great royal consort Nefertiti of the Aten, my father, in Akhetaten in this place. I build a jubilee temple for the Aten, my father, on the island of the Aten in Akhetaten in this place ... I build for myself palaces for the pharaoh, and I build a harem for the royal consort in Akhetaten in this place. I have a tomb built in the mountain of Akhetaten, where the sun rises, where I shall be buried after the millions of years' reign, that the Aten, my father, has allocated to me.*[12]

The 'great temple' for the sun god was aligned on an east–west axis. The 'palaces for the pharaoh', during his earthly life, had outdoor courts and gardens. They were

3.20 The temple of 'Glorious Seti in the West of Thebes' was restored by the German Archaeological Institute after 1972. A canal linked the temple to the Nile and it was the first halt in the procession from Karnak to the temples of the West Bank ('the Beautiful Feast of the Valley').

3.21 Dancers and musicians from the tomb of Nebamun.

distributed along a 5 km south–north Royal Road which was also a Sacred Way. It was used for the king and queen's chariot ride, south to the ceremonial area of the Central City. This area had a King's House and a Great Palace with sunken garden courts, pools and overhead shading. The walls were painted and, in peristyle areas, so were the pavements. The King's House had a Window of Appearance from which he and Queen Nefertiti could show themselves and distribute gifts.[13] A bridge crossed the Royal Road to a harem palace.

'Harem' derives from an Arabic word, meaning prohibited, and acquired its exotic association with sexual delight at a later date. In Egypt, a harem was a residential palace for women and children. Life was precarious and kings needed many wives because they needed many children, in whose veins ran the blood of gods. When his son, the future Ramesses II, came of age, Seti presented him with a delicious harem of 'female royal attendants who were like unto the great beauties of the palace'.[14] Ramesses was able to boast of fathering 79 sons and 59 daughters, four of whom he married (since royal daughters could not marry commoners, this may have been an act of charity). A harem palace was a safe residence for the royal women, their children, the old and the unmarried. It was a dormitory establishment with fertile women, productive gardens, fields and orchards. Dwellings within the harem compound had internal courts, often with plants and pools:

> *The physical setting of the more modern harem was very firmly focused inwards towards the central open space which became the scene of the daily activities of the harem-women. Here food was prepared, cosmetics applied, and the days and evenings were spent singing, dancing and telling stories.*[15]

The royal harem was also the most important school in Egypt. It was run by the Teacher of the Royal Children and attended by children of noble families. Officials boasted of having been 'a child of the Palace of the Royal Harem'. Garden courts in royal palaces were used for official gatherings, receptions, teaching and private life. Christian Jacq turned his imagination to an exotic garden scene:

> *The twelve dancers had chosen a vast lotus pond as their torchlit backdrop. Wearing pearl-studded netting beneath short tunics, triple-braided wigs, strands of beads and lapis lazuli bracelets, the young women swayed suggestively ... Suddenly, the dancers discarded their wigs, tunics and netting. Hair in a strict chignon, bare-breasted, clad in a wisp of kilt, they each tapped their right foot, then executed a breathtaking back flip, perfectly timed. Arching and bowing gracefully, they performed more acrobatic feats, all just as spectacular.*[16]

The most famous Egyptian garden painting was found, by an Italian Egyptologist in the nineteenth century, in the funerary chapel above Sennefer's burial chamber (Tomb 96 in the Western Valley). Today, the chapel is closed and the painting destroyed. Fortunately, a careful copy was made. Sennefer was an important man, 'Mayor of the Southern City' (Thebes) and 'Overseer of the Gardens of Amun', but it is not likely that the painting

3.22 The most famous painting of an Egyptian garden. Sennefer was responsible for the garden but is not thought to have been its owner. As a type, it is astonishingly similar to a modern domestic garden in a hot country.

depicts his private garden. More probably, Sennefer had responsibility for the garden's care, and perhaps its design, as part of the Karnak temple complex. A pharaoh could have used it during his afterlife but would have needed a similar space for his bodily life. The plan shows an enclosed court bounded by a mud-brick wall topped with glazed tiles. Gothein analysed the plan as follows:

> *You enter from the front by a large entrance gate, or by one of two side wicket-gates. A shady avenue follows the outside wall, and a canal, outside that; this adds to the feeling of complete seclusion which the picture suggests. You step through the door straight into the house, which is shown much too large in comparison with its surroundings, the doors being the only break in the façade. No doubt the artist wished to suggest that the owner was a very rich person, by emphasising the beauty of his front gate. Here too was the porter's lodge, perhaps also a reception-room for such visitors as were not allowed in the main building, which was hidden away in the garden. Between the gate and the house,*

3.23 The island of Philae was said to be so sacred that birds did not fly over it (painting by David Roberts).

> *occupying the whole of the middle space, was the vineyard. It consisted of four arched arbours, their rafters supported by posts. A path is left open in the middle forming the chief approach to the house from the gate; and from this path two side-walks lead directly to the covered ways.*[17]

Gothein writes as though it were a private garden. Wilkinson believes it to have been a temple garden.[18]

Temple and tomb gardens

Origins

The oldest religious site in Egypt is the stone circle at Nabta Playa (*c.*4500 BCE).[19] In a part of the Sahara which once had water, 100 km west of the Nile, it appears to have been used for astronomical observations and it is probable that this was combined with a religious role. The oldest temple to a known god is that of Neken in the 'city of the falcon', Hierakonopolis in Southern Egypt.[20] It was an enclosure containing a paved floor and a flagpole. Settled societies require cohesive beliefs and customs to maintain order. In Egypt this was provided by an integrated system of religion, government, laws and defence. Cities allowed protection and communication. Modern societies maintain a separation of powers but in the ancient world they were fused. Egypt's hierarchy of power had a god-king at the top and slaves at the base. Priests, scribes, soldiers, craftsmen and farmers occupied intermediate ranks. During his bodily life, a pharaoh's duty was discharged from a string of palaces along the Nile. During his afterlife, the duty was performed from a tomb-temple. At the transition from bodily life to afterlife a pharaoh changed from one incarnation of a god to another, just as the land he ruled changed with the annual cycle of inundation. A New Kingdom pharaoh was Horus in his earthly life and Osiris in his afterlife.

When royal tombs are distinguished from temples, it is more a matter of emphasis than essence. In the Old and Middle Kingdoms, the mortuary role appears stronger because the dominant structure was a pyramid. In the New Kingdom, the ceremonial role was emphasised, with tombs placed in the Valley of the Kings for security against tomb-robbers. The Egyptian word for all types of temple was *hut* ('mansion'). Cult temples were known as 'mansions of the gods' and mortuary temples as 'mansions of millions of years'. Cults were systems of worship expressed through ceremony. Gods were expected to inhabit their mansions for millions of years. For three millennia, extending through the Old, Middle and New Kingdoms, the planning of tombs and cult temples was governed by a creation myth inspired by Egypt's unique landscape.

When the flood reached its zenith, the Nile valley became a serene composition of water, trees and desert. Swirling currents produced uneven surfaces. As the flood ebbed, mounds appeared before flats and hollows. Everything was coated in black mud. Then the land was replanted and repopulated. The creation myth held that the earth itself was formed in this way: after the primal mound emerged from the waters, a reed grew and a falcon, representing Horus, landed. Divine powers, not unlike 'laws of nature', ruled the world. Concepts and aspects of the creation were represented by a family of gods with

3.24 Hieroglyph for a burial mound, planted with sycamores and with ideograms for flag, building and Osiris inside.

3.25 a–e Hieroglyph for a city, perhaps symbolising the need for protection and communication. The *niwt* symbol is a determinative. When used with other symbols, it names a specific city.

3.26 The Nile in the flood season with a village to the left and the pyramids in the distance (painted by A. MacCullum in 1880).

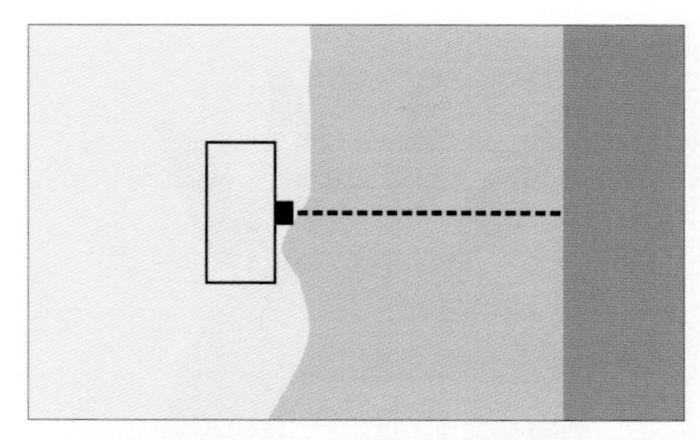

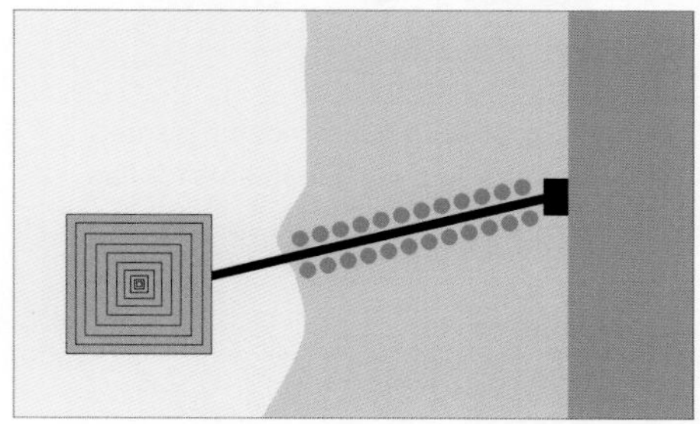

3.27 a, b, c Diagrams of an Osirian Temple in Pre-dynastic Egypt (top), the Old Kingdom (centre) and the New Kingdom (bottom).

3.28 Borchardt's drawing of the pyramid at Abusir shows a processional route to a 'valley temple' beside the Nile during the period of inundation.

overlapping roles. Atum was father of the gods. Amun was king of the gods. Ptah was creator of the universe. Nun, being the god of the primordial waters, was old and wise. Re was father of mankind and, as Amun-Re, identified with the sun god. Osiris was the giver of civilisation, ruler of the dead and god of fertility. Osiris' son by Isis was Horus. Osiris' family extended from the father of the gods to the 'Living Horus', Egypt's reigning pharaoh. The word for god (*netjer*) used a hieroglyph of a flag, which was derived from the flags that were always placed at entrances to shrines and temples.

Osiris' tomb (Figure 3.24) was made of sycamore wood and shaded by sycamore trees. The sycamore fig (*Ficus sycomorus*) was the abode of Hathor. The figs grow directly on branches. Botanically they are inside-out flower clusters that depend on a pollinator wasp. Without fertilisation, the fig falls to the ground and shrivels. The tree can bear up to seven crops a year – a good symbol for a fertility god. Sycamore wood, which is easy to work, was used for making royal coffins.

An eighteenth-dynasty hymn to Osiris celebrates his powers:

> *Thou hast made this earth by thy hand, and the waters thereof, and the wind thereof, the herb thereof, all the cattle thereof, all the winged fowl thereof, all the fish thereof, all the creeping things thereof, and all the four-footed beasts thereof. O thou son of Nut, the whole world is gratified when thou ascendest thy father's throne like Ra. Thou shinest in the horizon, thou sendest forth thy light into the darkness, thou makest the darkness light with thy double plume, and thou floodest the world with light like the Disk at break of day. Thy diadem pierceth heaven and becometh a brother unto the stars, O thou form of every*

god. Thou art gracious in command and in speech, thou art the favoured one of the great company of the gods, and thou art the greatly beloved one of the lesser company of the gods.[21]

The central feature of a temple sanctuary was first an Osirian mound (*benben*), then a pyramid and then a 'mansion'. Each was a house of Amun. Temples were not places for the faithful to gather and pray, as in synagogues, churches and mosques. They were exclusive places in which high priests performed sacred rites. Statues of gods were dressed, anointed and given food and drink, at fixed times determined by the sun. Priests, some full-time and many part-time, provided assistance. They helped to predict floods, resolve disputes and regulate water by forming basins and opening dykes. A temple door keeper was the 'Door Opener of Heaven'.[22]

Development

In the Old and Middle Kingdoms the features of a sanctuary were:

- a significant place in the landscape;
- a protective wall, often wavy in plan to symbolise the primordial waters;
- a sacred mound or pyramid, to symbolise the emergence of land from water;
- a path from the mound to water.

The New Kingdom was established after an Intermediate Period in which Egypt had been ruled by an Asiatic people, probably from Palestine. The Hyksos are thought to have introduced the horse and chariot to Egypt.[23] A 'standard' temple layout developed, redeploying the above symbolic elements as follows:

- a small 'valley temple' beside the water, to house a barge, used for the pharaoh when he died and for transporting effigies of gods at subsequent festivals;
- a ceremonial route from the water (river, pool, or T-shaped canal end) to the temple along which gardens could be made;
- an outer wall of mud brick, bounding the temple compound; the latter contained a lake, a grove, a mansion of god and stores;
- a pylon gateway marked by flagpoles and leading to the mansion itself;
- an open peristyle court, to admit the sun;
- a hypostyle hall, to symbolise the created world;
- the holy of holies (an inner sanctuary with a plinth for the god's statue).

Later temples were sited on the margin of life and death: the edge of the floodplain. Ceremonial routes were then walled, roofed, planted, lined with sphinxes, or given significance by colossal statues. Pylon gates were positioned so that the sun rose between the towers, creating the hieroglyph for horizon. A sacred lake and a sacred grove were contained within the sanctuary. The grove was planted with sycamore fig, native to

3.29 Steps to the sacred lake at Karnak, with an egret about to enter the water.

3.30 Ancient Egypt: map of the Red Land and the Black Land.

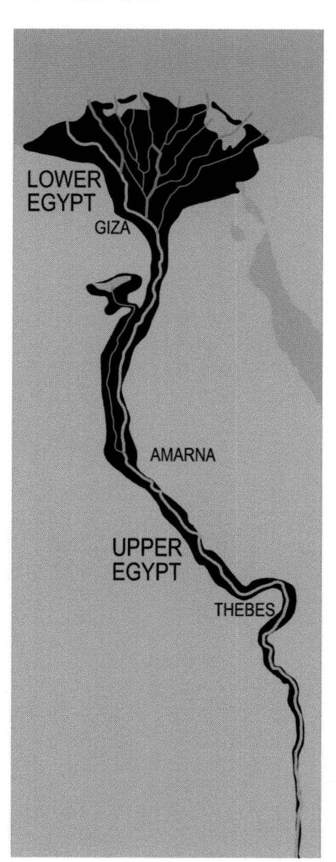

water margins, and tamarisk, native to desert margins. A flight of steps led into the water from the temple side of the lake. It was a place for priests to bathe at dawn and purify themselves. The sacred lake at Karnak had a tunnel from which geese, symbolising Amun, would emerge onto the water surface, as Amun himself had done at the beginning of time. The pharaoh, an incarnation of Amun and of Horus, was rowed on the lake.

At Malkata, near Medinet Habu, Amenhetep III made a ceremonial lake (2 km by 1 km) and shaped the spoil into 'rows of artificial hills'.[24] Kemp describes Malkata as 'Egypt's largest earthwork' and the mounds as an 'early example of landscaping'. They stood at the meeting point of the Nile floodplain and the desert. At royal jubilees (*Sed* festivals), the lake was traversed by Morning and Evening Barges, representing the journeys of the sun god. A New Kingdom temple was a model of the creation. Ceilings represented the sky; columns represented plants; the floor, occasionally flooded by the Nile, represented the primordial waters from which land emerged. The processional axis lay along the sun's daily path from east to west. The inner sanctuary was at the point nearest the setting sun. The temple compound was a meeting place of heaven, earth and underworld. It was a gate, allowing gods and kings to move between the here-and-now and the hereafter. Blank doors defined exit and entry points. Temples were tombs; tombs were temples.

Location and planning

At Thebes, New Kingdom temples for state gods were placed on the east bank of the Nile, the side over which the sun rose. They were built on levees and on the remains of older buildings. Temples for gods of the afterlife were placed on the side of the Nile over which the sun set. They could be on mounds or, as with Hatshepsut's temple, on the border of the Red Land (*Deshret*, desert) and the Black Land (*Kemet*, agricultural land). Floods were welcomed as symbols of the primal conditions from which the earth emerged. Temples were planned in relation to significant landscape features (cliffs, mountains, buildings, springs, etc.), on places associated with myths and traditions (e.g. a god's birthplace) and on lines of sight to other temples. They were connected to the Nile by a canal ending in a T-shaped dock. The T-shape was also used for pools containing pure water for rituals[25] and probably represented quays used by sacred barges. Temples owned fleets. Ships brought construction materials and the produce amassed within temple compounds. Stores filled up if there were 'seven fat years' and emptied in periods of 'seven lean years'.

Some temples (e.g. Elephantine) were aligned with the stars. Slots were made in walls and slits in roofs so that sunlight illuminated significant features. A temple's location was fixed at a foundation ceremony which included 'stretching the cord' (*pedj-shes*). This involved laying the first bricks and placing ritual offerings in foundation pits. North–south was favoured for the temple's short axis and east–west for the long axis. Prime axes could be fixed in different ways and a slightly new line was often adopted

3.31 a, b Photographs of Egypt's Red (desert) Land and the Black (agricultural) Land.

when a new king extended an old temple. Most temples used east–west as the long axis so that the sun arose over the pylon and set over the sanctuary of a departed pharaoh-god.

Temples were dimensioned in cubits. The Egyptian royal cubit was equal to the length of a god-king's forearm (524 mm). Multiples of ten cubits (5.24 m) were preferred for key temple dimensions. Subsidiary dimensions were one finger, two fingers, three fingers and a hand. Temples had large land holdings, from which they drew tribute. In the time of Ramesses III, the Domain of Amun had over 2,300 sq km of land and 80,000 personnel, most of whom were engaged in agriculture and horticulture. It is recorded that in a period of 1,057 days a total of 4,786,184 floral offerings were made in the Temple of Amun at Karnak.[26] Such a tribute implies the existence of many skilled gardeners.

Festivals

The Domain of Amun united the world of the living (the east bank) with the world of the departed (the west bank). Festivals marked seasonal and mythological events. The Festival of Opening the Dykes took place when the flood arrived and refilled pools. There were three seasons, related to the agricultural cycle:

1. Inundation (*Akhet*): the flood lasted approximately mid-July to mid-November.
2. Growing (*Peret*): the winter growing season was from mid-November to mid-March.
3. Drought (*Shemu*): the dry summer period was from mid-March to mid-July.

3.32 Looking across the Nile from Luxor to Western Thebes.

Memphis was an administrative capital. Thebes (now Luxor) was a religious capital and a festival city. It was called Waset and described simply as 'The City':

> *Waset is the pattern for every city. Both the flood and the earth were in her from the beginning of time. The sands came to delimit her soil, to create her ground from the mound when earth came into being. Then mankind came into being within her. To found every city in her true name (The City), since all are called 'city' after the example of Waset.*[27]

Like its temples, Luxor was inspired by the Osiris myth. The temple of Karnak is built on a Nile levee and the mound of the pre-New Kingdom city. It was planned on what Nims calls 'river north', a theoretical north–south line but actually a north-east–south-west line at a right angle to the Nile.[28] The inner sanctuary, or 'holy of holies', housed the divine boat-shrine and a statue of Amun. Carved reliefs show him, as Amun-Min, with penis erect to create the world. A T-shaped quay and canal led to the Nile. Festivals were occasions when the gods from the east bank of the Nile (both pharaohs and statues) visited the departed gods on the west bank. Processional routes, often paved and lined with statues, defined the Domain of Amun. From Karnak, routes led over the river to Western Thebes and up the river to Luxor.

The Festival of the Valley took place in the second month of summer, at the time of the new moon. Amun dwelt at Karnak. At the start of the Festival his statue, in its ship,

3.33 The modern road from the Nile to the Temple of Queen Hatshepsut and the Valley of the Kings is not far from the alignment of the old processional route.

was carried from its home by torchlight procession, escorted by priests, dancers, musicians and incense-bearers. He followed a processional route to the Nile, crossed the river and travelled by canal to a small temple on the edge of the Libyan Desert. Another processional route, centred on Karnak and lined with pairs of painted sphinxes, led to Hatshepsut's Temple, then known as Djeser-Djeseru ('Holiest of the Holy'). The temple compound was surrounded by a thick limestone wall:

> *Once through the gate, Amun passed immediately into a peaceful, pleasantly shaded garden where T-shaped pools glinted in the sunlight and trees – almost certainly the famous fragrant trees from Punt – offered a tempting respite from the fierce desert sun. Looking upwards, Amun would have seen the temple in all its glory; a softly gleaming white limestone building occupying three ascending terraces set back against the cliff, its tiered porticoes linked by a long, open-air stairway rising through the centre of the temple towards the sanctuary. Amun's route lay upwards. Passing over the lower portico he reached the flat second terrace where his path was marked out by pairs of colossal, painted red-granite sphinxes, each with Hatshepsut's head, inscribed to 'The King of Upper and Lower Egypt Maatkare, Beloved of Amun who is in the midst of Djeser-Djeseru, and given life forever'.*[29]

Festivals thus joined temple compounds to the wider landscape. They are the ancestor of garden avenues and town avenues in the modern world.

3.34 a, b, c The temples of Mentuhotep and Queen Hatshepsut are the oldest masterpieces of landscape architecture. Some of the tree pits from their sacred groves, marked in red, have been found and are the oldest known planting positions in the world.

Plant and animal collections

Temples owned gardens, outside their wavy walls. Productive gardens had orchards, pools, vineyards, vegetables and flower gardens. Ornamental gardens were often located on processional routes. Special gardens had names.[30] Aten was the solar disc and Akhenaten's garden at Amarna was 'The Seeing-Place of the Aten'. The garden to a shrine on the processional route between Karnak and Luxor was called 'Hatshepsut is united with the perfection of Amun'. A pyramid had a grove called the 'the soul of Sahure appears in splendour'.

Animals with symbolic significance were kept in temple and palace gardens. Carved lions decorated the king's throne and live lions were kept in cages at the entrance to the gardens at Karnak. Paintings show pharaohs being presented with giraffes, monkeys and tigers. Plants with symbolic significance were grown. At Pi-Ramesse there was a large garden filled with plants and animals, on a similar principle to contemporary Mesopotamian gardens (see Chapter 2):

> *The abundant supply of water allowed Pi-Ramesse to become a garden city, planted with pomegranate and date orchards and vineyards. Around the royal palace were ornamental gardens, a lake and even a zoo; lion, giraffe and elephant bones have all been discovered in the remains of the grounds.*[31]

Sycamore fig and tamarisk were grown within temple compounds because of their symbolic significance. The Egyptian Lotus (*Nymphea lotus*) was sacred to the goddess Isis

3.35 a, b Sacred lakes at Medinet Habu and the Temple of Mut at Karnak. Mut's lake surrounds the temple on three sides and is called the Isheru.

and appears in more tomb pictures than any other flower. Girls gathered flowers in the marshes, to place on banqueting tables, in vases and in their hair, or to offer as gifts to their gods and their husbands.

The influence of Egyptian gardens

Archaeology reveals the garden tradition of Ancient Egypt to have developed over 3000 years. One cannot detail its influence on Europe, but nor can one doubt it. The features listed below are common to the Egyptian and Graeco-Roman traditions. Some may have originated in Mesopotamia and some may have been reinvented:

- sacred lakes and groves;
- processional avenues;
- peristyle courts with fresco decoration;
- columns inspired by plant forms;
- terracing;
- rectangular pools and plant beds in walled enclosures;
- symbolic plants;
- stone and terracotta pots;
- vine pergolas;
- plant and animal gardens.

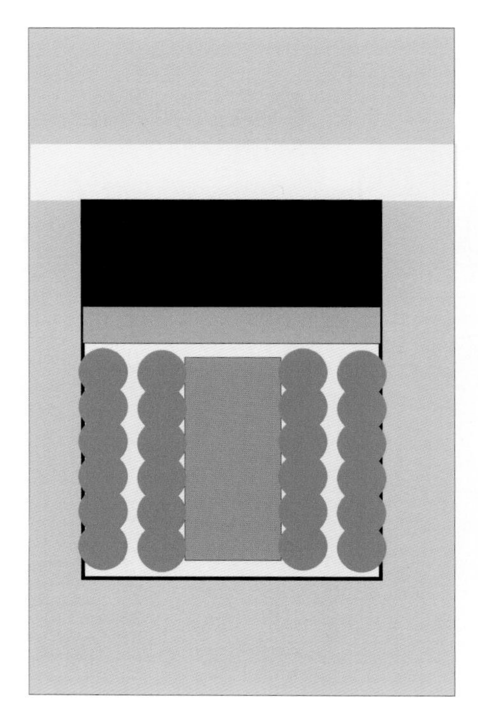

3.36 Egyptian domestic garden.

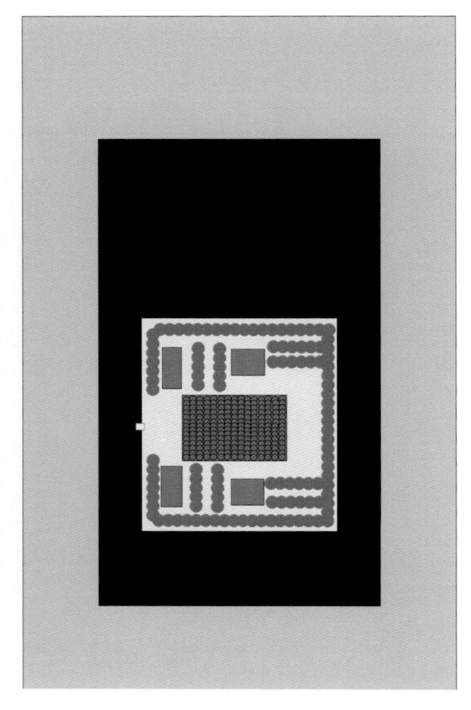

3.37 Egyptian palace garden.

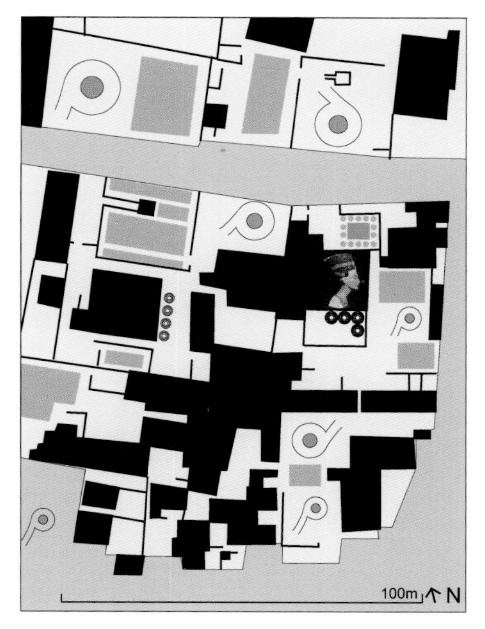

3.38 The famous head of Queen Nefertiti is positioned over the house of the sculptor in which it was found.

Types and examples

Domestic gardens

Use: Small domestic gardens functioned as part of the dwelling, meriting the description 'outdoor rooms'. Garden pools held fish and served as a water supply. Climbers and trees were needed for shade.

Form: House and garden walls were made of mud brick. Outdoor stairs led to flat roofs with rush sunshades. The roof space could be used for cooking, eating and sleeping. Since dwellings were on higher land, to avoid the floods, water had to be carried in or drawn from wells.

Amarna, 1350 BCE

Amarna is one of the few Ancient Egyptian settlements to have survived. The layout of dwellings, garden walls and wells was excavated by Barry Kemp. Nothing is known about the planting of its gardens. One of the dwellings belonged to the sculptor who made the famous bust of Nefertiti and it is likely that most of the spaces shown on the plan were working yards for craft and horticultural activities.

Palace gardens

Use: Egyptian palace gardens appear to have been more domestic than courtly. They were used for relaxation, outdoor eating, children's play and the cultivation of plants, both beautiful and edible. Our knowledge of palace gardens comes from tomb paintings, made so that pharaohs could enjoy in the afterlife comforts similar to those enjoyed in the earthly phase of their existence.

Form: Palace compounds, like temple compounds, were rectangular enclosures bounded by high walls. Tomb paintings show gardens with fruit trees, flowers, pools, pot plants, vine-clad pergolas and places to sit in winter sun or summer shade. Excavations reveal substantial buildings with internal courts that are likely to have been treated in this way. The geometry of gardens is more symmetrical than that of temples but this may indicate only the way they were drawn: regularity comes naturally to the draughtsman

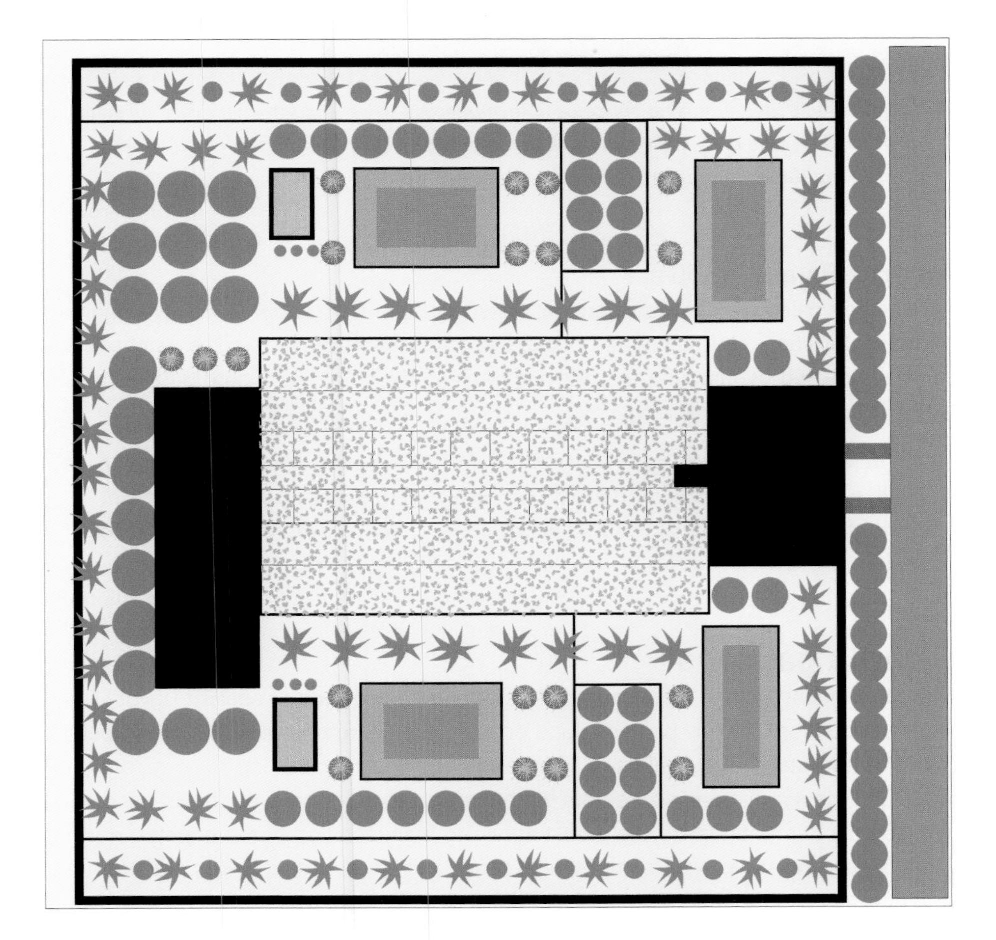

3.39 Sennefer's garden.

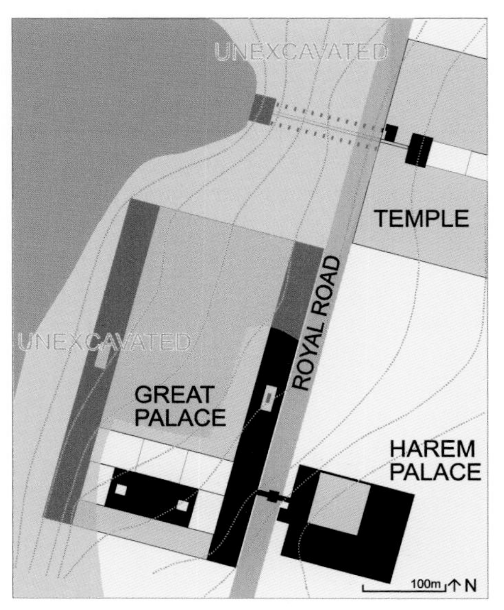

3.40 Akhenaten's palace at Amarna.

and less easily to those who work directly on the ground. The diagram shows a building with an internal court.

Sennefer's garden, 1400 BCE

The most famous painting of an Egyptian garden was found in the funerary chapel of Sennefer, above his burial chamber (Tomb 96 in the Western Valley). Sennefer lived in the reign of Amenophis II and is more likely to have been designer than owner of the garden, which is palatial in scale and may have belonged to a pharaoh. The original painting has been lost but a careful copy was made in the nineteenth century. Buildings and trees are drawn in elevation, as though flat on the ground, but other features are shown in plan. The garden is surrounded by a high mud wall capped with clay tiles, which are represented by hoops on the plan. Visitors could arrive by boat at the garden entrance, which is shown on the right of the drawing. A causeway leads to a gate lodge with a decorated door; one passed through this to a central, vine-shaded court. The master's house, shown with three rooms, is on the opposite side of the garden from the entrance. There are lines of palm trees on the other two sides. Four small garden pools can be seen, with ducks and flowers in their midst; two of these pools are overlooked by shelters with clumps of lotus flowers, possibly in pots, nearby.

> *Its mile-long canal, imposing entrance gate, numerous trees, and large vineyard all suggest great wealth ... the roof of the villa is shaded by awnings, and small garden pavilions overlooking the storage pools invite relaxation.*
>
> (Julia Berral)[32]

Amarna Palace, 1350 BCE

Akhenaten's palace and garden were excavated by Barry Kemp after 1977, revealing the layout of buildings, courtyards and pools, but not planting. Something of its character can be imagined by inserting the drawing of Sennefer's garden (Figure 3.38) into the layout uncovered by archaeology.

> *The desolate and deserted appearance of the plain of el-Amarna should not deceive the modern visitor, however. In the days of Akhenaten, this was a vast garden, dotted with plants, flowers, splendid palaces with magnificent painted decorations depicting natural subjects, and even a lake.*
>
> (Alberto Siliotti)[33]

Temple gardens

Use: The oldest 'garden' survivals are the temple compounds of ancient Egypt. They were sanctuaries used by pharaohs and priests, though some members of the public might be admitted on festival days. The design of temples explained the nature of the world and the social order, as we now do through science, religion, art, history and politics. Temple compounds are the oldest surviving manifestation of the quest to design outdoor space as what we now call works of art. Sacred groves and lakes were formed within temple compounds.

Form: Axial lines were used but the overall geometry was non-symmetrical. Temples were built in compounds bounded by wavy walls. The internal space was in part ceremonial and in part laid out in gardens. Temples were linked by avenues, lined with trees, sphinxes and statues. The line of the avenue ran into the compound and led through a series of processional gates to a hypostyle hall and then an inner sanctum, the holy of holies. Much of the enclosed land was used to accommodate storehouses. Compounds also held sacred lakes, pools, statues, shrines, flower and vegetable gardens. The construction material was stone, not mud brick.

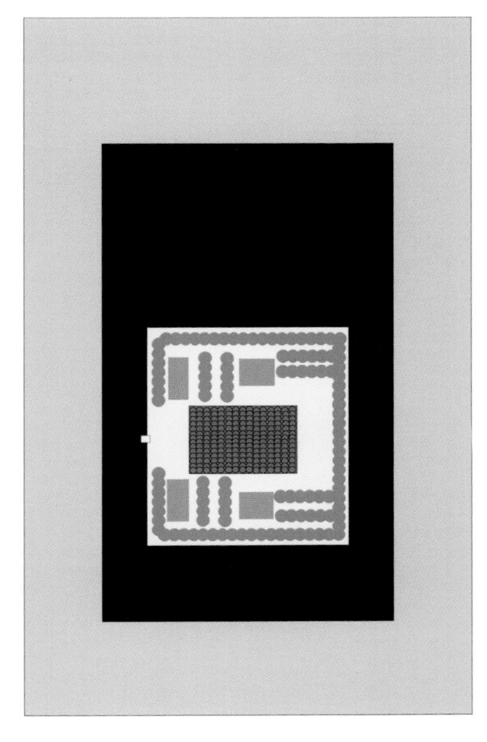

3.41 Egyptian sanctuary.

Temple of Mentuhotep, 2065 BCE

The Temple of Mentuhotep at Dêr el-Bahari was made for the pharaoh who re-united Egypt and established the Middle Kingdom. Described as 'entirely novel in its multi-level construction',[34] Mentuhotep's Temple has a forecourt, once planted with trees, and a ramp leading to a platform on which stood a temple with a view over the Nile Valley (see Figure 3.42). A decoy burial chamber was dug beneath the Temple and the king's actual burial chamber was dug into the cliffs.

> *Its unknown architect showed a remarkable eye for the picturesque exploitation of a site with his use of terraces and colonnades.*
>
> (Cyril Aldred)[35]

Temple of Queen Hatshepsut, 1450 BCE

The Temple of Queen Hatshepsut is the first masterpiece of Western landscape architecture: structure and setting are united. It was known as Djeser-Djeseru (Holiest of the Holy) to the Ancient Egyptians and is now known as Deir el-Bahri (Monastery of the North), after the Coptic monastery which occupied the site from the fifth century to the nineteenth century. Queen Hatshepsut (also known by her throne name Maat-ka-Re, 'Justice is the soul Re') ruled from 1479 to 1458 as 'God's Wife' (high priestess) of Amun. Her tomb and mortuary temple are in different locations. The tomb, where the treasure lay, is the oldest dateable tomb (KV 20) in the Valley of the Kings. Her temple was probably designed by Senenmut, governor of the Domain of Amun. If so, Senenmut deserves, among other distinctions, to be remembered as the first great landscape architect known to history. The Temple has three large rectangular courts, connected by ramps and commanding outward prospects. A handrail in the form of a serpent with a falcon's head followed the ramp. Tree pits in the lower court reveal the outline of a sacred grove which had two T-shaped pools abutting the central path. *The Book of the Dead* (Chapter 186) shows Hathor, as a cow, coming from a sacred mound in a clump of papyrus, representing the margin between life and death.

A processional route to the Nile, used for the Festival of the Valley, was lined with sphinxes placed at 10 m intervals; each of these was 3 m long and 1 m high. Napoleon's experts saw traces of their positions, so that 'approaching from the valley up a processional way lined with sandstone sphinxes, the visitor would have been conscious from

3.42 Queen Hatshepsut's Temple (1450 BCE), built beside the Temple of Mentuhotep (2065 BCE).

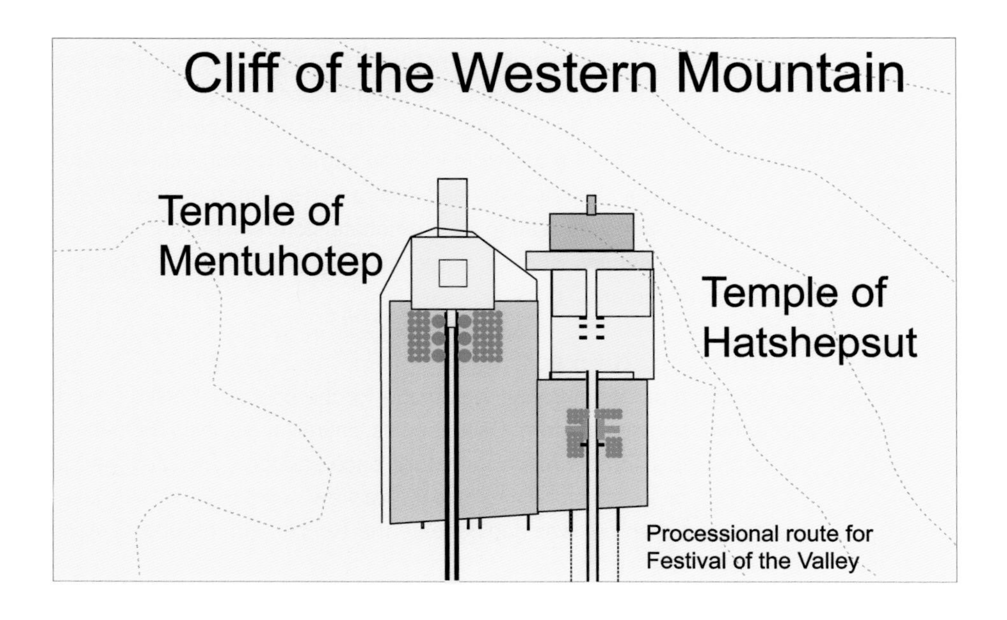

far away of the great painted limestone Osiride statues of the queen fronting the colonnade of the upper terrace'.[36]

Djeser-Djeseru is a deeply symbolic place:

> *Here there stands out for the very first time in the history of art a most magnificent idea – that of building three terraces, one above the other, each of their bordering walls set against the mountainside and made beautiful with pillared corridors.*
>
> (Marie-Luise Gothein)[37]

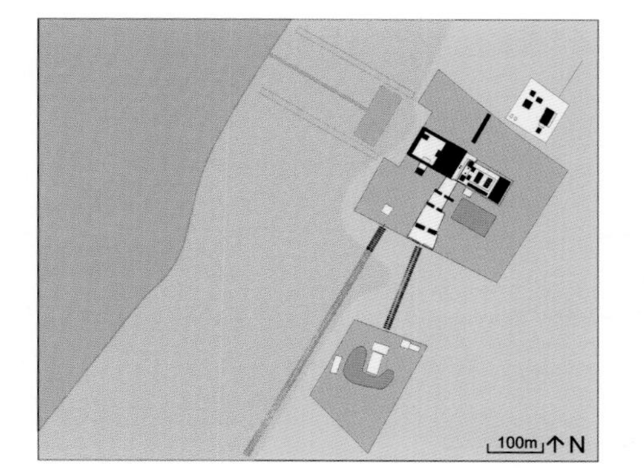

3.43 The Temple of Karnak and precinct of Mut.

Karnak, 1350 BCE

The temple precinct of Karnak is on the east bank of the Nile in the town known today as Luxor. It had a ceremonial dock for use during festivals but the layout shown on the diagram is conjectural.

Temples were used by priests and pharaohs for the religious and sexual rites on which the continued stability of the world was believed to depend. Pharaohs did not live in temples, but, being gods, had a central role in religious rites. The outer walls gave secrecy and mystery to the proceedings. Internal walls articulated the space and created compartments for different activities. Within the precinct, some of the land was managed as a sacred garden, but no details of this have survived. A 'holy of holies' lay at the centre. The sacred lake was a symbol of the eternal ocean from which the earth was created; the priests of Amun purified themselves in holy water. Avenues of sphinxes linked temple compounds.

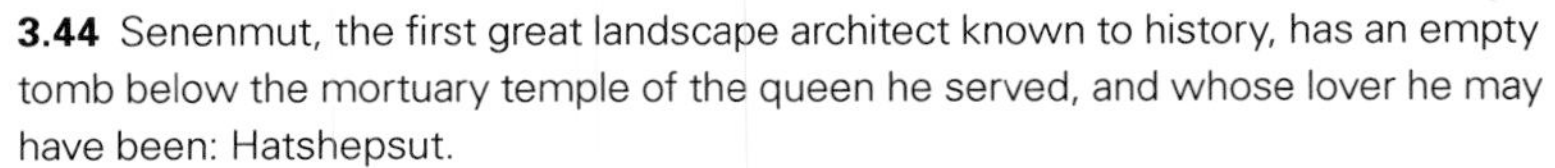

3.44 Senenmut, the first great landscape architect known to history, has an empty tomb below the mortuary temple of the queen he served, and whose lover he may have been: Hatshepsut.

3.45 Porphry statue of Senenmut, kneeling behind a pharoah's cartouche.

3.46 A right-angle square from Thebes with a broken ebony cubit rod, from the tomb of Sennefer.

The processions of images of the holy family of Thebes and of other sanctified beings (including statues of kings of olden times) setting forth from the huge, brightly painted temples, and making their slow progress along formally arranged avenues with carefully stage-managed halts at intermediate stations, and the occasional excitement of a 'miracle': all this brought to the city as a whole spectacle and munificence which regularly reinforced the physical and economic dominance of the temples.

(Barry Kemp)[38]

Temple of Ramesses II (Ramesseum), 1200 BCE

The temple and palace of Ramesses II (Ramesses the Great) was the greatest project of one of Egypt's greatest builders. His throne name, User-Maat-Re, was rendered by Diodorus Siculus as 'Ozymandias' and used by Shelley in his famous lines, 'My name is Ozymandias, King of Kings: Look on my works, ye Mighty, and despair'.

Much of the temple's structure has decayed: stone was removed for building, statues were smashed, the site was used as a church, and foundations were undermined by the Nile floods. Yet the layout and some of the structures survive. In plan, the temple is a parallelogram, not a rectangle, and half the space is occupied by storerooms. It had a palace and several garden courts and probably a sacred lake within the temple compound. A garden illustrated in the tomb of Nezemger (TT 138), 'Overseer of the Garden in the Ramesseum in the Domain of Amun', shows what these gardens may have contained.

The decoration of the site celebrates the arts of war and of peace: Ramesses led the charge at Kadesh on the River Orontes. It changed the course of history, and details of his victory are emblazoned on the Ramesseum. The 'astronomical room' shows the night sky and is decorated with scenes from the 'Beautiful Feast of the Valley'. There is a drawing of a sacred *ished* tree. The scale of the site remains impressive. The head of an enormous statue, with a nose the size of a grown man, lies on the ground. This colossus was cut from a single block of limestone, brought from Aswan, 400 km away. Another colossus from this site was taken to the British Museum.

The Ramesseum ... Most noble and pure in Thebes as far as great monuments are concerned.

(Jean-François Champollion)[39]

Temple of Ramesses III at Medinet Habu, 1150 BCE

As the last great king of the New Kingdom, Ramesses III revived Egypt's glory. There are remains of houses and vaulted stores built of mud brick. The eastern perimeter wall is battlemented and there is a palace beside the temple. A contemporary account describes a sacred pond: 'In front of it [the temple] I dug a pool copious with water, planted with trees and verdant as the Delta ... It was surrounded by arbors, courtyards, and orchards laden with fruit and flowers for thy [Amon's] countenance. I built there pavilions ... and I excavated a pool before them, adorned with lotus blossoms.'[40]

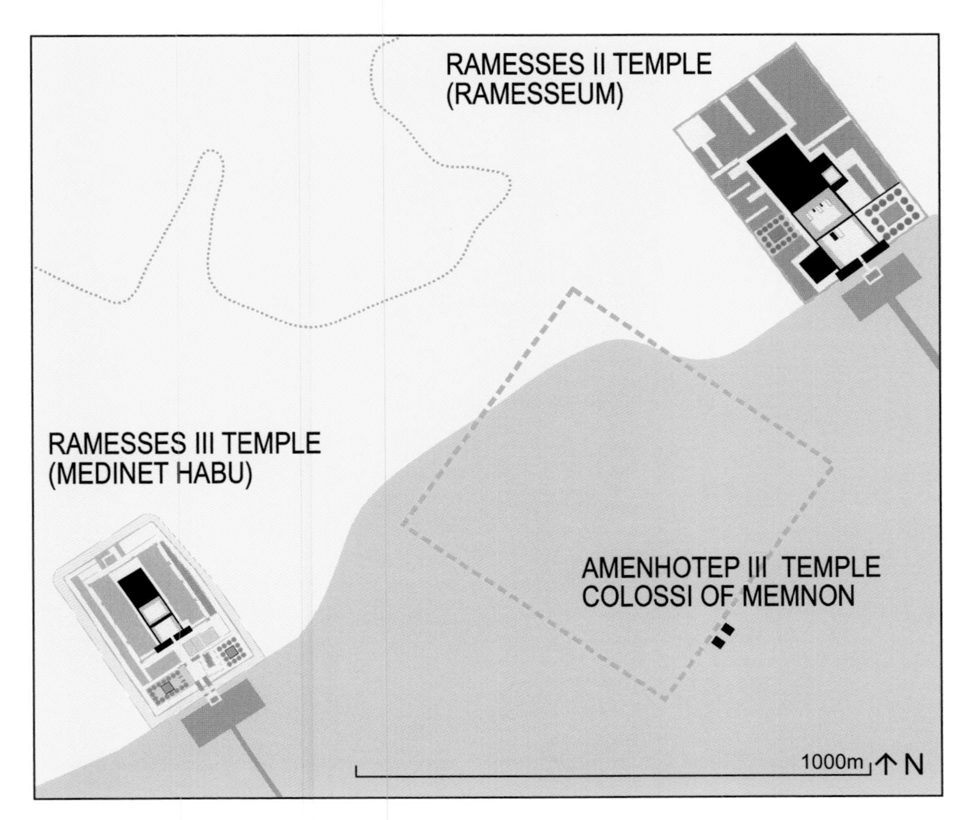

3.47 a, b Temple of Ramesses III and Temple of Ramesses II (Ramesseum), above; Colossi of Memnon and site of Temple of Amenhotep III, below.

3.48 The Temple of Ramesses III at Medinet Habu.

Ramesses' sacred pond lay where the ruined Saite Chapels are today. Another sacred pond, made after 330 BCE, still contains water and gives life to the temple compound. One can see the distinctions between temple, palace, citadel and garden starting to dissolve. A ceremonial route, used for the festival of Amun of Opet, led from Luxor to Medinet Habu. The sites and design of the canal and dock are conjectural.

> *Medinet Habu is no more than a tourist attraction today. It has long since stopped functioning in any of its past roles as fortress, shrine, or administrative headquarters. Yet, with imagination, the place can fleetingly live again. Here, in the city of the dead, silent with the memories of over five millennia, we can re-create the bustle of a living community of priests, workmen, and officials, whose everyday transactions, preserved in the surviving ostraia and papyri, speak to us today with a refreshing and poignant directness.*
>
> (William J. Murnane)[41]

Domain of Amun, 1100 BCE

The Domain of Amun comprised land on both sides of the Nile. It was a sacred landscape with cult and mortuary temples linked by processional routes. Festival

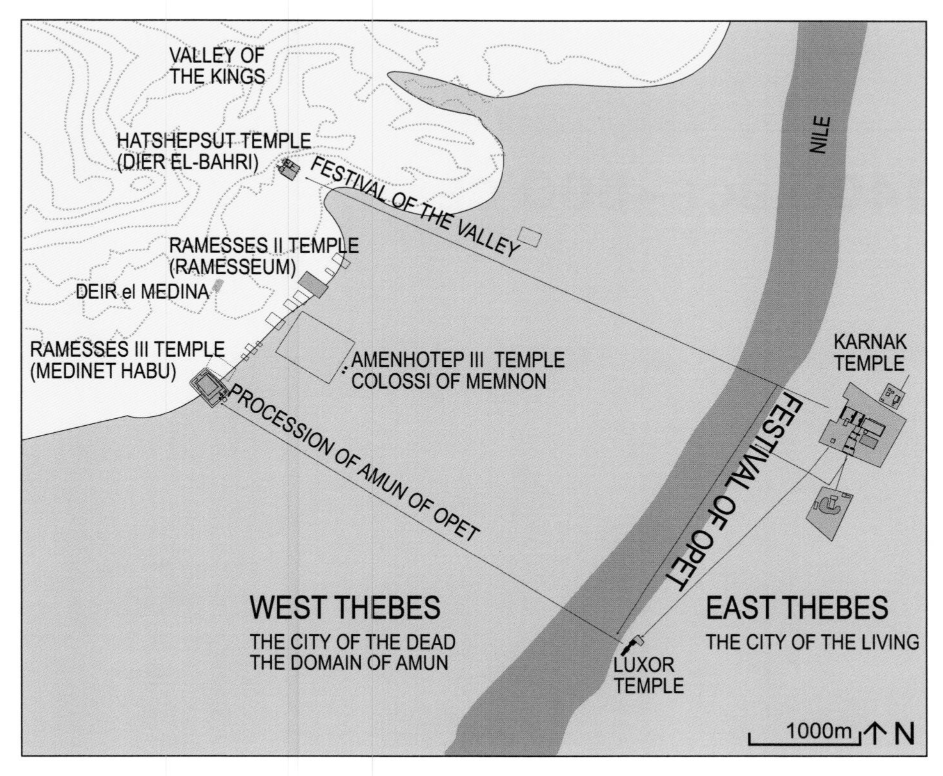

3.49 The Domain of Amun.

processions began in the land of the living, on the east bank of the Nile, crossed the river by royal barge and visited the mortuary temples in the land of the dead, on the west bank. Routes were treated in various ways: canals, roofed causeways and pavements lined with trees and statues. Temples were built on the margin of the Red Land (mountain and desert) and the Black Land (agricultural land within the flood zone).

> *On the western bank of the Nile, dominated by the Sacred Peak, devoted to the goddess Meretseger, 'She Who Loves Silence', stretched the great necropolis of Thebes, the final resting place for all eternity of kings and royal princes and princesses, of functionaries and courtiers. Here, between the Nile and the Mountain, every pharaoh ordered the construction of a 'Temple of Millions of Years', for the celebration of his cult. Each year, the god Amun paid a visit, in solemn procession, on the occasion of the 'Beautiful Feast of the Valley'.*
>
> (Alberto Siliotti)[42]

CHAPTER 4

Classical gardens, 1400 BCE–500 CE

4.0 Greece influenced the making of Roman and later European gardens through colonial sanctuaries, like Paestum, and as a result of the Romans' conquest of Greece.

History and philosophy

Greece

H.J.S. Maine believed that 'except the blind forces of Nature, nothing moves in this world which is not Greek in its origin'.[1] His belief in the primacy of Greek culture is typical of the nineteenth century – and mistaken. Historians now believe that Greek civilisation flourished in the context of West Asian trade and civilisation. Neolithic technology, Indo-European culture and the architecture of a palace civilisation came from lands to the east. The Minoans, on Crete, established a maritime kingdom which functioned as a stepping-stone between the already-ancient civilisations of West Asia and the emergent civilisations of mainland Europe. By 600 BCE, the Greeks had acquired a phonetic alphabet, from the Phoenicians, and were familiar with the Egyptian use of stone for sculpture and temple building. The defeat of the Persians at Marathon in 490 BCE led to a surge of confidence, and Pericles' leadership, from 444 to 429 BCE, saw Greek civilisation reach its apex.

Classical Greece did not enjoy settled times of the kind which had let garden-making flourish in Egypt. Though its plains were rich and its seas convenient for navigation, the geography of Greece did not lend itself to the centralisation of power. It had high mountains, steep valleys and rocky islands. Cities were well able to maintain their

4.1 Greece had many good sites for settlement and farming but did not lend itself to the centralisation of power (Meteora).

4.2 The city of Acrocorinth, on top of a 575 m hill, had a supply of water but was unsuited to garden making. Classical Corinth lies below the hill, in the foreground.

4.3 The Greek Gods were believed to live on Mount Olympus in Northern Greece, much as the Hindu gods lived on Mount Sumeru.

independence and were as often at war with each other as with invading armies. For safety, people lived in walled towns and kings lived in palaces within the city walls. The hill of Acrocorinth, inhabited for some 5000 years, was impregnable as a fortress but, though it had a supply of water, was not favourable to cultivation. Farmers commuted from walled towns to the fields and enjoyed a countryside where, in peaceful times, they could escape the restraints of city life. Pastoralism and the joy of being a 'happy husbandman' were celebrated in prose and poetry. Flowers were loved and garlands made.

Religious beliefs were a bond between warring city states. In the early days, Greek gods were symbolised by natural objects, including plants and animals. Later, they took human forms and a pantheon of gods was assembled. With Zeus as father of the family, they were believed to live on Mount Olympus in Northern Greece, as the Hindu pantheon lived on Mount Meru. Gods could symbolise both concepts and forces of nature. Homer and Hesiod explained their roles and relationships. Gods were more powerful than men but had human characteristics – and, like humans, they appreciated gifts. The places with which they were associated became sacred. According to Vincent Scully:

> *All Greek sacred architecture explores and praises the character of a god or a group of gods in a specific place. That place is itself holy and, before the temple was built upon*

4.4 Places with rocks, caves, springs and particular groupings of hills were regarded as sacred, leading to the placement of altars, statues and temples. In 2007, the EU declared the Athens Acropolis to be Europe's most significant cultural monument.

> *it, embodied the whole of the deity as a recognised natural force ... Therefore, the formal elements of any Greek sanctuary are, first, the specifically sacred landscape in which it is set, and, second, the buildings that are placed within it.*[2]

Temenos, the Greek word for a sanctuary, has the literal meaning 'cut out' (i.e., from the landscape) for a sacred or other purpose.[3] Sanctuaries were marked by boulders, cliffs or walls and used for ceremonies and animal sacrifices. Temples housed cult statues, not congregations. Altars were located out of doors so that smoke could rise to the realm of gods. The most sacred landscapes, taken by Scully to symbolise the sexual anatomy of the Earth Mother, had pure springs arising from deep caves framed by horned hills. Important sanctuaries became walled compounds with temples and treasuries. They had something of the visual character of a nineteenth-century European cemetery. There is some evidence that sanctuaries in Greece had ornamental planting and 'the adornment

4.5 The Temple of Apollo in Delphi has an altar, beyond the columns, and overlooks a landscape which was sacred before the Temple was built.

4.6 The Sacred Lake on the island of Delos may have been near a sacred grove and both features would have had a particular significance on such a small, dry, windy, sun-baked island.

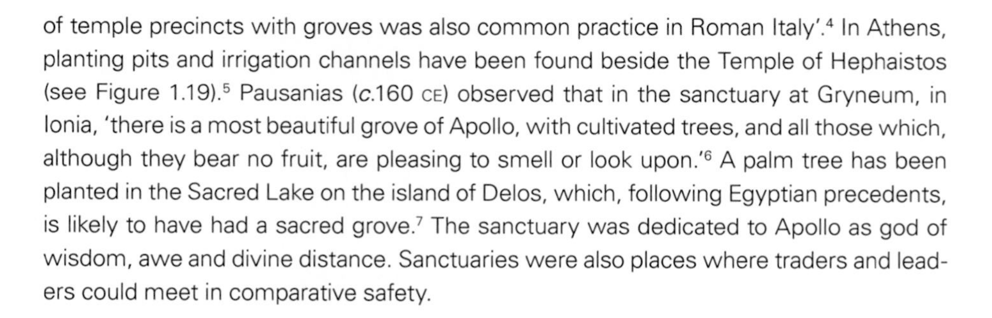

of temple precincts with groves was also common practice in Roman Italy'.[4] In Athens, planting pits and irrigation channels have been found beside the Temple of Hephaistos (see Figure 1.19).[5] Pausanias (*c.*160 CE) observed that in the sanctuary at Gryneum, in Ionia, 'there is a most beautiful grove of Apollo, with cultivated trees, and all those which, although they bear no fruit, are pleasing to smell or look upon.'[6] A palm tree has been planted in the Sacred Lake on the island of Delos, which, following Egyptian precedents, is likely to have had a sacred grove.[7] The sanctuary was dedicated to Apollo as god of wisdom, awe and divine distance. Sanctuaries were also places where traders and leaders could meet in comparative safety.

Christians described ancient Greek beliefs as 'pagan', referring to their association with the countryside (*pagus*, country district), but the term came to have a pejorative connotation which modern inter-faith dialogues would not support.

4.7 A stampede of Greek Gods, at Charlottenburg in Berlin.

Ancient Greek religious rituals included 'processions, dances, dramatic performances and athletic contests'.[8] Sanctuaries and gods were associated with particular cities. The sanctuary of Athena was in the centre of Athens, surrounded by a town and a prosperous agricultural zone. Delphi and Delos developed as towns because they were sacred to Apollo. Festivals were held with a presiding deity: Dionysus for the wine harvest, Artemis for hunting, Aphrodite for love. Statues were placed in sanctuaries. The Romans removed statues from Greek sanctuaries, took them to Italy and placed them in gardens. Copies of Greek statues can still be found in most of Europe's historic gardens and even in modern garden centres, often with their Roman names:

- Athena (Roman name, Minerva): goddess of wisdom and learning;
- Artemis (Diana): goddess of hunting;

4.8 Plato is famed for teaching philosophy in a garden, as shown on a tiled mural at Evora.

4.9 Plato believed the geometrical forms must exist before they can be re-created on Earth.

- Poseidon (Neptune): god of the sea;
- Dionysus (Bacchus): god of wine, feasts and revelry;
- Demeter (Ceres): goddess of earth and agriculture;
- Aphrodite (Venus): goddess of love and beauty.

Aphrodite's lover was Adonis, a youth of exceptional beauty whose life and death symbolised the cycle of the seasons. Girls sowed seeds in pots to watch the cycle:

> *At the festivals of Adonis, which were held in Western Asia and in Greek lands, the death of the god was annually mourned ... At Alexandria images of Aphrodite and Adonis were displayed on two couches; beside them were set ripe fruits of all kinds, cakes, plants growing in flower-pots, and green bowers twined with anise. The marriage of the lovers was celebrated one day, and on the morrow women attired as mourners, with streaming hair and bared breasts, bore the image of the dead Adonis to the sea-shore and committed it to the waves. Yet they sorrowed not without hope, for they sang that the lost one would come back again.*[9]

The Adonis cult is one of the few scraps of evidence for plants having been grown in pots within walled towns, probably on flat roofs and in paved yards.

The intervention of human-like Gods in everyday affairs directed philosophers' attention to the nature of the relationship between man and the external world. This was of fundamental importance for the advance of European civilisation. Plato, in *The Republic*, argued that the often-immoral behaviour of Homeric gods set a bad example to the

4.10 The walking place (*peripatos*) in Plato's Academy, outside the walls of Ancient Athens.

young. His Theory of Forms identified abstract concepts, rather than anthropomorphic gods, as the fundamental means of explaining nature. Reason began to challenge tradition and belief as the ultimate criterion of truth. Mathematics was developed and applied to practical affairs, including art and architecture. Groves outside cities became significant meeting-places in which to debate relationships between man, nature and the gods. Plato's Academy was in an olive grove, near a sanctuary and a gymnasium. Greeks also took to the sea, studied geography, and established colonies in the lands around the shores of the Mediterranean. They traded in knowledge as well as in material goods.

Alexander the Great was born in Macedonia in 356 BCE and extended the Greek empire to the borders of India before dying at the age of 33. He and his generals saw the luxurious gardens of West Asia; they found exotic parks, rich palaces and gardens with flowers, succulent fruits and graceful women. Commanders rode home with dreams of sumptuous palace gardens, beyond anything they had known in Greece. Their foot soldiers struggled home with booty. Towns grew, and as security improved, Macedonian nobles began making palaces outside their town walls. These palaces are thought to be the first European examples of what became a predominant urban form: a country estate on the edge of town, with house, garden, farm and woods. The Romans called it a villa.

Greek gardens

Less is known of Greek gardens in the Golden Age than of Egyptian gardens from a thousand years earlier. This is partly because Greek towns were constantly rebuilt and partly because so little Greek painting has survived, except on ceramics. The archaeological evidence for sculpture having been used in Greek domestic gardens is 'virtually non-existent'.[10] Yet Pierre Grimal felt able to write that 'no garden art worthy of the name could have developed in Rome without Greek influence'.[11] Homer, the father of Greek literature (and thus of European literature), is the key to the paradox.

Homeric groves, courts and gardens

Homer describes three categories of designed outdoor space: groves, courts and gardens. His poems, believed to have been written *c.*800 BCE, were set in the Heroic Age of Mycenae, Troy, Agamemnon and Ulysses. This was the period in which Indo-European migrants, the Dorians, ended the Mycenaean Bronze Age, giving Greece a Dark Age (*c.*1200–800 BCE) and then a Golden Age (*c.*500–338 BCE), in which Classical literature, philosophy and architecture flowered. Greek schoolchildren learned history from the *Iliad* and *Odyssey*. Virgil (70–19 BCE) based the *Aeneid* on these poems and they were learned anew in Roman times and from the Renaissance until the twentieth century. Since Greek civilisation drew upon that of Egypt, Mesopotamia and Crete, it is likely that we are reading, in Homer, about how outdoor spaces were conceived and used in earlier cultures with a less extensive literary heritage. George Steiner wrote that 'what is inescapable in the *Odyssey* is a sense of the Oriental. That the poet knew the Babylonian Gilgamesh epic is probable'[12] (see p. 42).

A selection of Homeric references to groves, courts, gardens and forests is given in Table 4.1. Though few, they are among the most influential garden comments in the entire corpus of European literature. Sacred groves are associated with gods, altars, offerings, nymphs, burials, caves, springs and the drawing of water. Palace courts are outdoor rooms associated with domesticity (and with threats to domesticity). Productive gardens, outside town walls, are used to grow fruits and flowers. Hunting forests are associated with masculinity, excitement and mountains. Homer's account of the garden of Alcinous – a palace court within a citadel, with productive gardens below its walls – 'became famous in antiquity as the ideal'.[13] Neglecting the Homeric distinctions between types of outdoor space leads to confusion about Greek 'gardens'.

Table 4.1 Homeric references to groves, courts, gardens and forests

Sacred groves	
Iliad Book VI	When he had burned him in his wondrous armour, he raised a mound over his ashes and the mountain nymphs, daughters of aegis-bearing Jove, planted a grove of elms about his tomb.
Iliad Book XX	There was not a river absent except Oceanus, nor a single one of the nymphs that haunt fair groves, or springs of rivers and meadows of green grass.
Iliad Book VIII	After a while he reached many-fountained Ida, mother of wild beasts, and Gargarus, where are his grove and fragrant altar.

Iliad Book XXIII	I returned home to my loved native land … to sacrifice to you there at your springs, where is your grove and your altar fragrant with burnt-offerings.
Odyssey Book XVII	When they had got over the rough steep ground and were nearing the city, they reached the fountain from which the citizens drew their water. This had been made by Ithacus, Neritus, and Polyctor. There was a grove of water-loving poplars planted in a circle all round it, and the clear cold water came down to it from a rock high up, while above the fountain there was an altar to the nymphs, at which all wayfarers used to sacrifice.
Iliad Book II	Holy Onchestus with its famous grove of Neptune;[14] Arne rich in vineyards; Midea, sacred Nisa, and Anthedon upon the sea.
Odyssey Book VI	As the sun was going down they came to the sacred grove of Minerva,[15] and there Ulysses sat down and prayed to the mighty daughter of Jove.

Palace courts

Iliad Book IX	Nine whole nights did they set a guard over me taking it in turns to watch, and they kept a fire always burning, both in the cloister of the outer court and in the inner court at the doors of the room wherein I lay; [the Penguin translation is 'and keeping two fires burning, one under the colonnade of the walled yard, and the other in the forecourt'[16] but when the darkness of the tenth night came, I broke through the closed doors of my room, and climbed the wall of the outer court after passing quickly and unperceived through the men on guard and the women servants.
Odyssey Book VI	If, therefore, you want my father to give you an escort and to help you home, do as I bid you; you will see a beautiful grove of poplars by the road side dedicated to Minerva; it has a well in it and a meadow all round it. Here my father has a field of rich garden ground, about as far from the town as a man's voice will carry. Sit down there and wait for a while till the rest of us can get into the town and reach my father's house. Then, when you think we must have done this, come into the town and ask the way to the house of my father Alcinous. You will have no difficulty in finding it; any child will point it out to you, for no one else in the whole town has anything like such a fine house as he has. When you have got past the gates and through the outer court, go right across the inner court till you come to my mother. You will find her sitting by the fire and spinning her purple wool by firelight. It is a fine sight to see her as she leans back against one of the bearing-posts with her maids all ranged behind her. Close to her seat stands that of my father, on which he sits like an immortal god. Never mind him, but go up to my mother, and lay your hands upon her knees if you would get home quickly. If you can gain her over, you may hope to see your own country again, no matter how distant it may be.

Odyssey Book XXII	As for Melanthius, they took him through the cloister into the inner court. There they cut off his nose and his ears; they drew out his vitals and gave them to the dogs raw, and then in their fury they cut off his hands and his feet.
Iliad Book XXIV	She went to Priam's house, and found weeping and lamentation therein. His sons were seated round their father in the outer courtyard, and their raiment was wet with tears.

Productive gardens	
Iliad Book XXI	As one who would water his garden leads a stream from some fountain over his plants, and all his ground-spade in hand he clears away the dams to free the channels.[17]
Odyssey Book VI	You will see a beautiful grove of poplars by the road side dedicated to Minerva; it has a well in it and a meadow all round it. Here my father has a field of rich garden ground, about as far from the town as a man's voice will carry.
Odyssey Book VII	Outside the gate of the outer court there is a large garden of about four acres with a wall all round it. It is full of beautiful trees – pears, pomegranates, and the most delicious apples. There are luscious figs also, and olives in full growth.

Hunting forests	
Odyssey Book XVII	This was Argos, whom Ulysses had bred before setting out for Troy, but he had never had any work out of him. In the old days he used to be taken out by the young men when they went hunting wild goats, or deer, or hares.
Odyssey Book XX	And indeed as soon as she began washing her master, she at once knew the scar as one that had been given him by a wild boar when he was hunting on Mount Parnassus with his excellent grandfather.
Iliad Book XXIII	Achilles was still in full pursuit of Hector, as a hound chasing a fawn which he has started from its covert on the mountains, and hunts through glade and thicket.

4.11 Mount Parnassus is mentioned by Homer as a place with good hunting.

4.12 a, b Tiryns was a citadel with a coastline to the south and productive gardens to the north.

Homer's words probably relate to the Mycenaean towns of mainland Greece and Ionia – the west coast of modern Turkey, including Troy, where Homer is thought to have lived. Tiryns and Mycenae, which flourished until the twelfth century BCE, are hill-top citadels with Cyclopean outer walls. Gated paths led to outer and inner colonnaded courts of the types described by Homer, though only their foundations survive. Tiryns had an inner palace and court, assumed to be the women's quarters, where one could expect to follow the instructions given to Ulysses, to 'go right across the inner court till you come to

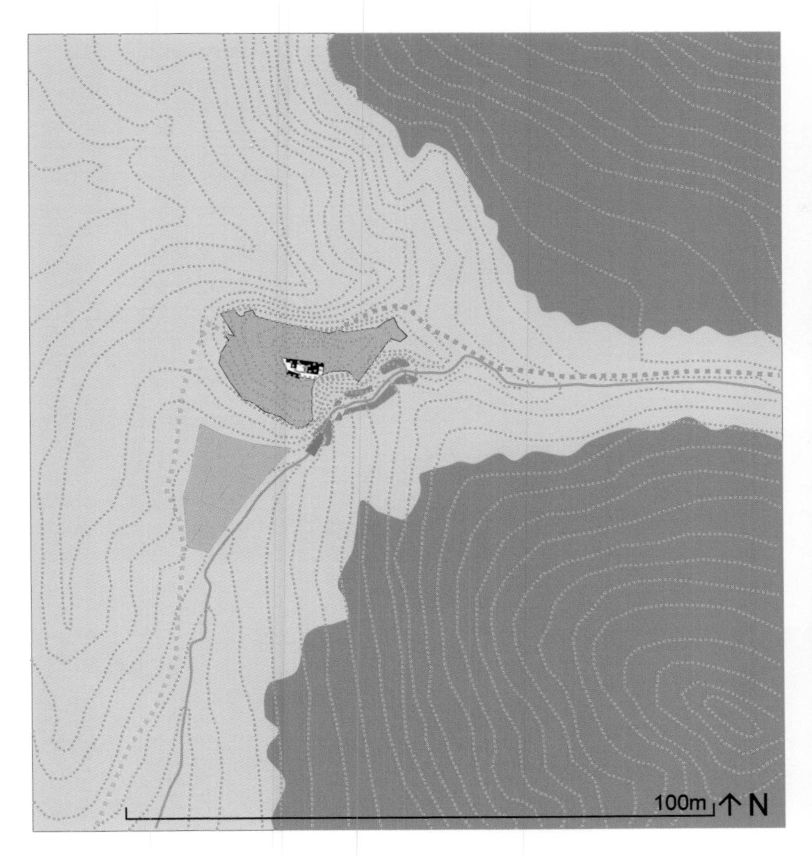

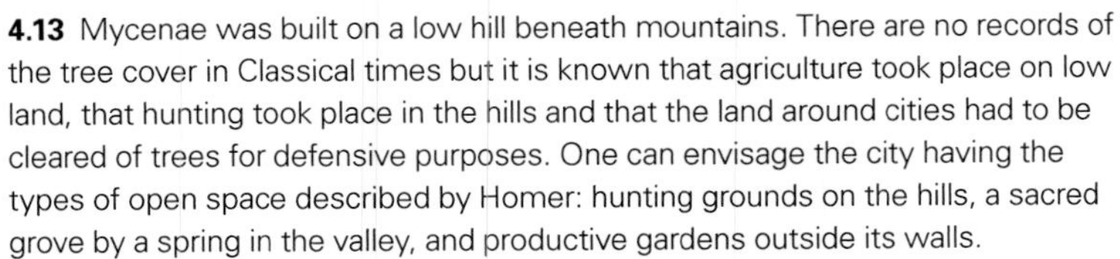

4.13 Mycenae was built on a low hill beneath mountains. There are no records of the tree cover in Classical times but it is known that agriculture took place on low land, that hunting took place in the hills and that the land around cities had to be cleared of trees for defensive purposes. One can envisage the city having the types of open space described by Homer: hunting grounds on the hills, a sacred grove by a spring in the valley, and productive gardens outside its walls.

4.14 Mycenae: looking out from the palace court to the Argolid Plain.

4.15 Mycenae: looking up the valley to the palace walls, with probable garden sites on the valley floor.

my mother' (see Table 4.1 excerpt from *Odyssey* Book VI). Looking over the Argolid plain from either citadel, seeing productive groves and hazy mountains, one can populate the landscape with rich gardens, sacred groves, satyrs and departing heroes. Physically and conceptually, this was the seedbed of European garden design. But the types of space Homer knew do not equate to modern gardens.

From Tiryns, it is 12 km to Mycenae and 140 km to Athens. Settlements developed into fortified towns as Western civilisation trod this path. An acropolis is a town on a hilltop (from *akron*, summit and *polis*, town). The most famous acropolis, in Athens, began as a fortified settlement on a plateau and became a religious sanctuary with a walled town beneath its walls. Caves and springs round the Acropolis became shrines. In the town,

4.16 Grand houses on the island of Delos had peristyle courtyards paved with mosaic tiles, often with a water tank beneath the paving.

4.17 Greek towns had productive gardens outside their walls (a vegetable garden on Mykonos).

4.18 The Roman Agora in Athens was a peristyle court, probably used as a meeting place and market place.

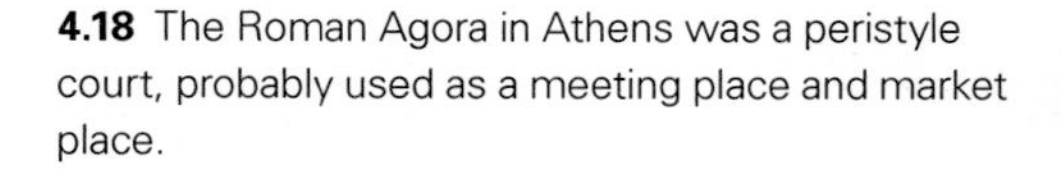

4.19 An artist's reconstruction of a sacred grove. Temples were built to house statues of gods and goddesses, not as places for congregations.

houses opened onto paved internal courts for living and working. The courts may have had pot plants and statues but no physical evidence for this survives. Few Greek houses survive, because they were built of mud brick. At Delos, Olynthos and Prienne, there are stone houses with small rooms and paved outdoor yards. At Delos many of the yards drain to underground cisterns, so that they could not have had trees or shrubs. Towns also had a public space, the *agora*, for meetings and markets. Many of these had roofed colonnades and were planted with trees beneath which philosophers could sit while formulating the concepts which led to the development of Western civilisation. In Athens,

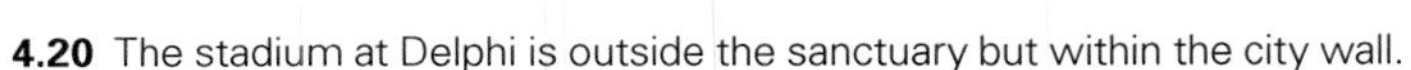

4.20 The stadium at Delphi is outside the sanctuary but within the city wall.

4.21 Olympia was a sanctuary with a stadium, temples and treasuries – but without an adjoining settlement.

the Greek Agora had colonnades attached to individual buildings (*stoas*) and the Roman Agora had a continuous colonnade enclosing an outdoor space.

Sanctuaries

In Classical times, the Greeks continued to use land outside fortified towns in the ways described by Homer. Individual landowners commuted to their fields and gardens, some only 'as far from the town as a man's voice will carry'. Young men hunted in woods and on the hills. A good spring 'from which the citizens drew their water' often became a sacred grove with a 'fragrant altar'. One could find 'a beautiful grove of poplars by the roadside dedicated to Minerva' with 'a well in it and a meadow all round'. Ornamental orchards were made outside walled towns. Both Greeks and Romans had sanctuaries for Isis, wife of the Egyptian god Osiris. Conjecture provides the following development path for Classical sanctuaries:

- The idea of a sacred grove derives from the religious sanctuaries of Mesopotamia (see Chapter 2) and Egypt (see Chapter 3) – and conceivably from the Indo-European homeland in Central Asia.
- Springs and caves were especially valued, because the water was fresh, pure, cool, healthy – and miraculous.
- Groves associated with a presiding god were marked by boundary stones.
- Offerings were made at outdoor altars.
- Statues were erected and treasuries built to house gifts.

- Shelters built to protect statues became temples.
- Boundary walls provided security.
- Sacred groves outside walled towns became places of resort for exercise (gymnasiums) and rest (*stoas*).
- Philosophers and students came to these places to experience nature and learn about the natural order.

This evolution took place as the Homeric Age was succeeded by the Classical Age. Two-and-a-half thousand years later the sacred grove evolved into the English landscape garden, laying the basis for the natural parks and national parks of the modern world.

The sacred groves of Greece had some characteristics in common with modern sports parks and universities. Olympia had the most famous games and Delphi the most famous oracle; Sparta emphasised physical prowess; Athens stressed intellectual skills. Glistening young men, clad only in oil, exercised in groves which became known as gymnasiums (from the Greek *gumnos*, naked and *gumnazo* exercise). Wrestling schools (known as *palaestra*, from the Greek *palaio*, to wrestle) were established, stadiums were built for races, and shelters, baths and specialised yards were added. Open colonnades provided for summer shade and winter exercise.

A gymnasium had moral, therapeutic and educational roles. Plato wrote that for a citizen to tell a lie is 'a more heinous fault than for the patient or the pupil of a gymnasium not to speak the truth about his own bodily illnesses'.[18]

Philosophers seeking conditions more suited to calm reflection than those offered by a public *agora* turned to quiet groves. Most famous is the Academy founded by Plato among the olive trees some 2 km from the walls of Athens. It was a sanctuary named after Academus and became the original 'grove of Academe'. Aristotle, himself a 'pupil of a gymnasium', was peripatetic: he walked his grove while discoursing on philosophy. This grove was called The Lyceum, from (*Lukeion*, an epithet of Apollo) and may have been near the site now occupied by Syntagma Square.[19] There are fine examples of gymnasiums at Delphi, Delos, Ephesus and Pergamon. European high schools continue to be known as gymnasiums, academies and *lycées*. One regrets their lack of contemplative groves.

4.22 Ninfa Egeria.

In Ancient Greece, the curriculum centred on gymnastics, poetry, rhetoric and music. Theophrastus is famed for teaching philosophy in a garden and wrote in his will: 'The garden and the *peripatos* and the buildings adjoining the garden I leave to my friends, named below, who wish to pursue the study of philosophy together.'[20] A *peripatoi* was a colonnade. Diogenes described Epicurus as 'A philosopher and a great lover of gardens'.[21]

Grottoes

> *Water is best, and gold, like a blazing fire in the night, stands out supreme of all lordly wealth.*[22]

Essential for life on earth, water is most pure and most fascinating when it springs from rock. Caves were associated, as in Neolithic times, with the Earth Mother, Gaia. According to Hesiod, life originated from a union between Gaia and the sky god, Uranus.

4.23 a–h From Greece to Rome, the grotto evolved from a sacred cave to a garden feature.

a The grotto on the island of Delos.

b The Caves of Apollo and Pan on the north slope of the Acropolis.

c The sacred cave at Eleusis.

d The Castalian Spring at Delphi.

e Looking outward from one of Hadrian's grottoes at Tivoli.

f Fountain of Peirene at Corinth.

g The so-called 'Villa of Tiberius' at Sperlonga has a seaside grotto.

h The sculpture it contained, montaged onto the photograph, was found in the pool.

4.24 Relief showing a young man placing a wreath at a temple beside a sacred tree.

4.25 This relief, found on the north slope of the Acropolis, is thought to have come from the Cave of Pan and to show the rural god with three nymphs.

Nymphs lived in caves, Naiads lived in springs, Dyads lived in trees. Zeus was said to have been born in a cave grotto (still a tourist attraction on Crete). Thus, caves were places in which one could reflect on the creation and make offerings to the gods. Marble statues of gods, dwarfed by the powers of nature, were placed in small temples outside caves, and wreaths were laid.

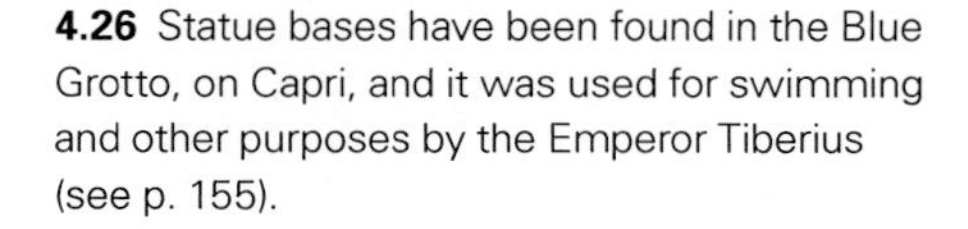

4.26 Statue bases have been found in the Blue Grotto, on Capri, and it was used for swimming and other purposes by the Emperor Tiberius (see p. 155).

4.27 The hot spring at Bath, England, was dedicated to Minerva (Athena).

There are sacred caves at Eleusis, Delos and in the cliffs round the *peripatis* of the Acropolis. Hadrian was initiated into the mysteries at Eleusis and, at his Villa outside Tivoli, made both a sacred cave and an underground room overlooking the Canopus. Remains of antique statues were found in the Blue Grotto on Capri.

Since we return to Mother Earth at the end of our days, a grotto could also be a gateway to the underworld, ruled by Hades. Caves were used for burials.[23] Offerings were made for proud mothers, newborn children and departed spirits. Later, the Romans used family shrines in gardens for these purposes. Cicero planned a shrine to his daughter, Tullia, who died in February 45 BCE, 'to ensure her apotheosis'.[24]

Caves might also house medicinal waters. The Romans valued mineral springs and hot springs. Bath, in England, has a sacred healing spring dedicated to Minerva from which water bubbles out at 46°C.

Caves are the origin of garden grottoes: the word 'grotto' derives from the Greek *kruptos* (hidden), as does the word 'crypt'. Let us hope that James Lovelock's Gaia Hypothesis[25] revives interest in the design of grottoes.

Hellenistic gardens

Greek cities lost their independence to Macedonia in the Hellenestic Period (332–30 BCE) but saw their culture influence a geographical area extending from France to India. Macedonia had the land, wealth and security which garden-making requires. Gothein sees this period as 'the beginning of garden craft in Greece' and notes that 'the raids of Alexander the Great opened to the Greeks the whole of Asia and all its elaborate garden culture'.[26] Longus' story *Daphnis and Chloe*, written *c.*200 BCE, linked gardens with rustic romance.

4.28 Longus' tale of Daphnis and Chloe, written in the second century CE, helped associate gardens with the pastoral dream of shepherds and shepherdesses living in harmony with nature.

Longus' story of Daphnis and Chloe is set on the isle of Lesbos during the second century CE, where Longus is thought to have lived. It tells of two young lovers' enjoyment of a pastoral idyll, and each other. An old man tells them:

> *I have a garden that I tend with my own hands – it has been my pride and joy ever since I gave up being a cowherd because of old age. All things that the Seasons bring forth, this garden bears in each several season. In spring there are roses and white lilies and hyacinths and both kinds of violets, in summer poppies and wild pears and every sort of apple, and, at the present season grapes and pomegranates and green myrtle-berries. Every morning flocks of birds foregather in this garden, some feed, some to sing; for the trees make a canopy overhead, and there is pleasant shade, and water comes from three springs; take away the boundary-wall, and you would think that you were looking at a woodland grove.*[27]

The old man then sees a beautiful and naked young man who, he fears, has come to steal his fruit. He turns out to be a god who bestows fertility on the garden and on lovers.

4.29 The Roman villa at Oplontis has a peristyle and a gymnasium-style pool.

Macedonians placed residential palaces in 'a commanding position above the city'[28] with 'enclosed gardens in the courtyards'.[29] Owners wanted to view their fields and gardens, together with the city, its temple and gymnasium. The Romans were profoundly influenced by this approach to residential planning and used it in all parts of their empire. One need look no further than the suburbs of any modern city to find estates of this type. They may still have outdoor courts, flower-filled urns, ornamental ponds, vegetables, woods and, if the owner can afford it, a gymnasium with a hot tub and a cold plunge pool. Great cities with gardens began to develop throughout the Hellenistic world, including Byzantium, Syracuse, Naples, Marseilles, Pergamum, Alexandria and Antioch.

Rome

The glory that was Greece
And the grandeur that was Rome.[30]

The glory of Greece lay in original thought, the grandeur of Rome in the vast application of new ideas to the establishment of a civil society under the rule of law. The two cultures were linked, first by Greek settlements in Italy, later by Roman annexation of the Hellenistic empire. In the period of Greek supremacy, Italy had a relatively primitive society and 'no Homer or Hesiod to tell us what men, their dwellings, and their altars, were like'.[31] The Romans undertook wholesale adoptions of Greek religion, philosophy, art, architecture and literature. Initially, they even wrote in Greek. The lack of information on pre-Roman Italy is consequential upon the lack of literature, though something is known of the Greek-influenced Etruscan culture.

Legend dates the foundation of Rome to 753 BCE. A republic was declared in 509 BCE and the rapid expansion of Roman power began. The Etruscans were defeated by 273 BCE. Carthage and Greece became provinces in 146 BCE. Spain fell in 133 BCE, Syria in 64 BCE and Egypt in 30 BCE. Rome became the great cultural melting pot. The rule of Augustus, from 27 BCE to 14 CE, saw the end of the republic but also the birth of a new Golden Age. In Roman eyes, it stood comparison with Greece's Age of Pericles. Suetonius records Augustus' justifiable boast that 'I found Rome built of sun-dried bricks; I leave her clothed in marble.'[32] The Roman Empire was marked by extravagant excess with intervals of reform, brilliance, chaos, madness, lust and terror. Hadrian, a Spanish emperor who ruled from 117 to 138, loved peace, architecture, religion and gardens. His *pax Romana* allowed extensive building, including the construction of Rome's most famous temple, the Pantheon, and his own palace-garden at Tibur (Tivoli), 40 km from Rome. Rome was sacked by Alaric in 410 and the last Western Emperor was deposed in 476. The Western historical tradition, heavily influenced by Gibbon, still tends to view the empire's decline and fall as a triumph of 'barbarism and religion' over a classic period of political, intellectual and religious freedom.[33]

The ancient religion of Italy was more practical than that of Greece but equally polytheistic. Strict observance of ritual (*pietas*) fostered a sense of awe (*religio*) and was expected to result in timely and practical divine assistance. Mythology, ethics and metaphysics had minor roles. The spirit (*numen*) which inhabits a place and the procreative

4.30 The Emperor Hadrian may have designed both the Pantheon and the villa at Tivoli. The Pantheon was a temple for the gods of Rome, who were related to the Greek gods.

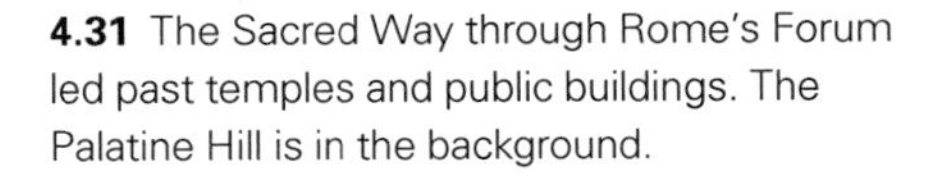

4.31 The Sacred Way through Rome's Forum led past temples and public buildings. The Palatine Hill is in the background.

4.32 A recreated Etruscan temple in the garden of the Villa Giulia, Rome.

power (*genius*) which sustains a family were revered. A spirit associated with a particular place, such as a river or wood, was known as a *genius loci* ('genius of the place'). Providing rituals were observed, the Romans were a tolerant people and found it easy to import religious and other ideas from around the empire. The Greek pantheon of personal gods was renamed and adopted, as were Greek statues and the idea of making sacred ways and temples. Caesars became gods, as pharaohs had been. Statues were erected to the *genius* of the nation and its leader.

Small gardens contained shrines. Every substantial house in Pompeii had such a place, used for offerings and prayers to mark family events. The Isis and Mithras cults, deriving from Egypt and Persia respectively, brought sacramental and mystery elements to Roman religion. Public temples were erected in towns, following Etruscan and Greek precedents. The Roman Forum had a shrine to Janus. London had a temple to Mithras. *Lares* (Roman household gods) were worshipped at property boundaries and crossroads. The circular temple of Vesta, goddess of the hearth, contained an eternal fire attended by the vestal virgins. Hercules had a Great Altar in Rome's cattle market. Ancestors were revered and entombed. Statues imported from Greece, and having lost their original significance, were used as ornaments on the Palatine and in lavish villa gardens.

Roman civilisation established garden design as a pan-European art. Those famous roads helped transmit knowledge throughout the empire. Near towns, roads were lined with tombs, so that they resembled sacred groves. Roman governors made gardens wherever they were posted. This required a vocabulary, which also travelled. The Latin word *topiarius* is used for a workman employed in an ornamental garden. In modern English 'topiary' is used to describe clipped plants thought similar to those in aristocratic Roman gardens. *Hortus* was the Latin word for a planted garden, as opposed to a

4.33 The Vestal Virgins had a garden beside the Sacred Way in the Roman Forum.

4.34 Pagan shrines placed in gardens resembled the wayside shrines still found in Roman Catholic countries. House of the Neptune and Amphitrite Mosaic Atrium. In Roman mythology, Amphitrite was the consort of Neptune and thus a symbol of the sea. Mosaic was used, in place of paint, when the walls were not protected by a peristyle.

4.35 A famous garden painting from the House of Livia at Prima Porta. Livia was the wife of Emperor Augustus. The painting shows the mix of fruiting and flowering plants which is likely to have been grown in the courtyard gardens of Roman palaces.

paved court. *Hortus* probably derives from the Greek *chortos*, meaning an enclosed place for growing food, and could refer to anything from a vegetable garden to an imperial park.[34] The art of growing plants in gardens came to be described, in English, as horticulture. '*Hortus conclusus*' is used by garden historians to mean 'an enclosed garden' in contrast to an open estate garden. Though the Egyptians also made enclosed domestic gardens, the modern garden as a place with multiple objectives appears to be a Roman invention. They made gardens for private pleasure, spiritual solace and gastronomic delight.

Roman gardens

Few Roman gardens have been excavated and those that have appear to show that gardens throughout the empire made little response to local conditions: regularity was always the Roman way. One can, however, distinguish between palace gardens, villa gardens and town gardens.

Palace gardens

The word 'palace' derives from the Palatine Hill, where the Emperors Augustus, Tiberius, Caligula and Domitian built palaces and gardens, creating a citadel with open courts:

4.36 A wayside shrine in Poland.

4.37 A model of the Palatine Hill with the Circus Maximus in the foreground. Several garden courts, with colonnades and fountains, have been excavated and now have inappropriate lawns of mown grass.

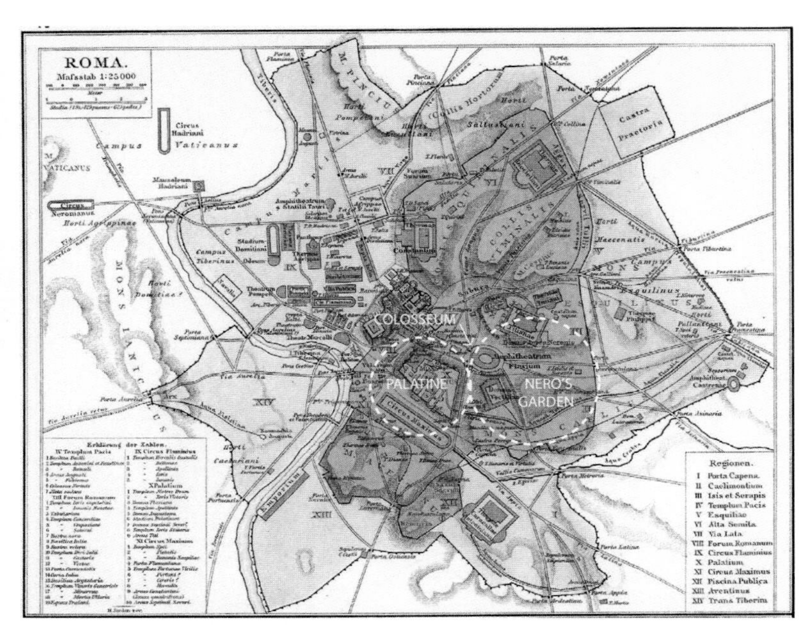

4.38 A plan of Rome in antiquity showing the garden of Nero's Golden House, east of the Palatine Hill.

Source: Droysen, G., *Professor G. Droysens Allgemeiner Historischer Handatlas in Sechsundneunzig Karten mit Erläuterndem Text*, Leipzig: Velhagen & Klasing, 1886.

4.39 Looking across the Circus Maximus, still used as an exercise ground, to the remains of the Palace of the Emperors on the Palatine Hill.

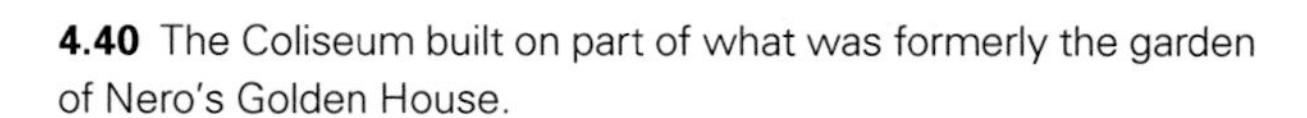

4.40 The Coliseum built on part of what was formerly the garden of Nero's Golden House.

> *The predominating characteristic of the whole palace was the close association – interpenetration is a better word – of house and gardens. The great open courtyards, with their fountains and flower beds, were evidently used as out-of-doors saloons merging, through porticoes and colonnades, into the rooms themselves.*[35]

One can reconstruct their character, in one's imagination, by remembering Pompeii (see pp. 133–4) and strolling through the archaeological wastes of the Palatine.

The house of Augustus (now called the House of Livia) confirms this interpretation. There are paintings on the walls and Suetonius wrote that 'In summer [Augustus] slept with the bedroom door open, or in the courtyard beside a fountain, having someone to fan him.'[36] Augustus watched official games from the palace windows, walked in the grounds and played hand-ball with his friends.[37] Livia's own villa, at Primaporta, is famous for its paintings of what we might call a wildlife garden.

Nero's Golden House resembled a modern dictator's palace or billionaire's retreat. It was 'a fanciful landscape garden' with a lake, open glades, groves, statues and numerous buildings: a *rus in urbe*'.[38] After his death, the Coliseum was built on the site of Nero's 'sea' and the Imperial Baths on the site of his Golden House, a fragment of which has been excavated.

Villa gardens

Emperors also had country villas, which can be viewed as privatised Greek sanctuaries and gymnasiums. The best surviving example is Hadrian's Villa at Tivoli. Though the site has been pillaged down the centuries, enough survives to reveal the immensity of the emperor's ambition. In our terms it was a museum complex, a sculpture park, a sports park, a banqueting suite and a vast pleasure ground with water features and sacred caves. Pliny believed that the taste for large estates ruined Italy; Gibbon observed that: 'The rich and luxurious nobles, ... as long as they were indulged in the enjoyment of their baths, their theatres, and their villas, ... cheerfully resigned the more dangerous cares of

4.41 a–d Hadrian planned and built the largest and most opulent of all Roman villas on a low hill near Tivoli. Much survives – but the planting shown on the model is speculative.

4.42 Paul Getty commissioned a re-creation of the Villa dei Papiri from Herculaneum. The architecture is based on archaeological research but the Renaissance parterre is an anachronistic figment of the designers' historical imagination.

empire to the rough hands of peasants and soldiers.'[39] The amazing opulence of such villas may have contributed to the decline and fall of the Roman Empire.

The urban villa (*villa urbana*) was 'urban' in the sense of 'civilised' rather than in terms of location. It was a comfortable place for a comfortable life. Scipio's villa at Liternum, often cited as the earliest example of the type, was made with detailed knowledge of Egyptian civilisation. Urban villas with luxurious rooms and gardens have been excavated in and around Herculaneum, with the Villa at Oplontis the most fully researched example. The suburban villa (*villa suburbana*), as the name suggests, shared characteristics with urban and rural villas. Seaside villas were popular on the coasts south of Rome and Naples.

4.43 a, b Villa di Plinio at Laurentum. The identification of the site has been challenged but Pliny's Laurentian Villa was built on sandy soil, near the sea among maquis vegetation (see p. 144).

The rural villa (*villa rustica*), exemplified by Virgil's retreat in the Sabine hills, was a farm which provided some urban refinements, but with less extravagance. Virgil shared the Greek dream of a happy husbandman retreating to a life of rural bliss, caring for his bees, his grapes and his soul. It was a pagan dream, in the religious sense and also in the physical sense that it was set 'in a country district'. Cato used *hortus* to mean the part of a farm which was watered and used for growing vegetables.[40]

The freshest picture of how villa gardens were used comes from the letters of Pliny. His uncle, Pliny the Elder, had written a treatise on natural history. Pliny the Younger had a villa at Laurentum on the coast south of Rome. The following quotations in Table 4.2 reveal his delight in villa life. He speaks of modesty but was immensely rich.

Table 4.2 Pliny's references to villa gardens

Letter III to Caninus Rufus	How is that sweet Comum of ours looking? What about that most enticing of villas, the portico where it is one perpetual spring, that shadiest of plane-tree walks, the crystal canal so agreeably winding along its flowery banks, together with the lake lying below that so charmingly yields itself to the view?
Letter XXIII to Gallus	You are surprised that I am so fond of my Laurentine, or (if you prefer the name) my Laurens: but you will cease to wonder when I acquaint you with the beauty of the villa, the advantages of its situation, and the extensive view of the sea-coast ... My villa is of a convenient size without being expensive to keep up. The courtyard in front is plain, but not mean, through which you enter porticoes shaped into the form of the letter D, enclosing a small but cheerful area between. These make a capital retreat for bad weather, not only as they are shut in with windows, but particularly as they are sheltered by a projection of the

Letter XXIII to Gallus *(cont.)*	roof. From the middle of these porticoes you pass into a bright pleasant inner court, and out of that into a handsome hall running out towards the sea-shore … The gestatio [an avenue for exercise either on horseback on in a horse-drawn vehicle] is bordered round with box, and, where that is decayed, with rosemary: for the box, wherever sheltered by the buildings, grows plentifully, but where it lies open and exposed to the weather and spray from the sea, though at some distance from the latter, it quite withers up. Next the gestatio, and running along inside it, is a shady vine plantation, the path of which is so soft and easy to the tread that you may walk bare-foot upon it. The garden is chiefly planted with fig and mulberry trees, to which this soil is as favourable as it is averse from all others. … Before this enclosed portico lies a terrace fragrant with the scent of violets, and warmed by the reflection of the sun from the portico, which, while it retains the rays, keeps away the north-east wind; and it is as warm on this side as it is cool on the side opposite: in the same way it is a protection against the wind from the south-west; and thus, in short, by means of its several sides, breaks the force of the winds, from whatever quarter they may blow.
Letter LII to Domitius Apollinaris	You descend, from the terrace, by an easy slope adorned with the figures of animals in box, facing each other, to a lawn* overspread with the soft, I had almost said the liquid, Acanthus: this is surrounded by a walk enclosed with evergreens, shaped into a variety of forms. Beyond it is the gestatio laid out in the form of a circus running round the multiform box-hedge and the dwarf-trees, which are cut quite close. The whole is fenced in with a wall completely covered by box cut into steps all the way up to the top. On the outside of the wall lies a meadow that owes as many beauties to nature as all I have been describing within does to art; at the end of which are open plain and numerous other meadows and copses.
Letter XXXIX to Mustius	I shall perform an act both of piety and munificence if, at the same time that I build a beautiful temple, I add to it a spacious portico; the first for the service of the goddess, the other for the use of the people. I beg therefore you would purchase for me four marble pillars, of whatever kind you shall think proper; as well as a quantity of marble for laying the floor, and encrusting the walls. You must also either buy a statue of the goddess or get one made; for age has maimed, in some parts, the ancient one of wood which stands there at present.

Note:
* Pliny uses the word *pulvinus*, translated as 'lawn', but it is not clear what character it had or how it differed from an open space (*spatium*).[41] The Latin word *pulvinus* means 'cushion' and is used in medieval texts for beds of flowers.[42] Pliny is no more likely than his medieval successors to have had a 'lawn' in the modern sense of an area of close-cut grass.

Town gardens

Roman town houses, unlike their Greek predecessors, had sufficient outdoor space for horticulture. This is best seen at Pompeii and Herculaneum. Drawing on Etruscan, Samnite, Greek and West Asian precedents, they provide much of our knowledge of

4.44 Though over 2000 years old, Herculaneum resembles the towns found in Mediterranean countries even today. The top right corner of the photograph shows the cliff of the volcanic debris which secured its preservation.

Mediterranean garden culture. To a greater degree than anywhere else in the ancient world, these towns give one the sense of visiting a garden in the owner's temporary absence.

Pompeii is a walled town with stone-paved streets, raised sidewalks, stepping stones and deep grooves cut by chariot wheels. When it rained, the streets must have been torrents of liquid filth. Pompeian dwellings were windowless for reasons of security, privacy and stench-avoidance. Many of the internal courts were surrounded by colonnades (peristyles) which acted as ventilated corridors between rooms and courts. Vitruvius specifies the correct proportions for such colonnades as follows:

> *Peristyles, lying athwart, should be one third longer than they are deep, and their columns as high as the colonnades are wide. Intercolumniations of peristyles should be not less than three nor more than four times the thickness of the columns. If the columns of the peristyle are to be made in the Doric style, take the modules which I have given in the fourth book, on the Doric order, and arrange the columns with reference to these modules and to the scheme of the triglyphs.*[43]

Within the scheme of proportions described here with such precision, garden courts were richly coloured, well-planted and intensively used. The *atrium* was a family space in which the central portion of the roof was open to the sky. Larger dwellings had a paved enclosure surrounded by a row of columns, known as a peristyle, which integrated

4.45 The *atrium*, in the foreground, was a small paved court which allowed light and water to enter. There is a peristyle beyond the *atrium* (Pompeii).

4.46 A peristyle garden with fresco painting, used to increase its apparent size (Pompeii).

4.47 A *hortus*, or *xystus*, was an ornamental area used to grow fruit and vegetables (Pompeii).

4.48 A bronze garden statue in a peristyle court (Pompeii).

indoor and outdoor space. The peristyle court was used for outdoor living and entertaining. Even larger town houses also had a rectangular space at the rear, known as a *hortus*, or *xystus*, used for vegetables and flowers. Sometimes the *hortus* became a private pleasure garden with statues, grottoes and topiary, as at the house of Loreius Tiburtinus (see Figure 4.58, p. 142).

Shrines to family gods (*aediculae*), were decorated with mosaic tiles. When dedicated to a nymph the shrine was known as a *nymphaeum*. Fountains were fed by lead pipes, which permitted larger and more complex designs than could be achieved in the earlier civilisations which had used terracotta ducts. Grottoes were made on large estates, the best surviving examples being those associated with Tiberius, including the Blue Grotto on Capri and the wonderful seaside grotto at Sperlonga (see Figure 4.23 g and h).[44]

Marble, bronze and terracotta statues were extensively used in Roman gardens. Cicero wrote of a villa that had 'Greek statues soon to be gardeners themselves, offering their ivy for sale.'[45] His own villa was at Pompeii,[46] where statuary was of 'garden centre' quality; the Oplontis villa, which is thought to have belonged to Nero's wife Poppaea Sabina, had much better statues.[47] The typical subjects for garden sculpture were Greek gods: Ceres, Venus, Flora, Bacchus, Cupid, Diana, Apollo and Pan. Sundials were decorative and functional. Paintings of garden scenes on the walls of colonnades enlarged the apparent size of peristyle courts: frescos show men in togas, dancing girls, fountains, trellis-work, pergolas, nymphs, flowers, children playing games and parents offering wine to visitors. Plant pots with drainage holes have been found. Birds were prized, whether painted, wild, caged, cooked or as a source of manure.[48] Fish were kept in pools and eaten.

Stone seats and tables were used for outdoor meals. They look harsh without cushions but most of us would find more comfort in a small Roman court than in the typical suburban garden of today. They were secure and sheltered. Plants were grown: for the kitchen (e.g. cabbage, parsley, fennel), for making medicines (mustard), for making drinks (grapes, apples, medlars), for feeding bees and keeping them healthy (rosemary), for making perfumes (roses), for making garlands (ivy, myrtle), for decoration (acanthus, periwinkle, laurel, rose) and for shade (pine, cypress).

Byzantine gardens

Byzantium was founded as a Greek colony, *c.*660 BCE, at the point where Europe meets Asia. Emperor Constantine named the city Constantinople and it became the capital of his empire in 330 CE. Greek remained the official language and Constantinople became the most resplendent city in the Western hemisphere. Its prosperity enabled its Classical traditions, art and books to survive the Dark Ages of Northern Europe. To travellers from the benighted north, Constantinople was amazingly large, beautiful, bureaucratic and opulent. Like a pot of gold, it attracted visitors – and invaders. The latter were resisted with strong walls, sea power, military governors and occasional help, or hindrance, from the Crusaders. By the eleventh century, Constantinople was little more than a fortified zone but within its walls the old tradition of garden-making survived and prospered. Indeed, the city survived as an outpost of Graeco-Roman culture until it fell to the Turks in 1453; it is now Turkish-speaking Istanbul.

Constantine ordered the building of the first church of St Peter in Rome (330), on the site of the present St Peter's. It had a large peristyle entrance court, originally planted as a garden and later paved. The great domed church of St Sophia in Constantinople, begun in 532 and known as Hagia Sophia, also had a peristyle court. The Palace of the Emperors had a garden which included the site of what is now the Blue Mosque and

4.49 a, b The murals and the surroundings of the Church of St. Savior in Chora (Istanbul) give some indication of the character of Byzantine gardens.

4.50 a, b Gardening continues on Mount Athos and, as may often have been the case in Classical gardens, the emphasis is on growing things to eat.

extended from the Hippodrome to the Sea of Marmara. These projects influenced the Islamic gardens discussed in Chapter 5.

MacLagan writes of the Emperor's Palace in Constantinople that 'efforts can be made to reconstruct the sites of some of the main features, but nothing will fully recreate the courtyards and the fountains, the corridors and vaulted chambers'.[49] The only area to have been excavated has 'a large cloistered courtyard' with floor mosaics. Information on other Byzantine gardens is mainly literary and difficult to interpret. Irrigation channels encouraged the planting of flowers and shrubs in rectangular blocks. Paths appear to have alternated with lines of vegetation and water. Changes of level were utilised to create terraces and sunken gardens. Flowers (rose, violet, lily, iris, narcissus) were cherished, as were evergreens (ivy, myrtle, box, bay), fruit trees (apple, pear, pomegranate, fig, orange, lemon, grape) and shade trees (pine, palm, oak, elm ash). As in Pompeii, the sounds of birds, fountains and rustling leaves were much appreciated.

Since Byzantine culture continued to flourish through the Dark Ages, future archaeology is the best hope of discovering more about this large missing section in the history of garden design. Something of Greek Orthodox garden culture survives on Mount Athos. Venice was the port through which Byzantine influence entered Europe; as Byron and Rice argued in 1930, Byzantium was the source of many Renaissance ideas.[50]

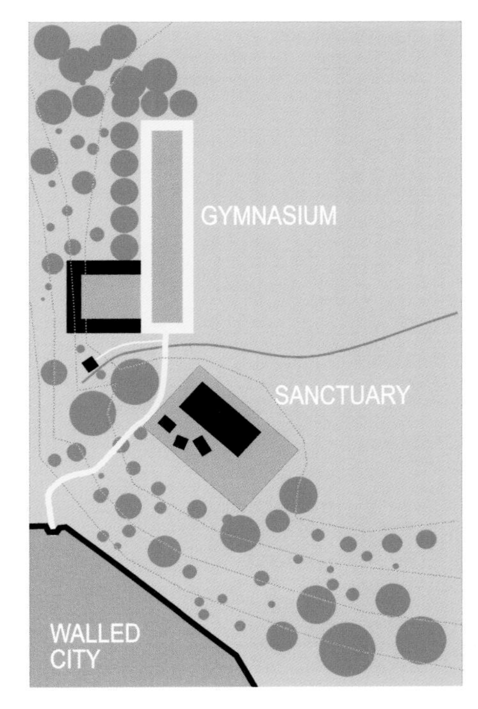

4.51 Greek sanctuary.

Types and examples

Sacred groves

Use: Believing that gods intervene in daily life, Greeks and Romans bestowed gifts, either in gratitude or in the hope of securing good fortune. In Greece, sacred landscapes were places to make offerings and sacred precincts were defined by boundary stones or walls. A grove for discussion, education and exercise, such as a gymnasium or *palaestra*, would often be created near a sanctuary. As places of spiritual enlightenment, Greek sanctuaries are related to the temple compounds of Egypt. Roman sanctuaries were usually within towns and shrines were often within gardens.

Form: The first sacred grove was probably an altar in a wood, perhaps near a cave with a clear spring. Groves were later furnished with a statue of the god and architectural elements, including temples and treasuries to contain gifts. Important groves became walled sanctuaries. There is textual and archaeological evidence that sanctuaries had ornamental planting. A settlement might develop near a sanctuary or a sacred grove might be established outside an existing town. A *palaestra* or gymnasium might have a roofed colonnade (peristyle) enclosing a rectangular court and a stadium for races. There were rooms, pools and lines of trees. Seats were placed in alcoves (*exedra*). Philosophers used the gardens for teaching.

Classical Athens, 400 BCE

The Acropolis was a fortified settlement in Mycenaean times. The caves and springs below its cliffs became the shrines which were later dedicated to Apollo and Pan. In Classical times, the plateau became a sanctuary and a walled city developed beyond the cliffs. The Walls of Themistocles enclosed what Herodotus called a 'wheel-shaped city'. It had a diameter of less than 2 km, with one spoke extending to the port of Piraeus and another, the Sacred Way, proceeding west through the Agora to the Dipylon Gate and Eleusis. Academy Way branched north, through Kerameikos, to Plato's Academy. Trees grew in the Agora and the surrounding buildings had roofed colonnades (*stoas*). The three famous gymnasiums with their associated schools of philosophy, and gardens, were outside the city walls. We can guess that olives grew on the drier land and that the moister land, near the rivers, was used for productive horticultural gardens. Structures were placed in relation to landform and, since statues, columns and walls were painted, there was no distinction between the arts which later became sculpture, painting,

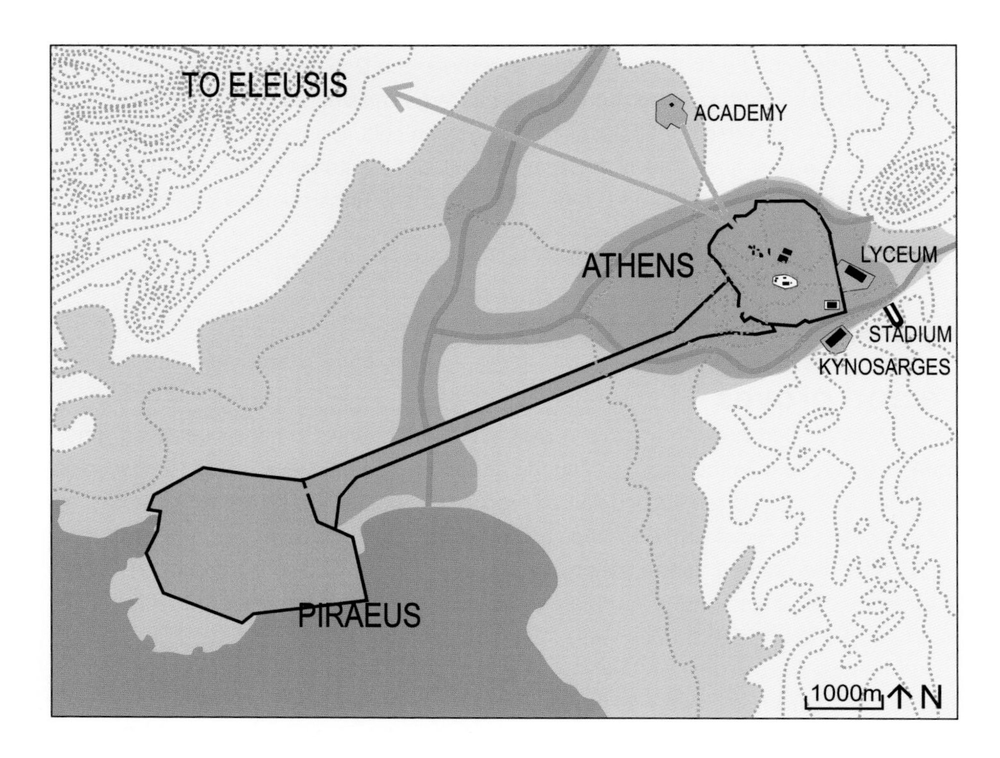

4.52 Classical Athens.

architecture, landscape architecture and town planning. Knowledge (*techne*) of their practice was simultaneously technical and artistic.

> *In the end the forms in the landscape there cannot be spoken of in terms of action or of time. Because of this it is possible they cannot be spoken of at all ... There is only being and light.*
> (Vincent Scully) [51]

Delphi, 400 BCE

Delphi occupies an extraordinary site: a cleft in the mountains beneath the horned cliffs of Phaedridae. As Vincent Scully has observed, the 'entrance by land into the citadel of Parnassos involves passage between horned cliffs ... a fastness is being penetrated'.[52]

The Sanctuary of Apollo is 600 m above the Gulf of Corinth and 1855 m below the peak of Mount Parnassos, although neither of these features is visible from the site. The aim, as with coquetry, was both to conceal and reveal. Apollo was the god of divine distance, light and wisdom. A sacred spring, dedicated to the Earth Mother, Ge, in Mycenaean times and now known as the Castalian Spring, was probably the landscape feature which led to the site being chosen. Even today, local drivers stop to fill their bottles with its health-giving water. Delphi was known as the centre of the world, its navel (*omphal-*

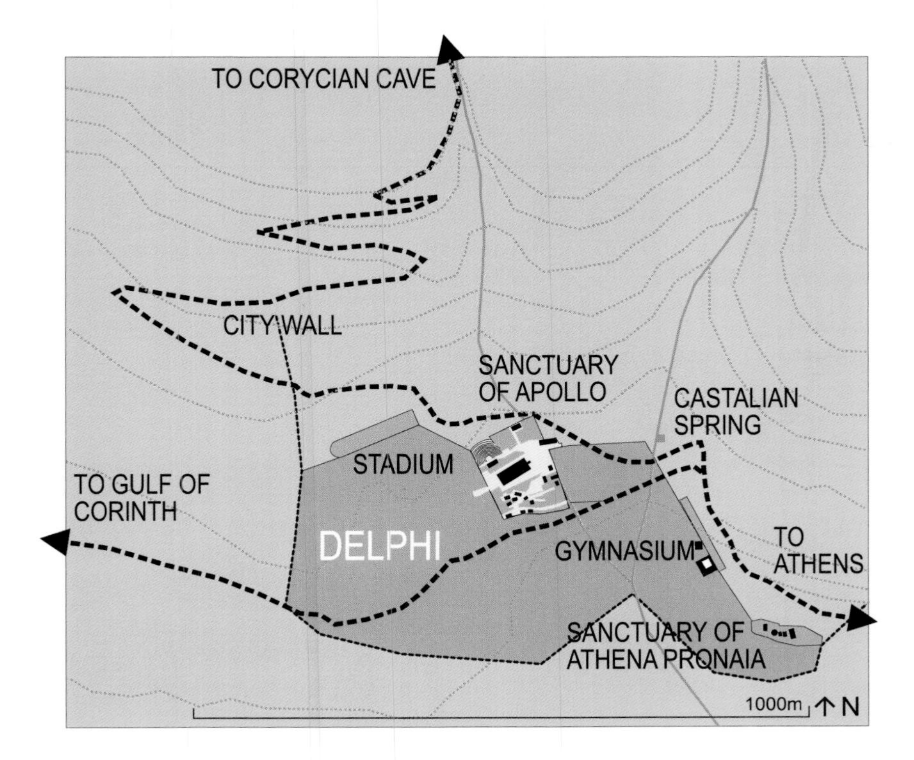

4.53 a Plan of Delphi, **b** Sanctuary of Athena Pronaia.

odes), a place of encounter between humankind, wisdom and Earth. Delphi remains a place of calm mystery, and – like a human navel – a reminder of the original creative drama. The Oracle's pronouncements were swathed by smoke from the sacred fire and profoundly ambiguous. The walled sanctuary contained a Temple of Apollo, an altar, a Sacred Way lined with Treasuries and a Theatre. Outside lay a Stadium, a town and a second Sanctuary, dedicated to Athena Pronaia. After the Acropolis in Athens, Delphi is the most visited archaeological site in Greece.

> *Delphi must therefore have seemed to the Greeks the place where the conflict between the old way, that of the goddess of the earth, and the new way, that of men and their Olympian gods, was most violently manifest.*
>
> (Vincent Scully)[53]

Olympia, 400 BCE

Olympia lies among wooded hills and near two rivers, the Alpheus and Kladeos, which have changed course. The oldest remains at Olympia date from 2000 BCE. Religious ceremonies later took place in a walled compound known as the *Altis*, or sacred grove of Zeus. It contained the Temples of Zeus and Hera and the Prytaneum with its perpetual fire and fountain. The inner Sanctuary of Pelops was a walled garden with trees and statues. Phidias the sculptor had his workshop at Olympia.

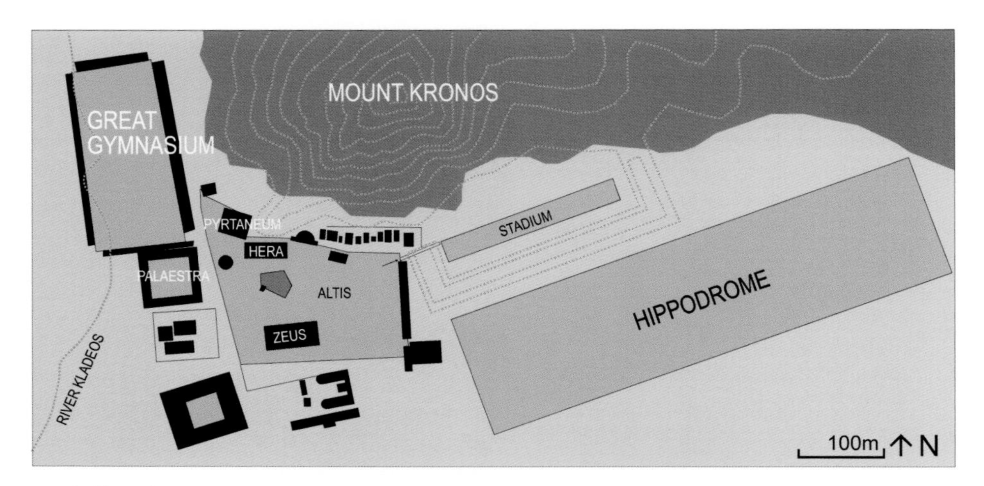

4.54 Olympia.

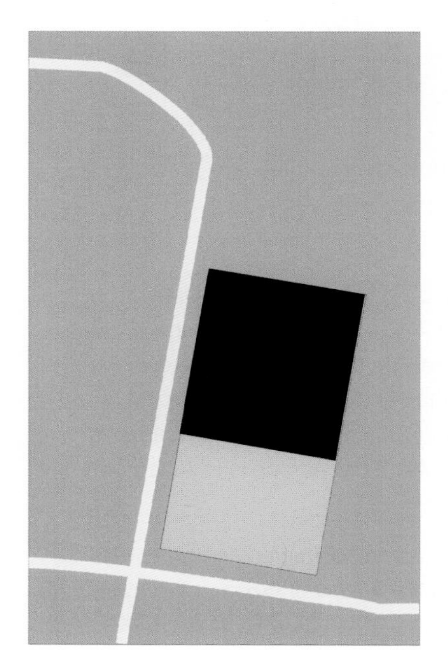

4.55 Greek court.

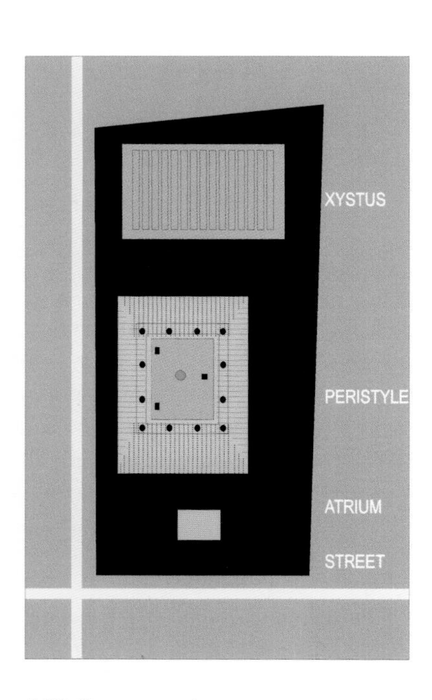

4.56 Roman court.

The Olympic Games were famed throughout the Hellenic world and held every four years from the eighth to the fourth century BCE. A covered entrance used by athletes led from the *Altis* to the oldest stadium in Greece. Spectators sat on earth embankments, which survive. They probably slept in tents or in the open. Only men and unmarried girls were allowed to watch the naked athletes. Horse races took place in the hippodrome, south of the stadium. The Romans continued to use the Olympic site after their conquest of Greece in 146 BCE. Nero built a small palace between the stadium and the hippodrome. Athletic facilities, sculptures and baths later became features of Roman villa gardens. Visitors may find it interesting to compare Olympia with the sports stadiums and park designed for the 1972 Munich Olympic Games (see p. 374). Great sports parks, whether from the fifth century BCE or the twentieth century CE, demonstrate a harmony of intellectual, artistic and physical concerns. The modern series of Olympic Games began in 1896.

> *The Spartans were the first to play games naked, and to rub themselves down with olive oil after their exercise. In ancient times even at the Olympic Games the athletes used to have coverings for their loins.*
>
> (Thucydides)[54]

Classical courts

Use: Space within walled cities was valuable: emperors had palaces with outdoor courts; wealthy nobles had houses with outdoor rooms; poor families lived in single, windowless rooms with doors opening onto narrow streets. In Greece, domestic courts were unroofed living rooms. In Roman Italy, courts were also used to house shrines, to grow plants and to display statuary and fountains. In towns, courts were enclosed by high walls for security and privacy.

Form: The Romans made three types of courtyard and some homes had one of each:

1. a yard (*atrium*) in the centre of the dwelling giving access to other rooms and to the street. The *atrium* served as a lightwell and ventilation shaft. It was paved or slightly recessed to catch rainwater, which was stored in a cistern.
2. a colonnaded yard (peristyle) ornamented and used as an outdoor living and dining room. The roofed colonnade on the perimeter functioned as a corridor giving access to bedrooms and living rooms. The enclosed yard had pools, fountains, shrubs, flowers, statues and a small shrine. Evergreens were favoured: bay, myrtle, oleander, rosemary, box and ivy. Among flowers, the Romans liked the rose, iris, lily, violet, daisy, poppy and chrysanthemum.
3. a horticultural space (*xystus*) was used for flowers and vegetables and might be decorated with statues, a pavilion and a water feature.

Delos, 400 BCE

The best-preserved examples of Ancient Greek domestic housing are at Olynthos in Northern Greece, Delos, an Aegean island, and Priene, in modern Turkey. At Delos, most of the houses comprise a room and an outdoor court, often with a cistern under the paving to store collected rainwater. The grandest houses at Delos have mosaic paving and elegant peristyles. They do not have any horticultural space but it is probable that plants were grown in terracotta pots.

4.57 Houses on Delos.

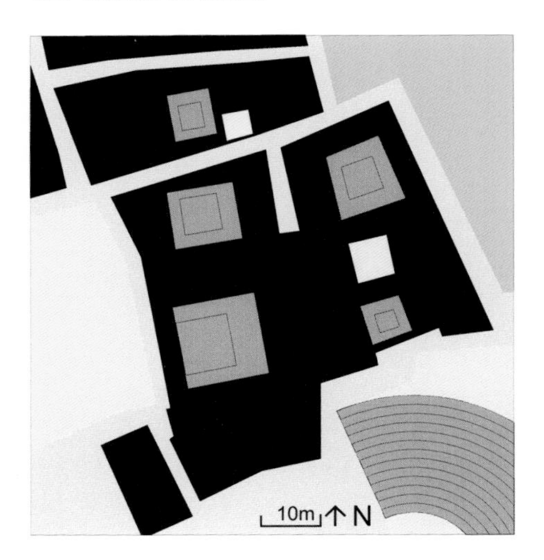

The better houses had a considerable number of rooms, some of them spacious and richly adorned, built round an elegant peristyle court ... But there were many poorer simpler houses. The site on which most of the houses were built is irregular, sloping and rocky; and the narrow streets are very irregular.

(Richard Wycherley)[55]

Pompeii, 79 CE

Pompeii lay 10 km from the summit of Mount Vesuvius and 3 km from the sea. The eruption of Vesuvius in 79 CE was a disaster for the citizens of Pompeii but a boon for garden historians, since about 500 domestic gardens were preserved under the volcanic ash. The 1942 bombing of Pompeii, the post-war usage by tourists and the urbanisation of the Bay of Naples have been unmitigated disasters. Nevertheless, much survives and more is excavated every year. Pompeii had been a Greek city and a Samnite city before it was colonised in 80 BCE by another Italian tribe, known to us as the Romans, and many Pompeian buildings pre-date the Roman conquest. Wall paintings (frescoes) were used to make small gardens appear large, often with a trellised fence in the foreground suggesting a barrier between the real garden and the garden painting.

You then pass through the ancient streets; they are very narrow, and the houses rather small, but all constructed on an admirable plan, especially for this climate. The rooms are built round a court, or sometimes two, according to the extent of the house. In the midst is a fountain, sometimes surrounded by a portico, supported on fluted columns of white stucco; the floor is paved with mosaic.

(Percy Bysshe Shelley)[56]

4.58 Pompeii.

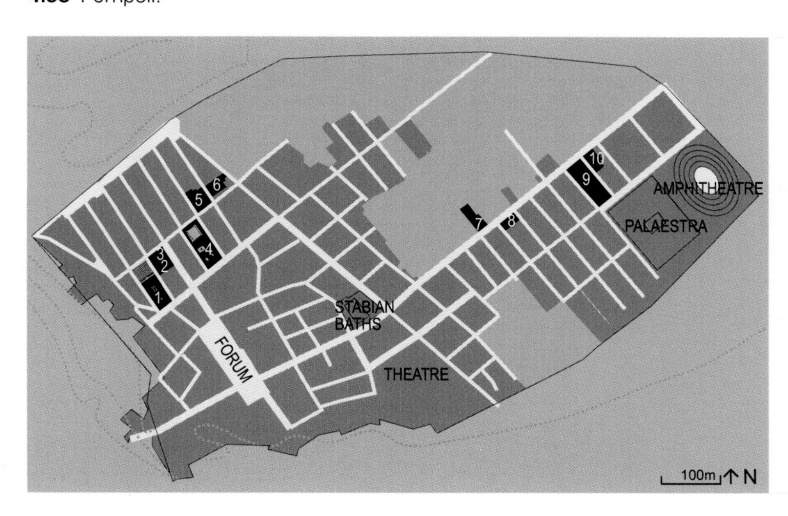

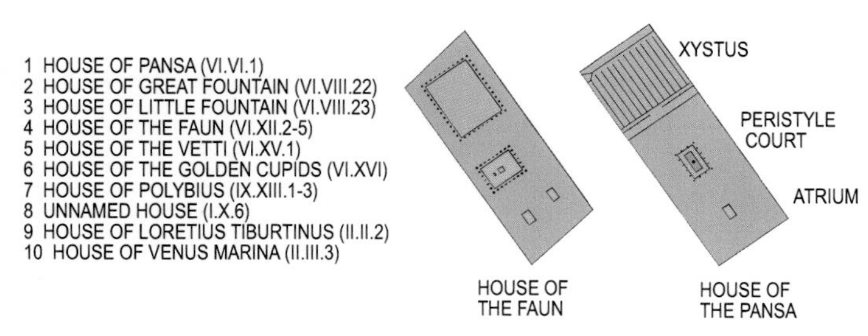

Palace of the Emperors, Palatine Hill, Rome, 100 CE

Several Roman emperors built palaces on the Palatine Hill. Deriving from earlier palaces in Macedonia, Mycenae, Crete and West Asia, the Emperors' Palace was a complex of interpenetrating buildings, roofed colonnades and outdoor courts. The courts were the grandest gardens in Rome. Small patches of mosaic paving and the brilliant quality of the sculpture in the Palatine Museum give an idea of their ancient quality. Most of the statues were copies of Greek originals found in sanctuaries. The surviving courts are among the most easily identifiable features among the ruins of the Palatine:

- Augustus Court, in the House of Livia;
- the oval Nymphaeum in Augustus' palace, originally one of a pair;
- the Labyrinth Court, occupied by a maze-like garden feature;
- the Fountain Court, now viewed from above, with semicircular inner canals surrounded by a rectangular outer canal;
- the two Peristyle Courts, one of which contained a pool and fountain;
- the large Hippodrome, which may have been used as a stadium.

> *In the centre was an octagonal fountain, on the west side there were grottoes, where cool water flowed continuously into ornamental basins. Parallel with the great building devoted to the Emperor's private life stood a second [court], facing south and descending by two terraces to the edge of a huge amphitheatre. You can still see that in the upper peristyle was a rectangular sheet of water, in the middle of which stood a little temple joined to the land by a small bridge with seven arches. Round the lower peristyle was a maze of rooms, staircases and gardens, whose ornate fountains are now bare of the statues and white marble that once decorated them.*
>
> (Pierre Grimal)[59]

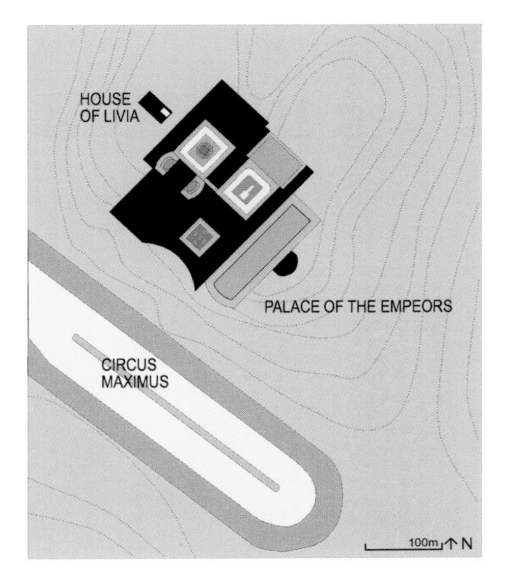

4.59 The Palatine Hill, Rome.

Villas

Use: Roman villas were palatial estates with dwellings, gardens and numerous subsid-iary buildings. Both rural and urban villas were built. Their owners used them as places in which to relax, exercise, entertain friends and conduct pleasant business – or, in Hadrian's case, run an empire. The villa incorporated elements from earlier outdoor enclosures: a domestic courtyard, a gymnasium (sacred grove), a temple garden (many emperors were considered gods), a park and grottoes.

Form: Buildings and gardens were grouped together within protected enclosures. The spaces adjoining individual buildings were axially planned but, by the standards of Renaissance villas, the lack of an overall controlling axis is surprising: structures were scattered like boxes on a table. The villa format was a persistent one: in Southern Spain (*c.*1250) the Moors built palatial villa-gardens, planned like their Roman predecessors but also drawing upon the Eastern tradition of paradise gardens.

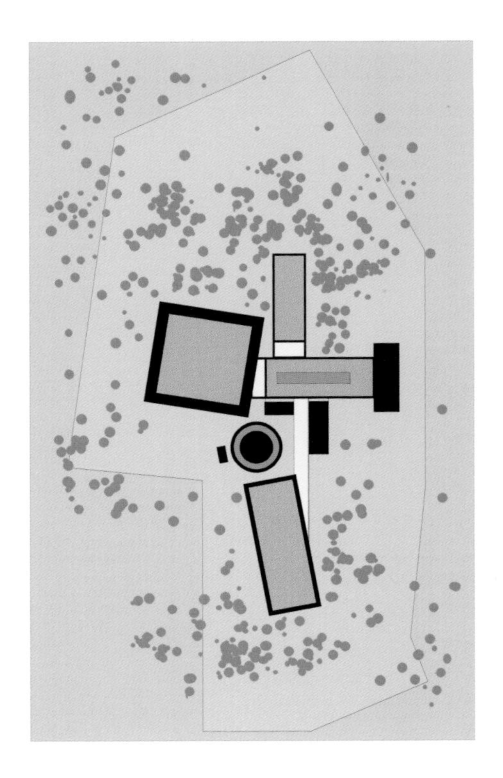

4.60 Roman villa.

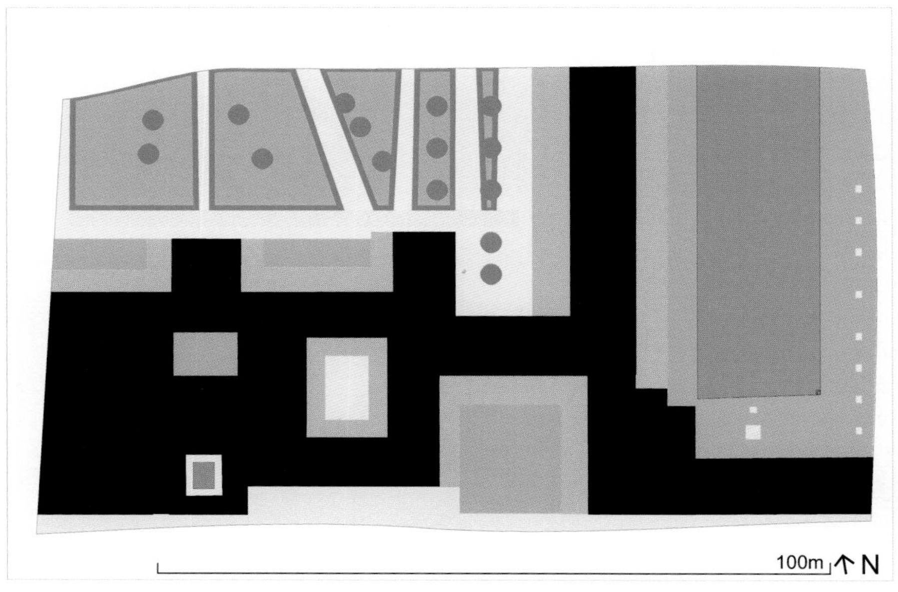

4.61 Poppaea's villa at Oplontis.

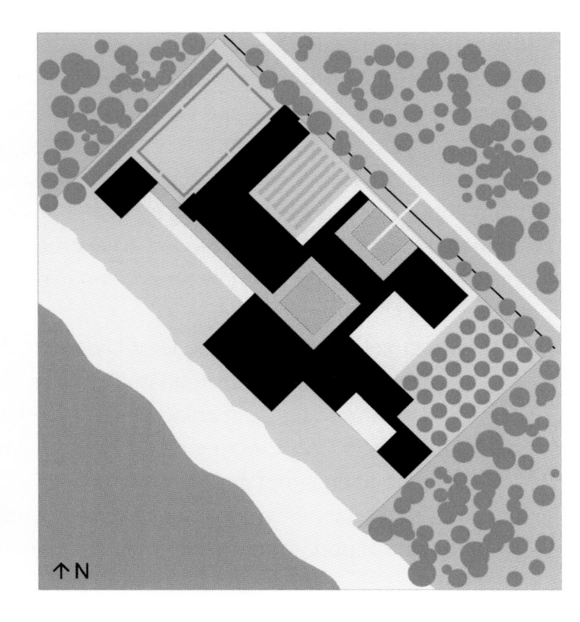

4.62 'Villa di Plinio', Laurentum.

Poppaea's villa, 79 CE

A once-luxurious villa with extensive gardens has been excavated since 1974, with great attention paid to the gardens by Wilhelmina Jashemski. Soils were investigated to find planting positions and replanting has taken place. There were internal courts, a swimming pool and an external garden. Ownership of the villa is attributed to Nero's wife, Poppea, who was said to keep 500 asses to supply milk for her bath. The site is now hemmed in by cliffs of volcanic debris topped by ugly apartment blocks.

> *Most important is the way in which the villa opened to the countryside, not only utilising the magnificent views of the sea and mountains but also looking out on its own parklike setting, embellished with formally planted exterior portico gardens that beckoned the visitor from both land and sea.*
>
> (Wilhelmina Jashemski)[58]

Pliny's villa, 100 CE

Pliny the Younger wrote about a seaside villa at Laurentum, east of Rome, and many authors have drawn garden plans based on his words. A possible site was found at Castel Fusano in 1935 and excavated. It is still marked on local maps as Villa di Plinio, and although it does not fit Pliny's words, it is of a similar age and type. The site contains features that evoke Pliny's words: sea air, sandy soil, a spring, pine trees and myrtles. In 1982, Ricotti argued that the real site of Pliny's villa is on the other side of Laurentum.

He writes of garden practices, site planning, plant materials, and the enjoyment of leisure at that time. Pliny owned five hundred slaves divided between his town house and his two country places.

(Julia Berral)[59]

Hadrian's villa, 130 CE

This is the most complete estate to have survived the fall of Rome. It is a larger and immensely grander version of the type of layout praised by Pliny the Younger. Though ruthless, Hadrian was a great emperor, an intellectual, a poet and a designer. His nickname 'Greekling' reflects his admiration for the source of Roman culture. Hadrian was probably born in Spain, near Seville, and, having travelled more extensively than any of his predecessors, made eclectic garden features representing places he had visited. In Greece, he could see the villas made after Alexander the Great's conquest of the East. In Egypt, he could admire the 'land of wonders'. His own villa made lavish use of water. The Canopus is a pool representing a branch of the Nile, used for summer banquets and dedicated to Serapis, an Egyptian who was licentiously worshipped by the Romans. The Maritime Theatre is ringed by Ionic columns and a circular canal. A lyceum and academy were inspired by Athens. A stadium, like the hippodrome which Pliny describes, was used for state banquets. The Piazza d'Oro is a peristyle garden which was lavishly adorned with fountains and statuary. Hadrian also had baths, theatres, libraries and apartments. Most of the sculpture was removed during the Renaissance, when the site was excavated, but enough remains to enable visitors to appreciate the magnificence of a Roman imperial garden. Some spaces are enclosed and some give views over the surrounding countryside. The villa had six grottoes and occupied an area 1 km in length and 0.5 km in width.

Hadrian's villa was really not a villa at all: it was a small town that had to contain everything that a great capital could offer. It was a dream translated into solid stone and marble, a miracle created by an emperor who was also an architect and an artist.

(Eugenia Ricotti)[60]

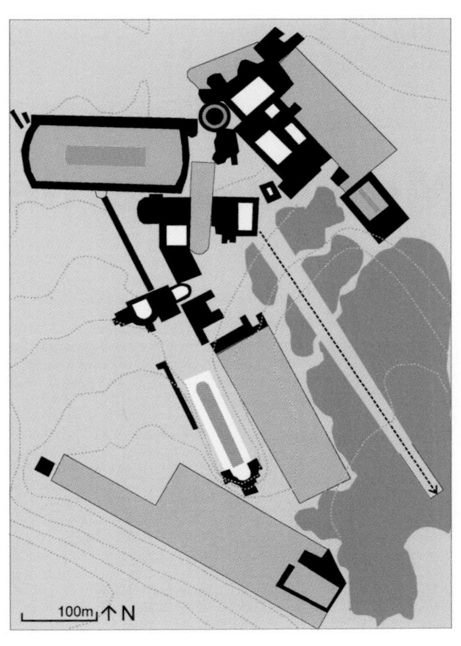

4.63 Hadrian's villa, Tivoli.

CHAPTER 5

Medieval gardens, 600–1500

5.0 Re-creations of medieval gardens tend to have more charm than authenticity (Bois Richeux Medieval Garden in France). There is no evidence for medieval gardens having had stone-edged mown grass paths.

History and philosophy

The medieval period is one of the most interesting in garden history, but frustrates the analyst on several counts. First, 'The present sum of all our fragments of knowledge does not reveal the configuration of an actual medieval garden, other than a few Hispano-Arab ones.'[1] Second, the re-creations which might contribute to our understanding of medieval gardens lack the qualities, and the excellence, shown in illustrations. Third, most historical illustrations of medieval gardens date from the Renaissance and after. We must therefore turn to general history, art history, texts and archaeology for information, never forgetting that symbolism lay at the heart of medieval culture.[2] Re-created medieval gardens tend to be 'rustic', which seems correct for vegetable gardens but incorrect for ladies' herbers within castle walls.

'Middle Ages' began as a pejorative label for the millennium covered by this chapter, signifying its inferiority to the old glory of Classical times and the new glory of the Renaissance. Scholars subsequently identified an Early Middle Age, or Dark Age (500–1000 CE), a High Middle Age (1000–1300) and a Late Middle Age (1300–1500). Although the adjective 'medieval' derives from 'middle age', it seems less pejorative. The relationship between Innsbruck and Ambras Castle in Austria (Figures 5.1 and 5.2) represents conditions at the close of the period.

After the collapse of Roman power in the West, Europe became a continent of warring tribes. Lack of records made the age 'dark' for historians, though research is lightening their gloom. The five centuries after 476 CE can be seen as an Age of Faith in which

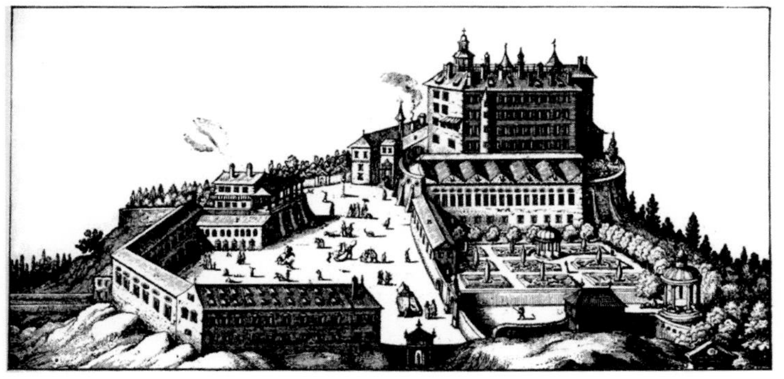

5.1 Innsbruck *c.*1600. The Braun and Hogenberg drawing shows a compact town overlooked by Ambras Castle (left, above town) with houses and gardens spreading beyond the medieval defences (right, below town).

5.2 A 1649 drawing of the old garden at Ambras Castle, showing the bustle of the yard and the seclusion of the herber.

5.3 Ambras Castle: a re-created herber nestling between the castle and the castle walls, with the mountains beyond.

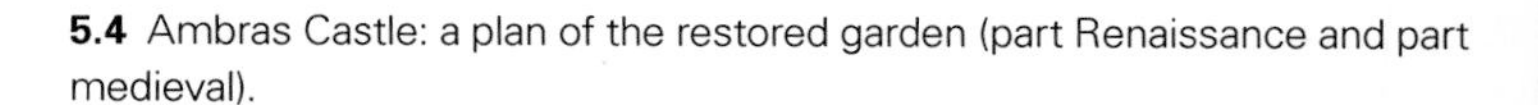

5.4 Ambras Castle: a plan of the restored garden (part Renaissance and part medieval).

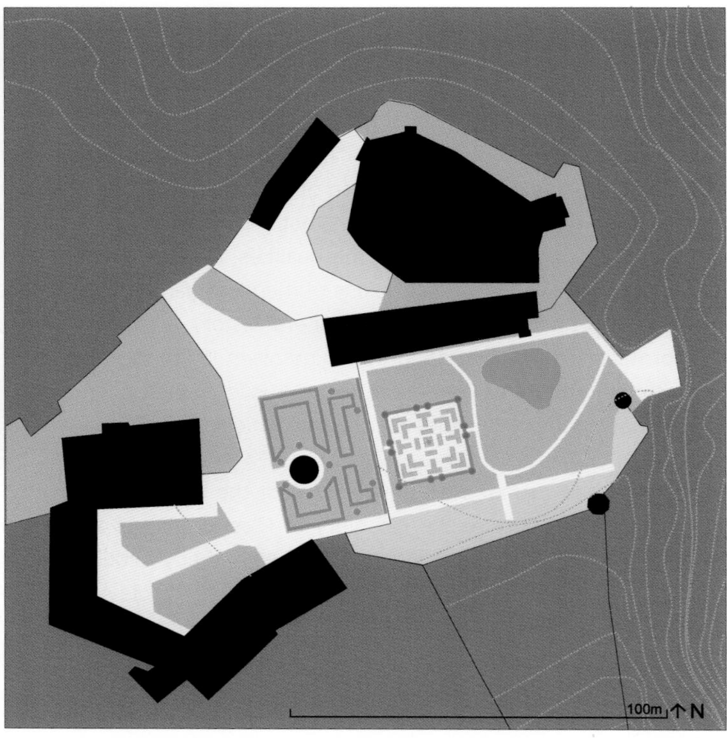

religion provided the test of truth and reason little more than an argument for faith. Individual opinion was discouraged and 'innovation was a sin'.[3] Christianity had spread from West Asia, through Rome, to the cities and then the country districts of North Europe. The Roman Catholic Church was the only institution to survive from ancient times until modern times. It was also the only international organisation, the arbiter even of trivial land disputes in Scotland. The rawness of medieval life made it easy to believe that paradise, which had not been offered in pagan times, would be superior to life on earth. Hell, for sure, would be worse. Preachers informed their congregations in plain terms about the conditions in hell: 'The horrible cold, the loathsome worms, the stench, hunger and thirst, the darkness, the chains, the unspeakable filth, the endless cries, the sight of demons.'[4] Densely populated cities gave residents some experience of these conditions.

Gardens symbolised heaven but the early Church Fathers had an ambivalent attitude, fearing that beauty, like luxury, would imperil the soul. Sacred painting, sculpture, literature and, to a lesser extent, gardens, were, however, valued as aids to private contemplation and doctrinal exegesis. Plotinus, a pagan philosopher, and Augustine of Hippo, a Christian saint, were the thinkers who did most to promote a symbolic art, glorying in the unseen order of an awesome universe.

5.5 Fra Angelico's *Last Judgement* shows the wicked on their way to hell (right). The virtuous are shown (left), being led by angels from a paradise garden to heaven's gate, represented by an opening in a castle wall.

5.6 The densely populated hill-towns of medieval Europe lacked space for gardens within their walls and, when suffering hunger or plague, gave a foretaste of hell. When safe, the countryside was more like heaven.

Plotinus (205–270) was born at Assiut in Upper Egypt, a capital city during the Middle Kingdom and famous for the worship of Osiris in Hellenistic times. Plotinus moved to Rome and became the key figure in developing a Neoplatonic theory of art. He equated the Form of the Good (see Chapter 1) with a supreme being who could be mystically sensed but not directly known. Plotinus believed the Forms to be 'fully organised into a

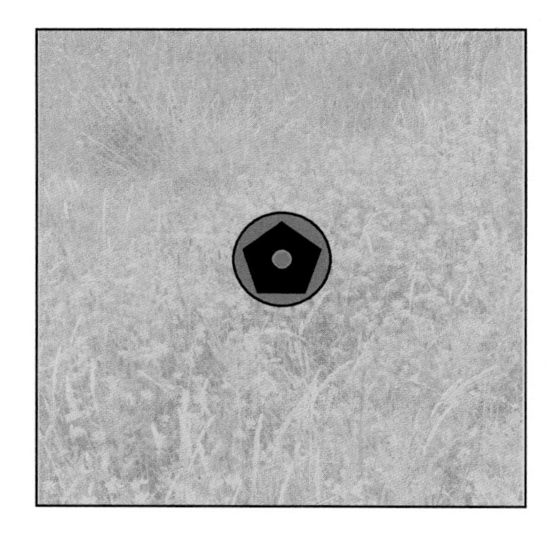

5.7 Pentads, including fountain basins and roses, could symbolise the five books of Moses, the five wounds of Christ or the Pentateuch.

coherent general scheme of things', a scheme that became known as 'the great chain of being'.[5] It had a hierarchical structure: from God at its head, through angels, saints and mankind to the animal kingdom. Everything in the visible world was believed to be formed in the image of an eternal Form. Each rose, for example, was thought to be shaped from the universal 'Rose Form', which must have existed before any particular rose could be made and which would still exist if roses became extinct on earth.

Medieval enthusiasm for symbols derived from philosophy: 'nature appeared to the symbolical imagination to be a kind of alphabet through which God spoke to men and revealed the order of things'.[6] Herbs were seen as beautiful, because they are green. A vase of red and white roses with thorns could be viewed as martyrs and virgins surrounded by their persecutors.[7] The five petals of the rose symbolised the five books of Moses (the Pentateuch), the five wounds of Christ and other pentads. In colours, white symbolised virginity, red symbolised the blood of Christ, blue, as in ancient Egypt, symbolised truth and justice.[8] A rose could symbolise life on earth. It 'flowers in early

5.8 Red and white roses symbolised the blood of Christ and the purity of the Virgin Mary.

5.9 The north window at Notre Dame in Paris, later described as a rose window, has the Virgin Mary at its centre and she is surrounded by prophets and saints.

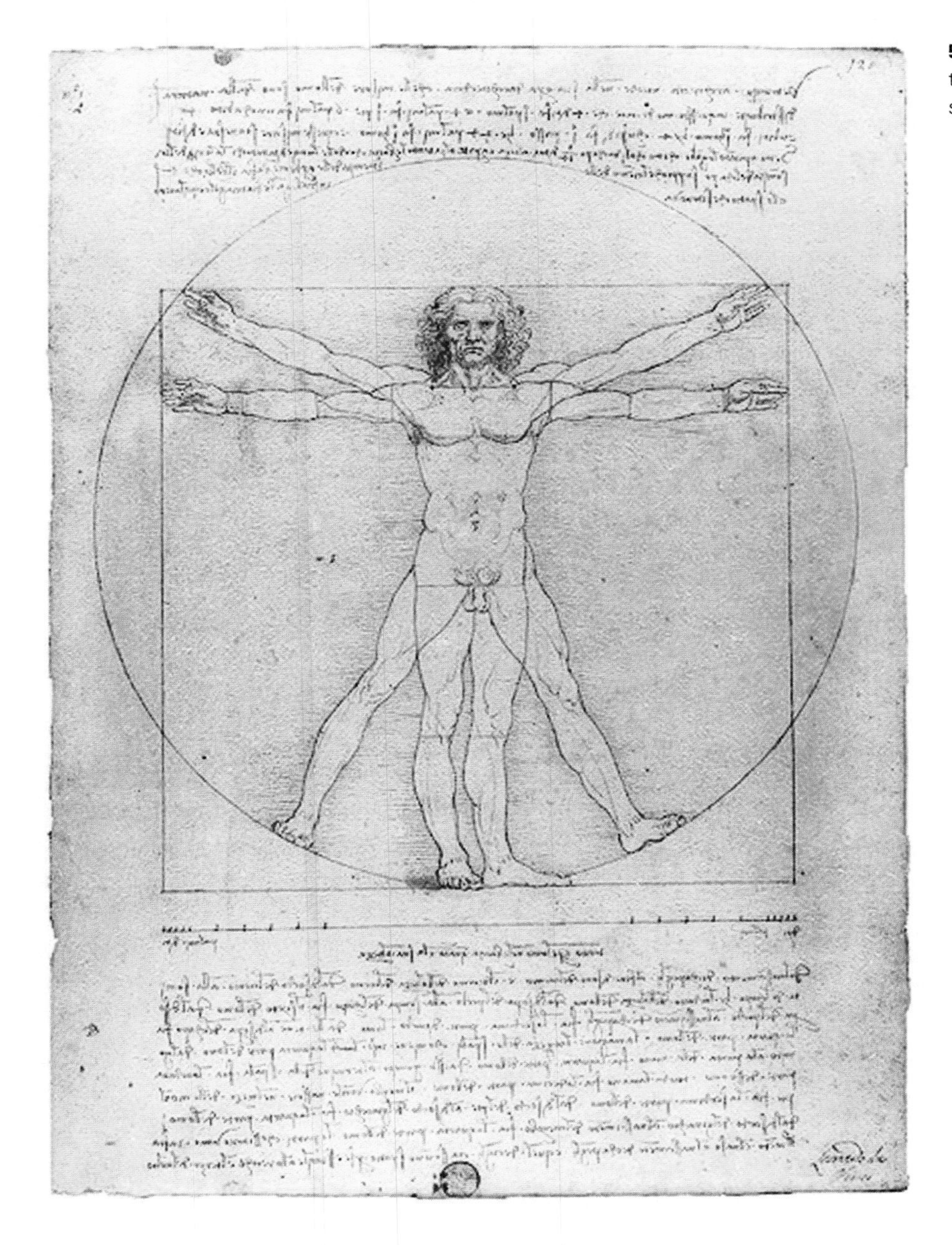

5.10 Leonardo's diagram (*c.*1492), inspired by Vitruvius' text, shows the relationship between the forms of the square, the circle and the human body.

morning' and fades 'in the evening of our age'.[9] The tortured flesh of a Christian martyr could symbolise his 'brilliant interior beauty'.[10]

In his tract, *On Intellectual Beauty*,[11] Plotinus explained how the Forms inspire the work of designers. When a block of stone is 'wrought by a craftsman's hands into some statue of god or man', its beauty comes from 'the Form or Idea introduced by the art', which 'is

Utriusque Cosmi
MAIORIS scilicet et MINORIS METAPHYSICA, PHYSICA
ATQVE TECHNICA
HISTORIA
In duo Volumina secundum COSMI differentiam diuisa.
AVTHORE ROBERTO FLUD
Tomus Primus
OPPENHEMII

5.11 Medieval and Renaissance thinkers were fascinated by the relationship between microcosm and macrocosm.

Source: Fludd, R., *Utriusque Cosmi majoris scilicet et minoris metaphysica atque technica historia in duo volumina secundum cosmi differentiam divisa*, Oppenhemii, 1617.

in the designer before ever it enters the stone'. Likewise, 'music does not derive from an unmusical source': it comes from the eternal and mathematical Forms of Rhythm and Harmony. Therefore beauty derives from the Platonic Forms and art should imitate the forms. Imitation should not be disparaged, despite Plato's critical remarks on the subject:

> *The arts are not to be slighted on the ground that they create by imitation of natural objects; for, to begin with, these natural objects are themselves imitations; then, we must recognise that they give no bare reproduction of the thing seen but go back to the Ideas from which Nature itself derives ... Thus Pheidias wrought [his famous statue of] Zeus upon no model among things seen but by apprehending what Form Zeus must take if he chose to become manifest to sight.*[12]

To the Emperor Gallienus, Plotinus proposed a city constituted on Plato's *Laws* 'to be called Platonopolis'.[13] It was a hint that Neoplatonic ideas could be applied to physical design projects, and indeed, such ideas later influenced architecture and gardens. Neoplatonism was transmitted to medieval and Renaissance art by St Augustine (396–430), another son of Graeco-Roman Africa and the greatest Christian thinker of antiquity. Augustine was Bishop of Hippo Regius (the modern city of Annaba in Algeria). His father was a passionate pagan and his mother a passionate Christian. The son reconciled his parents' beliefs, showing that pagan philosophy could illuminate Christian thought: first, by using reason to reveal the unseen order of God's Creation and second, by infusing order into works of art.

St Augustine thus became the steersman for medieval aesthetics and, as will be explained below, for a Christian approach to gardens. His key aesthetic concepts were order, unity, equality, number and proportion. 'Examine the beauty of bodily form', he wrote, 'and you will find that everything is in its place by number.'[14] Number gives rise to order. Order gives rise to symmetry. Design, when orderly and symmetrical, shares formal characteristics with the universal Forms. The principle that good designs are microcosms of the macrocosm underlies the sacred geometry of Christian and Islamic architecture. 'Vitruvius taught that four was the number of man, because the distance between his extended arms was the same as his height – thus giving the base and height of a square.'[15] Squares manifest the relationship between Man and God. Cathedral design is based on mathematical symbolism. A thousand years after Augustine, mathematical order provided the basis for 'formal' gardens, in the sense of gardens embodying the Platonic Forms. Wittkower explains the geometrical ideas of Pythagoras and Plato, commenting that, 'Generally speaking, equilateral triangle, square and pentagon formed the basis of medieval aesthetics.'[16] Though documentary evidence is lacking, mathematical symbolism can also explain the use of square plans for Islamic courts and Christian cloister garths:

> *Medieval symbolism found a particularly large field of application in the very rich Christian liturgy, chiefly in fact in interpreting religious architecture ... It is easy to*

> *understand that the round church was the image of the perfection of the circle, but it must be realised that the cross-shaped plan did not only represent Christ's crucifixion, but rather was the* ad quadratum *form, based on the square, designating the four points of the compass and epitomizing the universe. In both cases the church was a microcosm.*[17]

The Dark Ages were a period of migration for peoples, as well as ideas, and geometrical perfection became characteristic of religious space from India to Europe. Latin, Persian and Arabic became the languages of scholarship and diplomacy, as Greek had been in Hellenistic and Roman times. Much that the Romans created in Western Europe had fallen into decay, and learning Latin helped scholars to understand the old civilisation.

North Europeans were not uncultured, either before or after imperial times. The structure of the medieval household was directly descended from 'the classical Roman empire, and the peoples, whom the Romans called barbarians'.[18] Medieval gardens share these parents, as Classical ideas were adopted by tribal societies and Christianity modernised ancient beliefs. The end of slavery and the Church's insistence on monogamy[19] diminished the Classical role of gardens as places for social opulence: compared to their Roman predecessors, Frankish gardens were simpler and more spiritual.

5.12 Geometrical perfection was a goal of medieval art (the cloister at Mont St Michel in France).

Charlemagne, King of the Franks, became Holy Roman Emperor in 800 CE. When not on campaign, he lived at Aachen in North Germany. He introduced the tithe, whereby one-tenth of a peasant's income went to the Church. His concern for religion was matched by his passion for gardens: his court compiled a list of plants, issued as the *Capitulare de Villis*, for use in royal gardens. A few years after the king's death, his court sent instructions for an exemplary monastery to be designed in Switzerland, at Reichenau. The design, described below as the St Gall plan, is Europe's oldest drawn plan for a building project. It is of interest that the text of Vitruvius found in 1415 was also in the St Gall library.[20]

Charlemagne's empire scarcely outlived its founder. Power became local and nation-states in the modern sense were slow to develop, with Britain one of the first. France became a great feudal power but not until after the Renaissance did it become a unitary power. Power in Italy and the German-speaking lands remained regional until the nineteenth century. An un-Roman chasm yawned between the Eastern and Western worlds, which became the worlds of Christ and of Muhammad. For all these reasons, monasteries, castles and walled towns became the social organisations which exercised power in medieval Europe.

Medieval gardens

Lasting for a thousand years, Europe's Middle Age had intervals of peace and prosperity which could have been used to make great gardens. The leaders of the ninth-century 'renaissance' associated with Charlemagne, and of the twelfth-century 'renaissance' associated with cathedral-building, had all the necessary skills and resources. Castles and towns lacked internal space, but extensive gardens could have been made outside

5.13 Jesus and his disciples assured a place in Christianity for gardens by spending the night before the crucifixion in the Garden of Gethsemane at the foot of the Mount of Olives.

5.14 St Augustine renounced lust in a small garden in Milan (illustration from a stained glass window in Norwich Cathedral).

fortifications, as the gymnasiums and groves of Ancient Greece had been. Religion favoured gardens: Eden had been a garden; the Jewish *Song of Songs* (see p. 63) laid the foundation for Christian gardens of love.

Jesus spent the night before his arrest in the Garden of Gethsemane; the first mosque was a garden; the scene of St Augustine's conversion in Milan took place in a garden. Yet medieval gardens were small, because a different attitude to faith produced a different attitude to gardens. Cathedrals satisfied the ritual and ceremonial aspect of religion, as temple sanctuaries had done in Egypt, Greece and Rome. Christian gardens therefore became places for meditation, even if, despite the prevailing asceticism, people dreamed of romance.

St Augustine wrote of his wanton youth: 'I could not discern the clear brightness of love from the fog of lustfulness. Both did confusedly boil in me, and hurried my youth, unfastened, over the precipice of unholy desire.' He therefore cherished the calm sanctuary where, with tumult in his breast, he renounced sexual passion:

> *A little garden there was to our lodging, which we had the use of, as of the whole house; for the master of the house, our host, was not living there. Thither had the tumult of my breast hurried me, where no man might hinder the hot contention wherein I had engaged with myself, until it should end as Thou knewest, I knew not. Only I was healthfully distracted and dying, to live; knowing what evil thing I was, and not knowing what good thing I was shortly to become. I retired then into the garden.*[21]

Augustine also turned against the pagan gods he identified as 'malignant and deceitful demons'.[22] Had he read Suetonius' account of Tiberius' dealings with pagan gods in groves and grottoes, his revulsion from this aspect of his father's religion would be all the more comprehensible:

> *A number of small rooms were furnished with the most indecent pictures and statuary obtainable, also certain erotic manuals from Elephantine in Egypt ... [Tiberius] furthermore devised little nooks of lechery in the woods and glades of the island, and had boys and girls dressed up as Pans and nymphs posted in front of caverns or grottoes; so that the island was now openly and generally called 'Caprineum', because of his goatish antics. Some aspects of his criminal obscenity are almost too vile to discuss, much less believe. Imagine training little boys, whom he called his 'minnows', to chase him while he went swimming and get between his legs to lick and nibble him.*[23]

The cavern of Eros and Cupid is identified with the Blue Grotto, under Capri (p. 122), though it is said that Suetonius exaggerated Tiberius' evil. Augustine was by no means the first to condemn pagan statues and sacred trees. *On the Life of St Martin*, who died in 397, records him speaking of 'a moral necessity why the tree should be cut down, because it had been dedicated to a demon' and of 'the crowds of heathens [who] looked on in perfect quiet as he razed the pagan temple even to the foundations, he also reduced all the altars and images to dust'.[24] St Martin nearly perished on both occasions but was saved by divine intervention. Everything connected with paganism was anathematised and destroyed.

5.15 Christianity supported the making of ideal places. The illustration is from an 1868 edition of Bunyan's *Pilgrim's Progress*.

Source: Bunyan, J., *Pilgrim's Progress*, Glasgow: William Collins, 1868.

Architecture and gardens, however, could be designed in perfect accord with St Augustine's *City of God*. The book opens as follows:

> *The glorious City of God is my theme in this work ... a city surpassingly glorious, whether we view it as it still lives by faith in this fleeting course of time, and sojourns as a stranger in the midst of the ungodly, or as it shall dwell in the fixed stability of its eternal seat, which it now with patience waits for, expecting until 'righteousness shall return unto judgment,' and it obtain, by virtue of its excellence, final victory and perfect peace ... the King and Founder of this city of which we speak, has in Scripture uttered to His people a dictum of the divine law in these words: 'God resisteth the proud, but giveth grace unto the humble.'*[25]

Augustine prompted medieval garden-makers to abjure earthiness and look heavenward for inspiration for their designs. A perfect square with a round pool and a pentagonal fountain became a microcosm, illuminating the mathematical order and divine grace of the macrocosm (the universe). Numbers were symbolic. Quadrads (designs based on the number four) might represent the four winds, the four seasons or other sets of four. 'The very regularity of the Gothic garden defies the romantic notion of Gothic irregularity and mystery.'[26] Religion and romance were intertwined. Flowers communed with the soul. Even in pagan times, the rose had been sacred (to Venus). Roses and lilies had grown on the tomb of the Virgin Mary after she went to heaven:

5.16 The Virgin Mary, reading on a flowery mead in a paradise garden with saints, flowers and birds. One can identify the Madonna lily, peonies, columbine, strawberries, roses, sweet rocket, lilies of the valley, violets, cowslips, hollyhocks, irises, bergamot, hoopoe, golden oriole, tomtit and woodpecker (painting by a German master *c.*1410).

> *These two famous flowers should call to our mind*
> *The two greatest gifts of the Church to mankind.*
> *In the blood of her martyrs she plucks a red Rose,*
> *And in sign of her faith a white Lily she shows.*
> *O virginal mother! O store of ripe seed!*
> *Inviolate maid, wed to Heaven indeed.*[27]

The Madonna lily, *Lilium candidum*, seen by Crusaders in the Holy Land, produced the epithet 'lily-white'. In 1213, the Abbot of Cirencester wrote:

> *The stalk of the lily, when it is green, produces a most splendid flower, which changes from green to white. So must we persevere in the best of behaviour so that, immature plants as we are, we may attain to the whiteness of innocence.*[28]

The rose was an adored theme of Islamic and Christian art. Edward I took 'England's rose' as his insignia, and countless medieval love poems took the rose as their theme. Most famed was the *Roman de la Rose*, expressing the inextricable bonds between faith, chivalry, gardens and eroticism, of which Huizinga wrote: 'Few books have exercised a more profound and enduring influence on the life of any period.'[29]

The *Roman de la Rose* stimulated the imagination of medieval Europe concerning the treasures within castle and garden walls. Readers could learn how to court a lady and,

5.17 a–f Details from *Les Très Riches Heures du Duc de Berry*: **a** and **b** are scenes of castle life; **c** and **d** show horticultural plots; **e** shows peasants harvesting grapes and **f** shows grain being harvested on a horticultural scale.

through a thinly veiled subtext, how to seduce her. The *Roman* opens with the Lover approaching the wall of the garden of love. It climaxes with 'plucking the rose':

> *Dame Leisure opens the gate for him, Gaiety conducts the dance, Amor holds by the hand Beauty, who is accompanied by Wealth, Liberality, Frankness, Courtesy, and Youth. After having locked the heart of his vassal, Amor enumerates to him the blessings of love, called Hope, Sweet Thought, Sweet Speech, Sweet Look. Then, when Bel-Accueil, the son of Courtesy, invites him to come and see the roses, Danger, Malebouche, Fear, and Shame come to chase him away ... Virginity is condemned, hell is reserved for those who do not observe the commandments of nature and of love. For the others the flowered field, where the white sheep, led by Jesus, the lamb born of the Virgin, crop the incorruptible grass in endless daylight. At the close Genius throws the taper into the besieged fortress; its flame sets the universe on fire. Venus also throws her torch; then Shame and Fear flee, the castle is taken, and Bel-Accueil allows the lover to pluck the rose.*[30]

Medieval society only provided the necessary level of security for gardens of love in or near castles, fortified towns or monasteries.

Castle gardens

The organisation of warfare was one of the skills which dwellers in northern forests learned from the Romans. This led to a need for residential castles. Forts, on the Roman

5.18 Burg Eltz, built in the twelfth century as a family home. It has small areas of green space with the fortifications and may have had a herber outside the walls.

model, had been occupied only by soldiers enforcing the will of a distant emperor who used roads to dispatch reinforcements. When power became local, residential castles replaced forts and warfare became more domestic. Castles developed as crowded homes for a lord, his wife, his family, armed retainers and, in times of danger, the local populace.

For us, castles symbolise the society of the High Middle Ages (1000–1350). When called, a knight rode forth in his lord's or lady's service, clad in armour and mounted on a warhorse. Making boasts and taking vows, he lived and died by a code of chivalry. Since trade would have been unchivalrous, a rich wife, or a ransomable prisoner, were his chief means of advancement. Marriage was no love affair: it was a serious business with dynastic implications. Though fair maids might dream of love, as chatelaines they had to breed families and run great estates in their lords' absence. In peacetime a young wife might have leisure to sew, make a garden, listen to minstrels or conduct an illicit romance. Sitting on a flowery mead to make daisy chains was an approved pastime. As adults, medieval women became domestic stalwarts with more knowledge of medicinal herbs, horticulture and gardens than other castle residents.

Castle-building developed rapidly in Europe after the ninth century, especially in France. Castles often began as a stockade on conical mounds (*mottes*) with a ditch at the foot of the slope. Later castles were built in stone, often with a nearby garden and orchard. When outer curtain walls and moats were added, garden plants could be tended within the fortified zone. In times of siege, villagers would take refuge within the bailey, trampling everything, and ladies could take exercise only on the ramparts. Symbolic illustrations, like those in *Les Très Riches Heures du Duc de Berry* (*c.*1410) allow, in what are 'virtually colour-photographs',[31] glimpses of ornamental gardens occupying land within curtain-walled enclosures. They correlate with the garden descriptions in the *Roman de la Rose* and with the numerous illustrations from the late-medieval period, drawn to accompany the poem and reproduced in books on medieval gardens. We see flowery

5.19 Outside the walls of Whittington Castle is a mount which overlooked a medieval garden.

5.20 An orchard at Penshurst Place.

5.21 A perfect herber (*c.*1465) from the *Mystical Marriage of St Catherine.*

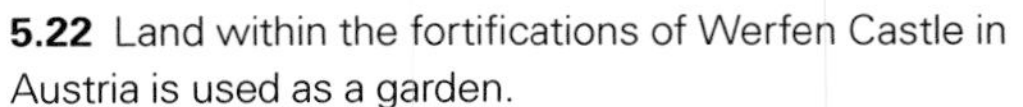

5.22 Land within the fortifications of Werfen Castle in Austria is used as a garden.

5.23 a, b Castle ramparts and yards could be used as garden space in peaceful times (Salzburg).

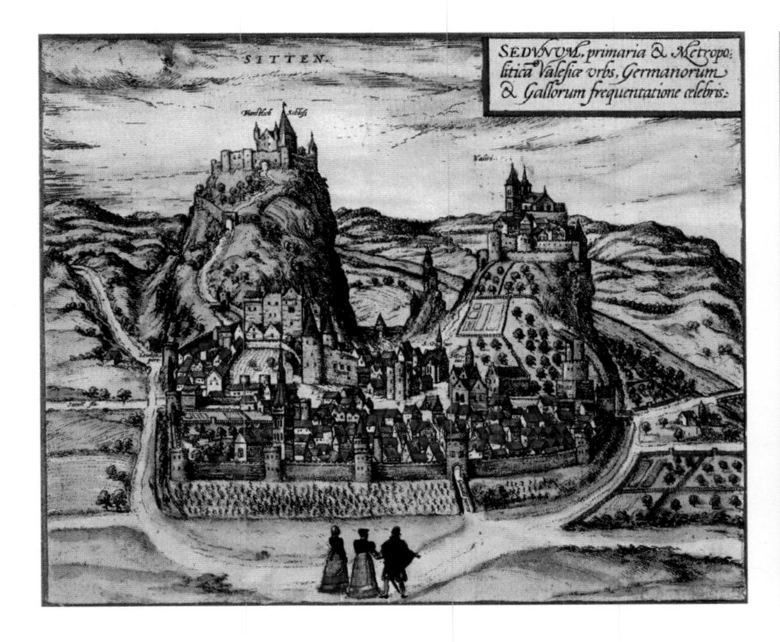

5.24 a, b Sion (Sitten), Switzerland. Medieval cities often had a herber inside the bailey, a *pleasance* near the curtain walls and horticultural plots outside the city walls. The Valère Basilica (on the left peak) is a fortified church with greenspace within the walls and Tourbillon (on the right peak) is now a ruined castle (drawing by Braun and Hogenberg, 1572).

lawns, basins, turf seats, summer houses, flowers, neat trees, trellis-work and rose arbours in which maidens could steal a forbidden kiss from a 'veray parfit gentil knight'.[32] Who would not seek relief from the stench, noise and lack of privacy within the keep, or from the excrement-strewn mud of the bailey and barnyard?

St Albertus Magnus explained how to make a 'pleasure garden', in 1206 – although it unlikely that he ever made such a garden for the Dominican monastic order to which he belonged. He was the son of a wealthy German lord and was probably describing

5.25 a, b Pre-Raphaelite paintings may represent the planting in medieval gardens with more accuracy than modern re-creations of medieval gardens. The paintings of The Enchanted Garden, in Boccaccio's *Fifth Day*, are by Marie Spartali Stillman (1889) and J .W. Waterhouse (1916).

5.26 a, b Saumur Château, *c.*1410 and today, showing the accuracy of the Limbourg brothers' paintings, new roofs and new fortifications at ground level.

the kind of garden he had known as a boy. His teacher, St Thomas Aquinas, had developed St Augustine's ideas on aesthetics, stressing the role of cognition in perceiving transcendental beauty. Albertus referred to Aristotle as his chief authority on science, and would have understood the significance of geometry in Christian design. He, and his English contemporary, Henry the Poet,[33] wrote about 'square' gardens. Here are Albertus' instructions for a perfect 'green cloth' framed by 'a bench of turf' and 'every sweet-smelling herb':

The whole plot is to be covered with rich turf of flourishing grass, the turves beaten down with broad wooden mallets and the plants of grass trodden into the ground until they cannot be seen or scarcely anything of them perceived. For then little by little they may spring forth closely and cover the surface like a green cloth. Care must be taken that the lawn is of such a size that about it in a square may be planted every sweet-smelling herb such as rue, and sage and basil, and likewise all sorts of flowers, as the violet, columbine, lily, rose, iris and the like. So that between these herbs and the turf, at the edge of the lawn set square, let there be a higher bench of turf flowering and lovely; and somewhere in the middle provide seats so that men may sit down there to take their repose pleasurably when their senses need refreshment. Upon the lawn too, against the heat of the sun, trees should be planted or vines trained, so that the lawn may have a delightful and cooling shade, sheltered by their leaves.

5.27 A re-created medieval seat, in Sissinghurst Castle garden.

Figure 5.28 shows a reconstruction, based on Albertus' text and on symbolic paintings in medieval manuscripts. The following points can be noted:

- Medieval garden illustrations were as diagrammatic as those of buildings.
- Despite their simplicity, medieval gardens surely had the high quality we find in medieval buildings.
- Albertus' mention of a square plan implies a wider use of geometry, as in religious architecture.
- Albertus' delight in flowers and scents implies the riches of a millefleurs tapestry, which is difficult to show on a diagram.

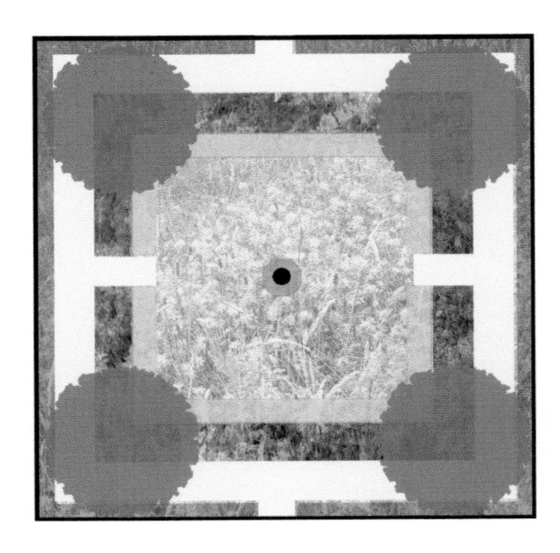

5.28 A reconstruction, based on St Albertus Magnus' account of how to make a pleasure garden.

Most reconstructions of medieval gardens treat the grass as a mown lawn despite the fact that textual and visual sources reveal it to have been what modern authors call a 'flowery mead'. Lawns maintained by modern 'lawn experts' with chemicals and machines will never have the quality of a hand-weeded, beaten and scythed 'flowery mead': it is the difference between chipboard and oak.

Gardens were also made outside curtain walls. Areas of woodland were fenced for country pleasures, as in ancient Mesopotamia. Wooded pleasure parks can be distinguished from hunting parks but the roles overlap: a *pleasance* (pleasure-ground) might have a *gloriette* (pavilion) where the ladies could eat while watching men hunt, fish or joust. The word *gloriette* comes, via Spain, from West Asia.[34] A *pleasance* was a place of resort. In *Mai and Beaflore*, the prince banquets in 'a little garden of trees full of white-rose bowers under the castle. Many were sitting there on seats; poor and rich ate together.'[35] Nobles maintained extensive hunting parks, subject to forest laws:

A forest is a certain territory of woody grounds and fruitful pastures, privileged for wild beasts and fowls of forest, chase, and warren, to rest and abide there in the safe protection of the king ... And therefore a forest doth chiefly consist of these four things: of vert and venison; of particular laws and proper officers.[36]

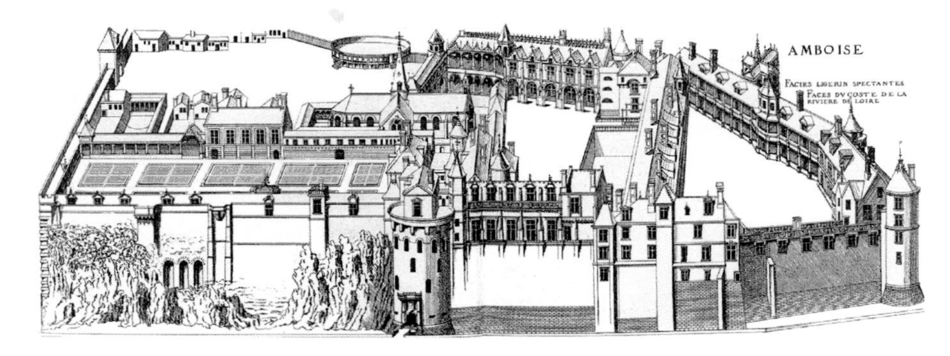

5.29 a, b Du Cerceau's drawing of Château Amboise in the 1570s shows a Renaissance parterre on what may have been the site of a medieval herber.

The rights of peasants to exploit the resources of a hunting park were carefully defined: they might graze livestock and collect fallen wood, but were subject to mutilation or execution if caught poaching game or felling trees.

Some information about castle gardens can be gleaned from Renaissance plans, such as Du Cerceau's drawing of Montargis, in *Les Plus Excellents Bastiments de France* (1576). It shows a herber within the castle walls and extensive orchard and vegetable gardens outside the curtain wall. Du Cerceau was a Protestant refugee who lived at Montargis for a time (see p. 176).

Kings had grander gardens than nobles but they were similar in kind. Because his empire was secure, Charlemagne did not need to build his palaces and gardens behind fortifications. His palace at Aachen (*c.*780) was near a hot spa and had a courtyard like a Roman villa. His successors had less security and found it necessary to live behind fortifica-

5.30 A sundial at Penshurst Place in a re-created garden.

5.31 The King's Knot, viewed from Stirling Castle.

tions and to make their gardens in the woods – or, if space allowed, within the bailey. Massive castles were built in Northern France; Vincennes and St Germain had space for gardens, but these are likely to have been small.[37] Henry III of England had gardens outside the fortifications of Windsor Castle and created the post of Royal Gardener in 1268.[38] Edward I made a garden for the Palace of Westminster on his return from the Crusades in 1272. It was fortified and the herber occupied 'about half-an-acre of the Palace precinct'[39] (and a fragment survives). The King's Knot and the parterre beneath Stirling Castle 'occupy the site of a great garden which was probably laid out by James I of Scotland soon after 1424, in imitation of the King's Garden below Windsor Castle where he had first seen his queen'.[40] At the Louvre 'the great garden of the palace was connected to the Petit Jardin on the other side of the street by a private arched bridge',[41] which is reminiscent of Amarna (see pp. 78–9 and p. 83). Sundials are one of the few surviving features of medieval castle gardens.

5.32 a, b Prague Castle stood, as it still stands, on a hill outside the medieval city. There are still gardens on the slopes outside the walls of Prague Castle.

With the deployment of cannon in the fifteenth century, it became easier to smash castle walls. It was then necessary to have an army for defence and a centralised government to organise the army. Many castle owners developed their gun platforms, ramparts and bailies into Renaissance gardens of the kind discussed in the next chapter. Prague has a royal garden north of Hradschin Castle and aristocratic gardens on its southern ramparts.

Monastery gardens

Though a life of retreat offers various joys,
None I think will compare with the time one employs
In the study of herbs, or in striving to gain
Some practical knowledge of nature's domain.[42]

Monasteries compare with the temples of the ancient world, which often had resident priests. Regularity lay at the heart of the monastery and members of the public were excluded unless it had a public church, an infirmary or a school. But monastic gardens were contemplative and functional, never pompous. While knights devoted themselves to war, the arts of civilisation were kept alive by the clergy, mostly from the upper classes. The Knights Templar were an aristocratic order with both monastic and military roles. Taking their name from Jerusalem's ancient Temple, they fought to protect Christian pilgrims visiting shrines in the Holy Land.

Christian monasticism originated in Egypt, possibly as a result of the contacts between Alexandria and the East. Early monks (from *monos*, meaning single) lived in self-denial and poverty, following Christ's example. St Anthony of the Desert, an early monk, was

5.33 St Anthony's is the oldest Christian monastery and is 2 km from the cave where St Anthony lived, in Egypt.

5.34 Jan Brueghel's painting of a paradise garden.

5.35 Manual labour in a garden was regarded as devotional and cloisters became places to combine use with beauty and work with contemplation (San Lorenzo, Rome).

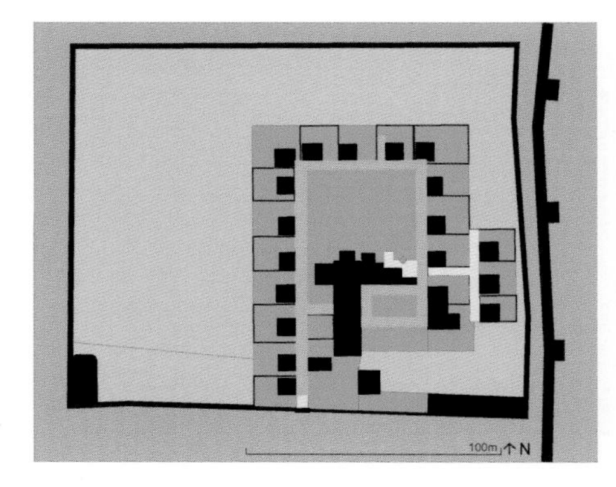

5.36 Diagram of a Carthusian monastery, each cell with its own garden.

5.37 Cloister arcades were busy places. Westminster Cathedral cloister in London is now used as a café.

an Egyptian who lived from 251–356 CE. He gave his father's estate to the poor and 'shut himself up in a remote cell upon a mountain' where he 'cultivated and pruned a little garden', his heart 'filled with inward peace, simplicity, goodness'.[43] Christian monastic communities developed and the movement spread round the shores of the Mediterranean in the fourth and fifth centuries. The Roman Empire supported Christianity after 313 CE and when the Western Empire collapsed, three centuries later, the Church became reliant on monasticism. Pope Gregory, himself a monk, sent his brethren on evangelical missions to former outposts of empire. Monasteries became repositories of Classical civilisation, like pools in the bed of a dried-up river. By Charlemagne's time, some of these pools had become enviably deep and well-stocked, thereby sowing the seeds of their destruction.

Manual labour was regarded as devotional and garden work especially so, for 'the Lord God took the man, and put him into the Garden of Eden to dress it and to keep it'.[44] The *hortus delicarum* (garden of delights) became an artist's theme, contrasting with paintings of hell.[45] St Benedict's Rule (*c.*540) stated that 'Whenever possible the monastery should be so laid out that everything essential, that is to say water, mills, garden and workshops for the plying of the various crafts, is found within the monastery walls.'[46] Brothers were reminded that 'idleness is an enemy of the soul'. The Carthusians, founded as a solitary order, gave each monk a cell, a workspace and a private garden. Vegetables were grown for the table, herbs for the hospital. Flowers were cherished like religious icons. Cultivation of choice fruits was a favoured pastime. The day was divided into 'hours' for prayer, reading, work, eating, meditation and sleep. Books of Hours, like *Les Très Riches Heures du Duc de Berry*, illustrated the tasks.

5.38 Many cloister garths, like this example at Salisbury Cathedral, have been planted as gardens.

5.39 San Giovanni, in Rome, has a beautifully calm cloister marred by thoughtless planting.

5.40 The cloister from St Michel de Cuxa, in France, has been moved to New York and has what its creators described in 1927 as a living millefleurs tapestry.

5.41 'Though the stem of the Chervil be straggly and weak ... it ... freely bestows of its comfort and cheer on the poor.'

Cloisters were intrinsic to monasticism. The word 'cloister' means 'enclosed' and describes that part of a monastery from which the public is excluded. In communal orders, the cloistered area had a colonnaded court which became known as *the* cloister. Its form derived from Roman peristyle courts which, as noted in Chapter 4, frequently contained shrines. The cloister lawn was known as a 'garth'. Later authors wrote of cloister 'gardens'. 'Garden' is cognate with 'garth', but now implies the presence of ornamental plants, which, unless in the grass, were rare in medieval cloisters. The garth often had a roofed fountain to supply water for washing, either in the centre or at the edge. Arcades were busy places, used as covered paths, for reading, for teaching, for exercise in bad weather and for work. Adjoining the arcade were rooms in which to eat, cook, sleep, read and store provisions. Umberto Eco explained the importance of a garth: 'The green turf which is in the middle of the material cloister refreshes encloistered eyes and their desire to study returns.'[47]

John Harvey found no evidence for cloisters having been planted, but, since there is no evidence for their having being mown, their character may have been what is now called a wild-flower meadow (Figure 5.40).[48]

Some monasteries, especially in England, were also cathedrals (i.e. they had a church with a bishop's throne) and many cathedrals had cloisters even if there was no resident community. Alec Clifton-Taylor offers a reason:

> *For monastic cathedrals [cloisters] were indispensable, and they were felt to be such an agreeable accessory that several of the non-monastic cathedrals added them, for the sheer pleasure they provide: and what better reason can be imagined?*[49]

The earliest document to mention the building of a European cloister is the Life of St Philibert, Abbot of Jumièges (*c.*655). He studied the design of 'all monasteries in the bosom of France and Italy' but does not name their designers. Works of art were unattributed for the reason given in Chapter 57 of St Benedict's Rule:

> *If any (craftsman) be puffed up by his skill in his craft, and think the monastery indebted to him for it, such a one shall be shifted from his handicraft, and not attempt it again till such time as, having learnt a low opinion of himself, the abbot shall bid him resume.*

St Philibert's biographer therefore wrote:

> *Divine Providence built battlemented ramparts rising up in a massive square ... The cell of God's Saint himself looks out from the south, adorned with an edging of stone. Arcades accompany the laboriously stone-built cloister; the soul is delighted by varied decoration and girt about with bubbling waters.*

This is in line with St Augustine's beliefs: the monastery was viewed as a creation of Divine Providence, working through the hand of St Philibert and using the square as a symbol of God's perfection. Mention of the cloister being 'girt about with bubbling waters' is of great interest: 'bubbling' implies moving water and 'girt about' suggests a

5.42 a, b The Templars' monastery (founded 1172, Coulommiers, France) has a re-created medieval cellarer's garden, probably in its original location. Wattle fencing protected the crops from animals.

greater extent of water than in a fountain basin, either in channels of the type used in West Asian paradise gardens or outside the garth.

The oldest cloister plan was drawn some 175 years later, by Abbot Haito of Reichenau for Abbot Gozbert of St Gall. Haito had been to Constantinople and had supervised the design of a church. He asked Gozbert to dwell upon the plan 'in spirit', reminding him that 'we drew it through the love of God out of fraternal affection, for you to study only'. It was thus presented as an Augustinian (Platonic) Form – not a plan for a real place – and it was mathematically composed. Medieval schoolmen liked Plato's argument that reason implies the existence of a perfect world. Columns, arcades and buttresses are planned according to the proportion of the Golden Section.[50] The cloister has a quadripartite plan with crossing paths, the oldest representation of a four-square plan of the type discussed in the previous chapter. There are two semi-circular spaces labelled 'paradise', at the east and west ends of the church, confirming the influence of West Asia on the St Gall plan. The word 'paradise' 'entered Christian Church history as the name for the porticoes adjoining the oldest Byzantine basilicas, planted as gardens'.[51] In Europe, the quadripartite plan symbolised both the four points of the Holy Cross and the Four Rivers of Eden. The cloister garth is marked with the words *semitae* (footpaths) and *savina* (juniper) in the centre. Juniper, which symbolised the Tree of Life and therefore paradise,[52] had a liturgical role: its branches were used to sprinkle holy water. The only other monastery plan to have survived, for Christ Church, Canterbury, was drawn in 1160 and,

5.43 a, b An obedientary garden at Klosterneuberg in Austria, for office holders.

like the St Gall plan, shows domestic accommodation and a church adjoining the cloister, together with a fountain, a fishpond, a cemetery, a herbarium, an orchard and a vineyard.

One of Haito's pupils, Walafrid Strabo, reveals an expert knowledge of plants in the poem from which the quotation at the start of this section is taken. *Hortulus* ('The Little Garden') was 'a bestseller throughout the Middle Ages'.[53]

Of heroical deeds, do not scorn my desire,
But this my poor vegetable epic inspire!
Though the stem of the Chervil be straggly and weak,
And its seed mean and paltry, not easy to seek
In the thick of the leaves, it is green all the year
And freely bestows of its comfort and cheer
On the poor.

Landsberg distinguishes the following monastic horticultural types:[54]

- *Cemetery orchard*: the St Gall cemetery orchard would have contained tombs and fruit trees. It symbolised paradise.
- *Infirmary garden*: used to grow medicinal plants.
- *Green court*: an area of grass and trees, used for grazing horses and for other incidental functions.

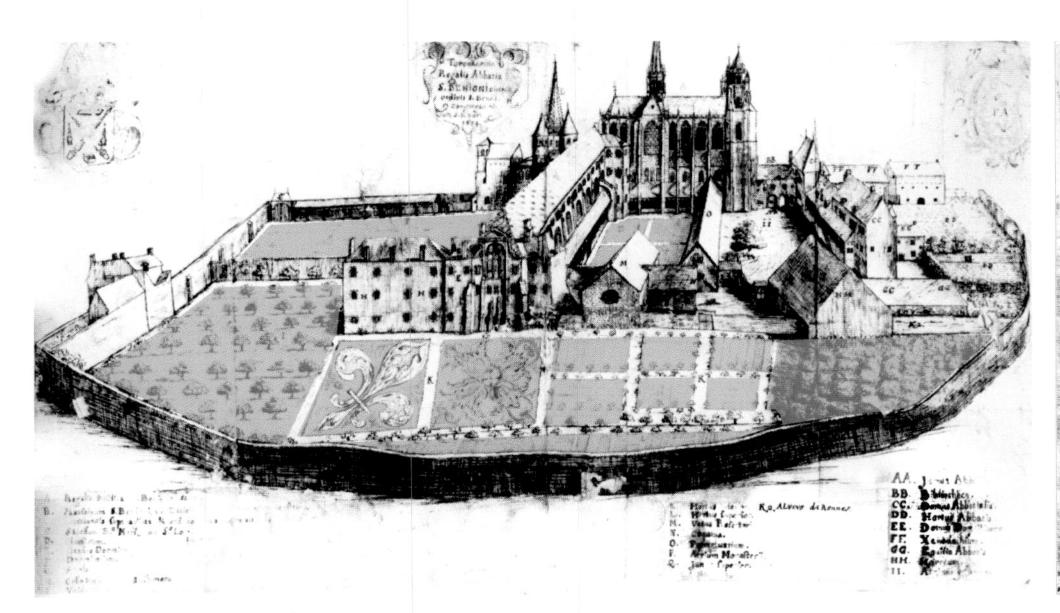

5.44 A seventeenth-century drawing of St Bénigne shows lily and rose decoration in the *hortus superior.*

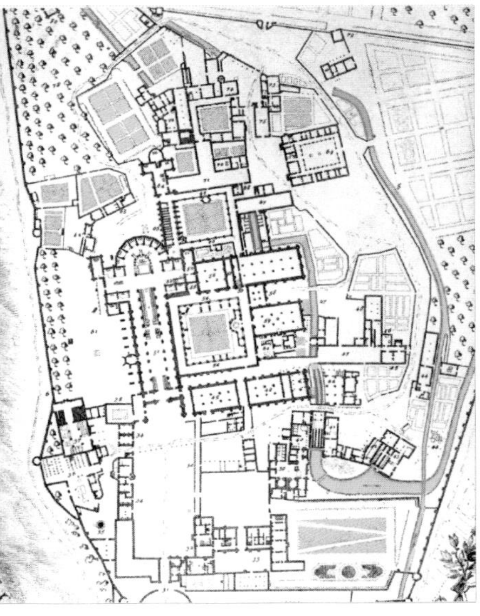

5.45 The 1708 drawing of Clairvaux shows a profusion of small rectangular gardens.

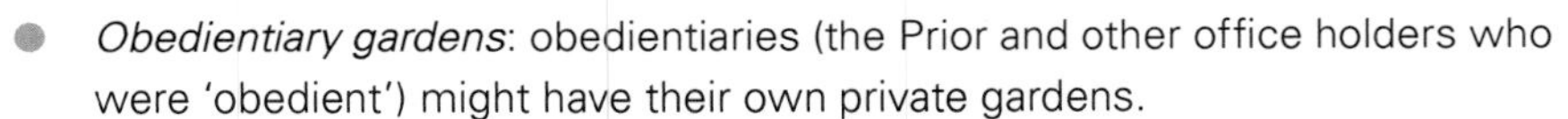

- *Obedientiary gardens*: obedientiaries (the Prior and other office holders who were 'obedient') might have their own private gardens.
- *Cellarer's garden*: for growing vegetables, culinary herbs and other utilitarian plants (e.g. Covent Garden in London, which later became a vegetable market).
- *Herber*: a small enclosed garden containing a lawn and herbaceous plants.
- *Vineyard*: the Domesday Book (1086) records 38 vineyards in England.
- *Kitchen garden*: used to grow both food and medicinal plants.

Monastic foundations became repositories of wealth. This was virtually unavoidable, since knowledge, education and skill made monks the best gardeners, the best farmers and the best industrialists of their age. Benefiting also from gifts and legacies, monasteries became opulent. Their churches came to rival cathedral churches and the old virtues of self-denial and manual work vanished. Architectural historians classify the style of the Early Middle Ages as Romanesque and that of the Late Middle Ages as Gothic, with sub-divisions to suit different countries.

Garden historians, having less evidence, can distinguish usefully only the symbolic purity of the Early Middle Ages and the comparative luxury of monastic gardens during the Renaissance. The employment of professional gardeners led to the replacement of herbers, orchards and cloister garths with elaborate parterres, clipped hedges and

5.46 Westminster Abbey. The Little Cloister was an infirmary garden before it became an ornamental space.

5.47 Monasteries and cloister garths became places of luxury. **a** Certosa di Pavia, Italy; **b** Jerõnimos Monastery, Belém, Portugal.

5.48 A modern interpretation of a paradise garden at Stift Melk (Melk Abbey) in Austria.

ornate fountains. At the abbey of St Bénigne, the rose and the lily were used as patterns for parterres. Envy replaced admiration. Tales of vice spread abroad, Charlemagne himself noting that monks are too often 'found to be sodomites'.[55] The scene was set for a tragedy. Braunfels describes: 'the great onslaught on the monasteries, prepared by the Enlightenment and released by the French Revolution' in which 'the idealism of the monks was impugned, their treasures were barbarously scattered and destroyed, their monasteries sold, their churches deconsecrated, and many of the finest of them torn down'.[56] It parallels the ruthless vigour with which St Martin and his contemporaries had destroyed the sacred trees, statues and sanctuaries of the detested pagans.

5.49 Medieval towns sometimes had space for gardens inside city walls and normally had space for gardens outside the walls. There are still gardens of this type outside the city walls of Constantinople though their presence is illegal. The city's name was changed to Istanbul in 1930.

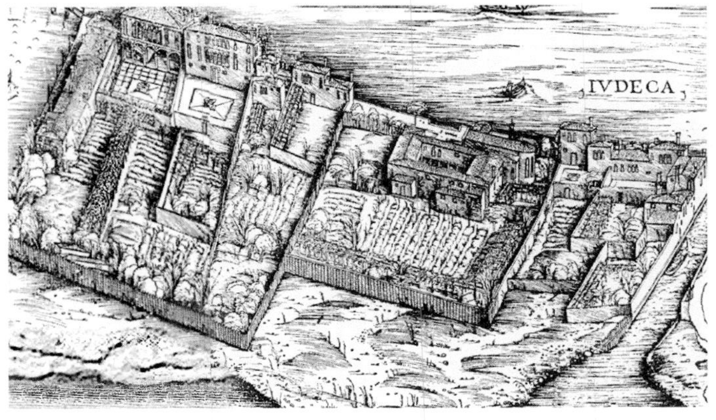

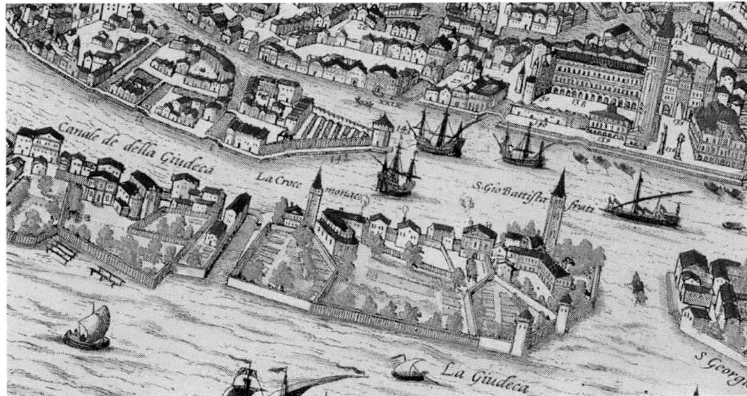

5.50 a, b These drawings (by Jacopo de' Barbari *c.*1500 and by Braun and Hogenberg *c.*1600) show the garden island of Guidecca, which is across the canal from St Mark's Square.

Town gardens

The only generalisation that can be made about medieval cities is that it is impossible to generalise about their form, since 'medieval towns and cities came in all shapes and sizes, adapting themselves freely to every geographical and economic circumstance'.[57]

Settlements were large and small, bonded and free, chartered and unchartered, walled and unwalled, on hilltops and in valleys. Some had space for gardens, others did not. The first topographical maps showing details of gardens were produced in Italy. Venice was drawn by Jacopo de' Barbari *c.*1500 and by Braun and Hogenberg *c.*1600. The details in Figure 5.50 show the garden island of Guidecca, across the canal from St Mark's Square. Barbari shows most of the land used for productive horticulture but there are ornamental courtyard gardens near the villas and tunnel arbours for grapes between the horticultural plots. Venice was one of the wealthiest and most powerful cities in Medieval Europe but lost its position after Constantinople fell to the Turks in 1453.

North Europe had many unwalled settlements belonging to feudal lords or monastic foundations. The tenant's oath of loyalty was a contract between free men. He then became a bondsman holding land in return for services owed to his lord – military, agricultural and domestic. Village houses were placed beside roads. Farmland was ploughed in long thin strips by ox-drawn ploughs. Smaller areas were cultivated by gardening techniques or un-wheeled ploughs. Plants were cultivated for their usefulness, although some were also valued for their beauty. Even the lily and rose had medicinal uses. Legal reports provide the information that house doors were frequently open so that 'while the baby of the family slept in its cradle by the open hearth, chickens, pigs and the family cat rooted in the straw'.[58]

Every feature of a medieval village was multi-functional. No plans survive but archaeology has yielded some information and will surely yield more. Laxton, the best example in England, was first mapped in 1635. Village gardens were enclosed by earth banks, hedges, ditches, walls and fences. The house and its surrounding land were known as a close, a toft, a croft or a messuage. Rectangular plant beds, of a size which could be reached from paths without trampling on plants, were used primarily for vegetables but also for growing some decorative herbs and flowers. The commonest vegetables were kale, leeks, parsley, parsnips, peas and beans, all of which could provide food in winter. Homes with only one room had another use for gardens. Mumford writes that late medieval astrological calendars 'show lovers having intercourse in the open ... erotic passion was more attractive in the garden and the wood, or under a hedge, despite stubble or insects, than it was in the house'.[59]

Towns were constituted on a different basis. Typically, house-owners were freemen: merchants, craftsmen and professionals who needed the protection of town walls because they had no lord. Burghers made features resembling those in castle gardens:

- *Covered walks*: pergolas were used to create shady walks. Vines and roses were the favoured plants.
- *Arbours*: semicircular arbours were used to shelter seating areas.
- *Seats*: these were often covered in turf, herbs, stone or timber, and usually lacked a back support.
- *Plant beds*: these might be raised or sunken.
- *Turf and flowery meads*: both pure grass and flowery lawns were valued.
- *Boundaries and fences*: hedges were used to keep out cattle and other animals. Walls and fences made from wattle and boards were also used.

5.51 a, b A modern re-creation of a medieval garden at Bois Richeux, France, has a vine arbour, raised beds and plants from the *Capitulare de Villis*.

- *Fountains*: many medieval illustrations show fountains, which are often set in pools.
- *Moats, rivers and pools*: used for fish and as boundaries.
- *Baths*: ladies would refresh themselves before a meal by washing their feet.
- *Fishponds*: known as 'stews', fishponds were popular and useful features of the medieval garden.
- *Dovecots*: ornamental, as well as an important source of food.

The walled towns of North Europe were often better suited to garden-making than those of South Europe, because they were not on dry rocky hills. However, not all Mediterranean settlements were densely-built hill-towns; some had space for both functional and ornamental gardens. Renaissance maps and drawings show these gardens to have been surprisingly similar to those of Northern Europe.

The Middle Ages did not, of course, come to a sudden end in 1500. Adoption of Renaissance urban patterns, if rapid in the great commercial cities, took centuries to reach the backward regions of backward countries. When armies, instead of fortifications, became the means of protecting towns, living in country villas became sufficiently safe to make the great villa gardens which will be discussed in Chapter 6.

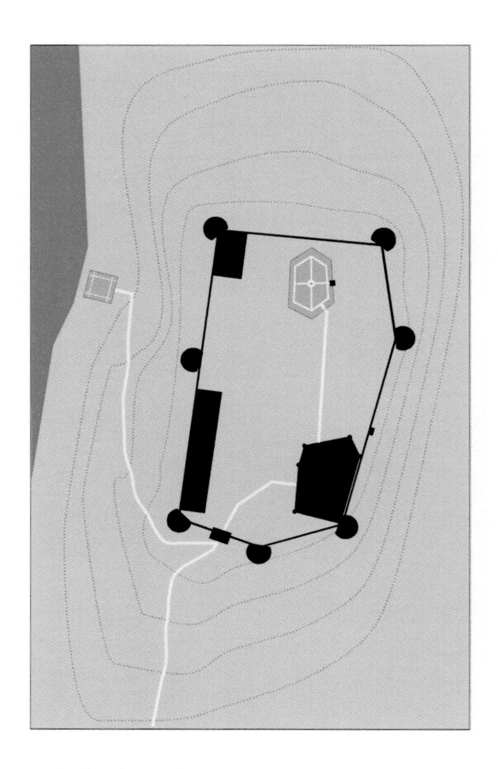

5.52 Castle garden.

Types and examples

Castle gardens

Use: Forts had been occupied only by soldiers. A castle was a place for a lord to live with his family, dependants and retainers. Castle gardens were sometimes within the fortifications and sometimes outside. In both cases they were primarily for the use of ladies, children, swains and troubadours. In times of siege, an army, or the whole population of the surrounding area, might occupy the space inside the outer fortifications and trample the garden to mud.

Form: A garden could be a small hexagonal, rectangular, or irregular enclosure, within or near the fortified area. No examples survive but a good idea of their appearance can be gained from the symbolic illustrations in medieval books, which show flowery lawns, trellis fencing, turf seats, tunnel-arbours and a profusion of sweet-scented flowers. Castles also had orchards, pleasure parks and hunting parks outside the fortified zone. There are many surviving castles where one can imagine castle gardens within the inner or outer bailey, and there are some sixteenth-century plans and records of castles with knot gardens.

Montargis, 1560

Louis XII of France (1462–1515) invaded Italy and arranged for his daughter, Renée, to marry Hercules d'Este of Ferrara. Following d'Este's death in 1560, Renée returned to

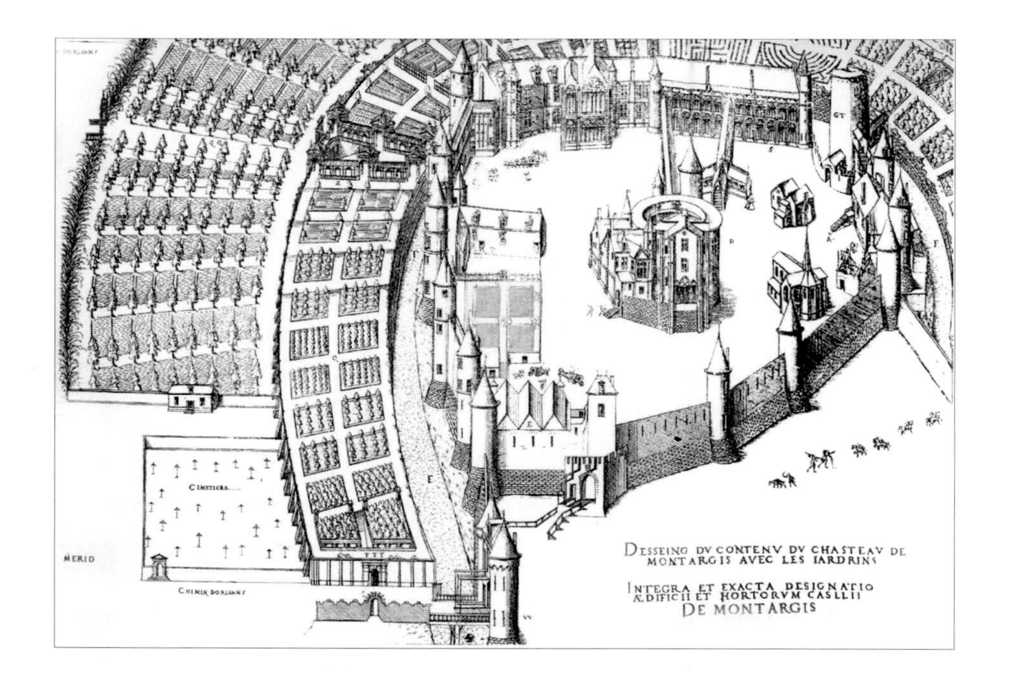

5.53 Montargis.

France and lived in the hilltop castle of Montargis. As a Protestant, she had been unhappy in Italy, but had come to love Italian gardens. The hilltop castle to which she returned had a donjon protected by a turreted outer wall. Du Cerceau was employed to rebuild the castle and lay out a garden on the slope beyond the walls. His drawing also shows a small herber in just the place where one would expect to find a medieval garden: within the fortifications. It may well have been a survival from the castle's medieval period. The old castle was demolished after the French Revolution but has been partly rebuilt.

> *Most gardens were divided into enclosed rectangular pleasaunces ... Almost the only exception is in the semicircular gardens of Montargis, planned by du Cerceau in a radiating scheme, with the castle as centre, and trellis arbours as rays.*
>
> (William H. Ward)[60]

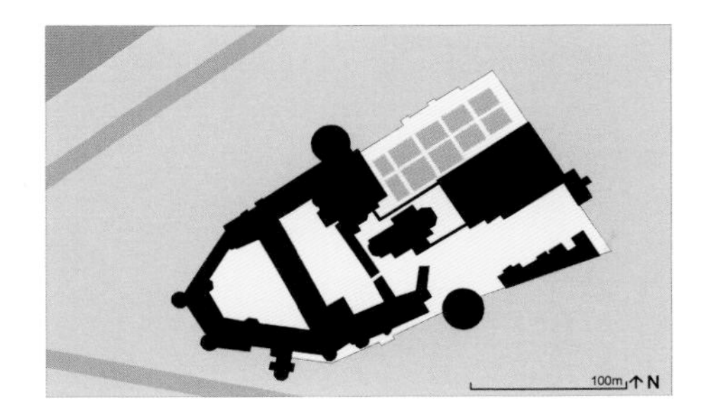

5.54 Amboise.

Amboise, 1576

The Early Renaissance castle garden as it exists today is similar to the garden shown in the Du Cerceau drawing of 1576. Before that, Amboise probably had a small enclosed herber containing a lawn and herbaceous plants. The castle is on a rocky plateau with spectacular views of the River Loire.

> *The platforms, the bastions, the terraces, the high-niched windows and balconies, the hanging gardens and dizzy crenellations, of this complicated structure, keep you in perpetual intercourse with an immense horizon.*
>
> (Henry James)[61]

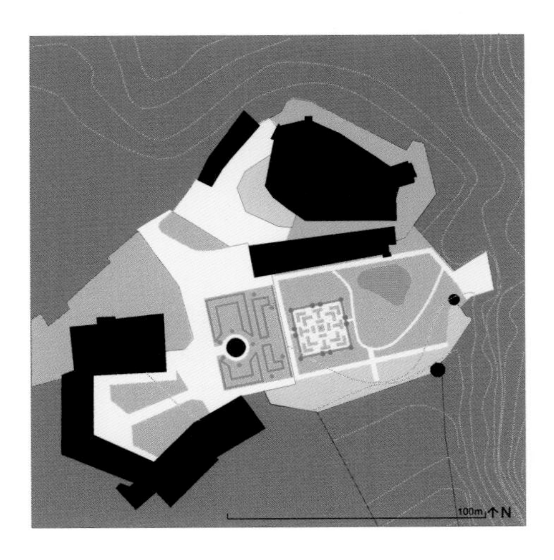

5.55 Ambras.

Ambras Schlosspark, 1570

Ambras was converted from a fortress to a palace when it was acquired by Archduke Ferdinand II in 1564. It now has re-created medieval and Renaissance gardens. The castle is now surrounded by a large landscape park in the English style, and woods hide the castle in a way which would not have been allowed when the defences were in good order. But when the castle is floodlit, and one looks across Innsbruck from the northern side of the valley, it is still possible to see how Ambras commanded the heights above Innsbruck.

> *The castle at Ambras was built on the hill, 'in magnificence excelling the finest villas of the ancients.' In the women's part the visitor first saw hanging gardens and wired aviaries, but it is not clear whether by this is meant real roof-gardens or high terraces, for the gardens proper are at the foot of the hill.*
>
> (Marie-Luise Gothein)[62]

5.56 Cloister garth.

Cloister gardens

Use: Cloister courtyards, used for walking, reading and working, were at the heart of monastic communities. They gave access to the adjacent buildings: the refectory, dormitory and cellar, where food was stored. Another door led to the church. The garth (lawn) was an aid to contemplation.

Form: The typical cloister is a square courtyard surrounded by a covered walk, similar in plan to the Greek and Roman peristyle courts from which they derive. Early cloisters may have contained herbs and shrubs but there are no medieval records of their having contained vegetation other than close-scythed grass. During the Renaissance, princes of the church became leaders in the art of garden design and many simple plats of grass were transformed into ornamental gardens. In the nineteenth century some became Gardenesque, with herbaceous plants and shrubs. Monastries also had flower, vegetable and orchard gardens, but no medieval examples of these survive.

St Gall, 820

The famous St Gall Plan was drawn by Abbot Haito of Reichenau (763–836), who resigned as abbot, at the age of 56, to live in simple conformity with St Benedict's Rule. A love of regularity pervades his plan: the cloister is exactly 100 feet square and the placing of elements is symmetrical (using a 40:40 module). The plan includes an infirmary garden, a cemetery garden and a gardener's house.

> *The most astonishing document of early medieval Benedictine monastic architecture is the plan of an ideal Carolingian monastery preserved in the library of St Gall. It represents the only architectural drawing antedating the thirteenth century in Europe to reveal the exercise of powers of planning.*
>
> (Wolfgang Braunfels)[63]

5.57 St Gall.

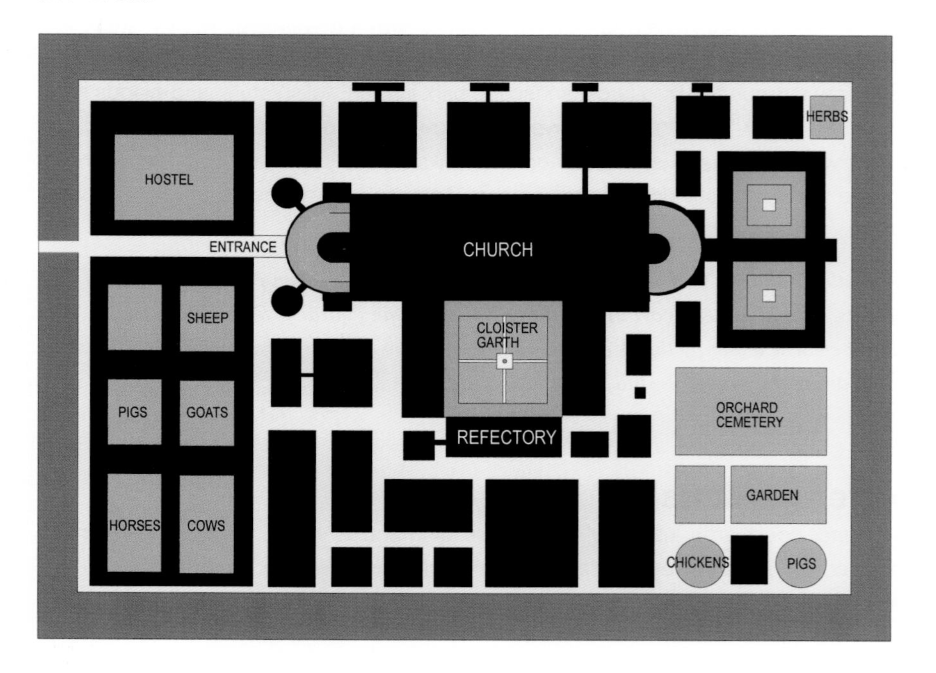

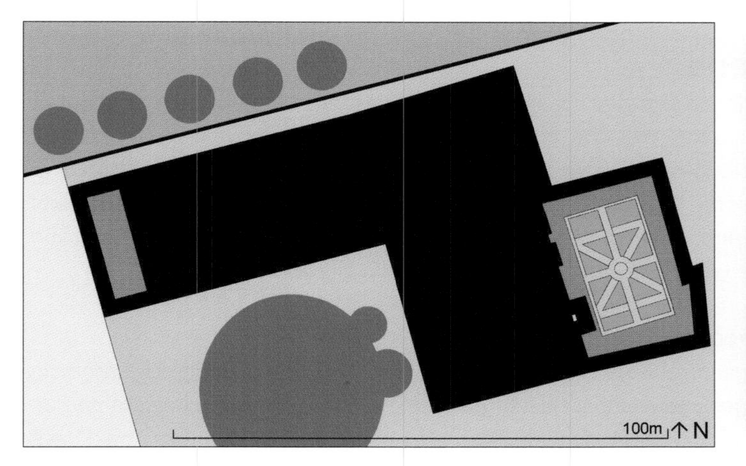

5.58 San Lorenzo fuori le Mura, Rome.

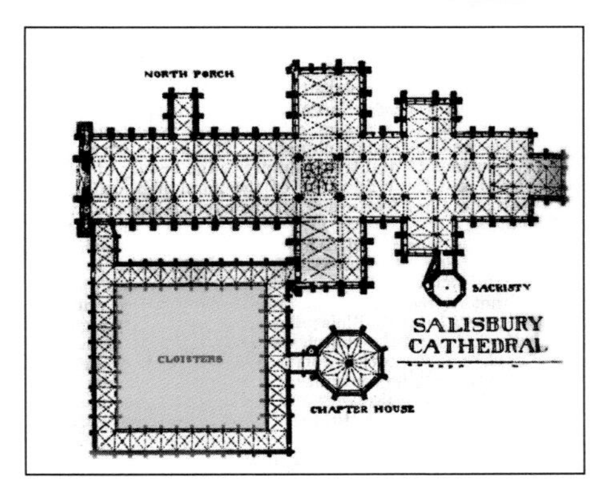

5.59 a, b Salisbury Cathedral, England.

San Lorenzo fuori le Mura, Rome, 1200

The north part of the church was built in the sixth century, above a catacomb that houses San Lorenzo's tomb. The south section of the church, on a different alignment, was built in the twelfth century. The two parts were joined in 1216. The 'simple, very austere'[64] cloister, of *c.*1190, has an unusually intimate scale. An illustration from 1924 shows it with a Renaissance pattern of gravel and low box hedging. The pattern has been retained and the cloister is now stocked with flowering herbaceous plants, creating a fresh and sweet atmosphere.

> *In the garden the peace of past centuries still fills its surrounding arcades while shafts of sunlight stream down between the classical and medieval columns, which are so appropriately mingled in this place where memories of pagan, early Christian and medieval Rome are fused together.*
>
> (Georgina Mason)[65]

Salisbury Cathedral, 1260

Salisbury Cathedral is a prime example of the Early English Gothic style, splendidly placed in an open landscape. It was built 1220–1258. The graceful, arcaded cloister contains what would have been a plain square of grass in the Middle Ages but now has a great tree and is managed like a suburban garden. Clifton-Taylor admires the cedars but does not mention the scruffy foundation planting:

> *These are the largest and, with the exception of Gloucester, the finest cloisters in England, as well as being the earliest to survive in their present form. Four spacious walks, all with simple quadripartite vaults, open upon a garth in which today grow magnificent cedars.*
>
> (Alec Clifton-Taylor)[66]

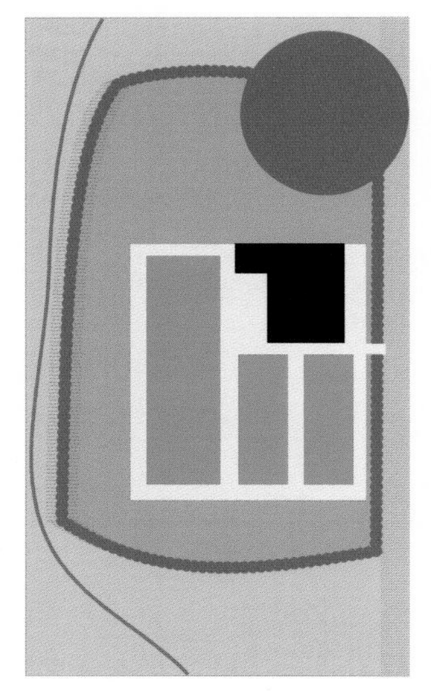

5.60 Medieval town garden.

Town gardens

Use: Lack of evidence besets the study of every aspect of medieval gardens but it seems fair to surmise that the gardens of wealthy burghers near town centres were used like castle gardens while the poor used what land they had for culinary and medicinal plants, some of them decorative. The gardens of the middle classes must have ranged between those of the rich and the poor, with much depending on the availability of space within the walls of a particular town at a particular time.

Form: Evidence from archaeology and from Renaissance maps of medieval towns shows that many gardens were irregular in shape, with boundaries made by buildings, walls, fences, hedges and ditches. Beaten-earth and gravel paths were used to demarcate planting beds. Such gardens are unlikely to have had lawns, as these would have wasted space, fostered weeds and required laborious care.

Bruges, 1500

Bruges became the largest trading city in North Europe. Its walls enclosed 3 ha in the ninth century, 86 ha in the eleventh century and 400 ha in the fourteenth century. Space

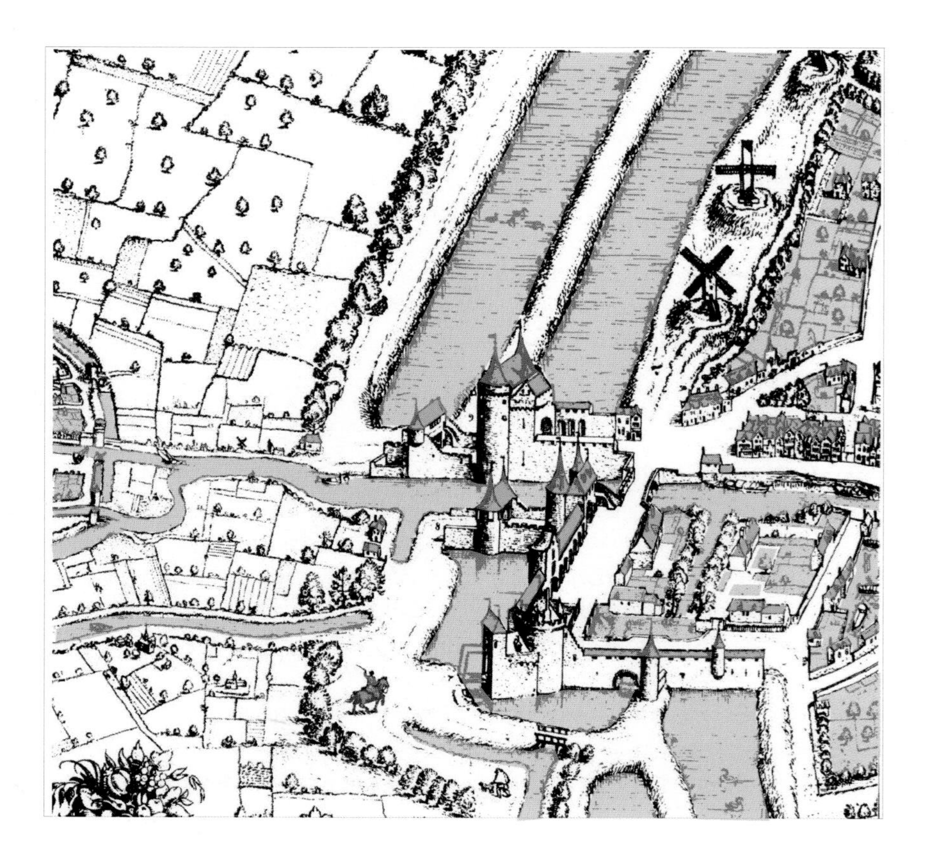

5.61 Town gardens inside the gates of Bruges (from the 1562 plan by Marcus Gerards).

was scarce before each expansion and relatively abundant afterwards. Wealthy burghers lived near the market square, in tall terraced houses with small courts and yards. Poorer folk, who lived near the town walls, had vineyards, small fields and what we would call market gardens. There was a vast uncovered area on the western fringe of Bruges, used for the traditional Friday market fair. It was partly planted with trees and flanked by a navigable canal.[67] Wealthy burghers also owned orchards and vineyards in the suburbs, as did their Ancient Greek predecessors.

5.62 Much of the fabric of medieval Bruges survives.

CHAPTER 6

Renaissance gardens, 1350–1650

6.0 Renaissance garden design began when princes felt secure enough to build villas outside the medieval walls of Florence and other cities.

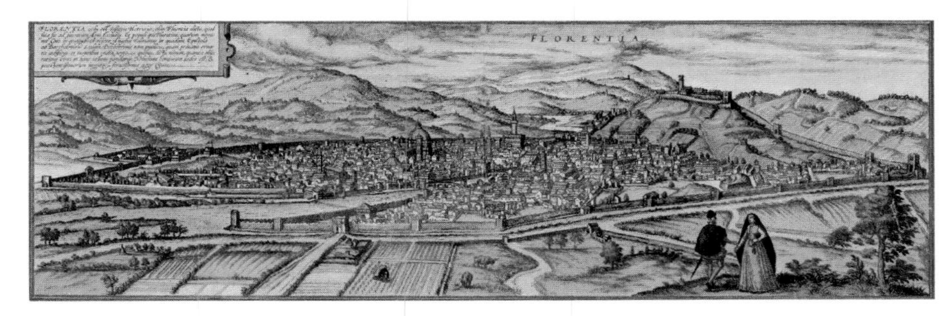

6.1 a, b Florence in 1600, with Fiesole on a prominent hill overlooking the city (Braun and Hogenberg). The photograph looks more westerly than the drawing.

History and philosophy

The physical landscape of Italy in the fourteenth century, as today, had rugged mountains, deep forests, intensively cultivated farmland and dramatic building sites. But the political landscape was different. There was no national government and scarcely a national language. Settlements, subject to attack from neighbours and foreigners, had to be defended. Great cities, like Rome, Naples, Venice, Milan and Florence could hold their own against each another but fell to invading armies like flies to a frost. Wealthy nobles therefore lived behind high walls. Some built castles on isolated peaks; others integrated their defences with the towns they ruled. Rather than live in unprotected farmsteads, farmers made daily journeys to cultivate their fields. Dense towns were often built on hilltops where space was limited and water scarce. Such conditions were not conducive to garden-making.

Italy's most celebrated nineteenth-century author, Alessandro Manzoni, paints a vivid picture of late-medieval life in his historical novel *The Betrothed*.[1] It is a tale of two young lovers from a small town. A robber baron from in a local castle plans to abduct the girl, with romancing the rose far from his thoughts. He bullies a local priest to delay the girl's wedding, leading her mother to put the girl in a convent for safety. Her swain sets off to beg help from a trusted cleric but was caught first in a riot and then in a plague outbreak. The book has a happy ending but these social conditions, like the settlement patterns, were unsuited to garden-making. Dreams of an earthly paradise were, however, stirring anew.

6.2 Boccaccio's *Decameron* tells of a party of young men and women playing in a garden.

Boccaccio's *Decameron*, completed in 1353, tells of a party of young men and women sojourning in the countryside while their city endured an outbreak of the plague. The youths tell saucy tales and relish the health-giving air of a delightful garden on a forested hill outside Florence. I did not read the garden descriptions when passed a grubby copy of *The Decameron* at school, but now appreciate their value as accounts of Early Renaissance gardens:

> *In the midst of the garden was a plot of very fine grass, so green that it seemed well nigh black. It was embellished with perhaps a thousand kinds of flowers and enclosed with the greenest and lustiest of orange and lemon trees. The trees bore at once old fruits and new flowers. They not only afforded the eyes a pleasant shade, but were no less pleasingly scented. In the midst of the grass was a fountain of the whitest marble, enchased with wonder-goodly sculptures. A great jet of water spring from a statue, that stood on a column in its midst. The water which overflowed the full basin issued forth from the lawn by a hidden pipe. It came to light encompassed by very goodly and curiously made channels. But before reaching the plain it turned two mills with exceeding power, to the no small advantage of the lord. The sight of this garden, its fair order, the plants and the fountain and the rivulets, pleased the ladies and the three young men. They all of one accord said that if a Paradise might be created upon earth, they could not conceive any form, other than that of this garden, which it might have. Nor what further beauty might possibly be added.*[2]

The young men and women of *The Decameron* had left castle life behind them. Their joy, freedom and optimism infused the *quattrocento*; Boccaccio and other scholars knew that their country had been home to a great civilisation which had declined and fallen into a Dark Age; they dreamed that the darkness would lighten and that the civilised glories of ancient Rome would be recovered. Signs of progress were abundant: trade was reviving and new ideas were flowing into Italy from every direction. Merchant sailors told of Spain's Islamic gardens. Christian scholars, fleeing Constantinople as the Turkish conquerors drew nigh, carried knowledge of ancient and Classical civilisations. In Italy, they found a culture already interested in its origins. Renaissance leaders shifted the focus of their curiosity from Ancient Rome to Ancient Greece and then to the Bible lands. They were fascinated by the culture of Constantinople – Roman, but Greek-speaking. A rebirth of Classical learning contributed to a new interest in gardens, now viewed as places of luxury and integrated works of art.

One family, the Medici, and one city, Florence, can be used to illustrate the times. The Medici became successful bankers, and established a gold currency, but they were of peasant stock from a village north of the city. Giovanni (1360–1429) was famed for his simple tastes and immense wealth. His son, Cosimo the Elder (1389–1464), died at Careggi, the richest man of his age. Money brought political power to the family and in 1469 Lorenzo, aged 20, became head of the family. His patronage of the arts made him Lorenzo the Magnificent. Later members of the family included grand dukes, popes and a queen. When the 'Last of the royal Medici line', as inscribed on her tomb, died in 1743, the family pursuits had continued through four centuries: scholarship, the arts, architec-

6.3 a, b Cosimo di Medici's loggia looked over his garden, at Careggi, and the Florentine landscape, presumably without trees obscuring the view.

ture and garden design. It has been suggested that the Medici love of gardens derived from a never-forgotten rural background.

The Medici family villas on the wooded hills around Florence (see p. 18) were enjoyed something in the manner of family-owned country retreats in the modern world, say, the Kennedy Compound at Hyannis. A young man might go there with a group of friends, or a young lady, for healthy exercise. Fashionable society might call to admire the family art collection and the garden statues. An ageing aunt might spend time in the country to recoup her health. The association of Renaissance gardens with art, scholarship, health and nature was a key factor in their development.[3] Medieval gardens had been ladies' work and monks' work, with individual plants cherished for their medicinal and symbolic qualities. Renaissance gardens became works of art, scholarship and male pride. This is possible only in civilised times, such as those enjoyed by Florentine society during the Medici ascendancy. Gardens integrated architecture, landscape and society.

Symbolically, the key event in the development of Renaissance gardens took place on a summer's day in 1439, in a hilltop garden at Careggi, 5 km from the centre of Florence. Cosimo de Medici assembled a group of scholars. Conferring on the art and philosophy of the ancient world, they re-forged the link between garden design, the humanities and architecture. Medieval philosophy had been dominated by religion, as had monastic gardens. Renaissance philosophy set reason on a course to recover its Classical position as the ultimate criterion of truth, instead of merely a support for dogma. Humanism, as an educational programme, affected every branch of art and knowledge:

> *It is credited with the concept of human personality, created by the emphasis on the uniqueness and worth of individuals. It is credited with the birth of history, as the study of the processes of change, and hence of the notion of progress; and it is connected with the stirrings of science.*[4]

6.4 Ovid's *Metamorphoses* tells of Acteon metamorphosing into a stag and being hunted by Diana. The sculpture is at Fontainebleau.

The honoured guest at Cosimo's garden party was Marsilio Ficino, founder of the new Platonic academy, translator of Plato and Plotinus, author of the *Theologica Platonica*. The grand master of Western philosophy, Plato, began to emerge from Aristotle's shadow. The Neoplatonic theory that 'art should imitate nature' (see p. 23) took on a new life, though it had not slept through the Middle Ages. Ficino believed the soul could engage in rational contemplation of the Platonic forms and that this was the condition in which artistic creation takes place. Experiencing beauty demands reflection as well as observation. Animals, for example, may observe more than humans but are unable to appreciate art because they cannot engage in rational contemplation of the forms. Artist-scholars therefore applied reason to the fine arts, resulting in a series of books: Leonardo wrote on painting, Alberti on architecture, Dürer on geometry, perspective and human proportions.

Mathematics was seen as fundamental to perception and representation. It was basic to the theory of linear perspective, as discovered during the Renaissance and used to unify both paintings and construction projects. Nature was conceived to be mathematically ordered, as though God had himself been a mathematician. Vitruvius, rediscovered in 1415, was studied for his remarks on the mathematics of proportion. A translation of Euclid from Arabic to Latin, in 1482, gave designers a geometrical understanding of the Golden Section.[5] Circles, squares, proportions and mathematical patterns were used in design. Perspective was used to integrate buildings with gardens.

The essential nature of the world was also interpreted culturally. Homer and Ovid, neglected by medieval thinkers on account of their paganism, re-entered the curriculum.

Greek myths became a source of inspiration for painting and garden sculpture. The story of Diana and Actaeon from Book III of Ovid's *Metamorphoses* provides an example.[6] The writing is graphic, the scene delightful, and the incident thought-provoking: should girls be pleased that men are attracted to their nudity, or should they be affronted by the threat to their virginity? Actaeon's metamorphosis from a man into a stag, exemplifies truths about nature and gardens: seeds become flowers; flowers decay; boys become men; men decay; mould becomes soil; life is renewed. Ovid's *Metamorphoses* regained the position it holds to this day as one of the most popular works by any Latin author.

Alberti applied these ideas to the design of villas. His *Ten Books on Architecture*, written in 1452 and published in 1485, had a profound influence on both architecture and gardens.[7] Though modelled on Vitruvius, 'Alberti's ultimate model is neither contemporary nor ancient architecture, but nature itself.'[8] The art of villa design, lost after the death of Charlemagne, was rediscovered. Pliny's famous letter on his Laurentine Villa (No. XXIII, see pp. 131–2) praised 'the beauty of the villa, the advantages of its situation, and the extensive view of the sea-coast'. Italy was rich in such sites and, it now being safe to build outside town walls, Alberti recommended sites that 'overlook the city, the owner's land, the sea or a great plain and familiar hills and mountains', adding that 'in the foreground there should be a delicacy of gardens'. Alberti also wrote about Ovid and about the desirability of building urban squares.

It was thus that garden design rejoined the fine arts. Dwellings were located in estates, as they had been in the suburbs outside Rome. Hunting parks were formed. Pagan statues were put back on their pedestals. Roman gardens were excavated, surveyed and pillaged. Plant collections linked artistic, scientific and religious interests. The use of terraces and topiary, which Pliny loved, was re-explored. The study of Euclid fostered an enthusiasm for geometry and the first accurate drawings of European towns and gardens date from this period.

Antique, architectural and botanical interests were brought together in a brilliant illustrated book, *The Dream of Polyphilus*.[9] Believed to have been written by Francesco Colonna, a Dominican monk, it is un-monkish in its association of passionate love with gardens and pagan imagery. *The Dream of Polyphilus* contains the oldest drawings of knot gardens, and, two centuries later, it influenced the making of sacred groves in England; William Kent is known to have owned several copies.[10]

Joscelyn Godwin has made a significant contribution to garden history by translating Colonna's *Dream* into English[11] and surveying its influence on Renaissance, Baroque and Romantic art and gardens. It was a dream 'that used the imagery of Greco-Roman paganism to enrich the surface of things, to nourish the imagination, and to convey an esoteric message'.[12] The Neoplatonic and Heremetic ideas underling the *Dream* linked Christianity to the philosophy and imagery of the ancient world. The text and woodcuts contain so many design ideas that Alberti has been claimed as the book's author.[13] Amongst

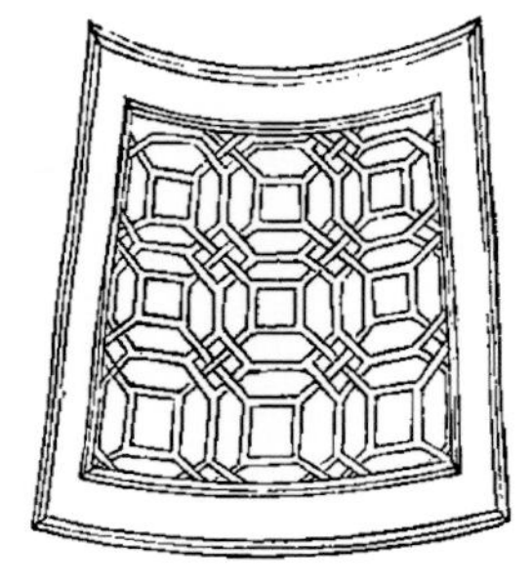

6.5 a, b, c Drawings from the *Hypnerotomachia Poliphili* (*The Dream of Polyphilus*) help bridge the visual gap between medieval and Renaissance gardens by providing some of the oldest illustrations of garden features, including knot gardens and vine arbours.

these designs are the oldest representations of Renaissance planting, described as 'little square gardens of marvellous work, showing arrangements of various edible plants' with comprehensive information on their design, construction and planting:

> *The first quadrangle was defined by the paths on either side, which caused it to be an irregular square. It had a four-sided lineament of knot-work three palms wide, made out of bunches of flowers ... The loops of the first band open out inside the second square to make a circle that filled it. ... in the middle of that circle was an eight-petalled rosette. In the centre of this was set a hollow round altar of yellow Numidian stone with three ox-skulls ... the first band was densely planted marjoram, the second with aurotano, the third with ground-pine, and the lozenge with mountain thyme.*[14]

This description is of the patterned garden shown in Figure 6.5 a. The 'bands' which make the pattern are made of 'simples' (herbs). A second patterned garden, Figure 6.5 b, shows 'a marvellous distribution of plants and a splendid knot-design picked out by the colours of various simples':

> *The lines of the pattern were made with bands of white marble fixed in the ground, four and a half inches wide on their surface and bordered on either side with simples. Within the boundaries of this stone enclosure there grew various little herbs, dense and level ... By Jupiter, it was a wonderful exhibition, giving great delight to the senses! ... Every free square was covered with flowering cyclamen, and their bands were of myrtle.*[15]

The typical use of flowers in Renaissance gardens in Italy was in patterned compartments:

> *These gardens with ornamental designs, planted with simples and flowers, were not identified by the term parterre, used in France from the mid-sixteenth century but not in Italy until long after.*[16]

These arrangements can be seen on Utens' paintings (see Figure 7.6 b, p. 227). Some compartments were enclosed by box hedges and used for geometrical patterns of flowers and herbs (simples) planted in geometrical beds separated by ribbons of gravel. Other compartments were used to make labyrinths, either with low herbaceous plants or tall trees and shrubs trained on trelliswork. The patterns were 'never of box as they were in later gardens'.[17] Clipped box patterns probably originated in France.

The origin of what came to be called 'knot gardens' in England remains a matter of conjecture. The idea of patterned planting in compartments surely came to England from Italy but the idea of making 'knot' patterns may have come from elsewhere. Gothein comments that:

> *We know how widespread the fashion for tree-clipping had become in the days of later Roman antiquity, but still the art had been so perfected (as we see it in the Quaracchi gardens) that it is impossible to think it is derived from faint indications in Pliny and other*

6.6 The Pazyryk Carpet (*c.*500 BCE) is the world's oldest carpet and has a design which could be related to garden design.

> *ancient writers; rather it must be due to long practice in the Middle Ages, and never since abandoned, although the threads are hard to follow.*[18]

Persian or Turkish carpets, made by knotting, are a possible source for the idea. None survive from the period but patterns made by knotting rope were used as a decorative motif in Sumerian, Persian, Roman and Islamic designs. The Pazyryk Carpet, dating from the fifth century BCE and thought to be Persian, has a floral grid as its central motif, with borders of antelopes and horsemen.[19] By the seventeenth century 'knot garden' had become a general term for square gardens with clipped box, sand, gravel, pebbles and flowers. They were made in enclosed castle gardens and expansive villa gardens with outward views. Artificial mounds (mounts) with spiral paths were made to allow views of garden compartments and of the surrounding scenery.

The physical divide between the inward-looking medieval enclosed garden and the outward-looking Albertian villa garden symbolises the social and intellectual chasm between the two eras. Instead of making sequestered gardens for their womenfolk,

6.7 The Medici villa at Fiesole looks outward with the Renaissance garden.

6.8 An Albertian view of Florence from La Petraia.

noblemen began making palace gardens in the manner of their Roman ancestors. Old castles, like Careggi itself, grew into proud villas. In the early years, gardens were sited in and near towns. Another Medici villa, on the edge of Fiesole, has outward-looking terraces that resemble castle ramparts. Later, it became safe to build villas in hilly locations, away from towns and the diseases associated with them, with fresh, cool and healthy air. Visitors to Florence can experience the change by journeying from the city centre, with its hard narrow streets, small courts and high façades, to a villa made by a later Medici prince, Cosimo I, at Castello. From the rear terrace one looks down to the Renaissance garden, still enclosed but with very open views, or up and over the palace roof, to Florence and its southern hills.

A typical Renaissance garden in the closing years of the fifteenth century had:

- clipped hedges;
- a rectangular shape;
- a geometrical relationship with the house to which it belonged.

As the Renaissance gathered momentum, other aspects of humanism influenced gardens:

- excavation of ancient Roman gardens;
- restoration of pagan stories and pagan images to their Classical place in the fine arts;
- a resurgent challenge from reason to faith as the ultimate criterion of truth.

The first phase of the Renaissance is closely associated with the arts and architecture of Florence. By 1500, Renaissance practice was spreading, at various speeds, to other arts, other parts of Italy and other countries. Dates and categorisations can only be arbitrary, but the following are typical:

- Early Renaissance (1300–1480);
- High Renaissance (1480–1520);
- Mannerism (1520–1580);
- Baroque (1580–1750).

As for Western civilisation as a whole, the period was formative. Shortly after 1500, Renaissance leadership passed from Florence to Rome and patronage from princes to popes.

Italy

On his deathbed in 1455, Pope Nicholas V urged his cardinals to re-establish Rome as the greatest city in the world. Remembering his predecessor's wish when he became Pope in 1503, Julius II commissioned Bramante to design a new Basilica of St Peter, Michelangelo to paint frescoes on the Sistine Chapel and Raphael to decorate his private apartments. To outshine Florence, Julius assembled the noblest display of antique sculpture since the Fall of Rome, one thousand years earlier. Though pagan, the statuary was

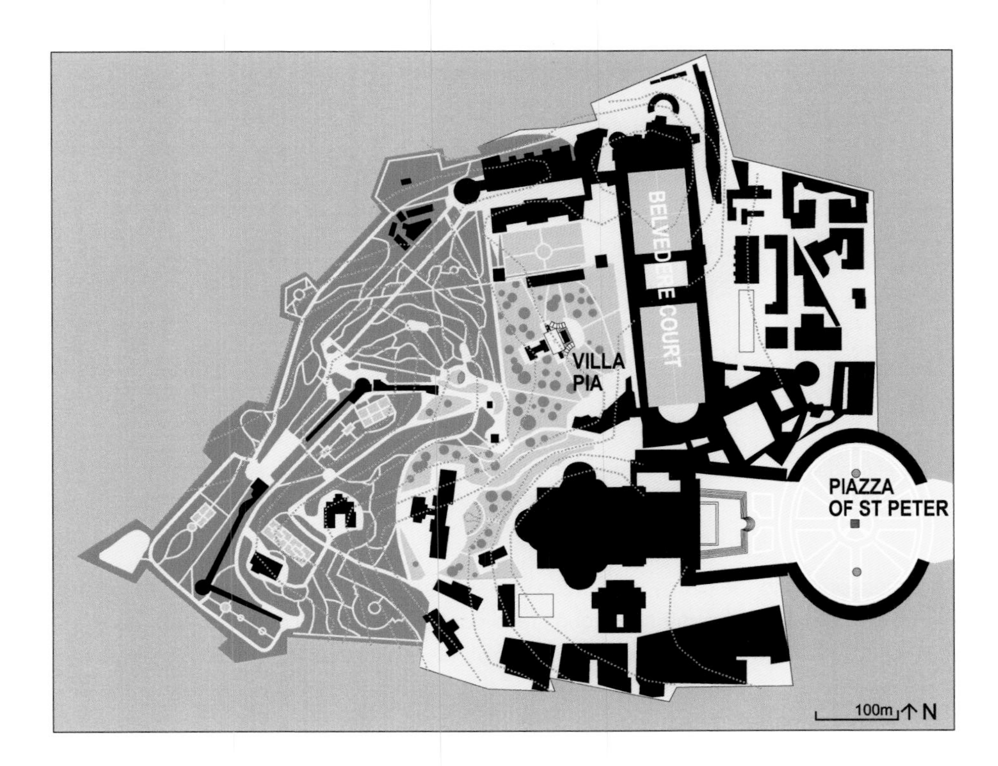

6.9 Plan of the Vatican, showing Bramante's Belvedere Court garden bisected by a subsequent structure.

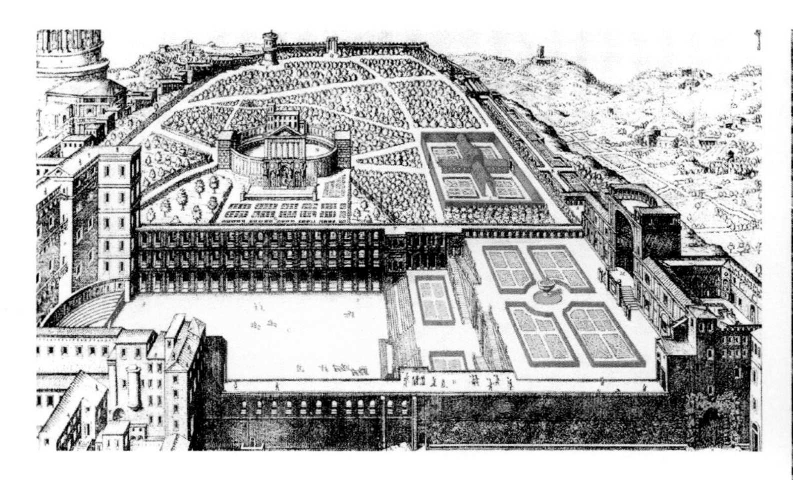

6.10 The Vatican's Belvedere Court in 1579 with steps on the land which is now a library and a ceremonial court on the lower level. A small enclosed Renaissance compartment can be seen beyond the Belvedere. The Villa Belvedere is in the bottom right corner of the drawing and the top left of Figure 6.11.

6.11 Bramante's Belvedere Court 'dictated the basis of European garden design' for 200 years, but fell to the austerity of the Counter-Reformation: it was bisected by a library. One part of the court survives; another is used as a car park. The Vatican should restore the Lower Court and encourage priests to ride bicycles, so that the car park becomes redundant.

6.12 The Villa Lante shows a perfect integration of architecture and landscape on a central axis.

6.13 The Medici villa at Castello is aligned with the garden, though the axis does not point to a significant feature of the building.

made acceptable to the clergy by treating Classical myths as moral allegories: Venus, for example, could stand for the sensuous life in contrast with the contemplative life.[20] As in St Augustine's time (see Chapter 4), Neoplatonism assisted the fusion of pagan and Christian ideas.[21] The sculpture displayed in the Vatican attracted visitors from all over Europe. To house it, Bramante designed the Belvedere Court (*c.*1505). The design for

6.14 The Villa Pia decorates and defines an outdoor space.

6.15 The Villa Madama has sculpture, niches and porticos on an architectural scale.

6.16 a, b Villa Medici in Rome used to be enclosed by walls but is now open to Rome (treating St Peter's almost as a garden ornament).

this space 'dictated the basis of European garden design for more than two centuries to come'.[22] Gombrich has suggested that Bramante conceived the court as a sacred grove inspired by the *Hypnerotomachia Poliphili*.[23] On a sloping site, the garden court joined the main Vatican Palace to the Villa Belvedere. The characteristics of Bramante's design were:

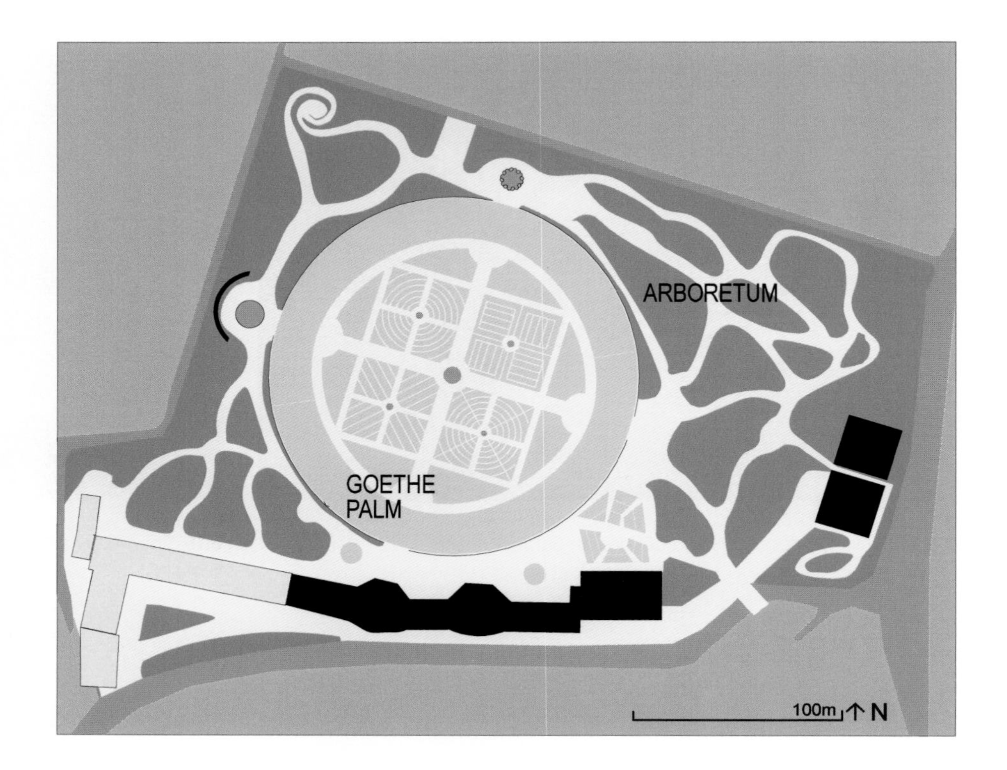

6.17 a, b Padua's Botanical Garden had scientific objectives and an intricate geometrical plan based on circles within squares within circles.

- a dominant central axis;
- full integration of garden and architecture;
- terraces linked by great flights of steps;
- a garden theatre;
- the use of Classical (pagan) statuary;
- niches for fountains (they had been central elements on medieval lawns).

Sadly, the progenitor of High Renaissance garden design fell victim to the Counter-Reformation. After Pius V ascended the papal throne, in 1565, a stern reforming spirit led the Church of Rome. Catholicism, challenged by Protestantism, became austere. The free spirit of the Roman republic, and Boccaccio, was cast into the shade. Theatrical displays in gardens were discontinued; pagan statues were banished once more; a theological library was built in the Belvedere Court, destroying Bramante's composition. Other Roman gardens inspired by Bramante were also destroyed. Fragments, such as the loggia of the Villa Madama, survive in Rome, but one must look further afield to see Bramante's principles preserved on any large scale.

Examples of integrated architecture and landscape can be seen at Villa Castello and Villa Lante (Figures 6.12 and 6.13). At the Villa Pia, in the Vatican Gardens (Figure 6.14), one cannot say whether the oval court was made as a setting for the building or the building as an ornament to the garden. At the Villa Lante (Figure 1.25, p. 17), instead of one large palace, two small palaces were built, which had the character of garden pavilions. At the Palazzo Farnese, a summer-garden was laid out on one flank of the pentagonal palace and a winter-garden on the other. From the summer-garden, a path leads to a *casino* (little house) in the woods, which is fully integrated with the surrounding landscape. Most Renaissance garden designers followed Bramante in their dramatic use of geometrically integrated terraces, steps, water, and sculpture. The study of perspective and optics nurtured the taste for vistas. Plant collections for scientific and medical purposes were geometrically planned, as in the Orto Botanico (Botanical Garden) in Padua.

Spain

Arab culture was a strong influence on Spain during the Middle Ages, allowing a fusion of Islamic and Christian ideas; Moorish features retained or adapted in post-Islamic Spain, were described as *mudejar*. Both cultures made enclosed rectangular gardens, but Renaissance fountains, parterres and other features were grafted onto Islamic gardens, as at the Alcazar in Seville. It had been a great Moorish garden, and in the sixteenth century Charles V added Renaissance ornament to the enclosing wall and made a labyrinth on the lower terrace. He also built a Renaissance villa on the Alhambra plateau (his troops having inspected the architecture and gardens of Rome as they sacked the city in 1527).

6.18 a, b The character of the gardens of the Alcazar in Seville is predominantly that of the Renaissance. The use of fruiting plants in gardens is both Moorish and Italian.

6.19 a, b The Escorial lies below the Guadarrama mountains like a galleon before a storm. The richness of the garden, controlled by geometry, contrasts with the rugged hills.

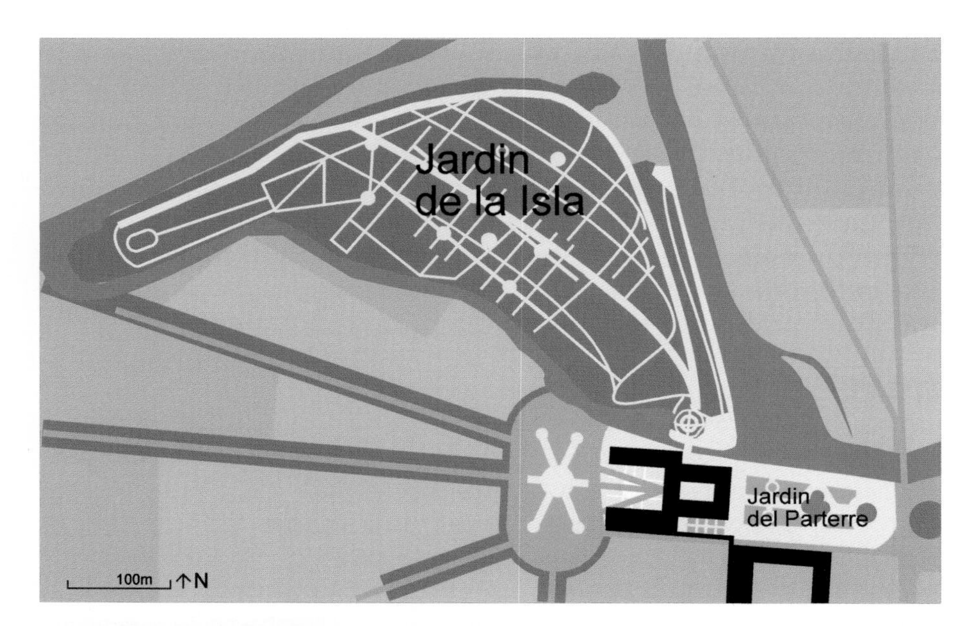

6.20 a, b, c The parterre garden at Aranjuez is separated from the palace by a river, more in the style of the Early Renaissance than the High Renaissance. The trees are a sensible response to the local climate.

Charles V's son, Philip II, implemented his father's will by building a great Renaissance palace and monastery: the Escorial. Its gardens, like its architecture and its owner, have been judged gloomily morbid at the bar of history, partly influenced by fact that Philip II launched the Spanish Inquisition, the Spanish Armada and other offensives. Yet he had a softer side and loved gardens. The garden he commissioned as a summer retreat, at Aranjuez, was almost cheerful, making good use of the River Tagus and the Ria Canal.

Having been reared in the Spanish Netherlands, his tastes were more Dutch than Italian. Philip's successors introduced Baroque avenues and fountains to Aranjuez.

Portugal

In Portugal, Italian ideas were adapted to suit the Moorish tradition of water tanks and brightly coloured tiles. Alfonso d'Albuquerque visited Italy as a young man and, remembering its charms, made the first Italian-influenced garden in Portugal, the Quinta da Bacalhoa. It has rectangular courts and a large water tank overlooked by three small

6.21 a, b, c Despite having been made in the 1660s, Palacio de Fronteira has a Renaissance layout, well adapted to Portugal by the inclusion of a tank garden with ceramic tiles. It is shown **a** before and **b** after repainting.

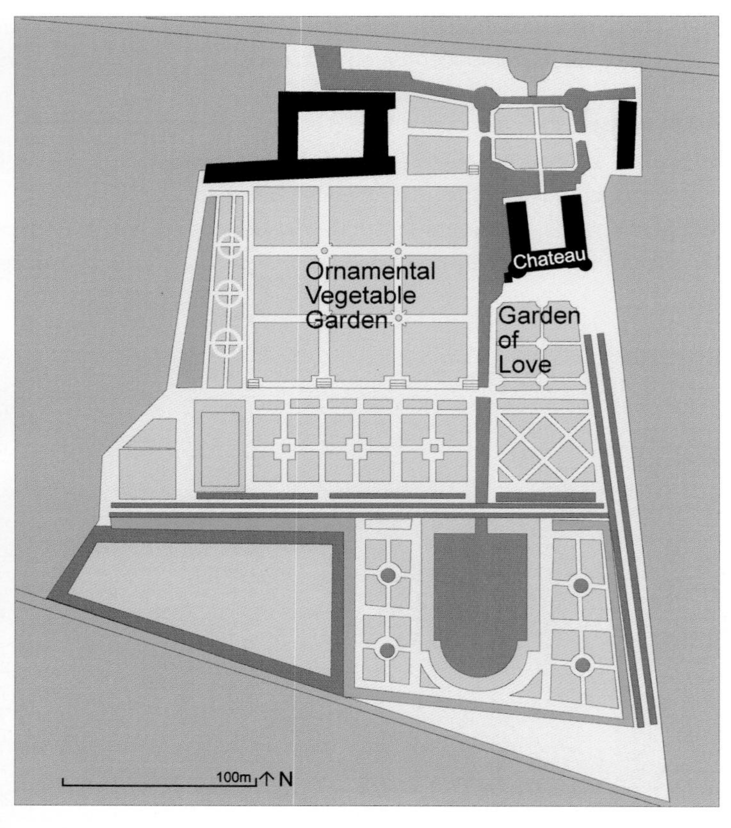

6.22 a, b, c The garden at Villandry is an extravagantly romantic re-creation of an Early Renaissance garden.

pavilions. The garden of the Palacio de Fronteira, made over a century later, is famed for a great rectangular water tank flanked by a pavilioned wall. The latter is decorated with beautiful panels of glazed tiles. They depict the medieval knights who fought for Christendom, though the use of tiles was inspired by Islamic gardens.

France

Charles VIII of France invaded Italy in 1494, claiming the Kingdom of Naples as his inheritance. While there, he and his generals saw the expansive glory of Italian Renaissance gardens and compared them with the cautious medieval gardens of France. Like other conquerors, Charles returned home with his head full of dreams and his wagons full of statues. It was by such means that the Renaissance style of garden design crossed the Alps. Charles took a garden designer and 21 other artists back to France. The

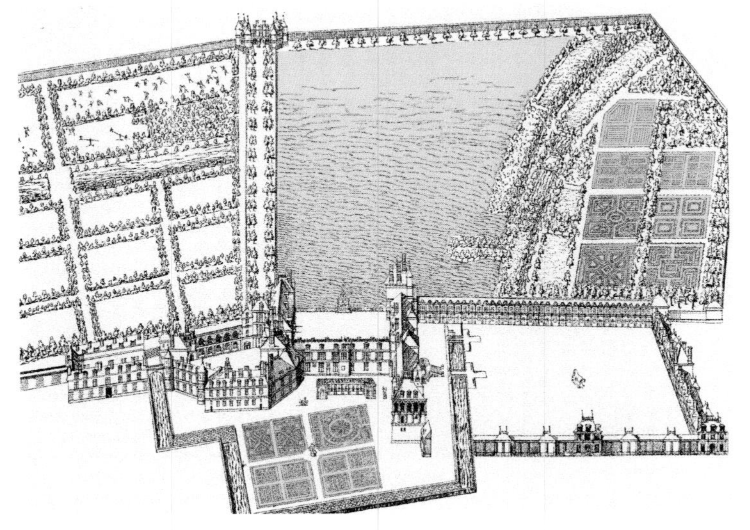

6.23 a, b Fontainebleau as a Renaissance garden (drawing by Du Cerceau *c.*1560) and as it is today (see Figure 7.7, p. 227 for Fontainebleau as a Baroque garden).

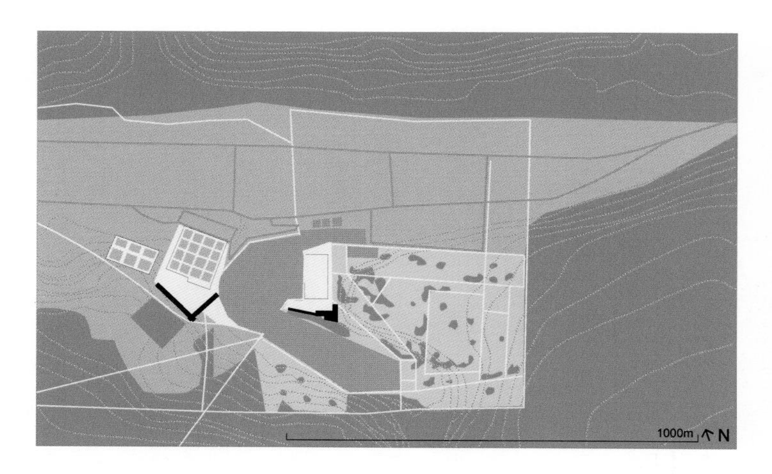

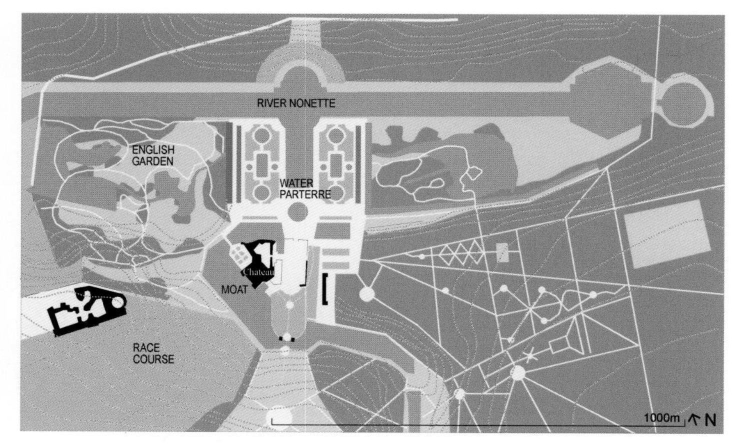

6.24 a, b The Renaissance garden at Chantilly (left) was later converted to the Baroque (right) as described in Chapter 7.

6.25 The medieval moat at Chantilly survives as the setting for a Baroque garden and château.

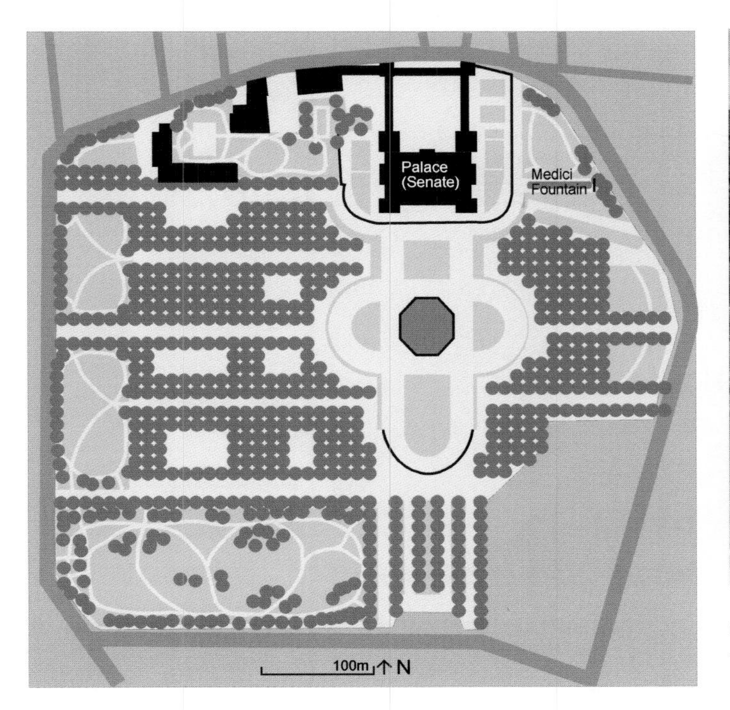

6.26 a, b The Luxembourg Gardens was one of the first gardens in North Europe to come fully under the influence of Renaissance ideas.

designer worked first at Amboise and then at Blois. Neither garden survives in its original form. They were castle gardens with high walls and geometrical compartment gardens. Neither survives in its original form but at Villandry, a garden with something of this character was made in the twentieth century, beside an old moated castle. The garden at Fontainebleau, commissioned by Francis I, had walled compartment gardens around the château. It was the greatest Renaissance garden north of the Alps.

Other castle grounds were adapted to suit Renaissance principles, creating a series of romantic water castles in the lowlands of Northern Europe. Old moats were used in garden designs. New moats were made as garden features. The château at Chantilly, though substantially rebuilt, remains surrounded by a moat. At Chenonceaux, the parterre garden is itself moated. Books with plans showing how to design parterres were published by Mollet and Boyceau.

A further step in the introduction of Renaissance ideas to France was taken by Marie de Medici, Queen of France, at the Luxembourg Gardens in Paris. A Medici by birth, she asked the architect Salomon de Brosse to reflect the spirit of the Boboli Gardens, which she had known as a child in Florence. Boyceau designed the parterre, which was aligned with the axis of the queen's palace. As at the Boboli, there are two axes at right angles. At one stage in his career, André le Nôtre, who became Europe's most famous garden designer, was the head gardener at the Luxembourg Gardens.

6.27 Vredeman showed how perspective could be used to compose gardens with architecture.

6.28 The Dutch Classical Garden was designed with circles and squares (Honselersdijk).

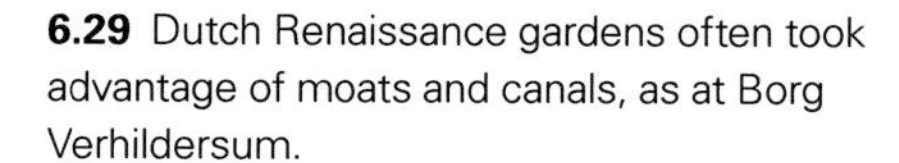

6.29 Dutch Renaissance gardens often took advantage of moats and canals, as at Borg Verhildersum.

Holland

Erasmus, a Renaissance scholar born in Rotterdam in 1466, gave a description of an ideal garden in *The Godly Feast* (1522).[24] It was influenced by his stay in Italy but retained a strongly Christian spirit, mentioning religious instead of pagan statuary. The garden was a medieval square, enclosed by galleries and trelliswork. Vredeman de Vries interpreted and illustrated gardens of this type in the first pattern book to treat garden design as a fine art. The *Hortorum viridariorumque elegantes et multiplicis formae* was published in 1583.[25] His last book, *On Perspective*, showed how lines of perspective could be used to compose architecture with gardens.[26]

After 1609, when Holland won its independence from Spain, a distinctively Dutch type of Classical garden emerged, based on Neoplatonic principles. Canals and trees defined a strict rectilinear framework. Within the enclosure were perfectly square and circular spaces bounded by clipped hedges, trees and trelliswork. The designers were interested in Renaissance botany, geometry and science. No examples survive but the growth-point of European garden design was shifting, with that of European trade and culture, from the Mediterranean to the North Sea and the Atlantic Ocean.

England

Compared with the countries discussed above, few records, and even fewer examples survive of the gardens made in England during the Renaissance. One civil war opened the period; another closed it and since then, Britain's zest for garden-making has laid change upon change. Yet England did have Renaissance gardens. At Hampton Court, Henry VIII sought to outshine Francis I's Fontainebleau estate. He made rectangular gardens and ornamented them with knots and heraldic beasts set high on coloured poles.

At Nonsuch, Henry made a palace intended – as the name implies – to exceed all others. It was loved by his daughter, Elizabeth I, but no trace of it now remains. Theobalds, another great palace, was made by William Cecil, Lord Burghley, who was Elizabeth's

6.30 A modern interpretation of Henry VIII's heraldic beasts in the reconstructed Renaissance garden of Penshurst Place in Kent.

6.31 a, b The drawing of Boscobel, done because Charles II hid here, was used to restore a modest, northern Renaissance garden.

first minister. Bounded by a canal, it had two large square gardens: a Privy Garden to the west and a Great Garden to the south. It too has gone.

When James VI of Scotland became James I of England, after the death of Elizabeth in 1603, there was more intercourse with continental Europe. Salomon de Caus, a French architect-engineer, was invited to work in England. His designs for Anne of Denmark, James I's queen, at Somerset House and Greenwich, were influenced by his travels in Italy: house and garden were aligned with one another, and fountains in Renaissance style were made. Advantage was taken of another continental skill, copperplate engraving, to illustrate de Caus' design for Wilton House. The garden has been changed, but the book survives as the fullest record of an Early Renaissance garden in England. It had *parterres de broderie*, and the statuary included copies of the Borghese *Gladiator* and other cultural icons of the Renaissance.

In 1642, a civil war ended the domestic peace which had prevailed since the Wars of the Roses. Boscobel House in Shropshire is the most interesting survival from the pre-1642 period. The design of the garden was unremarkable and the site would never have been remembered or maintained, but for a dramatic incident in 1644. Charles Stuart, the future Charles II of England, having been defeated by Cromwell, hid in a tree outside the enclosed garden at Boscobel. This incident led to full records being made of the garden, which made possible a reconstruction in the twentieth century. It is a modest, rural, North European interpretation of the Italian Renaissance style. The garden is enclosed by a fence, divided into compartments and aligned with the geometry of the house. An

6.32 The lawns at Ham House were formerly occupied by a Renaissance parterre.

6.33 Though the planting dates from *c*.1960, Edzell is a prime northern example of an enclosed castle garden in the Early Renaissance style.

artificial mount allowed the wide views, sun and air which Alberti considered essential in the making of good gardens.

Scotland

The influence of the Renaissance upon Scotland's gardens was somewhat delayed, but sharp and clear when it arrived. Scotland's climate is colder than Italy's, but its rugged terrain and unsettled social conditions had some similarities with the country in which the Renaissance was born. Two fascinating examples of Scottish Renaissance gardens survive from the seventeenth century: Edzell in Angus and Pitmedden in Aberdeenshire have rectangular enclosures protected by sandstone walls. They were replanted by Scotland's Department of Antiquities in the twentieth century, without as much archaeological investigation as would now be the norm.

Germany

After the Peace of Augsburg established a religious truce, in 1555, the German Lands were set fair to become Europe's leading region. Noblemen, artists, doctors and scientists travelled to Italy, spent time there, and returned home with a desire to make new gardens. German was spoken in much of Central and North Europe, though there was no unitary state with a royal court to promote the art of garden design, as in Spain, France and England.

Wealthy burghers made gardens within city walls. Often, they were sober versions of Italian Renaissance gardens, with particular collections of medicinal plants. The nobility

6.34 a, b, c Even in its ruined state, the Hortus Palatinus (Heidelberg) remains the foremost Renaissance garden in Germany.

made gardens beside their castles. Ferdinand I's wife made a Renaissance parterre at the medieval castle of Ambras in the Austrian Tyrol (see p. 177). Ferdinand's brother, Maximilian II, employed Italian craftsmen and designers to help make the Neugebaude palace and gardens in Vienna. An Italian gardener was employed to lay out the gardens of the Belvedere Palace outside Prague Castle (Figure 6.36).

Germany's greatest Renaissance garden was the Hortus Palatinus, 'the Garden of the Palatinate' in Heidelberg, taking its name from the Palatine Hill in Rome (see pp. 127–8). The garden was planned for the Protestant Frederick V, after his marriage to Elizabeth, daughter of James I of England. She invited her former tutor, Salomon de Caus, to design and supervise the work. It was a magnificent garden in a dramatic situation, rich in parterres, grottoes and waterworks. The designer has been criticised for not learning more from Alberti about the use of an axis and well-proportioned flights of steps to integrate garden enclosures, and it is true that the garden has an Early Renaissance plan, despite its large size and late date. Work on the garden stopped when Frederick V became a Protestant commander at the outbreak of the Thirty Years War, in 1618. The Hortus Palatinus was then trampled by the Four Horsemen of the Apocalypse: war, starvation, disease and death. Today, it is a romantic ruin and one of Germany's leading tourist attractions.

Czech Republic

Wallenstein, a Catholic commander during the Thirty Years War, began to make a garden in Prague in 1623. The Wallenstein Garden was dominated by a loggia, reminiscent of

6.35 a, b The Wallenstein Garden in Prague has medieval seclusion and a Renaissance layout.

6.36 Prague's Royal Garden and singing fountain were made outside the old fortress of Hradschin.

the Villa Madama in Rome, facing onto a parterre with a fountain. Much of the garden survives. Though clearly inspired by Italian villas, it lacks their informal charm – a consequence perhaps of its northerly location, or of its owners' military preoccupations. Wallenstein was defeated by Gustavus Adolphus and murdered by his own officers in 1634.

Mannerism

'Mannerist' began as a derogatory term for artists who, lacking personal greatness, could be derided for working 'in the manner' of greater masters. Medieval designers would have taken this as a compliment but the individualism of the Renaissance led men to think otherwise. 'Mannerist' is now used as a term of praise to describe art and design of the six decades between High Renaissance and Early Baroque, when artists, showing more personal vision, drifted away from the Classical ideals of stasis and perfection. The distinction between High Renaissance and Mannerism can be seen by comparing two paintings of the same subject. Leonardo's *Last Supper* (1495) is calm, symmetrical and balanced. Tintoretto's *Last Supper* (1592) bustles with energy and directional thrust. A comparison of the gardens of the Villa Medici at Fiesole (*c.*1458) and the Villa d'Este at Tivoli (*c.*1560) reveals a serenity in the former and an energetic bustle in the latter. The Flemish sculptor, Jean de Boulogne, known in Italy as Giambologna, was famous for his Mannerist statuary, including *The Rape of the Sabines*. There are examples of his work at Pratolino, the Boboli and other gardens. The most famous Mannerist architects were Palladio and Vignola. Palladio used the natural landscape as a setting for his villas. Vignola worked on the Palazzo Farnese at Caprarola and the Villa Lante at Bagnaia.

The Villa d'Este, made by Cardinal Ippolito d'Este, is one of the most popular gardens ever made. Controlled by powerful intersecting axes, the garden sparkles with drama.

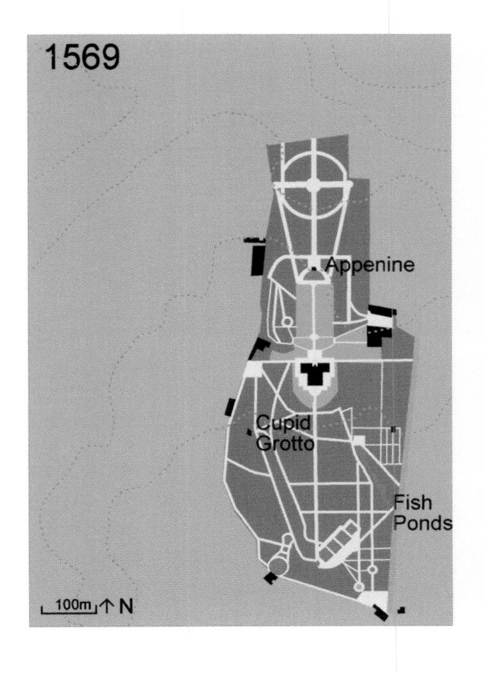

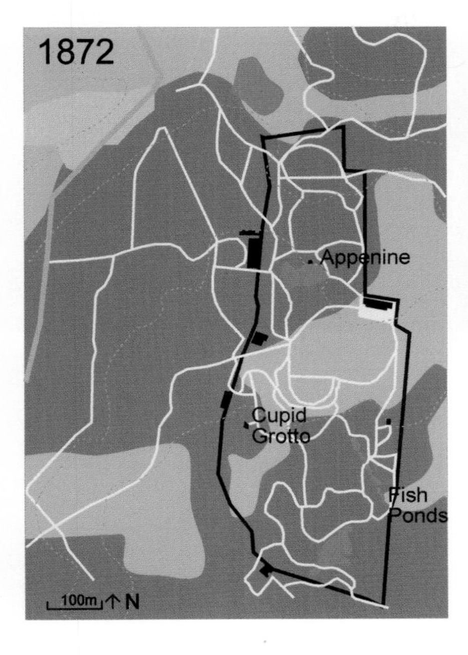

6.37 a, b Pratolino in 1569 and after conversion to the Picturesque style in the nineteenth century.

6.38 Giambologna's statue of Appenina, at Pratolino, is the most dramatic extant feature in what was once a great Mannerist garden.

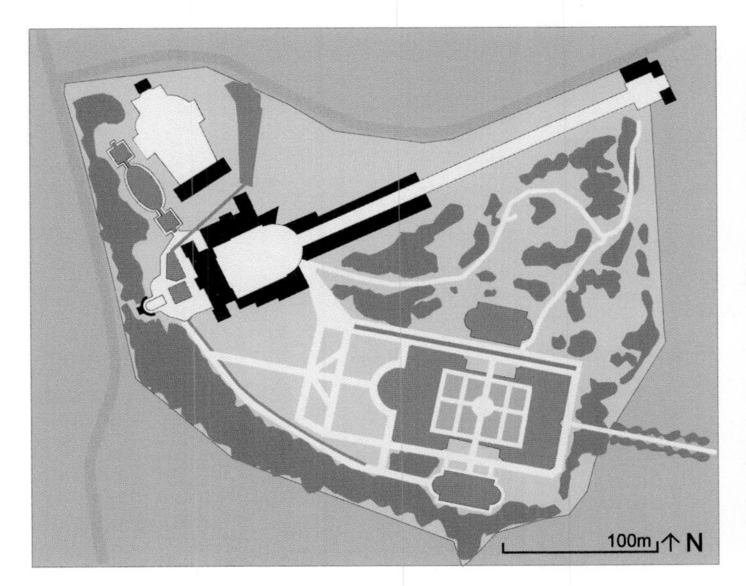

6.39 a, b At Hellbrun, the Mannerist parterre is surrounded by water and is not aligned with the house.

It has myriad fountains, a water theatre, statues and other icons, all telling the glorious history of the Este family and its Herculean ancestry. The transition between Renaissance and Baroque gardens is evident in the plan: the avenues, though still confined within the garden enclosure, are gaining strength and pushing against the boundaries. Subsidiary avenues throb for release. Yet the garden remains a mannered and

6.40 a, b, c Gamberaia brings the surrounding landscape into composition with the garden.

6.41 Caprarola has a Mannerist pleasure garden in the woods behind its fortified palace.

6.42 a–d The Villa d'Este has a long axis, a cross-axis and Mannerist waterworks. It is one of the most popular gardens ever made.

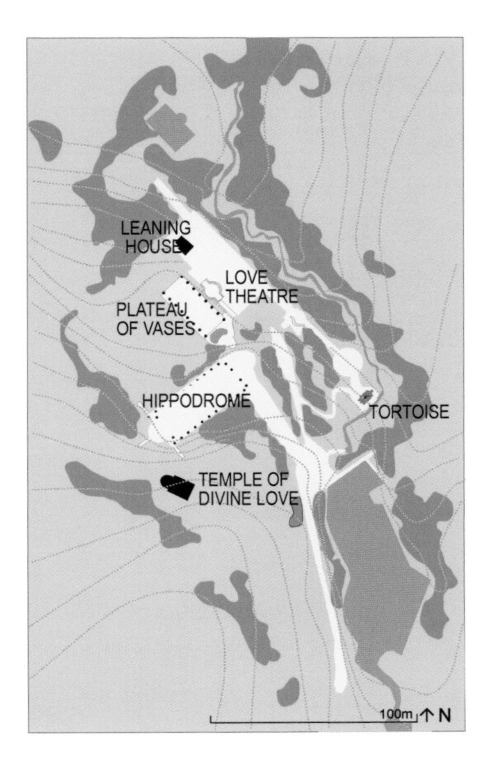

6.43 a–d The Sacro Bosco ('Sacred Wood'), at the Villa Orsini outside Bomarzo, is a mannered departure from ideal perfection.

light-hearted place, always bubbling, like the Villa Lante, with entertainment, novelty and invention.

The Sacro Bosco at Bomarzo (1552) was started just after the Villa d'Este. Its owner and designer, Duke Vincino Orsini, shared an interest in Ovid, Ariosto and Classical mythology with Ippolito d'Este but made an utterly different garden. The first explanation

6.44 a, b Hellbrunn has the best surviving hydraulic marvels anywhere and is the finest example of a Mannerist garden north of the Alps.

of Bomarzo's unique character comes from its name: Sacro Bosco. 'Sacred wood' is a literal translation but 'sacred grove' conveys the meaning with greater precision in English. The idea of the sacred grove comes from the ancient world (see Chapter 4); this example was inspired by Homer's *Odyssey*, Virgil's *Aeneid*, and Ariosto's romantic epic *Orlando Furioso*. If the early Christians had not been so efficient in destroying pagan sanctuaries, the Sacro Bosco would not be quite such a startling place, though it would remain bizarre. The second explanation of its character may be found in Ariosto's interest in the struggle between Christians and pagans. Duke Orsini had been a soldier and, seeing a new and dangerous world opening before him, used mythology to explore the paradoxical relationships between life, death, man, religion and nature. The garden is a 'mannered' departure from Classical perfection.

The Bishop of Salzburg made a garden at Hellbrunn in 1613–1615. His family had close links with Italy and the garden drew inspiration from that country. The garden was sited near the hills, outside the town, like a Medici villa. It had two water parterres, one of which survives, and a range of typically Italian automata and water devices, which survive today in good condition. Hellbrunn also has a dramatic outdoor theatre in a quarry.

6.45 Early Renaissance garden.

Styles and examples

Early Renaissance

Use: Renaissance gardens developed by stages from their medieval precursors. Noblewomen continued to use gardens to take the air in safety, but men resumed their involvement with gardens – and more resources became available. The principles of ancient garden design were rediscovered and combined with new artistic and scientific ideas about the 'nature of the world'. As in Roman times, Renaissance gardens were used for social gatherings and great occasions.

Form: As castles evolved into fortified manor houses, more space became available for gardens. Square and rectangular planting beds were laid out like carpets, so that their unity, order and regularity could be viewed from upper windows. Crusaders may have seen Eastern gardens with geometrical beds of flowers, or traders may have seen them in Muslim Spain. Patterns, taking their name from carpet patterns, were used in the design of what became known in England as 'knot gardens'.

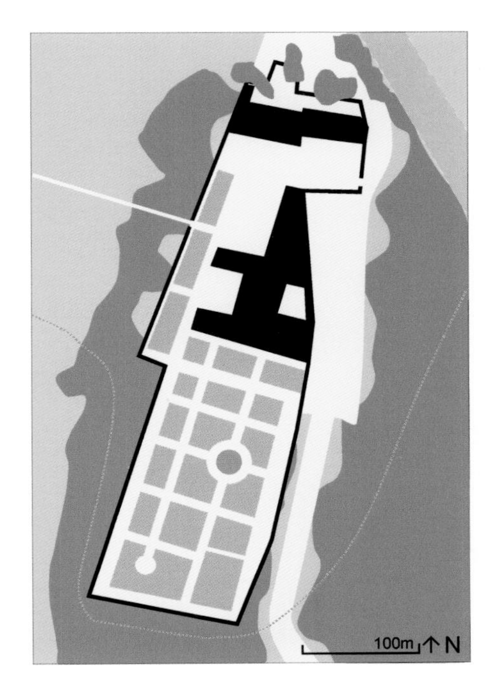

6.46 Careggi, Florence.

Careggi, 1450

'Two miles from Florence [Michelozzo Michelozzi] made the palace of the Villa di Careggi, which was a rich and magnificent structure. Michelozzo brought water to it in the fountain which may be seen there at the present time.'[27] Vasari describes how Michelozzi was employed to transform a medieval fortified manor house into a comfortable residence with elegant loggias. The garden nestles behind a high wall and is famed as the place where Cosimo de Medici assembled his Platonic academy. The garden was laid out in imitation of a Roman villa with space for outdoor living, of the type described by Pliny. A drawing of 1636 shows the house and garden much as they are today, though without the circular pool. The original planting was more botanical, with 'countless specimens of trees and shrubs'.[28] Cosimo also employed Michelozzi to work on the Villa Medici at Fiesole. Careggi looks inward, with the Middle Ages. Fiesole looks outward, with the Renaissance.

> *Yesterday I came to the villa of Careggi, not to cultivate my fields but my soul. Come to us, Marsilio [Ficino], as soon as possible. Bring with you our Plato's book* De Summo Bono, *which I presume you have now translated into Latin according to your promise; for there is no employment to which I so ardently devote myself as to discover the true road to happiness.*
>
> (Cosimo de Medici)[29]

Villa Medici, Fiesole, 1450

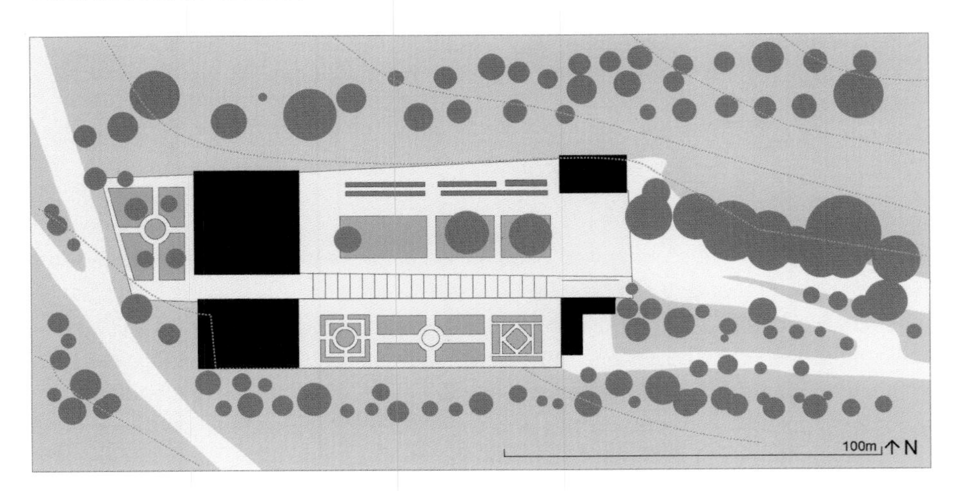

6.47 Villa Medici, Fiesole.

The villa has a hillside site and gracious terraces, as Alberti recommended in his treatise of 1452. There are panoramic views of the River Arno and Florence. Giovanni de Medici, Cosimo's overweight, libidinous favourite son was a child of the Renaissance. He lived for art, music and beauty. After Giovanni's early death, the villa was inherited by Cosimo's grandson, Lorenzo the Magnificent. Had it been built 50 years earlier, the garden would surely have been walled in the medieval manner. Had it been made 50 years later, the terraces would surely have been joined with great flights of steps in the style of Bramante. It is likely that the upper terrace was originally used as an extension of the house and the lower terrace as a vegetable garden. Today, they have tree-shaded walks, lawns and parterres. Cosimo's Platonic academy was moved from Careggi to Fiesole.

> *Such a villa, designed solely to provide luxurious mental refreshment, and placed in the most beautiful situation of any round Florence, could not fail to attract scholars for the interchange and acquisition of knowledge ... As a work of garden architecture, it was a thoroughly sound conception, and one of the most important foundations of future garden design.*
>
> (Geoffrey Jellicoe)[30]

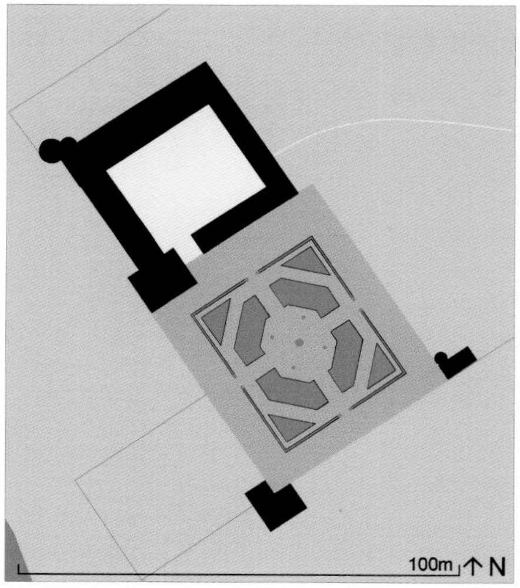

100m N

6.48 Edzell Castle, Angus.

Edzell Castle, 1604

The plan shows a castellated house integrated with a Renaissance castle-garden, in the foothills of the Scottish Highlands. The layout was probably the work of its owner, Sir David Lindsey, Lord Edzell. The square garden is enclosed by massive but well-proportioned red sandstone walls with astrological carvings of the planetary deities. Alternating niches may have been used for flowers and nesting birds. Nothing is known of the original planting. The parterre installed in the 1960s is pleasant but ahistorical. The castle and garden gave protection in the medieval manner while encouraging the family to take an interest in Renaissance art and science. 'Delicat' plants, including fruit, flowers and herbs, required protection from animals, men and the weather.

> *It is ane excellent dwelling, a great house, delicat gardine, with wall sumptuously built of hewen stone, polisht, with pictures and coats of armes in the walls, with a fine summer house with a hous for a bath on the south corners thereof, far exceeding any new work of our times.*
>
> (Ouchterlong of Guinde)[31]

Heidelberg, 1614

Only the bones survive of what was once famed as 'the eighth wonder of the world'. It was made by Frederick V and his wife Elizabeth, daughter of King James I of England. A devoted couple with a shared love of the arts, they fled to exile in Holland in 1620, after the Battle of the White Mountain. The Hortus Palatinus (Garden of the Palatinate) was designed by Elizabeth's drawing master, Salomon de Caus. A famous garden designer, author and hydraulic engineer, he also wrote a book (*Hortus Palatinus*) on the garden. The surviving terraces allow one to see the structure of the Renaissance garden but

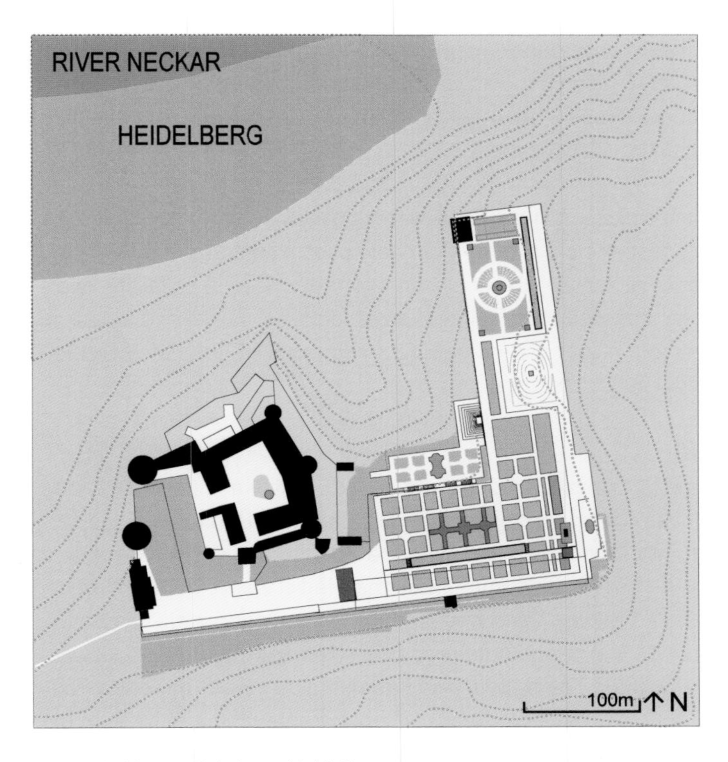

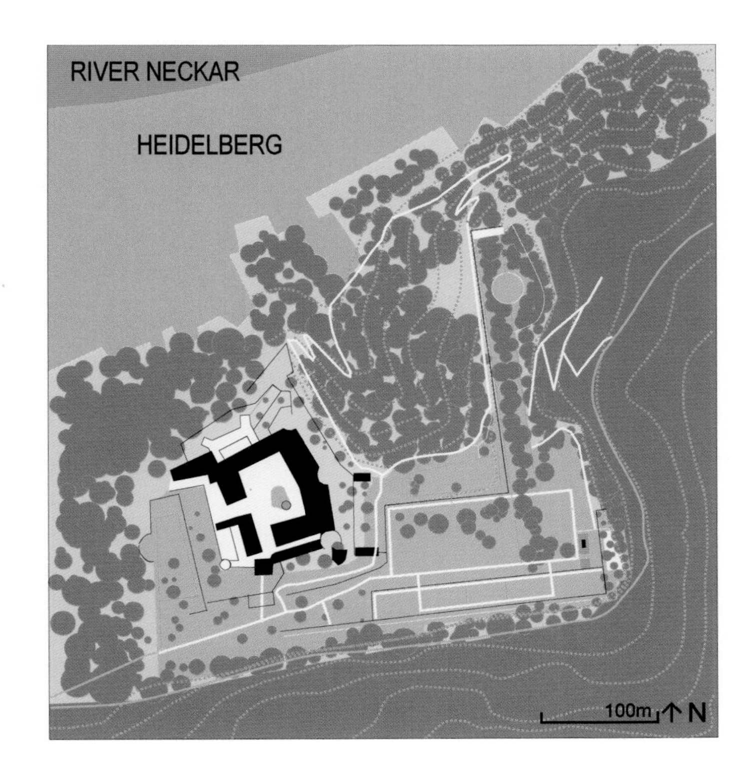

6.49 a, b Hortus Palatinus, Heidelberg.

the Mannerist water tricks, games, musical devices and parterres were destroyed during the Thirty Years War (1618–1648). It did not have a High Renaissance central axis.

> *The ascent is long and steep, the way plain, and no guide needed ... and there, among treasures of art, decaying and decayed, and the magnificent bounties of nature, the stranger may wander the day through.*
>
> (Dorothy Wordsworth)[32]

> *There is scarcely a building in the whole world which has excited admiration of so varied and so critical a kind.*
>
> (Marie-Luise Gothein)[33]

High Renaissance

Use: Alberti advised making

> *Open places for walking, swimming, and other diversions, court-yards, grass-plots and porticoes, where old men may chat together in the kindly warmth of the sun in winter, and where the family may divert themselves and enjoy the shade in summer ... and have a view of some city, towns, the sea, an open plain.*[34]

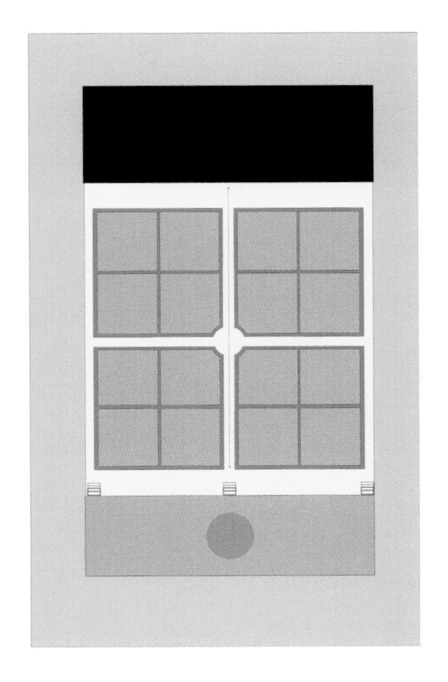

6.50 High Renaissance garden.

Medieval gardens had been inward-looking places, physically and spiritually. High Renaissance gardens began to reach outward, physically and intellectually. Displaying a collection of antique statuary became an important garden use – a way of connecting with history, the fine arts and the landscape.

Form: The organising principles of High Renaissance gardens were developed by Bramante, following a suggestion from Alberti. Bramante used a central axis to integrate house and garden. A series of rectangular enclosures with terraces at different levels was thus fused into a single composition. Flights of steps, alcoves, niches and fountains were disposed in relation to the axis and embellished with statues, fountains and terracotta pots containing flowers and fruit trees.

Villa Madama, 1518

The Villa Madama became influential because of its superb quality and because it was designed by Raphael, whose painting was seen as the pinnacle of Renaissance perfection, before its 'descent' into Mannerism and Baroque. Madama was one of the first High Renaissance villas to be built outside Rome. Like the Medici villas outside Florence, it was conceived as a villa of the type described by Pliny the Younger in his garden letters. The distinction between inside and outside was blurred and there is an outward view from the terrace to the Tiber. The original plan included a courtyard, a monumental flight of steps, a circular court, an open-air theatre, a hippodrome, and a terrace. In the woods there is a grotto. The famous Elephant Fountain by Giovanni da Udine survives in an alcove. The villa was conceived more as a place to entertain than a place to live. Its scale is monumental but there is a perfect balance between architecture, garden and landscape.

> *If fate had allowed the building to proceed, a jewel comparable with anything the Renaissance can offer would be now before our eyes, but changes of fortune have left only the ruins of a fragment.*
>
> (Marie-Luise Gothein)[35]

6.51 Villa Madama, Rome.

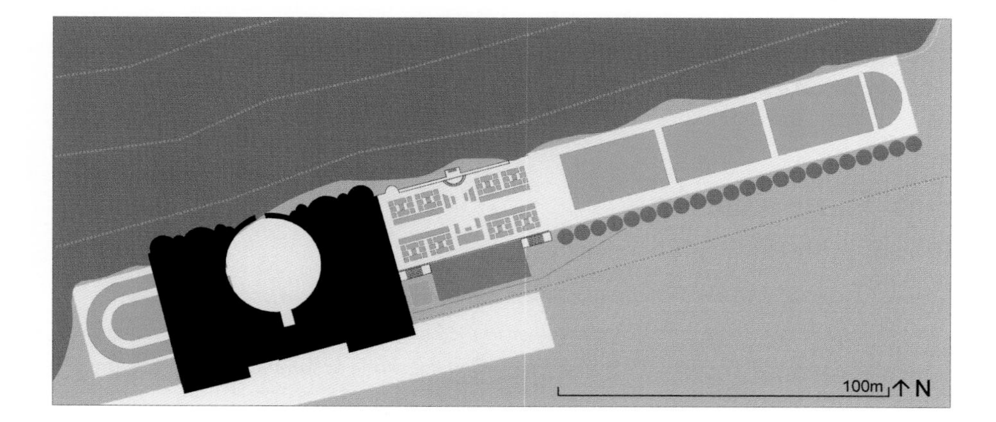

The existing fragment is, however, well worthy of study, for the purity of its plan are in marked contrast to the complicated design and overcharged details of some of the later Roman gardens.

(Edith Wharton)[36]

Villa Medici at Castello, 1537

Though cold, secretive, moody and despotic, Cosimo I, Grand Duke of the Medicis, was a generous patron of the arts. He employed a sculptor, Niccolò Tribolo, to design the garden of his villa at Castello. The plan shows spacious terraces on several levels, arranged around a central axis. There is a fine grotto, set into the garden wall, inspired by Cosimo I's love of hunting. Tribolo's sculpture follows an iconographical theme, drawn from Ovid's *Metamorphoses*, celebrating the greatness of the Medici family. Much of the original garden decoration described by Vasari has gone. A lunette of the garden, painted in 1599, shows the garden layout much as it is today, but the planting has been thinned and the garden does not have as much charm as one feels it could have. After a visit he made in 1580, Montaigne described the garden with his customary freedom from prejudice:

The house itself is not worth looking at; but there are several gardens admirably laid out, all of them on the slope of a hill, so that all the straight walks are upon a descent, but a very gentle and easy one; the cross walks are level and terraced. In every direction, you see a variety of arbours, thickly formed of every description of odoriferous trees, cedars, cypresses, orange trees, lemon trees and olive trees ... We went to look at the principal fountain, which discharges its contents through two large figures in bronze [Hercules and Antaeus], *the lower of which has taken the other in his arms, and is squeezing him with all his might; the latter, almost senseless, has his head thrown back, and discharges the water from his mouth; and the machinery is so powerful that the fountain rises to a height of 222 feet above the figures, which themselves are 20 feet high ... There is also a very handsome grotto, in which are to be seen all sorts of animals, sculptured the size of life, which are sprouting out water, some by the beak, others by the mouth, or the nails, or the nostrils.*

(Michel de Montaigne)[37]

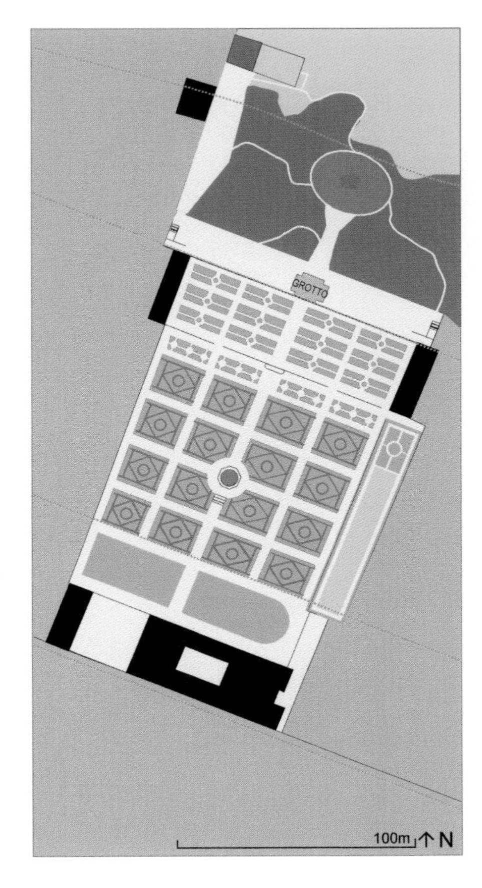

6.52 Villa Medici, Castello.

Palazzo Farnese at Caprarola, 1550

The plan shows a Renaissance castle garden to the south and a Mannerist pleasure garden to the north, separated by woods. The Renaissance parterres flank a great pentagonal fortress at the head of the town. Their layout has changed but they remain impressive, if somewhat formalistic. The garden retreat in the woods, designed by Vignola, is a richly integrated Mannerist composition. Known as the Casino del Piacere (Little House of Pleasure), it hides in a glade at the end of a long path. There is a water staircase, fountains, terraces, a *casino* and loggia used as a private retreat by Cardinal Odorado Farnese.

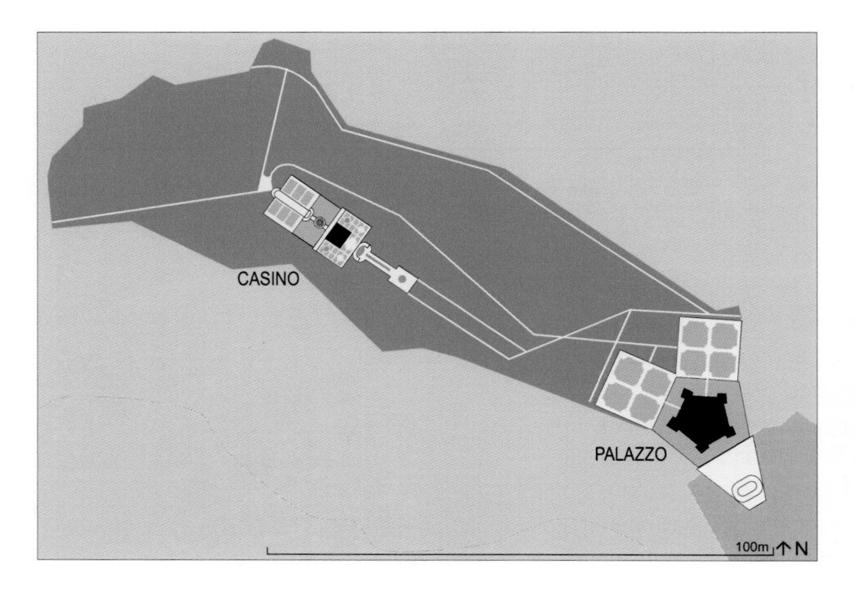

6.53 Palazzo Farnese, Caprarola.

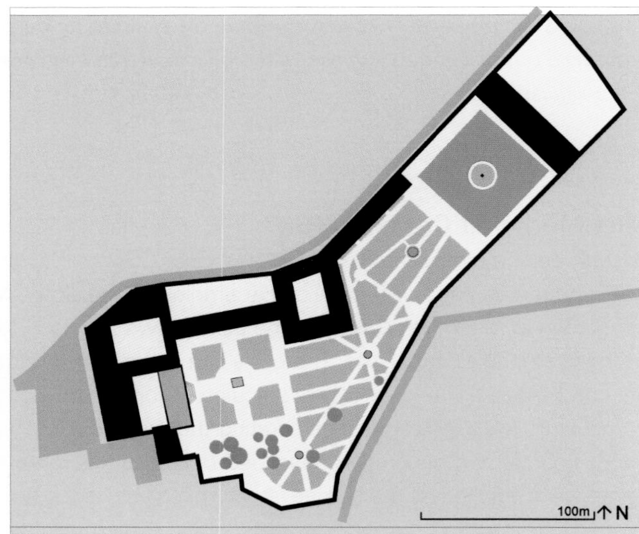

6.54 Valdstejn Garden, Prague.

It is like a fortress, with a winding staircase outside and a moat and drawbridge, in a new style and fine invention. The gardens are filled with rich and varied fountains, graceful shrubberies and lawns, and every requisite for such a royal villa.

(Giorgio Vasari)[38]

Valdstejn (Wallenstein) Garden, 1614

One of Europe's greatest military commanders had a sector of medieval Prague destroyed to make his palace and garden. Wallenstein was cold, egotistical, avaricious and autocratic, though he had studied in Padua and admired the Italian Renaissance. The scale and character of his garden compare with the Villa Madama, but it is shut off from the town in the medieval style – one senses the hard defensiveness of a man whose life was spent in war. A monumental loggia overlooks a disciplined parterre. Hercules, symbolising power, stands in a large tank of water. Other bronze statues, lining the main axis, are copies of originals taken as war booty to Drottningholm by the Swedish general, Gustavus Adolphus, who led the Protestant forces against Wallenstein in the Thirty Years War.

The house was no ordinary nobleman's mansion, a slice of autonomous territory rather, amidst the patchwork of the city, a miniature realm enclosed by outbuildings and a park wall like a circumvallation. When Wallenstein's coach had rolled into the courtyard to the left of the front, he had all that he needed – a chapel, a riding-ground at the lower end of the park, and (the absolute essential) a bathing pool, in a grotto bedizened with crystals, shells, and stalactites, as well as walks between statues and fountains.

(Golo Mann)[39]

Palacio de Fronteira, 1660

This garden is distinguished by its great stairways, water tanks, *azulejos* (coloured glazed tiles) and decorative parterres. From the plan, one might think it a Renaissance garden inspired by Du Cerceau and dating from the 1550s. In fact, as the exuberant detailing reveals, the garden was made in the 1660s. The water tanks have panels decorated with glazed tiles, plaques and busts, adding brilliant hues to the composition: terracotta, indigo, cerulean, turquoise, lemon-yellow. The Chapel Walk is an outdoor gallery with tiled panels showing allegories of the arts and sciences. Fronteira exemplifies a uniquely Portuguese approach to garden design: comfortable, grand, lush, intimate and brilliantly coloured.

> *The eye is arrested by something new and strange, a basin lying at the side, which occupies nearly the whole length of the garden. In the water stand two statues, and there are two little flowery islands in it, while the high wall that supports a narrow terrace is articulated with three doors, between which are twelve panels with the figures of knights made in faience. The wall of the narrow upper terrace has no plants, but is decorated with plaques and also has five niches containing the portrait busts of Portuguese kings.*
>
> (Marie-Luise Gothein)[40]

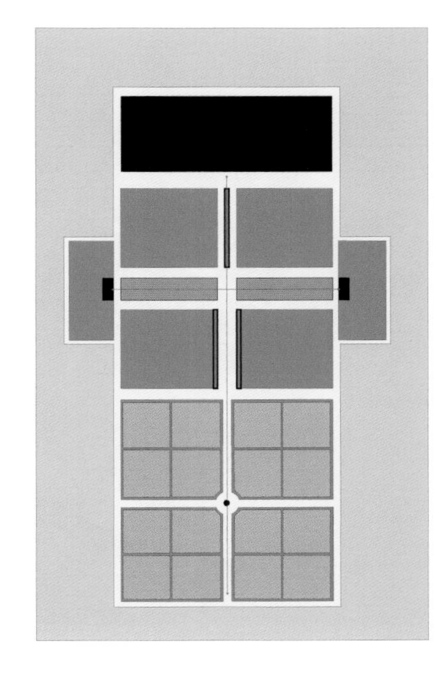

6.55 Mannerist garden.

Mannerist

Use: When Renaissance art was thought to have reached its peak of perfection, designers and their clients became attracted by surprise, novelty and allusion. Gardens were furnished with dramatic features for outdoor masques and parties. Virtuoso water displays were admired and the creation of garden features to impress one's friends became a design objective.

Form: The characteristics of Mannerist painting and sculpture – movement and drama – became important in gardens. Hydraulic marvels and elaborate water features were driven by streams flowing through gardens. Streams also had an allegorical role. It was as though designers had taken heed of Leonardo's remark that 'it is a wretched pupil who does not surpass his master'. Dramatic sites were chosen and embellished with exotic sculpture. There was a new interest in Classical literature and, with Palladio, a Neoplatonic respect accorded to circles and squares. Houses became ornaments in great outdoor compositions.

Villa d'Este, 1550

The plan shows a highly developed Renaissance plan with a central axis stepping down a terraced hill. The Ville d'Este is an important Mannerist garden, verging on the Baroque. 'If we drew up a list of the seven wonders of the gardening world, this villa might well rank as the first', declared Jellicoe in 1937.[41] Cardinal Ippolito d'Este, as proud as he was rich, ensured that no other garden has such spectacular waterworks. Visitors entered at the lowest point of the garden. As they ascended the hill, the water marvels were revealed and the story of the family's illustrious ancestors (including Hercules himself)

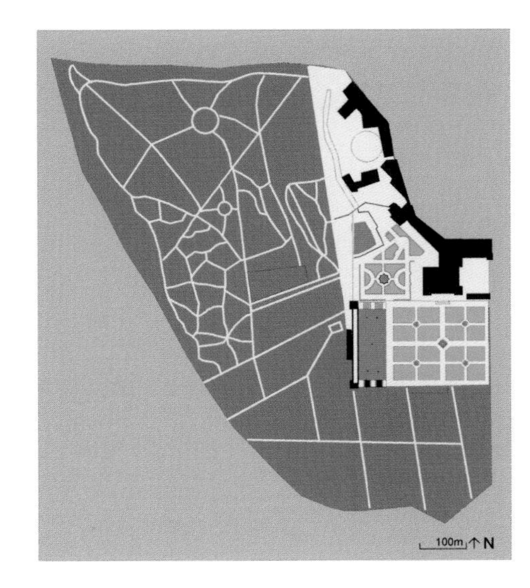

6.56 Palacio de Frontiera, Lisbon.

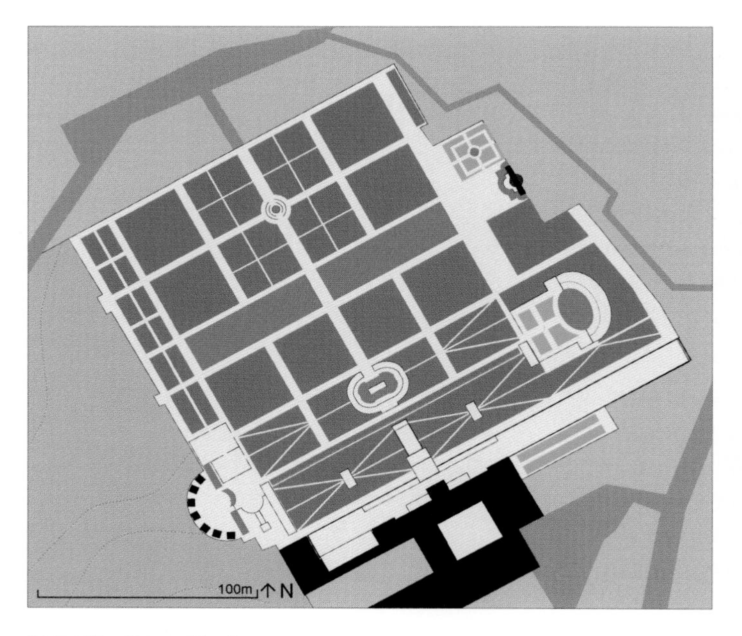

6.57 Villa d'Este, Tivoli.

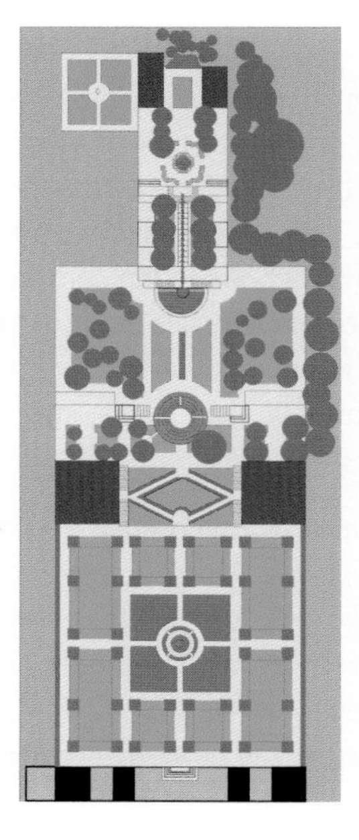

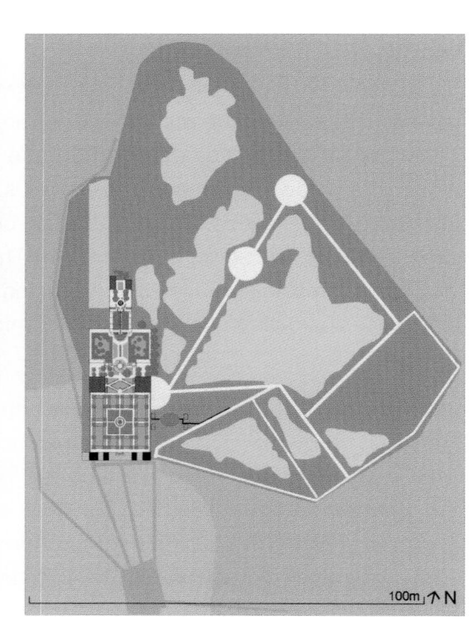

6.58 a, b Villa Lante, Bagnaia.

unfolded. The garden contains many references to Ovid's *Metamorphoses*. Detours were necessary to see the garden's different sections but if everything went according to plan, one arrived at the top believing the Estes to be the most brilliant family in history. The Aniene River supported the story by supplying the fountains and, with the aid of a water organ, a musical accompaniment. Many of the statues were obtained from Roman sites. Pirro Ligorio supervised the excavations and supplied the erudition and imagination behind the conception of the garden. The Rometta Fountain is a miniature representation of Rome, topped by a statue of Romulus and Remus.

> *There are such depths of mystery in the infinite green distances and in the cypress-shaded pools of the lower garden, that one has a sense of awe rather than of pleasure in descending from one level to another of darkly rustling green.*
>
> (Edith Wharton)[42]

Villa Lante, 1573

'A place not of grandeur or tragedy but of enchanting loveliness'[43], the garden of the Villa Lante is 'a perfect thing of the imagination'.[44] It has a perfectly balanced plan with rich embellishment. In the eyes of many, it is the best example of the best period in garden design – the Mannerist phase of the Italian Renaissance.

It was conceived by Cardinal Gambara, who had a modern taste for outdoor living, and the overall design is attributed to Vignola. Buildings are treated as garden ornaments, illustrating a good principle – that of making architecture subservient to garden designs. The circle and square are prominent in the layout: a square terrace is subdivided into smaller squares, and there are circular and semi-circular pools. The water parterre has a central fountain. The design was inspired by earlier projects: the geometry of the plan by Bramante's Belvedere; the use of water by the Villa d'Este; the circular island either by Hadrian's 'marine theatre' at Tivoli or the *isolette* in the Boboli Gardens. The echo of the Temple of Queen Hatshepsut in the terraces that command views down a sloping hillside, however, is entirely coincidental.

A river of delight flows from a grotto at the summit of the hill but does not stick to the central axis. Symbolically, the garden represents the tale of humanity's descent from the Golden Age described in Ovid's *Metamorphoses*. Paths lead to an outdoor dining area with a fountain table and to other enclosures. The Water Chain is the best and earliest example of a stepped cascade. The Villa also has a park with the character of a hunting park, but too small for anything but a ring hunt with already-captured animals.

> *A gentle and pretty maiden, well adorned with varied and sumptuous clothes and also with jewels on her fine head, pearls in her ears, and many rings on her well-kept hands.*
>
> (Agostino del Riccio)[45]

CHAPTER 7

Baroque gardens, 1600–1750

7.0 Drama became the essence of Baroque gardens. Louis XIV saw himself as the Sun King, Apollo, and the Apollo Fountain at Versailles represents the god in his chariot being pulled by horses representing force, ardour and the power which gives life to all things.

7.1 a, b The greatest Baroque garden, Versailles, was designed for drama. On a quiet day it is like an empty theatre.

History and philosophy

'Baroque', like many of the labels used by art historians, began as a term of abuse. Baroque art was seen as imperfect in comparison with the perfection of the High Renaissance. Bazin suggests that the word derives from *barocco*, meaning an 'irregular pearl'.[1] But he admires Baroque art and sees the years from 1600 to 1750 as 'the period of Western civilisation that is richest in expressive variety'. Bazin distinguishes Baroque from Classical as follows:

> *Classical compositions are simple and clear, each constituent part retaining its independence; they have a static quality and are enclosed within boundaries. The Baroque artist, in contrast, longs to enter into the multiplicity of phenomena, into the flux of things in their perpetual becoming – his compositions are dynamic and open and tend to expand outside their boundaries.*[2]

Bazin's main interests were painting, sculpture and architecture but his comment fits Baroque gardens exceptionally well. They integrate a 'multiplicity of phenomena' (land-form, water, vegetation, sculpture, fountains, terracing, roads, paths, steps, bridges and architecture); they are 'dynamic and open', with avenues piercing garden boundaries as effectively as cannon pierced city walls in the Baroque era; their dramatic water features create a 'flux of things' in 'perpetual becoming'. Drama is their essence.

Baroque art is associated with the Counter-Reformation and the rise of science in seventeenth-century Europe. The forces of attack gained an ascendency over those of defence: after the deployment of cannon there was less point living in walled cities.

7.2 The Baroque period gave Europe its most dramatic garden sculpture and fountains, as in the Boboli Gardens.

7.3 Astronomy became a royal enthusiasm in the Baroque period. The Observatory in Greenwich Park is seen here with the neglected remains of the Le Nôtre parterre and the Giant Steps which once carried the Baroque axis up the escarpment.

Instead of city-states, it became necessary to have regional powers, with symbols of their capacity to project power. It was also necessary to train, equip and organise armies. The armies made it safe to live in large villas outside the towns. Baroque art is associated with absolutist government. Louis XIV was the leading patron of the arts but, as the favoured style of kings and nobles, Baroque art affected all Europe, including the Protestant countries. The speed with which the new style was adopted varied according to political, economic and religious circumstances, but where and whenever they emerged, Baroque gardens shared many common features.

Should one seek a prime cause for the changes which affected Europe during the Baroque age, the best candidate is the rise of science and consequent weakening of Church authority. The arguments of Copernicus (1473–1543), Kepler (1571–1630), Bacon (1561–1626), Galileo (1564–1642) and Newton (1642–1727) were, slowly and reluctantly, accepted by the Church. Galileo was the first to use a telescope to study the geometry of the universe, bringing him into conflict with religion. Catholics and Protestants fought each other but accepted the use of reason, as did armies, philosophers, politicians, industrialists and artists. The resultant changes are described as the Enlightenment because the 'light of reason' illuminated, and thus undermined, the dogma of earlier times. Kings acquired telescopes and espied for themselves a place in the majestic structure of the universe: a god-given right to rule. Mathematics helped to explain the universe and was linked ever more closely with natural philosophy and the fine arts. In this, Descartes (1596–1650) was the key thinker.

Though Descartes did not write on aesthetics or gardens, the term 'Cartesian garden' is often applied. It points to the rationalist philosophy on which the Baroque age was founded and reminds us of Descartes' personal contribution to geometry – we still speak of 'Cartesian' co-ordinates. In philosophy, Descartes' *Discourse on Method* proposed the application of 'systematic doubt'.[3] It would, he argued, tell us what knowledge men can have which is certain beyond the possibility of doubt. His conclusion was that we cannot doubt either the truths of mathematics or the existence of God – and these two categories of truth came to dominate design. Descartes' *Discourse* inspired artists and authors to emphasise certainty in human affairs. Scientists looked for 'laws of Nature', a phrase invented by Descartes, and critics looked for 'rules of taste' to distinguish good art from bad art. The rules appealed to long-accepted standards, such as formal poetic structures. Even the greatest scientist of his age, Newton, believed himself to be rediscovering truths known to the ancients.[4] Rules of taste were examined for their antiquity and their mathematical foundation. The Golden Section passed both tests, having been explained by Euclid.[5] Sculptural themes were drawn from the Classics and used to represent Christian truths. Alexander Pope equated the 'rules of old' with a Newtonian conception of Nature.[6] He advised artists to follow:

> *Those Rules of old discover'd, not devis'd,*
> *Are Nature still, but Nature Methodiz'd.*[7]

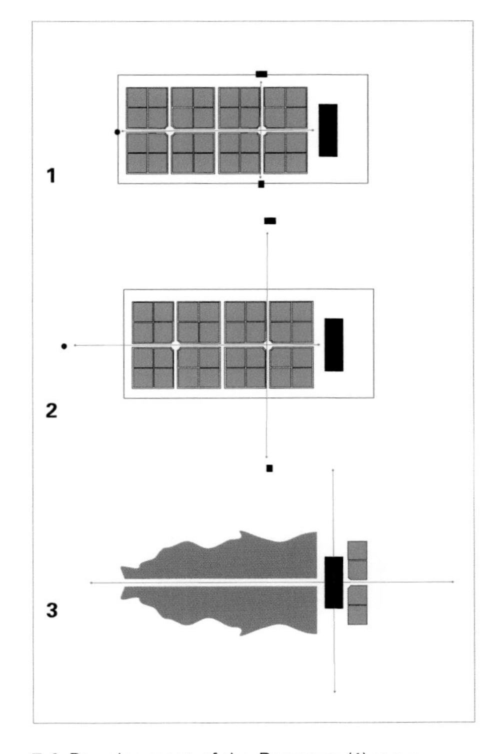

7.4 Development of the Baroque: (1) axes within gardens; (2) axes aimed on landmarks outside gardens; (3) axes projecting beyond gardens.

Geometry was the branch of mathematics with the most obvious relevance to garden design. Axes, as introduced to gardens by Bramante, became their dominant feature. The stages in the advance of axes were as follows:

- single axis, within boundaries (Belvedere Court, Vatican, 1505);
- transverse axes, using focal points within boundaries (Villa Castello, 1538; Villa d'Este, 1550; Villa Lante, 1566);
- transverse axes, projecting to remote focal points (Villa Mattei, 1582; Villa Montalto, 1585);
- long axes projecting through the landscape to churches and distant focal points (Villa Aldobrandini, 1589; Villa Torlonia, 1621);
- radiating axes, within boundaries (Boboli Gardens, 1549–1620; Luxembourg Gardens, 1612);
- radiating axes, projecting beyond boundaries (Vaux-le-Vicomte, 1656; Versailles and Paris, after 1665);
- radiating axes, projecting through cities (Karlsruhe, Germany, 1715; Washington DC, USA, 1791; New Delhi, India, 1911).

Axes could integrate gardens, architecture and landscapes into unified geometrical compositions. The principal features of Baroque gardens were:

- avenues;
- canals;

7.5 Avenues became the most characteristic feature of Baroque gardens. **a, b** Long avenues at Versailles and Windsor Great Park; **c** cross-avenues at the Luxembourg Gardens.

- parterres;
- green structures formed by hedging;
- buildings on axes;
- focal points within gardens (e.g. fountains);
- focal points outside gardens (e.g. churches);
- axially coordinated steps, water features and statues, as pioneered by Bramante;
- integration with the surrounding landscape.

Baroque ideas influenced the planning of avenues in the princely environs of capital cities: at Frascati outside Rome; at Versailles outside Paris; at Potsdam outside Berlin; at Hampton Court outside London; at the Peterhof outside St Petersburg. The guillotines which decapitated the French aristocracy after 1793 cooled Europe's enthusiasm for the style, though it was applied to the layout of Paris itself after the failed revolution of 1848. The military idea behind this – which proved successful in the 1871 Paris Commune – was that revolutionaries could be chased down boulevards and shot like beasts in a nobleman's park.

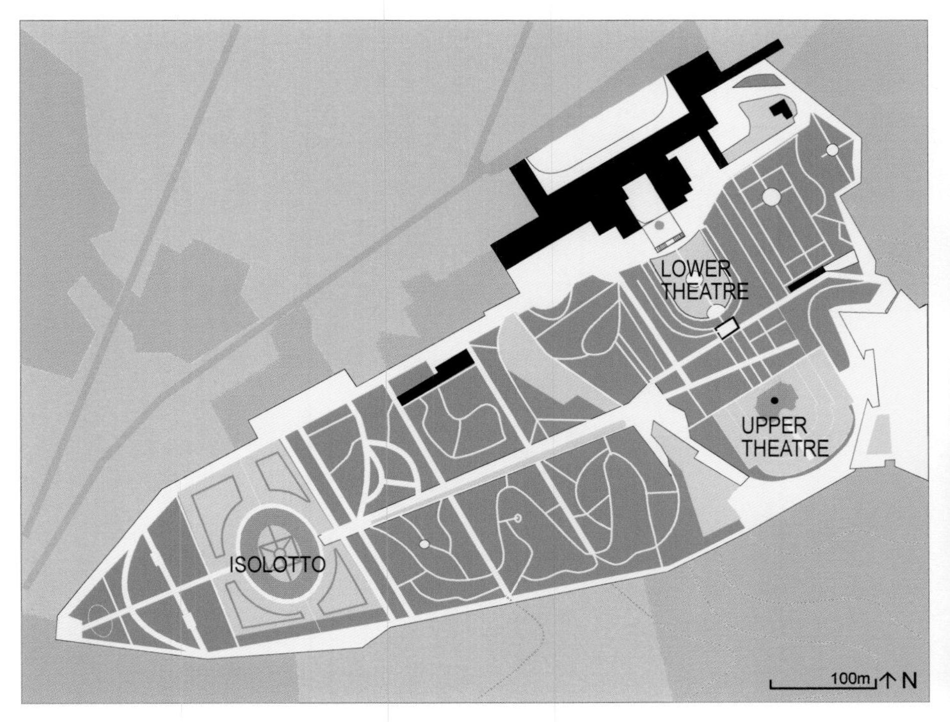

7.6 a, b, c The avenues are contained within the boundaries of the Boboli Garden in Florence.

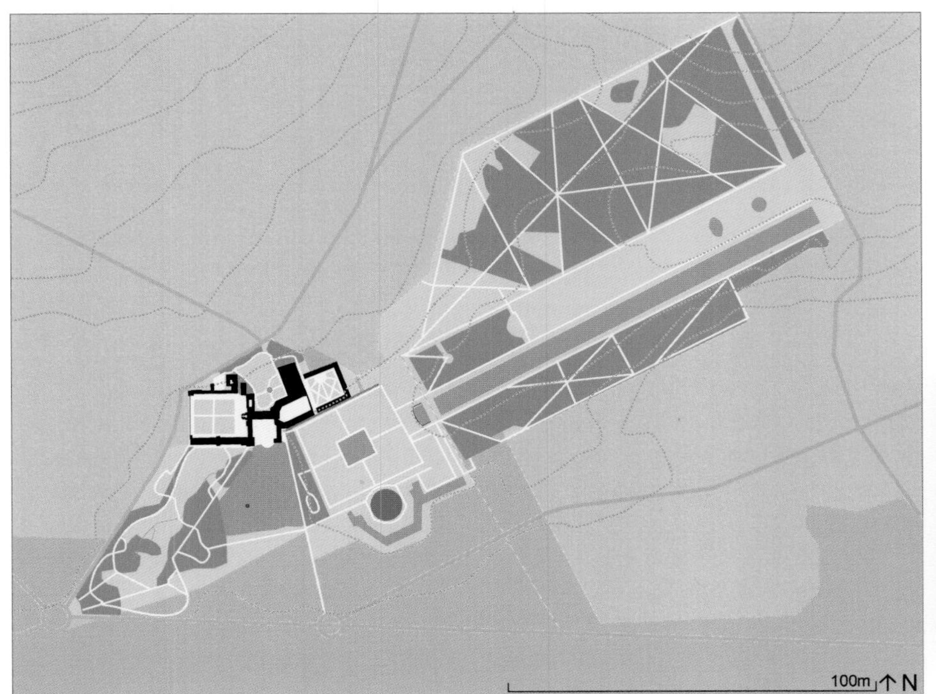

7.7 a, b Fontainebleau has a Renaissance core (see p. 199) to which Le Nôtre made Baroque additions.

7.8 Bernini's piazza in front of St Peter's is bounded by a peristyle, curved but derived from rectangular peristyle courts built for cloisters since the early days of Christianity.

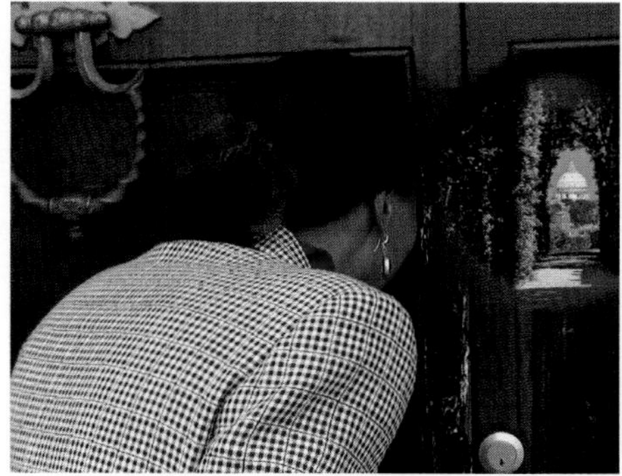

7.9 There was a Baroque fashion for focusing garden views on the dome of St Peter's. The inset view is through a keyhole in a door to the garden of the Knights of Malta in Rome.

The characteristics of Baroque parks and gardens varied with the circumstances of the countries in which they were made. Bazin remarks that it was 'the moment at which each of the peoples of Europe invented the artistic forms best fitted to its own genius'.[8] Books on French, Italian, Spanish, German and English gardens concentrate on styles which originated between 1550 and 1750. Taking a broader view, one can distinguish an Early Baroque period in Italy, when the tendency began, a High Baroque period in France, when a climax was reached, and a Late Baroque period when the style was adopted, with different accents, throughout Europe. A distinction can also be made between gardens, with a domestic space related to the dwelling, and parks, integrated with the surrounding landscape. A few Baroque projects, including Isola Bella and

Drottningholm, achieved both objectives. Mirabelle in Salzburg and Queluz in Portugal are gardens. Versailles, near Paris, and Caserta in Italy are primarily parks. The Baroque style also had a powerful influence on town planning in capital cities (Rome, Paris, Berlin, Washington DC) and elegant resorts (Versailles, Potsdam, St Petersburg, Aranjuez).

Early Baroque in Italy

Italy was dominated by Spanish influence during the reign of the Hapsburgs (1525–1700), although some areas, including Venice, the Papal States, Tuscany and Genoa, retained nominal independence. It was a period of relative economic decline as the hub of world trade and industry shifted from the Mediterranean to the Atlantic. But it was also a period when Rome briefly recovered its former role as the centre of Western civilisation: the place which every artist and every tourist felt compelled to visit. Visitors were interested both in ancient remains and new projects. Leading Baroque projects were initiated by the Church; the greatest of all was the completion of St Peter's, by Madero and Bernini (1605–1666). This included a giant oval piazza, inspired by the peristyle court of Old St Peter's.

The use of focal points in garden design was first seen at two proto-Baroque villas in Rome: Montalto (*c.*1570; demolished) and Mattei (*c.*1582).[9] The Villa Montalto belonged to Sixtus V before he became Pope. It was designed, with Domenico Fontana's help, to have a network of avenues, some projecting beyond the garden boundary towards Roman landmarks. The garden was 'adorned with choice works of ancient art, although

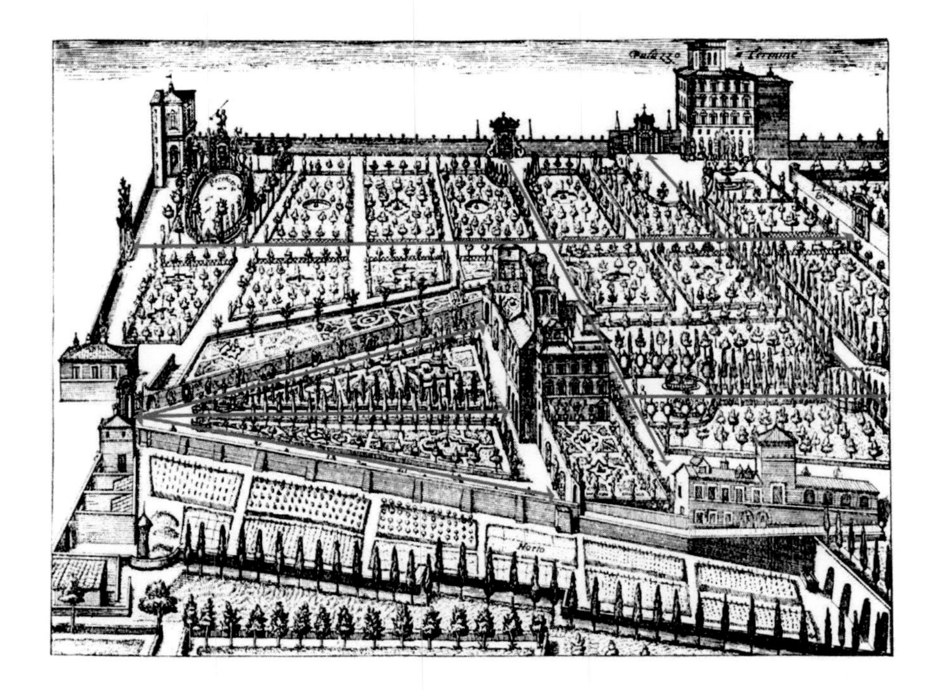

7.10 The Villa Montalto, which belonged to Pope Sixtus V, had avenues with focal points, as did his subsequent plan for the glorification of Rome. Subsequently, the land was used for a railway station.

7.11 The Villa Aldobrandini has a long avenue running 'through' the centre of the villa.

7.12 The avenues at the Villa Ludovisi (Torlonia) are now recovering from the damage they suffered in the Second World War.

7.13 The garden of the Villa Garzoni does not have the owner's house as a focal point but forms a splendid prospect from the road. It was built on the site of a castle which protected the village of Collodi before the age of cannon.

at one time he [Sixtus] had scornfully opposed the cult of antiquity'. The most significant feature of the garden was that:

> *Here for the very first time the artist is working in a larger style with perspective. Long avenues are made with definite endings, architecture or sculpture ... Villa Montalto had not only its own* points de vue *to rejoice in, but also the help of buildings outside.*[10]

It was at Villa Montalto that Sixtus developed an enthusiasm for building which he later applied to the whole city of Rome. In 1588, he began to build Baroque axes to run between focal points in the city. A number of other Early Baroque gardens were also made in Italy but the economy was in decline, partly because Sixtus preferred to hoard gold in the Castel Sant'Angelo, instead of allowing it to circulate. 'Cash starvation dealt a death blow to commerce and industry'.[11]

Frascati has a group of Baroque gardens which, as Steenbergen and Reh have shown, were aligned on the dome of St Peter's.[12] Many were damaged by allied bombing in the Second World War and have been restored. The Villa Ludovisi in Torlonia is now a public park and retains a quiet dignity. The Villa Mondragone is larger but less dramatic. Villa

7.14 Isola Bella is an island garden, integrated with a landscape in the Baroque manner.

Aldobrandini dominates the small town of Frascati, with the palace as its focal point. On the town front, Frascati occupies the foreground and Rome the background. On the garden front, there is a water theatre, a cascade and a shaft of space projecting uphill into dark woods. Grandeur and drama surround the place.

The garden of the Villa Garzoni at Collodi, in Tuscany, does not use the house as a focal point but the garden is very much a place of show. Italian gardens were often open to visitors, and this is one that can be appreciated as a spectacle from outside the gates. From the entrance, a strong central axis draws the eye, and then the visitor, into the garden, up the cascade and through the woods. A colossal terracotta statue of Fame waves to spectators from on high. The garden is a boastful stage, not a place of Renaissance seclusion. At Isola Bella on Lake Maggiore, the garden occupies a whole island: the waters of the lake, framed by the surrounding hills, become an immense garden feature. They provide a visual feast with 'the unceasing change of the water's surface, shut in by towering hills'.[13] As at Collodi, the garden is a focal point in the landscape and the landscape is part of the garden. The 'beautiful isle' has dramatic hanging gardens, a harbour, grottoes, statues and a villa rising directly from the lakeshore. The natural landscape had no place within Renaissance gardens. In Baroque gardens, the demarcation lines between landscape and garden were blurred: gardens merged into forests, lakes and hills. Yet the landscape of Italy was not so well suited to the full development of

7.15 a, b, c Vaux-le-Vicomte, by Andre Le Nôtre, looks empty without an audience.

7.16 a, b Versailles was conceived as a place from which the Sun King's power would radiate across Europe – and as a place to be appreciated from a horse or carriage.

this style as the rolling hills and forests of Northern Europe. Nor was Italy as wealthy as France became during the seventeenth century.

High Baroque in France

France suffered from devastating religious wars in the sixteenth century but reached a settlement, embodied in the Edict of Nantes, in 1598. The Edict laid the foundations for the most brilliant period in French history, though it was revoked in 1685. With Germany in ruins, England kingless and Italy dominated by Spain, France assumed a position of political and cultural pre-eminence which continued until 1815. Under Louis XIV (1661–1715) the fine arts flourished as an instrument of state policy.

It was a high official in Louis' court who set the course of garden design. Nicolas Fouquet commissioned Le Vau, Le Brun and Le Nôtre to design his château and garden at Vaux-le-Vicomte. This first great work of the French Baroque remains the example most admired by design critics. Historians write of 'the style of Louis XIV' but, in gardens, it might be more accurate to say 'the style of Nicolas Fouquet'. Grander in scale than any of its Italian predecessors, Vaux-le-Vicomte overtly demonstrates its artistic, political and geographical roots. Artistically, it is a product of the High Baroque enthusiasm for drama. Politically, it relates to the wealth and power of a unified state with global ambitions. Geographically, it suits the landscape of Northern France – gently rolling country, rich in billowing woods and flowing water, through which it is comparatively easy to cut avenues and canals. Gothein sees Vaux as a balance between two tendencies: on the one hand, order, discipline and proportion, and on the other, variety and change.

Vaux-le-Vicomte is theatrical: a spectacle to be viewed from the house but with many surprises for the energetic visitor. To inaugurate the garden, Fouquet held a famous

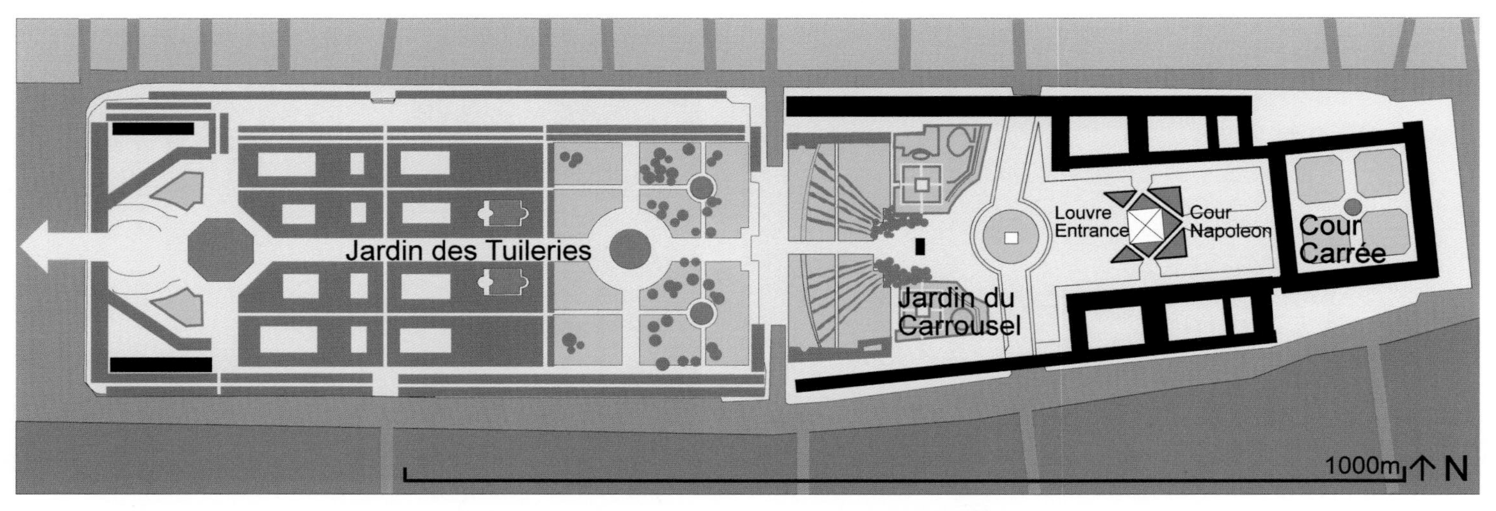

7.17 a, b, c André Le Nôtre, like his father and grandfather, worked in the Tuileries Gardens. André re-designed the garden and began the outward extension of an axis which, over four centuries, projected to the Arc de Triomphe and the Grand Arche – and now beyond.

party. Louis XIV loved the party, admired the design, imprisoned the owner and took the design team to create what became the most celebrated royal estate in Europe: Versailles.

In 1668, Louis XIV came under the influence of a woman, who, like himself, was in the full tide of youth:

> *His love for Madame de Montespan gave the inward stimulus to his being; she was the woman who supplied what in these years he wanted. She was beautiful, proud, self-willed, and full of spirit and fun, a nature which wanted to rule and gave in to him alone.*[14]

7.18 a, b Versailles was conceived from the outset as a dramatic palace estate for a Sun King with dramatic views radiating in every direction; **c** Chantilly was a Renaissance garden to which Le Nôtre added a Baroque garden.

Louis XIV became known as the Sun King (*le Roi Soleil*) and this metaphor provides the simplest way of interpreting the plan of the grounds at Versailles. Whereas Renaissance castles had been sited at the edges of their gardens, the palace of Louis XIV, like the Villa Aldobrandini, was at the heart of the realm. Axes radiate towards the furthest corners of France – and beyond. Versailles has a sun plan for a Sun Prince. Thompson sees Louis as the producer-director and Le Nôtre as the creative-director.[15] It was more a government centre than a garden as we now understand the term and one needed horses to enjoy the scenery. A century later, Versailles inspired Pierre L'Enfant's plan for another government centre, Washington DC; two centuries later it inspired the axial planning of

7.19 a, b, c Chenonceaux, like all the best Baroque gardens, draws upon the characteristics of its setting.

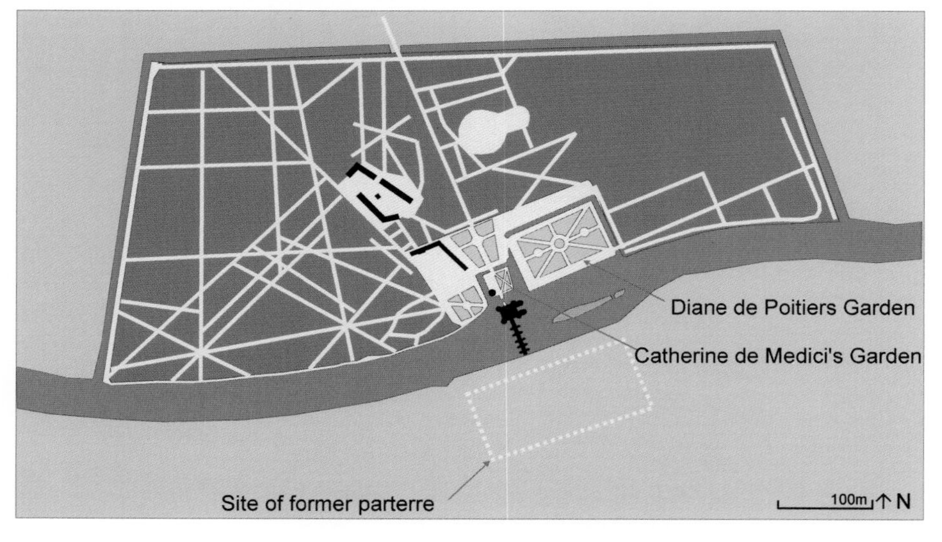

New Delhi; three centuries later it influenced the axiality of Brazilia and other capital cities in developing countries.

Versailles was immediately seen as the grandest, if not the most charming, of gardens – and it retains this status. The villas of the ancients and all Renaissance villas were cast into the shade by its audacious scale. First, the French nobility, then the kings of Europe took their lead from Versailles. Le Nôtre undertook some commissions himself and passed others to assistants. Chantilly was one of Le Nôtre's favourite projects and one of his first for the nobility. The moated medieval château was given a breathtaking water garden. At Fontainebleau, the Renaissance layout was remodelled in the Baroque style. Le Nôtre also worked at Meudon, Saint-Cloud and Marly-le-Roi. The Grand Trianon at Versailles was designed as a retreat for Madame de Maintenon.

In keeping with the spirit of the age, Baroque gardening dynasties branched outward. Jacques Mollet became head gardener to Henri IV in 1595. His son, Claude, and one of his grandsons, André, published books on garden design. Other grandsons, and some great-grandsons, became gardeners in their turn. André Le Nôtre's grandfather (Pierre, d. 1610) had worked for Catherine de Medici. André's father (Jean, d. 1655) lived and worked in the Tuileries Garden and in due course gave up his job to André (d. 1700), who worked in the Luxembourg Gardens and at Fontainebleau before joining the design team for Vaux-le-Vicomte. In 1657, André went to work for Louis XIV. Louis funded his dreams and, in 1693, awarded him the Order of Saint-Michel; but above all he gave him affection. André died in 1700, the most distinguished landscape architect since Senenmut.

7.20 Chenonceaux at night.

High Baroque outside France

The glare of Versailles was brightest on the rolling hills and plains of North Europe, but its rays also shone across the Alps, the Baltic and the Atlantic. Many observers, especially those from England, found it too bright. Except when large fêtes were in progress, the gardens seemed too large, too empty, too grandiose. These seemed simple errors to avoid. Later monarchs also found something excessive about Louis XIV's absolutism and imagined they could run 'enlightened' despotisms at home. If money were no object, it was in fact rather easier to make a Versailles than a Villa Lante. Not only were the principles clear and flexible, but also a professional staff, trained by Le Nôtre, was available for hire. There was also a book, *The Theory and Practice of Gardening*, by Dézallier d'Arganville, which set forth the principles on which Versailles was based.[16]

The first of d'Arganville's principles was that a single grand idea should unify the design, with sufficient variety to charm and surprise the visitor. Palatial buildings were sited on raised terraces overlooking parterres. Water features – simple, powerful and with balanced proportions – were set among great trees. Secret gardens were made in woodland compartments (*bosquets*), to surprise the visitor. Avenues ran through forests and projected beyond estate boundaries to increase their apparent size. Statues and water features were made by the best artists and technicians of the day.

Although the schema is simple, Baroque gardens took different forms, influenced by social and physical geographies. The High Baroque worked best in those parts of North Europe with undulating land, copious water and deciduous forests. On flat land, it was difficult to achieve drama and variety. In mountainous country, there was likely to be too much variety and not enough unity. In hot, dry climates, it was difficult to make sufficiently large areas of wood and water to bring the composition into balance. The style also required lavish resources directed by royal and princely powers – on a scale unavailable in the first of the countries we will consider.

7.21 a, b Hampton Court has both a privy garden and a Baroque park.

English Baroque

England, protected from continental wars by her choppy seas and rugged navy, nevertheless experienced internal strife from the start of the Civil War in 1625 to the restoration of Charles II in 1660. The subsequent period of rapid economic and cultural change was associated with anti-Baroque tendencies: liberalism, empiricism and the Industrial Revolution. A dalliance with Baroque garden design lasted for a few decades and ended with a Romantic passion for Dame Nature. In the eighteenth century, London's palace gardens, including Greenwich Park and Kensington Gardens, were touched by the Baroque but did not become prime examples of the style.

Before ascending the English throne in 1660, Charles II had spent 16 years of exile in France. His memories of England, and of the enclosed Renaissance garden at Boscobel (see p. 204), were none too happy. Having some enthusiasm for Louis XIV's approach to autocratic government and absolutist design, Charles made England one of the first countries to follow the path of Le Nôtre. His mother Henrietta Maria, a French princess who had been present at the opening of Vaux-le-Vicomte, came to live at the Queen's House in Greenwich Park and Charles invited Le Nôtre to design a parterre for her (see Figure 7.3). It was Le Nôtre's only English project – a Baroque park to help the dowager queen feel at home in England. It did not work and she returned to France. Charles also employed André Mollet to design canals and avenues for St James' Park, perhaps to make himself feel more at home in England.

7.22 An avenue in Claremont.

Outside London, avenues became the most popular aspect of the High Baroque style. Not only were they fashionable, and even useful, they could also be attached to

7.23 An avenue in Greenwich Park.

England's Late Renaissance gardens without undue expense. A close examination of Kip and Knyff's copperplate engravings of English estates in the early eighteenth century reveals a profusion of avenues tacked onto Renaissance layouts.[17] Perhaps 'Low Baroque' could serve as a name for this design approach but some of the avenues, such as that at Levens Hall, Cumbria, have an informal charm.

Dutch Baroque

Holland experienced a Golden Age from 1609 to 1713, in which the country was wealthy, Protestant and independent. Despite wars with Spain, England and France, Holland took a leading role in the arts. William III, Stadholder of the United Provinces after 1672 and King of England from 1688 to 1702, favoured a modified absolutism in government and

7.24 a–d The garden at Het Loo was made by William and Mary. In 1688, they took the English throne and moved to Hampton Court. Het Loo was restored for its 300th anniversary in 1984.

a modified Baroque style in garden design. The gardens he commissioned for Het Loo in Apeldoorn and Hampton Court in London reveal this taste.

As a nation, the Dutch had no reason to like Louis XIV. But the cultural influence of so powerful a neighbour could not be resisted: William and Mary's garden at Het Loo became known (unfairly, because it is more Dutch and less grandiose) as 'the Dutch Versailles'. At Honselersdijk, William made another garden, with a more interesting and distinctively Dutch design (see Figure 6.28). The avenues outside the garden, not shown on the drawing, were lines of trees projecting into agricultural land. This garden, which no longer exists, would have been a much more interesting subject for a restoration project than Het Loo. Dutch Baroque gardens were also made at Enghien and Neuberg. The country had a great deal of water but, especially in the polder lands, a shortage of forests.

German Baroque

When the Thirty Years War ended in 1648, large sections of Germany were devastated, and theological and territorial disputes continued to make a political union impossible. For garden designers, this was an advantage: there were more court gardens to be made. Each state had a palace and most were touched by the rays which shone from Versailles. Germany was rebuilt, but it lacked experienced designers; often, the princes and prince-bishops employed an Italian architect and a French garden designer. Many of the places they made are original and eccentric, fertile ground on which, in time, the Baroque could evolve into the graceful curves and rich decoration of the Rococo. Rococo is the name for a style that originated in Paris in the early eighteenth century, partly as a reaction to the ponderous grandeur of Versailles. It was popular in the courts of Southern Germany and Austria.

Sophie, daughter of the king who made the Hortus Palatinus (see pp. 206–7), commissioned a student of Le Nôtre to design the Grosser Garten at Herrenhausen, Hanover,

7.25 a, b Nymphenburg, outside Munich, has a great Baroque garden, set in a forest with outward views.

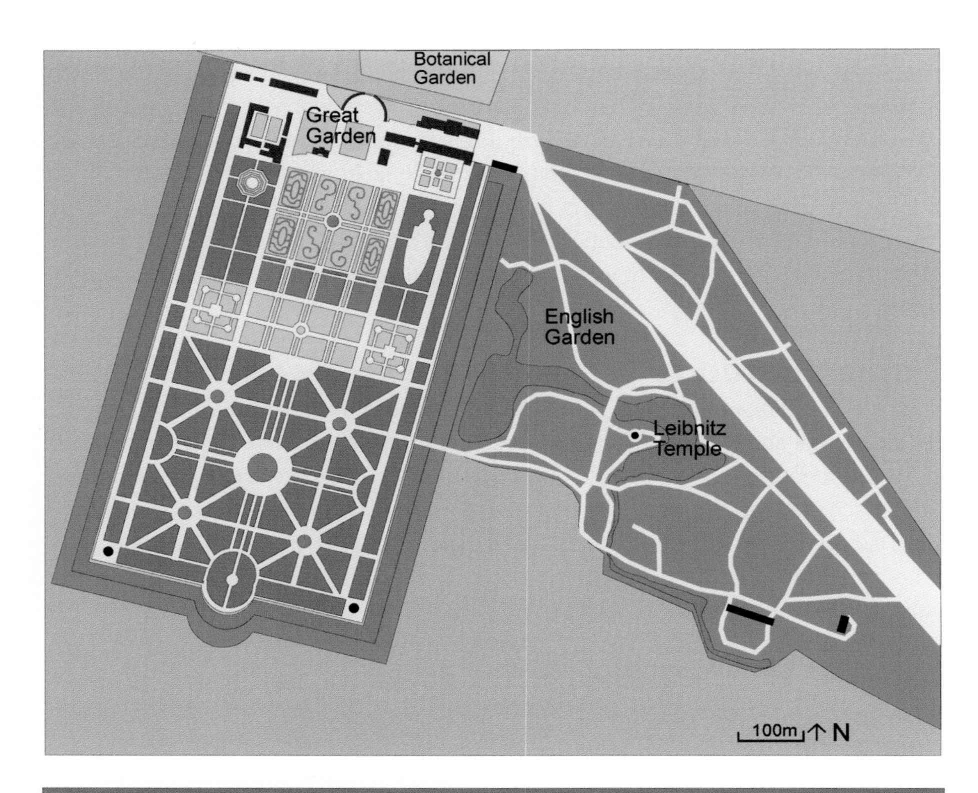

7.26 a, b, c Herrenhausen has a disciplined Baroque garden, bounded by a canal in the Dutch manner – with a serpentine park outside.

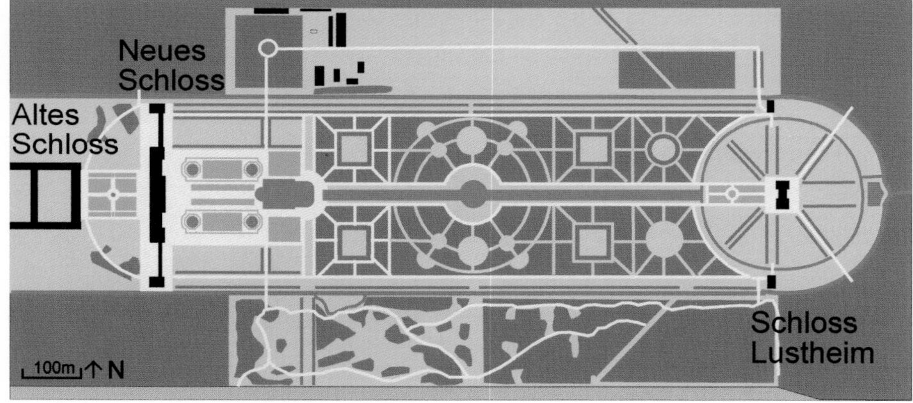

7.27 a, b Schleissheim, in South Germany, has an Early Baroque garden inspired by North Italian precedents.

in 1666. It was a textbook example of regularity in the relationship of house to garden. Sophie had spent her youth in Holland and remembered the geometrical discipline of Dutch gardens. Since Herrenhausen's avenues do not project beyond its canal, this regularity is even more pronounced than at Versailles. Another German prince, the Elector Max Emanuel, returned from a period of exile in Paris with a taste for French gardens. At Nymphenburg, he made great flower parterres, canals and avenues around the focal point provided by the castle.

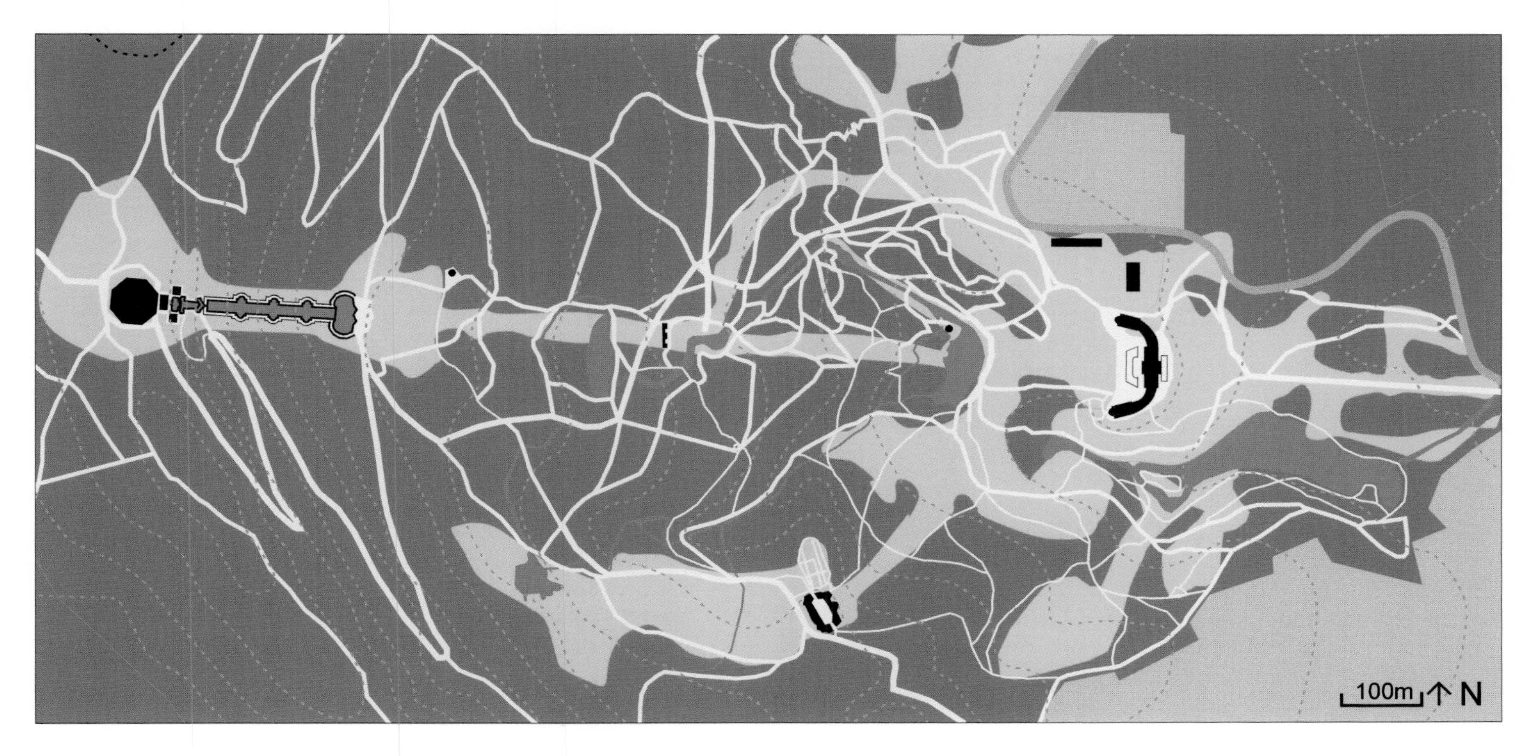

7.28 Though much of the park is now Romantic, the Wilhelmshöhe Bergpark has a colossal axis. Made after 1701, it runs for 7 km from the Hercules fountain to the centre of Kassel.

7.29 The Hercules fountain and cascade in Wilhelmshöhe Bergpark.

7.30 Looking east from the Hercules cascade.

At Karlsruhe in South West Germany, the idea of radiating avenues was developed in a way never before seen in France, or any other place. A hunting-tower was used as the node for a star of 32 avenues. Façades of buildings were planned to create unified frontages onto avenues with parterres behind. At a later date the garden plan was transformed into a town plan. Another distinctive design, made for the castle of Wilhelmshöhe at Kassel, is more Italian than French in its use of rugged scenery. Only the upper part of the cascade was completed, but even this fragment is vast and dramatic.

In the mid-eighteenth century, confidence in enlightened despotism and enthusiasm for the High Baroque waned together, leading to Rococo gardens and, as discussed in

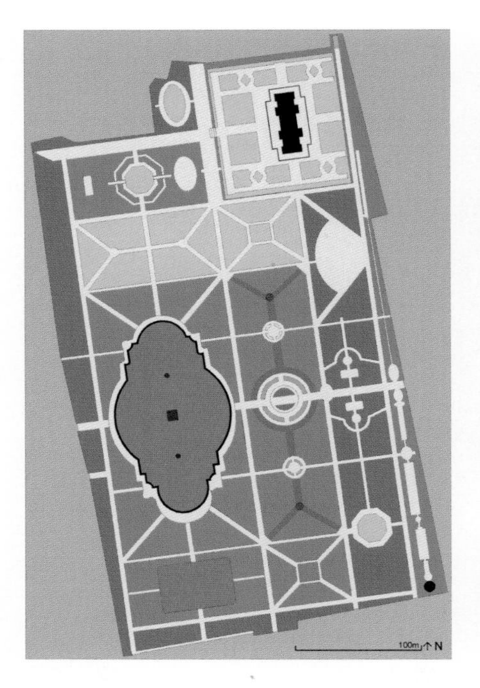

7.31 a, b Veitshöchheim Hofgarten. In Germany, the Baroque evolved into the Rococo.

Chapter 8, to landscape gardens. The formal garden at Schwetzingen, made after 1753, is less axial and more compartmentalised than High Baroque designs. Other German gardens tended towards the Rococo. Socially, their function was for gay events rather than displays of raw power. This translated into outdoor rooms with comparatively weak overall plans. The Ermitage at Bayreuth, made after 1735, has a theatre in the form of a Roman ruin, made for outdoor opera. Veitshöchheim, near Wurtzburg in Bavaria (*c.*1763), has numerous hedged garden rooms with mischievous Rococo statuary and other relaxed details – the bishops who made this garden must have been more inclined to aestheticism than asceticism.

Austrian Baroque

Austria, though the centre of the Holy Roman Empire, could not undertake major building projects during most of the seventeenth century. It was restrained by the Thirty Years War in the first half of the century and by the Turkish threat until 1688. Following the return of peace, fine gardens were built. Gardens were made in and near Vienna, at Belvedere, Schwarzenberg, Liechtenstein, Schloss Hof and Schönbrunn. Hungary was part of the empire, and a great Baroque garden was made at Esterhazy.

The Belvedere Garden, just outside the walls of Vienna, was inspired by the palace of Versailles and laid out by a French designer. Its scale is closer to that of an Italian garden than a French park, befitting its intended use for high society. There was no forest and the water features are too small for boats. Schönbrunn, made by the great Empress

7.32 a, b, c The Belvedere Palace, built outside Vienna's medieval walls, has an imposing pool to the south and a large parterre garden overlooking the city to the north.

Maria Theresa, is the Versailles of Austria. In a reversal of the standard Baroque plan, the palace stands at the foot of the hill and there is a *gloriette* where the palace 'should' be. Paintings and photographs showing the garden from the *gloriette* do not do justice to Fischer von Erlach's imperious design; the scale of the parterres needs the balance provided by the spectacular fountain and the *gloriette*-topped hill.

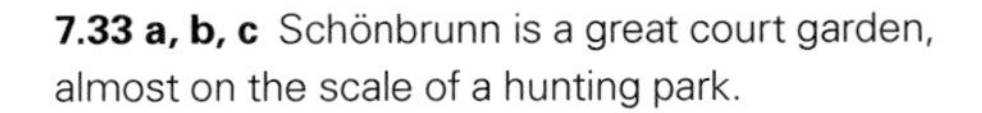

7.33 a, b, c Schönbrunn is a great court garden, almost on the scale of a hunting park.

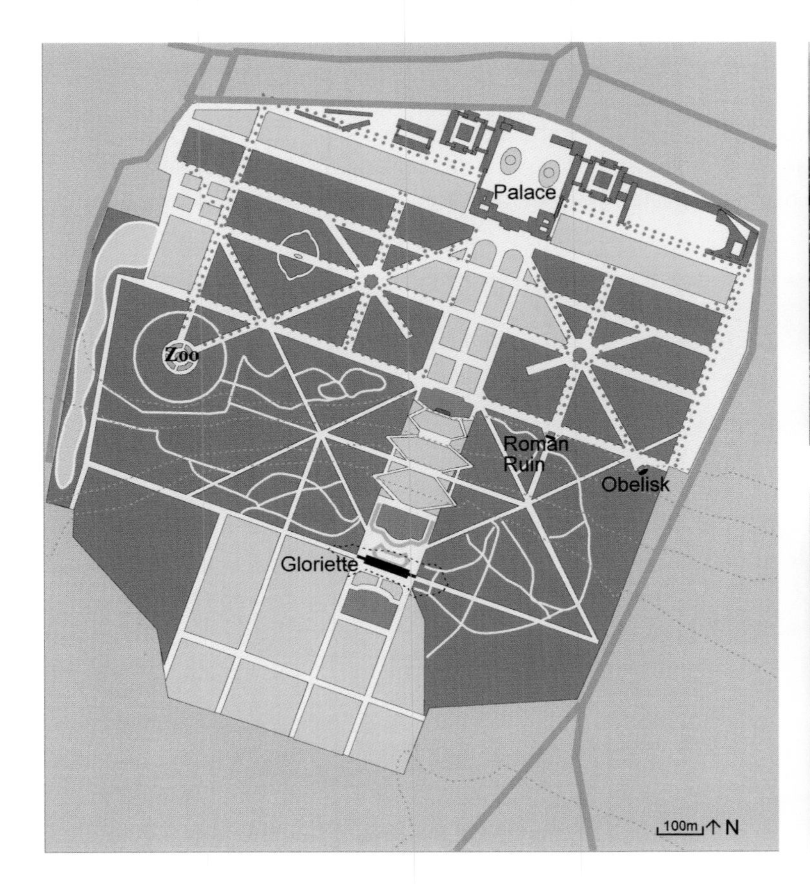

7.34 a, b Mirabelle, with the gaiety of a Mozart opera, retains the air of a court garden better than any of its counterparts.

7.35 a, b, c Drottningholm is proudly at home in a northern landscape, with statues taken from the Wallenstein Garden in Prague (see plan on p. 258).

Hellbrunn (1615), the country retreat of a prince archbishop, falls into the same stylistic group as the Villa Aldobrandini (1598) and the Boboli (1620) – but retains a Mannerist light-heartedness. It has two axes, it takes advantage of the landscape and it has elaborate water features. Salzburg, the city which gave birth to Mozart in 1756, has a garden with some of the character of his music. Mirabelle is a court garden in the midst of a city. Its prime axis is aligned with Salzburg's castle. The garden is gay and has an outdoor theatre beautifully suited to a performance of *The Magic Flute* or *The Marriage of Figaro*. Today, the garden is understandably popular with young couples and wedding photographers.

Scandinavian Baroque

Sweden enjoyed an Age of Greatness in the seventeenth century. Its king, Gustavus Adolphus II, was the leading Protestant commander in the Thirty Years War. After taking Prague he transported the statues from his adversary's garden to Drottningholm (1665–1700). But 'for fashion and etiquette, for architecture and art, the Court of Louis XIV provided the divine archetype'.[18] Gustavus' daughter, Queen Christina, summoned French designers to Sweden and the dowager Queen Hedvig Eleonora planned a full-blown Baroque garden at Drottningholm. It is the best example of the Baroque style in a cold climate. The garden itself may have been designed under Le Nôtre's personal supervision, in France by Nicodemus Tessin.

A wise and loved Queen, Hedvig Eleonora tried to restrain her grandson, Charles XII, from the military campaign which ended so disastrously for Sweden. Her garden at Drottningholm has avenues and fine parterres, aligned with a frontage on Lake Mälaren

7.36 A lake separates the parterre at Frederiksborg from its castle (see Figure 8.48, p. 300).

and a focal point on a hill. It is a national symbol, drawing from Europe's history but fully adjusted to, and at home in, the Swedish landscape. In commemoration, Emanuel Swedenborg wrote a *Sapphic Ode*:

> *Sweden, of ancient Goths thou parent land,*
> *Weep! Nurse of nations and of warriors brave,*
> *With locks and garments torn by frantic hand,*
> *Weep o'er yon grave!*[19]

King Frederick IV of Denmark visited Paris in 1700 and returned with a penchant for the Baroque. This resulted in the parterre garden at Frederiksborg and the radiating avenues at Fredensborg. At Frederiksborg, it is a pleasure to find a Baroque garden where the designer, instead of attempting yet another Versailles, drew upon Chantilly.

7.37 a, b The Peterhof was built as a symbol of Russia's ambition to be a great European power (see Figure 7.52).

7.38 The Catherine Palace at Tsarskoe Selo overlooks a Baroque parterre (see also p. 297).

Like medieval French lowland castles, Frederiksborg Castle is in the middle of a lake (Figure 7.36). It was used as a summer residence for the Danish royal family before becoming a national museum. The castle is arranged on three islands with its main axis projecting over a fourth island and across the moat-lake. A canal penetrates the lakeshore and the axis ascends a terraced hillside to an oval pond, defined by clipped box and pleached limes. A restoration programme was started in 1995. Departing from the axis to walk round the lakeshore gives one a different prospect: what looks like a Baroque garden from within the castle becomes a fairytale park containing a romantic castle on a lake isle (see p. 300).

Russian Baroque

Russia was a backward country from the Time of Troubles (1606–1613) until the reign of Peter the Great (1689–1725). Peter won great military victories and opened Russia to the art and technology of Europe. Baroque town planning and garden design were among his imports; St Petersburg and the Peterhof are the spectacular results. Peter was a marginally enlightened despot with a savage streak of cruelty. Apart from the unintended symbolism of a poor country pouring gold into a northern ocean, and Samson savaging the lion, one can read little of Peter's barbaric personality, drunkenness or fondness for torture. Instead, one sees the enlightened side of his character. The Peterhof was severely damaged in the Second World War and then rebuilt, possibly with Soviet imperialists admiring Baroque imperialists.

Iberian Baroque

Spain was ruled by the Habsburgs from 1516 to 1700, leading to protracted European wars. This assisted the influx of artistic ideas to Spain but all the gold of South America was not enough to secure victory in these wars. Military overreach ended Spain's domination

7.39 The Royal Palace in Madrid was commissioned by Philip V. Born in Versailles, he was Spain's first Bourbon king.

7.40 Aranjuez was designed as a retreat from the heat of summer and the walks are shady.

7.41 a, b, c Queluz has a Baroque layout on a domestic scale and with the richness of a southern landscape.

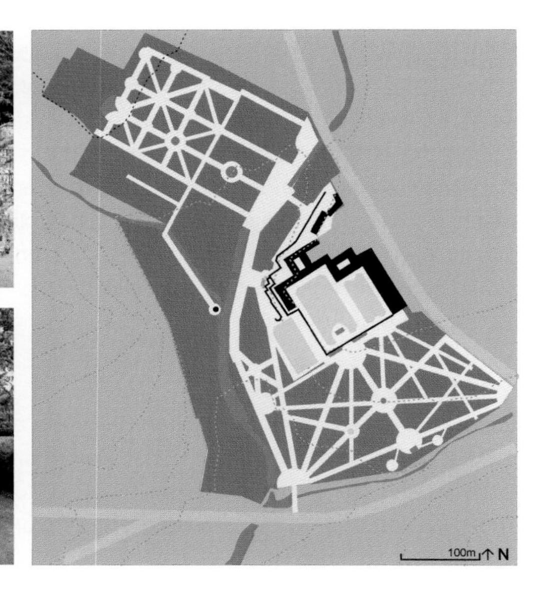

7.42 a–e La Granja, outside Sevovia, follows Baroque practice in drawing upon the characteristics of the local landscape. It is a southern garden with a northern tint.

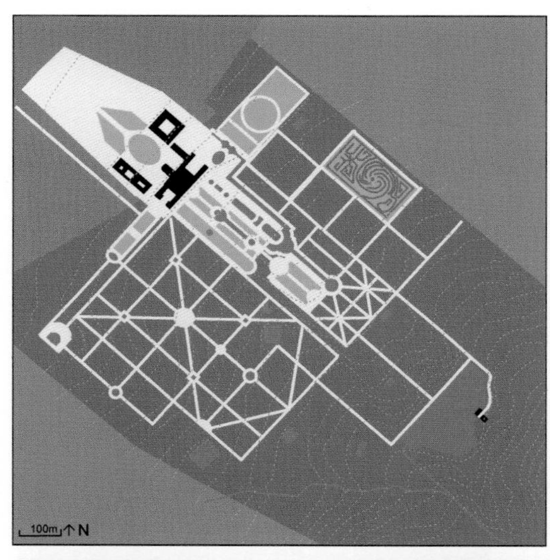

of Europe by 1630. The Habsburg dynasty, worried that its right to rule was less secure than formerly, indulged in displays of power that made them feel important. Buying Baroque art reassured the Habsburg dynasty that it was doing its duty for the Holy Roman Empire and the Catholic faith. After the House of Bourbon took the Spanish throne, in 1700, Baroque gardens were made at Aranjuez and La Granja. The latter, benefiting from the un-Mediterranean climate of Central Spain, is an exceptionally fine example of the style. The glistening white of the sculpture coordinates with the snow-capped peaks, the marble cascade and the whitish bark of the trees.

Late Baroque in Italy

7.43 a–d The great Baroque axis at Caserta. There is a scene from Ovid at the foot of the upper cascade.

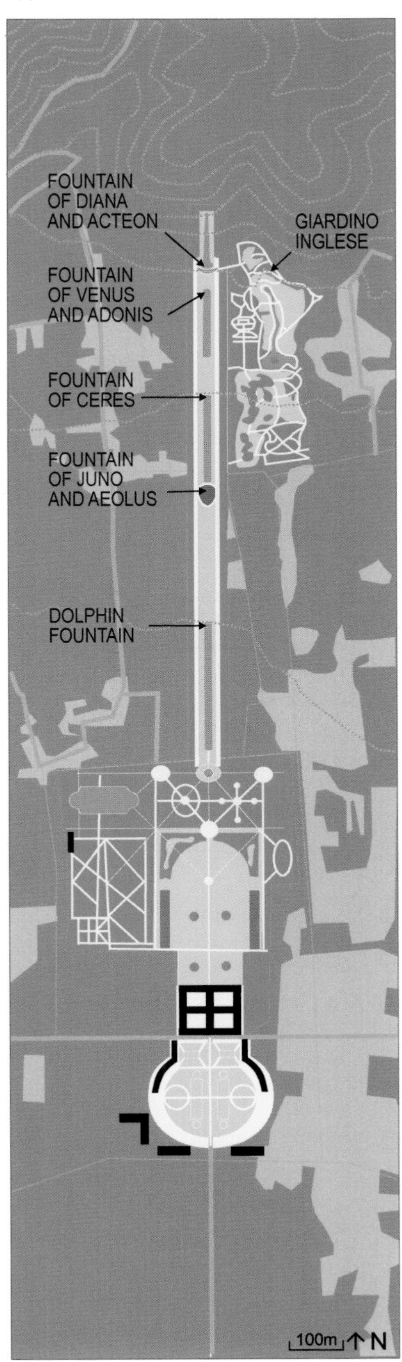

Having originated in Italy, developed in France, and spread through Europe, the Baroque style returned to influence its homeland. It had some success on the flat lands of Northern Italy (e.g. at Monza), to which it was not unsuited. The most significant 'Versailles of Italy' was attempted at Caserta in 1752, by a Bourbon prince, Charles III, who had spent his youth at La Granja. The longest cascade in Europe emerges from the palace and flows 3 km into a vast canal. It is awe-inspiring, as one would expect of the Late Baroque, but it lacks the sense of proportion which guided the best Italian and French designs of earlier periods.

Styles and examples

7.44 Early Baroque garden.

Early Baroque

Use: Early Baroque art is associated with the Counter-Reformation and the quest to re-establish the power of prelates and princes. Garden layouts became a means of advertising power. Since physical security now rested more on guns and armies than fortifications, rural life became as safe (or unsafe) as town life. The villas of Frascati were built with their lines of sight trained on the dome of St Peter's in Rome. Pope Sixtus V used Baroque ideas, drawn from garden design, to glorify Rome. Vistas were fixed on obelisks and spires. Courtly gatherings took place in Baroque gardens.

Form: The Baroque style began with the projection of axes beyond the boundaries of enclosed Renaissance gardens. In towns, the avenues focused on church domes and other features. Outside towns, they pushed into the landscape, bringing mountains, lakes and forests into composition with gardens. The results were dramatic. Lines of view projected ever-outwards. Enthusiasm for the discoveries of geometry, optics and perspective influenced garden design. The avenue became the most characteristic feature of Baroque parks and gardens. It began life as a shady walk on the edge of a square medieval plat. Then:

- Bramante used an axis as the central feature in a garden layout.
- Avenues projected towards garden features.
- Avenues projected towards features outside the garden (e.g. the dome of St Peter's).
- Avenues began to radiate in all directions, to the greater glory of their owners.

Villa Aldobrandini, 1600

This is the best-known example of the Early Italian Baroque style. Instead of standing on the fringe of the garden, the palace is its centrepiece, theatrically set into a wooded hill and, like the other Frascati villas, casting an eye over the landscape towards the dome of St Peter's in Rome. Every aspect of the place is aristocratic. It was designed for a 'nephew' of a Pope (a euphemism for a papal child) in an imposing situation with a broad

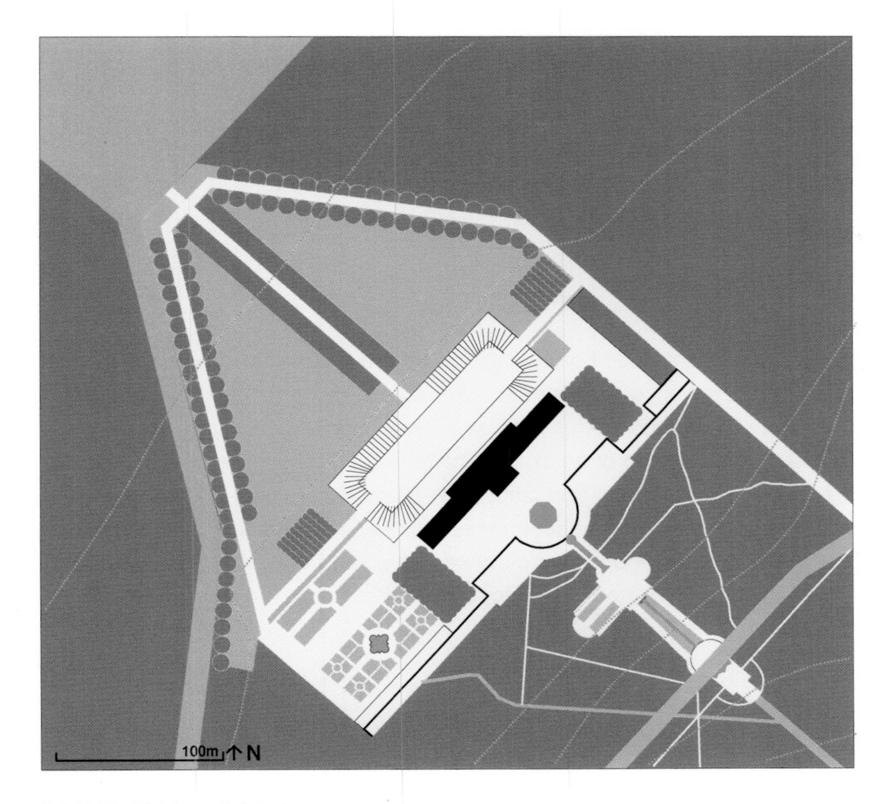

7.45 Villa Aldobrandini, Italy.

terrace dominating Frascati. To the rear, there is a water theatre with niches for statues and fountains. Atlas holds a globe in the central niche. Behind the theatre, an avenue with a central water cascade pushes upwards into the oak and chestnut woods. There are garlanded Pillars of Hercules. Work on the garden began in 1598 and was finished in 1603. The Villa Aldobrandini was badly damaged during the Second World War and subsequently rebuilt. Many of the statues have gone and the fountains that used to soak and delight unsuspecting visitors were not working at the time of writing.

> *In my opinion [one of] the most delicious places I ever beheld for its situation, elegance, plentiful water, groves, ascents, and prospects. Just behind the Palace (which is of excellent architecture) in the centre of the enclosure, rises a high hill, or mountain, all over clad with tall wood, and so formed by nature, as if it had been cut out by art, from the summit whereof falls a cascade, seeming rather a great river than a stream precipitating into a large theatre of water, representing an exact and perfect rainbow, when the sun shines out.*
>
> (John Evelyn)[20]

> *A baroque villa without water is almost unthinkable ... At the Villa Aldobrandini the water appears high at the top in an untamed, natural setting as a* fontanone rustico*; it falls*

straight down between hemispherical boulders, gathers, falls again over a high wall into a pool, disappears and reappears, alternates again between falling and gathering in a pool. Now the structure becomes more definite: the water falls again over a wavy, sharply inclined ramp, and finally the cascade appears as the centrepiece of the teatro behind the villa.

(Heinrich Wölfflin)[21]

Villa Garzoni, 1652

The villa provides an ornamented Baroque spectacle in a bucolic valley, with its garden standing apart from the house and its medieval village. Guests reached the garden by walking through shady woods from the house. They burst into the glare of the mid-seventeenth century at the top of an axial cascade. False perspective on the cascade exaggerates its length when seen from above and its drama when seen from below: it narrows as it descends. A heroic terracotta statue of Fame waves gaily from the upper garden. Behind her is a bath-house which once had a music room and every kind of luxury for male and female bathers. They could chatter without, it is said, being able to

7.46 a, b Villa Garzoni, Italy.

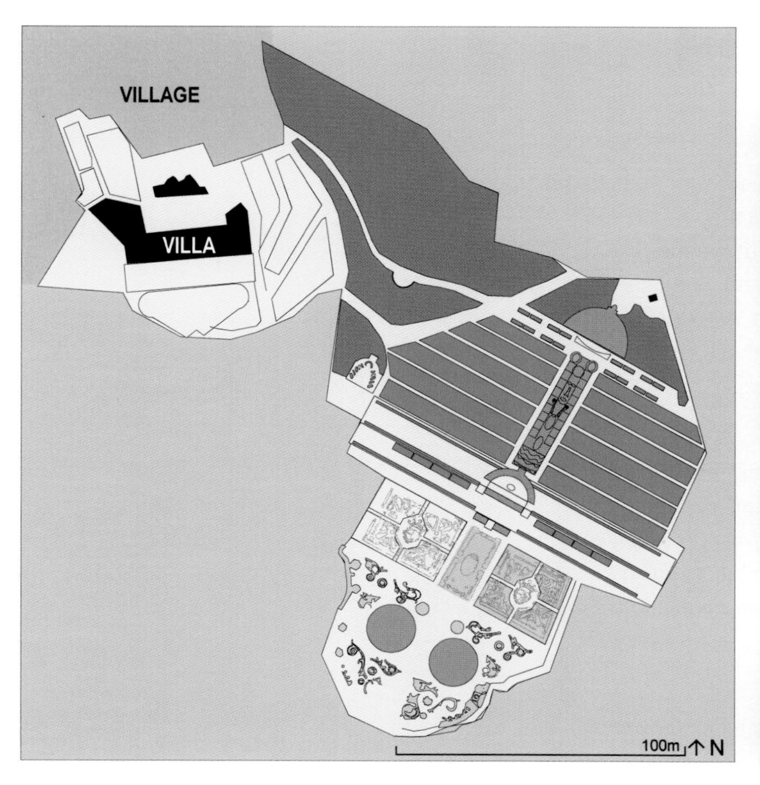

see one another. The cascade flows down the terraces to a semi-circular parterre. The garden design reveals itself to passers-by in the valley below, unlike a secluded Medici garden.

> *Here ... is one of the most spectacular baroque gardens of Italy, whose layout makes the fullest use of a precipitous hillside site in a manner that is usually associated with Rome.*
>
> (Georgina Masson)[22]

Isola Bella, 1630

A small rocky island in Lake Maggiore is wholly occupied by the Borromeo villa and its garden extravaganza. Local legend relates that the Borromeo ladies asked the Count to build the house on an island so that they would not have to listen to the screams of prisoners in the dungeons of his mainland castle. Like a flower-strewn barge, the island appears to drift among the snow-capped mountains of the lake, belying the gruesome motivation behind its creation, and the labour involved in transporting the soil and stone to the site. Isola Bella uses the lake and mountains as garden ornaments in a vast

7.47 Isola Bella, Italy.

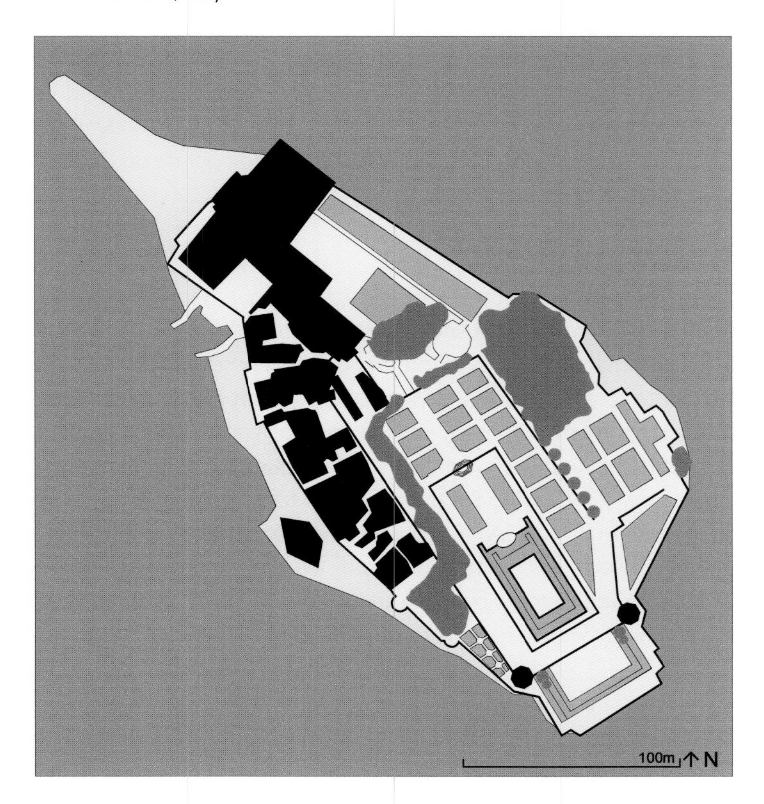

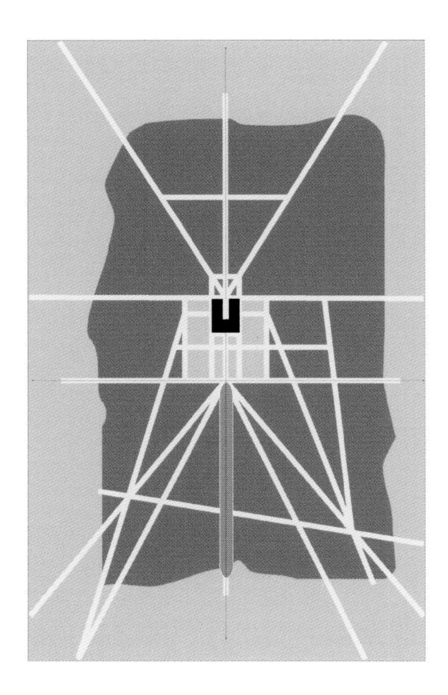

7.48 High Baroque garden.

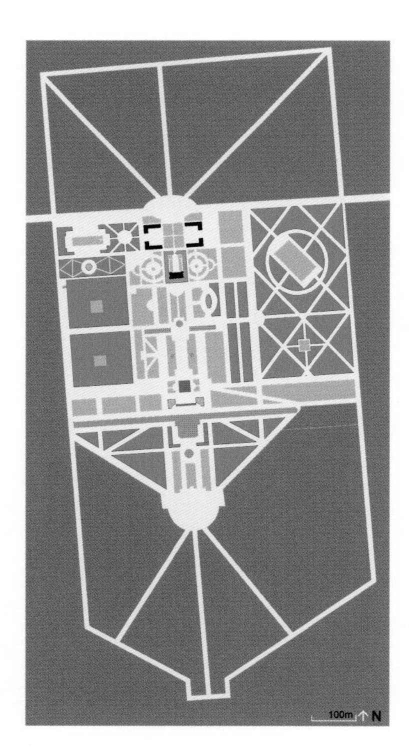

7.49 Vaux-le-Vicomte, France.

composition: axes join the house to the scenery. The stepped terraces remind one of painters' interpretations of the Hanging Gardens of Babylon.

> *The whole island is a Mount, ascended by several Terraces and walks all set about with oranges and citron trees, the reflection from the water rendering the place very warm, at least during the summer and autumn.*[23]
>
> (John Evelyn)

High Baroque

Use: Baroque gardens became increasingly haughty, as did their owners and their guests. Estates became a physical expression of the owner's status. France was the leading country in the development of High Baroque gardens and they were associated with an autocratic style of government. The palace and garden of Versailles were freely open to gentlemen, providing they carried swords, and the crowds would part admiringly when Louis XIV made a stately progression through his park, perhaps accompanied by its designer, André Le Nôtre. The forest rides were used by hunting parties.

Form: Designers drew upon developments in mathematics and science, using 'Cartesian' geometry to lay out avenues that drew the surrounding landscape into the composition. The characteristic features of High Baroque gardens were: a centrally positioned building, extensive avenues, elaborate parterres, fountains, basins and canals. Lines of perspective integrated residential architecture, garden architecture, sculpture, fountains, cascades, planting and other features. Command of the waters was essential and in many gardens there were so many fountains that they could be operated only during a social event. These days, in gardens open to the public, they tend to operate on Sunday afternoons.

Vaux-le-Vicomte, 1656

The most elegant and geometrically harmonious of all High Baroque gardens was designed by Le Nôtre and Le Vau. Their composition is mathematically proportioned: its axial principle derives from Bramante and was recommended by André Mollet. At Vaux, the axis passes through parterres, over basins of water, and into forest compartments. Brilliant use of landform allows many surprises, yet the composition is balanced from every point of view. The estate belonged to a rich financier, Fouquet, and had many statues. Louis XIV removed them after throwing the owner into jail for being over-ambitious. Vaux was designed as a place of show, and remains splendid for a day's promenade. It was not designed, or ever used, for domestic pleasure. Vaux fell into disrepair after Fouquet's arrest. Eventually, it was restored by Henri and Achille Duchêne, after 1875. It remains a showpiece, a splendid location for a day's promenade.

> *In order to clear the ground for the castle, garden, and a proper open space round them, it was necessary for Fouquet to buy three villages, and to pull them down. The place grew with astonishing quickness over its foundations. The powerful financier had inexhaustible*

wealth at his disposal, so he pressed on the work eagerly. It is said that at times as many as eighteen thousand labourers were employed together, and the cost was computed at sixteen million livres.[24]

(Marie-Luise Gothein)[24]

Plans and aerial views of Vaux do little to advance our understanding; like all Le Nôtre's compositions it has to be seen on the ground. And it takes time; it cannot be seen at a glance; it grows in the mind.

(Kenneth Woodbridge)[25]

In some of the great French gardens, at Vaux and Versailles for example, one is conscious, under all the beauty, of the immense effort expended, of the vast upheavals of earth, the forced creating of effects.

(Edith Wharton)[26]

Versailles, 1661

Versailles was conceived as a palatial centre of government for an absolute monarch, Louis XIV. It is the prime example of the French Baroque style, and has the most famous garden in the world. Andre Le Nôtre worked on the design from 1661 to 1700. Yet

7.50 Versailles, France.

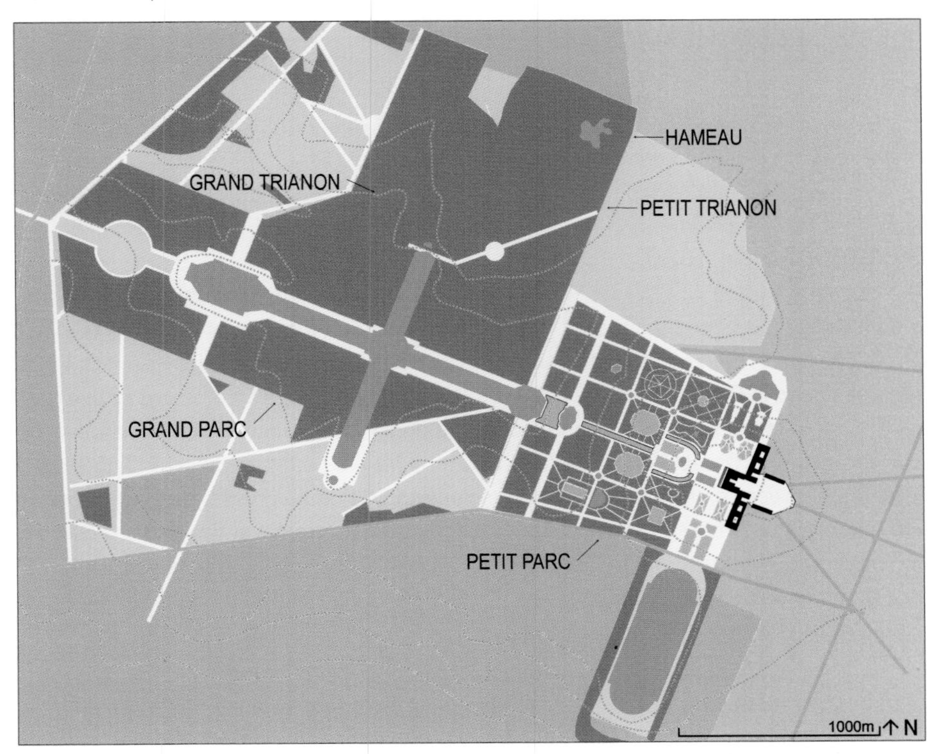

'garden' is scarcely the right designation. The scale is monumental and there is no sense of enclosure. Nor is it a friendly place: 'overbearing' is a common English response to this site, and critics have often been disenchanted. Horace Walpole saw Versailles as 'the gardens of a great child'.[27] Andre Le Nôtre worked on the estate from 1661 to 1700. Avenues project ever-outward to distant horizons, integrating the royal palace with the town, the parterres, the forest and the hoped-for empire. There are great basins, immaculate parterres, an orangery, a vast collection of outdoor sculpture and some of the grandest fountains ever made.

> *When Versailles became the official residence of the court, the gardens lost any privacy they may have had, and became an instrument of propaganda demonstrating to all Europe the superiority of French gardening. Louis himself wrote instructions on how tours should be conducted.*
>
> (Kenneth Woodbridge)[28]

> *Gray the poet was struck with their splendour when filled with company, and when the water-works were in full action. Lord Kaimes says only they would tempt one to believe that nature was below the notice of a great monarch, and therefore monsters must be created for him, as being more astonishing productions. Bradley says 'Versailles is the sum of every thing that has been done in gardening.' Agricola, a German author, declares that the sight of Versailles gave him a foretaste of Paradise. Our opinion coincides with Gray's: 'Such symmetry' as Lord Byron observes, 'is not for solitude.'*
>
> (John Claudius Loudon)[29]

> *The palace of Versailles ... is not in the least striking: I view it without emotion: the impression it makes is nothing.*
>
> (Arthur Young)[30]

Drottningholm, 1680

The summer palace of Sweden's royal family stands on an island in Lake Mälaren, known as the Island of the Queen. Hedwig Eleonora was the wife of one warrior king, Charles X, and the grandmother of another, Charles XII. The garden is thought to have been designed in France under Le Nôtre's supervision but, like all the best Baroque gardens, it exploits the surrounding landscape. The design 'embodied in stone the ideals of Sweden's Age of Greatness'. The prime axis runs from a harbour with a landing stage. Behind the palace lie elegant Baroque parterres and an avenue pressing into the woods. The garden is ornamented with sculpture taken as booty from the Wallenstein garden in Prague and Frederiksborg in Denmark. A Chinese summer house was built in 1753, as a birthday present for another queen, Louisa Ulrika (1720–1782). Drottningholm has examples of Baroque, Rococo and Romantic taste.

> *Hedwig Eleonora ... found a medieval castle on one of the islands in Lake Mälaren, and she began to make alterations in 1661. This castle also stood on a raised terrace, and its*

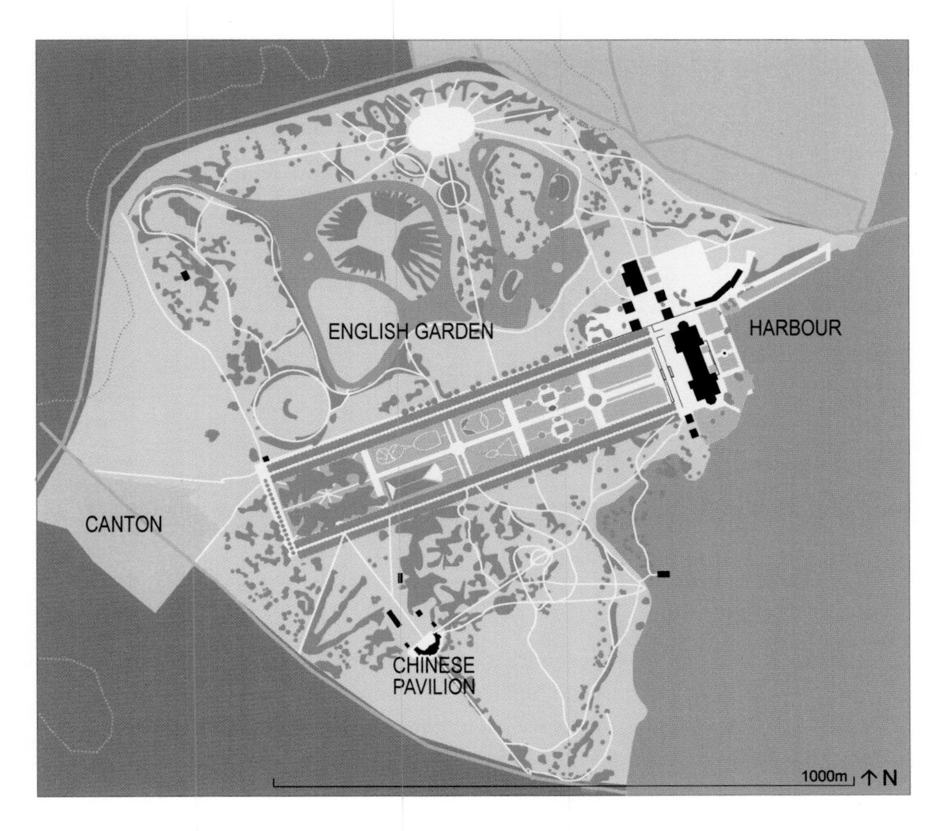

7.51 Drottningholm, Sweden.

> *approach was by water from an oval-shaped harbour. The garden lay towards the south, and showed the influence of Versailles more than any other in Sweden; its fine parterre was laid out in patterns of box, with a border of clipped trees and flowers. In the centre, steps in the open mount up by a wide middle walk to a basin with a Hercules fountain.*
>
> (Marie-Luise Gothein)[31]

Peterhof, 1716

Russia's most important Baroque garden, attached to Peter the Great's summer palace, was inspired by Versailles and designed by Jean-Baptiste Le Blond, a pupil of Le Nôtre. There is a good water supply and the palace stands on a natural terrace overlooking the Baltic. A fabled marble cascade lined with gilded statues flows from the palace to the sea, along the Samson canal (see Figure 7.37). It symbolises Russia's conquest of the Baltic coast in the Great Northern War. One hundred and seventy-three fountains line the canal and ornament the woods. On the south front of the palace are parterres, allées, grass plots, basins, fountains and statues. Like St Petersburg itself, the Peterhof is a symbol of Peter's desire to build Russia into a sophisticated European power:

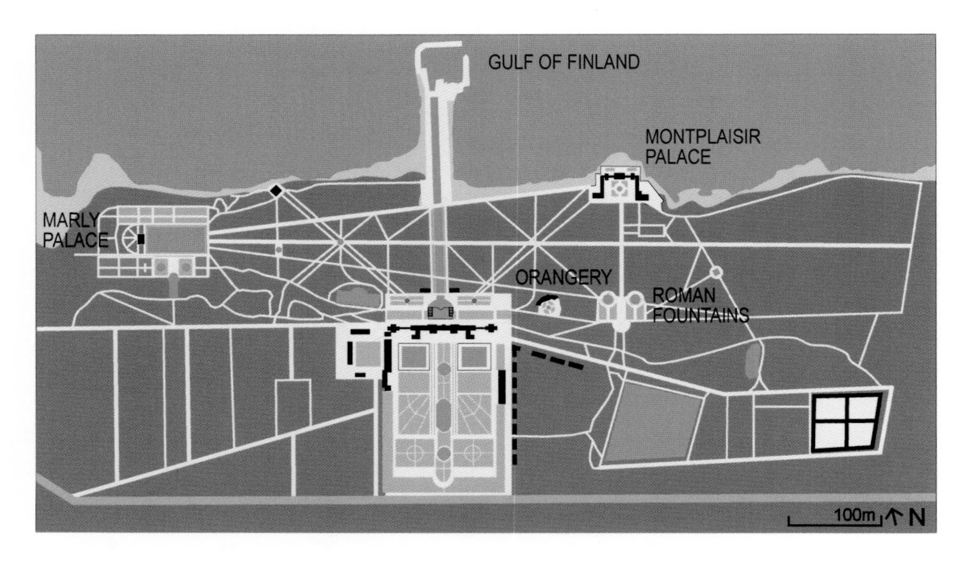

7.52 Peterhof, Russia.

> *Peterhof, in respect to situation, is perhaps unrivalled. About five hundred fathoms from the sea-shore this region has a second cliff, almost perpendicular, near twelve fathoms high ... The declivity from the back-front of the palace towards the sea has two magnificent cascades, rolling their streams over the terraces into large basins, and beneath which the visitor may walk as under a vault, without receiving wet, into a beautiful grotto.*
>
> (John Claudius Loudon)[32]

> *Every night during the festival the gardens of the palace were illuminated, Russians said that there were ten millions of lamps ... rows of lamps were placed, over which the fluid rushed from the cascade like a shower of diamonds, whilst the flashing lights beneath had an indescribably brilliant effect; the fine bronze figures untarnished glittered like statues of gold in the rays of thousands of beaming stars.*
>
> (Anonymous, 1855)[33]

CHAPTER 8

Neoclassical and Romantic gardens, 1700–1810

8.0 Classical landscapes became symbols of the Enlightenment, as in Catherine the Great's garden at Tsarskoe Selo.

8.1 a–d The Rococo aspects of Sanssouci provide the best indication of how gardens might have evolved if a radical departure from the Baroque had not occurred.

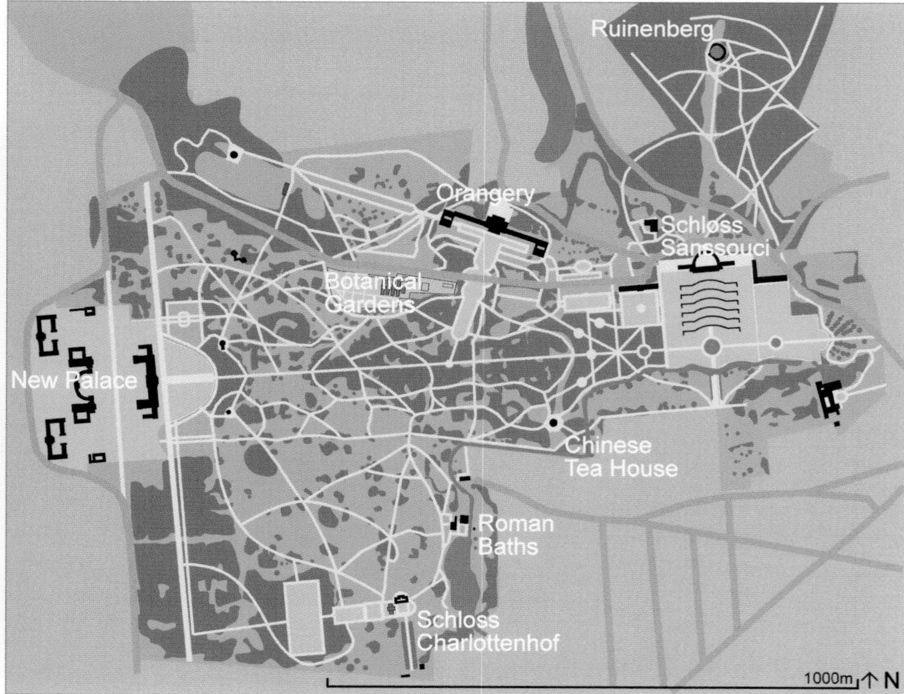

History and philosophy

Even in the Protestant countries, Baroque gardens continued to be made during the eighteenth century. But a radically different style also became established, eventually described as the landscape garden. Historians enjoy tracing its origins. There are many candidates for the role of prime cause and it is unlikely that agreement will ever be reached. The position I took in 1986 was that the departure resulted from a coalition of six key ideas: empiricism, Neoplatonism, constitutional democracy, landscape painting, rural retirement and Chinese gardens.[1] I now view empiricism as the prime minister and rationalism as the finance minister.

The role of political parties in representing coalitions of interest was devised in the eighteenth century and came to be regarded as the most reasonable and natural form of government. Conversely, the divine right of kings to stand above the law, taxing, imprisoning and torturing their subjects, came to be seen as unreasonable, unenlightened and unnatural. Paintings of idealised landscapes incorporating Classical subjects were admired as representations of a harmonious calm between mankind, nature and the gods. Therefore Roman ruins were venerated. Men dreamed that adherence to natural law would allow god-fearing shepherds, charming shepherdesses, landed improvers and rational gentlefolk to enjoy peace on earth. The English Civil War had given the leading political theorist of his day, Thomas Hobbes, personal experience of a 'state of nature' with 'a condition of war of everyone against everyone' and with the life of man 'solitary, poor, nasty, brutish and short'.[2] Advocates of the new style planned for a better world, symbolised by ideal landscapes adorned with Classical figures. The four phases in the development of these ideal landscapes will be categorised as Augustan, Serpentine, Picturesque and Landscape, with the fourth of these phases discussed in the next chapter. These phases were influenced by the Enlightenment response to the Baroque, known as Neoclassicism, and by the growth of the Romantic movement.

The term 'English landscape garden' does not place the new ideas in an art-historical context. Opinions vary as to which of the categories of eighteenth-century art – Neoclassical, Rococo and Romantic – provides the most appropriate label for the new movement in garden design. Bazin, whose precise summary of the Baroque was quoted at the start of the previous chapter, sees the landscape garden as 'in fact the principal contribution of Great Britain to the Rococo style'.[3] Gombrich associates the new style with the Classicism of Claude and Palladio.[4] Pevsner sees it as 'a truly Romantic conception'.[5] Jansen (with whom I agree) identifies the artistic parents of the new approach as Classicism and Romanticism:

> *Long regarded as opposites, the two seem today so interdependent that one name would serve for both, if we could find it. ('Romantic Classicism,' which has been proposed, has not won wide acceptance.) The two terms are too unevenly matched – like 'quadruped'*

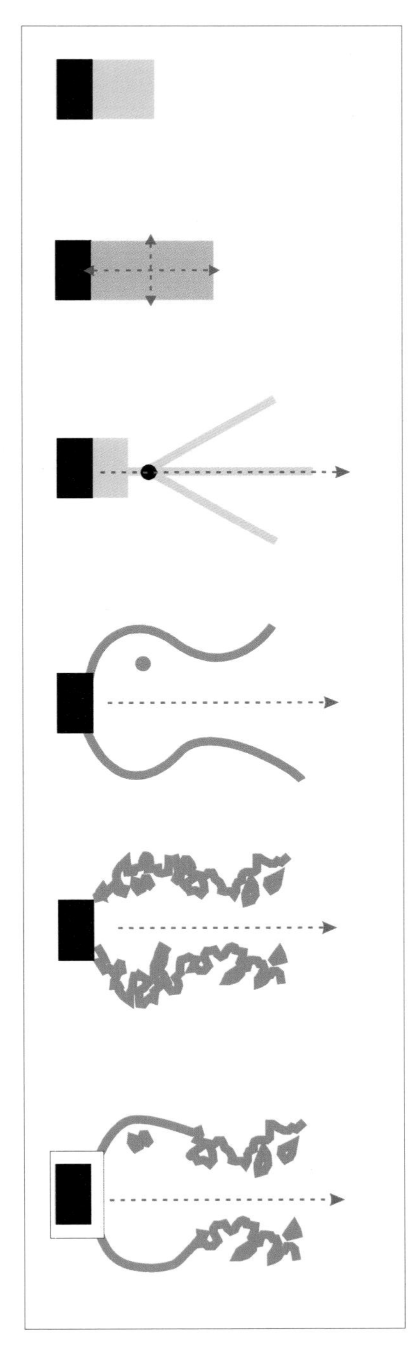

8.2 Thumbnail diagrams showing the geometrical evolution of garden plans after the Renaissance.

8.3 a, b, c Chiswick House and park, designed by Lord Burlington and William Kent, is a statement to their love for Classical landscapes in general and Palladio's Villa Rotunda in particular.

> *and 'carnivore.' Neoclassicism means a new revival of Classical antiquity, more consistent than earlier classicisms, while Romanticism refers to an attitude of mind that may reveal itself in any number of ways. The word derives from the late-eighteenth-century vogue for medieval tales of adventure (such as the legends of King Arthur or the Holy Grail, called 'romances' because they were written in a Romance language, not in Latin).*[6]

The first work discussed in Part 4 of Jansen's *History of Art* is Chiswick House in London, inspired by an Italian architect's vision of the ancient world. Andrea Palladio (1508–1580) was inspired by reading Vitruvius and sketching Roman ruins. He developed a simple Classicism which appealed equally to the wealthy farmers who were his clients and, two centuries later, to their English counterparts. Landowning farmers in the Veneto and in England wanted open views of their fields uncluttered by expensive gardens and Renaissance frippery.[7] Claude Lorrain (1600–1682), who has 'at all times been considered the greatest of landscape painters',[8] drew antique and ideal landscapes. The mythological scenes identified by his titles are 'the primordial element, from which the entire composition is conceived'[9] and, in the greatest of his paintings, the themes were drawn from Greek myths told in the *Metamorphoses* of Ovid or of Apuleius. Claude depicted a Romantically Classical world adorned with temples and populated by gods, heroes, shepherds and shepherdesses.

Claude's world drew upon the landscapes of Greece and Rome, but not from their gardens. Comparing his paintings with the quotations from Homer in Chapter 3 reveals this: we see no walled cities, palace courtyards or productive gardens with 'beautifully

8.4 Claude Lorrain's *Landscape with the Father of Psyche Sacrificing at the Temple of Apollo* (1662) reveals his interest in mythology, architecture and Classical landscapes.

arranged beds of flowers that are in bloom all the year round' (*Odyssey* Book VIII). Instead, Claude painted antique landscapes with sacred groves and mythological events which resonate with their Indo-European heritage. The subject of Claude's *Landscape with the Father of Psyche Sacrificing at the Temple of Apollo* (1662; Figure 8.4) comes from Apuleius. Venus, jealous of Psyche's wonderful beauty, asked Cupid to make her fall in love with a detestable man. Psyche's father learned of his daughter's fate at an altar outside a temple in a grove sacred to Apollo. In Renaissance Italy the story was given a Neoplatonic interpretation. It became an 'account of the progress of the soul in its search for, and ultimate union with, divine Beauty'.[10] Such were the scenes Claude painted. Many are their delights.

The respective roles of gardens and groves were as separate in the ancient world as they became in eighteenth-century Europe. Though not without a spiritual dimension, the primary roles of French Baroque estates were courtly gatherings and deer hunting. The roles of English landscapes were agricultural and, at a spiritual level, to provide a balm for the soul. In his *Essay … on the Use of Studying Pictures, for the Purpose of Improving Real Landscape* (1794), Sir Uvedale Price wrote:

> *The peculiar beauty of the most beautiful of all landscape painters is characterised by* il riposo di Claudio, *and when the mind of man is in the delightful state of repose, of which*

8.5 *Il riposo di Claudio*, with Duns Castle in the middle ground.

> *Claude's pictures are the image – when he feels that mild and equal sunshine of the soul which warms and cheers, but neither inflames nor irritates – his heart seems to dilate with happiness, he is disposed to every act of kindness and benevolence, to love and cherish all around him.*[11]

Kenneth Clark described this as 'the most enchanting dream which has ever consoled mankind'.[12] Imagine stepping out from a frenzied baroque ballroom to view the sun setting over a valley and stars appearing in the night sky: this contrast represents the psychological divide between Baroque gardens and landscape gardens. Inside, everything is sprightly. Outside, the soul yearns to fathom the mysterious yet ordered nature of the universe with whatever help can be obtained from reason, imagination, empirical observation or the lips of one's partner. Landscape gardens evolved during the eight-

8.6 a, b The Temple of Eternity at Bomarzo, in Italy, and the Venus Vale at Rousham, in England, have a shared ancestry in the sacred groves of ancient Greece and Rome.

eenth century, in step with the progression from Neoclassicism to Romanticism. The closest forebear of Chiswick House, artistically, conceptually and chronologically, is the Sacro Bosco which Duke Vincino Orsini made in the valley beneath the walled city of Bomarzo (see pp. 211–12). I would like to know whether the designers of Chiswick House knew this place.

There is a tendency for British garden historians to view the inception of the landscape garden through the distorting glass of patriotism. Plucky British designers, they say, spurned autocracy and, motivated by high ideals drawn from poetry, painting, reason, nature and democracy, originated a glorious new style which conquered first Britain, then Europe and then the world. French historians like Bazin, tend to see matters through a different lens, finding *le style Anglo-Chinois* to be an effete scion of the Baroque, pushing out baleful tentacles from the long shadow of Chinese art.

The characteristic which landscape gardens unquestionably shared with Baroque gardens, and Classical art, was dependence on the axiom, derived from Plato's Theory of Forms, that 'art should *imitate* nature'. It is embodied in the following quotations:

- Aristotle: 'Epic poetry, tragedy, comedy, lyric poetry … are, in the most general view of them, modes of imitation.'[13]
- Cicero: 'I follow Nature, the best of guides, as I would a god.'[14]
- Plotinus: 'What is beyond the intellectual principle we affirm to be the nature of Good radiating beauty before it.'[15]
- Du Fresnoy: 'A learned Painter should form to himself an Idea of perfect Nature.'[16]
- Dézallier d'Arganville: 'If one wishes to lay out a garden it must be borne in mind that one must stay closer to nature than to art.'[17]

- Salmon: 'The work of the painter is to express the exact imitation of natural things; wherein you are to observe the excellencies and beauties of the piece, but to refuse its vices.'[18]
- Temple: 'Greater sums may be thrown away without effect or honour, if there want sense in proportion to money, or if Nature be not followed; which I take to be the great rule in this, and perhaps in everything else.'[19]
- Pope: 'First follow NATURE, and your Judgment frame/By her just Standard, which is still the same.'[20]
- Walpole: 'Kent ... had followed nature, and imitated her so happily, that he began to think all her works were equally proper for imitation.'[21]
- Reynolds: 'The great style in art, and the most perfect imitation of nature, consists in avoiding the details and peculiarities of particular objects.'[22]
- Dryden: 'Those things, which delight all ages, must have been an imitation of Nature.'[23]
- Downing: 'By Landscape Gardening, we understand not only an imitation, in the grounds of a country residence, of the agreeable forms of nature, but an expressive, harmonious, and refined imitation.'[24]

What did change in eighteenth-century England was the predominant interpretation of the axiom. 'Nature', in Neoclassical art theory, meant the world of the universal forms. In Romantic art theory, 'Nature' meant the world of the particulars. It was a change from the '*nature* of the world' to the 'world of *nature*'. The period 1780–1830 saw the flood tide of Romanticism, but the movement began softly, rose to a torrent, and subsided gradually, leaving permanent tidemarks on the world's psyche. This chapter deals first with England and then with other parts of Europe.

Pre-1700

According to Pevsner, European Romanticism began with a hint from Sir William Temple:

> *What I have said of the best forms of gardens, is meant only of such as are in some sort regular; for there may be other forms wholly irregular, that may, for ought I know, have more beauty than any of the others ... something of this I have seen in some places, but heard more of it from others, who have lived much among the Chinese; a people, whose way of thinking seems to lie as wide of ours in Europe, as their country does.*[25]

Using vivid purple ink, Pevsner wrote that:

> *This passage is one of the most amazing in the English language. It started a line of thought and visual conceptions which were to dominate first England and then the World for two centuries. It is the first suggestion ever of a possible beauty fundamentally different from the formal, a beauty of irregularity and fancy.*[26]

Pevsner specifically identified a winding stream south-east of Temple's walled garden at Moor Park, outside Farnham in Surrey, as the first hint of Romanticism in the visual arts (see Figure 8.7). After being involved as a diplomat in the murky religious wars of the

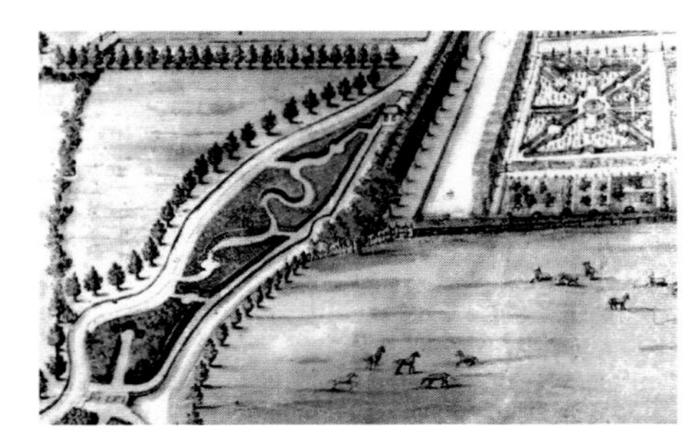

8.7 a, b According to Pevsner, Moor Park in Surrey was the first designed landscape to have a deliberately serpentine line.

seventeenth century, Temple retired to Moor Park to reflect on his experience of life, to compose some of the best English essays of the period and to cultivate his garden. He had two Classical predecessors: Horace, who withdrew from the civil strife of Rome to savour the pleasures of country life, and Epicurus, the Greek philosopher who withdrew to a 'grove of academe' (see p. 112) to teach the value of simple pleasures as compared with the deceits of glory and power. Temple's essay *Upon the Gardens of Epicurus* may have been in Voltaire's thoughts when he had Candide conclude, '*il faut cultiver notre jardin*' ('we must cultivate our garden'), in the sense of 'mind our own affairs'.

1700–1750

The advance of Romanticism, which saw enclosed gardens evolve into open landscapes, was traced with great skill by Christopher Hussey.[27] An early step was the layout of estates in what Switzer described as a 'forest style',[28] using the geometry of the Baroque but for a life of rural retreat and practical husbandry. The next steps were pragmatic acceptances of landscape features: the retention of Wray Wood and the design of Henderskelf Lane, both at Castle Howard. Hussey commented that the low hill on which they lie is 'historic ground, since it became the turning-point of garden design not only at Castle Howard but in England'.[29]

In 1700, Wray Wood was a stand of mature beech trees on a low hill east of Castle Howard. George London and Stephen Switzer were advising Lord Carlisle on the layout of his estate. London wished to drive an avenue along the north front of Castle Howard and then up the hill to make Wray Wood a star of Baroque avenues. Switzer

8.8 Cirencester Park is the best example of the Forest style of estate layout. It has radiating avenues but was a forestry project.

8.9 a, b, c Castle Howard represents a Classical landscape, with a temple, a mausoleum, an obelisk, a Roman bridge, 'city' walls, a pyramid and even a long straight Roman road with triumphal arches.

8.10 Instead of driving into Wray Wood, the straight path in front of Castle Howard swings south on the empirical line of Henderskelf Lane.

8.11 Henderskelf Lane at Castle Howard (**a**) and the terraces at Duncombe (**b**) and Rievaulx (**c**) are classic examples of the serpentine line.

8.12 The Serpentine in London takes its name from its serpentine curve.

8.13 a, b Rousham has England's most perfect example of a serpentine line.

wrote, in 1718, that George London's proposal 'would have spoil'd the Wood, but that his Lordship's superlative genius prevented it'.[30] Wray Wood was retained and furnished with labyrinthine paths and waterworks to make what Switzer judged an 'incomparable Wood the highest pitch that Natural and Polite Gardening can possibly ever arrive to'. Hussey suggests that since Switzer was an expert in waterworks, it may in fact have been he, rather than Lord Carlisle, who had the 'superlative' notion of conserving Wray Wood. If so, it was an elegant way of clothing a boast in flattery of a patron.

Henderskelf Lane is the path which skirts the southern flank of Wray Wood and joins Castle Howard to the Temple of the Four Winds. This ancient track, according to the logic of the Baroque, should have been straightened or eliminated (Figure 8.10). Instead, it was made into a serpentine walk commanding a prospect of the Neoclassical landscape which Lord Carlisle created. Henderskelf Lane has a family resemblance with the serpentine grass terrace at nearby Duncombe. Its owner had married a member of the Howard family and planned to extend the terrace for three miles along the hillside to join a third serpentine walk, made at Rievaulx in the 1740s – a very Romantic conception.

8.14 Middleton Place in Virginia belongs to the same group as Rousham and Studley Royal.

Some of the other famous steps in the evolution of landscape gardens are as follows:

- Vanbrugh's proposal, which was rejected, for saving £1000 by keeping Old Woodstock Manor in Blenheim Park as a picturesque feature in the view. It was also a historic site, home to Henry I and birthplace of the Black Prince.
- The acceptance of site irregularities at Bramham Park, Yorkshire, to create a garden axis independent of the house axis.
- Formation of the irregular grove at Melbourne, Derbyshire, which Hussey describes as 'the classic example in England of the first movement away

8.15 a, b Stourhead and Studley Royal have a Classical perfection.

from an entirely regular conception of garden-design which eventually led to landscape'[31] (as at Bramham, the axis of the garden was not related to the house axis).

- The use of the accidental diagonal provided by an old lane at Stowe, Buckinghamshire, to form the 'Great Cross Lime Walk' (it crosses at 70° instead of the usual 90°).
- Extensive use of the ha-ha (sunk fence) at Stowe to bring the view of the countryside into the garden.
- Charles Bridgeman's design for joining up a series of small ponds in Hyde Park, London to form the large lake which is known, eponymously, as 'the Serpentine' (Figure 8.12).

Each of these examples marks a progression from:

- regularity to irregularity;
- rationalism to empiricism;
- Neoclassicism to Romanticism;
- formal (in the Platonic sense) to informal (in the Romantic sense).

A remark by A.O. Lovejoy, read by Frank Clark to his class of 1969, inspired the above analysis and my approach to the analysis of gardens:

> *In one of its aspects that many-sided thing called Romanticism may not inaccurately be described as a conviction that the world is an* englischer Garten *on a grand scale.*

8.16 The Grecian Vale at Stowe is an eighteenth-century 'sacred grove', and all the more interesting for not being described as Roman. One can imagine a grove peopled by young athletes outside the walls of Athens.

> *The God of the seventeenth century, like its gardeners, always geometrized; the God of Romanticism was one in whose universe things grew wild and without trimming and in all the diversity of their natural shapes.*[32]

Some of the best eighteenth-century English gardens were made under the auspices of both Gods. Duncombe Park, Yorkshire (1713–1750), Studley Royal, Yorkshire (1715–1730), Rousham, Oxfordshire (1726–1739), Stourhead, Wiltshire (1726–1739), and Middleton Place, South Carolina, USA (1741) are brilliant examples of the way in which a classically-ordered concept, rich in allegory, can develop from an imaginative response to the genius of a place. The Latin phrase *genius loci* meaning 'the guardian spirit of a place' probably derives from the animist and Indo-European idea that places are inhabited by forces or spirits or gods. English designers used 'genius of the place' to mean 'the essential character of a place', but were pleased to erect statues of Greek and Roman gods in their Romantically Classical groves.

1750–1783

These dates cover the independent career of Lancelot 'Capability' Brown. Brown's career reached a peak in the 1770s and he died, in 1783, the most celebrated landscape and garden designer of the eighteenth century. Then the criticism began. By 1793, his reputation was besmirched – and remained so until he was reassessed and then rescued by Marie-Luise Gothein after 1913. Brown was then restored, like a pagan statue, to an honoured place in the sacred grove of garden heroes.

In 1751, Brown had been head gardener at Stowe for ten years and had seen great works executed under the overall direction of William Kent. It is thought that Brown and Kent

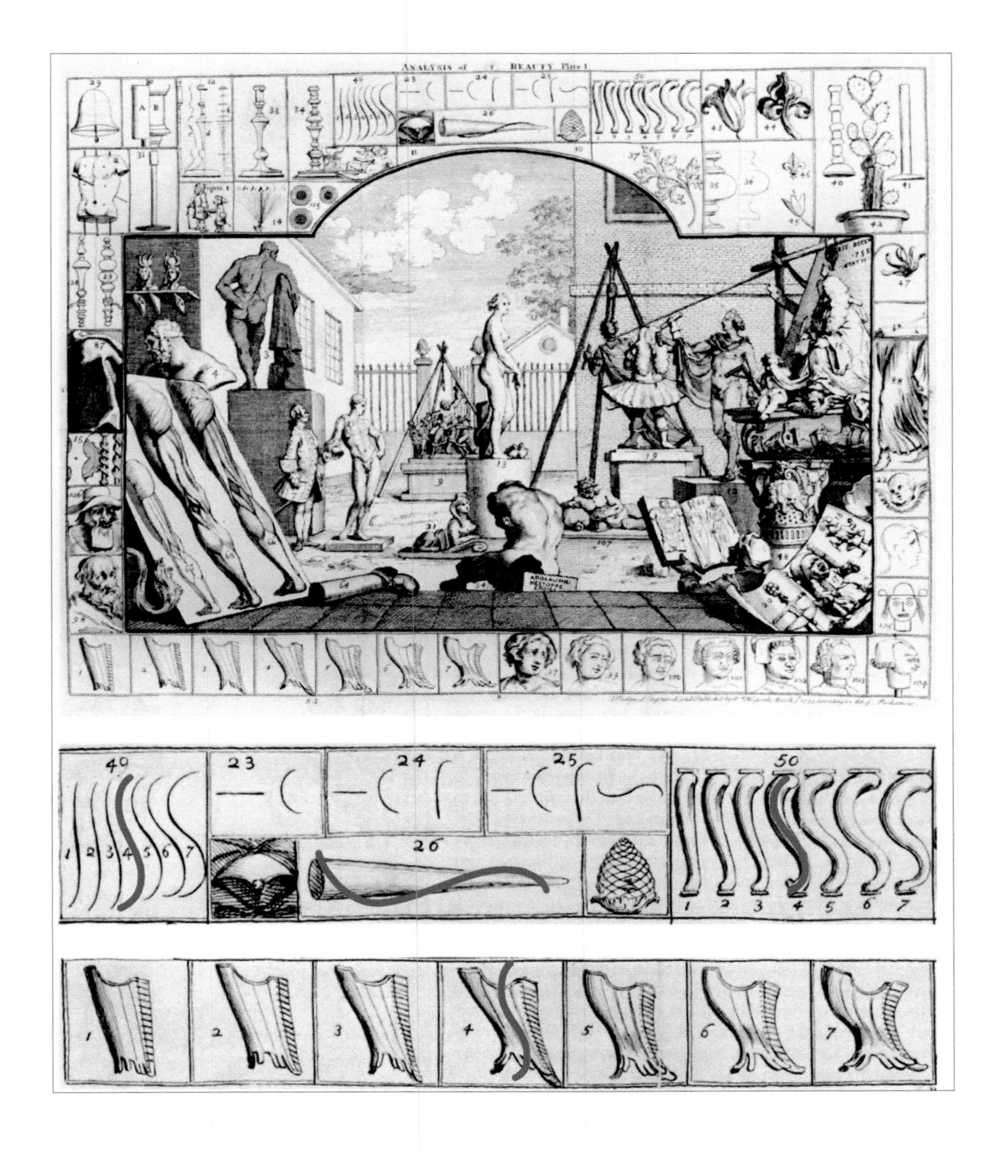

8.17 Hogarth's line of beauty, marked by red lines.

were jointly responsible for the Grecian Vale, one of the last projects at Stowe. It had classical overtones but was executed with more feeling for the composition of landform and woods than is shown in Kent's drawings for other projects. Serpentine lines became Brown's trademark after he left Stowe. He was not averse to the occasional temple, when it improved the composition, but there is no reason to think he had any taste for allegory, symbolism or the landscapes of antiquity. One could describe his style as nature-like, or nature-esque.

During the 32 years of his career as an independent designer Brown's style hardly changed. The characteristic features of his work are circular clumps of trees, a grassy

8.18 a, b Lancelot Brown used earthworks and planting to convert the surroundings of Alnwick Castle into a serpentine park.

meadow in front of the house, a serpentine lake, an enclosing belt of trees and an encircling carriage drive. Hussey remarks that Brown was 'a practical man in the grip of a theory'.[33] The diagram (Figure 8.60, p. 307) shows the theory. Brown's interest in serpentine shapes was quickly recognised, and comparisons were drawn between Hogarth's line of beauty, the outline of a woman's body and a Brownian park. The editor of *The World* wrote, in 1753, that 'a young lady of the most graceful figure I ever beheld' came to London

> *'To have her shape altered to the modern fashion'. That is to say, to have her breasts compressed by a flat straight line. I protest, when I saw the beautiful figure that was to be so deformed by the stay maker, I was as much shocked, as if I had been told that she was come to deliver up those animated knowls of beauty to the surgeon – I borrow my terms from gardening, which now indeed furnishes the most pregnant and exalted expressions of any science in being. And this brings to mind the only instance that can give an adequate idea of my concern. Let us suppose that Mr Brown should, in any one of the many Elysiums he has made, see the old terraces rise again and mask his undulating knowls, or straight rows of trees obscure his noblest configurations of scenery.*[34]

The comparison between serpentine lines and women's stays comes from Hogarth's *Analysis of Beauty*, first published in 1753.[35] Hogarth observed 'an elegant degree of plumpness to the skin of the softer sex', and drew diagrams to show how closely an ideal stay resembles the line of beauty. The beautiful Lady Luxborough, banished by her boorish husband to his Warwickshire estate near a celebrated *ferme ornée* (The

Leasowes – see p. 278) borrowed a copy of the book. In her correspondence with the owner of The Leasowes, the poet and gardener William Shenstone, she envied the shape of the letter with which Shenstone's name began, regretting that 'I have not now an S in my name to claim any share in it.'

Dorothy Stroud attributes 211 designs for English parks to Brown. A surprisingly large number of his landscapes remain in good condition, often because they have been adapted to modern use as public parks, farms, golf courses and schools. The best of them are magnificent, probably more so today than when they were seen by Brown's critics in the 1790s. My favourites are the Arcadian glade at Prior Park, Somerset, the Grecian Vale at Stowe, the lakes at Luton Hoo, Sherbourne Castle, Blenheim Park, the embankment outside Alnwick Castle, the riverside scenery at Chatsworth, Derbyshire, and the grand views at Petworth, Sussex and Harewood, Yorkshire, which J.M.W. Turner loved to paint. Many other Brownian designs are disappointing, possibly because they were not fully implemented or have not been maintained.

Some of Brown's other designs are so 'natural' and so 'English' that it is difficult to appreciate them without a survey of the pre-existing site and a plan of the executed works. His lakes sit in comfortable depressions, his woods clothe hills which would resist the plough and his green pastures roll to the rhythm of the English countryside. A large collection of Brown's professional papers, which might have provided more information on what he actually did, was given to Repton by Brown's son and subsequently disappeared.

8.19 Petworth has a classic serpentine lake.

8.20 a, b, c Shenstone's ornamental farm, now a golf course, had fields, ponds, a grotto and seats with poetic inscriptions. The seat was part of a restoration scheme and the poem was supplied by the photographer.

A variant of the Serpentine style, known as the *ferme ornée*, is of particular interest to historians of rural retirement. Maren-Sofie Røstvig comments that 'Instead of penning yet another version of Horace's second epode, Southcote translated the literary ideal into a living reality'[36] at Woburn Farm (*c.*1735). It was a working farm ornamented with trees, shrubs and temples. 'Ideal farm' would be a good description. In 1746, a poet and gardener, William Shenstone, called his estate at The Leasowes a *ferme ornée*, but he did not include the term in his 1764 classification of garden types. This may be because he had read Burke's argument that beauty does not arise from utility. Burke observed that the wedge-like snout of a pig and the bared teeth of a wolf are useful but not beautiful.

Horace Walpole's essay *On Modern Gardening* (1780) was brilliant, witty, short and misleading. It ends with the tongue-in-cheek remark that his successors should 'observe *as strict* impartiality' (my italics): Walpole was the relentlessly partisan son of an outstanding Whig politician. Hunt writes that: 'Walpole's achievement has to be saluted all the more when it is realized that single-handedly he determined (or distorted) the writing of landscape architecture history to this day.'[37] The distortion of most concern is revealed by this famous passage:

> *But the capital stroke, the leading step to all that, has followed, was (I believe the first thought was Bridgeman's) the destruction of walls for boundaries, and the invention of fosses – an attempt then deemed so astonishing, that the common people called them Ha! Ha's! to express their surprise at finding a sudden and unperceived check to their walk ... At that moment appeared Kent, painter enough to taste the charms of landscape, bold and opinionative enough to dare and to dictate, and born with a genius to strike out a great system from the twilight of imperfect essays. He leaped the fence, and saw that all nature was a garden ... Kent, like other reformers, knew not how to stop at the just limits. He had*

followed nature, and imitated her so happily, that he began to think all her works were equally proper for imitation.[38]

In this paragraph, Walpole distorts historical fact for the convenience of his argument, as follows:

- Baroque gardens were not contained within boundaries. They reached into the surrounding landscape and were scenically integrated.
- The English did not invent 'Ha! Ha's!' Sunk retaining walls were used to allow outward views from Baroque gardens.
- Kent did not *originate* the 'system' of 'imitating nature' – it can be traced back to Plato.

Walpole commented on Kent's successor:

It was fortunate for the country and Mr Kent, that he was succeeded by a very able master; and did living artists come within my plan, I should be glad to do justice to Mr Brown; but he may be a gainer, by being reserved for some abler pen.[39]

Saying he *may* be the gainer could be sarcasm. Always attuned to the tides of taste, Walpole may have realised that Brown's work was not 'natural' in what was becoming the 'modern' sense.

8.21 The Reverend William Gilpin awakened tourists to the scenery of the Wye Valley and the fact that its character resembled a Brownian park – but was on a grander scale and more rugged.

8.22 a, b William Hearne's engravings, from Knight's *The Landscape*, contrast the smoothness of the Serpentine style with the irregularity of the Picturesque style.

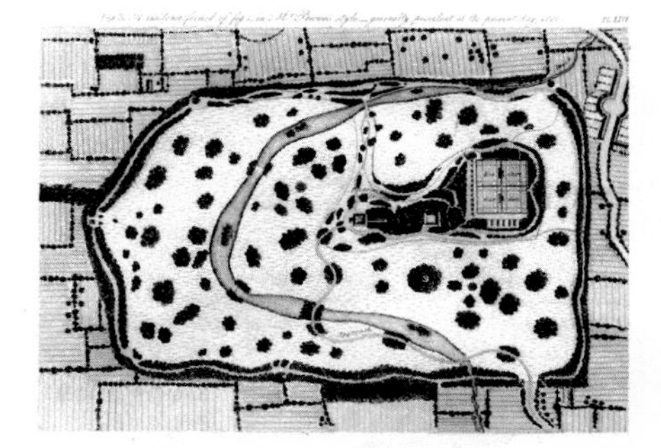

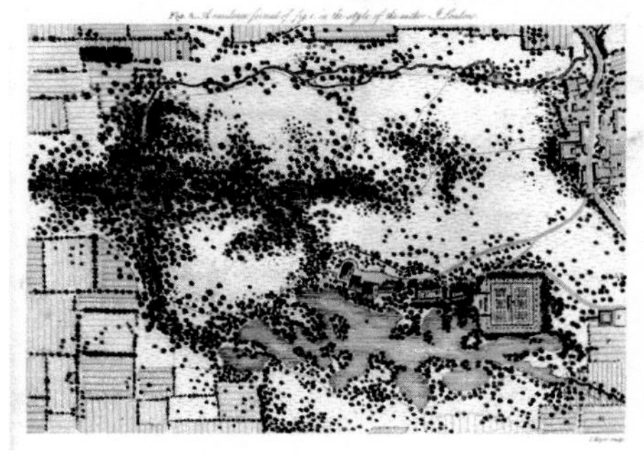

8.23 a, b Loudon's diagrams of the Serpentine and Picturesque styles, which he described as 'Mr Brown's style' and 'the style of the author, J. Loudon'.

1783–1813

It is no surprise that the next step on the road to Romanticism was taken by a vicar. Theologians, also influenced by empiricism, increasingly saw 'the wonder of creation' as being the visible world, rather than the abstract realm of the Platonic Forms. William Gilpin (1724–1804) was described as 'Master of the Picturesque and Vicar of Boldre'.[40] His essay *On Prints* (1768) and his series of Picturesque *Tours*, published between 1782 and 1809, awakened British tourists to the natural delights of the River Wye, North Wales and 'the Mountains and Lakes of Cumberland and Westmoreland'. He then wrote three *Essays* on what had become the heart of eighteenth-century garden theory: landscape painting and the appreciation of nature.[41] Gilpin reveals a passion for rough, shaggy scenery, commenting that although 'the picturesque traveller is seldom disappointed with pure nature, however rude' he is 'often offended with the productions of art' and 'frequently disgusted' by the timidity of modern gardens: 'How flat, and insipid is often the garden scene, how puerile, and absurd! The banks of the river how smooth, and parallel! The lawn, and its boundaries, how unlike nature!' For Brown's style, this was a death sentence.

Gilpin said that if a modern landscape painter were to attempt a garden scene he would need to consult Claude on how to

> *Turn the lawn into a piece of broken ground: plant rugged oaks instead of flowering shrubs: break the edges of the walk: give it the rudeness of a road: mark it with wheel-tracks; and scatter around a few stones, and brushwood; in a word, instead of making the whole smooth, make it rough; and you make it also picturesque.*[42]

8.24 A picturesque view of Downton Castle – now fronted with Reptonian terraces.

8.25 A picturesque view from the site of Uvedale Price's house at Foxley.

Sir Uvedale Price applied Gilpin's idea to landscape design in *An Essay on the Picturesque, as Compared with the Sublime and the Beautiful; and, on the Use of Studying Pictures, for the Purpose of Improving Real Landscape*. Price echoed Gilpin's opinion that 'whoever views objects with a painter's eye, looks with indifference, if not disgust, at the clumps, the belts, the made water, and the eternal smoothness and sameness of a finished place'. Price jested that Brown would consider the 'finest composition of Claude' to be 'rude and imperfect', with some 'capability' for improvement[43] – which was like saying Brown would remove the blood and nails to 'improve' a *Crucifixion*. Though Price did not argue for gardens to be wholly Sublime, in Burke's sense of 'fitted ... to excite the ideas of pain and danger',[44] his *Essay on the Picturesque* incited readers to make gardens Picturesque in the sense of rough, varied, and intricate.

Price's friend and neighbour, Richard Payne Knight, possessed the incautious hauteur of an immensely wealthy man. Downton Castle, five miles west of Ludlow in Herefordshire, was designed with a Classical interior and Gothic exterior. Then: 'large fragments of stone were irregularly thrown amongst briers and weeds, to imitate the foreground of a picture'.[45] Repton believed this to be a temporary 'experiment' but John Claudius Loudon observed their presence a decade later, adding that the rocks were 'quite unconnected with each other'.[46] Downton Vale was rich in Gilpinesque, Christian, thorns. The young Loudon was an ardent admirer of Price, Knight and Romantic irregularity. His first book told the world that:

> *I believe that I am the first who has set out as a landscape gardener, professing to follow Mr Price's principles. How far I shall succeed in executing my plans, and introducing more of the picturesque into improved places, time alone must determine.*[47]

8.26 Like other circular temples, the design of St Bernard's Well, built in Edinburgh in 1789, relates to the Temples of Vesta in Tivoli (Figure 8.29) and Rome and to the Temple of Athena Pronaia at Delphi (Figure 4.53, p. 138).

Loudon was correct about time determining the issue. He arrived in England at the age of 20 and within a decade had given up the attempt to establish himself as a landscape gardener. From the surroundings of Edinburgh he remembered the naturally picturesque valley of the Water of Leith and an unnaturally hideous park designed by a pupil of Brown's. The brook running through the park had, Walter Scott later observed, been 'twisted into the links of a string of pork-sausages'. He too was a disciple of the Herefordshire squires.

Loudon's early work shows the influence of Price and Knight's plea for the Picturesque. The sketches and plans published in *Country Residences* (1806) contrast 'Mr Brown's style' with 'the modern style' as practised by Mr Loudon (see Figure 8.23). It is plain that 'the modern style' is more deserving of the description 'irregular' than any other style in garden history. Little survives of Loudon's built work from this period but in the grounds of Barnbarrow (now Barnbarroch) in Wigtownshire, Scotland, natural regeneration has created some of the effects which Loudon sought to attain by art.

The year 1813, chosen to end this period, is marked by two events discussed in the next chapter – Repton's conversion to the Mixed style, and Loudon's European tour, which led him to question and then adapt 'the principles of Mr Price'.

England

It is as well to begin with a comment on the use of the word 'landscape' joined to 'gardens'. Timothy Nourse associated the two words in 1699. Addison was the first, in 1712, to speak of 'making' a landscape. Shenstone was the first, in 1754, to speak of a 'landscape gardener'. Lancelot Brown, now the most famous 'landscape gardener',

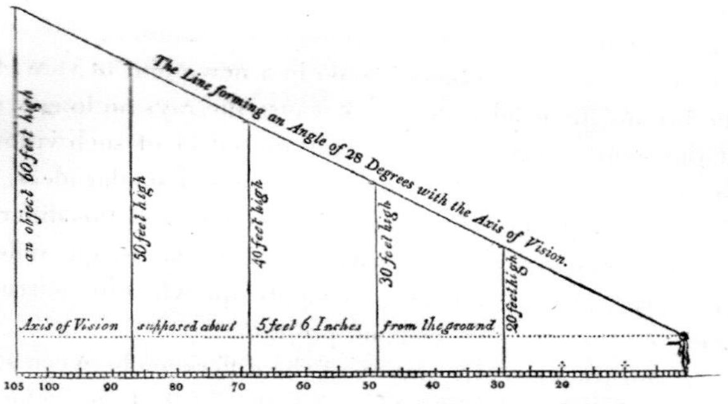

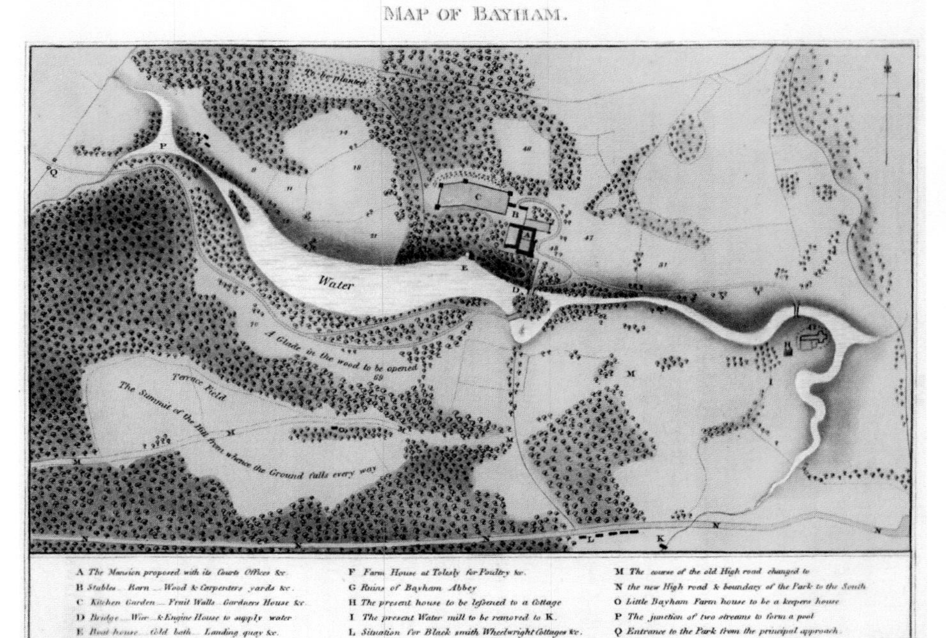

8.27 a–e Humphry Repton was the first man to use the term 'landscape gardener' and had an admirably professional approach, using surveying equipment to draw accurate plans, cross-sections, line-of-view projections and careful before and after sketches.

in fact called himself a 'place-maker' (*c.*1760); Humphry Repton was the first professional designer to call himself a 'landscape gardener' (*c.*1794) but often used 'improver' as an alternative. The nineteenth century was the heyday of landscape gardening as a professional activity. In 1986, these considerations persuaded me to avoid the word 'landscape' in connection with styles of garden design.[48] But I have changed my mind. 'Landscape garden' is used in this chapter as a general term for the set of styles which originated in the eighteenth century and 'Landscape style' is used, in the next chapter, for a specific style which integrated three distinct eighteenth-century styles of garden design: Augustan, Serpentine and Picturesque.

8.28 a, b, c Repton's before and after drawings of West Wycombe and a recent photograph, with Repton's foreground added.

The first generation of English landscape gardens was inspired by a vision of the landscape of antiquity, shaped by landscape paintings, Grand Tours and dreams of Classical antiquity. Italian scenery dominated the vision because Greece, then part of the Ottoman Empire, was hard to visit. Naming the style 'Augustan' follows the use of this term for the Augustan poets who, like Pope, wished to recreate the glory of Rome in the age of its first emperor, Augustus (27 BCE–14 CE). Chiswick, Claremont, Rousham, Stowe, Castle Howard, Painshill and Stourhead are the most important Augustan landscapes. The leading designers were the garden owners themselves, with professional assistance from William Kent, Stephen Switzer and Charles Bridgeman (see p. 278) They are Classical landscapes with statues, grottoes, temples and roofed bridges. The bridges were inspired by the work of Andrea Palladio (see Chapter 6).

8.29 The Temple of Vesta (*c.*100 BCE) was admired by eighteenth-century English visitors, partly for its picturesque location beside the falls of the River Aniene in Tivoli.

The second generation of English landscape gardens, described as 'Serpentine', showed less concern for the romance of antiquity and more for the naturally flowing geometry of landform, woods and lakes. It was as well suited to England's geography as Renaissance gardens had been to Tuscany and the High Baroque to Northern France. All the important examples – Blenheim, Petworth, Prior Park, the changes at Stowe and some 40 other estates – were designed by Lancelot 'Capability' Brown. Many of his lesser projects have become golf courses, which tell us something about their mock-Arcadian character. The principal features were a serpentine tree belt, circular clumps, a naturalised body of water and curvaceous lawns sweeping up to the windows of Palladian mansions.

8.30 a, b The wavy and serpentine lines of the lake at Stowe (above) and the woods at Prior Park (left) form a pleasing contrast with their Palladian bridges.

8.31 The amphitheatre at Claremont was intentionally Classical.

8.32 Brown's lake, at Blenheim, has a flowing geometry.

The third generation of English landscape gardens is described as 'Picturesque' with a capital 'P' to mark its use as a specialised aesthetic term for a type of scene midway between Burke's concepts. 'Sublime' and 'Beautiful' are also written with capital letters when used as specialised terms. In England, Picturesque gardens involved 'heroine worship': of Mother Nature. She was displayed in all her natural glory, unadorned by temples or follies. It was a type of 'natural' scenery well suited to city-centre parks. In continental

8.33 St James' Park was converted from the Baroque to a Picturesque composition, with a capital 'P', which remains a surprise and a delight in the heart of a capital city.

Europe the making of natural landscapes with Romantically pagan temples became a badge of support for Enlightenment values.

France

Louis XVI loved country pursuits and was sympathetic to the calls for reform from the *philosophes*. His journey to the scaffold in 1793 was a consequence of his failure to persuade the nobility and clergy to pay taxes or accept change. Louis' gloomy awkwardness affected his marriage to Marie Antoinette. Marie was the fourteenth child of the Empress of Austria and had lived at Schönbrunn (see p. 245). 'Her tragedy was that

8.34 a, b, c The eighteenth-century additions to Versailles included a Romantic grotto (left), a Temple of Love (top) and an ornamental farm, the Hameau de Trianon (above).

she had to be a queen. Nature had made her a brave, charming, warm-hearted, and indiscreet girl, who only wanted to be happy and to make others happy.' But in France, 'Her slightest indiscretion was magnified into a scandal, her mildest witticism into an insult.'[49] Between 1774 and 1784, Louis allowed her to create an expensive but delightful retreat: the landscape garden and Hameau de Trianon at Versailles. To the King, it was a fashionable gift, perhaps symbolic of the more natural approach to life, society and government he favoured. To the Queen, it was a place to escape from the intrigues and formalities of palace life. To Parisian journalists, it was wanton royal profligacy, a place for the Queen to enjoy the pornographic adventures of which she was so often accused. To some historians, it was 'the first distinctly English landscape garden on the Continent'.[50]

The new garden at Versailles was made beside an older garden and building, the Petit Trianon. Marie Antoinette chose the English fashion for her garden, which was made in two stages. First, Madame de Pompadour's Baroque garden was complemented with an informal layout of walks, streams and woods, embellished with a circular Temple of Love. Second, the informal layout was extended, between 1778 and 1782, and provided with a fashionable accessory: an ornamental hamlet (*hameau*). Antoine Richard, its designer, had travelled in England and visited both Stowe and Kew. The hamlet has a bucolic group of thatched buildings beside a small lake. There is a dairy, a fisherman's house, a mill and a house for the Queen:

> *Here Marie Antoinette trifled away the last years of her glory with her ladies and cavaliers. No threatening voice of the coming revolution penetrated to that rippling lake, where they played blind-man's-buff on the banks; or to the beautiful round temple, whence the little god of love looked down on their happy games. The noble groups of trees that were set round the lake were calmly growing higher and higher; men who were used to this pretty little place shuddered to think of the long broad avenues at Versailles, where one was lost and felt so small. Versailles slept the sleep of the giant, slept through every danger that threatened, until the day of its awakening came.*[51]

Marie Antoinette's garden is a convenient symbol of the days before 14 July 1789 but the French royal family, like Britain's, had lost its leading role in the art of garden design. The author of a careful study, *The Picturesque Garden in France* wrote that: 'The first irregular French garden has yet to be identified. One of the earliest, however, is Ermenonville.'[52] Ermenonville's owner and designer was the Marquis de Girardin, who had been a French officer during the Seven Years War. Like many French intellectuals, he hastened to visit England after the Treaty of Paris ended hostilities in 1763. Girardin found much to admire, and was particularly struck by William Shenstone's *ferme ornée* at The Leasowes. Girardin's writings on garden design were published in English in 1783 as *An Essay on Landscape, or on the Means of Improving and Embellishing the Country round Our Habitations.* He wrote:

> *This change of things then, from a forced arrangement to one that is easy and natural will bring us back to a true taste for beautiful nature, tend to the increase of agriculture,*

8.35 At Chantilly, an uninspired *jardin anglais* was added to the Baroque park (see p. 235).

8.36 Jean-Jacques Rousseau's tomb and the Ile des Peupliers at Ermenonville.

> *the propagation of cattle, and, above all, to more humane and salutary regulations of the country, by providing for the subsistence of those, whose labour supports the men of more thinking employments who are to instruct, or defend society.*[53]

A distinctive feature of Ermenonville was the owner's determination to combine 'use with beauty': Girardin was both a scenic and an agricultural improver. His *hameau* was a working model farm, not a model of a working farm. Another much-admired *hameau*, preceding Marie Antoinette's, was made at nearby Chantilly.

Ermenonville drew upon ideas propagated by the Enlightenment philosophers who paved the road to the French Revolution: Montesquieu (1689–1755), Voltaire (1694–1778) and Rousseau (1712–1778). Montesquieu and Voltaire favoured constitutional monarchy on the English model. They saw, admired and praised English gardens. Rousseau believed all men should be free, equal and virtuous. His famous words, in *Du contrat social,* proclaim: 'Man was born free, and everywhere he is in chains.' In *Emile*, a man explains that he has to write because he has to live and an aristocrat replies, 'I fail to see why.' In Rousseau's *Nouvelle Héloïse* (1761) Julie took her lover into a wilderness with no trace of artificiality. Unlike Marie Antoinette, Rousseau married for love, choosing an illiterate chambermaid. His call for natural rights was heard throughout Europe: men, children and gardens should be allowed to express their inner natures – with the 'nature' in question being discovered through empirical observation. Kant interrupted his fixed routine to read about Julie's romantic nature. In 1778, Rousseau was buried on an island at Ermenonville which became a place of pilgrimage to be copied elsewhere.

Though influenced by the same coalition of ideas as Britain, the weighting of its constituents and the resultant design style differed in France and in those parts of Europe which saw England through a French glass. The Augustan phase of the landscape garden and its supposed Chinese origin were the dominant influences, William Kent and William Chambers the leading innovators. Stowe and Kew were the most admired gardens. The Serpentine phase of the landscape garden, as pursued by Brown, received little attention in France. French landscape gardens were characterised by a profusion of small buildings and the avoidance of straight lines. But 1763–1789 was too short a period for the style to reach maturity. The Parc Monceau in Paris, a prime example, is rich in small buildings but weakly composed; buildings, landform, woods, water and paths are spotted about. French gardens decayed during the revolutionary period (1789–1815). When the old families recovered their property, they had neither the wealth nor the inclination to repair the ancestral symbols of aristocratic privilege. Instead, they turned to a Mixed style of informal planting and building styles (see Chapter 9).

Germany

A love of forests and nature has run deep in German culture since pre-Christian times (see pp. 66–7). Under the influence of the Romantic movement, it burgeoned. Poets wrote of it. Thinkers thought about it. Princes used landscape gardens as evidence for their despotism being enlightened. In the eighteenth century, Germany came under the domination of Prussia's Hohenzollern kings: Frederick-William I (1688–1740) and his son, Frederick II (1712–1786), called Frederick the Great. Frederick-William I, a mountain of efficiency, left Prussia with a brimming treasury, a highly trained army and a son reared in a blisteringly un-Enlightened manner. In 1730, aged only 18, the boy was accused of 'deserting' his militaristic home, court-martialled, imprisoned in a dank cell and made to watch his best friend being executed as a 'co-conspirator'. The experience contributed to Frederick II becoming the first of Europe's enlightened despots. Unfortunately, he also wished to shine in battle. To learn about war, Frederick read history. To learn about the Enlightenment, he turned to Voltaire. To learn about culture and the arts, he turned to the *ancien régime* that Voltaire despised. Frederick spoke French better than German and loved the literature, painting, music, architecture and gardens of France.

Frederick-William I, also a Francophile, had employed a pupil of Le Nôtre to design the first Baroque palace garden in Germany, the Charlottenburg. Frederick II associated the site with brutality, and decided to make a new house and garden in the relaxed lakeside suburb of Potsdam. His project was influenced by French Rococo ideas and its name, Sanssouci ('without care'), reveals both the design aim and its inspiration. As a poet, a philosopher and a gardener, Frederick wanted his home to evoke that of a Roman poet, not a Caesar. He told Ligne that 'I used Vergil's *Georgics* as a gardener's Guide.'[54] Sanssouci, planned as a rural retreat, was never the hub of a groaningly sybaritic court.

There were other departures from Baroque practice: first, the house was set to one side of the prime axis, instead of being a focus for radial avenues (see p. 262). Second,

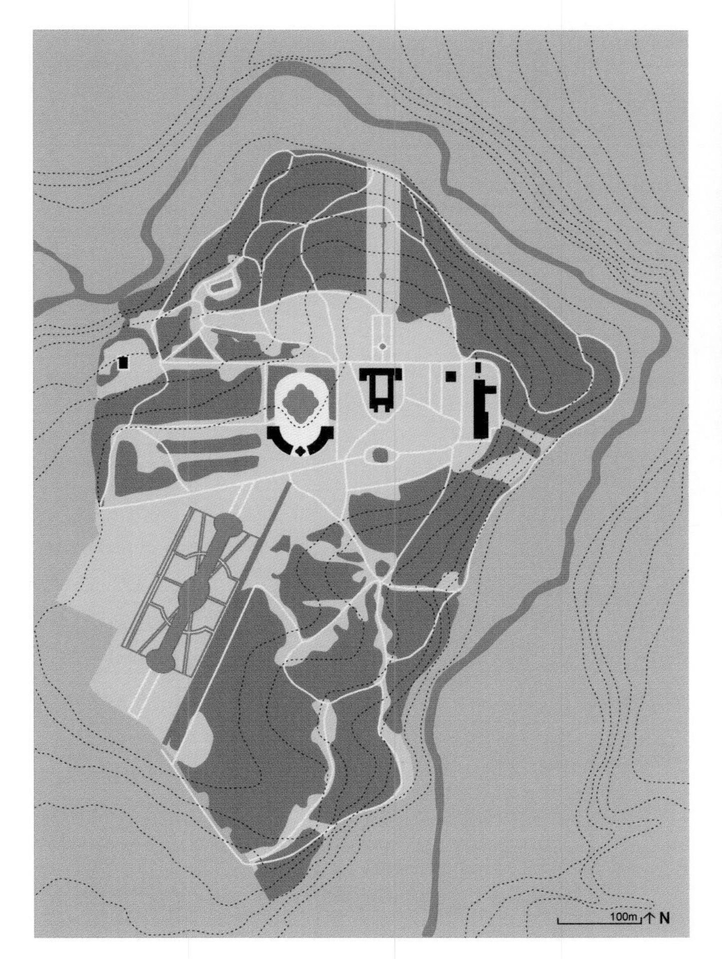

8.37 a, b The great Rococo fountain at the Ermitage, which belonged to Frederick the Great's sister.

Frederick placed a wine-hill-terrace in front of the palace windows, instead of an embroidered parterre. It was a most unusual feature, functional, curved and glazed with French windows. Third, the Tea Pavilion was Rococo. Fourth, the owner's enlightened submission to the rule of law was demonstrated by allowing a miller to bring a suit against him to prevent the removal of his mill. It survives. Frederick also abolished torture. His garden is unique but something can be done to set its design in a context.

Frederick did not see the famous gardens of Italy or France, because his foreign 'travels' were always with an army. The gardens he knew belonged to German courts. Of these, the Ermitage, made by his favourite sister, is likely to have been the most influential. As its name suggests, it was a retreat, and it had features in common with Sanssouci: it is Rococo; it is on a hilltop; it has axes at right angles to one another; it has a gay spirit; it contains a collection of Classical structures. Another sister added Chinese buildings to

8.38 The landscape park at Wörlitz is dominated by water.

Drottningholm (see below). For Sanssouci, Frederick commissioned features in Classical and Romantic styles: busts of Roman Emperors (1744), an Egyptian obelisk (1747), a Neptune grotto (1751), a Chinese tea pavilion (1754), and, most appropriately, a Mount of Ruins. During the Seven Years War (1756–1763), Prussian estate owners became as interested in English gardens, as they were in the English gold that filled Prussia's war chest. *La Nouvelle Héloïse* fanned the flames of enthusiasm for Dame Nature.

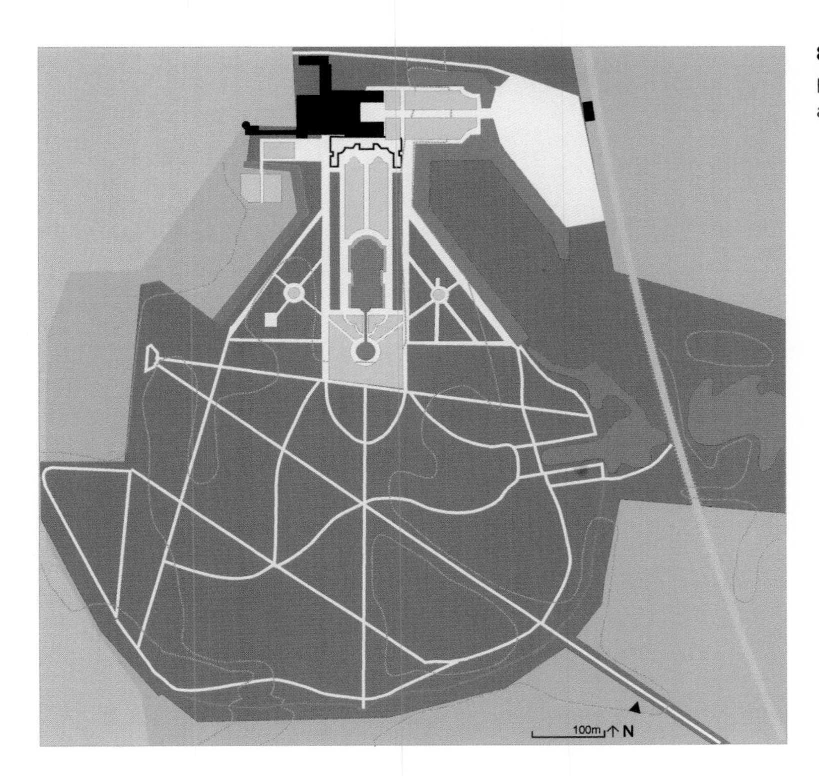

8.39 Peter Joseph Lenné designed a landscape park around the Baroque gardens of Augustusburg and Falkenlust.

Sanssouci and Stourhead were both made between 1745 and 1785, and the ideas that led to their creation are not so far apart as one might suppose. *Compare and contrast Sanssouci and Stourhead* would be a useful essay question. The owners of both were attracted by landscape painting, rural retirement, Classicism, rationalism and empiricism. Bankers like Hoare, the creator of Stourhead, favoured constitutional democracy. Enlightened despots like Frederick, considered democracy unworkable. Both agreed that 'art should imitate nature'. We thus have a list of similarities. The differences were that Frederick looked to modern France rather than Ancient Rome to learn about 'nature', and that he preferred the landscape paintings of Watteau to those of Claude or Poussin. In art-historical terms, the Rococo garden at Sanssouci and the landscape garden at Stourhead are both departures from the Baroque style. By the 1770s, the Baroque was 'dying in the climate of rationalism'.[55] Had the landscape garden not been devised, Sanssouci might have been the seminal garden design of the period.

The first Romantic landscape garden in Germany was made at Wörlitz by Prince Franz von Anhalt-Dessau, between 1765 and 1817. Though surrounded by Prussia, the Prince retained his independence. He admired the English gardens which were also admired in France. They belonged to the Augustan phase of the landscape garden: Claremont, Stourhead and Stowe. But Wörlitz was low-lying and flood-prone, unlike the English sites. This was turned to great advantage: nature's flood was allowed to enter the garden.

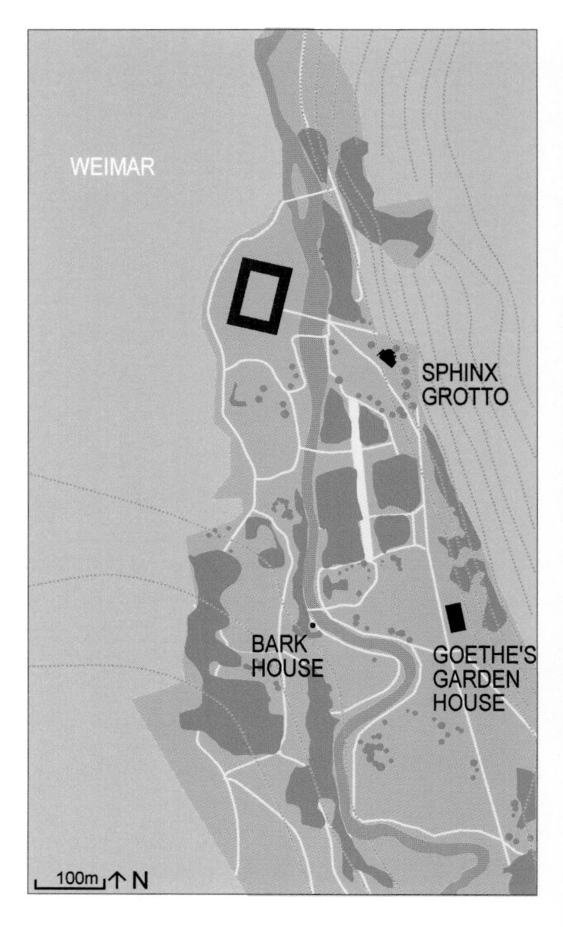

8.40 a, b Goethe's work at the Ilm Park did much to popularise Romantic gardens in Germany.

Water dominates the design and visitors have to choose between a long walk and a series of short boat trips. The buildings that populate the garden are in Classical and Romantic styles, with the choice of Classical structures influenced by Winckelmann. Taking a Platonic view, Winckelmann found in Greek art a 'noble simplicity and supreme calm'.[56] Wörlitz has a Palladian villa, an Elysium and a Temple of Venus. The Romantic features include a Gothic House, a Swiss Bridge and a symbolic Isle of Poplars to commemorate Rousseau's tomb at Ermenonville. The Georgium, with Wörlitz part of Prince Franz's 'garden kingdom', is a landscape park with artificial ruins and a Classical temple.

Use of Classical and Romantic elements became characteristic of German gardens. A Danish Professor of Philosophy and Aesthetics at Kiel University, Christian Hirschfeld, published a *Theory of Garden Design* in 1779, recommending 'both the English land-

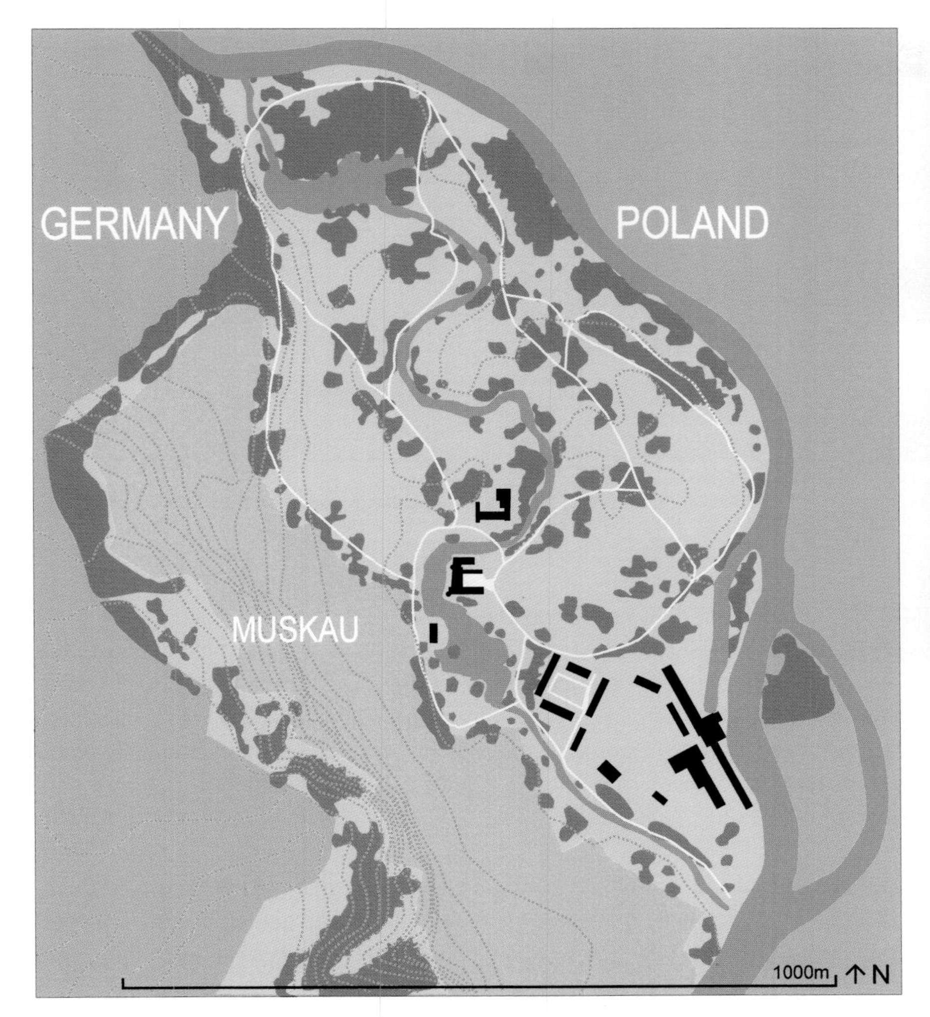

8.41 a, b, c Muskau had one of Europe's largest landscape parks.

scape garden that was popular at the time and the French Baroque garden, in order to create a specifically German garden'.[57] In England, Baroque gardens were destroyed. In Germany, Baroque gardens were modernised by surrounding them with landscape parks. There were many happy marriages, with good examples at Schwetzingen, Nymphenburg and Herrenhausen. The designers of completely new gardens turned to Hirschfeld for advice on landscape gardens. He recommended use of the 'strict English line' of Lancelot 'Capability' Brown, meaning the serpentine line, hitherto unused in Germany. Though Hirschfeld advised self-restraint with regard to the use of small buildings, they were prominent in his illustrations.

Hirschfeld's *Theory of Garden Design* and the Wörlitz landscape garden attracted the attention of Germany's leading poet and writer. Johann Wolfgang von Goethe

8.42 The Baroque garden at Nymphenburg (see p. 241 and p. 347) was ringed with a Romantic park.

8.43 Munich's Englischer Garten was designed by Friedrich Ludwig von Sckell.

(1749–1832) balanced the Romantic and Classical in his thoughts, always seeking both the unity and the individuality of nature. In 1777, the Duke of Saxe-Weimar asked for help with the layout of the Ilm Park in Weimar, beside which Goethe lived. In the spirit of Hirschfeld, it is a Brownian composition of woodland and grassland with a minimum of Classical allusion. Order restrains chaos. The River Ilm provides a serpentine water feature and there is no trace of the Rococo. Goethe's endorsement of the new approach was extremely influential in Germany.

Prince Pückler-Muskau (1785–1871) inherited a large estate at Muskau and purchased additional land, in what is now Poland, to create a landscape garden of 6 sq km with 27 km of paths. The topography has a rolling character and the style is Serpentine. The design was highly regarded by the American historian, Norman T. Newton:

> *The whole scheme was tied together with a flowing system of roads, paths, and bridges that provided routes of great variety and ingenuity as described by Pückler in 'the three carriage drives' on which he conducts the reader in his book. The crowning glory of the park, however, is the firm integrity of its magnificent pastoral spaces. Here Pückler seems to have revealed most clearly the innate understanding of spatial structure – the awareness of spaces as components of design – sought in vain among the usual English landscape gardening works.*[58]

Pückler-Muskau had toured English gardens and regarded himself as more a follower of Repton than Brown. In my view, Pückler-Muskau's first project, Muskau, was more Brownian and his second, Branitz, more Reptonian. Neither project belongs to the Picturesque phase of the landscape garden. The natural landscape at Muskau was well suited to the creation of 'magnificent pastoral spaces'. At Branitz, because of the smaller and flatter site, it was easier for Pückler to create the Mixed style effects associated with

Repton's later writings and nineteenth-century projects (see Chapter 9). Branitz has a Pyramid Lake, a Serpentine Lake, a Blue Garden, a Smithy Garden, a Rose Mount, a Moon Mount and Island of Venus, an iron Kiosk and a series of waterways.

Pückler-Muskau was an owner-designer and author. The leading professional designers of German landscape gardens were Peter Josef Lenné (1789–1866), who designed the Potsdam landscape, and Friedrich Ludwig von Sckell (1768–1834), who surrounded Schwetzingen with a landscape garden and made the famous Englischer Garten in Munich.

Russia

Catherine the Great (1729–1796) introduced the landscape garden to Russia. She was Prussian by birth and had attracted the admiration of Frederick the Great, who, when Catherine was only 14, insisted on her attendance at a court dinner. Frederick supported her marriage to Peter III and concluded a vital alliance with her after the Seven Years War. Like him, she preferred to speak French and, for artistic and intellectual guidance, always looked abroad. To Diderot, she sighed:

> *All your work is done upon paper, which does not mind what you do to it: it is all of a piece, pliable, and presenting no obstacles either to your pen or to your imagination. But I, poor Empress, must work upon the human skin, which is terribly ticklish and irritable.*[59]

Landscape design, which compares with drawing on 'the bark of a tree',[60] appealed to Catherine as a symbol of how an Enlightened Empress should conduct her affairs. Politically, she was an autocrat who questioned and then extended the practice of

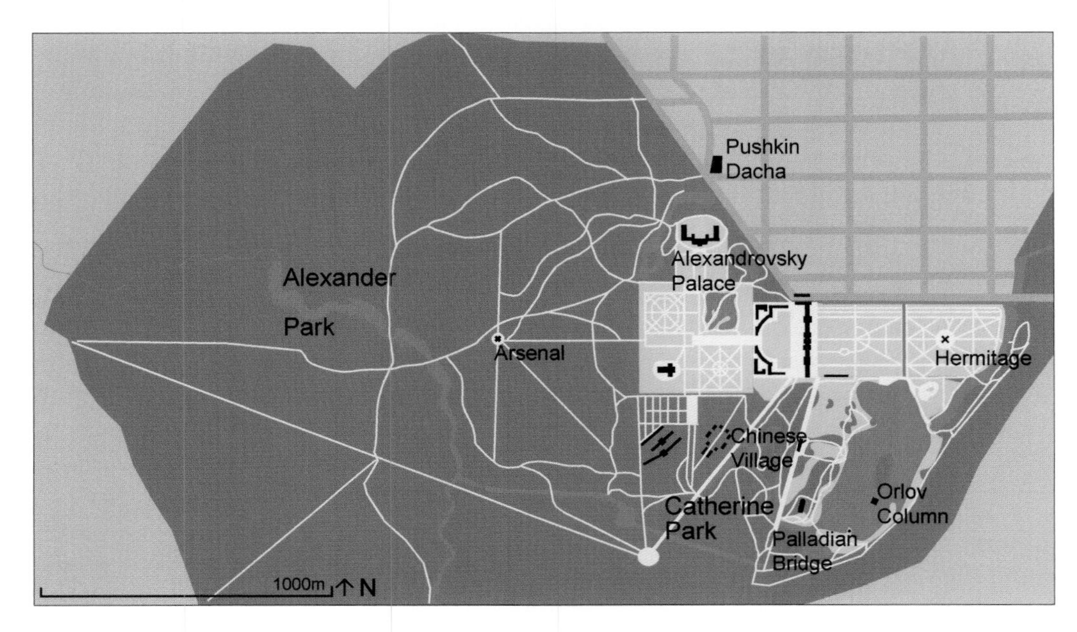

8.44 Catherine the Great commissioned the first landscape park in Russia for the Royal Village (Tsarskoe Selo).

8.45 a, b The Cameron Gallery at Tsarskoe Selo overlooks a landscape park and a Baroque parterre (see p. 248). From the woods, the Catherine Palace forms part of a scenic composition.

8.46 The Palladian bridge at Tsarskoe Selo was a symbol of Catherine's enlightenment.

serfdom. Culturally, she had a liberal enthusiasm for the Enlightenment. Sexually, she chose young men. Catherine commissioned landscape parks for herself, at Tsarskoe Selo, and for her son, at Pavlosk.

The landscape garden made for the Catherine Palace at Tsarskoe Selo (*c.*1770) is separated from an older, Baroque garden (*c.*1750) by a covered walk, known as the Cameron Gallery. From it, Catherine could view both gardens, symbols of old and new Russia. She employed a German-born, English-trained landscape designer (John Busch) for the new park. For the buildings she employed a Russian, Vasily Neyelov, whom she sent to visit England, and a Scotsman, Charles Cameron, who married Busch's daughter.

The setting of the Palladian Bridge was inspired by Stowe. There are excellent Chinese pavilions and a Chinese Village. Since it was made for an Empress, Tsarskoe Selo has an opulent grandeur uncommon in landscape parks. The Orlov Column in the lake commemorates Catherine's most dashing lover. The park was given the name Pushkin by the Soviets, in 1937, to mark the 100th anniversary of the death of Russia's great Romantic poet, who also loved the park. The family of Russia's last Tsar, Nicholas II, lived in the Alexander Palace before being exiled and shot in 1917. Despite Catherine's modernising liberalism, Tsarskoe Selo played the role of Russia's Versailles.

Pavlovsk was designed by Charles Cameron for Grand Duke Pavel, whose German wife was the chief influence on the design. The Duke resented his mother's involvement but

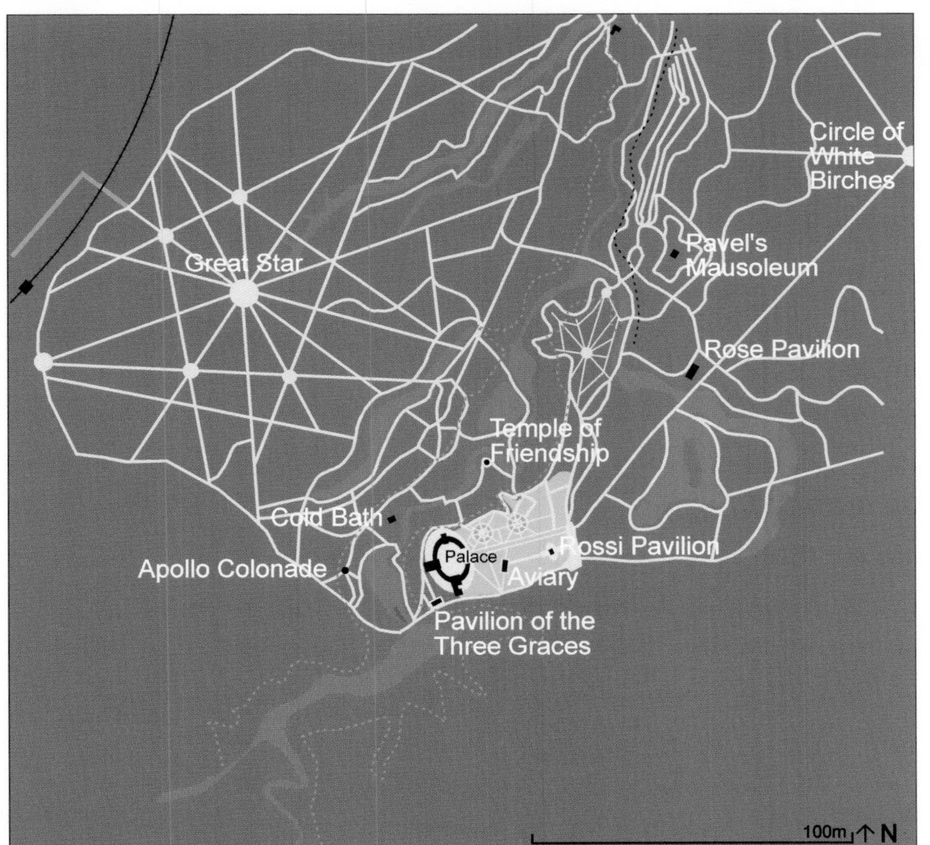

8.47 a, b, c Pavlovsk was designed by Charles Cameron for Catherine the Great's son and his German wife, Sophie of Wurttemberg-Stuttgart.

the Duchess adored the landscape garden. The Temple of Friendship, built to please her mother-in-law, was the first of some 60 garden buildings in a park of 10 sq km. The River Slavyanka was dammed and bridged. Lakes were dug. The Apollo Colonnade was made into a real ruin by a great storm in 1817. There is a Temple of the Three Graces, a thatched

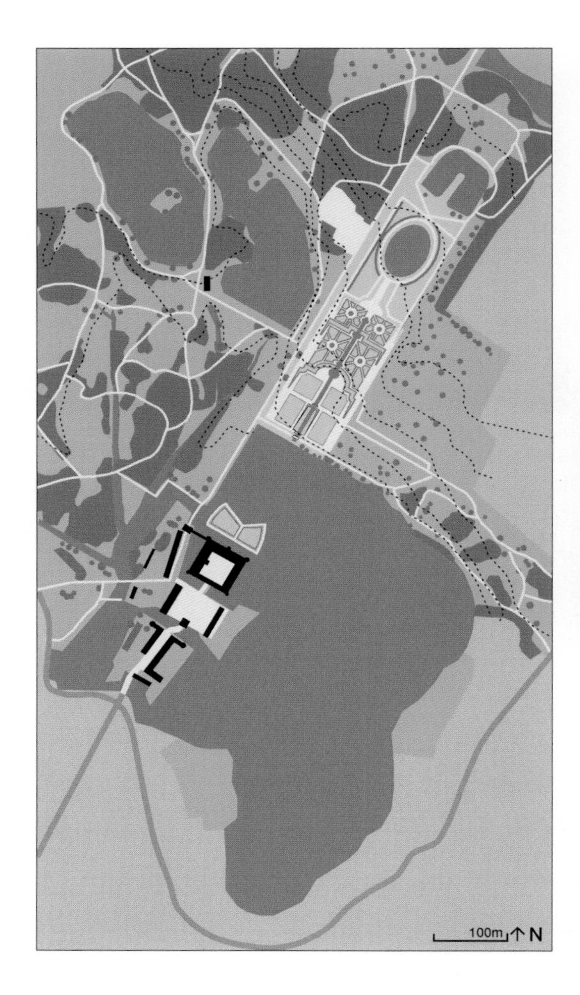

8.48 a, b The Frederiksborg castle, in Denmark, is now surrounded by a Romantic park.

dairy, a hermit's cell and a Mausoleum for the Emperor Paul. Loudon visited Pavlosk in 1812 and judged it the best design of its type in Russia. He believed Lancelot Brown had 'furnished a design', which is unlikely. The profusion of small buildings in diverse styles suggests Cameron was most interested in the Augustan phase of the landscape garden.

Scandinavia

In Denmark, some Baroque gardens, including Fredensborg, Glorup and Frederiksborg, were remodelled in the Landscape style. In Norway, a landscape garden was made at Bogstad Manor outside Oslo *c.*1780. In Sweden, a landscape garden was added to the royal estate at Drottningholm, where Frederick the Great's sister had built a Chinese pavilion after her country made peace with Prussia in 1763. The siblings were energetic and ambitious. Louisa Ulrika was queen during the Period of Liberty (1718–1772). Her son, Gustavus III, reverted to despotism but, wanting to represent himself as enlightened, employed F.M. Piper to design landscape parks at Drottningholm and Haga. Gustavus was a theatre-loving aesthete. Haga was planned on a dramatic scale in dramatic scenery, drawing upon both the Augustan and Serpentine phases of the landscape garden. It has a Neoclassical Royal Pavilion, built after an Italian tour undertaken by Gustavus in 1782, a 'Roman battle tent', designed in 1790 by Jean-Louis Desprez, (1737–1804), a Chinese Pagoda, a Turkish Pavilion and a brightly coloured Ekotemplet used as a summer dining room. Gustavus III was assassinated by a nobleman who thought him too despotic. His son, who built Haga Slott in 1802, was deposed for the same fault. Mere symbols of enlightenment were no longer sufficient.

8.49 Haga Royal Park has a large landscape park in dramatic surroundings.

Southern Europe

The Landscape style had some influence on Southern Europe. Irrigation and intensive care allowed the creation of gardens with a serpentine form but dry rocky hills were unsuited to the formation of large serpentine parks. Usually, an English garden was an addition to a Baroque park, as at Caserta in Italy and Aranjuez in Spain. Where larger projects were instigated, as at the Pena Palace in Portugal, they were Romantic developments of the Picturesque phase of the landscape garden. At the Villa Borghese in Rome, Edouard André helped transform a Baroque garden into a landscape park. At Ninfa, a ruined village provided the picturesque buildings around which planting was arranged in a Picturesque style.

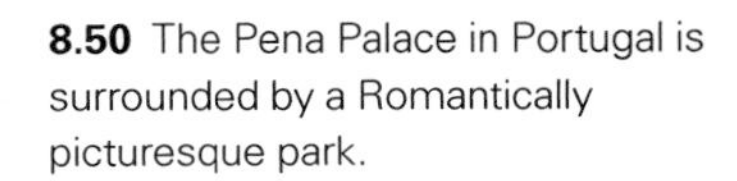

8.50 The Pena Palace in Portugal is surrounded by a Romantically picturesque park.

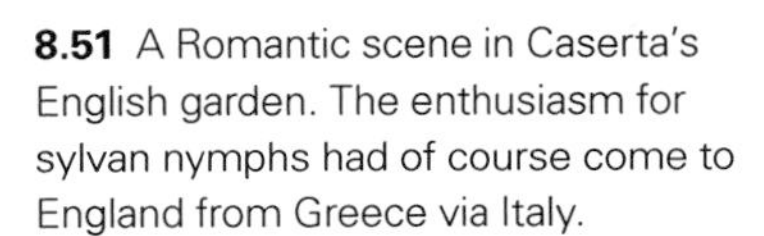

8.51 A Romantic scene in Caserta's English garden. The enthusiasm for sylvan nymphs had of course come to England from Greece via Italy.

8.52 The Villa Borghese in Rome became a *giardino inglese* in the nineteenth century.

8.53 Ninfa has a picturesque composition of ruined buildings with Romantic planting.

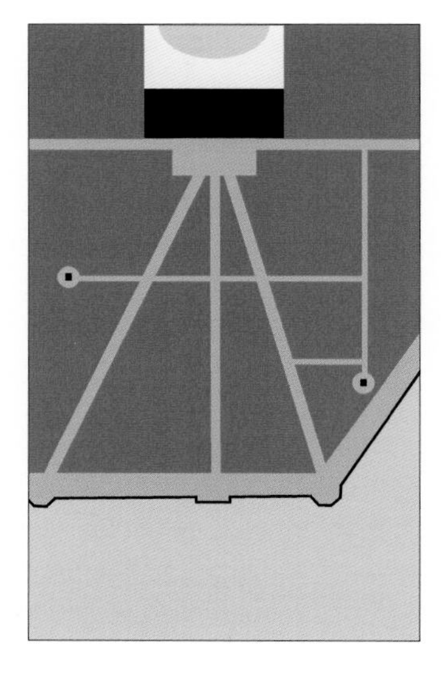

8.54 Forest style.

Styles and examples

Forest style

Use: The view of gardens as rural retreats grew in deliberate contrast to their High Baroque role. Owners shunned courtly life, with the proud aim of imitating Virgil's example by making places which are simultaneously useful and beautiful. Agriculture and forestry became important land uses. Avenues were made by planting new forests, not by cutting rides through existing forests. The name 'Forest style' comes from Stephen Switzer. He also called it 'rural' and 'extensive' gardening.

Form: The radial geometry was carried over from the High Baroque. Boundaries were often low retaining walls with bastions at turning points giving views over the surrounding countryside. There was an interest in lines of view, sometimes emphasised by low hedges on the inside margins of avenues, meeting the estate boundary at bastion points.

Cirencester Park, 1715

As it is 8 km long and 4.8 km wide, the leading example of the English Forest style requires an informed eye and an enthusiasm for walking. Stephen Switzer may have advised on the design. Pope came here over a 30-year period and invested money in Lord Bathurst's forest enterprise. It has a Baroque goosefoot of avenues, but the intention was to make a Sabine farm, not to impress visitors with the owner's wealth, power or fashionable taste. The best view of the park is from the top of Cirencester's church steeple, not from the great man's house.

> *Alexander Pope was closely connected for thirty years with Lord Bathurst's creation of Cirencester Park, or rather the series of conjoined parks that stretches from the town*

8.55 Cirencester Park, England.

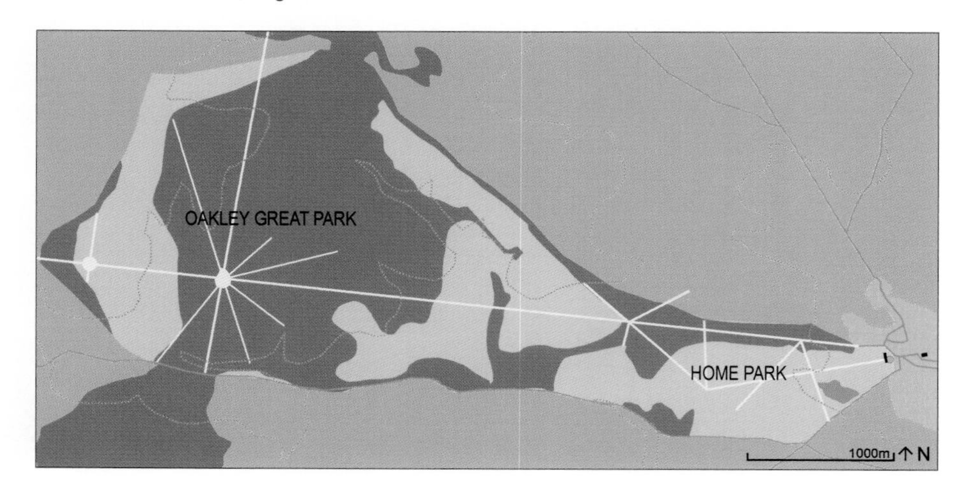

of Sapperton, five miles to the west. The outcome is the largest and most impressive example surviving of 'extensive or forest gardening' – as Stephen Switzer in 1714 termed the earliest kind of landscape gardening ... The creation of the great park at the geographical and historical focus of the Cotswold uplands, on what had previously been predominantly open sheepwalks, was an undertaking as visionary as sustained.

(Christopher Hussey)[61]

Augustan style

Use: Owners looked back, before the Baroque, before the Renaissance, before the Middle Ages, to the Roman roots of Western culture. They wanted gardens which recalled the Classical landscape of antiquity, suitable for use as places to reflect on literature, history, natural science and the affairs of the day. Discussions with friends might take place while strolling through the grounds or taking tea on a well-placed garden seat. Classical ornament and allusion contributed to the theme. For landowners who had been on a Grand Tour, an Augustan garden became a symbol of their travels and a place to display souvenirs, including urns, statues and quotations from Roman poets.

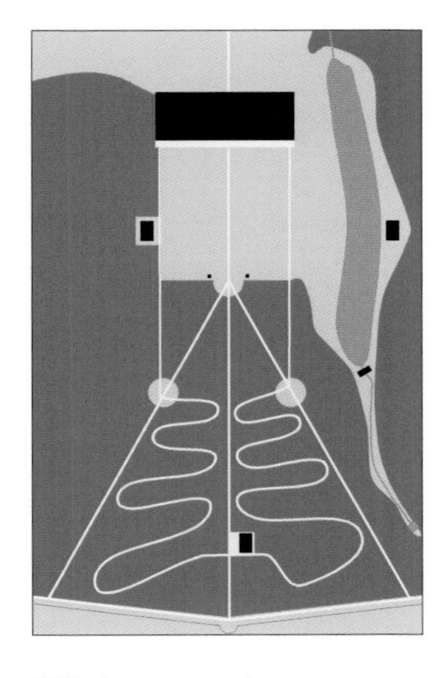

8.56 Augustan style.

Form: The first 'landscape gardens' in England drew upon visions of Rome's landscape in the time of the Emperor Augustus. They were Classical groves with woods, water, grass and small temples, as in Graeco-Roman sanctuaries. William Kent was the first professional designer to give physical form to this vision. The diagram shows part of the garden as a carry-over from the Baroque and part as an early exercise in the re-creation of a Classical Italian landscape. Between 1720 and 1745 the placing of temples and statues was more important than the plan geometry.

Chiswick, 1725

'Chiswick is a prime example of Palladio made to speak good English – the architectural equivalent to what Pope was doing for Homer in the 1720s.'[62] Indeed, the garden at Chiswick was sufficiently changed by 'landscape' ideas for Pope to see it as the first garden in which 'the genius of the place' had been duly consulted. Lord Burlington, the owner and chief designer, was assisted by Charles Bridgeman and William Kent. They aimed to make an Augustan villa, but with the architecture modelled on Palladio's Villa Rotunda of 1550. Buildings and obelisks were placed at the termination of avenues, in the Baroque manner. Classical busts, sphinxes, columns and an *exedra* evoked the landscape of antiquity. William Kent helped with the Classical allusions, designed a rustic cascade and gave the canal a mildly serpentine shape. The area between the canal and the house, occupied by a maze in 1730, was the first to be treated as a Classical landscape. Since Kent's style became influential, we are fortunate that it survives.

The garden was in poor condition when Frank Clark (quoted below) saw it but has been restored. This was a difficult task because of the five important stages in the garden's evolution:

1. A 1707 drawing by Knyff showed a simple Renaissance garden with grass plats and knots. This has gone, except for the path on the north front of the house.
2. By 1730, Lord Burlington had made a 'Roman' garden, which drew something from the Baroque and something from Robert Castell's *Villas of the Ancients*.[63] It had avenues, geometrical pools, an amphitheatre, a maze and several small pavilions.
3. By 1733, William Kent was recognised as having introduced a 'natural taste in gardening', probably in the area between the house and the canal. A maze was removed and the area treated in a manner which was to become famous as 'the English style'.
4. By 1753, the year of Lord Burlington's death, the *exedra* was planted, an orangery built and more of the land fronting the canal 'naturalised' by removing the basins of water.
5. By 1858, several Dukes of Devonshire had made further changes to the estate. These included demolition of the old house and some of Burlington's temples. A conservatory and an 'Italian' garden were added.

The gardens of Chiswick Park are now a public park. They are, or they should be, a public monument. Here lies buried under bamboo, rhododendron and worn turf, the first of the experimental irregular gardens. The grounds are rich in association and historical memories.

(Frank Clark)[64]

8.57 a, b Lord Burlington's villa in 1736 and 2003.

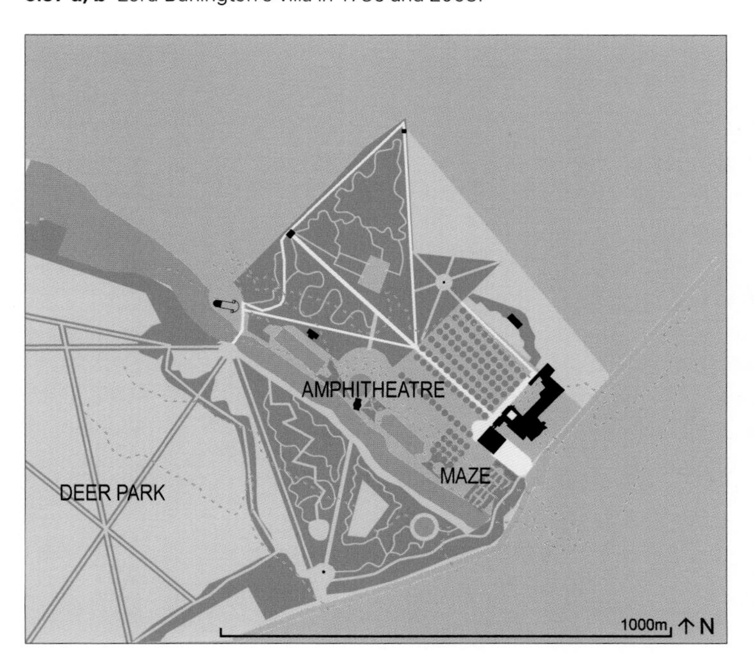

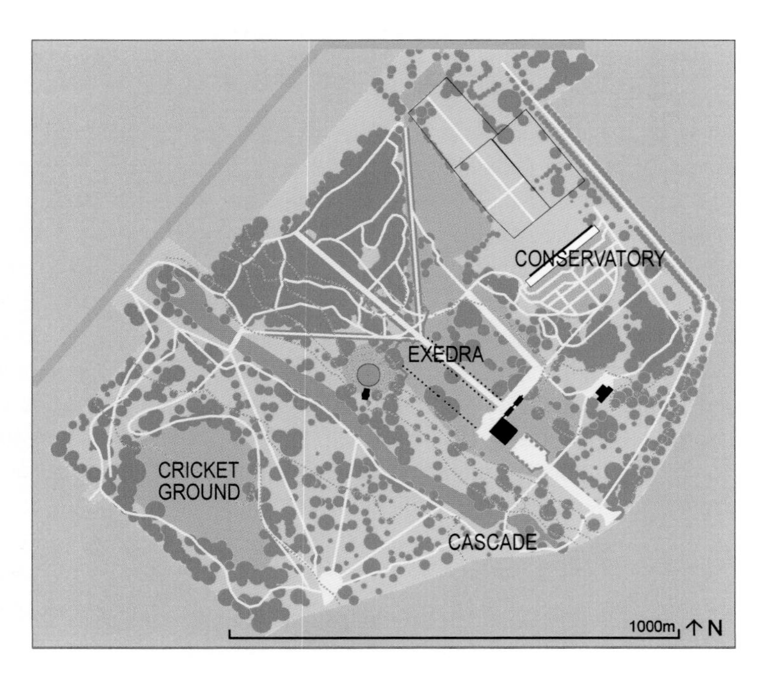

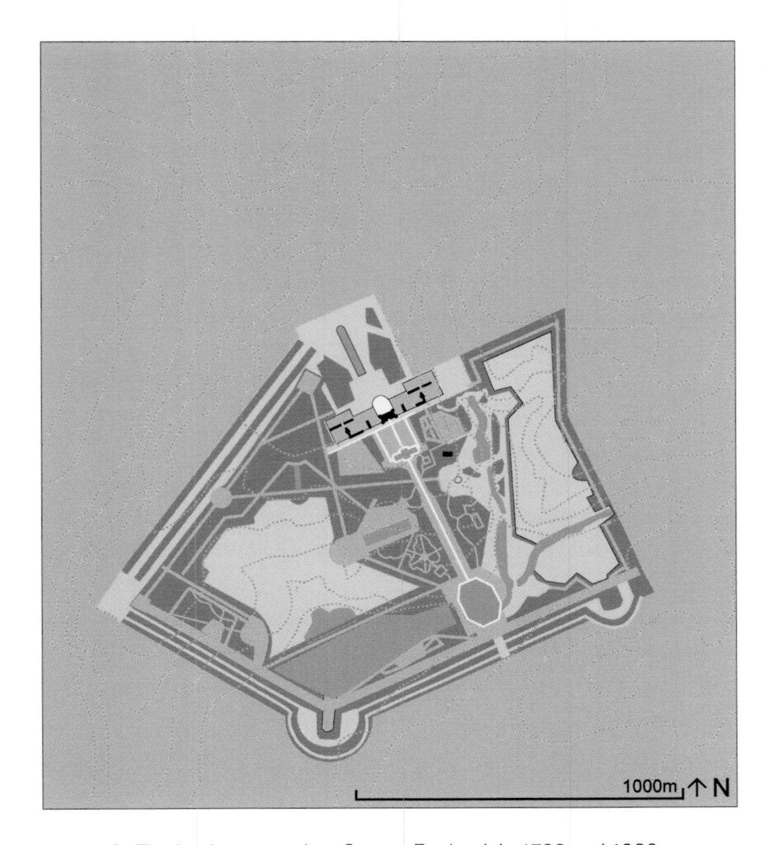

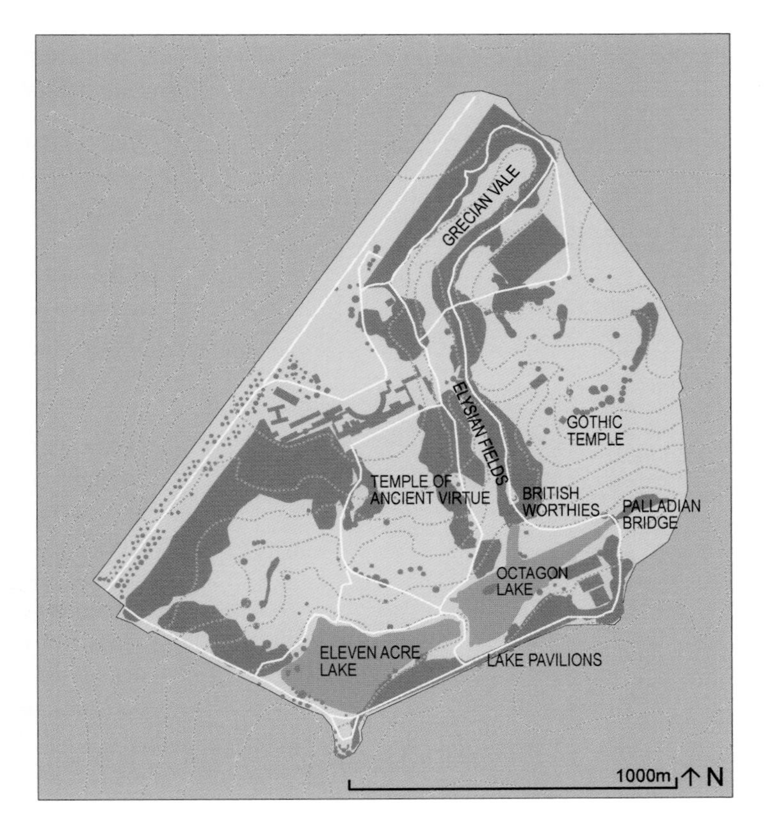

8.58 a, b The landscape park at Stowe, England, in 1739 and 1980.

Stowe, 1730

Stowe has many beautifully composed Classical scenes. It lacks cohesion but the design history is intriguing:

- In the 1690s Stowe had a modest, Early Baroque parterre garden, owing more to Italy than France.
- After 1710, Charles Bridgeman, as garden designer, and John Vanbrugh, as architect, designed a Baroque park, inspired by the work of the famous garden designers, London and Wise.
- In the 1730s, William Kent and James Gibbs were appointed to work with Bridgeman. Stowe began to evolve into a series of Classical scenes to be appreciated from a perambulation rather than from a central point.
- Brown made a Grecian Vale.

Kent's Temple of Ancient Virtue (1734) looks across the Elysian Fields to a Shrine of British Worthies. A Palladian Bridge was made in 1744. Lancelot 'Capability' Brown was appointed head gardener in 1741. He worked with Kent until the latter's death in 1748 and his own departure in 1751. Bridgeman's Octagonal Pond and Eleven Acre Lake were given a 'natural' shape and Brown contributed the Grecian Vale.

> *Stowe appears to have been the first extensive residence in which the modern style was adopted ... Kent was employed ... in the double capacity of architect and landscape-gardener; and the finest buildings and scenes there are his creation. The character of Stowe is well known: nature has done little; but art has created a number of magnificent buildings by which it has been attempted to give a sort of emblematic character to scenes of little or no natural expression. The result is unique; but more, as expressed by Pope, 'a work to wonder at', than one to charm the imagination.*
>
> (John Claudius Loudon)[65]

> *Landscape design can be said to have originated at Stowe and Castle Howard ... The outstanding monument of English landscape gardening is also its most complete 'living document': a visual epic of social and political as well as of aesthetic history. Soon after its inception Pope considered the new garden 'a place to wonder at' and by the mid-century its scenery was generally accepted as the finest physical expression of the age's aesthetic concept of Ideal Nature. This was the more influential owing to Stowe's being the chief seat of the Whig political establishment ... Stowe's scenery remained almost as influential in shaping the continental conception of* le jardin anglais *as had been Versailles for that of the Grand Manner.*
>
> (Christopher Hussey)[66]

Wörlitz, Germany, 1765

The first landscape park in Germany was inspired by Prince Franz Anhalt-Dessau's visits to Claremont, Stourhead and Stowe. It forms part of a collective project covering a 25 sq

8.59 Wörlitz, Germany.

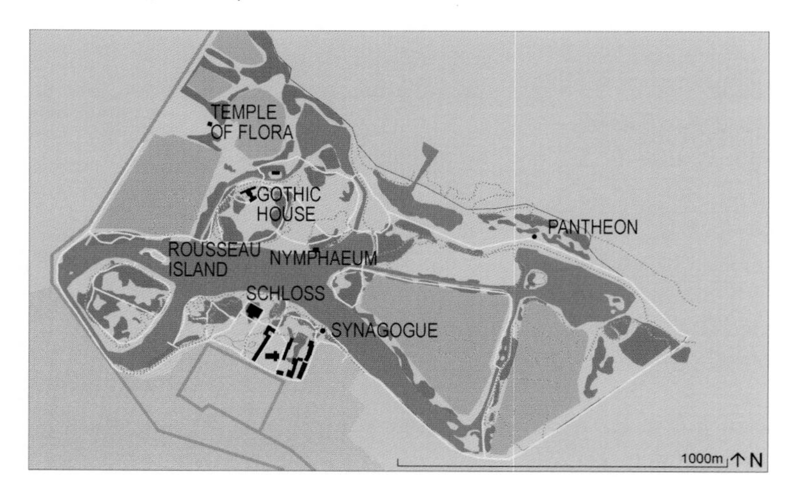

km area. There is a Temple of Flora, a Temple of Venus, a Gothic House, a Nymphaeum, a Classical Bridge and a Rousseau Island. The estate can be divided into five sections:

1. the Schloss Garten, modelled on Stourhead but intended as a private garden;
2. the Neumark Garten, with a canal, islands and a circular building modelled on a temple at Stowe;
3. the Schloss Garten with a Gothic House, a Temple of Venus and a Temple of Flora;
4. the garden on the north-east shore of the lake;
5. the New Gardens, with mementoes of Italy.

Wörlitz has many interesting scenes, which can be enjoyed like a postcard collection.

> *It is beautiful without end here. Yesterday, as we walked by canals and groves it touched men how the Gods could allow the Prince to create such a dream around himself. Travelling through, it seems like a fairy-tale and has the character of Paradise.*
>
> (Johann Wolfgang von Goethe)[67]

Serpentine style

Use: A circumferential track allowed owners to enjoy what Hussey, quoting Burke, described as the 'sense of being swiftly drawn in an easy coach on a smooth turf, with gradual ascents and declivities'.[68] Parkland was used for grazing, allowing visitors to note that, although the owner was extremely rich, his resources were used productively instead of being wasted on boastful display. In continental Europe, writers, including Goethe and Rousseau, admired the naturalness of the style. Its adoption became a badge of an estate-owner's support for Enlightenment values.

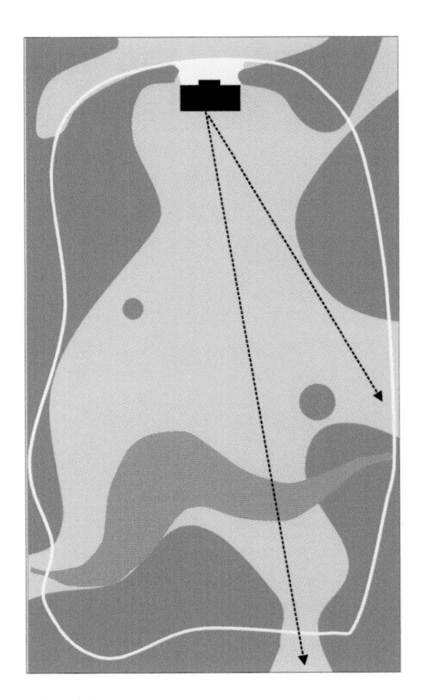

8.60 Serpentine style.

Form: The hallmarks of this style were a lawn sweeping to the house front, circular clumps, a serpentine lake, an encircling tree belt and a perimeter carriage drive. This combination is sometimes known as the 'English landscape garden' or 'Brownian' style. The adjective 'serpentine' draws attention to use of a free-flowing 'line of beauty'. Lancelot Brown's approach was significantly more abstract than the Augustan style, making less use of garden buildings and more use of serpentine lines in the design of lakes and woodlands.

Blenheim Palace, 1760

The palace, designed by Vanbrugh *c.*1705, was the nation's reward to the first Duke of Marlborough for his victories against Louis XIV. Henry Wise, working with Vanbrugh, designed the garden in an Anglo-Dutch style with military overtones – mock fortifications and regimented parterres. The first Duke died in 1722. During the 1720s, his wife, Sarah, canalised the River Glyme and spanned it with a triumphal bridge. In 1764, the 4th Duke

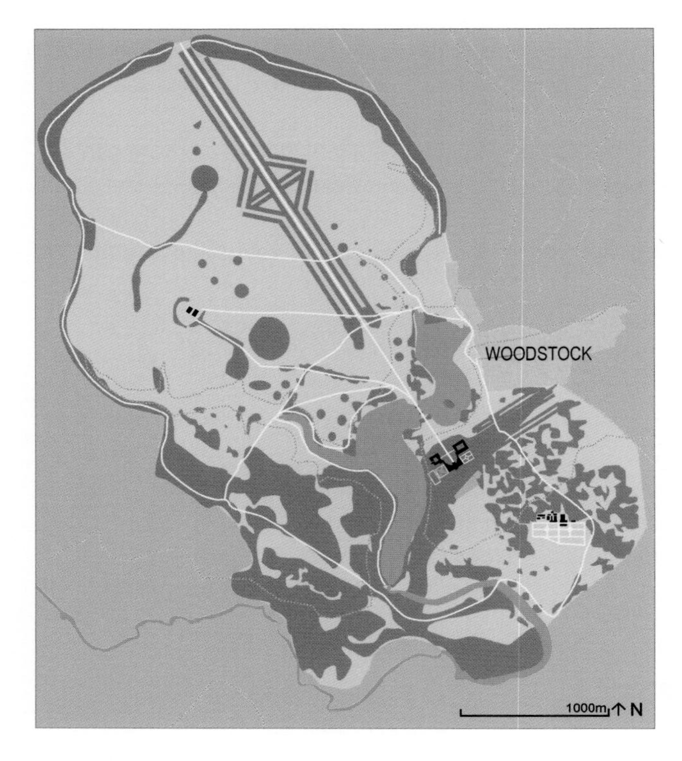

8.61 Blenheim, England.

commissioned Lancelot Brown, then at the apogee of his fame. Brown transformed the canal into a serpentine lake. He also naturalised the woods, designed a cascade and placed clumps of trees in strategic positions.

The ninth Duke commissioned Achille Duchêne in the 1930s to design a terrace and water parterre as transitional features between the palace and its landscape setting.

> *Blenheim, leaving its size and classic garb out of the question, is moulded to produce a varied and intricate impression on the eye, by masses of light and shade, and a dramatic outline built up like an apotheosis of Rubens, the modern 'dwelling' is given features that appeal to the common mind as being in themselves picturesque.*
>
> (Christopher Hussey)[69]

Bowood, 1761

Lancelot Brown's design for the park at Bowood, Wiltshire, was a clear example of his style, with circular clumps, an encircling tree belt and a serpentine lake. The plan of the park today shows that the principle of his design has survived. The lake discharges via a cascade designed by Charles Hamilton of Painshill and there is a small Doric

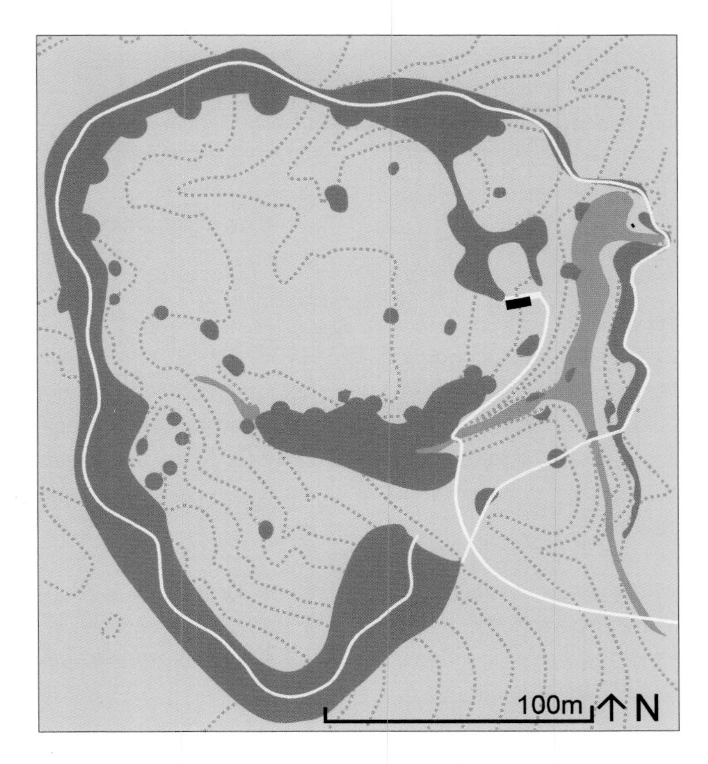

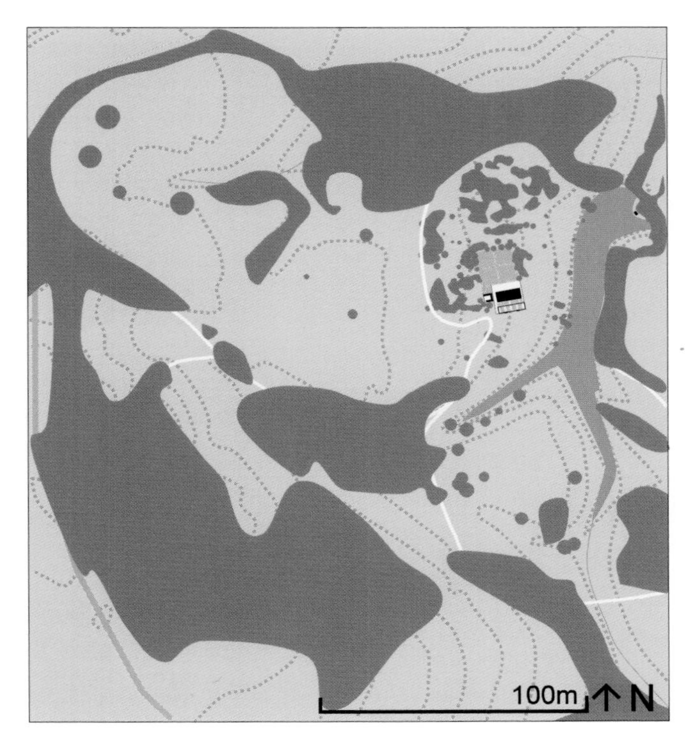

8.62 a, b Bowood, England, as designed by Brown and in 2000.

temple beside the lake. In order to create a landscape transition, George Kennedy was asked to design an 'Italian garden' in 1851. It has terraces, balustrades, urns and steps. The north section of the park is now a golf course, which retains its structure but mars its texture.

> *[Brown's] bill for this work, £4,300, included such common trees and shrubs as ash and hawthorn – twelve thousand hawthorns cost him £50 – but his client had to pay extra for some exotic trees. Bowood Park has not been much altered since Brown worked on it, and is one of the best places now left to us where his style can be studied.*
>
> (Edward Hyams)[70]

Englischer Garten, Munich, 1789

The oldest public park in Germany was promoted by Count Rumford, an American, and designed by Friedrich von Sckell. The central feature is the circular Monopteros Temple. It stands on a mound and overlooks a grass meadow with a lake. Von Sckell was the court gardener to Elector Carl Theodor. He designed a people's park for the purpose of exercise and recreation. It is one of Europe's largest city parks (5 km by 1.5 km) and a popular area for nude sunbathing, contributing to its Arcadian ambience in summer.

8.63 The Englischer Garten, Munich.

[Von Sckell] walked through the terrain in person indicating where the pathway should go, in order to be sure that walkers would be able to see ... 'the city of Munich in the foreground and the age-old Hirschanger wood in the barkground along with the other beauties of nature'. Crown and countryside, the spheres of courtly and rural society, were to be linked by means of curving paths of this kind.

(Ehrenfried Kluckert)[71]

Picturesque style

Use: Picturesque estates were designed to stimulate the mind with scenery composed according to the principles of landscape painting. They were not intended for domestic pleasure, social gatherings or hunting. Spelt with a capital 'P', the Picturesque was primarily an aesthetic conception. Clients, one must suppose, can have found few other uses for parks and gardens designed in this manner, but their maintenance budgets would have been gratifyingly low.

Form: Enthusiasm for the Picturesque resulted in the most irregular plans in garden history. As advocated by Gilpin, Price and Knight, and as illustrated by the drawings in Loudon's *Country Residences*, they were jagged in every detail, except for the kitchen ground. The style is best viewed in elevation.

8.64 Picturesque style.

Hawkstone, 1790

The design history of Hawkstone awaits further investigation but it appears to have been conceived under the torrent of Picturesque enthusiasm unleashed by Gilpin in the late eighteenth century. The park was made by Sir Roland Hill and his son in dramatic countryside with hills, woods and rocks. *Rhododendron ponticum*, introduced to Britain *c.*1770, has overrun the site.

8.65 Hawkstone, England.

8.66 a, b Barnbarrow, Scotland.

> *In the eighteenth and nineteenth centuries it was ranked as one of the principal attractions of England ... When Dr Samuel Johnson visited Hawkstone in 1774 he wrote 'By the extent of its prospects, the awfulness of its shades, the horrors of its precipices, the verdure of its hollows, and the loftiness of its rocks, the ideas which it forces upon the mind are the sublime, the dreadful and the vast'.*
>
> (Dennis McBride)[72]

Barnbarrow, 1806

Loudon published his designs for converting the house and estate to the Picturesque style. They were not fully implemented but the house and garden fell into a ruinous condition and one could scarcely hope to find a better example of the character which Loudon intended.

> *Rocks may be shewn by removing earth, and forming breaks and abruptnesses in the surface. This may be done in several ways; but those are to be preferred which shew a perpendicular surface, or upright front of rock ... Many examples of this kind occur in the different parts of Barnbarrow.*
>
> (John Claudius Loudon)[73]

CHAPTER 9

Eclectic gardens, 1800–1900

9.0 The Castle Gardens at Schwerin use an eclectic mix of design ideas from French châteaux, Italian villas and English landscape parks, including work by Peter Joseph Lenné (1789–1866). They were restored to their 1857 condition as part of the German Federal Horticultural Exhibition, BUGA 2009.

History and philosophy

About 1800, garden design theory struck a problem which, even today, is scarcely resolved. Gothein's analysis was that practitioners had ceased to 'look for art at all',[1] so that, 'the whole of the nineteenth century must complete its tale of sins before the foundations are shattered'.[2] Nineteenth-century architecture suffered a comparable fate. It was seen, with less clarity, as the dilemma of which historic style to choose. Artists also turned to historic themes but some individuals, less dependent on patronage than designers, were able to chart their own futures. This often involved starving in a garret but it allowed the realisation of a personal vision. Gombrich commented that 'it was only in the nineteenth century that the real gulf opened between the successful artists – who contributed to "official art" – and the nonconformists, who were mainly appreciated after their death'.[3] Garden designers, like architects, and 'successful' artists, gave up the quest for art which imitates 'the nature of the world'. They turned to exoticism and eclecticism.

Quatremère de Quincy, an astute French critic, was one of the first to appreciate the problem facing garden designers. In 1823, he explained the dilemma facing the 'irregular system of landscape gardening' as follows:

> *What pretends to be an image of nature is nothing more or less than nature herself. The means of the art are reality. Everyone knows that the merit of its works consists in obviating any suspicion of art. To constitute a perfect garden, according to the irregular*

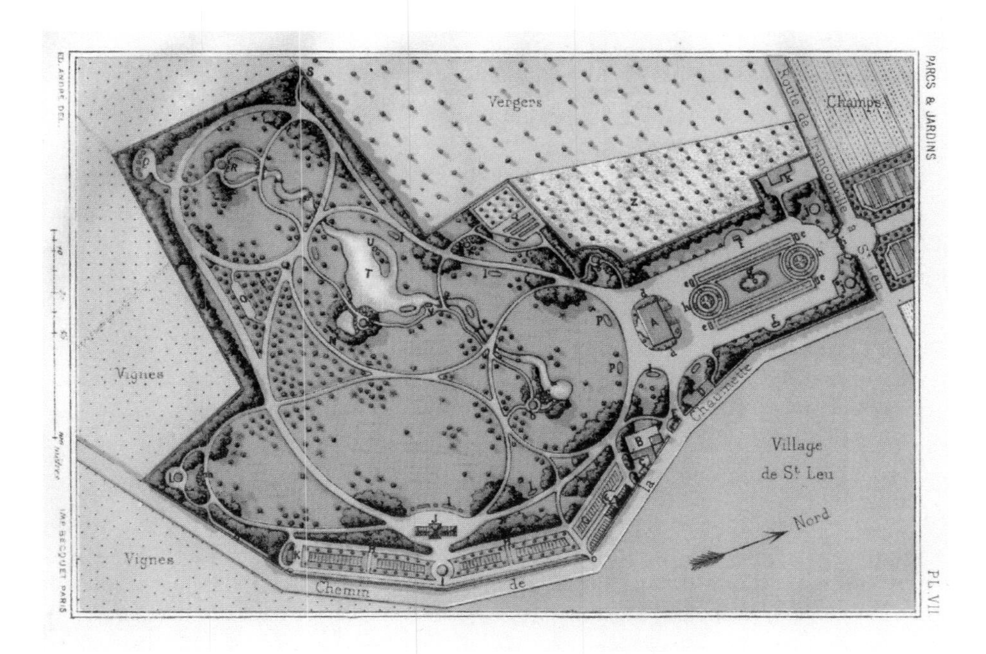

9.1 A typical plan from Édouard André's *The Art of Gardens* , with an 'informal' area (*jardin paysager*) and a 'formal' area for floral bedding (*jardin regulier*).

9.2 This is art, because it was designed by Lancelot Brown, but one could mistake it for 'nature'. The lake lies below Blenheim Palace.

> *system of landscape gardening, we must not have the least suspicion that the grounds have been laid out by art.*[4]

What could an unfortunate designer do? It appeared that, to be works of art, gardens must imitate nature – yet, if they imitate nature, gardens cannot be works of art.

The first proposition, that art should imitate nature, had been agreed by all since ancient times and was the foundation of Neoplatonic aesthetics. The second proposition arose from the empiricist aim, explained in the previous chapter, of creating 'natural' gardens using native plants, rocks, water and jagged lines. Picturesque gardens, with a capital 'P', became indistinguishable from Mother Nature herself: romantic, wild, unadorned, intensely desirable – and impossible to live with. In Britain, and elsewhere, garden design reached an impasse which cannot be explained with the usual British design-historical categories of 'Stuart' 'Georgian' and 'Victorian' Gardens. These labels inspire royal devotion in some and republican dismay in others but do not illuminate the whys or wherefores or garden history. Royal leadership in garden design had, in any event, died with the Stuarts.

When there was no obvious way forward, most designers turned back: they reproduced ancient styles and combined them in new ways. A Great Debate led to a Great Turning Point and a number of approaches:

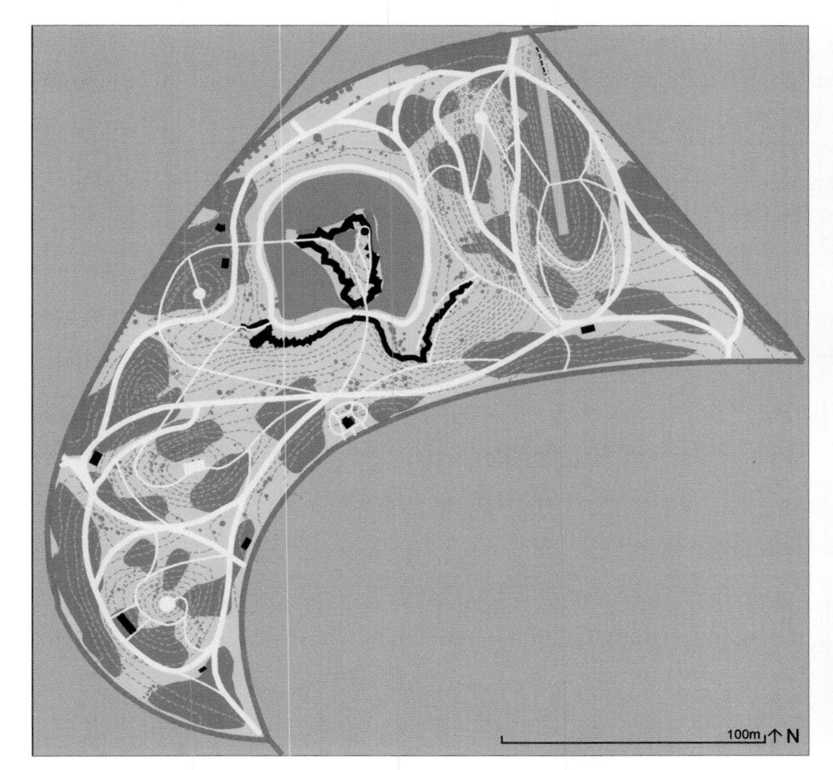

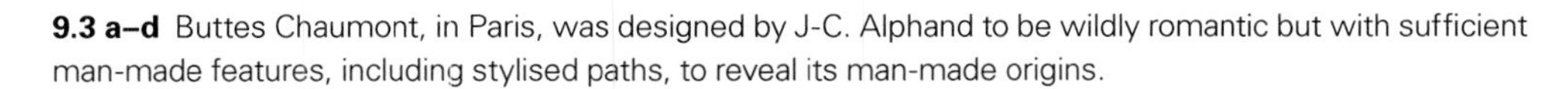
9.3 a–d Buttes Chaumont, in Paris, was designed by J-C. Alphand to be wildly romantic but with sufficient man-made features, including stylised paths, to reveal its man-made origins.

- *the Landscape style*: using ideas selected from the past in a structured sequence;
- *the Mixed style*: using design styles selected from other countries and displayed as if in a museum;
- *the Formal-Informal style*: using rectilinear and curvilinear elements;
- *the Gardenesque style*: using plants selected from favourite regions of the world and arranged to display their individuality;
- *nationalistic styles*: using design ideas selected from glorious eras in the histories of the nations in which the gardens were made.

The word 'selected' is used in each of the above accounts to underline what they have in common. 'Eclectic' derives from the Greek *eklektikos*, meaning 'to select or pick out'.

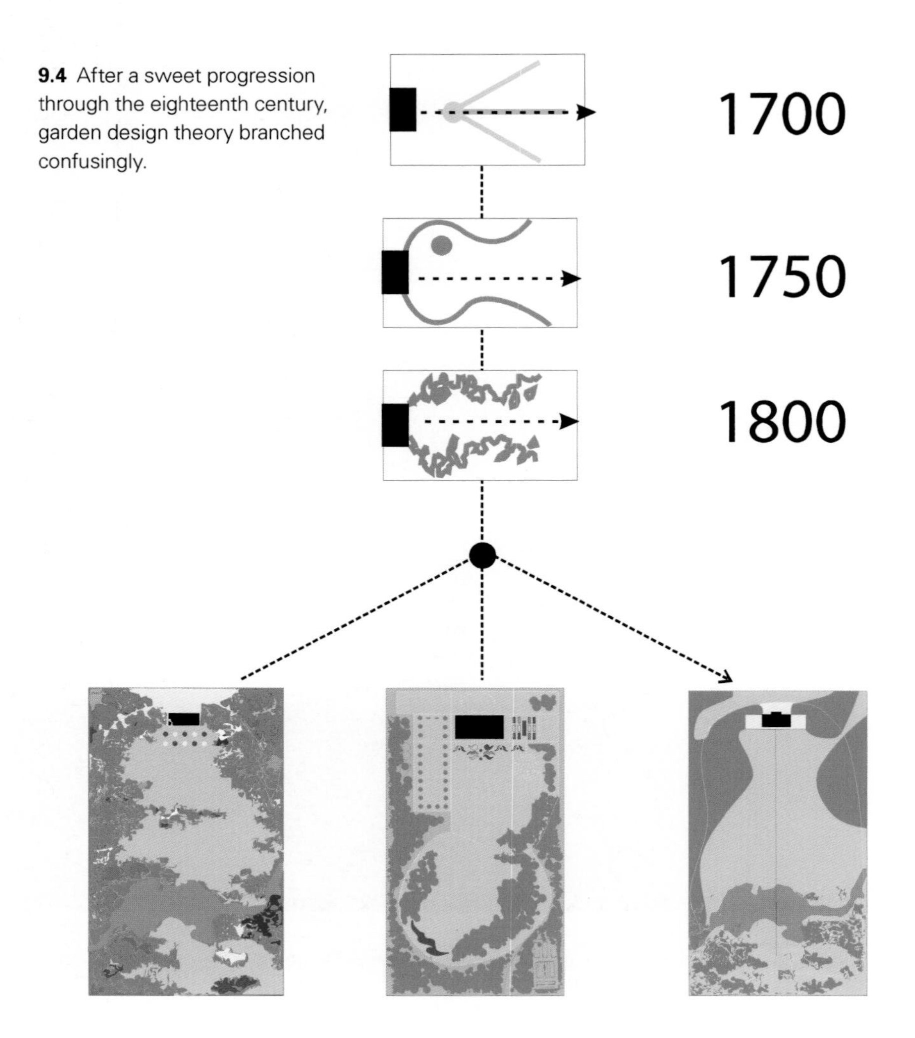

9.4 After a sweet progression through the eighteenth century, garden design theory branched confusingly.

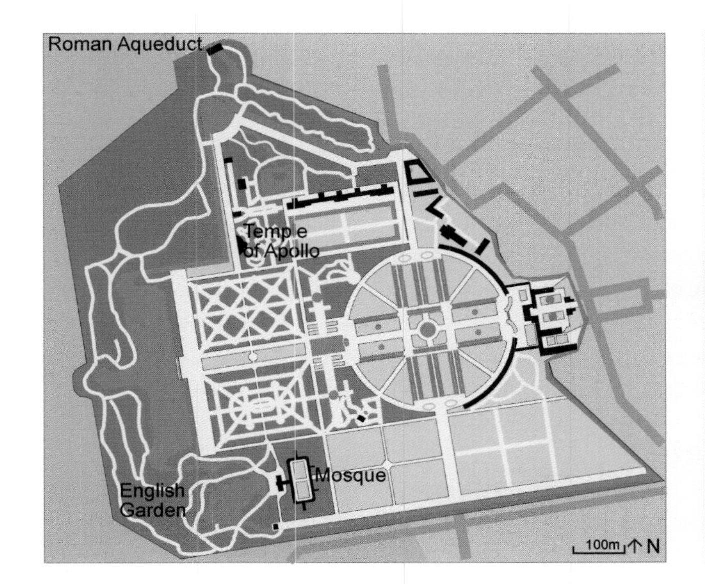

9.5 a, b, c Friedrich Ludwig von Sckell encircled Schwetzingen's Baroque garden with a landscape park. The garden has Classical statuary, a mosque, an obelisk and a Roman aqueduct.

In Ancient Greece, the Eclectics were philosophers who, on principle, selected and combined the best ideas from every source. Systematic philosophers disdain the practice but most of us do it to a greater or lesser extent.

In the absence of a workable design theory, eclecticism ran amok in the gardens of nineteenth-century Europe. The Landscape style was most popular in Britain and

Germany. In Britain, it led to the addition of terraces and woodland gardens to Brownian parks; in Germany, picturesque parks were wrapped round Baroque gardens. The Mixed style was popular in most parts of Europe and also in North America. The Gardenesque style affected botanical gardens everywhere and private woodland gardens in Britain. Nationalism affected most countries. Before examining these approaches in detail, one point should be emphasised: some of the resulting gardens were of high quality. One may find them lacking in a spiritual or artistic dimension but this is akin to criticising Berlioz for not being Bach, or a house for not being a church. The four approaches rested on a sophisticated theoretical debate, which also created the modern profession of landscape architecture and helped split it from garden design. In the longer term, the ideas were of more importance than their design consequences.

The Great Debate

Between 1793 and 1815, while continental Europe was in thrall to Napoleon, three English squires – Sir Uvedale Price, Richard Payne Knight, and Humphry Repton – conducted a discussion of garden theory. Most nineteenth-century garden theorists, including John Claudius Loudon, Prince Pückler-Muskau, Frederick Law Olmsted and Gertrude Jekyll, took this debate as the starting point for their own deliberations. It also had a deep influence on twentieth-century town and country planning. The principles of Mr Price,[5] the theories of Mr Knight, the reputation of Mr Repton and the phenomenal literary output of Mr Loudon spread round the world, aided by the industrialisation of book production and distribution. The debate centred on the classic themes of utility, firmness and beauty (see Chapter 1).

Knight was a wealthy dilettante, the grandson of an ironmaster and the brother of a famous horticulturalist. He opened the debate with a Gilpinesque attack on Brown's style of landscape gardening.[6] The illustrations supporting his argument showed Brown's work as 'bald and shaven' in contrast with the romantic charm of Dame Nature. A jibe against Repton was included, because he had proclaimed himself Brown's successor. Repton was both hurt and worried that his business might suffer. He entered the debate, emphasising utility, and poked fun at Knight for placing picturesque rocks on his front lawn at Downton Castle (see p. 281). Price agreed this was impractical but joined Knight in writing lyrically about Dame Nature's seductive beauty and her affinity with the masculinity of Classical architecture. A compromise was reached, in the best tradition of English diplomacy.

In 1986, albeit unrequested, I put my services as a technical editor at the disposal of the departed squires by writing a collective opinion for them to give to a client who wished to 'improve his estate'.[7] Their collective opinion was based on the following principles:

1. There should be a grand transition, both philosophical and visual, from the realm of art to the realm of nature.
2. The foreground, near the dwelling house, should be the realm of art.

9.6 a, b, c King Ludwig is unlikely to have been directly influenced by the three English squires but his Romantic love of scenery and history produced a similarly eclectic enthusiasm. Linderhof has a transition from art to nature, a terrace for social events, a serpentine park, a Sublime background and exotic buildings in various styles.

9.7 The Devil's Bridge, Teufelsbrücke, on the St Gothard Pass provided Grand Tourists with a famously Sublime experience.

3 Exotic plants should be used near the dwelling but not elsewhere in the estate.
4 The design should be based on nature's compositional principles, as illustrated in the work of the great landscape paintings of Italy.
5 The design should respond to the character of the locality in terms of climate, materials and design traditions.

In time, the first of these principles led to the Landscape style, the second to the Mixed style and the third to the Gardenesque style. The fourth principle led to the term 'landscape architecture'. The fifth principle influenced nationalistic approaches to design and to the inception of the Arts and Crafts movement. Had the principles been better understood by their protagonists and the public, they might have resulted in even better gardens. But scale was a problem. The five ideas worked well on the 300 ha estates typical of royal and aristocratic gardens. They were less companionable in the small suburban estates of the rising middle class.

The debate is often described as the 'picturesque controversy', because it centred on the relationship between landscape paintings and landscape design, but this label does little justice to the participants. Knight and Price had a keen interest in aesthetic theory. Repton cared about every aspect of the relationship between landform, water, planting, buildings and gardens. All three wished to see a just balance between the Vitruvian values.[8]

Landscape style

Knight, Price and Repton used initial capitals for the words Beautiful, Sublime and Picturesque to mark their use as part of a specialised aesthetic vocabulary. As explained by Edmund Burke, 'Beautiful' meant smooth, flowing, like the body of a beautiful woman. 'Sublime' meant wild and frightening, like a rough sea or the views that might be obtained while crossing the Alps on a rocky track in a horse-drawn coach. 'Picturesque' was an intermediate term, introduced after Burke, to describe a scene with elements of both the Beautiful and the Sublime. Without its initial capital, 'picturesque' means 'like a picture'. In what is called the Landscape style in this book, picturesque gardens have a sequential transition from a Beautiful foreground through a Picturesque middle ground to a Sublime background. Composing gardens like paintings integrated the design ideas of the eighteenth century to create a landscape design concept of significant grandeur and exceptionally wide application.

The Landscape style is the chief support for the claim that British designers made a unique contribution to Western culture during the eighteenth century. In his 1955 Reith Lectures, Nikolaus Pevsner used the term 'English picturesque theory' for what he described as an 'English national planning theory' (see p. 336).[9] Pevsner stated that it 'lies hidden in the writings of the improvers from Pope to Uvedale Price, and Payne Knight' and that it gave English town planners 'something of great value to offer to other nations'. He then asked whether the same can be said 'of painting, of sculpture, and of architecture proper'. His answer was that Henry Moore and other sculptors had 'given England a position in European sculpture such as she has never before held', but that English painting and architecture of the period were of markedly inferior quality. By the end of the twentieth century, Moore was still regarded as a great artist and the importance of the landscape planning theory identified by Pevsner had taken on a global relevance.

9.8 Beautiful and Sublime – a nymph in the garden of York House in London.

9.9 a, b Sheringham exemplifies Repton's use of terraces to create garden-to-park transitions (see p. 3).

9.10 Brown's serpentine park at Harewood House was adapted to the Landscape style by adding a terrace (designed by Charles Barry).

Partly inspired by Pevsner, I wrote in *Landscape Planning and Environmental Impact Design* that:

> *The idea of forming a graded transition from art to nature remained at the heart of English garden design from 1793 until 1947. When the 1947 Town and Country Planning Act imposed a squeeze on garden size, the transition idea leapt the garden wall and took*

9.11 Lancelot Brown's parks at **a** Bleiheim, **b** Castle Ashby and **c** Longleat were furnished with terraces and formal gardens in the nineteenth century.

> *over the country. Planners became enthused with the notion that towns should be tightly urban in character and surrounded by a Brownian agricultural hinterland, itself giving way to wildly irregular National Parks and Areas of Outstanding Natural Beauty. Strict planning controls were imposed on developments in the green belt, so that towns would become denser and the spaces between buildings could develop a townscape character, with urban squares and circuses like those of Renaissance towns.*[10]

It provides a sound theoretical base for the profession of landscape architecture (see p. 337).

The transition idea also appeared in France. Edouard André advocated a style 'in which the *jardin paysager* followed a *jardin regulier* as an ideal expression of the transition from architecture to nature'.[11] Similarly, Duchêne sought an 'undisrupted harmony' in the flow from a geometric pool to a picturesque river; using this sequence to link the resident to

9.12 a, b, c Charlottenburg, in Berlin, has a transition from a 'formal garden' to a 'romantic park'.

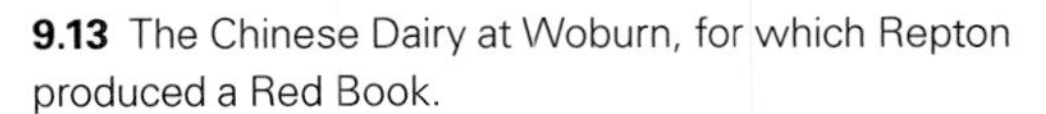

9.13 The Chinese Dairy at Woburn, for which Repton produced a Red Book.

9.14 a, b Alton Towers was sharply criticised by Loudon for its eclecticism, though it is often associated with his name.

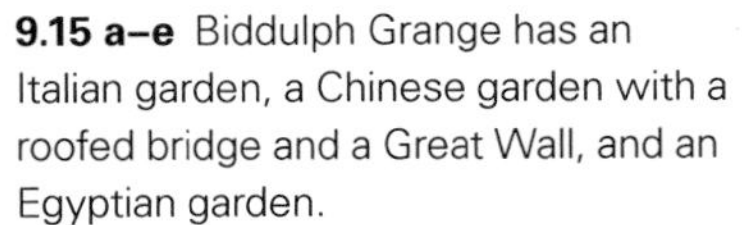

9.15 a–e Biddulph Grange has an Italian garden, a Chinese garden with a roofed bridge and a Great Wall, and an Egyptian garden.

9.16 a, b Branitz was designed by Prince Pückler-Muskau, who admired Repton. It has an ornamented terrace near the house and an exotic pyramid tomb in the lake.

9.17 Guildford Castle, in England, was once a royal residence. It was bought in 1885, 'dedicated to the use of the public for ever', and subsequently used for carpet bedding.

9.18 Insel Mainau, Lake Constance, Germany, became an arboretum in the mid-nineteenth century and a full Mixed style garden in the twentieth century.

9.19 The Pfaueninsel ('Peacock Island'), Berlin-Wannsee, Germany, was laid out by Peter Joseph Lenné, after 1818, with exotic plants, animals and a rose garden.

9.20 The Japanese garden at Courances was made in the early twentieth century.

9.21 Repton's design for a rose garden at Valleyfield.

the forest, he appeared to combine the syntax of both the regular and Landscape styles. Towards the end of his career, Duchêne made more 'architectural' gardens, because his clients had less money and land, but he did not become a Modernist.[12]

Mixed style

The nineteenth century was a time more of industrial than agricultural revolution. Fortunes were made and eighteenth-century parks were adorned with costly gardens surrounding mansions. The three squires' original idea had been to make a realm of art (e.g. a terrace) near the house, presumably so that families could enjoy the utilitarian pleasure of afternoon tea while watching children in sailor suits gambol on perfect lawns. Repton's imagination leapt the terrace. He began recommending a rich mixture of different types of garden. With commendable clarity he argued that:

> *There is no more absurdity in collecting gardens of different styles, dates, characters, and dimensions, in the same enclosure, than in placing the works of a Raphael and a Teniers in the same cabinet, or books sacred and profane in the same library.*[13]

This became the Eclectics' Charter, providing a logical foundation for what Edward Kemp was later to call the Mixed style. Repton was the first theorist to advocate collections of gardens in diverse styles. He saw himself as a successor to Brown, which, in terms of professional status, he was. Later commentators saw Repton as a stylist in the manner of Brown, which he was not. They also saw Loudon as an advocate of the Mixed style, which he never was.[14] Confusion reigned, both theoretical and visual.

The eclectic trend which Repton began soon led to whole gardens being laid out in styles associated with particular countries: Chinese gardens, Japanese gardens, Swiss gardens, Indian gardens, American gardens, Italian gardens and English gardens. Sometimes the styles were used in compartments. Sometimes they were very mixed. Italian gardens were the most popular. The introduction of exotic plant species from all over the world assisted the mixture of styles. Two of the best eclectic gardens in England – Biddulph Grange and Alton Towers – were in the English Midlands, an important manufacturing region. It may be that manufacturers had the most money or it may be that they had the most interest in foreign parts. At Biddulph Grange, brilliant use is made of tunnels to keep the stylistic zones apart. In other gardens the search for variety and contrast was assisted by elaborate bedding arrangements. Edward Kemp's account of the Mixed style supports Gothein's opinion that designers forgot to 'look for art at all':

> *Serpentine or wavy lines may be regarded as the characteristic features of the mixed style. Its object is beauty of lines, and general variety. Roundness, smoothness, freedom from angularity, and grace rather than dignity or grandeur, are among its numerous indications. It does not reject straight lines entirely near the house, or in connexion with a flower-garden, or a rosary, or a subordinate building (as a greenhouse) that has a separate piece of garden to it. Nor does it refuse to borrow from the picturesque in regard to the arrangement and grouping of plants ... It has all the grace of nature without its ruggedness, and the refinement of art apart from its stiffness and severity.*[15]

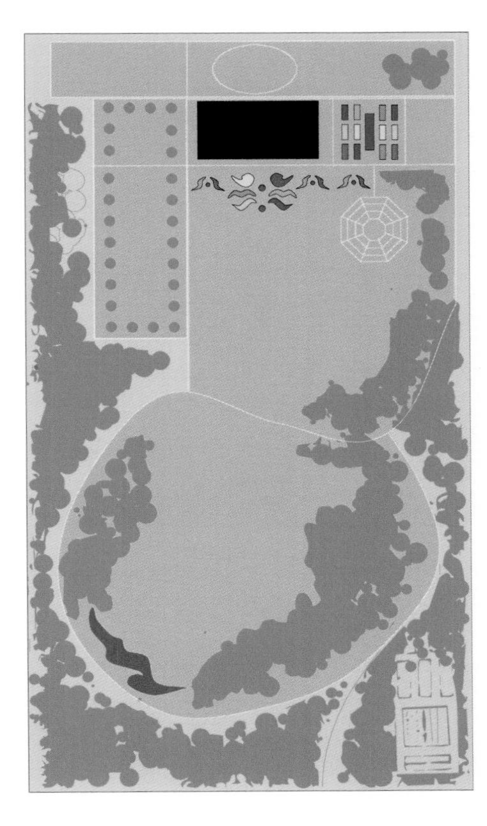

9.22 Diagram of Mixed style, applied to the area near the house.

In considering how the chaste manners of the eighteenth century evolved into the nineteenth-century's promiscuous eclecticism, one should remember both Repton's theoretical position and the different circumstances of our predecessors. Should you or I wish to see foreign gardens or exotic plants, we can use the web to find a thousand images or book a flight. Our predecessors heard travellers' tales of astounding places but had to rely on engravings and bric-a-brac to learn more. Bombay could not be a holiday destination when the ship went via Cape Town, took three months and exposed travellers to hellish tropical diseases. To modern eyes the eclecticism of Victorian gardens may be excessive.[16] Norman Newton used 'Single Track Eclecticism Takes Over' as a chapter title.[17] To Victorian eyes, it expressed a multicultural enthusiasm and was a means of transporting the imagination to far-away places and far-off times. It should also be remembered that the Augustan style had itself used an eclectic range of garden 'follies'. They, and the Mixed style, were products of Romanticism.

9.23 Repton conceived Brighton's Royal Pavilion and Nash executed the design.

9.24 The Roman Baths at Potsdam, designed by Karl Friedrich von Schinkel.

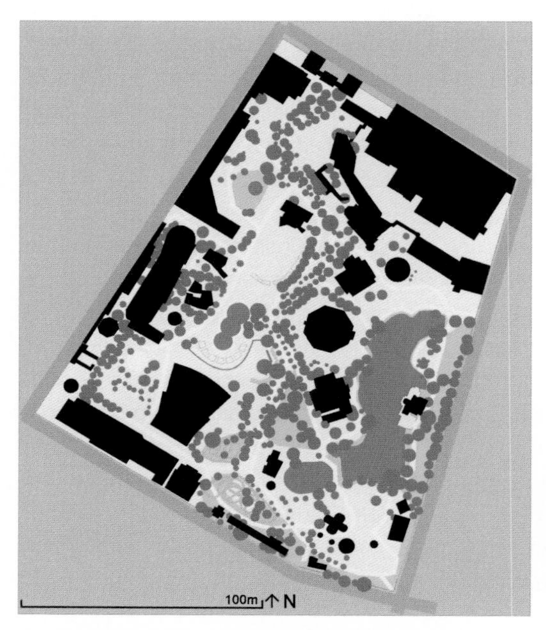

9.25 a, b, c The Tivoli Garden in Copenhagen was opened in 1843 and continues to be managed in the Mixed style.

9.26 The Villa Monastero, Lake Como, Italy, was furnished with a Moorish loggia in the nineteenth century, and then with a botanical garden.

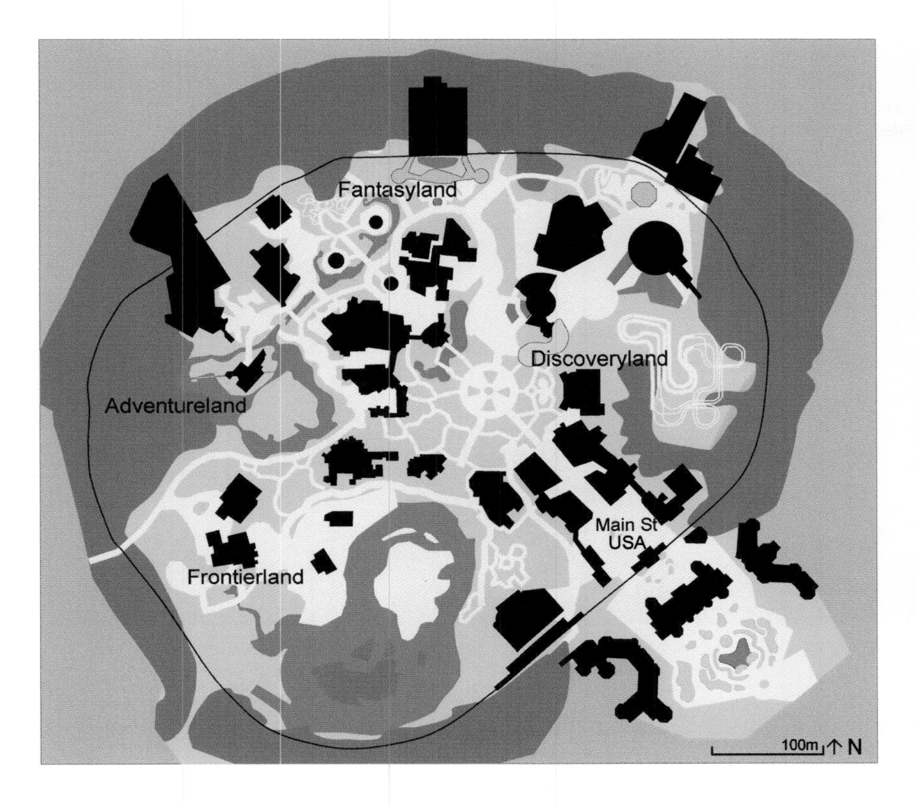

9.27 a, b, c Disneyland Paris opened in 1992 and was designed in the Mixed style. The Sleeping Beauty Castle is believed to have been inspired by King Ludwig II's Schloss Neuschwanstein (below).

When Ancient Egypt was uncovered by Napoleon, there was a craze for Egyptology: Biddulph has an Egyptian garden. When serious excavations began at Pompeii, there was craze for Roman gardens: Schinkel added a Roman Garden to the Potsdam landscape. When plant collectors returned from the mountains, everyone wanted an 'Alpine' garden. Many of the best and worst nineteenth-century gardens were in England, because of the maritime origins of her wealth. Others were in America, like the Du Pont family's Longwood Gardens in Pennsylvania (1907). Also popular for commercial parks and exposition grounds, the popularity of the Mixed style did not end with the nineteenth century. In the twentieth century it was used for theme parks. The original Disneyland, in California, let visitors taste the romance of the Old World and the Wild West without a passport. Disneyland Paris was located outside an Old World capital but its Magic Kingdom was inspired by nineteenth-century Romanticism: the Neuschwanstein of 'mad' King Ludwig II of Bavaria, or the rebuilt castle of Segovia in Spain. Alton Towers was a fine example of the Mixed style before it became, very appropriately, the location of Britain's largest theme park.

Postmodernist theory did much to legitimate the theoretical basis of eclecticism. The argument, in short, was that Modernism was elitist and autocratic; it prescribed a single approach, the International style, as morally and aesthetically acceptable.

9.28 Longwood Gardens, Pennsylvania, designed by the co-owner of a chemical company. Pierre S. Du Pont was a meticulous engineer with a special interest in fountains. He was inspired by visits to French gardens.

Postmodernism boasts of being multicultural and multi-ethnic, arguing that East is as good as West, women are as good as men, black is as good as white, Hindu is as good as Christian and eclecticism is as good as rationalism. Repton might well have agreed and it is a pity that this aspect of his legacy is not better remembered. He was, for exam-

9.29 Crystal palaces were built to house exotic plants from exotic lands (Buen Retiro in Madrid).

ple, responsible for persuading the Prince of Wales to build an Indian Pavilion in the heart of Britain's most Georgian seaside town: the Royal Pavilion in Brighton.[18]

Gardenesque style

John Claudius Loudon began his career with a gutter-low opinion of Repton and no appreciation of the Landscape style. He was determined to follow 'the principles of Mr Price' (see Chapter 8), and his lavish two-volume work, *Country Residences*, of 1806,

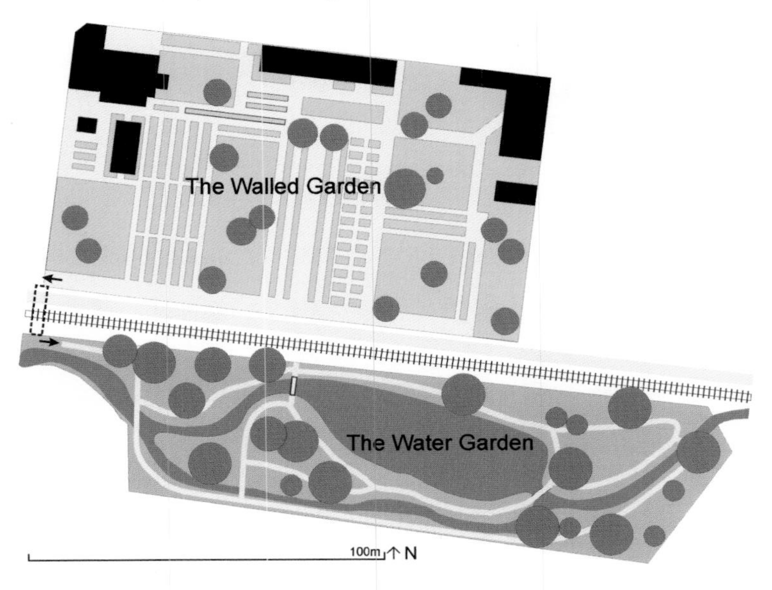

9.30 Monet's planting design at Giverny is gardenesque: **a** garden plan, **b** the Water Garden, **c** the walled garden.

9.31 Trebah in Cornwall has an exotic woodland garden.

9.32 a–d Kew is a botanic garden with Gardenesque planting.

9.34 a, b Circular beds in Greenwich Park.

9.33 Cragside, in the north of England, is immediately 'recognisable' as a work of man, rather than 'wild nature'.

was full of proposals for converting estates laid out in the manner of 'Capability' Brown to 'Mr Price's principles', meaning Picturesque irregularity.[19] One has to doubt the popularity of this style with clients: from the illustrations, it looks as though Loudon specialised in converting fine parks to tracts of weeds.

Ill-health terminated Loudon's Picturesque quest in the 1810s. But in the 1820s Loudon returned to landscape gardening, this time as an author with a full appreciation of the logical impasse. Drawing intellectual support from Quatremère de Quincy, Loudon proposed that gardens in the irregular, or Picturesque, style should be planted with exotic species, to make them 'recognizable' as works of art entirely distinct from unadorned nature.[20] This aspect of the Gardenesque, which Loudon named the Principle of Recognition, was constant. But Loudon spread confusion by using the term in different ways on different occasions. Circular beds could be Gardenesque, if they displayed a gar-

9.35 The garden in the style of Louis XIV, at Champs-sur-Marne, was designed by Henri Duchêne and Achille Duchêne after 1895.

dener's skill.[21] An arboretum could be Gardenesque, if it showed the individual character of each specimen to best effect. In my view, the best application of the idea was in composing exotic plants in the 'natural' arrangements characteristic of landscape paintings. This led to a genuinely original nineteenth-century idea, one that remains popular today: the woodland garden. It works particularly well in the warm, wet conditions that favour the naturalisation of rhododendron species, including the cypress swamps of the southern United States and the woodland valleys of South West England. Exotic plants can be composed with the eye of an artist, as Monet showed at Giverny (after 1883) and as Jekyll showed at Munstead Wood (after 1895).

Nationalistic styles

Nationalism blew through nineteenth-century Europe. It affected gardens, garden owners and garden designers. Despite the fact that Romantic garden theorists, like Christian

9.36 Duchêne's recreation of the style of Le Nôtre, at Courance, has an elegant charm scarcely found in the master's own work.

9.37 Cecilienhof, designed by Paul Schultze-Naumburg in the manner of an English country estate, was the last Hohenzollern palace and the location of the 1945 Potsdam Conference.

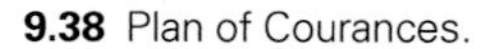

9.38 Plan of Courances.

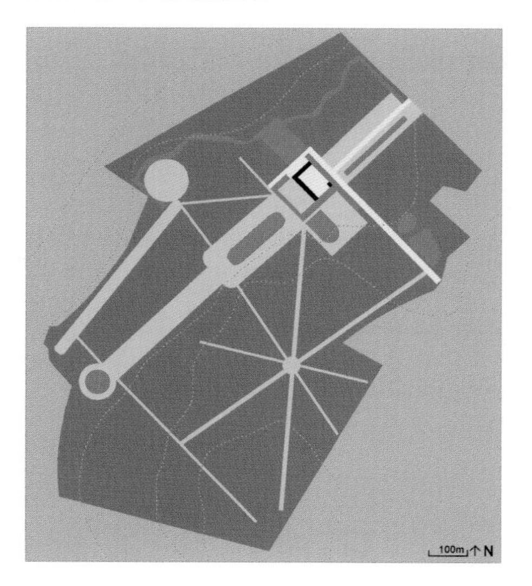

Hirschfeld[22] in Germany and John Claudius Loudon in Britain, had cautioned against mixing styles, their writings fuelled eclecticism. As the nineteenth century drew to its close, writers and designers saw nationalism as a potentially purifying force. Garden historians tend to welcome the influence of nationalistic movements on the appreciation of old gardens, but to lament the more speculative and inaccurate 'restorations' of gardens carried out in the nineteenth century – rather as Victorian architects have been castigated for imaginative 'restorations' of medieval churches. A different complaint is made about present-day reconstructions: with their emphasis on archaeological and documentary evidence, they can be so accurate that they are boring.

France, after the 1870 war with Prussia, was one of the first countries to be touched by artistic nationalism. French critics found fault with German music for aesthetic and nationalistic reasons. The 'Anglo-Chinese' style of garden design was seen as a foreign invader which could be expelled rather more easily than the German army. The France of Louis XIV was revered as a triumphant example of the national genius. Henri Duchêne set up his office in 1877 and his son, Achille, joined him at the age of 12. Their first great project, for a wealthy and patriotic industrialist, was the restoration of Le Nôtre's design at Vaux-le-Vicomte. It was successful and the office prospered. In addition to restoring other Le Nôtre Parks (e.g. Champs-sur-Marne, Le Marais and Courances), they designed new parks somewhat in the style of le Nôtre. These included Voisins in France and the water parterre at Blenheim Palace in England (Figure 9.11 a).

Germany had various reasons for a nationalist approach to landscape. First, a love of German soil, and forests, had been present in the culture since Celtic times. Second, the

9.39 Jac P. Thijsse overlooking his wildflower garden.

9.40 The cover of Thijsse's book *De bloemen in onzen tuin door* [*The Plants in Our Garden*] celebrates native plants.

Romantic love of nature, fanned by Goethe, had grown strong. Third, the study of ecology and native habitats had originated in Germany, under the influence of Humboldt and Haeckel. Fourth, the nation unified in the 1870s took a new pride in its history. In *Heimatschutz* (*Homeland Protection*), published in 1901, Ernst Rudorff protested at the

9.41 Completed in 1936, Hearst Castle was inspired by Spanish and Portuguese villas. The Neptune Pool is surrounded by colonnades and one can't help thinking that Caligula would have appreciated the design.

destruction of nature and called for protected reserves. The architect Paul Schultze-Naumburg used these ideas in his books *Gärten* (*Gardens*, 1902) and *Die Entstellung unseres Landes* (*The Disfigurement of Our Countryside*, 1905). Willy Lange, often referring to Rousseau, Goethe, Schiller, and Humboldt, advocated nature gardens in his book, *Gartengestaltung der Neuzeit* (*Garden Design for Modern Times*, 1907). Such ideas were discredited after the Second World War because Hitler had supported them.

Holland developed an ecological approach to gardens under the influence of Jac P. Thijsse and others. The results can be seen at the Amsterdam Bos Park, the Jac P. Thijsse Park and the Thijsse Hof. Thijsse favoured the use of native plants in garden design.

England was influenced by nationalism in the late nineteenth century, for sentimental, patriotic and artistic reasons.[23] Writers and artists rebelled against High Victorian eclecticism and yearned for gardens to be as they had been in the merrie days of Bacon and Shakespeare. The restoration of Penshurst Place in the 1870s, based on an illustration from Kip, was an early product of this sentiment. Pre-Raphaelite painters dreamed of Olde England, and painted their visions. This contribution to the Arts and Crafts movement, which led in time to the establishment of Britain's National Trust (which has its own style of garden management), will be discussed in Chapter 10.

America was proud of its nationhood but always aware of its European roots. It was natural for designers to adopt an eclectic approach, based on paintings, drawings and plans from the Old World. Colonial gardens were often the work of immigrant designers and European influence remained strong in the work of Andrew Jackson Downing, Calvert Vaux, Frederick Law Olmsted, Charles Platt, Beatrix Farrand and others. Yet the twentieth century saw a growing demand for an American style.

Australia, largely peopled by British and Irish settlers, had a strong sense of 'the old country'. Colonists yearned for gardens and parks like those they had known in Victorian Britain. It was only towards the end of the twentieth century that Australian garden designers took an interest in the native flora and in the garden cultures of the other nations from which immigration was then allowed.

Landscape architecture

Repton, Price and Knight accepted the compositional principles of the great landscape paintings as an unimpeachable standard of good taste. Sir Walter Scott was of the same opinion and one of his friends took the idea further. Gilbert Laing Meason published 150 copies of a book on *The Landscape Architecture of the Great Painters of Italy* in 1828.[24] Meason advised designers to study relationships between buildings and their settings in the landscape paintings of Giotto, Titian, Poussin, Veronese, Claude, Tintoretto, Raphael, Domenichino, Michelangelo and others. Meason did not make a name for himself with this idea but the most prolific garden author of the day liked the title of his book. Loudon used the term 'landscape architecture' in his 1840 edition of Repton's

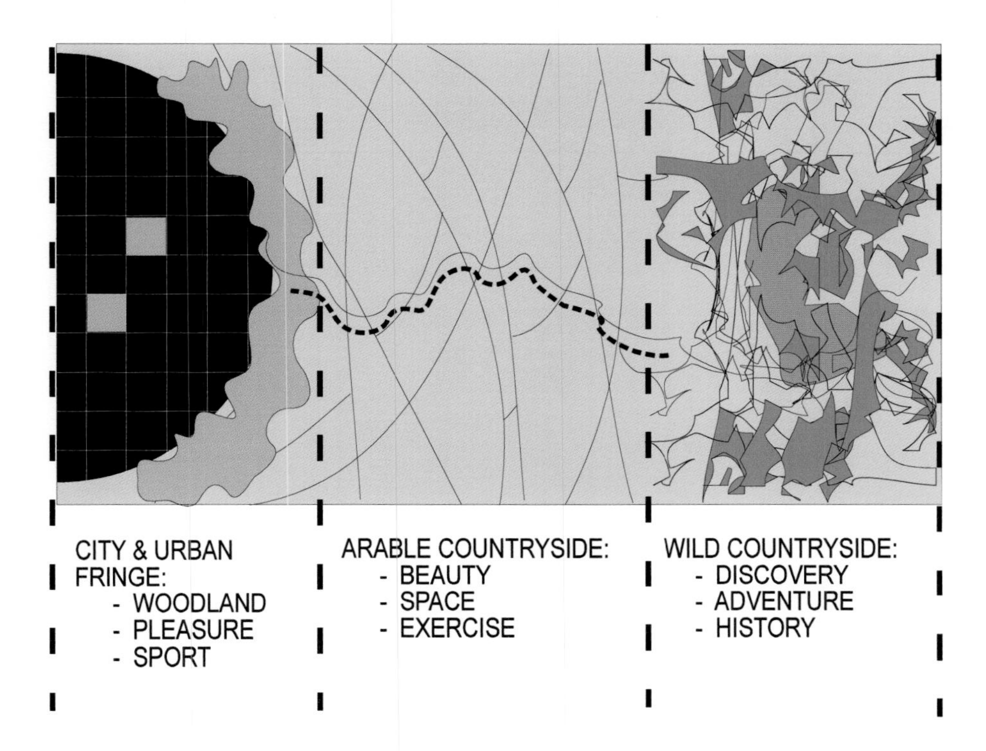

9.42 The Landscape style led, in the twentieth century, to the idea of planning compact towns, greenways through an agricultural hinterland and national parks in distant hills and valleys.

9.43 Meason's own house at Lindertis was an example of landscape architecture based on the great painters of Italy – and on a narrow definition could be regarded as the world's first landscape architecture project.

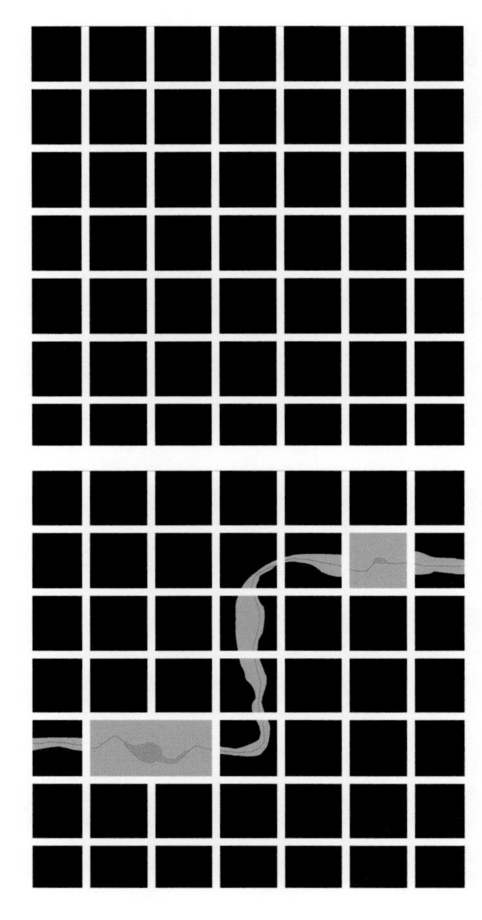

9.44 The profession of landscape architecture was founded, by Olmsted, on the brilliant idea of planning greenspace to run through America's gridiron cities.

9.45 Central Park, New York, inaugurated the modern profession of landscape architecture and remains the best example of what can be achieved by visionary landscape planning geared to urban design.

works: *The Landscape Gardening and Landscape Architecture of the Late H. Repton Esq.* It was then taken up by the American author, Andrew Jackson Downing, who considered Loudon 'the most distinguished gardening author of the age'.[25]

Calvert Vaux, a young architect persuaded by Downing to move from London to New York, also liked the term. When he collaborated with Frederick Law Olmsted on an entry for the Central Park competition of 1858, they described themselves as 'landscape architects'. Since Olmsted spent most of his subsequent career on parks and park systems, his chosen professional title became associated with public projects, as distinct from private gardens, and this remains its predominant use. The strengths landscape architecture draws from its garden design heritage include:

- the Vitruvian design tradition of balancing utility, firmness and beauty;
- use of the word 'landscape' to mean 'a good place' – as an objective for the design process;
- a comprehensive approach to open space planning involving city parks, greenways and nature parks outside towns;
- a planning theory about the contextualisation of development projects;

9.46 Olmsted's 'Emerald Necklace' starts in Boston Common and follows parkways to Franklin Park.

- the principle that urban development plans should be adapted to their landscape context;
- the professionalism associated with the roles of a 'co-ordinator', 'architect' and 'head of techniques' relating to outdoor design.

Landscape architecture is now an internationally accepted professional title for one of the world's most important professions. But its adoption caused garden design and landscape architecture to split apart, with significant damage to both activities. Landscape architects, though professionally trained, were deprived of a history or theory for their activity. Garden design suffered the same fate for a different reason: it became a branch of horticulture, supported by a largely scientific and technical education. After the establishment of the world's first landscape architecture course, at Harvard University in 1900, most education courses adopted this title during the second half of the twentieth century. The University of Greenwich tried to heal the breach at an educational level by establishing parallel degrees in Landscape Architecture and Garden Design. The former emphasised open space and public projects; the latter emphasised enclosed space and private projects. Technical and theoretical courses were shared.

Landscape architecture was often concerned with creating areas of natural scenery and public gardens in towns. The Olmsted and Vaux design for Central Park had areas equivalent to the stages of a transition from art to nature. Olmsted and Eliot applied the same idea of transition to the entire Boston metropolitan region. The first European to use 'landscape architect' as a professional title, Patrick Geddes, designed a park in Dunfermline and went on to become the most inspirational planning theorist of the twentieth century. Some of the best examples of landscape planning at the scale of an urban region are in continental Europe, including the cities of Stockholm, Stuttgart and Barcelona. In America, the Greenways movement has injected new energy into open space planning and new life into old cities.[26]

9.47 Gardenesque style.

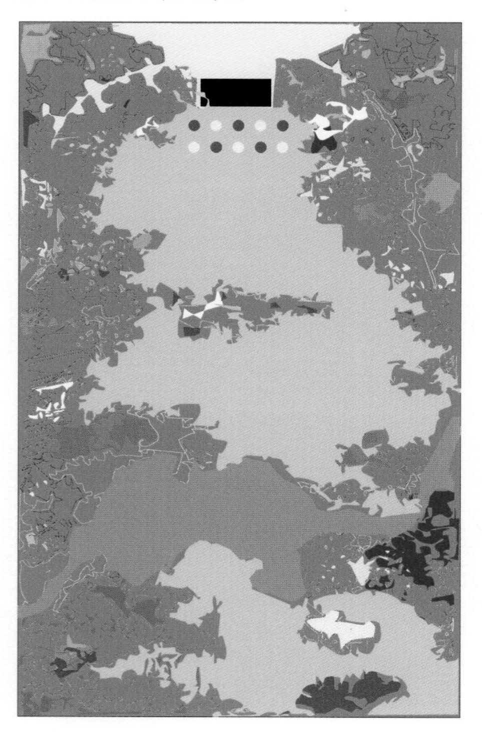

Styles and examples

Gardenesque style

Use: Picturesque gardens, of the type discussed in the previous chapter, came to be used for collections of exotic plants. Loudon, believing this should be a primary role of gardens, invented the term 'Gardenesque' to describe a Picturesque design which was 'recognisable' as a work of art because it incorporated non-native plants. He also argued that such places would help working men to educate themselves and thus improve their economic status.

Form: To begin with, few aristocratic owners were willing to surround their dwellings with wholly 'irregular' gardens. But in the second half of the nineteenth century many woodland valleys were converted into 'natural compositions' of exotics. Himalayan plants (e.g. rhododendrons and camellias) and North American plants proved particularly well suited to this idea. The diagram shows a Picturesque estate, converted to the Gardenesque by planting exotics. Loudon favoured circular beds because they allow plantsmen to show their skill in combining plants in schemes that look good from all angles. Such beds can still be seen in the flower garden at Greenwich Park (see Figure 9.32).

Kew Gardens, 1841

The original garden was created for Augusta, Princess of Wales, around Kew Palace. She was helped by Sir William Chambers, a sharp critic of Brown's vapidity and an admirer of Chinese gardens, who designed the Pagoda and other buildings for Kew. The estate was acquired by the nation in 1841, as a centre for horticulture, and now contains what is said to be the largest collection of plants in the world. The variety is overwhelming and designers complain about the lack of aesthetic order. But Loudon, one cannot doubt, would have seen it as a prime example of his Gardenesque principles. He would also have admired splendid examples of the building type he did much to promote in his youth: the glasshouse, used for tropical and sub-tropical plants.

At Kew, avenues of different species were planted in various parts of the grounds, taking their position from local features of ground and water without being aligned on one focus

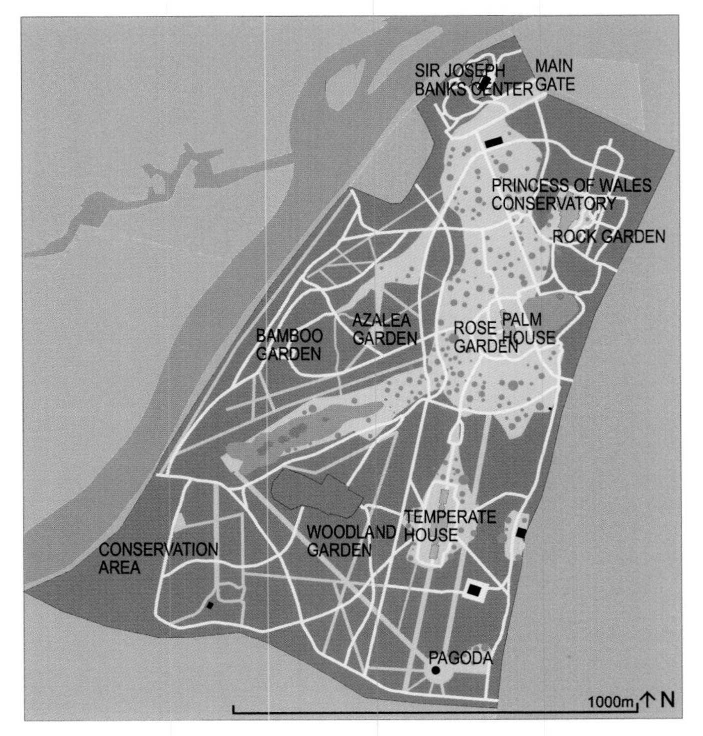

9.48 Kew Gardens, England.

or in a mutually symmetrical pattern ... when Nesfield proposed grading trees by height in the vistas at Kew, and abandoning rigorous botanical order, Glendinning accused him of sacrificing the object of an arboretum for the sake of appearance.

(Brent Elliott)[27]

Leonardslee, 1889

Leonardslee is a development of the planting ideas of Sir Uvedale Price, Richard Payne Knight and Loudon. It displays the Gardenesque principle of composing exotic plants in a picturesque manner, derived from landscape painting. Sir Edmund Loder bought the estate in 1888 and imported a herd of wallabies, whose descendants still thrive on the site. The garden lies in a sheltered valley with a string of ponds, made a century earlier to provide waterpower for the local iron industry. Being damp and slightly acid, the soil is well suited to rhododendrons, camellias and magnolias. Like Sir Edmund, one can walk through the garden imagining oneself in a misty Himalayan valley. Before visiting the garden one might read Sir Joseph Hooker's *Himalayan Journals*. Hooker, who collected *Rhododendron griffithianum*, a parent of the 'Loderi' hybrids, tells of high adventure and intrepid plant collecting. Lenordslee exudes the romance of travel and adventure.

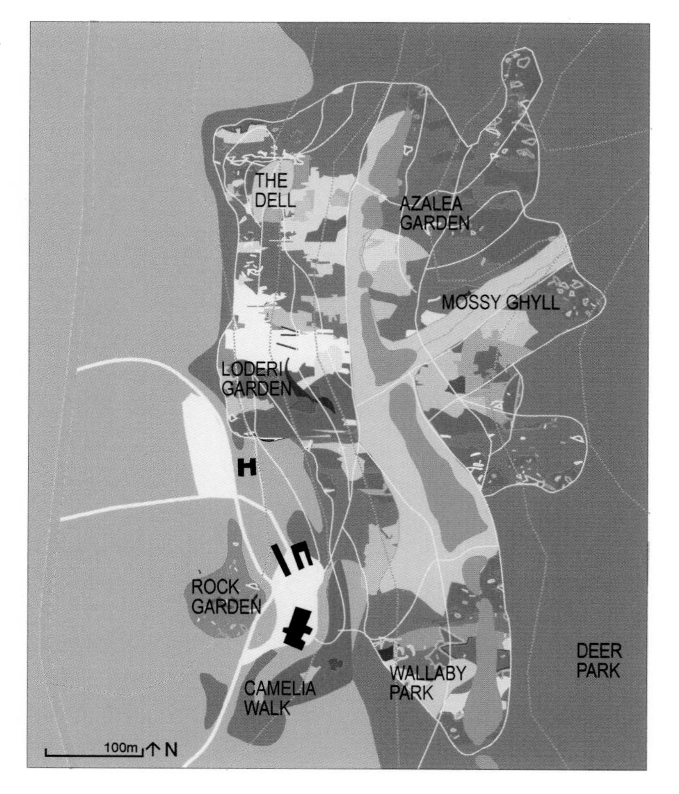

9.49 Leonardslee, England.

> *There must always have been forest here and so it is a perfect site for a woodland garden which is precisely what Sir Edmund Loder set out to create when he started planting in 1888. Within a few years he was raising new rhododendrons as well as buying existing ones. Many fine hybrids were produced by Sir Edmund and his successors, but none destined to have a greater impact on rhododendron breeding than Rhododendron loderi..*
>
> (Arthur Hellyer)[28]

Mixed style

Use: The Gardenesque taste for plant collecting developed into a wider enthusiasm for collecting styles of garden design. Collections helped their owners envision historically and geographically remote areas. As with the Landscape style, the area near the dwelling was used for domestic pleasure. Servants did the physical work of gardening. Owners would take tea, use their lawns for summer games and show visitors their exotic plant collections. Gardens slaked the nineteenth-century thirst for awe, landscape painting, travel, adventure and scientific knowledge.

Form: Towards the end of his career, Humphry Repton argued that there is no more absurdity in collecting styles in a garden than books in a library or pictures in a gallery. This led to a vogue for American, Chinese, Japanese, Italian and other eclectic gardens. Victorian gardens came to be characterised by their mixed collections of zones laid out in different styles, although as the century progressed, the 'Italian' style became the most popular. The diagram shows the style as it was used in suburban gardens. In large parks, there was scope for large collections of styles inspired by themes and countries.

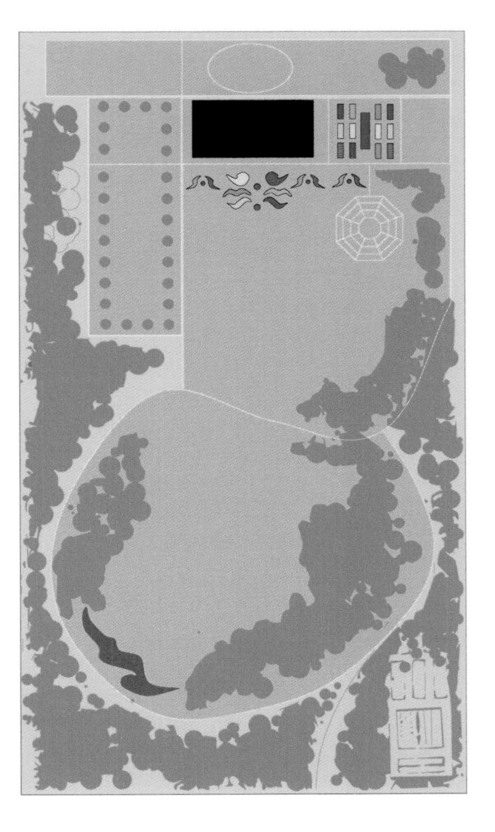

9.50 Mixed style.

Alton Towers, 1827

An early example of the Mixed style, Alton Towers became a popular theme park in the twentieth century. The garden was begun by the eccentric fifteenth Earl of Shrewsbury, who, Loudon relates, consulted every authority, only to avoid 'whatever an artist might recommend'. Loudon himself – and perhaps Repton also – was one of the artists, yet Alton Towers grew under the Reptonian principle that collecting design styles in a garden is no more absurd than collecting diverse pictures in a gallery or books in a library. There is a Swiss cottage, a Stonehenge, a Dutch garden, a Pagoda fountain, a Choragic monument copied from Athens and much else. The rides and slides of the modern theme park merely add to the eccentricity of an early nineteenth-century earl's fancy. He might appreciate them.

> *This nobleman, abounding in wealth, always fond of architecture and gardening, but with much more fancy than sound judgement, seems to have wished to produce something different from everything else. Though he consulted almost every artist, ourselves among the rest, he seems only to have done so for the purpose of avoiding whatever an artist might recommend.*
>
> (John Claudius Loudon)[29]

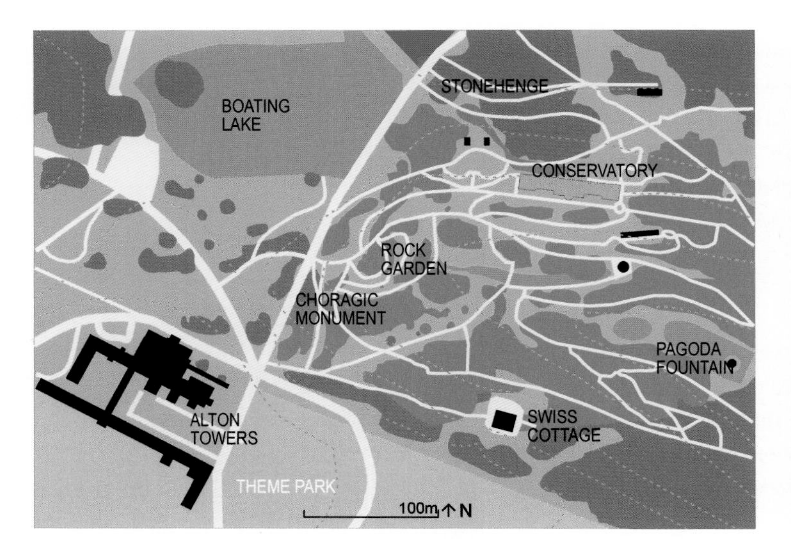

9.51 Alton Towers, England.

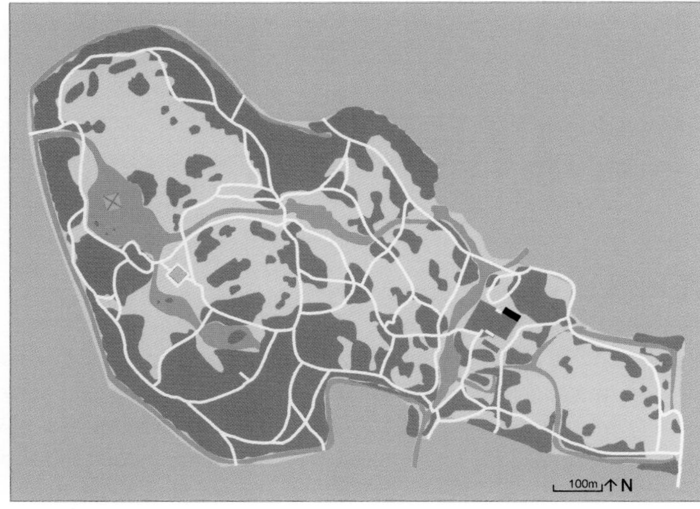

9.52 Branitz, Germany.

Branitz, 1846

This is the 'small' estate which Prince Pückler-Muskau bought when forced to leave Muskau (see p. 295). Still working with English precedents, he made a Serpentine Lake, a Pyramid Lake, a Blue Garden, a Smithy Garden, a Rose Mount, a Moon Mount and Island of Venus, a light iron Kiosk and a series of waterways. It is a good example of the Mixed style. The Prince and his wife lie at rest in a pyramid tomb, in a lake, with an inscription from the *Koran*: 'Graves are the mountain tops of a distant, lovely land'.

> *For the prince, an indispensable component of the artistic effect of the garden was its separation from the park. The garden was related to the castle, and was seen by him as an 'extended dwelling place', whereas he interpreted the surrounding park area as 'concentrated idealized nature'.*
>
> (Ehrenfried Kluckert)[30]

Biddulph Grange, 1860

Biddulph Grange epitomises the Mixed style as effectively as Vaux-le-Vicomte and Stourhead represent the styles of the preceding two centuries. The way in which funding was obtained for these representative projects is indicative of the way in which power moved: Vaux was made for a government minister, Stourhead for a banker, Biddulph for a manufacturer. If one does not admire eclecticism, one will not admire this garden.

> *The garden at Biddulph Grange, by evoking vanished and alien civilisations, served as an affirmation that the millennium was coming ... Bateman may well have overstretched his*

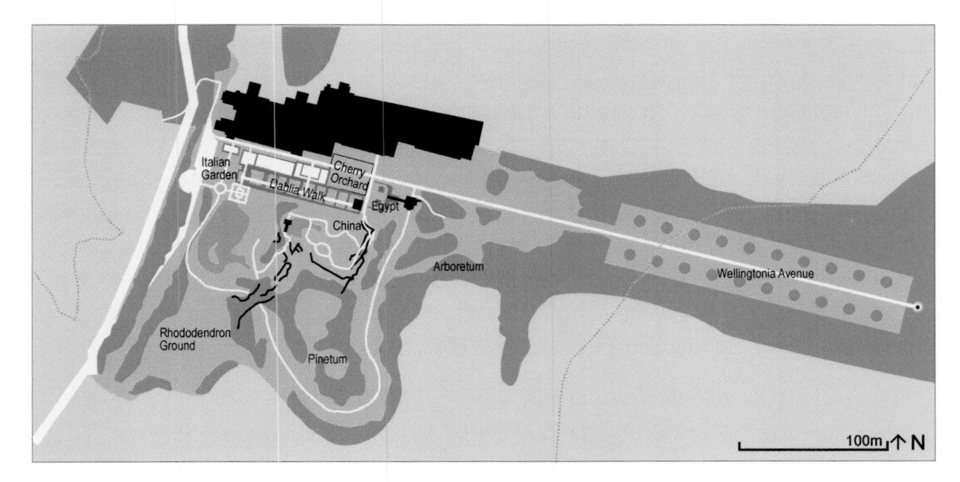

9.53 Biddulph Grange, England.

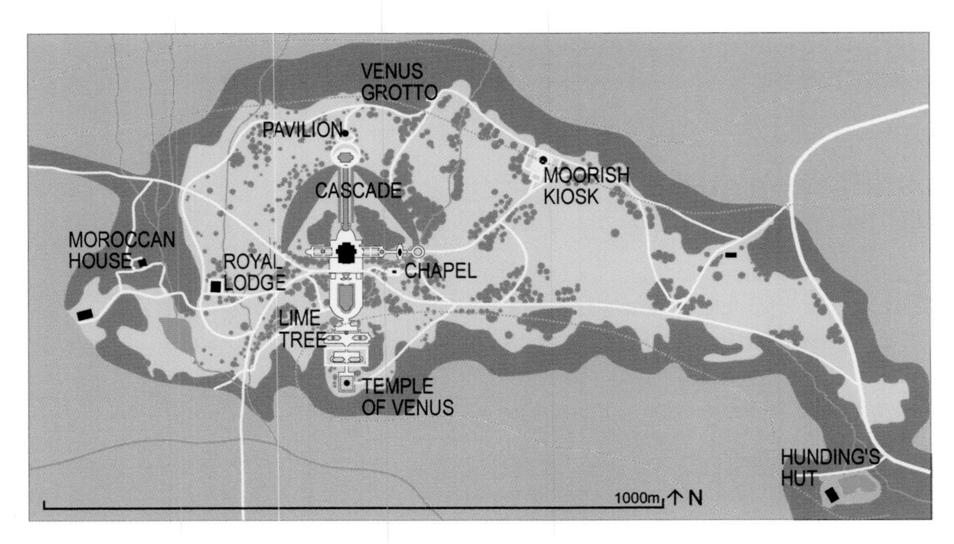

9.54 Linderhof, Germany.

> *resources in his works at Biddulph ... But by the time of Bateman's departure, the impact of Biddulph on the development of Victorian gardens had already been decisive.*
>
> (Brent Elliott)[31]

Linderhof, 1874

This garden, made for the 'mad' King Ludwig II of Bavaria, is a choice German example of the Romantic enthusiasm for mixing styles. After a lonely youth, Ludwig turned to fantasy, dreams, historical epics and wild buildings. His castle at Neuschwanstein is justly famous (see p. 329). It parodies European castle-architecture, just as Linderhof parodies palace-architecture. Ludwig, wanting to be an absolute monarch, thought of naming the place 'Meicost Ettal', an anagram of Louis XIV's epigram, 'L' état c'est moi'. Schloss Linderhof has a Neo-Rococo style. The garden was designed by the Bavarian Royal Garden Director, Karl von Effner. The ancient lime tree, after which the estate is named, is near the southern terrace. Linderhof has a sunken parterre with a 'French' pond and fountain. Beside the Schloss, 'Italian' garden rooms and water steps lead to a gazebo. The adjoining park, in the 'English' style, makes imaginative use of a valley in the foothills of the, real, Alps. The Venus Grotto, inspired by Ludwig's love of Wagner, has a shell-throne, a coral table and a mural depicting a scene from Act I of Tannhäuser. Hunding's Hut, twice destroyed and twice restored, was designed using the libretto from the *Ring of the Nibelungen*. Unquestionably, Linderhof is a product of the Romantic movement.

> *In the midst of the solitude of the Graswang Valley, he sought while smoking a chibouk in the Moorish Kiosk and in the Moroccan House to revive the fairytale world of the Arabian Nights; in Hunding's Cabin lying on bearskins with his retainers and drinking mead, he wanted to re-experience the mythical content of the Valkyrie; in the golden skiff on the lake of the Venus Grotto he desired to feel the enchantment of Tannhäuser and on the morning of Good Friday to sense the consecrating effect of Parsifal in Gurnemanz's hermitage.*
>
> (G. Hojer and E. Schmid)[32]

9.55 Landscape style.

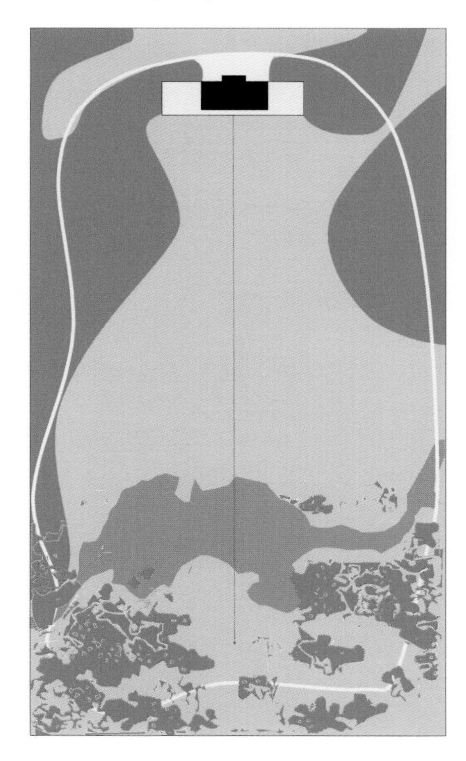

Landscape style

Use: The plan comprised three zones with distinct functions:

1. a zone near the house for the quiet enjoyments of polite society;
2. a park for farm animals and forest trees;
3. a scenic backdrop for the aesthetic pleasure of looking at nature.

Form: The form also comprised three zones:

1. a rectilinear or terraced zone with beds of colourful plants near the house;
2. a serpentine park with undulating ground, woods and water;
3. an irregular 'natural' area of woodland, mountain, coast, river or wild vegetation.

The estate was thus 'composed, like a landscape painting with foreground, middle-ground and background'. Repton, Price and Knight supplied the principle behind the style *c.*1794 and it was used throughout the nineteenth century. In England, there was generally a linear transition from foreground to background, while in Germany and other continental European countries, the transition was achieved by surrounding a Baroque garden with a naturalistic park.

Crystal Palace, 1852

The Crystal Palace was designed by Joseph Paxton for the Great Exhibition in 1851 and first erected on the exhibition site in Hyde Park. It was moved to Sydenham in 1852 and

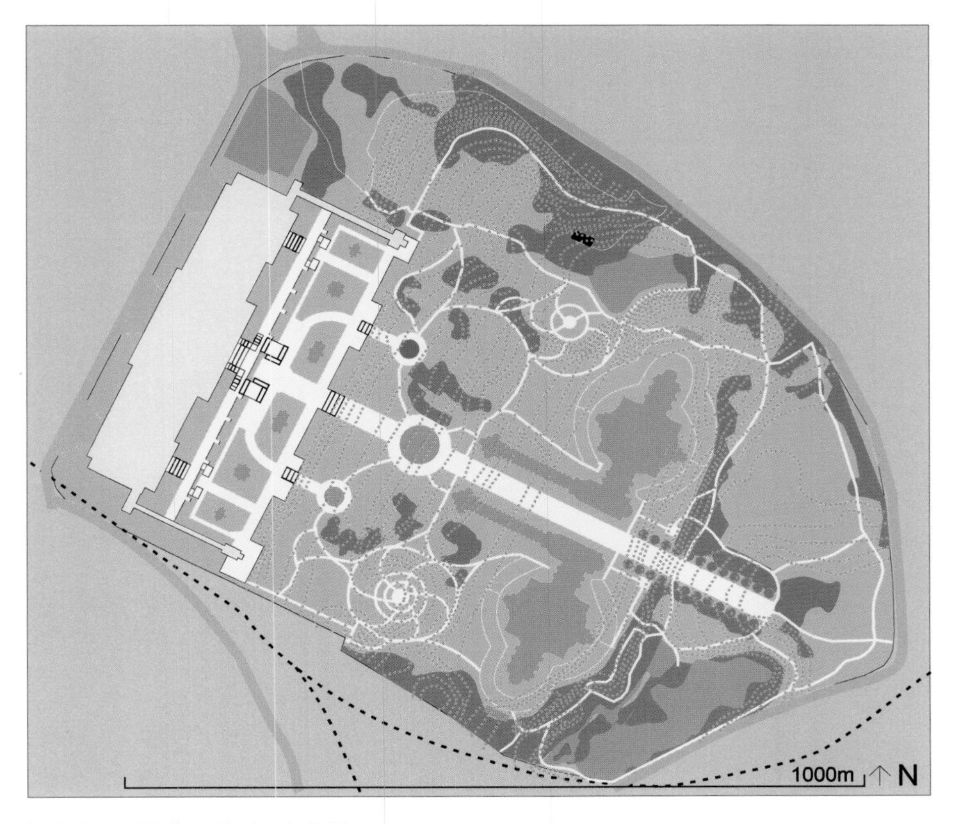

9.56 Crystal Palace, England, 1860.

set in a large Italianate park, also designed by Paxton. Most of the park has gone but one fine terrace survives, as do Paxton's extraordinary prehistoric monsters round the lake in the southern corner of the park. The central area of the site has been laid out as the National Sports Centre in a grim Soviet style.

> *Aside from the central axis and the waterworks, the layout of the park lost its formality after descending from the terraces, and the winding paths and woods of Paxton's landscape style superseded the Italianate features above them, although there were two further circular motifs, the maze and the rosary.*
>
> (George Chadwick)[33]

Nymphenburg, 1820

Maximilian Emanuel's park, 2 km from the centre of Munich, has a Baroque heart. Ludwig II lived here as a child and later remembered with distaste the formality of his surroundings, which was of a piece with the strictness of his upbringing. Like Schleissheim, it was designed by Zuccali and Girard with a central canal, on which a gondola service used to operate. Canaletto painted the garden in 1761. At the end of

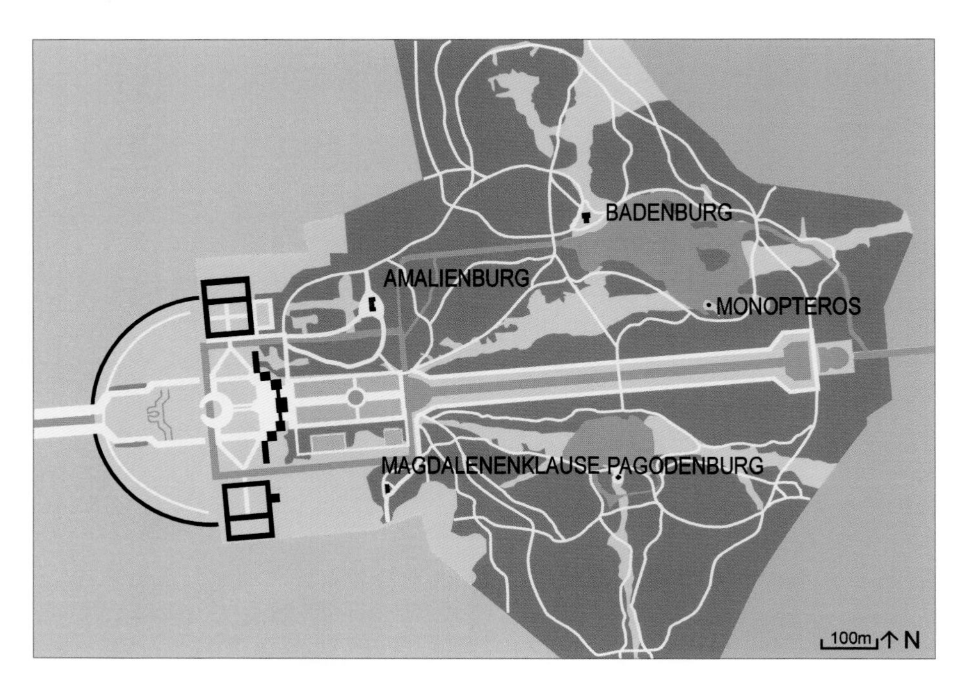

9.57 Nymphenburg, Germany.

eighteenth century, the Baroque garden was fringed with a landscape park. The Classical and Romantic geometries work well together. The three elegant Baroque pavilions once had geometrical gardens: the Pagodenburg (1716), the Badenburg (1719) and a hermitage known as the Magdalenenklause (1725). Today the temples stand in a landscape park designed (*c.*1800) by Germany's leading exponent of the Landscape style: Ludwig von Sckell. He has the credit of making an 'English garden' without destroying a Baroque garden. A circular temple, the Monopetros, was added in 1865. The canals often freeze in winter and are used by skaters and curlers.

> *Although Friedrich Ludwig von Sckell turned most of the garden into a romantic park with natural-looking lakes in front of two pavilions in 1804–23, he incorporated some elements of the baroque layout in his wider scheme, including the* basin *surrounded by fountains and the* parterre de broderie *under the west front.*
>
> (P. Hobhouse and P. Taylor)[34]

Landscape architecture

Use: When landscape architecture became an organised profession, first in America, then in Europe and then in the rest of the world, it led to the planning of open spaces with distinct uses:

- city parks and squares for urban uses;

- greenways, using coasts, river valleys and other corridors, for recreation: hiking, cycling, riding, organised games, water conservation, nature conservation, scenic preservation, historic conservation, etc.;
- protective ordinances and reservations in country areas – variously described as metropolitan parks, country parks, nature parks and national parks – for the enjoyment of nature and natural scenery.

Form: Landscape architecture was founded on the idea of using the compositional principles of the great landscape paintings of Italy to establish relationships between buildings and contexts. This led to the planning of foregrounds, middle grounds and backgrounds. Land use planning, zoning and environmental regulations were used to encourage the formation of compact cities with good open spaces; greenways and public open space corridors were used to provide natural areas within towns and links to the countryside, and conservation policies were used to provide public access and environmental protection for areas of farming, forestry and natural scenery.

Boston, 1890

When asked to advise on the selection of land for open space development in Boston, in 1880, Olmsted proposed a chain of parks which became world famous as Boston's 'Emerald Necklace'. It linked the 'foreground' of Boston Common to the 'background' of Franklin Park. In 1890, Charles Eliot extended Olmsted's scheme into a proposal for

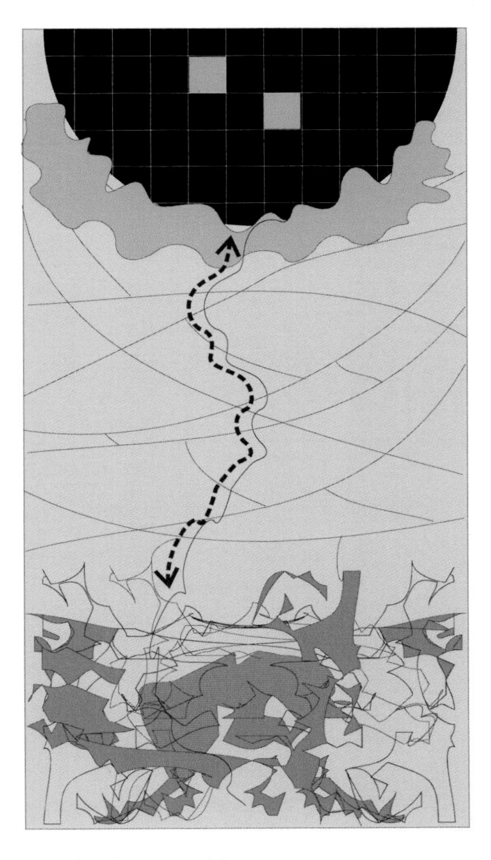

9.58 Landscape architecture.

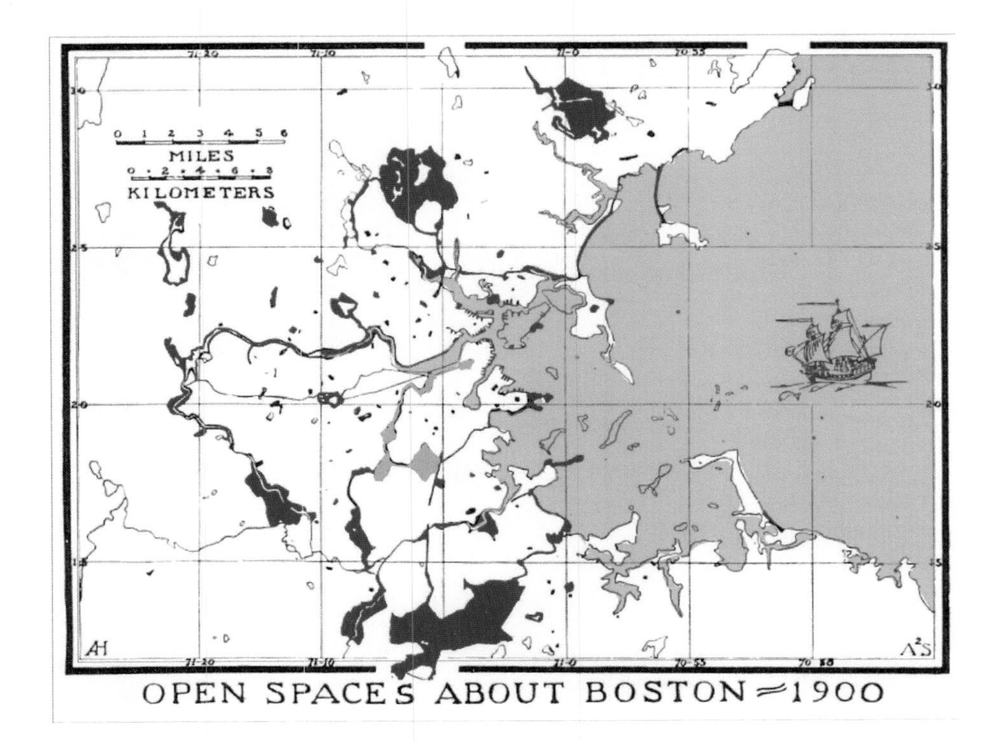

9.59 Boston's Open Space System in 1900, with Olmsted's 'Emerald Necklace' in light green and Charles Eliot's Metropolitan Open Space System in a darker green.

the Boston Metropolitan region. Eliot pressed, successfully, for legislation to establish the Trustees for Reservations, which protects historic spaces by holding them in trust for the nation:

> *[Eliot] suggested that 'for a district such as ours' the system as a whole ought to include five types of area: spaces on the ocean front, shores and islands of the inner bay, the courses of the larger tidal estuaries, two or three large areas of wild forest on the outer rim, and small squares, playgrounds, and parks in the densely populated sections, to be provided by the local communities.*
>
> (Norman T. Newton)[35]

Stockholm, 1938

Sweden's capital city developed one of the first modern park systems in Europe. Holger Blom took charge of the Parks Department in 1938, at the age of 31. He planned a park system which spread out from the old city centre, along the shore of Lake Mälaren and into the Stockholm region. Blom's designs for Norr Mälarstrand and Fredhällsparken became famous outside Sweden. He used natural materials and was a great advocate of children's play areas. One can visit the most interesting section by taking the metro to Kristineberg and walking back to the Stadshuset (City Hall).

> *Stockholm's parks are part of a very complete park system – not large segregated parks, but rather a system of linked strips – which is gradually being developed ... In almost every other city this lake front [on Lake Mälaren] would have been an urban promenade: here a natural and varied landscape has been created in which one can walk or stroll or picnic, where mothers can rest and children play.*
>
> (Peter Shepheard)[36]

Stuttgart, 1950

A series of garden shows held over 50 years has established a chain of green spaces in the form of the letter 'U'. It proceeds north from the city centre, reaches the River

9.60 Stockholm.

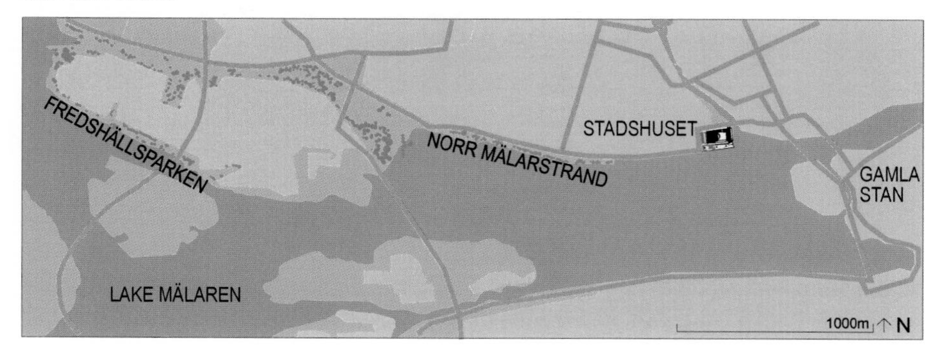

Neckar and then turns back on itself. Garden shows were held in 1939, 1950, 1961, 1977 and 1993. The 1939 and 1950 designs for the Killesberg quarry used a traditional approach with drystone walls and steps. Hans Luz and Partners, as landscape architects, were involved in four of the garden shows. The 1961 scheme for the Upper Schlossgarten is a prime example of rectilinear Abstract Modernism – the outdoor equivalent of a Cubist painting. The 1977 scheme can be categorised as curvilinear Abstract Expressionism. The 1993 design team, which included ecologists and social scientists, aimed at a more ecological approach for the Rosensteinpark, encouraging contact between people and nature. Walking from the city centre to the Rosenstein allows one to see textbook examples of design evolution from 1939 to 1993.

> *On both a citywide and human scale, the parks and working landscapes within and surrounding Stuttgart are among the most climatically functional, socially useful and aesthetically pleasing of any modern city in the western world.*
>
> (Michael Hough)[37]

9.61 Stuttgart.

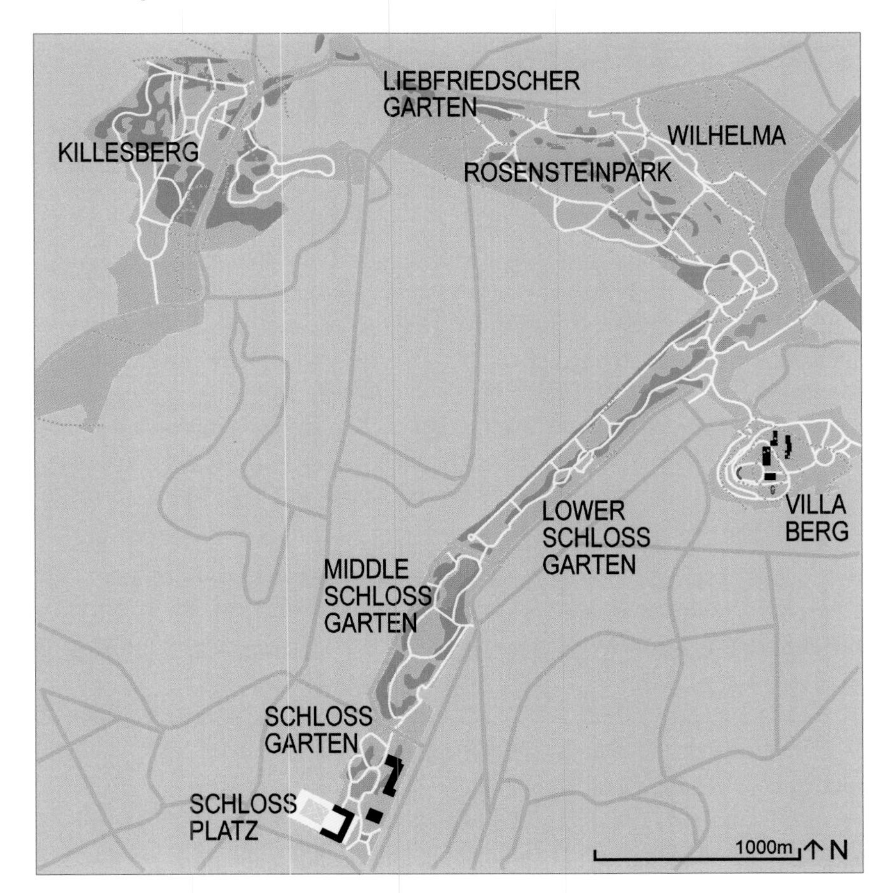

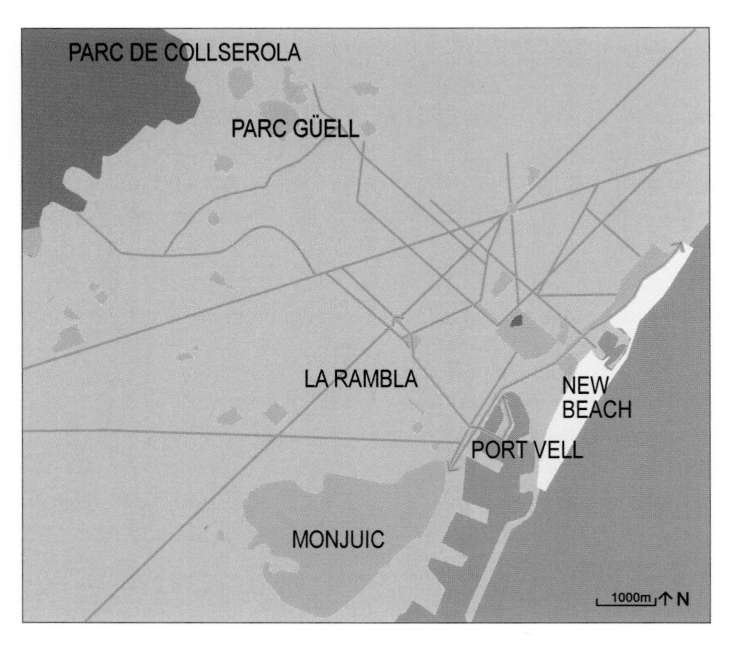

9.62 Barcelona.

Barcelona, 1992

Two events occasioned the outpouring of design energy which led to the planning of Barcelona's open space system: the death of General Franco in 1975 and the preparations for the 1992 Olympic Games. The General oppressed the city because it had opposed him in the Spanish Civil War. After he died, power was devolved to the region of Catalonia and a programme of civic improvements was launched. The Rambla was extended from the city centre to the old port (Port Vell) and a waterfront greenway leads to an extensive beach park and to Montjuic. In 1987, the encircling hills came under a management plan, as the Parc de Collserola. A swimming park (Parc de la Creueta del Coll) was made near the Parc Güell, where the hills touch the city. The dense urban fabric was enlivened with a series of new parks and squares designed by teams of sculptors and architects. Public art became a symbol of the city's renewal. Over 70 public gardens were made, with many successes and failures:

> *The great success of Barcelona is in the total acceptance of contemporary needs and values. For once the needs of the pedestrian and the inhabitant have been recognised ... 'No other metropolis has so cleverly utilized public space as a foundation for re-thinking the concept of the city.'*
>
> (*Domus Magazine*)[38]

CHAPTER 10

Abstract and Post-abstract gardens, 1900–2000

10.0 The Barcelona Pavilion by Mies van der Rohe.

10.1 Abstract garden design was characterised by clean lines and freedom from ornament: the Barcelona Pavilion, by Mies van der Rohe (see p. 387).

History and philosophy

Visually, it is easy to identify the arts, architecture and gardens of the twentieth century. They are startlingly different from the work of the nineteenth century. But the adjective 'Modern', used to describe this work, has surely passed its use-by date. A replacement is due and, in this chapter, 'Abstract' is used as an alternative. It pinpoints the key feature of twentieth-century gardens: the abstraction of universal principles from the everyday world. Artists and designers, admiring the way scientists abstracted the laws of nature and applied them in technology, sought an analogous design procedure. Painting, architecture, gardens, furniture and fashion design thus became characterised by analytically clean lines, freedom from ornament, simple colours, new technology and geometrical elegance.

10.2 Victorian gardens were criticised for their spottiness in the early twentieth century.

10.3 Post-abstract garden design saw a return to representation (Swarovski Crystal Worlds, Austria).

The central phase of High Modernism was followed by a period of diversity, currently described as Postmodern, though it would be odd if this term were to outlive its parent. 'Post-abstract', formed on the model of Post-Impressionist and Post-Expressionist, is more explanatory and implies a retreat from the clinical purity of abstraction and a return to the realm of stories, symbols and meanings. The designers of Hatshepsut's temple, Pompeii, cloister courts, the Villa Lante, Versailles and Stowe were more than familiar with using design to speak of other things: allegory was their preoccupation. The word derives from *allos* (other), and *-agoria* (speaking). Children, said the Victorians , should be seen and not heard. But why should gardens be silent? For two reasons: first, the deliberate rejection of symbols, allegory and literary themes in High Modernist design; second, the use of pesticides, as described in Rachel Carson's *Silent Spring*.[1]

The previous chapter began with Gothein's remark that the nineteenth century 'must complete its tale of sins before the foundations are shattered'. During the first half of the twentieth century the 'sin' of most concern to avant-garde designers was the very foundation of Victorian gardens: eclecticism. In 1938, Christopher Tunnard, in his book on *Gardens in the Modern Landscape*, charged that:

> *The unfortunate duality of temperament with which the Victorian garden was endowed was not an aid to its establishment as an artistic entity ... And what a glorious, gaudy blotch it made ... A cedar of Lebanon, a clump of plumous pampas grass and some pieces of rockwork were used to make a miniature landscape on the front lawn with a crescent moon and stars carved out of the turf for bedding at the back. The gross indecency of either act would not have been admitted then.*[2]

Tunnard believed that selecting plants and styles from everywhere had made gardens spotty, haphazard and amateurish. Garden ornaments, often inferior copies, were

10.4 a, b, c Though conceived nationally, Arts and Crafts gardens looked overseas and to the principles of composition. Hidcote was designed by Lawrence Johnston, an American.

10.5 Ditchley Park, Oxfordshire, on a wet day. Geoffrey Jellicoe drew upon the compositional principles of Italian gardens, but was less interested in their iconographical programmes.

collected like trinkets on a mantelshelf. Owners boasted about the brightness of their plants and the sizes of their forced pineapples. Modernist critics and designers raised their hammers, sharpened their pencils, charged their pens and screamed for reform. Order, they said, must be abstracted from chaos. Four approaches to abstraction are outlined below.

The first approach was nationalism (see Chapter 9). Reformists looked to heroic periods in their nations' histories and aimed to abstract stylistic essences. The problem was that every 'national' style had roots elsewhere. In their days of glory, Greece had drawn from West Asia, Italy from Greece, France from Italy, Spain from Italy and France. England, Germany and America drew from everywhere. Nationalism thus gave way to internationalism. A Zeitgeist with left-wing credentials entered the world of garden design.

The second approach was to abstract *design methods* from past times. Designers hoped that an artistic approach wedded to honest rough-hands craftsmanship, again as used in their nation's rose-tinted histories, would improve design standards. And it did. Arts and Crafts gardens were often excellent. One has to wonder how the principles were ever neglected, and why they still are. But the Arts and Crafts movement focused designers' attention on abstract design and became the seed bed from which Abstract Modernism arose.

The third approach was to abstract compositional principles from historic gardens. Edith Wharton explained the approach in 1904:

> *The cult of the Italian garden has spread from England to America, and there is a general feeling that, by placing a marble bench here and a sun-dial there, Italian 'effects' may be achieved ... The first lesson is that, if they are to be a real inspiration, they must be copied, not in the letter but in the spirit. That is, a marble sarcophagus and a dozen twisted columns will not make an Italian garden; but a piece of ground laid out and planted on the principles of the old garden-craft will be, not indeed an Italian garden in the literal sense, but, what is far better, a garden as well adapted to its surroundings as were the models which inspired it. This is the secret to be learned from the villas of Italy.*[3]

Geoffrey Jellicoe, writing 21 years later, agreed with this judgement and wrote that 'the bases of abstract design, running through history like a silver thread, are independent of race and age.'[4]

The fourth approach was to abstract concepts from history and themes from nature and the modern world. In the last quarter of the twentieth century, this led to the notion of double coding, characterised as Postmodern. Gardens can, for example, have a primary code legible to all observers and a historic, symbolic or literary or scientific code which can be read only with an educated eye. Every visitor can see the mound, trees and water in Jencks' design for the Scottish National Gallery of Modern Art. Only the extra-well-informed will understand their relationship with the nature of the cosmos. Postmodern designers have interests in ontology, epistemology, semiology, quantum mechanics, cosmogenesis and other recondite branches of knowledge.

10.6 Edith Wharton knew that Italian gardens must be treated as a source of inspiration and not copied. Her own garden at The Mount (Lenox, Massachusetts) has a Modern air and does not match the quality of the Italian gardens which inspired its design.

10.7 UEDA Landform: Scottish National Gallery of Modern Art, Edinburgh, by Charles Jencks.

10.8 Charles Jencks' garden, at Portrack, helps explain the Nature of the World.

Arts and Crafts style

Edith Wharton and Geoffrey Jellicoe both attempted Italian gardens and their attempts illustrate the difficulties in applying principles which have been abstracted from their original context. Wharton's garden at The Mount in Lenox, Massachusetts, despite her good intentions, showed little skill with 'the principles' of Italian gardens.[5] A harsh critic might compare it to a novel with a weak plot, poor characterisation and a lack of style. In later years Jellicoe used to chuckle that when younger 'I could do a *pretty good* classical garden'. This was true, but his Italian design for Ditchley Park is good rather than excellent.

Forward-looking critics and designers argued that work of the first quality could be produced only when artists were craftsmen and craftsmen were artists. John Ruskin was one of the first to advance this view. William Morris developed and implemented Ruskin's ideas. Morris was a craftsman, a poet, a painter and much else. He made

10.9 a, b Harold Peto, the architect son of a builder, used fragments collected in Italy to make his own garden at Iford Manor, including a terracotta urn made by Carlo Bitossi of Montelupo, a pottery town 20 km from Florence.

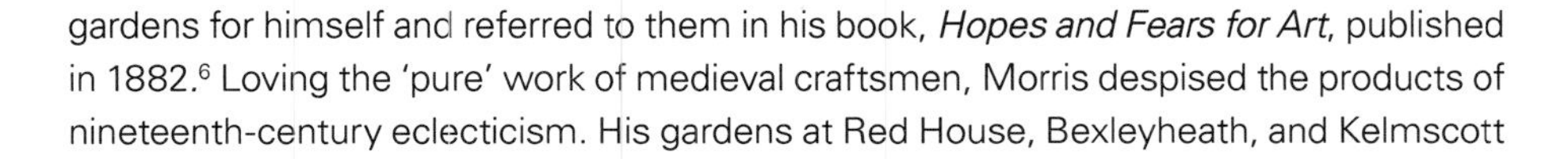

gardens for himself and referred to them in his book, *Hopes and Fears for Art*, published in 1882.[6] Loving the 'pure' work of medieval craftsmen, Morris despised the products of nineteenth-century eclecticism. His gardens at Red House, Bexleyheath, and Kelmscott

10.10 Axel Munthe, a Swedish author, made a popular Italian Arts and Crafts garden on Capri with extensive use of collected antiquities.

10.11 Harold Peto designed the garden of the Villa Ephrussi for Beatrix de Rothschild.

10.12 The Red House was William Morris' first garden design project.

10.13 An Arts and Crafts garden in London, designed by Margaret Turner.

Manor (the setting for *News from Nowhere*) were products of these tastes. They had neat enclosures, flowers and hedges. Morris was a founder of the Art Workers Guild, which young designers rushed to join. They reconsidered the art of design, the craft of making things, and the convenience of users. First cousins of the classic Vitruvian virtues ('firmness, commodity and delight'), these principles reshaped design theory and produced what became known as the Arts and Crafts style. It did not originate in gardens but it had a profound influence on them, re-shaping garden art. Marie-Luise Gothein, in 1914, felt able to look to the future with a new confidence: 'All garden lovers and artists may rejoice in the consciousness that in our own time a new development has come about, and one that is full of promise.'[7] Yet the promise was more of a better yesterday than a better tomorrow.

In England, the leading practitioners of Arts and Crafts gardens were Gertrude Jekyll, Edwin Lutyens, Reginald Blomfield and Thomas Mawson. The men were members of the Art Workers Guild, from which Jekyll was excluded on account of her sex. They produced some of the best and most popular gardens which have ever been made in England, most so popular with their owners that one can visit them only by special arrangement. Excellent examples of the style can, however, be seen at Sissinghurst and Hidcote.

Jekyll became the best known designer in the group, partly on account of her books. She practised many arts and crafts herself, and had excellent judgement as to what types of place it is good to have in gardens. On joint projects with Lutyens, I believe she

10.14 a, b Sissinghurst, Kent, made by Vita Sackville-West and Harold Nicolson, is perhaps the most famous garden made in the twentieth century. It demonstrates the popularity of the Arts and Crafts approach and the use of compartments.

was responsible for the design and he produced detail designs following her outline plan – although her 'plan' was a concept rather than a drawing on paper.

The Arts and Crafts approach was particularly suited to small gardens designed, built and maintained by their owners. Even large gardens, like Sissinghurst were treated as compartments. It was a Renaissance idea (see p. 188).

In France, garden designers sensed that the flow of private commissions for great estates was drying up and hoped that new work would come from the public sector. Duchêne wrote that:

> *Looking at the art of gardens from the social angle, we will create a new formula which will give birth to an art of great power put in the service of the community. Here luxury will cease to have an end in itself ... it must satisfy the aesthetic aspirations of the masses.*[8]

He was right to the extent that public commissions were to provide a source of new work and there was wide agreement that professional designers should satisfy 'the aesthetic aspirations of the masses'. Most designers did not, however, see Duchêne's approach, an Arts and Crafts gloss on the French Baroque, as being an appropriate style for the social circumstances of a new age. In most countries they adopted the name 'landscape architecture' for public projects.

In Germany, a revolt against garden eclecticism was led by the architectural profession. Hermann Muthesius delivered a series of lectures in 1904. In them, 'he attacked

10.15 a, b Jacques Majorelle's design for a garden in Marrakesh was an Arts and Crafts interpretation of the Arab culture he admired and painted. His father, Louis Majorelle, was a significant Art Nouveau furniture designer. The garden was restored by Yves Saint-Laurent and Pierre Bergé, who retained the *bleu Majorelle*.

landscape gardening on similar and often identical grounds with Blomfield, finding it still the leading fashion in Germany'.[9] Gothein emphasises that Muthesius' aim was not to adopt a Renaissance approach to geometry and ornament, as Blomfield and Peto had done. He wished to make outdoor living rooms in which 'the garden, the seats, the borders

10.16 a, b Parc Güell is the only major example of the Art Nouveau (Modernista in Catalan) style of garden design.

10.17 Dumbarton Oaks, Washington DC, designed by Beatrix Farrand, is an excellent American example of the Arts and Crafts style.

of hedge or pergola, the paths – all should show some likeness to the inside arrangements of a house'. She sees this as more akin to Greek and Roman courtyard gardens than to their Renaissance successors. Paul Schultze-Naumburg's book *Gärten* (*Gardens*),[10] showed how to design garden rooms in conformity with the principles of aesthetic art.

In America, Beatrix Farrand (Edith Wharton's niece) became a leading practitioner of the Arts and Crafts style in garden design. She admired Jekyll and purchased her planting plans, sold to raise funds for the war effort. Farrand was a founder member of the American Society of Landscape Architects, and her approach was highly professional. Whereas Jekyll only drew planting plans, Farrand drew all the plans and elevations for building work as well as planting work.

Abstract style

Modern architecture had become a recognised phenomenon by 1930. But Modern gardens, even today, are shrouded in mist. Did they really exist? If so, when and where did they originate? Who were the practitioners? Were Modern gardens as bare as Bauhaus architecture? Are they still being made? Despite writing a book entitled *Modern Gardens* in 1953, Peter Shepheard believed that it was almost impossible for Modern architecture to have a stable companion, because such modern materials as glass, steel and concrete were inherently unsuited to garden design.[11] The generally wise American historian, Norman T. Newton, in *Design on the Land*[12] (1971) had a blind spot concerning Modern gardens. Ignoring Fletcher Steele, a fellow Harvard man and America's pioneer Modernist, Newton contented himself with the remark that Church, Eckbo, Royston and Halprin, were 'inventive designers'. He failed to say what they invented.

10.18 Falling Water, designed by Frank Lloyd Wright in 1936–7, shows that he could have made a significant contribution to the development of Modern gardens.

Jane Brown introduced the subject as follows in her book, *The Modern Garden*, published in 2000:

> *The modern garden achieved stature in America, so much so that it tended to become an interpretation of the modern landscape, and it was re-exported to a rather mystified Europe in the 1950s. Within a decade it was dead, mainly through misunderstanding, and a smothering in historical revivals and rampantly eclectic postmodernism.*[13]

Yet her book is replete with examples of Modern gardens made after 1960 and their inclusion is surely correct. Modern art in general and Abstract art in particular continue to have a deep influence on gardens, which is best understood by looking beyond the garden wall.

The evolution of Modernist ideas was traced by Pevsner. He found the impetus to have come from William Morris, through the Arts and Crafts ideas outlined above.[14] They led to the principle that form should follow function. As framed by the American architect Louis Sullivan, this became the Modernist mantra. Sullivan's pupil, Frank Lloyd Wright, believed design should also draw on a scientific and aesthetic appreciation of nature, which he called 'organic'. The quotations below reveal his sensitivity to places, functions and organic form:

> *I chose Taliesin for a name – it means 'shining brow', and this place now called Taliesin is built like a brow on the edge of the hill – not on top of the hill – because I believe you should never build on top of anything directly. If you build on top of the hill, you lose the hill.*[15]

> *We see an airplane clean and light-winged – the lines expressing power and purpose; we see the ocean liner, streamlined, clean and swift – expressing power and purpose ... Why are not buildings, too, indicative of their special purpose? The forms of things that are perfectly adapted to their function, we now observe, seem to have a superior beauty of their own. We like to look at them. Then, as it begins to dawn on us that form follows function – why not so in architecture especially? ... Buildings are made of materials too. Materials have a life of their own that may enter into the building to give it more life. Here certain principles show countenance. It is the countenance of organic simplicity.*[16]

Had anyone asked him, Frank Lloyd Wright might have invented the Modern Garden in a morning: he was an astonishingly inventive designer. Most of his work was residential and he had an instinctive sense for relationships between indoor and outdoor space. At the Robie House (1908–1909), the abstract geometry of the building was projected into the garden plan. At Falling Water (1936–1937), a relationship between architecture and landscape is the leading idea: the house grows out of the land. But the America which had spurned Sullivan was not ready for Wright. Instead, it chose a Beaux Arts Renaissance revival. Wright therefore had little influence on American architecture in the first half of the twentieth century and even less influence on American gardens. He was, however, admired in Europe, which became the proving ground for Modernist designs.

The *de Stijl* movement in Holland, was excited by Wright's work and the cover of *De Stijl* magazine could be mistaken for – or used as – a garden plan. The *Exposition des Arts Décoratives Modernes* (which became known as the 'Art Deco Exposition'), held in Paris in 1925, showed work by Tony Garnier, Gabriel Guevrekian and André Vera. Guevrekian exhibited a Garden of Water and Light that inspired Charles de Noailles to commission

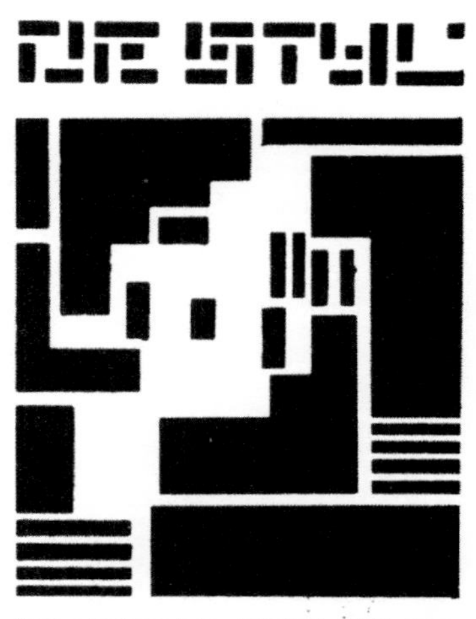

10.19 The front cover of *De Stijl* magazine reads '*The Style*: Magazine for the modern visual arts, Editor Theo van Doesburg with assistance from well-known national and international artists', Issue 10, 1917.

10.20 The cover of *De Stijl* could – and deserves to be – used as a garden plan.

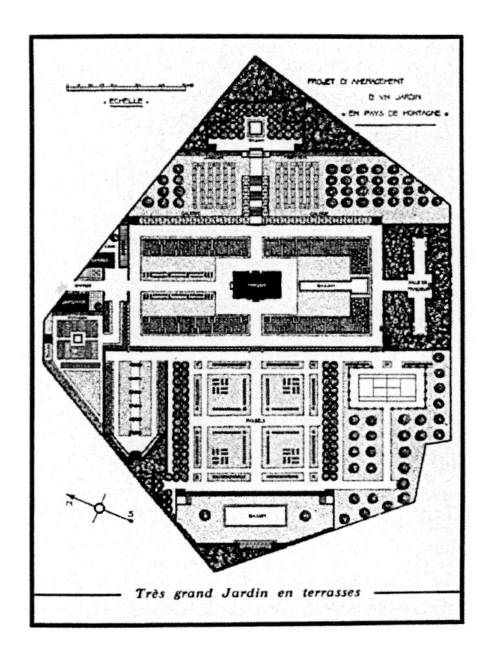

10.21 André Vera's design for a large terraced garden (1912) is an Abstract interpretation of the French garden design tradition.

10.22 The Villa Savoye in Paris, by Le Corbusier, is surrounded by vegetation but has a roof terrace instead of a conventional garden because the designer regarded grass as 'unhealthy and damp'.

a triangular, Abstract garden for his villa at Hyères in the South of France. Le Corbusier was also a creative influence on Modern gardens. A sculptor at heart, he cared about the relationship of buildings to sites and had the love of scenery one would expect in a child of the Swiss Alps. The Villa Savoye (1928–1931) has a garden terrace on the roof. A similar principle was used for the *Unité d'Habitation* (1946) in Marseilles, where the roof terrace is as much a garden as a Modern sculpture. Abstract designers looked back to the Classical principles of composition, often using primary colours and the primary geometrical forms.

In many parts of Europe, admiration for natural forms and flowing lines led to the development of a new style. It was known as Art Nouveau in England, *Jugendstil* in Germany and *Stile Liberty* in Italy. In Catalonia, which, in Gaudí's design for the Parc Güell, has the only major outdoor design in the style, it was called *Modernista*. Elsewhere, the word 'Modern' was used for the Abstract art and architecture of the twentieth century.

Another strand of influence on Modernism came from Germany. The Bauhaus was founded in Weimar in 1919 by combining the Art Academy with the Arts and Crafts school of design. Under its first director, Walter Gropius, the school aimed to integrate art, economics and engineering into a unified design process. Gropius wrote:

> *Let us create a new guild of craftsmen, without the class distinctions which raise an arrogant barrier between craftsmen and artist. Together, let us conceive and create the new building of the future, which will embrace architecture 'and' sculpture 'and' painting*

10.23 The Bauhaus in Dessau had a profound influence on the design of Modernist space around buildings. Blocks of grass, paving and planting were treated as components in an Abstract composition.

10.24 The Meisterhäuser in Dessau are Abstract white compositions, without gardens but built in a woodland framework.

> *in one unity and which will one day rise toward heaven from the hands of a million workers, like the crystal symbol of a new faith.*

The Bauhaus moved to Dessau in 1924 and to America in 1933. Gardens were not an interest of the school but the emphasis on design unity thrust Bauhaus principles into the landscape. Tall blocks were composed with rectangles of grass to create unitary Abstract compositions.

10.25 The Villa Noailles was inspired by the 1925 Art Deco World Fair (the Exposition Internationale des Arts Décoratifs et Industriels Modernes). One can relate the design to the Art Deco spire on the Chrysler building in New York.

In France, designers were pulled in two ways: by the desire to be Modern and by the desire to be true to the French tradition.

In Denmark, designers were less chauvinistic and happy to take inspiration from England and Germany.

In England, clients were slow to become interested in Modern gardens, probably because of their nostalgia for the imperial age then passing. Design schools, more open to the future, looked across the Atlantic and the Channel for inspiration. London's Architectural Association became a test bed for new ideas. Geoffrey Jellicoe, a student there in the 1920s, designed a strikingly Modern garden in 1933. Christopher Tunnard, also associated with the AA, wrote a book, *Gardens in the Modern Landscape* which, in the event, had more influence in America than England.[17] He looked to Japan, and sought to understand the compositional principles used in Japanese gardens, in a way that compares with Jellicoe's interest in Italy.

Fletcher Steele was the most important American designer to take an early interest in Modern gardens. During the 1920s his practice was sufficiently profitable to fund his regular European tours. These included a visit to the Art Deco Exposition in Paris in 1925. He met Guevrekian and visited the garden at Hyères. Steele admired Le Corbusier for his 'strikingly original ideas' and 'odd patterns of concrete walks' but criticised him for becoming 'banal'. Steele had good design judgement and his work was more Art Deco

10.26 Naumkeag was a successful translation of Art Deco ideas into garden design, by Fletcher Steele.

than Abstract. Writing in *Landscape Architecture* (October 1930), Steele gave his opinion that 'What a modernistic garden may be is everybody's guess. The reason is that it does not yet exist as a type.'[18]

'The International Style: Architecture since 1922' was the name of an exhibition organised by Henry-Russell Hitchcock and Philip Johnson. It was held in New York in 1932 and showed the work of Walter Gropius, Mies van der Rohe and Le Corbusier. In 1937, the Dean of the Graduate School of Design at Harvard invited Gropius, a refugee from Hitler's Germany, to America. Though not personally interested in the design of outdoor space, Gropius influenced garden designers through his advocacy of Bauhaus principles. Garrett Eckbo, James Rose and Dan Kiley were in the same Harvard class. They read *Gardens in the Modern Landscape* and two of the youngsters went to work for Thomas Church on the West Coast. Kiley remained on the East Coast and developed a practice with famous Modern movement architects: Eero Saarinen, Kevin Roche and John Dinkeloo.

Design slogans from the period provide a useful summary of International style principles. Designers were urged to:

- develop form by following function;
- express structure;
- be true to materials;
- use modern materials for modern construction;
- avoid stories and sentimentality;
- remember that the styles are dead;
- avoid decoration, because less is more.

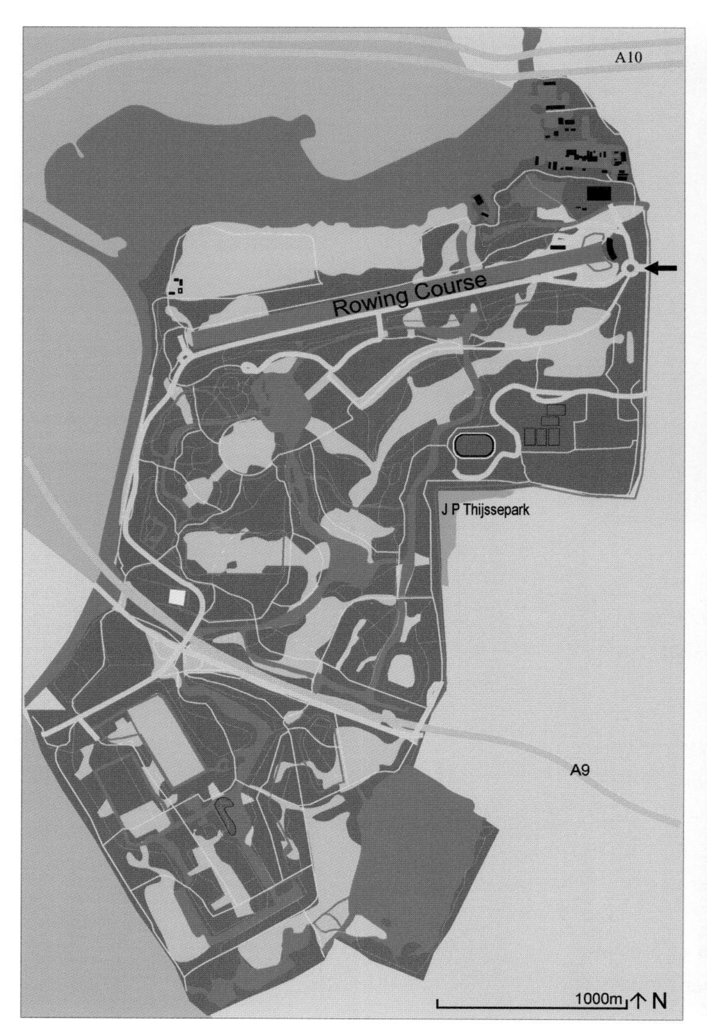

10.27 a, b The Bos Park in Amsterdam showed how the 'form follows function' principle could be applied to landscape design. Using ecological knowledge in the composition of water, landform and vegetation, it was designed to 'follow' the recreational patterns of Dutch people.

In parks and in gardens, these principles had the following consequences: nationalistic styles, stories and allegories were spurned; functional spaces for outdoor living were created; native plants were used to create natural habitats and wild-flower meadows; a new geometry inspired by Abstract art was employed. Often, the paved areas were rectilinear and the planted areas curvilinear. Concrete, glass and steel made an appearance. Apart from private and domestic gardens, the Amsterdam Bos was the first major example of how these principles could be used to design space on a scale comparable to that of the great estates which are the main subject of this book. (See Abstract style, p. 387.)

Roberto Burle Marx, a Brazilian designer, is perhaps the most representative designer of Modernist gardens. Born in 1909, his father (Marx) was German-Jewish and his mother

10.28 a, b Burle Marx designed an Abstract Modern garden and a ceramic fresco for the Moreira Salles house. Built 1949–1951, it is now the Instituto Moreira Salles, IMS, in Rio de Janeiro.

10.29 a, b Wildflower meadows, at Great Dixter and Iford Manor, were a twentieth-century approach to the imitation of nature.

(Burle) was French-Brazilian. The son developed a love for the native flora of Brazil. He studied fine art in Berlin and on returning home made friends with a group of Brazilian architects, all influenced by Corbusier: Oscar Niemeyer, Alfonso Reidy and Locio Costa. Burle Marx's Cubist paintings translated easily into garden designs for flat surfaces,

10.30 The park beside Lake Mälaren, in Stockholm, by Holger Blom.

10.31 a, b The Woodland Cemetery Skogskyrkogården, by Gunnar Asplund.

10.32 Ragnar Ostberg's design for Stockholm City Hall (Stadshuset) abstracts the Swedish character, the principles of design and the principles of craftsmanship.

10.33 The Louisiana Art Gallery, Humlebaek, Denmark, used the principles of Abstract design to integrate architecture and landscape.

especially near buildings. His use of native plants in gardens complies with Modernist principles: it is functional; it represents truth to materials; it relates to the structure of natural plant communities. Burle Marx's work with natural landform was less happy. As Marc Treib notes:

> *More often that not, he appears to blanket the contours in forms derived from his own flat artworks rather than from the lay of the land. Rarely is there any perceivable attempt to, say, derive a shape from the profile of the topography.*[19]

In the 1940s, when the progress of European garden design was interrupted by war, Sweden was neutral. Its relatively short summers had not favoured the development of a strong garden design profession but architects, imbued with Bauhaus principles, took a serious interest in outdoor design. The projects which became best known outside Sweden were Stockholm's park system and the Woodland Cemetery designed by Gunnar Asplund. Finland and Denmark adopted a similar approach, which came to be known by the catch-all description 'Scandinavian'.

Germany emerged from the Second World War with a strong desire to look forward and forget the past. West Germany became the richest country in Europe and East Germany the richest part of the Soviet Empire. Both Germanys adopted the Modernist approach that Hitler had discouraged.

10.34 Marx-Engels Platz in the former East Berlin. The figures, now objects of curiosity, were ideological patrons of functionalist design.

10.35 The Munich Olympiapark is the best example of curvilinear functionalism, integrating architecture and landscape in a manner bearing comparison with the Ancient Greek sanctuaries from which the Olympiapark derives.

10.36 Peter Walker's design for the Sony Centre Plaza, in Berlin, demonstrates his belief in the principles of Abstract composition using Minimalist shapes.

America became the world's largest economy in the 1950s and the Abstract approach to garden and landscape design was widely adopted. Dan Kiley was born in Boston in 1912 and studied landscape architecture at Harvard. In 1955 he worked with Saarinen on the Miller Garden in Columbus, Indiana. Inspired by Mies van der Rohe's Barcelona Pavilion and the *de Stijl* movement, it had a grid plan and full integration of indoor with outdoor space. There was also a picturesque transition from garden to meadow to wood. The design was widely acclaimed and became a key American example of the Abstract style, at once splendidly Modern and rooted in the landscape tradition. Kiley's subsequent projects include the United States Air Force Academy, the Oakland Museum, Independence Mall in Philadelphia, the Dallas Museum of Art, and Fountain Place in Texas. In her book *The Modern Garden*, Jane Brown rightly described Kiley as 'the supreme master of the modern garden'.[20]

Peter Walker belongs to a later generation than Kiley. The title of his book, *Minimalist Gardens*,[21] implies respect for those Minimalist painters who remained true to the principles of Abstract art, basing their work on the primary geometrical forms. The best of Walker's design work has this quality.

There were good and bad aspects to the International style as applied to garden design. One can understand why the nationalism over which nations fought lost its appeal to those who, like Gothein, had seen their children die in the First World War. But the modernist thirst for internationalism resulted in the loss of local identity now associated with the word globalisation. After the Second World War, Hitler's fondness for vernacular design and native plant species was seen as dangerously close to racism, leading to a

10.37 A sustainable 'form follows function' approach to water management is the central aspect of Herbert Dreiseitl's design for Hannoversch Münden, in Germany.

continued distrust of localism in design. Postmodern design philosophy therefore appeared to offer the desirable solution of keeping what was good about internationalism while bringing back localism and some of the other good things which had been jettisoned.

Post-abstract style

The closing decades of the twentieth century saw many artists turn away from abstraction. Poets and painters renewed their interest in figurative themes; musicians recovered an interest in melody; architects resumed their flirtation with the Classical orders; garden designers drew inspiration from meanings, iconography and allusion; wildlife and wild plants became a consideration in garden design.[22] Since all these developments came after the vacant phase of Abstract Modernism, it makes sense to classify them as Post-abstract or Postmodern. Modernists believed in purity, simplicity and abstraction from context; Postmodernists believed in complexity, pluralism, conceptualism, layering and recontextualisation.

Sir Geoffrey Jellicoe's career illustrates the relationship between Abstract and Post-abstract design. He opened his book on *Italian Gardens* with the remark that 'Pandora never loosed a livelier spirit than the one for ever parting Fancy from Design' and stated that the best gardens were made when 'Fancy and Design roam undivided'.[23] By 'Fancy', he meant imagination. His 1933 design for Ditchley Park was allegory-free but

10.38 a, b Geoffrey Jellicoe viewed his design for Kennedy Memorial in Runnymede, England, as his first allegorical project. The granite sets are an allegory for 'a multitude of pilgrims on their way upwards'.

his design for the Caveman Restaurant, in the same year, combined an allegorical theme with a Modernist composition in white concrete. Looking up through the glass roof and fish pond, visitors to the restaurant were challenged to speculate on man's evolution from the miasmal mire. In 1956, Jellicoe designed a magical roof garden for a department store in Guildford. Again, the composition appeared Abstract, but the design had meaning: the circular stepping stones and plant pots that orbited the rooftop pool were inspired by the launch of the first Russian satellite in that year.

In 1964, Jellicoe designed a memorial garden for President Kennedy. There was a Classical aspect to the Kennedy story – of a bronzed young hero, slain in his prime. Subsequent revelations about Kennedy's libido being unavailable, this reminded Jellicoe of *The Pilgrim's Progress* by Bunyan and of Bellini's *Allegory of the Progress of the Soul.* These works provided the theme for an exercise in allegory. Granite sets ascend the hill, an allegory for 'a multitude of pilgrims on their way upwards'. The difficulty of the journey is a preparation for the tranquillity of the sculptured stone memorial. The lettering reads as texture, as though 'the stone itself were speaking'.[24]

10.39 The Time Garden at the London home of Charles Jencks, a 'four-square window on the world'.

The Sutton Place project of 1980 was an opportunity to develop a Bunyan-Bellini allegory of Creation, Life and Aspiration. Creation was represented by the lake. Life was represented by the gardens, which, as in the Landscape style, adjoin the house. Aspiration was represented by the Nicholson Wall. When asked about the meaning of the Wall, Ben Nicholson replied, 'How should *I* know?'[25] He asked because he was an Abstract artist. Jellicoe, who was not, began to take an interest in Jung's theory of symbols as representations of the collective unconscious.

Charles Jencks, author of *The Language of Postmodern Architecture*,[26] borrowed the term 'Postmodern' from literary criticism and used it with brilliance in architectural criticism. He then designed three Postmodern gardens. The first was a Time Garden for his London home.[27] It is divided into four quadrants, representing the four seasons, and making play with a four-square window-on-the-world motif. Both house and garden have explicit iconographic programmes. Each detail contributes to the symbolic meaning of the whole. Belief, not eclecticism, guided their composition. After writing *The Architecture of the Jumping Universe*,[28] Jencks designed two gardens which draw upon a scientific understanding of nature: for his house in Dumfriesshire and for the Scottish National Gallery of Modern Art in Edinburgh. These projects can be seen as a return of garden design theory to its ancient theme: the imitation of nature – with nature used to mean the laws which govern the universe. Having lost its way in the 1790s, garden design theory returned to a historic path in the 1990s.

Speaking about his design for the Gallery of Modern Art, Jencks explained:

> *I am trying to create a new language of landscape. If you look at the way nature organises itself, it has inherent principles of movement. I wanted to design something that reflected*

10.40 a, b Little Sparta, the garden of Ian Hamilton Finlay, near Edinburgh, has a Postmodern garden, rich in allusion.

10.41 a, b, c Hundertwasser's approach is as much Postmodern as Anti-modern.

> *these natural forces but heightened them. The shapes have been partly inspired by two so-called 'strange attractors', one of them called the Ueda Attractor, named after the Japanese scientist that discovered it. These 'attractors' (weather systems, for example) create a series of self-similar curves that overlap but never repeat, and are attracted to a certain point or 'basin'. I think the landform will create a gateway to the area and identify the gallery from the road as a special place – the locus of contemporary art in Scotland.*[29]

Jencks' design was inspired by patterns of nature, from meteorological effects to chaos theory. 'I am trying to create a new language of landscape,' he stated. 'If you look at the way nature organises itself, it has inherent principles of movement. I wanted to design something that reflected these natural forces but also heightened them.'[30]

10.42 Duisburg-Nord seeks meaning in the site's industrial history.

One of the most intriguing Postmodern gardens in Britain lies about 20 km south of Edinburgh. It is the work of 'Scotland's leading concrete poet', Ian Hamilton Finlay. Concrete poetry is a genre that uses graphic effects to enhance the meaning of a poem. Originally, the effects were typographical, carrying echoes of the pattern poems of the Babylonians, Islamic calligraphy and the quotations which eighteenth-century landscape designers inscribed on temples and urns. A modern revival of the idea began with the

10.43 a, b Sudgelande Nature Park, Berlin, finds post-industrial meaning in pre-industrial fragments and rusting steel.

10.44 The Jewish Museum, Berlin, was deliberately Postmodern and Anti-modern.

work of a Bolivian-born Swiss poet, Eugen Gomringer, in 1951. A 1970 anthology of *Concrete Poetry* contained a quotation from Finlay:

> *My point about poems in glass, actual concrete, stone or whatever is – simply – that new means of constructing a poem aesthetically, ought to lead to consideration of new materials. If these poems are for 'contemplating', let them be sited where they can be contemplated.*[31]

From concrete poetry, it was a natural progression to think of gardens as places where words could be inscribed on stones, sculptures, posts and other objects. Concrete poetry works as code, leading the reader from surface structures to deep structures.

Peter Latz's design for Landschaftspark Duisburg-Nord represents another approach to meaning in outdoor design. Turning its back on mythological and poetic allusions, it refers instead to the site's industrial history: chemicals, steel, fire, blood and toil produced the site's character. A similar approach was taken at Sudgelande Nature Park in Berlin. These projects look forward to a more sustainable future and back, nostalgically, to the pre-post-industrial age. They are Postmodern and Anti-modern. Friedensreich Hundertwasser's radical integration of gardens with architecture is overtly Anti-modern.

The Jewish Museum in Berlin could serve a mausoleum for Abstract Modernism, a place to wail forever against functionalism, master planning and racial purity. The design abjures Cubism, truth to materials, expression of structure, curtain walls, doors, windows and every aspect of Modernism. Whether or not the architect, Daniel Libeskind, had them in mind, this project clearly has a relationship with the use of allegory at the Kennedy Memorial by Jellicoe, and the Vietnam War Memorial by Maya Lin. The Jewish Museum reminds us, in George Santayana's words, that 'Those who cannot remember the past are condemned to repeat it.'[32] Looking back is the necessary prelude to moving forwards.

Sustainable style

Can the first decade of the twenty-first century tell us anything about the future of garden design? My answer is based on a theory and will be illustrated with examples from the Chelsea Flower Show.

The theory was advanced with regard to urban design in *City as Landscape*:

> *Postmodern architecture can be seen as inherently trivial, glitzy and stunt-ish, appealing to the wallet, not to the mind and not to the soul. It belongs in shop windows and in cinemas, in Madison Avenue and in Tinseltown. No one who uses retail shops or watches movies should despise the great products of these great industries. But an 'anything goes' pluralist approach to urban design gives us the equivalent of a junk shop with, perhaps, an empty chocolate box, a kettle and an old TV set. Alone, each might be elegant, stylish or beautiful; together they are a jumble. As a direct consequence of pluralism, the postmodern city street resembles an out-of-step chorus line. If anything goes, then nothing goes.*
>
> *But there are signs of post-Postmodern life, in urban design, architecture and elsewhere. They are strongest in those who place their hands on their hearts and are willing to assert 'I believe'. Faith always was the strongest competitor for reason: faith in a God; faith in a tradition; faith in an institution; faith in a person. The built environment professions are witnessing the gradual dawn of a post-Postmodernism that seeks to temper reason with faith.*[33]

The beliefs influencing gardens relate to the most ancient pre-occupation of garden designers: the relationship between the works of man and the works of nature. After centuries of confidence about adapting wilderness to human needs, societies now have serious concerns about climate change, shortages of natural resources and rising sea levels. The extents to which human actions caused these problems and changes in

10.45 a–k CAT, the Centre for Alternative Technology, has a sustainable garden made with local plants, local materials, recycled materials, edible plants, animals and a great deal of rain. The design details and the design intention are something of a return to the gardens of the Middle Ages.

behaviour can resolve them, are un-provable and un-measurable. But the belief that 'something must be done' is having a visible influence on garden design:

- Green walls and green roofs are increasing the extent of horticultural activity.
- Sustainable water management is becoming a significant influence on garden design.
- Natural swimming ponds are replacing chemically filtered artificial pools.
- Gardens are becoming more practical, with function becoming an equal partner with beauty as a design objective. More land is used to grow food and more space is used for living with nature.
- Mere 'show' is coming to be seen as ostentatious.

The obvious description of these trends is that they represent a sustainable style of gardening.

The spread of gardening activity onto walls and roofs will contribute to the sustainability of cities by making them:

10.46 Walls, as well as roofs, are set to become gardens.

10.47 The 1-ha roof garden on Warsaw University Library also has green walls and green ramps (landscape architect Irena Bajerska, 2002). It has views of the River Vistula and the city.

- able to manage rainwater more sustainably (with rain gardens, detention ponds, infiltration ponds, etc.);
- better insulated, because soil and vegetation shield buildings from heat loss and solar gain;
- more productive, because roof and wall vegetation can produce food;
- quieter, because noise is reflected by hard surfacing and absorbed by soft surfacing;
- less dusty, because dust settles on vegetation and becomes soil when the vegetation decays.

So my prediction is that when a garden historian extends the history of garden design from 2010 to 2110, he or she will probably observe that while skyscrapers were the most dramatic feature of twentieth-century cities, sustainable roof and wall vegetation were the most significant changes in the twenty-first century.

Styles and examples

Arts and Crafts style

Use: Using one's hands came to be seen as a physically and spiritually rewarding activity. This gave wealthy owners a significant involvement in the maintenance of their own gardens – probably for the first time in European history. The poor must always have worked their own land and the rich sometimes had a dilettante involvement. But the hard

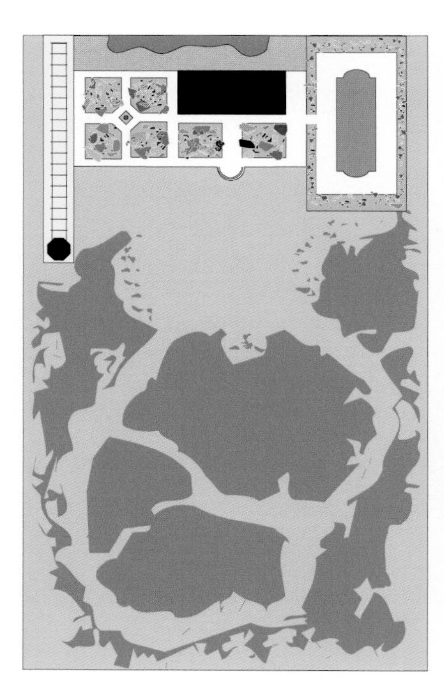

10.48 Arts and Crafts style.

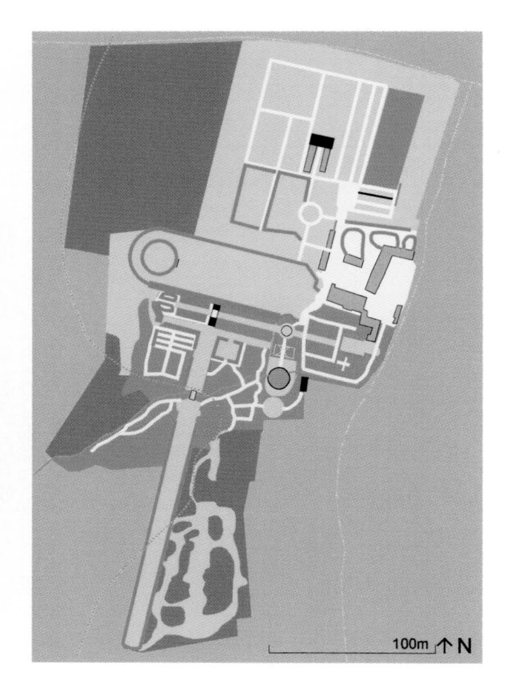

10.49 Hidcote Manor, England.

physical work had always been done by gardeners. Arts and Crafts admiration for the honesty of manual work led to a marriage of gardens with gardening.

Form: Led by Ruskin and Morris, designers sought a return to the principles of art and to the craft skills on which, it was held, true style must rest. Arts and Crafts gardens generally have a clear demarcation between an enclosed area, with geometrical compartments, and a naturalistic 'wild garden'. Refined discernment was exercised in the choice of good plants, fine building materials and craft-based construction.

Hidcote, 1905

Hidcote was made by an American owner-designer after 1905. Lawrence Johnston was a keen plantsman with a strong sense of artistic composition. He was reticent about his stylistic influences but his work sings of the Arts and Crafts movement. Yew, holly and beech hedges are used to define a series of garden rooms. A stream crosses the garden and one room is occupied only by a circular pool, perhaps the most beautiful bathing pool in England. Other garden rooms derive their character from the planting. The standard of craftsmanship is exceptional and the number of plants which have the varietal name 'Hidcote' point to Johnston's expertise with plants.

> *It appeals alike to the advanced gardener in search of rare or interesting plants, and on the aesthetic side to the mere lover of beauty, content to wander down broad grass walks*

flanked with colour, turning continually aside as the glimpse of little separate gardens lures him.

(Vita Sackville-West)[34]

Stockholm Stadshuset (City Hall), 1911

The City Hall, on the north shore of Riddarfjarden, exemplifies a Swedish Arts and Crafts approach, known as the 'national romantic style'. Both the Hall and its south-facing garden were designed by Ragnar Ostberg. They are well proportioned and beautifully detailed. The garden has a central lawn framed by a grid of stone paths with grass-filled joints. Water steps fall south and east into the lake, as though it were a vast lily-pond. The statues which flank the southward steps, by Carl Eldh, are of a man and a woman, dancing above the waters in a celebration of life. A small parterre and pleached limes close the space to the west.

The waters of Lake Mälar surround the Garden on three sides, washing, on the west, against the Wallenberg Wall. This wall ... surrounds a parterre which is embellished with fountains, greenery, ponds and sculptures. This sequestered spot enables the general public to enjoy in peace the beauties of the waterside, and has attractions for the little folks.

(Ragnar Ostberg)[35]

10.50 Stadshuset (City Hall), Stockholm, Sweden.

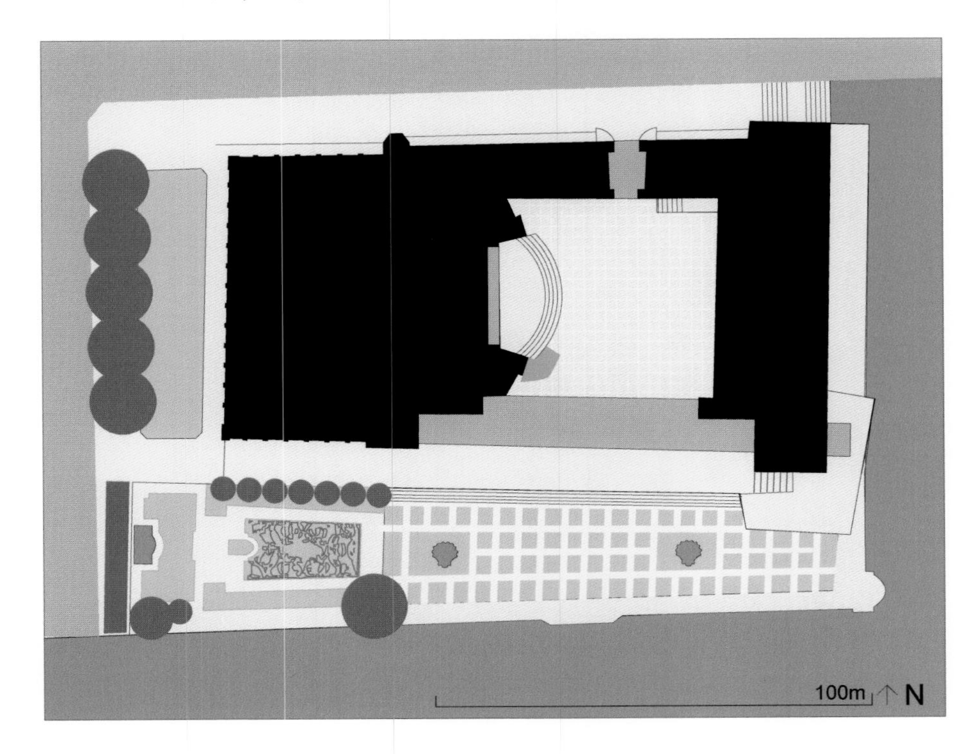

Sissinghurst, 1930

Sissinghurst was made amongst the remains of a fortified manor dating from the sixteenth century. This was a period admired by the Arts and Crafts movement. The garden was designed by its owners, who knew Jekyll and Lutyens. Harold Nicolson, a diplomat and author, laid down the main lines of the plan in the 1930s. Vita Sackville-West, a poet, a garden writer and Harold's wife, took responsibility for the planting. She worked as an 'artist-gardener'. Her planting design was brilliant and, though the garden is well maintained, those who knew it in the 1950s believe she achieved a quality which has not been equalled since her death. The historical importance of Sissinghurst comes from its role in transmitting the Arts and Crafts design philosophy to a host of visitors.

> *Sissinghurst seems to stand out for one particular quality; shades of its design and all its planting ideas might be found elsewhere, but where else was such a comforting, intimate garden? Even in this company of the great and good, Sissinghurst shone out for its quality of love.*
>
> (Jane Brown)[36]

10.51 Sissinghurst Castle garden, England.

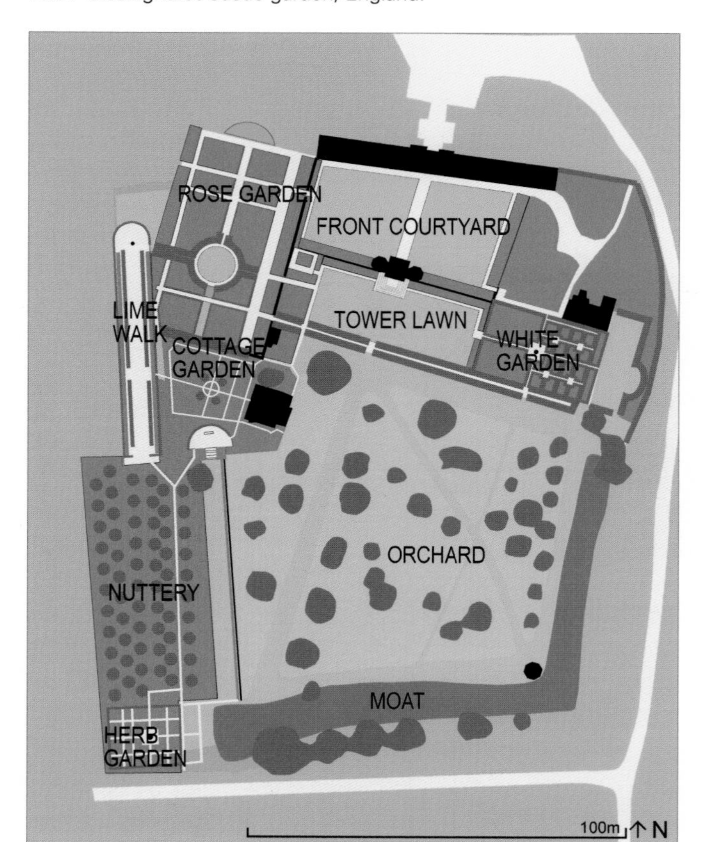

Abstract style

Use: The Abstract style of garden design, like the Modern movement in architecture, grew by degrees out of the Arts and Crafts movement. Corbusier said that a house should be a machine for living. Gardens were designed as space for outdoor living and exercise grounds for machines: mowers, pumps, cultivators, sprays and other gadgetry. This enabled owners to undertake as much of the maintenance work as they pleased, even in large gardens.

Form: Twentieth-century designs were inspired by the startling shapes and patterns of Abstract art. The rectilinear geometry of the *de Stijl* movement, Mondrian and Nicholson influenced the design of paving and walls; the curvilinear geometry of landform and planting has been influenced by Moore, Miro, Brancusi and Arp. New materials appeared in gardens: concrete, steel and glass. There was often a transition from rectilinear to curvilinear.

Barcelona Pavilion, 1929

Mies van der Rohe's German Pavilion for the 1929 Barcelona Exhibition 'became the true archetype of modernist spatial composition'.[37] The building and garden were designed for the Barcelona International Exposition of 1929, dismantled after the show and rebuilt in 1983, on the same site and using the same materials. They are a prime example of how the principles of Abstract, Cubist design can be applied to the

10.52 Abstract style.

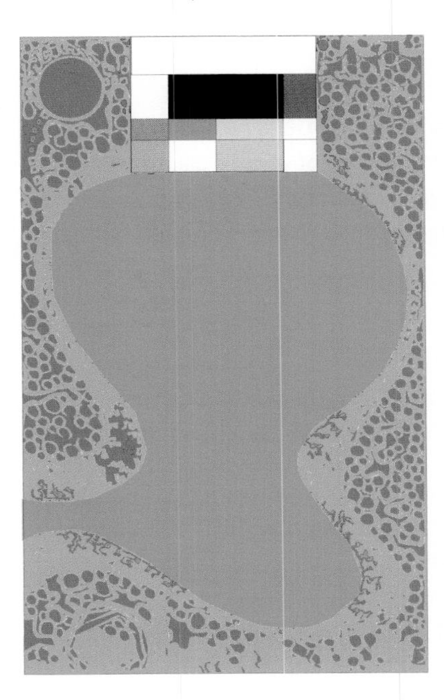

10.53 Barcelona Pavilion.

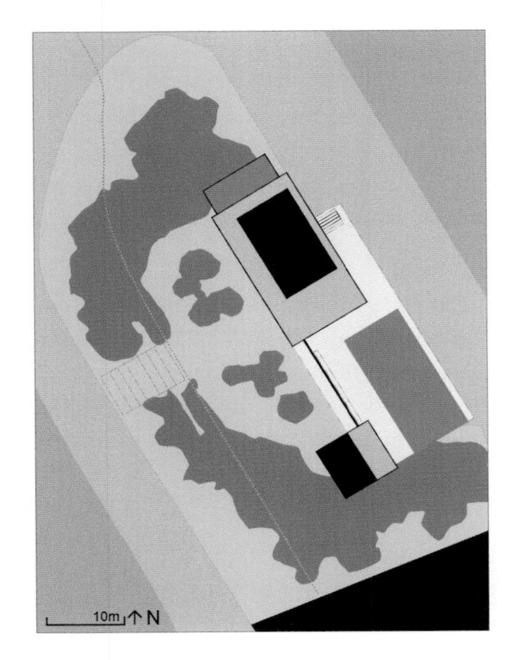

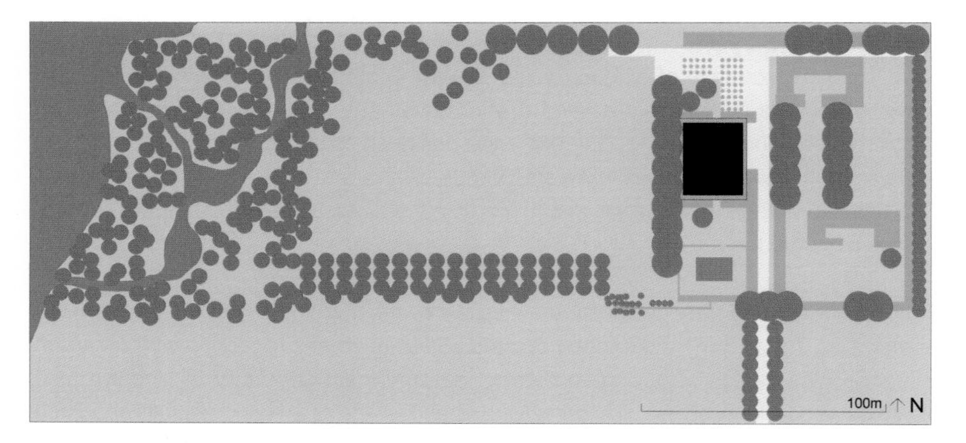

10.54 Miller Garden, Columbus, Indiana.

integration of outdoor and indoor space. The materials are sheet glass, polished steel, marble, travertine and onyx. Partly because of stone's exceptional colour and texture, partly because of the beautiful composition and partly because of the water and vegetation, the pavilion is vastly more appealing than most Modernist-Brutalist concrete structures which use related principles.

> *The German Pavilion – the Palace of Reflections – is the most authentic expression of Cubism, the chief manifestation of that dead, quartered aesthetic which Picasso invented one gloomy day.*
>
> (A. Mars and L. Marsillach)[38]

Miller Garden, Indiana, 1957

Dan Kiley traced the genesis of his design to the European gardens he had seen in 1945: 'From that point onward, I experimented with the translation of various classic elements into a modern spatial sensibility.'[39] The result is widely regarded as a classic: structures, planting, paving and pool are treated as compositional elements in a neoplastic composition.

> *The Miller garden, Kiley's masterpiece, was designed for a client rare in modern times, a real patron, Irwin Miller ... [It] does not shock or even amuse the eye. Rather it leads one gently from space to space through a witty and ambiguous game of discovery ... The spaces one moves through are clearly defined yet fluid, ever expanding outward from the house to the street and the river.*
>
> (P. Walker and M. Simo)[40]

Louisiana, 1958

Louise was the name of the owner's three wives. His nineteenth-century seaside house became a museum of painting, sculpture, graphics, architecture and landscape design.

10.55 Louisiana, Denmark.

The building and its landscape are a work of Modern art in their own right. Glass corridors join pavilions, creating an Abstract composition with an unusually successful fusion of indoors and outdoors. Louisiana has been greatly admired since its opening in 1958 and was particularly influential in the 1960s. The original landscape designers, Ole and Edith Norgaard, were followed by Lea Norgaard and Vibeke Holscher.

> *The new building is situated across the existing park where the view opens up to the sea but is connected with the old house by long twisting walkways. Sometimes these are closed in on both sides, with walls displaying works of art, sometimes one or both sides are glass from ceiling to floor. Thus a wonderful succession of glimpses of art and nature alternating has been achieved, and the landscape floats through the walkways.*
>
> (T. Hutton)[41]

Munich Olympiapark, 1972

Munich has a remarkable Modern landscape, made for the 1972 Olympics. Previously, the site was dull and flat, surrounded with ugly buildings and strewn with heaps of rubble cleared from the 1945 bombing. It was transformed into a sinuous web of tented structures, lakes and hills. The roof flows with the land and the landform sweeps into the water. Geometrically, there were two varieties of Abstract Modernism: rectilinear and curvilinear. The Olympiapark is the purest example of curvilinear international

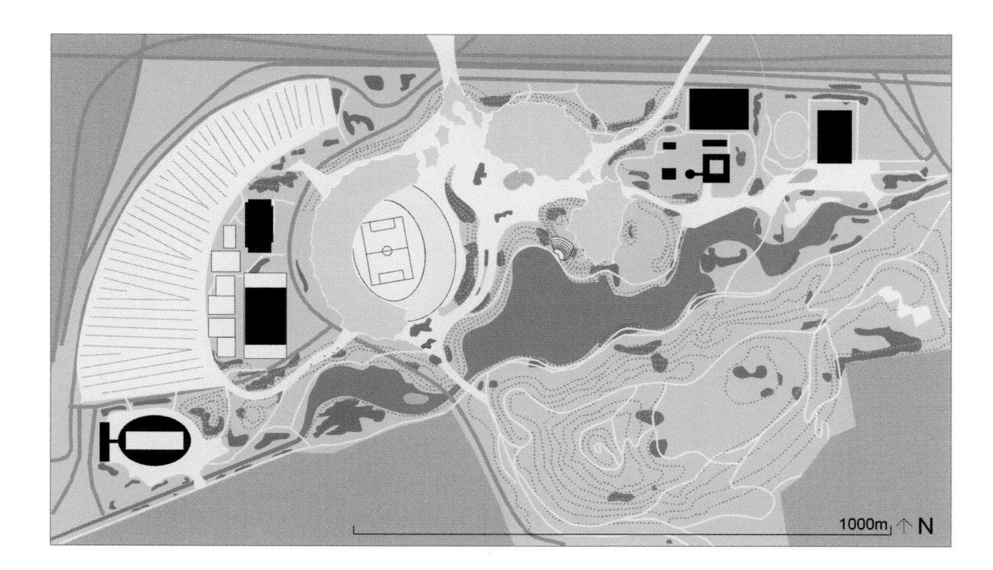

10.56 The Olympiapark, Munich.

Modernism. Behnisch were the architects, Frei Otto designed the tented structures, Günter Grizmek was the landscape architect – and they worked together. Of all the Olympic parks built in the twentieth century, this is the only one which has a landscape quality matching that of ancient Greek sanctuaries and stadia.

> *It was not to be a copy of nature; rather an imitation of nature in an architectonically conceived composition combining landform, buildings, water and plants.*
>
> (Michael Lancaster)[42]

Post-abstract style

Use: Postmodern ideas encourage garden owners to deconstruct their preconceptions, allowing experimentation with new materials, new geometries, concrete poetry, hot tubs, glass rooms, non-traditional plants and the transformation of pavements into water features. Above all, it can be used to overlay uses and ideas in a multifaceted Postmodern structural composition. Towards the end of the twentieth century, the style was used to win design competitions.

Form: Geometrically, Postmodernism is associated with layered, fractured and deconstructive geometries. Relationships are overturned. Rectangles clash with circles and are intersected by haphazard diagonals, as in Russian Constructivist art. Steel and concrete structures are painted in bright colours. Glass and other reflective surfaces help create illusions.

Parc de la Villette, 1982

Parc de la Villette, in Paris, was the first major landscape design to draw upon deconstructionist philosophy. It was the result of a competition won by Bernard Tschumi.

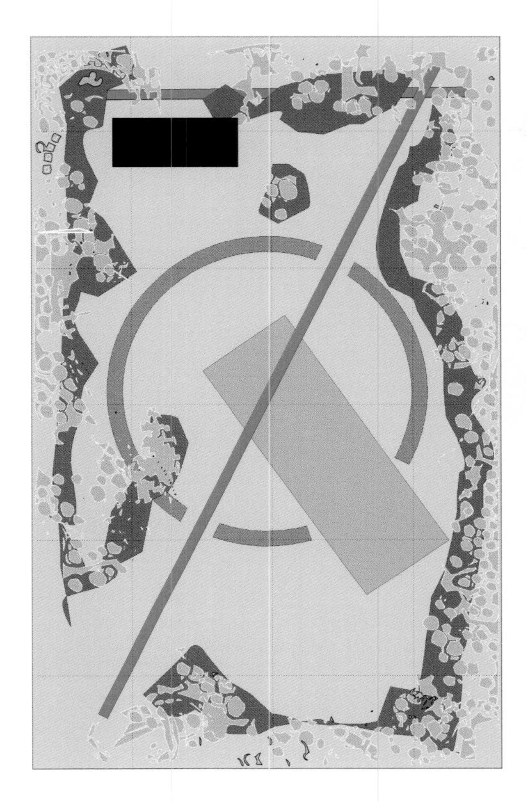

10.57 Post-abstract style.

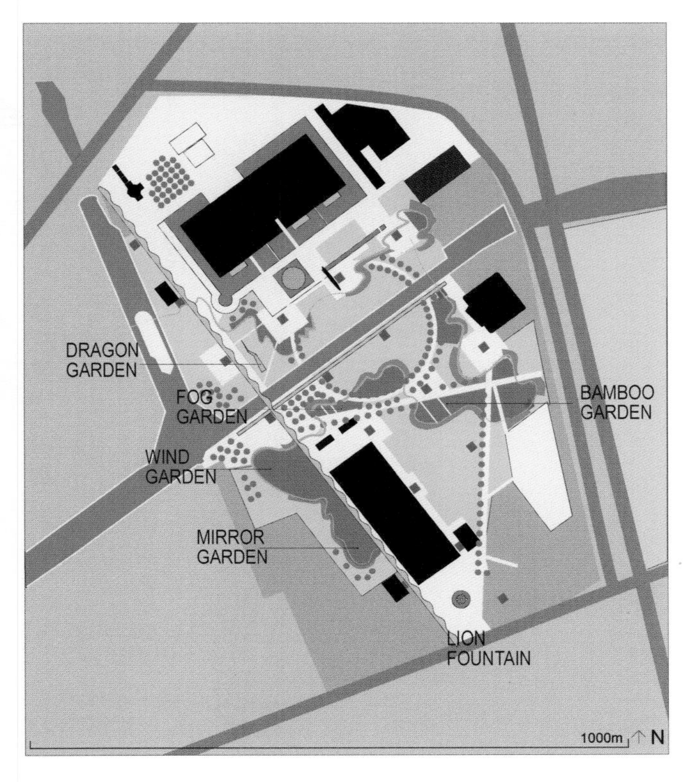

10.58 Parc de la Villette.

Rejecting the old idea of a 'park', Tschumi sought to create 'the largest discontinuous building in the world'. Jacques Derrida, the philosopher, encouraged him to determine the form *before* the functions: an Anti-modernist reversal of the traditional design procedure. Tschumi laid down three geometries: of points, lines and curves. Clashes were encouraged. The points took the form of a collection of steel pavilions, inspired by Russian constructivist art and painted red. The lines were not unlike traditional French avenues. The most dramatic curved feature was the Cinematic Promenade. Alongside the Promenade are a number of themed areas. Alexandre Chemetoff's Bamboo Garden is an exotic oasis. There is a Fog Garden (by Alain Pélisier), a Dragon Garden, a Mirror Garden (by Tschumi), and a Wind and Dune Garden. The public and the professions were puzzled by the original drawings but have come to admire the result.

> *'If this is a landscape design', one could hear the landscape designers thinking, 'then pink atoms will learn to yodel'. Now that Parc de la Villette is substantially complete, one can see that it was a landscape design, and that alternative readings of the scheme are possible ... Whether or not they appertain to the designer's intentions is, of course, strictly irrelevant in deconstructionist theory.*
>
> (Tom Turner)[43]

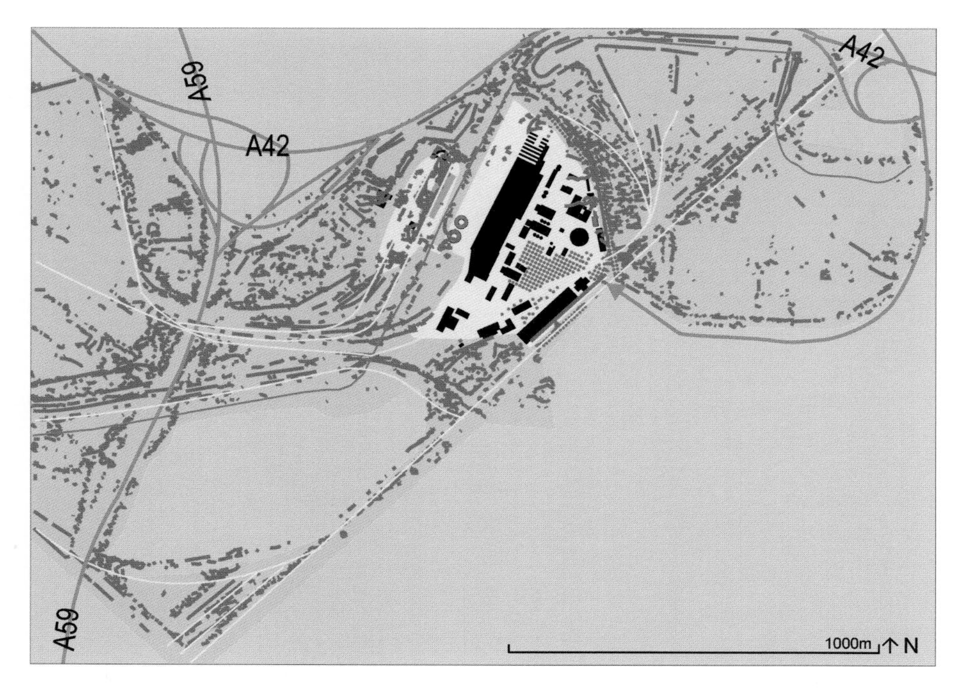

10.59 Landschaftspark Duisburg-Nord, Germany.

Landschaftspark Duisburg-Nord, 1991

The Landschaftspark in Duisburg-Nord is part of the 300 sq km Emscher Park system. It returns to an ancient principle: 'consult the genius of the place'. Since the local genius was a steelworks, the policy produced, for a park design, a wholly new range of features, shapes, forms and textures. Appearing in the guise of constructivist painting, the forms result from deconstructing the industrial facility: ugly becomes beautiful; wastes become productive; weeds become habitat; contaminated water becomes pure. The design is postmodern, Post-horticultural, post-machine-age – and very popular.

> *The aesthetic ambition calls for a revolution in one's thinking of what a park can be ... The design is based on an appreciation of the industrial inheritance: lines of old railway embankment are seen as a form of land art and will be managed as grassland. Visitors can wander through the site and from the embankments view the land around with a sense of liberation.*
>
> (Robert Holden)[44]

> *At Emscher Park, the idea of nature is not confused with that of landscape. For Latz, nature is usually something divorced from landscape: landscape exists as a cultural phenomenon, while nature is a self-determining force ... The Piazza (Metallica) also draws attention to two aspects of the nature of metal. The industrial infrastructure reminds the visitor of the creation, over many generations, of the solid, hardened product, a process*

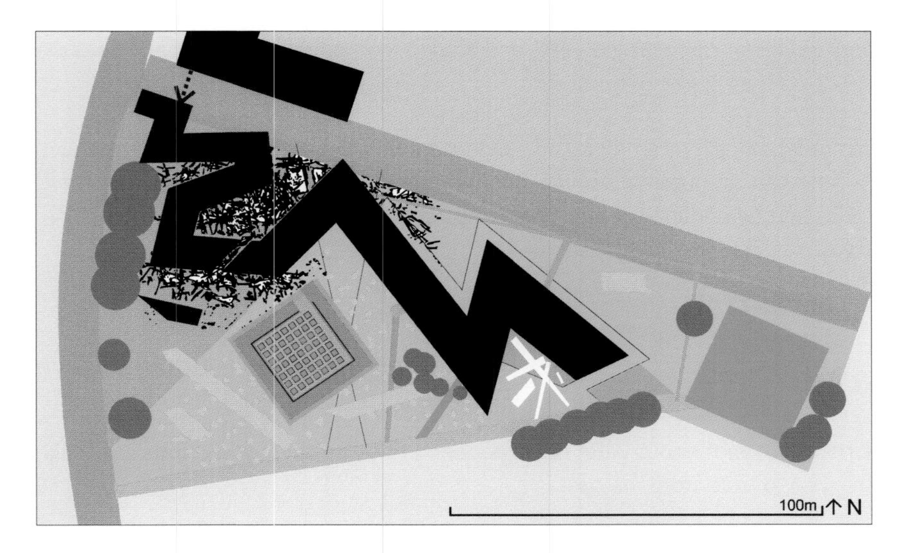

10.60 Jewish Museum, Berlin, Germany.

> *that demands temperatures of some 1300 degrees centigrade. Metal is also present in the eroded form, deprived by time of its molten, energizing force.*
>
> (Michael Spens)[45]

Jewish Museum, Berlin, 1998

The design of the museum is based on a burst Star of David, abjuring right angles, doors, windows and other architectural conventions. The notice beside the Garden of Exile (2002) states:

> *Here architect Daniel Libeskind asks us to think about the disorientation that exile brings. The 49 columns are filled with earth in which willow oaks grow. Forty-eight of the columns contain the earth of Berlin and stand for 1948 and the formation of the state of Israel. The central and 49th pillar is filled with earth from Jerusalem and stands for Berlin itself.*
>
> *References to the history of Berlin's Jews are implicit in the site's design – references which can be found, for example, in the composition of the paving, or the lines on the building, in the engraved stones and in the use of gravel to emphasize the 'voids' created by the forms of the building.*
>
> (Robert Holden)[46]

Sustainable style

Use: Sustainable gardens spurn the notions of 'art for art's sake', 'style for style's sake' and 'ornament for ornament's sake'. Instead, functions are emphasised. Vegetation is used, on walls and roofs, as insulation and for carbon sequestration. In place of 'expert

10.61 It is too early to represent sustainable gardens with a diagram. But we can expect garden designers to keep exploring the relationship between the nature of man and the nature of Nature. They may do so with regard to the functions, technology and aesthetics of outdoor space, including both Euclidean and fractal geometries.

lawns' and 'a blaze of colour all the year' land is used for production, beauty and outdoor living.

Form: No geometrical patterns can be associated with the style, as yet. But one can expect a renewed enthusiasm for the geometrical forms: circles, squares, triangles, straight lines and serpentine curves. They reflect a 'back to basics' ethos and combine naturally with vegetation.

What next?

There is much to learn about what could happen in the gardens of the future, should designers wish to learn from the past:

- From the ancient world they could relearn the twin arts of making outdoor rooms and using roof space as living space: the ground in modern towns lacks seclusion and is dominated by motor vehicles; roof space is delightful and would be more so if adorned with rush awnings and pot plants.
- From the Classical world, they could learn the outstanding merit of peristyle courts and of treating whole landscapes as sacred, in the sense of 'safeguarded or required by religion or reverence, or tradition, indefeasible, inviolable, sacrosanct'. To a degree, we do this in natural and national parks, but they are too often violated by tourist facilities, motor vehicles, folksy signage, litter and rangers in mock-military costumes.
- From the medieval world of Christianity and Islam, designers could learn to make gardens with an other-worldly perfection: quiet, calm, geometrically perfect and as carefully designed as illuminated manuscripts. The love of labour induces an appreciation of craftsmanship and a delight in economy.
- From the Renaissance, Baroque and Romantic periods, designers could learn first to integrate architecture with gardens, so that these arts compliment and complement one another. Second, they could learn to weld great and small building projects into the wider landscape. Third, they could relearn the skill of coordinating the arts (building, planting, painting, music, sculpture, etc.).
- From the nineteenth century, designers could learn that, on occasion, it is good to be bold, brash and colourful. Gardens can be different. There is much to be learned from other climes and other countries.
- From the twentieth century, designers could learn to employ the principles of Abstract design – and the pure fun of overthrowing them.
- From 50 centuries, we can learn about the close relationship between garden design and urban design, because both arts involve the composition of buildings with paving, landform, water, vegetation and climate.[47]

10.62 a–i Annual reviews of the Chelsea Flower Show, in London, lead to the following observations about early twenty-first-century trends in garden design: (1) Abstract Modernism, after a long delay, has become a significant aesthetic; (2) designers are exploring the aesthetic implications of sustainability; (3) the old quest to make comfortable space for outdoor life is alive and well; and (4) enthusiasm for colour and representation can be described as Maximalist (in opposition to Minimalist).

Having lasted for 5000 years, the use of natural materials to express ideas about nature may be expected to continue. The best garden designs are produced with an awareness of the art, science, history, geography, philosophy, social habits and construction techniques of their period. Furthermore, and especially on mass housing projects, it is necessary to plan gardens before dwellings.

Notes

Preface

1. Turner, T., *Asian Gardens*, London: Routledge, 2011.
2. Clark, H.F., *The English Landscape Garden*, London: Pleiades Books, 1948. I think Clark hoped to revise this book in the light of Lovejoy, A. O., *The Great Chain of Being: A Study of the History of an Idea*, Cambridge, MA: Harvard University Press, 1936, which he kindly lent me.
3. Loudon J.C., *Self Instruction for Young Gardeners*, London: Longman, 1845, p. 23.
4. Jellicoe, G.A., *Gardens of Europe*, London: Blackie & Son, 1937, p. 83.

1 Design philosophy

1. Repton, H., *Fragments on the Theory and Practice of Landscape Gardening*, London 1816, Fragment XXVII, Gardens of Ashridge.
2. Kipling, R., *The Elephant's Child*: 'I keep six honest serving men/(They taught me all I know);/Their names are What and Why and When/And How and Where and Who.' *The Collected Poems of Rudyard Kipling*, Ware, Hertfordshire, UK: Wordsworth Editions, 1994, p. 635.
3. Vitruvius, *The Ten Books on Architecture*, trans. M.H. Morgan, 1914, and reprinted London: Dover Books, Inc., UK edn, London: Constable & Co., 1960, p. 17.
4. Wotton, H., *The Elements of Architecture*, London, 1624.
5. Thompson, I., *Ecology, Community and Delight*, London: Spon, 2000.
6. Turner, T., *Asian Gardens*, London: Routledge, 2011, Chapter 1.
7. Vitruvius, op. cit., pp. 161–2.
8. Ibid., Chapter 4, p. 17.
9. Sullivan, C., *Gardens and Climate*, London: McGraw-Hill, 2002.
10. Masson, G., *Italian Gardens*, London: Thames & Hudson, p. 168.
11. Horace, *Ars Poetica*. The quotation and its translation are from Hussey, C., *English Gardens and Landscapes, 1700–1750*, London: Country Life, 1967, p. 11.
12. The practice has not entirely ceased: it was reported at the time of writing (*Sunday Times*, 27 July 2003) that Saddam Hussein's son, Uday, fed two men to lions, in Mesopotamia, because they had competed for his girlfriend's favours.
13. *The Bible*, Genesis 2:7–10 (Authorised version).
14. *The Koran*, Surah XIII, 2.
15. Smart, N., *The Religious Experience of Mankind*, London: Fontana, 1984, p. 15ff.
16. *Encyclopaedia Britannica*, Vol. 16, p. 123.
17. Ibid.
18. The term 'aesthetics' was coined by Alexander Baumgarten, a disciple of Leibniz, in his book *Aethestica* (Pt. I 1750, Pt. II 1758).
19. Russell, B., A *History of Western Philosophy*, London: Allen & Unwin, 1946, pp. 13–14.
20. Ibid., p. 54.
21. Ibid., p. 53.
22. Ibid., p. 136.
23. Murdoch, I., *The Fire and the Sun: Why Plato Banished the Artists*, Oxford: Clarendon Press, 1977.
24. Plato, *The Republic*, Book X, trans. B. Jowett.
25. Pliny, *Natural History*, Book XXXV, 64.
26. Panofsky, E., *Gothic Architecture and Scholasticism*, London: Thames & Hudson, 1957, pp. 44–5.
27. Wittkower, R., *Architectural Principles in the Age of Humanism*, London: Academy Editions, 1962, pp. 22–32.
28. Whitehead, A.N., *Process and Reality: An Essay in Cosmology*, New York: Free Press, 1985, p. 39.
29. Pope, A., *Essay on Criticism*, London, 1711.
30. Pope, A., 'On gardens', *The Guardian*, London, 1713.
31. Hunt, J.D., *Greater Perfections: The Practice of Garden Theory*, London: Thames & Hudson, 2000, pp. 32–75.
32. Huxley, T.H., *Evolution and Ethics and Other Essays*, London: Macmillan, 1893.
33. Wölfflin, H., 'Principles of art history' (1915), in D. Preziosi (ed.), *The Art of History*, Oxford: Oxford University Press, 1998, p. 115.
34. Kemp, B.J., *Ancient Egypt: Anatomy of a Civilization*, London: Routledge, 1991.
35. The Garden Finder section of the Gardenvisit.com website has maps of garden locations, aerial photographs of gardens, garden descriptions and biographies of garden designers.

2 Garden origins, 10,000–1000 BCE

1. Kramer, S.N., *History Begins at Sumer: Thirty-nine Firsts in Man's Recorded History*, Philadelphia, PA: University of Pennsylvania Press, 1981.
2. Turner, T., *Garden History: Philosophy and Design 2000 BC–2000 AD*, London: Spon, 2005, p. 1.
3. Darwin, C., *The Descent of Man*, London, 1890, p. 135.
4. Bard, K.A. and Blake Shubert, S. (eds), *Encyclopedia of the Archaeology of Ancient Egypt*, New York: Routledge, 1999, p. 1054.
5. Hancock, J.F., *Plant Evolution and the Origin of Crop Species*, Upper Saddle River, NJ: Prentice Hall, 1992, p. 162.
6. Levy, T.E., *Archaeology of Society in the Holy Land*, Leicester: Leicester University Press, 1998, p. 37.
7. Bradley, R., 'Architecture, imagination and the Neolithic world', in S. Mithen (ed.), *Creativity in Human Evolution and Prehistory*, London: Routledge 1998, p. 228.
8. Kenyon, K.M., *Archaeology in the Holy Land*, London: Thomas Nelson, 1985, p. 21.
9. Pogucki, P., *The Origins of Human Society*, Oxford: Blackwell, 1999, p. 161.
10. Mithen, S., *After the Ice: A Global Human History, 20,000–5000 BC*, London: Weidenfeld & Nicolson, 2003, p. 36.
11. Ibid., p. 59.
12. 'Reconstructing Landscapes and Environments of Archaeological Sites: Çatalhöyük, Opovo, and Chiripa', available at: http://www.mactia.berkeley.edu/tringham/Anthro2_Fall03_RET/04_landscape/sec110_lands_chilly_web.pdf.
13. McIntosh, J., *Ancient Mesopotamia*, Santa Barbara, CA: ABC-Clio, 2005, p. 154.
14. Gordon Childe's ten characteristics of the 'urban revolution' were: (1) cities; (2) advanced division of labor; (3) production of an agricultural surplus; (4) monumental public architecture; (5) a ruling class; (6) writing; (7) exact and predictive sciences; (8) sophisticated art; (9) long-distance trade; (10) an organised state. Childe, V.G., 'The Urban Revolution', *Town Planning Review*, 23 (1950): 3–17.

15 Sayce, Rev. A.H., Professor of Assyriology, Oxford, *The Archaeology of the Cuneiform Inscriptions*, 2nd edn, rev., 1908, London: Society for Promoting Christian Knowledge, p. 99.
16 Brusasco, P., *The Archaeology of Verbal and Non-verbal Meaning*, Oxford: British Archaeological Reports/Hadrian, 2007, p. 25.
17 Gates, C., *Ancient Cities*, London: Routledge, 2003, p. 33.
18 Finkel, I.L. and Seymour, M.J., *Babylon, Myth and Reality*, London: British Museum Press, 2008, p. 110.
19 Galpin, F.W., *The Music of the Sumerians and Their Immediate Successors the Babylonians and Assyrians*, Strasbourg: Librairie Heitz, Strasbourg University Press, 1955, p. 23.
20 Harding, A.F., *European Societies in the Bronze Age*, Cambridge: Cambridge University Press, 2000, p. 57.
21 Ibid., p. 60.
22 Ibid., p. 55.
23 Pryor, F.L., 'The invention of the plow', *Comparative Studies in Society and History*, 27(4) (1985), pp. 727–43.
24 Harris, D.R., *The Origins and Spread of Agriculture and Pastoralism in Eurasia*, London: Routledge, 1996, p. 3.
25 Pryor, F.L., op. cit., pp. 727–43.
26 Levy, T.E., op. cit., p. xviii.
27 Lerro, B., *Power in Eden*, Victoria, BC: Trafford Publishing, 2005, p. 29.
28 Ibid., p. 35.
29 Harris, D.R., op. cit., p. 554.
30 *Epic of Gilgamesh*, trans. M.G. Kovacs, 1998, http//www.ancienttexts.org/library/mesopotamian/gilgamesh/tab1.htm
31 Kramer, S.N., op. cit., p. 71.
32 Ibid., p. 69.
33 Potts, D.T., *Mesopotamian Civilization: The Material Foundations*, Ithaca, NY: Cornell University Press, 1996, p. 69ff.
34 *Kiru* is the nominative and *kiri* is the genitive of the Assyrian and Babylonian word for garden.
35 Wainwright, J. and Thornes, J.B., *Environmental Issues in the Mediterranean: Processes and Perspectives from the Past and Present*, London: Routledge, 2003, p. 241.
36 Bard, K.A. and Blake Shubert, S., op. cit., p. 124.
37 Shillington, K. (ed.), *Encyclopedia of African History*, London: Routledge, 2004, p. 416.
38 Halstead, P. 'The development of agriculture and pastoralism in Greece: when, who, why and what?', in Harris, D.R., op. cit., p. 296.
39 Ibid., p. 305.
40 Dietrich, B.C., *The Origins of Greek Religion*, Bristol: Bristol Phoenix Press, 1974, p. 36.
41 Milisauskas, S. (ed.), *European Prehistory: A Survey*, New York: Springer, 2002, p. 148.
42 Mallory, J.P. and Adams, D.Q. (eds), *Encyclopedia of Indo-European Culture*, London: Routledge, 1997, pp. 243–4.
43 Foxhall, L., *Olive Cultivation in Ancient Greece: Seeking the Ancient Economy*, London: Oxford University Press, 2007, p. 219.
44 Ibid., p. 222.
45 Isager, S. and Skydsgaard, J.E., *Ancient Greek Agriculture: An Introduction*, London: Routledge, 1995, p. 43.
46 Ibid., p. 46.
47 Harris, D.R., 'The origins and spread of agriculture and pastoralism in Eurasia: an overview' in D.R. Harris, op. cit., p. 559.
48 Fussell, G.E., *The Classical Tradition in West European Farming*, New York: Fairleigh Dickinson University Press, 1972, p. 12.
49 Henderson, J., *The Roman Book of Gardening*, London: Routledge, 2004, p. 6.
50 Ibid., p. 34.
51 Ibid., p. 39.
52 Scarre, C., *The Human Past*, London: Thames & Hudson, 2005, p. 398.
53 Hogg, A.H.A., *A Guide to the Hill-forts of Britain*, London: Paladin, 1984, p. xi.
54 Arnold, B. and Blair Gibson, D. (eds), *Celtic Chiefdom, Celtic State*, Cambridge: Cambridge University Press, 1995, p. 27.
55 Julius Caesar, *Commentaries on the Gallic War*, Hayes Barton Press, 1877, p. 113.
56 Ibid., p. 58.
56 Lieberman, P., *Uniquely Human*, Cambridge, MA: Harvard University Press, 1993, p. 162.
58 Ingold, T., 'Comment on "Beyond the original affluent society" by N. Bird-David', *Current Anthropology*, 33 (1992): 34–47.
59 Bradley, R., *An Archaeology of Natural Places*, London: Routledge, 2000, p. 147.
60 Khazanov, A.M., 'The spread of world religions in medieval nomadic societies of the Eurasian Steppes', in M. Gervers and W. Schlepp (eds), *Nomad Diplomacy: Destruction and Religion from the Pacific to the Adriatic*, Toronto: Joint Centre for Asia Pacific Studies, 1998, p. 12.
61 Anthony, D.W., *The Horse, the Wheel, and Language: How Bronze-Age Riders from the Eurasian Steppes Shaped the Modern World*, Princeton, NJ: Princeton University Press, 2008, p. 6.
62 Turner, T., *Asian Gardens*, London: Routledge, 2011.
63 Ibid.
64 Wikipedia http://en.wikipedia.org/wiki/G%C3%B6bekli_Tepe 15.4.2009
65 Diamond, J., *Guns, Germs and Steel*, London: W.W. Norton, 1997, Chapter 14.
66 Nemet-Nejat, K.R., *Daily Life in Ancient Mesopotamia*, Westport, CT: Greenwood Press, 1998, p. 19.
67 Leick, G., *Sex and Eroticism in Mesopotamian Literature*, London: Routledge, 1994, p. 13.
68 Black, J.A., Green, A. and Rickards, T. (eds), *Gods, Demons and Symbols of Ancient Mesopotamia: An Illustrated Dictionary*, Austin: University of Texas Press, 1992, p. 27.
69 Kramer, S.N., op. cit., p. 73.
70 Scully Jr, V., *The Earth, the Temple, and the Gods: Greek Sacred Architecture*, Addenda, 1964: Society of Architectural Historians.
71 Ibid., p. 1.
72 Fox, M.V. (ed.), Preface, *Temple in Society*, Winona Lake: Eisenbrauns, 1988, p. v.
73 Burl, A., *The Stone Circles of Britain, Ireland and Brittany*, New Haven, CT: Yale University Press, 2000, p. 75.
74 Gimbutas, M., *The Language of the Goddess*, London: Thames and Hudson, 1989, p. 131.
75 Lock, G., 'Wessex Hillforts after Danebury: exploring boundaries', in C. Gosden, H. Hamerow, P. de Jersey and G. Lock (eds), *Communities and Connections: Essays in Honour of Barry Cunliffe*, Oxford: Oxford University Press, 2007, p. 352.
76 Eph al, I., *The Ancient Arabs: Nomads on the Borders of the Fertile Crescent, 9th–5th Century BC*, Jerusalem: Magnes Press, 1982, p. 11.
77 Kramer, S.N., 'The temple in Sumerian literature', in M.V. Fox, op. cit., p. 12.
78 Postgate, J.N., *Early Mesopotamia: Society and Economy at the Dawn of History*, London: Routledge, 1992, p. 125.
79 Ibid., p. 306.
80 McIntosh, J., *Ancient Mesopotamia: New Perspectives*, Santa Barbara, CA: ABC-Clio, 2005, p. 154.
81 Dalley, S., *Mari and Karana: Two Old Babylonian Cities*, London: Longman, 2002, p. 12.
82 Oleson, J.P. (ed.), *The Oxford Handbook of Engineering and Technology in the Classical World*, Oxford: Oxford University Press, 2009, p. 291.
83 Dalley, S., 'Ancient Mesopotamian gardens and the identification of the Hanging Gardens of Babylon resolved', *Garden History*, 21(1) (1993): 1–13; and

'Nineveh, Babylon and the Hanging Gardens: cuneiform and classical sources reconciled', *Iraq*, LVI (1994): 45–58.

84 British Museum London (Room 89) WA124939. The caption, in 2002, read: 'An Assyrian park, with aqueduct, columned pavilion, and royal stella with altar in front. Assyrian about 645–635 BC, from Nineveh, North Palace.'
85 Wiseman, D.J., 'Mesopotamian gardens', *Anatolian Studies*, 33 (1983): 137–44, British Institute at Ankara. JSTOR.
86 *The Song of Solomon*, 4: 12.
87 *The Song of Solomon*, 4: 16.
88 Bergant, D., Cotter, D.W., Walsh, J.T., and Franke, C., *The Song of Songs*, Minneapolis, MN: Liturgical Press, 2001, p. 55.
89 Lemche, N.P., *The Old Testament Between Theology and History: A Critical Survey*, Louisville, KT: Westminster John Knox Press, 2008, p. 244.
90 Hafemann, S.J. (ed.), *Biblical Theology*, Illinois: Inter-varsity Press, 2002, p. 56.
91 Hamilton, V.P., *The Book of Genesis: Chapters 1–17*, Grand Rapids, MI: William B. Eerdmans Publishing Co., 1996, p. 154.
92 Johnston, S.I., *Religions of the Ancient World: A Guide*, Cambridge, MA: Belknap Press, 2004, p. 208.
93 Budin, S.L., *The Ancient Greeks: New Perspectives*, Santa Barbara, CA: ABC-Clio, 2004, p. 225.
94 Ibid.
95 Koch, J.T., *Celtic Culture: A Historical Encyclopedia*, Santa Barbara, CA: ABC-Clio, 2006, p. 1351.
96 Dietrich, B.C., *The Origins of Greek Religion*, Bristol: Bristol Phoenix Press, 2004, p. 65.
97 Allsen, T.T., *The Royal Hunt in Eurasian History*, Philadelphia, PA: University of Pennsylvania Press, 2006, p. 14.
98 Ibid., p. 12.
99 Ibid., p. 10.
100 Cohoon, J.W., *Dio Chrysostom, I, Discourses 1–11*, Cambridge, MA: Harvard University Press, 1932.
101 Orlin, L.L., *Life and Thought in the Ancient Near East*, Ann Arbor, MI: University of Michigan Press, 2007, p. 25.
102 Allsen, T.T., op. cit., p. 161.
103 Breasted, J.H., *History of Egypt from the Earliest Time to the Persian Conquest*, 1909, p. 350.
104 Richards, M.P., 'A brief review of the archaeological evidence for Palaeolithic and Neolithic subsistence', *European Journal of Clinical Nutrition*, 56 (2002): 1270–8.
105 Genesis 2:15.

3 Egyptian gardens, 2000–1000 BCE

1 Herodotus, *An Account of Europe: Being the Second Book of His Histories Called Euterpe*, Harvard Classics, 1909–14, paras 1–19.
2 Myer, I., *Oldest Books in the World: An Account of the Religion, Wisdom, Philosophy, Ethics, Psychology, Manners, Proverbs, Sayings, Refinement, etc., of the Ancient Egyptians*, London: Kegan Paul & Co.:1900, p. 150.
3 Wilkinson, A., *The Garden in Ancient Egypt*, London: Rubicon Press, 1998, p. 16.
4 McDermott, B., *Decoding Egyptian Hieroglyphs*, London: Duncan Baird Publishers, 2001, p. 43.
5 Ibid., p. 20.
6 Ibid., p. 38.
7 Malek, J., *In the Shadow of the Pyramids: Egypt during the Old Kingdom*, New York: Little, Brown & Co., 1986, p. 43.
8 Aufrère, S. and Golvin, J-C., *L'Egypte Restituée*, vol. 3, Paris: Errance, 1991, p. 236.
9 Wildung, D., *Egypt from Prehistory to the Romans*, Cologne: Taschen, 2001, p. 12.
10 Petrie, W.M.F., *Tell El Amarna*, London: Methuen, 1894.
11 Verner, M., *The Pyramids: Their Archaeology and History*, London: Atlantic Books, 2001, p. 23.
12 Wildung, D., op. cit., p. 121.
13 Kemp, B.J., *Ancient Egypt: Anatomy of a Civilisation*, London: Routledge, 1989, p. 276 ff.
14 Tyldesley, J., *Rameses*, London: Viking, 2000, p. 113.
15 Tyldesley, J., *Hatchespsut, the Female Pharaoh*, London: Penguin, 1998, p. 54.
16 Jacq, C., *Rameses, the Son of Light*, London: Simon & Schuster, 1997, p. 32.
17 Gothein, M-L., *A History of Garden Art*, London: J.M. Dent, 1928, pp. 9–10.
18 Wilkinson, A., *The Garden in Ancient Egypt*, p. 131.
19 Wilkinson, R. H., *The Complete Temples of Ancient Egypt*, London: Thames & Hudson, 2000, p. 16.
20 Ibid., p. 17.
21 An English translation was published in *Records of the Past*, 1st series, vol. iv., p. 99 ff.
22 Wilkinson, A., op. cit., p. 119.
23 Booth, C., *The Hyksos Period in Egypt* , Princess Risborough: Shire Books, 2005, p. 23.
24 Kemp, B.J., op. cit., p. 215.
25 Ibid., p. 214.
26 Wilkinson, R.H., op. cit., p. 97.
27 Nims, C.F., *Thebes of the Pharaohs: Pattern for Every City*, London: Elek, 1965, p. 69.
28 Ibid., p. 13.
29 Tyldesley, J., op. cit., pp. 170–1.
30 Wilkinson, A., op. cit., p. 8 and pp. 148–56.
31 Tyldesley, J., op. cit., p. 97.
32 Berral, J.S., *The Garden*, London: Thames & Hudson, 1966, p. 13.
33 Siliotti, A., *Egypt*, London: Thames & Hudson, 1994, p. 150.
34 Wilkinson, R.H. op. cit., p. 180.
35 Aldred, C., *The Egyptians*, London: Thames & Hudson, 1961, p. 132.
36 Smith, W.S., *The Art and Architecture of Ancient Egypt*, London: Pelican History of Art, 1958, p. 133.
37 Gothein, M-L., op. cit., p. 15.
38 Kemp, B.J., op. cit., p. 206.
39 Champollion, J-F., *Egypt Ancienne*, 1835, p. 291.
40 Papyrus Harris I.
41 Murnane, W. J., *United with Eternity: A Concise Guide to the Monuments of Medinet Habu*, Cairo: American University in Cairo Press, 1980.
42 Siliotti, A., op. cit., p. 161.

4 Classical gardens 1400 BCE–500 CE

1 Maine, H.J.S., *Village Communities in the East and West*, Rede Lecture, Oxford, 1876.
2 Scully, V., *The Earth, the Temple and the Gods*, New Haven, CT: Yale University Press, 1962, p. 1.
3 Carroll, M., *Earthly Paradises: Ancient Gardens in History and Archaeology*, London: British Museum Press, 2003, p. 124.
4 Ibid., p. 69.
5 Scully, V., op. cit., p. 189.
6 Pausanias, 1.21.7. Gryneum is in Asia Minor (modern Turkey).
7 Tomlinson, R.A., *Greek Sanctuaries*, London: Paul Elek, 1976, p. 16. The Greek word for a sacred grove was *alsos* and, as the English phrase implies, it was a wooded place with a sacred role as 'a natural and divine manifestation of a median place between two worlds'. (Bonnechere, P., 'The place of the Sacred Grove (Alsos) in the Mantic Rituals of Greece: the example of the Alsos of Trophonios at Lebadeia (Boetia)', p. 42 in Michel Conan, *Sacred Gardens and Landscapes: Ritual and Agency*, 2007). Temples were often built in

sacred groves, so that the temple and the grove became components of the sanctuary. There are known sites at Nemea.

8 Tomlinson, R.A., *Greek Sanctuaries*, London: Paul Elek, 1976, p. 16.
9 Frazer, J.G., *The Golden Bough*, London: Macmillan & Co, 1890, Ch. 32.
10 Ridgeway, B.S., 'Greek antecedents of garden sculpture', in *Ancient Roman Gardens*, Dumbarton Oaks: Harvard University Press, 1981, pp. 7–28.
11 Grimal, P., *Les Jardins Romains*, 2nd edn, Paris: Presses Universitaires de France, 1969, p. 63.
12 Steiner, G. and Fagles, R., *Homer: A Collection of Critical Essays*, Englewood Cliffs, NJ: Prentice Hall, 1962, p. 10.
13 Farrer, L., *Ancient Roman Gardens*, Stroud: Sutton Publishing, 1998, p. 5.
14 Rieu, E.V. (trans.), *Homer: The Iliad*, Harmondworth: Penguin Books, 1966, p. 53, has 'from holy Onchestus, with Poseidon's sacred wood'.
15 Lemprière, J., *A Classical Dictionary*, London: Routledge, 1904, p. 90: 'Athena, the name of Minerva among the Greeks; and also among the Egyptians, before Cercops had introduced the worship of the goddess into Greece (Pausanias 1, c, 2).
16 Rieu, E.V. op. cit., p. 173.
17 Ibid., p. 387, has 'like a gardener who is irrigating his plot by making a channel in among the plants with fresh water from a spring'.
18 Plato, *The Republic*, Book 3.
19 Wycherley, R.E., *The Stones of Athens*, Princeton, NJ: Princeton University Press, 1978, p. 228.
20 Ibid., p. 227.
21 Ibid., p. 231.
22 Pindar, *Olympian Odes*, I.
23 Miller, N., *Heavenly Caves: Reflections on the Garden Grotto*, London: George Allen & Unwin, 1982, Ch. 3.
24 Littlewood, A.R., 'Ancient literary evidence for the pleasure gardens of Roman country villas', in E.B. MacDougal (ed.), *Ancient Roman Villa Gardens*, Dumbarton Oaks: Harvard University Press, 1987, pp. 7–30.
25 Lovelock, J., *The Ages of Gaia*, Oxford: Oxford University Press, 1989.
26 Gothein, M-L., *A History of Garden Art*, London: J.M. Dent, 1928, vol. 1, p. 72.
27 Longus, *Daphnis and Chloé*, trans. R. McCail, Oxford: Oxford University Press, 2002, p. 25.
28 Nielsen, I., *Hellenistic Palaces, Tradition and Renewal*, Aarhus: Aarhus University Press, 1994, p. 81.
29 Ibid., p. 96.
30 Edgar Allan Poe, 'To Helen' in *The Works of Edgar Allen Poe*, New York: Widdleton, 1849, p. ix.
31 Böthius, A., *The Golden House of Nero*, Ann Arbor, MI: University of Michigan, 1960, p. 3.
32 Suetonius, *The Twelve Caesars*, London: Penguin, p. 66.
33 Gibbon, E., *The Decline and Fall of the Roman Empire*. The phrase is from the final chapter (LXXI).
34 von Stackelberg, K.T., *The Roman Garden*, London: Routledge, 2009, p. 9.
35 Masson, G., *Companion Guide to Rome*, Woodbridge: Companion Guides, 1998, p. 52.
36 Suetonius, op. cit., p. 95.
37 Ibid., p. 96.
38 Böthius, A., op. cit., p. 105.
39 Gibbon, E., *Decline and Fall of the Roman Empire*, Vol. 1, Ch. 10, Part III, 1776.
40 Farrer, L., *Ancient Roman Gardens*, Stroud: Sutton Publishing, 1998, p. 14.
41 von Stackelberg, K.T., op.cit., p. 131.
42 See http://www.doaks.org/publications/doaks_online_publications/Evelyn/evel009.pdf p. 203 (accessed 1.1.2009).
43 Vitruvius, *The Ten Books on Architecture*, trans. M.H. Morgan, 1914, and reprinted London: Dover Books, Inc., 1960. UK edn, London: Constable & Co., op. cit., p. 179.
44 Ricotti, E.S.P., 'The importance of water in Roman garden triclinia', in E.B. MacDougal, (ed.), op. cit., pp. 135–84. Ricotti believes Tiberius visited Sperlonga but was not the owner.
45 Littlewood, A.R., op. cit.
46 Ibid.
47 de Caro, S., 'The sculptures of the Villa of Poppaea at Oplontis: a preliminary report', in E.B. MacDougal (ed.), op. cit., pp. 77–134.
48 Littlewood, A.R., op. cit.
49 MacLagan, M., *The City of Constantinople*, London: Thames & Hudson, 1968, p. 67.
50 Byron, R. and Rice, D.T., *The Birth of Western Painting: A History of Colour, Form and Iconography, Illustrated from the Paintings of Mistra and Mount Athos, of Giotto and Duccio and of El Greco*, London: Routledge, 1930.
51 Scully, V., op. cit., p. 185.
52 Ibid., p. 108.
53 Ibid., p. 109.
54 Thucydides, *History of the Peloponnesian War, c.400*, trans. R. Warner, Harmondsworth: Penguin Books, 1954, p. 38.
55 Wycherley, R.E., *How the Greeks Built Cities*, New York: W. W. Norton & Co., 1976, p. 194.
56 Jones, F.L., *The Letters of Percy Bysshe Shelley*, Oxford: Clarendon Press, 1964, Letter of 26 Jan 1819.
57 Grimal, P., *Rome of the Caesars*, London: Phaidon, 1956, p. 24.
58 Jashemski, W.F., *Gardens of Pompeii: Herculaneum and the Villas Destroyed by Vesuvius*, New Rochelle, NY: Caratzas Bros, 1979, p. 314.
59 Berral, J.S., *The Garden*, London: Thames & Hudson, 1966, p. 41.
60 Ricotti, E.S.P., op. cit., p. 174.

5 Medieval gardens, 600–1500

1 Landsberg, S., *The Medieval Garden*, London: British Museum Press, 1995, p. 4.
2 Eco, U., *Art and Beauty in the Middle Ages*, New Haven, CT: Yale University Press, 1986, p. 52.
3 Le Goff, J., *Medieval Civilisation*, Oxford: Basil Blackwell, 1988, p. 325.
4 Huizinga, J., *The Waning of the Middle Ages*, London: Penguin, 1965 edn, p. 209.
5 Lovejoy, A.O., *The Great Chain of Being: A Study of the History of an Idea*, New York: Harper & Row, 1960, p. 61.
6 Huizinga, J., op. cit., p. 255.
7 Eco, U., op. cit., p. 55.
8 Hope, A. and Walsh, M., *The Colour Compendium*, New York: Van Nostrand Rheinhold, 1990, p. 281.
9 Alan of Lille, quoted in U. Eco, op. cit., p. 59.
10 Eco, U., op. cit., p. 9.
11 Plotinus, *The Enneads*, trans. S. MacKenna, London: Penguin, 1991, Vol. 8.
12 Ibid. (Note that MacKenna's original translation uses 'reason-principles' in place of 'ideas' in this quotation.)
13 Porphyry, 'On the life of Plotinus and his work', in Plotinus, op. cit., p. cxii.
14 St Augustine, *De Libero Arbitrio*, trans. Burleigh, II, xv1, 42.
15 Eco, U., op. cit., p. 35.
16 Wittkower, R., *Architectural Principles in the Age of Humanism*, London: Academy Editions, 1988 edn., p. 150.
17 Le Goff, J., op. cit., p. 333.
18 Herlihy, D., *Medieval Households*, Cambridge, MA: Harvard University Press, 1985, p. 1.
19 Ibid., p. 157.
20 Stierlin, H., *The Roman Empire*, Cologne: Taschen, 2002, p. 56.
21 St Augustine, *Confessions*, Book 8.
22 St Augustine, *The City of God*, Book IV.

23 Suetonius, *The Twelve Caesars*, Penguin, 1957, pp. 131.
24 Sulpitius Severus, *On the Life of St Martin*, trans. A. Roberts, New York, 1894.
25 St Augustine, *The City of God*, Book I.
26 Stokstad, M. and Stannard, J., *Gardens of the Middle Ages*, Kansas: Spencer Museum of Art, 1983, p. 31.
27 Walafrid Strabo, *Hortulus; or, the Little Garden etc*, trans. R.S. Lambert, Wembley Hill: The Stanton Press, 1924, p. 37.
28 Alexander Neckham, quoted in T. McLean, *Medieval Gardens*, London: Collins, 1981, p. 162.
29 Huizinga, J., op. cit., p. 105.
30 Ibid., p. 109.
31 Harvey, J., *Medieval Gardens*, London: Batsford, 1981, p. 98.
32 Chaucer, G., *Canterbury Tales*, Prologue, Line 72.
33 Harvey, J., 'The square garden of Henry the Poet', *Garden History*, 15(1) (1987): 1–12.
34 Harvey, J., *Medieval Gardens*, p. 44.
35 Gothein, M-L., *A History of Garden Art*, London: J.M. Dent, 1928, Vol. 1, p. 189.
36 Manwood, 1717, p. 143.
37 Gothein, M-L., op. cit., Vol. 1, p. 183.
38 Harvey, J., op. cit., p. 78.
39 Ibid., p. 82.
40 Ibid., p. 142.
41 Ibid., p. 75.
42 Walafrid Strabo, op. cit., pp. 11, 38.
43 St Athanasius, *Life of St Anthony*.
44 Genesis 2:15.
45 Ferzoco, G. and Muessig, C., *Medieval Monastic Education*, London: Leicester University Press, 2000, p. 96.
46 *Regula Sancti Benedicti*, Ch. 66.
47 Eco, U., op. cit., quoted in Landsberg, S., op. cit., p. 36.
48 Goode, P. (ed.), *Oxford Companion to Gardens*, Oxford: Oxford University Press, 1986, p. 364.
49 Clifton-Taylor, A., *The Cathedrals of England*, London: Thames & Hudson, 1967, p. 136.
50 Braunfels, W., *Monasteries of Western Europe: The Architecture of the Orders*, London: Thames & Hudson, 1972, p. 45.
51 McLean, T., op. cit., p. 16.
52 Genesis 2:8. I am grateful to Bettina v. Greyerz at Sankt Gallen for this information. See Sennhauser, H.R., in *St Gallen, Klosterplan und Gozbertbau*, vdf Hochschulverlag AG an der ETH: Zurich, 2001, pp. 23–8.
53 McLean, T., op. cit., p. 18.
54 Landsberg, S., op. cit., Ch. 1, 'Types of medieval garden', pp. 11–48.
55 *Capitulare de Villis*, in E.F. Henderson, *Select Historical Documents of the Middle Ages*, London: George Bell & Sons, 1896.
56 Braunfels, op. cit., p. 221.
57 Benevolo, L., *The History of the City*, London: Scolar Press, 1980, p. 308.
58 Hanawalt, B.A., *The Ties that Bound*, Oxford: Oxford University Press, 1986, p. 43.
59 Mumford, L., *The City in History*, Harmondsworth: Penguin, 1961, p. 330.
60 Ward, W.H., *The Architecture of the Renaissance in France*, New York: Hacker Art Books, Vol. 1, 1911, p. 180.
61 James, H., *A Little Tour of France*, London: Heinemann, 1900, p. 47.
62 Gothein, M-L., op. cit., Vol. 2, p. 12.
63 Braunfels, W., op. cit., p. 36.
64 Conant, K.J., *Carolingian and Romanesque Architecture 800–1200*, Harmondsworth: Penguin, 1959, p. 229.
65 Mason, G., *Rome*, Woodbridge: Companion Guides, 1965, p. 244.
66 Clifton-Taylor, A., op. cit., p. 136.
67 Benevolo, L., op. cit., p. 369.

6 Renaissance gardens, 1350–1650

1 Manzoni, A., *The Betrothed*, trans. C. Swan, 3 vols., Pisa: Niccolo Capurro, 1828. Italy's most celebrated nineteenth-century author, Manzoni paints a vivid picture of late-medieval life in this historical novel.
2 Boccaccio, G., *The Decameron*, London: Bibliophilist Society, 1918.
3 Edward Wright, D.R., 'Some Medici gardens of the Florentine Renaissance: an essay in post-aesthetic interpretation', in J.D. Hunt, *The Italian Garden: Art, Design and Culture*, Cambridge: Cambridge University Press, 1996.
4 Davies, N., *Europe: A History*, Oxford: Oxford University Press, 1996, p. 479.
5 Padovan, R., *Proportion: Science, Philosophy, Architecture*, London: Spon, 1999, p. 137ff.
6 Ovid, *Metamorphoses*.
7 Alberti, L.B., *Ten Books on Architecture*, London: Tiranti, 1955.
8 Padovan, R., op. cit., p. 220ff.
9 The book was published as *Hypnerotomachia Poliphili* and is attributed to Francesco Colonna. It was written in 1467 and published in 1499. An English interpretation is Fierz-David, L., *The Dream of Poliphilo*, New York: Bollingen, 1950, with an introduction by C.G. Jung.
10 Goode, P. (ed.), *Oxford Companion to Gardens*, Oxford: Oxford University Press, 1986, p. 268.
11 Godwin, J., trans., *Hypnerotomachia Poliphili: The Strife of Love in a Dream*, London: Thames & Hudson, 2005.
12 Godwin, J., *The Pagan Dream of the Renaissance*, Boston: Weiser Books, 2005, p. 237.
13 Lefaivre, L., *Leon Battista Alberti's Hypnerotomachia Poliphili: Re-Cognizing the Architectural Body of the Early Italian Renaissance*, Boston: MIT Press, 1997.
14 Godwin, J., *Hypnerotomachia Poliphili*, pp. 318–19.
15 Ibid., pp. 320–1.
16 Lazzaro, C., *The Italian Renaissance Garden*, New Haven: Yale University Press, 1990, p. 42.
17 Ibid., p. 52.
18 Gothein, M-L., *A History of Garden Art*, London: J.M. Dent, 1928, Vol. 1, p. 211.
19 Ayatollahi, H., *The Book of Iran: The History of Iranian Art*, trans. S. Haghshenas, Tehran: Centre for International Cultural Studies, 2003, p. 91.
20 Hall, J., *A History of Ideas and Images in Italian Art*, London: John Murray, 1983, p. 228.
21 Wind, E., *Pagan Mysteries in the Renaissance*, London: Faber & Faber, 1958.
22 Masson, G., *Italian Gardens*, London: Thames & Hudson, 1966, p. 123.
23 Gombrich, E.H., *Symbolic Images*, London: Phaidon, 1975, pp. 102–8.
24 Erasmus, *The Godly Feast*, 1522.
25 Vredeman de Vries, J., *Hortorum viridariorumque elegantes et multiplices formae*, Anvers: Philippe Galle, 1583.
26 Vredeman de Vries, J., *On Perspective*, Hendrik Hondius, 1605.
27 Vasari, G., *The Lives of the Painters, Sculptors and Architects, 1550*, London: J.M. Dent, 1963, Vol. 1, p. 321.
28 Burckhardt, J., *Civilisation of the Renaissance*, 1860, p. 176.
29 Letter from Cosimo de Medici to Marsilio Ficino, 1462.
30 Jellicoe, G.A., *Italian Gardens of the Renaissance*, London: Ernest Benn, 1925, p. 4.
31 Ouchterlong of Guinde, *c.*1722, quoted in G.A. Little, *Scotland's Gardens*, Edinburgh: Spurbooks, 1981, p. 184.
32 Wordsworth, D., *Journals of Dorothy Wordsworth*, New York: Macmillan, 1904, Journal IX.
33 Gothein, M-L., op. cit., Vol. 2, p. 37.
34 Alberti, L.B., op. cit.
35 Gothein, M-L. op. cit., Vol. 2, p. 231.
36 Wharton, E., *Italian Villas and their Gardens*, New York: The Century Co., 1904, p. 84.
37 M. de Montaigne, 1580. From his *Travel Journal*, trans, D.M. Frame, London: North Point Press, 1983.

38 Vasari, G., op. cit., Vol. 4, p. 95.
39 Mann, G., *Wallenstein*, London: Deutsch, 1976, p. 237.
40 Gothein, M-L., op. cit., Vol. 1, p. 383.
41 Jellicoe, G.A., *Gardens of Europe*, London: Blackie & Son, 1937, p. 125.
42 Wharton, E., op. cit., p. 144.
43 Sitwell, Sir G., *An Essay on the Making of Gardens*, London: John Murray, 1909.
44 Jellicoe, G.A., *Italian Gardens*, London: Ernest Benn, 1925, p. 27.
45 Riccio, 1595, quoted by C. Lazzaro, *The Italian Renaissance Garden*, New Haven, CT: Yale University Press, 1990.

7 Baroque gardens, 1600–1750

1 Bazin, G., *Baroque and Rococo*, London: Thames & Hudson, 1964, p. 6.
2 Ibid., pp. 6–7.
3 Descartes, R., *Discourse on Method, and Other Writings*, trans. with an introduction by F.E. Sutcliffe, Harmondsworth: Penguin Books, 1968.
4 Fauvel, J., *et al.*, *Let Newton Be!* Oxford: Oxford University Press, 1988, p. 187.
5 Padovan, R., *Proportion: Science, Philosophy, Architecture*, London: Spon, 1999, pp. 137–49.
6 Pope, A., *An Essay on Criticism*, 1711.
7 Ibid.
8 Bazin, G., op. cit., p. 8.
9 Gothein, M-L., *A History of Garden Art*, London: J.M. Dent, 1928.
10 Gothein, M-L., op. cit., Vol. 1, p. 305.
11 *NewAdventCatholicEncyclopedia*, http://www.newadvent.org/cathen/14033a.htm.
12 Steenbergen, C. and Reh, W., *Architecture and Landscape: The Design Experiment of the Great European Gardens and Landscape*, Amsterdam: Prestel, 1996.
13 Gothein, M-L., op. cit., p. 345.
14 Ibid., Vol. 2, p. 76.
15 Thompson, I., *The Sun King's Garden: André Le Nôtre and the Creation of the Gardens of Versailles*, London: Bloomsbury, 2006, pp. 5–6.
16 Le Blond, *The Theory and Practice of Gardening (of A. J. Dézallier d'Arganville)*, London: Lintot, 1728.
17 Kip, J. and Knyff, J., *Britannia Illustrata, or Views of Several of the Queen's Palaces, Also of the Principal Seats of the Nobility and Gentry of Great Britain*, 1707.
18 Hahr, A., *Architecture in Sweden*, Stockholm: Bonniers Boktryckeri, 1938, p. 37.
19 Swedenborg Digital Library, http://www.swedenborgdigitallibrary.org/ES/epic4.htm.
20 John Evelyn, 1645. The text is taken from William Bray's 1818 edition of Evelyn's *Diary*.
21 Wölfflin, H., *Renaissance and Baroque*, London: Collins, 1964, p. 157.
22 Masson, G., *Italian Gardens*, London: Thames & Hudson, 1961, p. 116.
23 John Evelyn 1646. The text is taken from William Bray's 1818 edition of Evelyn's *Diary*.
24 Gothein, M-L., op. cit., p. 52.
25 Woodbridge, K., *Princely Gardens: The Origins and Development of the French Formal Style*, London: Thames & Hudson, 1986, p. 188.
26 Wharton, E., *Italian Villas and their Gardens*, New York: The Century Co., 1904, p. 94.
27 Quoted in Hobhouse, P. and Taylor, P., *The Gardens of Europe*, London: George Philip Ltd., 1990, p. 89.
28 Woodbridge, K., op. cit., p. 213.
29 Loudon, J.C., *Encyclopaedia of Gardening*, London: Longman, 1822, p. 33.
30 Young, A., *Travels During the Years 1787, 1788, and 1789*, Bury St. Edmunds: Rackham, 1792–1794.
31 Gothein, M-L., op. cit., Vol. 2, p. 199.
32 Loudon, J.C., op. cit., p. 50.
33 Anon., *The Englishwoman in Russia: Impressions of the Society and Manners of the Russians at Home, by a Lady Two Years Resident in that Country*, London, 1855, p. 21.

8 Neoclassical and Romantic gardens, 1700–1810

1 Turner, T., *English Garden Design: History and Styles since 1650*, Woodbridge: Antique Collectors Club, 1986.
2 Hobbes, T., *Leviathan, or the Matter, Forme, & Power of a Common-wealth, Ecclesiasticall and Civill*, London: Andrew Crooke, 1651, Part I, Ch. 13.
3 Bazin, G., *Baroque and Rococo*, London: Thames & Hudson, 1964, p. 262.
4 Gombrich, E.H., *The Story of Art*, London: Phaidon, 1995, p. 460.
5 Pevsner, N., *An Outline of European Architecture*, London: Pelican, 1963, p. 350.
6 Jansen, H.W., *A History of Art*, London: Thames & Hudson, 1962, p. 453.
7 Ackerman, J.S., *Palladio*, London: Penguin, 1966, p. 78.
8 Röthlisberger, M., *Claude Lorrain*, New York: Hacker Art Books, 1979, p. 3.
9 Ibid., p. 23.
10 Hall, J., *A History of Ideas and Images in Italian Art*, London: John Murray, 1983, p. 265.
11 Price, Sir U., *An Essay on the Picturesque, as Compared with the Sublime and the Beautiful; and on the Use of Studying Pictures, for the Purpose of Improving Real Landscape*, London, 1794, p. 109.
12 Clark, K., *Landscape into Art*, London: Penguin, 1956, p. 67.
13 Aristotle, *Poetics*, trans. T. Twining, 1789.
14 Cicero, *Treatise on Old Age*. trans. E.S. Schuckburgh, New York: Collier & Son, 1909, para 2.
15 Plotinus, *The Enneads*, trans. S. MacKenna and B.S. Page, Sixth Tractate, 'On Beauty'.
16 Du Fresnoy, C.A., *The Art of Painting, translated by Mr Dryden*, 1695, p. XVI.
17 d'Arganville, D., *La Théorie et la Practique du Jardinage*, 1713. Quoted in Toman, R., *European Garden Design*, Cologne; Kömann, 2000, p. 228.
18 Salmon, W., *Polygraphice*, London, 1672.
19 Temple, W., 'Upon the gardens of Epicurus', in *Works*, London, 1814, Vol. III.
20 Pope, A., *An Essay on Criticism*, 1711.
21 Walpole, H., 'On Modern Gardening', in *Anecdotes of Painting in England*, 1780, Vol. 4.
22 Barrell, J., *The Political Theory of Painting from Reynolds to Hazlitt*, New Haven, CT: Yale University Press, 1986.
23 Quoted in Willey, B., *The Eighteenth-century Background: Studies on the Idea of Nature in the Thought of the Period*, Harmondsworth: Penguin, 1962, p. 26.
24 Downing, A.J., *Treatise on the Theory and Practice of Landscape Gardening Adapted to North America with a View to the Improvement of Country Residences*, New York: Moore & Co., 1859, Section II.
25 Temple, W., op. cit., Vol. III.
26 Pevsner, N., *Studies in Art, Architecture and Design*, London: Thames & Hudson, 1969, Vol. 1, p. 82.
27 Hussey, C., *English Gardens and Landscapes 1700–1750*, London: Country Life, 1967, p. 123.
28 Switzer, S., *Iconographia Rustica*, London, 1718, Vol. 1, p. 124.
29 Hussey, C., op. cit., p. 123.
30 Switzer, S., op. cit., Vol. 1, p. 124.
31 Hussey, C., op. cit., p. 61.
32 Lovejoy, A.O., *The Great Chain of Being*, New York: Harper Torchbook, 1960, p. 16.
33 Hussey, C., *The Picturesque*, London: Frank Cass, 1927, p. 137.
34 *The World* ,13 December 1753, no. 50.
35 Hogarth, W., *The Analysis of Beauty*, London: Strachan, 1753.
36 Røstvig, S.M., *The Happy Man: Studies in the Metamorphoses of a Classical Ideal*, Oslo: Norwegian Universities Press, 1962, Vol. 2, p. 42.

37 Hunt, J.D., *Greater Perfection: The Practice of Garden Theory*, London: Thames & Hudson, 2000, p. 208.
38 Walpole, H., op. cit.
39 Ibid.
40 Templeman, W.D., *The Life and Work of William Gilpin (1724–1804), Master of the Picturesque and Vicar of Boldre*, Urbana, IL: The University of Illinois Press, 1939.
41 They were entitled *Three Essays on Picturesque Beauty, on Picturesque Travel and on Sketching Landscape*, London, 1792.
42 Price, Sir U., op. cit., p. 9.
43 Ibid.
44 Burke, E., *An Essay on the Sublime and Beautiful*, 1898 edn., London, p. 44.
45 Loudon, J.C. (ed.), *The Landscape Gardening and Landscape Architecture of the Late H. Repton Esq*, London, 1840, p. 354.
46 Loudon, J.C., *Country Residences*, London, 1806, p. 371.
47 Loudon, J.C., *Observations... on the Theory and Practice of Landscape Gardening*, Edinburgh, 1804, p. 241.
48 Turner, T., op. cit., p. 43.
49 Gothein, M- L., *A History of Garden Art*, London: J.M. Dent, 1928, Vol. 2, p. 255.
50 Kluckert, E., *European Garden Design*, Cologne: Könemann, 2000, p. 208.
51 Ericson, C., *To the Scaffold: The Life of Marie Antoinette*, London: Robson Books, 2000.
52 Wiebenson, D., *The Picturesque Garden in France*, Princeton, NJ: Princeton University Press, 1978, p. 81.
53 Girardin, R.-L., *An Essay on Landscape, or On the Means of Improving and Embellishing the Country round Our Habitations*, London, 1783, p. 149.
54 Fraser, D., *Frederick the Great*, London: Allen Lane, 2000, p. 531.
55 Holborn, H., *A History of Modern Germany, 1648–1840*, London: Eyre & Spottiswoode, 1965, p. 322.
56 Ibid., p. 323.
57 Kluckert, E., op. cit., 2000, p. 406.
58 Newton, N.T., *Design on the Land: The Development of Landscape Architecture*, Cambridge, MA: Harvard Belknap Press, 1971, p. 237.
59 Thompson, J.M., *Lectures on Foreign History, 1494–1789*, Oxford: Basil Blackwell, 1962, p. 375.
60 Turner, T., *City as Landscape*, London: Spon, 1998, p. 38.
61 Hussey, C., op. cit., p. 78.
62 Hunt, J.D., *William Kent, Landscape Garden Designer: An Assessment and Catalogue of his Designs*, London: Zwemmer, 1987, p. 67.
63 Castell, R., *The Villas of the Ancients Illustrated by The Author*, London, 1728.
64 Clark, H.F., *The English Landscape Garden*, 1948, p. 37.
65 Loudon, J.C., *Encyclopaedia of Gardening*, 5th edn., 1835, p. 320.
66 Hussey, C., op. cit., p. 89.
67 Goethe, J.W., *Italian Journey*, 1778.
68 Hussey, C., Introduction to Stroud, D., *Capability Brown*, London: Faber & Faber, 1975, p. 31; Burke, E., op. cit., p. 170.
69 Hussey, C., op. cit., 1927, p. 186.
70 Hyams, E., *Capability Brown and Humphry Repton*, London: J.M. Dent, 1971, p. 42.
71 Kluckert, E., op. cit., p. 415.
72 McBride, D., *A History of Hawkstone*, Shrewsbury: MPS, 1987.
73 Loudon, J.C., op. cit., 1806, Vol. II, p. 369.

9 Eclectic gardens, 1800–1900

1 Gothein, M-L., *A History of Garden Art*, London: J.M. Dent, 1928, Vol. 2, p. 325.
2 Ibid., Vol. 2, p. 318.
3 Gombrich, E.H., *The Story of Art*, London: Phaidon, 1995, p. 503.
4 de Quincy, A.C.Q., *An Essay on the Nature, the End and the Means of Imitation in the Fine Arts*, trans. J.C. Kent, London, 1837.
5 Sir Uvedale Price was made a baronet in 1829.
6 Knight, R.P., *The Landscape: A Didactic Poem*, London, 1795.
7 Turner, T., *English Garden Design: History and Styles since 1650*, Woodbridge: Antique Collectors Club, 1986, p. 115.
8 Ibid., Ch IV.
9 Pevsner, N., *The Englishness of English Art*, London: Architectural Press, 1956, p. 168.
10 Turner, T., *Landscape Planning and Environmental Impact Design*, London: Spon, 1998, p. 92.
11 Imbert, D., *The Modernist Garden in France*, New Haven, CT: Yale University Press, 1992, p. 2.
12 Ibid., p. 5.
13 Loudon, J.C. (ed.), *The Landscape Gardening and Landscape Architecture of the Late H. Repton Esq*, London, 1840, p, 536.
14 Turner, T., 'Loudon's stylistic development', *Journal of Garden History*, 2(2) (1982): 175–88.
15 Kemp, E., *How to Lay Out a Small Garden*, London: Bradbury Evans, 1864, p. 117.
16 Newton, N.T., *Design on the Land: The Development of Landscape Architecture*, Cambridge, MA: Harvard Belknap Press, 1971, p. 337.
17 Ibid., p. 337.
18 Loudon, J.C., op. cit., p. 331 ff.
19 Picturesque improvement is the subject of the second volume of J.C. Loudon's *Country Residences*, 1806.
20 Loudon, J.C., *The Suburban Gardener and Villa Gardener*, London, 1838, p. 137.
21 Loudon, J.C., *Gardener's Magazine*, XVI, 1840, p. 622.
22 Hirschfeld, C., *Theory of Garden Art*, abridged and edited by Linda B. Parshall, Penn Studies in Landscape Architecture, Philadelphia: University of Pennsylvania Press, 2001.
23 Elliott, B., *Victorian Gardens*, London: Batsford, 1986, p. 162.
24 My copy of the book contains a letter, dated 28 May 1828, which includes the following: 'Mr Laing Meason requests Lord Granville will do him the honour of accepting a copy of a work which he has printed privately, and given only a hundred for sale to a bookseller, "On the Landscape Architecture of the great painters of Italy". Had Mr Meason had the opportunity of visiting Italy, and of comparing the remains of ancient country residences with the specimens to be found in the Italian pictures, the work might have been made more interesting, and more decisive on the artistry of those buildings.'
25 Downing. A.J., *A Treatise on the Theory and Practice of Landscape Gardening Adapted to North America*, New York: Putnam, 1850.
26 Fabos, J.G. and Ahern, J., *Greenways: The Beginning of an International Movement*, Amsterdam: Elsevier, 1996.
27 Elliott, B., op. cit., p. 118.
28 Hellyer, A., *The Shell Guide to Gardens*, London: Heinemann, 1977, p. 169.
29 Loudon, J.C., *Gardener's Magazine*, VII, 1831, p. 390.
30 Kluckert, E., *European Garden Design*, Cologne: Konemann, 2000, p. 436.
31 Elliott, op. cit., p. 106.
32 Hojer, G. and Schmid, E.D., *Linderhof Palace, München*, Munich: Bayerische Verwaltung der Staatlichen Schlosser, 1999.
33 Chadwick, G.F., *The Park and the Town*, London: Architectural Press, 1966, p. 92.
34 Hobhouse, P. and Taylor, P., *The Gardens of Europe*, London: George Philip Ltd., 1990, p. 268.
35 Newton, T., op. cit., p. 326.
36 Shepheard, P., *Modern Gardens*, London: Architectural Press, 1953, p. 120.
37 Hough, M., *City Form and Natural Process*, London: Routledge, 1995, p. 279.
38 *Domus Magazine*, 1992.

10 Abstract and Post-abstract gardens, 1900–2000

1 Carson, R., *Silent Spring*, London: Penguin, 1965.

2 Tunnard, C., *Gardens in the Modern Landscape*, London: Architectural Press, 1938, p. 49.
3 Wharton, E., *Italian Villas and their Gardens*, New York: Century Co., 1904, p. 12.
4 Jellicoe, G.A. and Shepherd, J.C., *Italian Gardens of the Renaissance*, London: Ernest Benn, 1925, p. 18.
5 For more information, visit: http://www.edithwharton.org/.
6 Morris, W., *Hopes and Fears for Art*, London: Ellis & White, 1882.
7 Gothein, M-L., *A History of Garden Art*, London: J.M. Dent, 1928, Vol. 2.
8 Woodbridge, K., *Princely Gardens: The Origins and Development of the French Formal Style*, London: Thames & Hudson, 1986, p. 291.
9 Gothein, M-L., op. cit., Vol. 2, p. 358.
10 Schultze-Naumburg, P., 'Kulturarbeiten Band 2', in *Gärten*, Munchen, 1902.
11 Shepheard, P.F., *Modern Gardens*, London: Architectural Press, 1953.
12 Newton, N.T., *Design on the Land: The Development of Landscape Architecture*, Cambridge, MA: Harvard Belknap Press, 1971.
13 Brown, J., *The Modern Garden*, London: Thames & Hudson, 2000, p. 8.
14 Pevsner, N., *The Sources of Modern Architecture and Design*, London: Thames & Hudson, 1968, p. 18.
15 Wright, F.L., *The Future of Architecture*, New York: Mentor, 1963, p. 21.
16 Ibid., pp. 142–3.
17 Tunnard, C., op. cit.
18 Steele, F., in *Landscape Architecture*, October 1930.
19 Treib, M., *Modern Landscape Architecture: A Critical Review*, Cambridge, MA: MIT Press, 1993, p. 53.
20 Brown, J., op. cit., p. 98.
21 Walker, P., *Minimalist Gardens*, Washington, DC, and Cambridge, MA: Watson-Guptil Publications and Hearst Books, 1997.
22 Baines, C., *How to Make a Wildlife Garden*, London: Elm Tree, 1985.
23 See discussion in T. Turner, 'Jellicoe and the subconscious', in S. Harvey (ed.), *Geoffrey Jellicoe*, Reigate: LDT Monographs, 1998,
24 Jellicoe, G.A., *The Guelph Lectures on Landscape Design*, Guelph: University of Guelph, 1983, p. 94.
25 Ibid., p. 194.
26 Jencks, C., *The Language of Postmodern Architecture*, New York: John Wiley & Sons, Ltd, 1977.
27 Jencks, C., *Towards a Symbolic Architecture*, London: Academy Editions, 1985.
28 Jencks, C., *The Architecture of the Jumping Universe*, London: Academy Editions, 1997.
29 Scottish National Gallery of Modern Art, Press Release 26 July 2002.
30 *National Galleries of Scotland Bulletin*, July and August 2002, p. 14.
31 Solt, M.E., *Concrete Poetry: A World View*, London: Indiana University Press, 1968.
32 Santayana, G., *The Life of Reason, or, The Phases of Human Progress*, New York: Charles Scribner's Sons, 1924, p. 284.
33 Turner, T., *City as Landscape*, London: Spon, 1996, p. 8.
34 Sackville-West, V., *Journal of the Royal Horticultural Society*, Vol. LXXIV, Part II, November 1949.
35 Ostberg, R., *Stockholm City Hall*, Stockholm, 1929, p. 35.
36 Brown, J., *Vita's Other World*, London: Penguin, 1987, p. 173.
37 Treib, M., op. cit., p. 43.
38 Marsa, A. and Marsillach, L, 'La montana iluminada', quoted (1929) in J. Quetglas, *Fear of Glass*, Barcelona: Actar, 2001, p. 15.
39 Kiley, D., *Dan Kiley: In His Own Words: America's Master Landscape Architect*, London: Thames and Hudson, 1999, p. 21.
40 Walker, P. and Simo, M., *Invisible Gardens*, Cambridge, MA: MIT Press, 1994, p. 191.
41 Hutton, T., *Journal of the Institute of Landscape Architects*, February 1961.
42 Lancaster, M., *New European Landscapes*, Oxford: Butterworth Architecture, 1994, p. 23.
43 Turner, T., *City as Landscape*, p. 208.
44 Holden, R., *International Landscape Design*, London: Laurence King, 1996, p. 13.
45 Spens, M., *Modern Landscape*, London: Phaidon Press, 2003, p. 40.
46 Holden, R., *New Landscape Design*, London: Laurence King, 2003, p. 114.
47 Study of this relationship is proceeding within the framework of 'landscape urbanism'. See http://en.wikipedia.org/wiki/Landscape_urbanism.

Illustration credits

The author and publisher wish to thank these individuals and organisations for permission to reproduce material. We are particularly grateful to NASA for making satellite imagery available. Other photographs are drawings are by the author. Every effort has been made to contact and acknowledge copyright holders, but if any errors or omissions have been made we will be happy to correct them at a later printing and on the companion website: http://www.gardenvisit.com/history_theory/european_gardens_companion

Frontispiece Margaret Turner

P.0 Onur Ersin/Dreamstime

1.2 JamesUK
1.5 Jesse Adams
1.6 Robwilson39/Dreamstime
1.10 Saints4757/iStockphoto
1.13 Bibliothèque National de France
1.14 Thomas Oswald, Munich
1.18 Ben Northrup
1.19 Skibreck/iStockphoto
1.20 Dr.Christoph Baron
1.21 Ben Bawden
1.25 Mario Carbone/Dreamstime
1.33 Didacus Valades, Rhetorica Christiana
1.34 b John Searle Plan of Mr. Pope's Garden
1.35 Alastair Diack

2.0 Conny Sjostrom/Dreamstime
2.5 John Cox Beidha
2.7 Zdj cie Wykonał A. Sobkowski/Wikimedia
2.9 Hélène David Cluny
2.10 Richard Lilly
2.12 Myshu
2.13 Lori L. Renner
2.14 Konstantina Karampetsou
2.22 Mark Nesbitt & Delwen Samuel
2.24 a Katie Swinford
2.24 b Katie Swinford
2.25 Roc8jas/iStockphoto
2.26 Robert Wallace
2.27 Dave Price
2.28 René Goguey and Daniel Beucher
2.30 Genevieve Carpentier Racine
2.31 M. Pushkarev/iStockphoto
2.34 Dalia Gheith
2.36 Anton Polsky
2.37 F.H. Mira
2.38 a Barry Hodges
2.39 Christine Howell
2.50 Ch.Pagenkopf
2.51 Dageldog/iStockphoto

3.1 Rraheb/Dreamstime
3.12 b Quintanilla/Dreamstime
3.14 British Museum
3.16 British Museum
3.17 Oleg Znamenskiy

4.0 Michele Stefanile/Dreamstime
4.1 Ollirg/Dreamstime
4.2 Philippehalle/Dreamstime
4.3 Piotr Tomicki/Dreamstime
4.4 BDphoto/iStockphoto
4.5 Natalia Pavlova/Dreamstime
4.6 Wallyg
4.9 Wikimedia Commons
4.11 Natalia Pavlova
4.12 b Lee Braverman
4.14 Natalia Pavlova
4.16 Christopher Biggs
4.18 Pavlos Rekas
4.23 f Miya Chan
4.23 g Jennifer Jordt
4.27 Library of Congress
4.29 Dale Morton
4.30 Norbert Rehm/Dreamstime
4.31 Xdrew/Dreamstime
4.32 François de Nodrest
4.33 Stefano Roverato
4.34 Jason Brooks
4.36 Emberiza/Dreamstime
4.40 Simone Manzoni/Dreamstime
4.41 b Valeria Cantone
4.41 c Paolo Cipriani
4.41 d Valeria Cantone
4.42 Andre Nantel/Dreamstime
4.45 Vladimir Khirman/iStockphoto
4.50 a Ferenc Macht/Dreamstime
4.50 b Helmut Flatscher
4.53 b Pronaia Ollirg/Dreamstime

5.3 Jonesfish
5.6 Trevi/Landscape Annual
5.12 Elena Elisseeva/Dreamstime
5.13 Xdrew/Dreamstime
5.14 Br Lawrence Lew O.P
5.16 Städel Museum Frankfurt
5.18 Alex.trefilov/Dreamstime
5.21 Mystical Marriage of St Catherine, Austrian National Library, Bildarchiv d. ÖNB, Österreichische Nationalbibliothek, Wein,
5.22 Gord Spence
5.23 a Andremichel/Dreamstime
5.23 b Mark Lijesen/Dreamstime
5.24 a Braun and Hogenberg
5.24 b Mihai Bogdan Lazar/Dreamstime
5.25 a Wikimedia Commons
5.25 b Wikimedia Commons
5.29 b Somatuscan/Shutterstock
5.31 D. Clarke

5.32 a Richard Turner
5.33 Michael Tyler
5.39 Mirek Hejnicki/Dreamstime
5.40 Steve Estvanik/Dreamstime
5.47 a Albo/Dreamstime
5.47 b Matt Trommer/Dreamstime
5.48 Brigitte Rieser

6.0 Panjuli/Dreamstime
6.1 a Braun and Hogenberg
6.1 b Steven Melanson/Dreamstime
6.4 Claudio Giovanni Colombo
6.11 Adam Mizrahi
6.12 Luca Chiartano/Dreamstime
6.14 Massimo Merlini/Dreamstime
6.19 a Somatuscani/Dreamstime
6.19 b Jorgefelix/Dreamstime
6.20 a Asturtom
6.21 b Danielle Kaufmann/Dreamstime
6.21 c Valeria Cantone/Dreamstime
6.23 a Darja Vorontsova/Dreamstime
6.25 Thomas Barrat/Dreamstime
6.29 Peter Wollinga/Dreamstime
6.33 Paul Butchard/Dreamstime
6.34 b Hansok/Dreamstime
6.34 c J0hnb0y/Dreamstime
6.35 a Nataliia Fedori/Dreamstime
6.35 b Petr Švec/Dreamstime
6.38 Antonio Scaramuzzino
6.39 b Steven R. Harvey
6.40 a Alberto Grazi
6.40 b Mmoraru3/Dreamstime
6.42 a Mario Carbone/Dreamstime
6.42 b Elen/Dreamstime
6.42 c Dimsle/Dreamstime
6.42 d Elen/Dreamstime
6.43 a Silvano Audisio/Dreamstime
6.43 b Silvano Audisio/Dreamstime

7.0 Alessandro Cucca/Dreamstime
7.2 Brechje Marechal/Andy Nelson
7.5 a Elena Elisseeva/Dreamstime
7.5 b Ji í Královec/Dreamstime
7.5 c Csld/Dreamstime
7.6 c Vladislav Gurfinkel/Dreamstime
7.7 b Darja Vorontsova/Dreamstime
7.8 Norbert Rehm/Dreamstime
7.13 Davide Romanini/Dreamstime
7.14 Federico Stella
7.16 a Albo/Dreamstime
7.16 b Sbolle/Dreamstime
7.18 c Jacques Rousseau/Dreamstime
7.20 Demid/Dreamstime
7.22 Andrea Poole/Dreamstime
7.24 b Jaap van 't Veen
7.25 a Janina Fiehl
7.26 a Jun Kwang Han
7.26 b Christian Hesse/Dreamstime
7.27 a Alexander Mertz/Dreamstime
7.28 Kassel Andreas Marx
7.29 Kassel Andreas Marx
7.31 b Eg004713/Dreamstime
7.32 a Natalia Belotelova/Dreamstime
7.32 b Jozef Sedmak/Dreamstime
7.32 c Natalia Belotelova/Dreamstime
7.33 b Daniele Dalledonne
7.34 b Sergey Borisov/Dreamstime
7.35 a Anna Yu/iStockphoto
7.35 b Steffen Højager/Dreamstime
7.35 c Anna Yu/iStockphoto
7.36 Leparu Fotolia
7.37 a Peter Zachar/Dreamstime
7.37 b Mikhail Kokhanchikov/Dreamstime
7.38 Korshunova
7.40 Adam Golabek/Dreamstime
7.39 Dbtale/Dreamstime
7.42 a Tomas1111/Dreamstime
7.43 a Gabriela Insuratelu/Dreamstime
7.43 c Danilo Ascione/Dreamstime
7.46 b Davide Romanin/Dreamstime

8.0 Afonskaya Irina/Dreamstime 13944973a.jpg
8.1 a Eg004713/Dreamstime
8.1 b Olga Zhuravlova/Dreamstime
8.1 c Mathias Kaden/Dreamstime
8.3 c Thomas Perkins/Dreamstime
8.4 Indianapolis Museum of Art
8.6 a Gianluca Carnicella
8.8 Paul Foye
8.10 Andrew Houghton/iStockphoto
8.14 Middleton Place Foundation, Charleston, South Carolina
8.21 Davidmartyn/Dreamstime
8.28 c John Griffiths
8.29 irakite/iStockphoto
8.34 b Alexandre Fagundes De Fagundes/Dreamstime
8.35 Jacques Rousseau/Dreamstime
8.37 b Pierre F.
8.38 Kay Friedlein
8.40 Alex Nikada/iStockphoto
8.41 c Karin Pospich
8.42 Elena Kouptsova Vasic/Dreamstime
8.43 Reiner Kaufmann/Dreamstime
8.45 a Daniela Staneva
8.45 b Korshunova/Dreamstime
8.46 Afonskaya Irina/Dreamstime
8.47 a Mikhail Kokhanchikov/Dreamstime
8.47 b Sailorr/Dreamstime
8.48 Kurtnielsen/Dreamstime
8.50 Rimaye Fotolia
8.52 Climberjk/Dreamstime
8.53 Marina Pykhova/Dreamstime

9.0 Harald Bolten/Dreamstime
9.3 b Alison Cornford matheson/Dreamstime
9.3 c Omers/Dreamstime
9.5 b Ingrid Balabanova/Dreamstime
9.5 c Zuboff/Dreamstime
9.6 a Center/Shutterstock
9.9 a Tim Caynes
9.9 b Dongyi Liu
9.10 Steven Feather
9.12 a Fabio Cardano/Dreamstime
9.12 b Wollemipine/Dreamstime
9.12 c Zemzina
9.18 Karin R. Hartman
9.19 Golli43
9.20 Marie France Durieux
9.25 b Kurtnielsen/Dreamstime
9.25 c Gary718/Dreamstime
9.26 Astra490/Dreamstime
9.27 b Victoria Simmonds
9.27 c Miklav/Dreamstime
9.28 Songquan Deng/Dreamstime
9.29 Kushnirov Avrhaam/Dreamstime
9.30 b Debra Law/Dreamstime
9.30 c Jaime Pharr/Dreamstime
9.35 Alain Michot
9.36 Alain Michot
9.37 Odoudo/Dreamstime
9.41 Ellen Golla/Dreamstime
9.45 Terraxplorer/iStockphoto
9.46 Gmiker/Dreamstime

10.0 Javier Gutiérrez Marcos
10.1 Javier Gutiérrez Marcos
10.3 Bruce Nguyen
10.4 a John Roger Palmour
10.4 b John Roger Palmour
10.4 c Allan Harris
10.6 Jason Malikow
10.7 Boon Low
10.8 Helen Nicol
10.10 Benjamin R. Jakabek
10.11 Djordje Jevtovic/Dreamstime
10.15 a David Lewis/Dreamstime
10.15 b Andrea Poole/Dreamstime
10.16 a Rui Caldeira/Dreamstime
10.16 b Kerstin Aust/Dreamstime
10.17 www.KarlGercens.com
10.18 Specialkrb/Flickr
10.22 Jesper Wiking
10.23 Dr. M. Hobl
10.24 Tarina Peterson
10.25 Martine Charmont
10.26 Kenneth G. Urquhart
10.27 a Sjors Grijpink
10.28 a Isabel Junqueira Loyola Brandao
10.28 b Chris Foster
10.31 a Peter Guthrie
10.31 b Marcin Kaminski/iStockphoto
10.32 Mark Ho
10.33 Kevin Walker
10.34 Iman M.P. Heijboer
10.35 Wilfried Maehlmann
10.36 Paulo Saldanha
10.37 Stefan Lehmann
10.38 a Judy Hitzeman
10.38 b gary shield
10.39 Margaret Turner
10.42 Rainer Junker/Dreamstime
10.44 Jeff Whyte/Dreamstime
10.47 Marcin Linfernum/Shutterstock

Index